W9-CCU-298

TEACHER'S ANSWER BOOK
HAYES INDIANA HISTORY

©Copyright Hayes School Publishing Co., Inc., Printed in USA

ANSWER KEY — PULL TO REMOVE

This Manual and Answer Book has been prepared for the purpose of assisting teachers who are using the INDIANA HISTORY Text-Workbook in their classes. It contains the answers to all the questions in the Study Exercises and in the Unit Tests. This is a teacher's book and should never be allowed in the hands of the students.

STUDY EXERCISES

UNIT 1. The Setting for Indiana History

Correct answers for the blanks.

1. (1) Location of the Northwest Territory, especially the part that became Indiana (2) Nature and physical features of this territory (3) People who lived here before and at the time of the white man's arrival (4) Reasons why white men came here (5) Reasons for delay in settlement of the territory (6) White men's struggle with the Indians for possession of the territory (7) Contest between English and French for control of the territory and the effects of these wars on the settlers (8) Efforts of the Americans to win this land from the English (9) How the pioneers lived (10) Growth and development of Indiana into one of the most important states 2. The "physical features" are the prairies, lakes, rocks, mountains, etc., or the kind of surface an area has 3. Northwest Territory 4. "Heartland of America" 5. North 6. The Ohio River 7. The Mississippi River 8. Ohio, Indiana, Illinois, Michigan, and Wisconsin 9. (1) Northern Moraine and Lake Region (2) Central Till Plain (3) Southern Uplands and Plains 10. "Indians' Ground" 11. Ohio River, Wabash River 12. Lake Michigan 13. 140 miles 14. 276 miles 15. Ice sheets or glaciers which came down from the north and covered the earth 16. Lake Wawasee, Cedar Lake, Lake James, Lake Maxinkukee 17. Any of the following: Wabash, White, Tippecanoe, Eel, Whitewater, St. Joseph, Elkhart, Mississinewa, Salamonie, Iroquois, St. Mary's, Patoka, Blue 18. hilly; Southern Uplands 19. It is a strip of level prairie land very suitable for farming; Central Till Plain 20. Part of it is level or gently rolling. There are many lakes and swampy regions. Part of the area is covered with sand dunes. Northern Moraine Region 21. Central Till Plain 22. Important things that were put here by nature and not man 23. Marengo and Wyandotte Caves 24. Strip of land between 2 rivers across which boats and supplies are carried 25. a. Where South Bend is now, between the St. Joseph and Kankakee Rivers b. Between the Maumee River and the Little River, which flows into the Wabash 26. "Mound Builders" 27. From the materials found in the mounds that have been excavated 28. Small hills filled with Indian relics such as stone axes, pottery, etc. 29. Southern part of the state - Angel Mounds near Evansville and Mounds State Park near Anderson 30. Articles made by primitive peoples 31. "Redskins" 32. (1) From Kentucky (2) By way of the Great Lakes (3) Down the Ohio River from western Pennsylvania

Map Exercises: 1. About 600 miles **2.** 36,205 square miles, 309 square miles of water

UNIT 2. The Indians in the Northwest Territory

Answers

1. Jesuit missionaries and a few fur traders 2. Scattered tribes of Indians 3. (1) Names of Indian tribes (2) Where each tribe was located (3) How the Indians felt toward the white man 4. Algonquin 5. Iroquois 6. Miami 7. "The most civilized of all Indians - neat of dress, splendid of bearing, haughty of manner, holding all other tribes as inferiors" 8. Little Turtle 9. Pontiac 10. Hostile 11. Shawnee 12. Bloodthirsty, cruel, treacherous 13. Prophet, Tecumseh 14. Tribe and Location:

Twightwees, near headwaters of Maumee River; Wea, near present city of Lafayette; Piankeshaw and Shockeys, western Indiana near Vincennes and eastern Illinois along Vermillion River 15. From southern Wisconsin into northern Illinois, around southern Lake Michigan, and northern Indiana 16. Fierce, murderous, drunken savages 17. Kekionga 18. They destroyed the Huron tribe completely in 1649. The Iroquois tribe weakened the Miami tribe with constant battles and other tribes moved in. 19. Southeastern Indiana 20. A pictorial record of the Delaware tribe 21. Along streams and lakes 22. Today we can find arrowheads, stone axes and other Indian relics there. 23. Either on foot or by small boats 24. Moved often 25. Arrowheads; Tomahawks 26. Bow and arrow 27. Hunting and cultivating small gardens 28. Smallpox 29. Skins and furs 30. Dugouts 31. Disease, Battles 32. Corn 33. They were rough tent-like structures with sides made of bark or skins. A few poles placed in the ground formed a circle and were tied together at the top. Skins or bark were then fastened to the poles and a hole was left at the top to let smoke escape.

Indian Names	What it is	Indian Meaning
1.	River	Father of waters
2.	City	Place of wild onions
3.	River	Blood root
4.	River	"I have spoken"
5.	region in N. Ind.	deep, still water
6.	River	Gleaming white
7.	City in Mich.	mouth of river
8.	City in Ind.	Black walnut
9.	River	Buffalo fish
10.	Menominee	
11.	State	men
12.	City of Mich.	Otter tail
13.	Lake in Ind.	full moon
14.	City	the claw
15.	Lake	big stone country
16.	River	much fall in the river
17.	River	standing rock
18.	City in Mich.	flat rock
19.	Indian tribe or fort in Ind.	round channel
20.	God of Indians	supernatural spirit

2. Answers will vary.

UNIT 3. French Explorations and Settlements in the Northwest Territory, 1634-1763

1. French 2. Priests, Jesuits 3. 1634 4. Converting Indians to Christianity 5. Among Huron Indians around Lake Erie 6. Up St. Lawrence River and down Great Lakes 7. None 8. Allouez; Dablon; Marquette; Hennepin 9. Appalachian Mts. 10. Furs 11. Little settlements which French fur traders set up 12. Coureuis-de-bois 13. Habitants 14. Knives, blankets, cotton, beads, whiskey 15. Control of fur trade 16. Build a chain of forts 17. La Salle

	Name	Location	Date
18.	Ft. Ouitenon	near Lafayette	1717 or 1722
	Ft. Miami	Ft. Wayne	
	Vincennes	on Wabash R.	1732
19.	Ft. Michilmackinac	between Lakes Huron & Mich.	1669
	Detroit	Central Mich.	1701
	Kaskakia	Lower Ill.	1695
	Cahokia	Opposite present St. Louis	
	Ft. St. Louis	Michigan	
	Ft. St. Joseph	Ill. River	1683

20. Vincennes 21. Ft. Miami 22. La Salle 23. 1770 24. La Salle 25. From Lake Mich. up St. Joseph R. near South Bend. Followed Kankakee River to its mouth and down Illinois R. to the Miss. River 26. From Lake Erie up Maumee R. then by portage to the Wabash R. and down the Wabash to the Ohio and Miss. Rivers 27. Cahokia — Along Mississippi River; Kaskaskia — At crossing of Miss. R. and Kask. R. in southern Ill. 28. A Jesuit priest who explored the Miss. R. in 1673 on behalf of France 29. French fur trader who accompanied Marquette on his journeys 30. Treaty of Paris gave England control of all French land in N.W. Territory 31. Answers will vary.

UNIT 4. Occupation of the Northwest Territory by the English, 1756-1778

1. 1763 2. England 3. Detroit 4. Vincennes; Ouiatenon; Ft. Miami 5. Pontiac; Ottawa 6. Pontiac's conspiracy 7. 1763 8. Murdered by another member of his tribe 9. Ft. Ouiatenon; Ft. Miami 10. Hostility of Indians; Proclamation of 1763 forbade English to settle west of Allegheny Mts. 11. Proclamation passed at end of French and Indian War 12. Annexed all lands north of Ohio R. and east of Mississippi R. to province of Quebec for purposes of government, 1774 13. Settlement slowed down 14. Kaskaskia; Cahokia 15. 1777 16. Governor Hamilton sent a representative to Vincennes to take possession and rebuild the fort there. 17. Indians were friendly toward the English and were rewarded for attacking Americans, discouraging Americans from settling in Indiana. 18. English are those loyal to England while Americans are those who came here from England but fought for their freedom in the Revolutionary War. 19. Kentucky

Correct paragraph answers.

A. Virginia, Northwest, Indians, Kentucky and Indiana, George Rogers Clark, Indian, American, states, Patrick Henry, Virginia, army, American, east, England, Henry

B. backwoodsmen, settlers, soldiers, Corn Island, Ohio, Louisville, Ky., Kaskaskia, rifles and knives, Indian fighting, hunting, wild, British, Kaskaskia, July 4, 1778

C. Sackville, Vincennes, Kaskaskia, Gibault, Catholic, English, Gibault, English, Vincennes, Clark, Vincennes, Cahokia

D. English, Henry, Hamilton, Detroit, Americans, Kaskaskia and Vincennes, Wabash, Vincennes, Corn, 2, Ft. Sackville, Hamilton's, Vincennes, Clark, English, 1778

UNIT 5. The Conquest of the Northwest Territory by the Americans, and the Immigration to this Territory, 1778-1800

1. Revolutionary War. To enable Americans to win freedom from England 2. Vincennes 3. Vincennes 4. English 5. English Governor of N.W. Terr. 6. Kaskaskia 7. Spanish trader; gave Clark information; loaned Clark money 8. March against Vincennes at once 9. It was mid-winter and land unfit for travel; Wabash River was flooded; constant danger of Indian attacks 10. 260 miles 11. 130 12. They were involved in the Rev. War 13. By a small gunboat 14. "Willing" 15. Wabash 16. Unfriendly 17. Because it was said he offered the Indians rewards for American scalps turned in. 18. Surrendered; Marksmanship of Clark's men and the fact that Clark's men scalped several Indians in full view of the English 19. Feb. 25, 1779 20. This could be considered the starting point of the history of Indiana and firmly established the claims of the Americans and the territory of Indiana. 21. Illinois country 22. Couldn't raise an army and was busy with Indian battles 23. Where Col. Laughery and his band of Indiana settlers were surprised and massacred by the Indians in 1781 24. Clark borrowed money to finance expedition and capture Vincennes expecting Virginia Colony to pay him back, but they didn't and he died a pauper. 25. Given large tract of land in southern Ind. 26. Vincennes; Clarksville 27. Deeded it to U.S. government 28. Public domain 29. Land ceded to government for public use 30. Unorganized Terr.; Organized

Terr.; State 31. Clarksville 32. 5 33. Size of territory made it hard to govern; Government not effective in scattered settlement 34. Vincennes; Kaskaskia; Detroit; Cincinnati 35. May 7, 1800

UNIT 6. Indiana as a Territory, 1800-1816

Correct answers for the paragraphs.

1. 1785; Land Ordinance of 1785; townships; 6; townships; sections; 640; 1 mile; $1.00; committees; 16; township; educational 2. Ordinance of 1787; governor; secretary; 3 judges; Congress; President 3. 1787; prohibited; speech and religion; Indians; consent; population; 5,000 people; legislature 4. 3; 5; states; 60,000; St. Clair; N.W. Territory; 1790; Knox, Indiana; Wis., Ill., Ohio and Mich.; Marietta

Correct words to complete the paragraphs.

1. England; Indians; N.W. Terr.; Little Turtle; Miami; Gen. Harmar; Indians; Kekionga; Americans 2. St. Clair; Indians; Ft. Recovery, Ohio; Americans; Washington; Wayne; Indians; Fallen Timbers; Americans; 1795; Wayne; Indians; Greenville, Ohio; Greenville; Ohio; Indiana; Ft. Wayne

Answers to fill-in blanks in paragraphs.

1. 1800; line from mouth of Kentucky R. to Ft. Recovery and then due North to Canada; Ohio R.; Mississippi R.; Lake Superior and Canada; 6500; Indians; southern; Ohio; Wabash; Whitewater and White; Vincennes; Clarksville; organized; hostile; unsettled; growing 2. Wm. H. Harrison; Ind.; 27; Indian; John Gibson (1) est. govt. for terr.; (2) deal with Indians and secure as much of their land as possible (3) survey land and grant titles to it 3. 2; Knox and St. Clair; Clark and Dearborn; Vincennes, Lawrenceburg, Clarksville, Madison, Corydon, Terre Haute; New Albany to Vincennes

Answers to fill-in blanks.

1. (1) Vincennes Tract - 1803 - line which extended from a pt. 12 miles above Vincennes to mouth of White R., from there to north part of Perry Co., then to Orleans, and back to start (2) southwestern Ind. - 1804; (3) southeastern Ind. and north bank of Ohio R. - 1805; (4) 1809 - land north and N.E. of Vincennes 2. It was called this because it was supposed to run in direction of sun's rays at 10:00 a.m. This was northern boundary of land acquired from Indians in 1809 treaty 3. Gov. Harrison 4. Because it deprived them of their best hunting ground 5. Tecumseh; Prophet; Shawnee 6. Tecumseh; Vincennes 7. Stop them 8. Harrison marched N. along the Wabash, stopping near T. H. to build a fort, crossed the Wabash there and continued along west bank to a place 8 miles N. of Lafayette (where Battle Ground) is located today; Harrison's Trail 9. Prophetstown, located along the Wabash R. 10. November 7, 1811 11. Indians attacked early in the morning and waged battle for 2 hours. Americans were completely victorious. 12. Deserted camp of Shawnees 13. Shawnee, Potawatomi, Chippewa, Winnebago 14. Prophet; Tecumseh 15. Monument 16. Pigeon Roost; Murdered 22 residents 17. Ft. Harrison; It was defended by the Americans and Indians defeated 18. All Indian villages along Wabash were destroyed South of Wabash River 19. People who settled on land before it was surveyed 20. 63,897 21. Large elm tree under which delegates met to form 1st constitution 22. December 11th

Correct answers for the blanks in paragraphs.

1. 1813; Vincennes to Corydon; center of the territory; John Gibson; Harrison; 1812; 1813; Posey; state; 1816 2. (1) Ind. made a territory separate from the N.W. Terr. in 1800 (2) In 1802, Ohio Terr. was separated from the Ind. Terr.; (3) In 1805, Michigan Terr. was separated from Ind.; Ind. Terr. advanced to one of a second grade and a terr. legislature and governor took control (4) In 1809, Ill. Terr. was separated from Indiana 3. Line drawn north from mouth of Great Miami River and then by a meridian line to Canada. Line drawn east and west 10 miles north of southern tip of Lake Michigan 4. Admission as a state; 1816; constitutional; Corydon; 13; constitution; constitution; state; December 11, 1816; 19th

UNIT 7. Pioneer Life in Indiana

Correct answers for blanks in paragraphs.

1. Kentucky; Ohio River; barrier; small boats, ferrying; horseback, foot and by wagons; rifles; protection; Indians, hunting, food; southern; heavy forest; roads, bridges, towns, stores; clearing; taking away underbrush; cutting down small trees; house; logs; planting crops; agriculture; provide 2. home; logs; 1 ft. (12"); logs; 20-25 ft.; sides; logs; diameter; ends; logs; log; notched; underneath; one; another; Poles; clapboards; clapboards; 4'; 6"; overlapping; nails; chimney; clay; fireplace; split logs; puncheon; clay; chinking; 3; open-faced; adz, axe, frow, pick; shelter 3. posts; poles; ropes; buckskin; poles; mats; benches; stools; chairs; bench; a table; iron or copper kettle; frying pan; pots and pans; iron or earthenware; heat and cooking 4. woman; clothing; farming; spinning wheel, thread; homespun; wool socks; underwear; mufflers; flax; thread; linsey-woolsey; vegetables or hulls of nuts

Correct answers for blanks.

1. Low and swampy land 2. Made soap 3. Corn and potatoes 4. Hogs 5. Deer; wild duck and geese; rabbits; wild turkey; squirrels; wild pigeons 6. Potatoes; radish; pickles; pumpkin; cabbage; beans; peppers; watermelons; onions; peas; turnips 7. Dried or stored in caves 8. Blackberries; grapes; wild haw; raspberries; crab apples; persimmon; mulberries; plums; paw paw 9. Put in salt water (pickled); Hickory smoked 10. Hickory; walnut; beechnut; chestnut 11. Sugar, salt and coffee 12. Had to be brought from elsewhere because soil in Ind. wouldn't grow it 13. Venison 14. Clothing from skin 15. Sap from maple trees 16. Wild honey 17. Salt springs 18. Parched corn or tree bark 19. Disease 20. Ague 21. Home remedies 22. 40 23. A watch

Correct answers for blanks

1. (1) Lack of sanitation; (2) Rough life and exposure to weather; (3) Swarms of flies and mosquitoes; (4) Impurity of water; (5) Lack of cleanliness in food handling 2. Cholera; morbus; diarrhea; flux 3. Cholera; smallpox; measles; diphtheria; typhoid; milk sickness; scarlet fever 4. Bloodroot; ginsing; rhubarb; bitter-root; yellowroot; slippery elm 5. Bottle of bitters 6. Goose grease 7. Sassafras tea 8. Severe intestinal spasms, craving for water, circulation slowed, eyes sunk 9. Eating too much fresh meat and improperly preserved foods 10. Lack of proper dental care 11. Erysipelas; the "itch" 12. Protestant 13. Preachers 14. Presbyterian, Methodist, Baptist, Christian 15. Meat or vegetables or what people raised 16. Rapidly 17. One million 18. Country crossroads; gristmill 19. Mill where corn and wheat were ground into meal and flour 20. Water 21. Agriculture 22. Oxen 23. Rail fence 24. Wedge and maul 25. Marketed it 26. Wheat; rye; wool; corn; corn meal; furs; flour; pork; hides 27. Wagons, then boats 28. New Albany; Madison 29. Ohio R. 30. Cincinnati; New Orleans 31. Brick; household furnishings 32. 1861

Correct answers for blanks

1. Tanned; buckskin; shoes; pants; shirts; gloves 2. Bears; grease; cooking; skin 3. Panther; panthers; hound dogs 4. Buffalo; first roads; buffalo; buffalo; 1798; starved; unusually severe weather 5. Heavy wool; sheared; washed; spun; wool; mill; cloth 6. 1787; knowledge; education; time; schools; tax; public schools; subscription; children; teacher; "boarding around"; 3 mos.; all; "one room"

UNIT 8. Political Development of Indiana, 1816 to the Present

Correct answers for the blanks.

1. 1850 2. November 1, 1851 3. Joseph A. Wright 4. Constitution of the U.S. 5. To set up basic laws for the state 6. 16 7. Bill of Rights 8. Freedom of religion and worship; freedom of speech; right of a public trial by jury; right of people to assemble in peaceful manner; right to be secure against unreasonable search and seizure 9. Legislative; executive; judicial 10. Executive 11. 4 yrs. 12. 2 13. General Assembly

14. Voters in their respective districts 15. Senate 16. 50 17. House of Representatives 18. 100 19. Every other year 20. Odd-numbered years — 61 session days; Even-numbered years — 30 session days 21. It is prohibited 22. Article 8 set up a permanent School Fund 23. Must be 21 24. Can be amended

Words to complete the paragraphs correctly.

1. Third; nineteenth; December 7, 1816; Jonathan Jennings; New Jersey; voters (people); governor; Jeffersonian Republican; 32; government; Constitution; Corydon; $1,000; 3; Jennings; Second; Jennings; Congress; Ratliff Boone; Indiana 2. Jennings; St. Mary's; Miamis; Wea; Potawatomi; Delaware; 1818; 8,000,000; central Wabash; Indians; New Purchase of 1818; settlement; rapidly; southern; New Albany; Corydon; Vincennes; college; newspaper; land office; library; Masonic Lodge; Vincennes; 150,000; Evansville; Terre Haute; Bloomington; Richmond 3. William Hendricks; Jeffersonian; Republican; 1822; resigned; Congress; northward; Corydon; edge of the state; 8; capital; Fall; White; Indianapolis; 1825; 1835; James B. Ray; Hendricks; 1825; Ray; roads; canals; railroads; internal improvements; Ray's; Wabash and Erie Canal; Michigan Road; Indian 4. Noah Noble; 1831; 1837; Andrew Jackson; prosperity; Noble; canals; railroad; Madison; Lafayette; bank; 13; David Wallace; internal improvements; Panic of 1837; Wallace's collapse; 13 million dollars; bankrupt; hard times; Wallace's; Indians; 1838; Potawotami 5. Whig; Democrat; William Henry Harrison; Whig; Samuel Bigger; Whig; James Whitcomb; 1843; Whitcomb; reducing credit; Mexican; 5,000; resigned; United States Senator; Paris C. Dunning

Correct answers for the blanks.

1. Glorious Fifties 2. Democrat 3. Willard 4. Peoples 5. Republican 6. Slavery 7. Republican 8. Underground Railroad 9. Henry S. Lane 10. Oliver P. Morton 11. Oliver P. Morton 12. North 13. Morton 14. J.F.D. Lanier 15. Prison camp 16. Indianapolis 17. 197,649 18. Lew Wallace 19. Morgan's Raid 20. Knights of the Golden Circle 21. Conrad Baker 22. Hendricks 23. Marshall 24. Williams 25. Willard 26-27. Hovey, Williams 28. 1878 29. 1888 30. Claude Matthews 31. James A. Mount 32. Winfield Durbin 33. J. Frank Hanly 34. Thomas Marshall 35. James P. Goodrich 36. Ku Klux Klan 37. Henry Schricker 38. George Craig 39. Henry F. Schricker and Otis R. Bowen 40. 40 41. Matthew Welsh 42. Roger D. Branigin 43. Edgar D. Whitcomb 44. Otis R. Bowen, M.D./Robert Orr 45. Answer will vary.

Correct answers for the blanks.

1. Caused the collapse of building programs 2. Provided for different county offices and specified their duties 3. 5; 5 4. Inheritance tax; primary election; vocational training; Workmens Compensation; Public Service Commission Law 5. Gross income tax law; Intangibles tax law; Excise tax law 6. Paul V. McNutt; Republican legislature 7. Ralph F. Gates 8. Gross income tax 9. The list will vary. 10. Answers will vary.

UNIT 9. The Development of Transportation Systems in Indiana

Correct answers for the blanks.

1. Traces, or buffalo traces 2. Buffalo herds and Indians 3. By cutting patches of bark off the trees along the trail, thus marking the path for other travelers 4. Buffalo Trace 5. By boat, on foot, and on horseback 6. So that wagons could be used to carry livestock and grain to market 7. By cutting down trees and removing the brush. The main drawback was the mud, especially in the winter and spring. 8. By felling trees and placing the logs crosswise on the road. One made by splitting logs into boards and making a road surface of the planks. The corduroy road held up well, but it was extremely rough, or bumpy; the plank road was smooth, but it needed repair most of the time. 9. Construction of railroads, canals, and roads 10. 1836; (1) The Whitewater Canal; (2) The Central Canal; (3) Completion of the Wabash and Erie Canal from Lafayette to the Central

Canal; (4) A railroad from Madison, through Columbus and Indianapolis to Lafayette; (5) A turnpike from New Albany to Vincennes; (6) A survey of the route from Jeffersonville to Crawfordsville; (7) A survey for a canal or a railroad from Fort Wayne to Lake Michigan; (8) The setting aside of $50,000 for removing obstructions from the Wabash River **11.** $13,000,000 **12.** The plan was too elaborate and costly to be financed by taxation, and with the beginning of the Panic of 1837, no money could be secured to carry out the construction. **13.** About $10,000,000 **14.** Potawatomi **15.** Michigan Road **16.** National Road

17.

	Michigan Road	**National Road**
(1)	1830	1827
(2)	Madison	Richmond
	Michigan City	Terre Haute
(3)	Versailes	Indianapolis
	Greensburg	Centerville
	Indianapolis	
	Logansport	
	South Bend	
(4)	421	40

18. Stage coaches; 7 or 8 miles per hour **19.** 1820; Louisville and Vincennes **20.** Madison and Indianapolis; Lawrenceburg and Indianapolis; Cincinnati and Indianapolis; Leavenworth and Indianapolis (by way of Bloomington); Lafayette and Fort Wayne **21.** (1) by state funds; (2) by counties; (3) by private companies **22.** By charging "toll" for use of the roads **23.** Because of bad weather and muddy roads **24.** They were bridges which were enclosed by a top and sides, like a tunnel. They were made of timber.

Correct answers for blanks in Column I, Trails and Traces.

1. Berry's Trace **2.** Wetzel's Trace **3.** Vincennes Trace **4.** Sac Trail **5.** Wea Trail **6.** Chicago Trail **7.** Wabash Trail

Correct information to complete the summaries.

I. Wabash and Erie Canal A. Lake Erie and Mississippi River B. 1832 C. 380 D. Lafayette, Terre Haute, Evansville E. Logansport, Peru, Lafayette, Attica, Williamsport, Covington, Terre Haute F. Carrying of farm produce to market G. Northern part, especially Wabash Valley H. Lack of funds I. It was operated for a time by private individuals but abandoned before completion of it.

II. Whitewater Canal A. 1836 B. Cambridge City, Brookville, Lawrenceburg, Cincinnati C. 76 miles D. From Brookville to Metamora

III. A. A wooden structure which carried the water of the canal across streams and rivers when it was necessary to cross to the other side B. A turning basin for boats traveling in canals C. The path along the canal bank. It was followed by horses or mules pulling canal boats D. A wide place in the canal, providing space for boats to turn around and return the way they had come E. Method of raising water level in canals to carry the canal boats over higher ground F. A flat bottomed canal boat pulled by a horse or a mule walking along a tow path; Usually used to carry freight.

Correct answers for Column I, Railroads.

1. Baltimore and Ohio **2.** Monon **3.** New York Central (Cleveland Division) **4.** Pennsylvania **5.** Nickel Plate **6.** New York Central (Cinn. Division) **7.** Wabash **8.** Pennsylvania

Words to complete the paragraphs correctly.

1. Canals; railroad; 1850; 1860; 200; 6,571 **2.** 1831; Madison; and Indianapolis; Madison Vernon; Indianapolis; internal improvement; private individuals; companies **3.** Monon; Ohio; Michigan; Michigan City; Lafayette; Crawfordsville; Salem (Others may be named.) **4.** Toledo, Wabash, and Western (Norfolk and Western); Wabash and Erie; Madison; Williamsport (Others may be named here.) Indianapolis **5.** Electric interurban; Alexandria; Anderson; Indianapolis; 600; 300; 2,168; (1) Union Traction Company; (2) The Terre Haute, Indianapolis and Eastern System; (3) The Interstate Company; South Shore

Correct answers for Column I, Highways.

1. No. 40 **2.** No. 465 **3.** No. 65 **4.** No. 50 **5.** No. 41 **6.** No. 74 **7.** No. 20 **8.** No. 30 **9.** No. 24 **10.** No. 421 **11.** No. 64 **12.** No. 52 **13.** No. 27/69 **14.** No. 70 **15.** No. 31 **16.** No. 136

Correct answers for the blanks.

1. Bus (or motor); railroads; It is fast and efficient. Freight can be delivered to the customer's door in less time and sometimes at less cost than by railroad. Bus lines connect all principal towns and cities, so that passengers can go almost anywhere in the state directly and at little expense. **2.** Greyhound Bus Line; Trailways; others **3.** So that they may more nearly bear their share of road costs **4.** Kentland, Sterling, Lafayette (Others may be named.) **5.** Highways built primarily to carry traffic from one state to another **6.** (1) A road built to carry through traffic around a city instead of through the business section; (2) A bridge for which a fee is charged to anyone who uses it; (3) An intersection of two highways where one highway crosses the other by means of an elevated bridge; (4) An intersection of two highways where one highway crosses the other by means of a passageway beneath the other. (Often used when a highway crosses under a railway.) (5) A highway constructed of a bed of broken stones covered with a hard, smooth surface material; (6) A method of entering or leaving a highway so that left-hand turns are eliminated; (7) Space between the two parts of divided lane pavements, arranged so that traffic in each part travels in only one direction; **7.** It is making it possible for modern highways to be built with private funds. Extending from the Ohio line to the Illinois boundary. 1956 **8.** State Highway Commission **9.** By money from gasoline tax and auto license fees. Also, the Federal government is assisting the state in the building of some highways **10.** Airplane; For passengers who wish rapid means of travel and for freight, especially for those kinds of goods which are perishable or for which there is a time limit on shipment **11.** American; TWA; Delta; Eastern; USAir; Ozark; United **12.** Weir Cook Airport; Indianapolis **13.** Water **14.** Ohio River; Lake Michigan **15.** Amtrak; Freight such as coal, oil, automobiles and other manufactured articles, iron ore, grain (Other items may be listed.)

Map C. State Highways

East & West - 20 - 30 - 24 - 40 - 52 (Also north and south - 136); North & South - 41 - 31 - 27

UNIT 10. The Growth of Education in Indiana

Correct answers for the blanks and charts.

1. Vincennes University; 1806 **2.** (1) Indiana University, Bloomington; (2) Purdue University, West Lafayette; (3) Ball State University, Muncie; (4) Indiana State University, Terre Haute **3.** Ball State Teachers College, Indiana State College **4.** (1) Butler University, Indianapolis, 1855; (2) DePauw University, Greencastle, 1837; (3) Earlham College, Richmond, 1847; (4) Franklin College, Franklin, 1834; (5) Hanover College, Hanover (Madison), 1827; (6) Indiana University, Bloomington, 1820; (7) Notre Dame University, South Bend, 1842; (8) Purdue University, West Lafayette, 1874; (9) St. Mary-of-the-Woods, Terre Haute, 1840; (10) Valparaiso University, Valparaiso, 1874; (11) Vincennes University, Vincennes, 1806; (12) Wabash College, Crawfordsville, 1832; (13) Indiana State University, Terre Haute, 1870; (14) Ball State University, Muncie, 1918; (15) Indiana Vocational Technical College, Indianapolis, 1963 **5.** (1) DePauw University, Methodist; (2) Earlham College, Quakers; (3) Franklin College, Baptist; (4) Goshen College, Mennonite; (5) Hanover College, Presbyterian; (6) Notre Dame University, Catholic; (7) St. Joseph's College, Catholic; (8) St. Mary-of-the-Woods, Catholic; (9) Valparaiso University, Quaker **6.** (1) Butler University, Original name: North Western Christian University; (2) Indiana State College, Original name: Indiana State Normal School; (3) DePauw University, Original name: Asbury University; (4) Evansville College, Original name: Moore's Hill College

ANSWER KEY — PULL TO REMOVE

(moved); (5) Franklin College, Original name: Indiana Baptist Manual Labor Institute; (6) Indiana University, Original name: Indiana State Seminary

Correct answers for the blanks.

1. On the Wabash River, about 30 miles above its junction with the Ohio River 2. 1814 3. Father George Rapp 4. Rappites 5. To all the people 6. Religion, hard work 7. Fruits; wine; cotton; wool 8. Sold them in outside markets 9. Sell out 10. Robert Owen 11. He wanted to establish a "community of equality." 12. New Harmony 13. Equality of work and equality of results of the work 14. (1) Educators and scholars; (2) the shiftless and lazy 15. William Maclure; Thomas Say; Charles A. Lesure; Joseph Neef 16. Kindergarten 17. Established libraries 18. It collapsed. There were too many nonworkers 19. Golden Raintree 20. Fauntleroy Home

Correct answers for the blanks.

1. It set aside one section of land (640 acres) in each township for school purposes. 2. It stated that education was necessary for free government. 3. General system of education from grade one through college at public expense 4. Means of raising money to carry on schools 5. Schools financed by taxes paid by all the people 6. Because they had no children. Also, because they thought free schools would encourage people to ask for other kinds of help at public expense. 7. (1) There were only a few children in each settlement; (2) There was no money to build schools or pay teachers; (3) The parents thought they needed the children to work at home. 8. One-room building 9. Men 10. Wanted to "run him out" 11. No special training 12. Benches and crude desks and a few books 13. readin', writin', 'rithmetic (reading, writing, arithmetic) 14. 8 15. A book of blank lines on which the pupils copied a sentence which was printed at the top of the page. This was thought to improve handwriting. 16. A contest to see who could spell the most words correctly. 17. Caleb Mills; Father of Indiana's Public Schools 18. A contest to see who could excel in getting correct answers to arithmetic problems. 19. McGuffey 20. Webster's 21. 1-8 22. The question of free public schools; Favorable 23. The power to provide money for free public schools. 24. 1852 25. (1) Established the state common school fund; (2) Levied a tax on property for the support of schools; (3) Established a State Board of Education 26. The Supreme Court of the state declared it unconstitutional. 27. County Superintendent of Schools; head of schools in county 28. 1873 29. Show that graduates were able to enter Indiana University 30. Real estate and personal property 31. Gross income tax (Perhaps from sales tax after 1963) 32. One to which pupils are transported from areas where other schools have been abandoned 33. Parochial 34. Catholic 35. Lutheran 36. No direct aid 37. Yes 38. Decreasing; because of consolidation 39. State Superintendent of Public Instruction 40. Constitution of 1851 41. Board of Education 42. Harold H. Negley 43. Voters in the state; four years 44. High School 45. Seven years and sixteen years 46. Attendance officer 47. White and black students attend the same schools; Supreme Court 1957 48-49. Answers will vary. 50. $2 billion

UNIT 11. Population Growth, Agriculture, Natural Resources, and Manufacturing in the State

Correct answers for the blanks.

1. The Crossroads of America 2. Its location, in the very center of the activities of the nation 3. Indiana; 1890; 1950 4. 147,178; 3,934,234; 5,193,669; 5,471,000 5. 6, 5

6.

	1970	1980
A.	Indianapolis	Indianapolis
B.	Fort Wayne	Fort Wayne
C.	Gary	Gary
D.	Evansville	Evansville
E.	South Bend	South Bend
F.	Hammond	Hammond
G.	Kokomo	Bloomington
H.	Bloomington	Kokomo
I.	Jeffersonville	Lawrence
J.	Connersville	Jeffersonville
K.	Goshen	Goshen
L.	Lawrence	Connersville
M.	Peru	Peru

7. Porter Marion

Correct answers for the blanks.

1. Agriculture (farming) 2. Natural resources 3. Manufacturing 4. Agriculture (farming) 5. Central 6. 88,000 7. 17.5 million 8. Almost $2 billion 9. Corn 10. Soybeans 11. Wheat 12. Oats 13. Hogs 14. Cattle 15. Tobacco 16. Spearmint 17. Peppermint 18. Apples 19. Peaches 20. Tomatoes 21. Corn 22. Peas 23. Purdue

Correct answers for the blanks.

1. Limestone 2. two-thirds 3. Lawrence; Monroe; Owen 4. Bedford; Bloomington; Oolitic; Elletsville 5. Goodland; Huntington; Wabash; Marion; Logansport (There are other places, too.) 6. Salt 7. French Lick 8. Timber (forest) 9. Water power 10. Turn mill wheels 11. A channel built for the water so that it would have more fall to turn a mill wheel 12. Yountsville 13. Tippecanoe 14. Monticello 15. Calumet 16. Gary 17. Answers will vary.

Words to complete the paragraphs correctly.

1. Was put there by nature; coal; oil; natural gas; limestone; lumber; natural gas; Grant; Howard; Hancock; Blackford; Tipton; Henry; Delaware; Hamilton; Madison; Rush; gas belt; grow rapidly; Marion; Muncie; Alexandria; Fairmount; New Castle; Hartford City; glassware; fail; 1900; close or move away; lose population 2. Natural; southwestern; Parke; Vigo; Vermillion; Clay; Sullivan; Greene; Knox; Davis; Gibson; Warrick; Pike; Vanderburgh; Terre Haute; Brazil; Clinton; Sullivan; Bicknell; Linton; Boonville; Petersburg; Oakland City; shaft mining; strip mining; A. On the decline B. To generate electricity 3. Oil; Terre Haute; oil; southwestern; Vigo; Sullivan; Pike; Posey; Gibson; Vanderburgh 4. Clay; shale; tile; brick; Bloomingdale; Clay City; Shoals; Martinsville; Veedersburg; Huntingburg; Bloomfield; Brazil; paving; building; cement; decreased; Brazil; Mecca; gypsum; building materials

Correct answers for the blanks.

1. 9th 2. 8,000 3. Whiting 4. Steel 5. Pork packing 6. Madison 7. Terre Haute 8. New Albany 9. Lafayette 10. Terre Haute (Logansport) 11. Gary 12. East Chicago 13. Hammond 14. Lafayette 15. Elwood Haynes 16. 1894 17. 208 18. More than 30 19. Indianapolis 20. One

Correct answers for the blanks.

1. Allen 2. Ohio 3. Marion 4. Ohio 5. Marion 6. Brown

Correct answers for the blanks.

1. City population 2. Country population 3. 2,500 4. Area around a city 5. Suburban 6. 3 7. 47

Ten largest cities in Indiana in 1980 and their population: (1) Indianapolis 700,801 (2) Fort Wayne 172,196 (3) Gary 151,953 (4) Evansville 130,496 (5) South Bend 109,727 (6) Hammond 93,714 (7) Muncie 77,216 (8) Anderson 64,695 (9) Terre Haute 61,125 (10) East Chicago 39,786

Chart 1. Population of Indiana by 10-Year Periods

See Appendix B, Table 1.

UNIT 12. Famous Persons, Places of Interest, and Miscellaneous Facts about Our State

Correct information for box.

1. 1816 2. Indianapolis 3. peony 4. Tulip tree 5. Redbird or cardinal 6. "On the Banks of the Wabash, Far Away" 7. Hoosiers 8. (1) A woodsman felling a tree (2) A buffalo running from the forest (3) The sun setting behind distant hills 9. Deep blue; gold 10. (1) Liberty and enlightenment, with their far-reaching influence (2) The original 13 states

(3) the 5 states admitted to the Union after the original 13 and before the admission of Indiana (4) Indiana 11. 21

Correct matching.

1. Brown County 2. Turkey Run 3. Pokagon 4. Mounds 5. Raccoon Lake 6-7. Wyandotte; Marengo 8. Spring Mill 9. Shakamak 10. Wawasee 11-12. Shafer; Freeman 13. Clifty Falls 14. McCormick's Creek 15. Dunes

Correct answers for the blanks.

1. 1917; 5 ft. 6 in. fly by 4 ft. 4 in. hoist 2. Yellow poplar; It grows large and straight, with deep green foliage and greenish-yellow flowers. 3. Zinnia; 1957 4. Constitution of 1851. As early as 1801, on the Seal of Indiana Territory. It is used on all official state documents. Two inches in diameter 5. A contraction of "Who is there?" 6. 92 7. Answers will vary. 8. Paul Dresser 9. Oh, the moonlight's fair tonight along the Wabash, From the fields there comes the breath of new-mown hay, Through the sycamores the candlelights are gleaming, On the banks of the Wabash, far away 10. 1816; In Spencer County, near Gentryville 11. His mother died. Nancy Hanks; Lincoln Memorial 12. 1830; In Illinois 13. See Famous Persons From Indiana in text material for this Unit. 14. John Clarke Ridpath; Charles A. Beard 15-17. See Famous Persons from Indiana in text material for this Unit.

Correct information for chart.

I. 1. Soldiers' and Sailors' Monument 2. World War Memorial (World War I) II. See list of State Memorials in text material for this Unit. III. See list of State Parks of Indiana in text material for this Unit. IV. Answers will vary.

UNIT TEST 1

Correct answers for the blanks.

1. Northwest Territory 2. artifacts 3. portage 4. Wyandotte or Marengo 5. natural resources 6. prehistoric 7. Wawasee 8. Mound Builders 9. (a) by way of Great Lakes (b) from Kentucky (c) down Ohio River 10. boat (water) 11. Appalachian Mts. 12. physical features 13. "Indian country"

Correct matching answers.

1. a 2. b 3. 1 4. e 5. o 6. v 7. i 8. h 9. n 10. w 11. t 12. s 13. x 14. r 15. c

UNIT TEST 2

Correct answers for the matching.

1. b; Little Turtle 2. c; Pontiac 3. b; corn 4. d; Potawatomi 5. d; Kekionga 6. b; smallpox 7. a; Wabash 8. c; Catholic priests 9. d; Shawnee 10. a; Manitou 11. c; Algonquin 12. b; the Prophet 13. b; hostile 14. d; lake or stream 15. a; Ouiatenon

Correct answers for the blanks.

16. Miami 17. Wawasee 18-19. fur & skins 20. Delaware 21. wigwam or tepee 22. women 23-24. by boat or on foot 25. dugout 26. Huron 27. Ouiatenon 28. Tippecanoe 29-30. tomahawk, bow and arrow 31-34. Twightwees, Piankeshaw, Shockney, Wea or Ouiatenon

UNIT TEST 3

Correct answers for the blanks.

1. France 2. habitants 3. Ouiatenon 4. Jesuit priests 5. Kaskaskia 6. LaSalle 7. 1732 8. England 9. Joliet 10. coureur-de-bois 11. Father Hennepin 12. Vincennes 13. Ft. Miami 14. St. Lawrence River & Great Lakes 15. Appalachian Mts.

True-false

1. False 2. False 3. False 4. False 5. True 6. True 7. False 8. True 9. True 10. False 11. True 12. False 13. False 14. True 15. True

UNIT TEST 4

Correct answers for the blanks.

1. Kaskaskia 2. French 3. Proclamation of 1763 4. Corn Island 5. Hamilton 6. Vigo 7. Father Gibault 8. Vincennes 9. backwoodsmen 10. Kaskaskia 11. Ft. Sackville (Vincennes) 12. Patrick Henry 13. Pontiac 14. Ft. Sackville 15. Pontiac's conspiracy 16. Kentucky 17. George Rogers Clark 18. opposition of Indians 19. Quebec Act 20. Virginia

Correct identification terms.

1. Ft. Sackville — the fort located at Vincennes which George Rogers Clark captured. 2. French & Indian War — ended in 1763, when control of the Northwest Territory passed from the French to the English. 3. Quebec Act — passed in 1774, gave all lands north of Ohio River and east of Mississippi River to province of Quebec to rule. 4. Virginia — leading English colony which claimed a large part of Northwest Territory. 5. Pontiac — Ottawa Indian who led an Indian uprising between 1760-63 and killed many white settlers. 6. Ouiatenon — Indian fort located on Wabash River, south of Lafayette.

UNIT TEST 5

Correct identification answers.

1. February 25, 1799 — Americans under George Rogers Clark captured Ft. Sackville. 2. Little Turtle — famous Miami chieftain who led successful attacks on settlers 3. section — Townships were divided into sections 1 mile square containing 640 acres. Sale price was $1.00 per acre. 4. Laughery Massacre — In 1781 the Indians surprised about 100 settlers and slaughtered them near the present city of Aurora. 5. Knox county — first county in Indiana, included all of present state of Indiana and parts of Illinois, Ohio, Wisconsin, and Michigan 6. organized territory — second stage of development of government; condition of land of Northwest Territory from 1787-1800 7. public domain — In 1784 Virginia deeded all Northwest Territory land to the U.S. 8. "Willing" — small gunboat built by men at Ft. Kaskaskia 9. St. Clair — first governor of Northwest Territory 10. Clarksville — first all-American settlement in the Northwest Territory, founded in 1784 and named for George Rogers Clark

Essay answers will vary.

Correct answers for the blanks.

1. Hamilton 2. Ohio River 3. Ordinance of 1787 4. section 5. Catholic 6. Vigo 7. St. Clair 8. Ft. Sackville 9. George Rogers Clark 10. Ordinance of 1785 11. Vincennes 12. unorganized territory 13. organized territory 14. state 15. Greenville 16. General Wayne 17. 1800 18. No less than 3 or more than 5 19. Clarksville 20-21. growth in population need for local government 22. Indians' consent 23. schools 24. slavery 25. grant of land

UNIT TEST 6

Correct answers for the blanks.

1. William Henry Harrison 2. Indian 3. John Gibson 4. 2 5. Knox 6. St. Clair 7. Clark 8. Dearborn 9. New Albany 10. Vincennes

Correct numbers and answers for blanks.

1. Shawnee, 3 2. Vincennes, 1 3. southern, 3 4. Clarksville, 3 5. Ohio, 4 6. 6500, 2 7. Nov. 7, 1811, 2 8. Battle Ground, 2 9. 1812, 1 10. Thomas Posey, 3 11. 13, 4 12. Corydon, 1 13. 19th, 2 14. 1809, 3 15. Pigeon Roost, 3

Correct answers for blanks.

16. east boundary of Indiana Territory 17. constitution 18. east boundary of state of Indiana 19. Corydon 20. Lake Superior & Canada 21. Tippecanoe 22. establish government 23. make treaties with Indians 24. survey land and grant titles 25. Dec. 11, 1816 26. Prophetstown 27. Harrison's Trail 28. Mississippi River 29. Tecumseh 30. Enabling Act

ANSWER KEY — PULL TO REMOVE

ANSWER KEY — PULL TO REMOVE

UNIT TEST 7

Correct matching answers.

1. honey 2. hickory 3. 1 million 4. Civil War 5. clapboard 6. wheat 7. blacksmith shop 8. potatoes 9. water was impure 10. maple sugar 11. buffalo 12. linsey-woolsey 13. deer 14. oxen 15. spinning wheel 16. puncheon 17. disease 18. wood ashes 19. blackberry 20. smoking 21. poisoning man's horse 22. axe 23. buckskin 24. ague 25. gristmill

Correct answers for the blanks.

1. Kentucky 2. Ohio River 3. barrier 4. boats 5. ferrying 6. southern 7. forest (trees) 8. clearing 9. farming 10. grow

Correct answers for blanks.

1. dried 2. tree bark 3. wood 4. raised 5. Methodist, Presbyterian, Baptist 6. rail fences 7. homespun 8. yellowroot 9. watch 10. milk sickness 11. salt 12. trees 13. water 14. rifle 15. fireplace

UNIT TEST 8

Correct answers and letters for blanks.

1. c, Corydon 2. a, 3 years 3. d, Vincennes 4. b, Ray 5. c, 1851 6. a, Whitcomb 7. c, Williams 8. a, Goodrich 9. d, Morton 10. b, Gross Income Tax 11. c, 1888 12. c, Mount 13. b, 1825 14. c, executive 15. a, 4 years

Correct answers for blanks.

1. Jennings 2. Dec. 11, 1816 3. too near edge of state 4. white 5. every year 6. Hendricks 7. Bill of Rights 8. prison camp 9. Noble 10. Welsh 11. Answers will vary. 12. Hendricks 13. Marshall 14. Ordinance of 1787 15. Answers will vary. 16. Republican 17. Schricker 18. Wright 19. Indiana Gazette 20. Potawatomi 21. voters 22. Morgan's Raid 23. General Assembly 24. Ralston 25. Internal Improvements 26. Joseph Wright 27. Glorious 50's 28-30. Corydon, Vincennes, New Albany

UNIT TEST 9

Any of the following can be listed:

1. Whitewater canal 2. Central canal 3. completion of Wabash & Erie canal 4. Railroad from Madison to Lafayette 5. Turnpike from New Albany to Vincennes 6. Survey of route from Jeffersonville to Crawfordsville 7. Setting aside $50,000 to remove obstructions from Wabash River 8. Survey for canal or railroad from Ft. Wayne to Lake Michigan

Correct answers for the blanks.

1. South Shore 2. corduroy 3. Whitewater 4. State Highway Commission 5. Weir Cook 6. Indianapolis 7. widewater 8. railroads 9. Wea Plains (Lafayette) 10. 1836 11. Madison & Indianapolis 12. Wetzel Trace 13. plank roads 14. Whitewater 15. 1850-60 16. toll 17. motor (cars, buses) 18. No. 40 19. traces 20. Wabash Trail 21-22. Lake Erie, Mississippi River 23-25. auto license fees; gas tax; Federal funds

Correct answers for the blanks.

1. 1831 2. Madison & Indianapolis Railroad 3. Madison 4. Vernon 5. Indianapolis 6. Monon 7. Ohio 8. Michigan 9. Michigan City

UNIT TEST 10

Correct matching answers.

1. consolidation 2. McGuffey 3. Vincennes 4. 1806 5. George Rapp 6. Board of Education 7. Caleb Mills 8. trustee 9. 1852 10. Owen 11. North Manchester 12. grades 1-8 13. Rappite 14. MacLure 15. kindergarten

College locations.

1. Greencastle 2. Franklin 3. Terre Haute 4. Indianapolis 5. Hanover 6. South Bend 7. Muncie 8. Bloomington 9. Crawfordsville 10. West Lafayette

Correct answers for blanks.

1. Webster's 2. Gross Income Tax 3. Asbury University 4. Ordinance of 1785 5. property tax 6. 7-16 7. Ball State University 8. Indiana State University 9. Harold H. Negley 10. Lutheran 11. Catholic 12. 1873 13. 1964 14-16. readin', 'ritin', 'rithmetic 17. parochial 18-21. Indiana State, Ball State, Indiana University, Purdue University, Vincennes University

UNIT TEST 11

1. Monroe Reservoir 2-3. Bedford & Bloomington 4. Elwood Haynes 5. Smithsonian Institute 6. Crossroads of America 7. steel 8. 14th 9. Ohio 10. northwest 11. Kokomo 12. corn 13. Allen 14. brick and tile 15. Whiting 16. Yountsville 17. French Lick 18. Madison 19. Ohio 20. natural gas 21. Tippecanoe 22. Purdue 23. 5 24. increased 25-27. natural resources; farming; manufacturing 28. coal 29. Gary 30. gas belt

Correct answers for the blanks.

1. was put there by nature 2. coal 3. oil or lumber 4. natural gas 5. limestone 6. natural 7. Southwestern 8. shaft mining 9. strip mining 10. generate electricity

Ten largest cities in order of size in 1980:

1. Indianapolis 2. Fort Wayne 3. Gary 4. Evansville 5. South Bend 6. Hammond 7. Muncie 8. Anderson 9. Terre Haute 10. East Chicago

UNIT TEST 12

Correct answers for blanks.

1. 1816 2. peony 3. cardinal 4. Indianapolis 5. tulip 6. on the Banks of the Wabash 7. 21 8. Crossroads of America 9. Hoosiers 10. 92

Answers for famous persons will vary.

Correct answers for blanks.

1. Dresser 2. 1917 3. Brown County 4. 19 5. Potato Creek 6. Wyandotte or Marengo 7. Clifty Falls 8. Wawasee 9. James Whitcomb Riley 10. Lake Maxinkukee 11. Maurice Thompson 12. Pokagon 13. Turkey Run 14. Lew Wallace 15. Soldiers & Sailors 16. deep blue 17. gold 18. Spring Mill 19. Theodore Dreiser 20. woodsman felling tree 21. buffalo running from forest 22. setting sun 23. 1816 24. 1830 25. Pigeon Roost 26. George Ade 27. Jennings 28. Sesquicentennial 29. Tarkington 30. McCutcheon

Indiana History

TEXT-WORKBOOK

By

Ardis Sanders
and
David McConnell

TABLE OF CONTENTS

© Copyright, 2001, Hayes School Publishing Co., Inc. Printed in USA. All rights reserved. The contents of this book are protected by the United States Copyright Law. This copyright fully protects the publisher and makes it illegal to copy or reproduce these lessons in any manner.

TO TEACHERS WHO USE THIS TEXT-WORKBOOK IN INDIANA HISTORY

This Text-Workbook is an instructional device and a study guide for use by teachers and students in classes in Indiana History. Since this book is a basic text as well as an exercise book, you should know the following things about it before you begin its use.

1. It is necessary for each student to have a copy of this Text-Workbook.

2. It is not necessary for students to have copies of other textbooks, too, because enough text material has been incorporated in the Text-Workbook to enable the pupils to get all the basic facts for each assignment from this source. This text material is given at the beginning of each unit under the heading of "Historical Survey of the Unit."

3. The Text-Workbook should be used as the basis for the course and the unit assignments should be made from it. The study exercise part of each unit furnishes an organized setup for the student's mastery of the text material. The study exercises are very comprehensive and appear in a variety of form.

4. A carefully compiled list of unit references is given at the end of each unit. This has been done to assist the student in further reading.

5. Tables of statistics and other valuable information are included in Appendix A, B, C, and D. Suggestions are given for the correlation of this material with that in the various units.

6. A set of unit mastery tests accompanies each copy of the Text-Workbook. These are in a separate booklet and will be found inserted in the middle of the Text-Workbook. It is suggested that the teacher collect these test booklets at the beginning of the course and keep them in her possession until needed. The pages of the booklets are perforated so that the tests may be detached as issued at the close of the respective units.

7. The Text-Workbook is very flexible and can readily be adapted to the amount of time available for the teaching of Indiana History.

SUGGESTIONS FOR USING THE TEXT-WORKBOOK

There are 12 large units in this Text-Workbook. In each unit, the assignment is represented by the content of the Historical Survey of the Unit. The members of the class should study this Historical Survey as the first step in the preparation of their lesson. If other books on Indiana History are not available, the Historical Survey in the Text-Workbook will provide enough material for an effective and comprehensive study of Indiana History in this course. If other books are available, the pupils should do further reading in them. On pages 5 and 6 of this Text-Workbook is a list of references which includes the most suitable publications which are available for the study of Indiana History. Specific references to these books are given at the end of each unit.

The questions which have been included in each unit under the heading of "Study Exercises" are intended for study-guide purposes. These questions have been carefully framed to call for answers which are as definite and as specific as possible. In some cases the correct answer may be stated in more than one way. The teacher should give full credit for any response which really answers the question correctly. The answers to the Study Exercises should be the basis for a class discussion of the important phases of each assignment. Practically all of the questions in the Study Exercises are answered by the text material in this book.

Each unit contains some "Topics for Discussion and Report" which will provide further topics for class recitation. Most of these topics will require reading in addition to the text material in this book. Some of the topics for report may call for rather extensive research from several sources. Most of the Units also contain one or more "Map Exercises" which correlate with the various topics.

The plan of the whole Text-Workbook provides for a very flexible course. The total amount of time which can be spent on Indiana History varies among schools. This Text-Workbook was arranged to take this into consideration.

Each Unit in the Text-Workbook should be assigned as a whole. The amount of time spent on each unit should be governed by the total amount of time which the school has to allot to that subject during the school year. No doubt each teacher will want to work out the exact details of allotting proportionate amounts of time for the reading of the references, the oral recitation, the Study Exercises, the special reports, and the other phases of the course.

TO THE STUDENTS WHO USE THIS TEXT-WORKBOOK

Every person is proud of his own state. Indiana is our state and we are proud of it. This Text-Workbook contains a history of our state and has been written to help you in the study of this history. You will be interested in it because it is about things which are familiar to you and to your friends. Each assignment is called a Unit. It will require several days for you to work out a Unit. Each Unit has a number of different kinds of study helps which have been put in the book to aid you in your work.

If you use this book in the way which your teacher tells you, and in the way which the author suggests, you will *like to study* Indiana History and also you will *know how to study it.* In order to get the most benefit, you should go at it in the following manner:

1. Look carefully at the title of the Unit so that you will know the general nature of the assignment.

2. Read the *Historical Survey of the Unit.* This is the Text material dealing with that Unit. It gives the important things connected with that particular period of Indiana History. When you use this Text-Workbook, it is not necessary for you to buy another textbook, too. However, if it is possible, you should do more reading than that included in the Historical Survey. Under the heading of *References* in each Unit there is a list of textbooks and reference books in which you may be able to find more complete information about your assignment. You will not be expected to read all that are listed there, but your classroom library, your school library, or the public library will have enough of these different books to enable you to have all the reference reading you can do. Remember that you should read the Historical Survey of the Unit in the Text-Workbook first but that you can prepare your lesson better if you do some further reading from these references which are listed. In order to save your time, the exact pages on which you will find the material for each Unit are given. If I were to answer the questions of just how much you should read on each Unit, I would say, "Read just as much as you possibly can." Each book may have something in it that the others do not have, and this "something" may be just the thing for which you are looking.

3. Answer the questions given under *Study Exercises.* These questions call for definite answers and they cover the important things in the Unit. They are given for the purpose of guiding you in your study. However, before attempting to answer them, be sure you have studied the Historical Survey of the Unit and, if possible, have read some additional reference.

4. Read the *Topics for Discussion and Report* and be able to answer these questions or make reports on these topics if you are called upon to do so. You cannot answer these questions very well unless you master thoroughly all the things which you are expected to read while you are preparing your lesson. Some of the questions call for rather long reports to the class. Each of these will require reading and research outside this Text-Workbook.

5. Most of the Units have one or more maps for you to complete. These are also study helps for you because locating places on a map and coloring the map to show certain things help you to learn about and to enjoy the historical events which you are picturing.

6. In the *References* there is a list of books suitable for the study of Indiana History. This list is rather long and it contains the best there is, but, of course, it does not include everything which has been printed about the history of this state. Each of you probably will be able to find other material which will be very valuable in the preparation of your lessons. Also, you may know of some older men and women who can tell you interesting stories about their experiences or the experiences of others in the pioneer days of Indiana. In different parts of the state there are a number of local Historical Societies and quite often these societies have collected material

of historical value and in some cases they have printed the most important part of it. If you have such a Historical Society in your county, you should find out whether or not it can help you.

7. You should read any good books of fiction which have a setting of Indiana History. Unfortunately, such books are few in number, but there are two or three with which every pupil should be familiar. If you do read such books you not only will find them interesting but will learn history in a way which you will never forget. Two such books you should all read are: *The Hoosier Schoolmaster* and *Alice of Old Vincennes*. *Alice of Old Vincennes* has recently been published in a new edition. Copies may be purchased from the Vincennes University Press, Vincennes, Indiana.

8. During all the time that you spend in the study of the history of the "Hoosier State" you should remember that the history of Indiana is only a small part of the history of the whole United States and that the things which happened here were largely influenced by all the things which happened in other parts of this country. That is the reason for the Historical Charts in different Units. As you study, you should constantly ask yourself, "What was happening in other parts of the United States at the same time these things were going on here in Indiana?" This will help you to appreciate local history more and also to better understand the history of the United States which you have studied.

If you will follow this plan which I have outlined for you, I am certain that you will thoroughly enjoy the history of our state of which you, and all of us, are so proud.

THE AUTHOR.

GENERAL REFERENCES FOR THE STUDY OF INDIANA HISTORY

(Specific page or chapter reference to most of the books in this list are found in various Units of the Text-Workbook.)

1. HISTORY OF INDIANA (School Ed.)
Logan Esarey
Harcourt, Brace and Co., 1922

2. INDIANA, ITS HISTORY, CONSTITUTION AND PRESENT GOVERNMENT
George S. Cottman
The Bobbs-Merrill Co., 1925, 1936

3. INDIANA
Thornton and Reade
Mentzer, Bush and Co., 1926

4. THE OLD NORTHWEST (Pioneer Period, 1815-1840) — 2 Vol.
R. Carlyle Buley
Indiana Historical Society, 1950

5. A HISTORY OF INDIANA (2-Volume Ed.)
Logan Esarey
W. K. Stewart Co., 1915 — B. F. Bowen and Co., 1918

6. A HISTORY OF INDIANA
John B. Dillon
Bingham and Doughty, 1859
(This is a history of the state from its earliest exploration by Europeans to the close of the Territorial government in 1816. It includes a general view of the progress of public affairs in Indiana from 1816 to 1856.)

7. HISTORIC INDIANA (Out of Print)
Julia Henderson Levering
G. P. Putman's Sons, 1910

8. INDIANA, ONE HUNDRED AND FIFTY YEARS OF AMERICAN DEVELOPMENT (5 Volumes)
Charles Roll
The Lewis Publishing Co., 1931
(Volumes I and II contain a complete general history of the state up to the date of publication.)

9. A BRIEF HISTORY OF INDIANA
Donald F. Carmony and Howard H. Peckham
Indiana Historical Bureau, 1947

10. THE INDIANA GAZETTEER OR TOPOGRAPHICAL DICTIONARY
John Scott, 1826
Reprinted from the Original Edition by the Indiana Historical Society, 1954.

11. THE INDIANA HOME
Logan Esarey
Indiana University Press, 1953
(This is a limited edition book of great value. A copy of it can be found in most public libraries in the state.)

12. THE STORY OF INDIANA
Ross F. Lockridge
Harlow Publishing Co., 1951

13. A HISTORY OF INDIANA LITERATURE
Arthur W. Shumaker
Indiana Historical Society, 1962

14. INDIANA
Prepared by direction of Governor Harry G. Leslie, 1930
(Contains a summary of different departments of the state government with brief historical sketches, and pictures of all the governors to that date. Only a limited number of copies were printed and additional copies are no longer available.)
Printed by State Board of Printing

15. THE LAND OF THE MIAMIS (Out of Print)
Elmore Barce
Benton Review Shop, 1922

16. STORIES OF INDIANA
Maurice Thompson
American Book Co., 1898

(The student should keep in mind that this book was written in 1898, long before most of the modern development had appeared.)

17. TRUE INDIAN STORIES (Out of Print)
Jacob P. Dunn
Sentinel Printing Co., 1900

18. INDIANA, A REDEMPTION FROM SLAVERY
Jacob P. Dunn
Houghton, Mifflin and Co., 1905

19. CONQUEST OF THE COUNTRY NORTHWEST OF RIVER OHIO, 1778-1783, AND LIFE OF GEORGE ROGERS CLARK (2 Volumes) (Out of Print)
William Hayden English
The Bowen-Merrill Co., 1897

20. HOW GEORGE ROGERS CLARK WON THE NORTHWEST (Out of Print)
Thwaites
(Gives a good account of Clark's conquest of the Northwest.)

21. INDIANA, A HOOSIER HISTORY
David Laurance Chambers
(This is a 48-page booklet issued by Indiana's Commission for a Century of Progress Exposition in 1933. Besides being a story of Indiana's early history and progress, it contains a reproduction of Thomas Hart Benton's mural paintings.)

22. PIONEER HISTORY OF INDIANA
William M. Cockrum
Oakland City Journal, 1907

23. The HOOSIERS
Meredith Nicholson
Macmillan Co., 1900

24. ECONOMIC GEOGRAPHY OF INDIANA
Stephen S. Visher
Appleton, 1923

25. WILLIAM HENRY SMITH
(The history of the state of Indiana from the earliest explorations by the French to the year of publication, 1903.)
Indianapolis' Western Pub. Co., 1903

26. READINGS IN INDIANA HISTORY (1914 Ed.)
Compiled and edited by a committee of the History Section of the Indiana State Teacher's Association.
Published by Indiana University, 1914
(This is a very interesting and valuable book. Although it is now out of print, copies of it are available in many libraries.)

27. READINGS IN INDIANA HISTORY (1956 Ed.)
Compiled by Gayle Thornbrough and Dorothy Riker, and published by the Indiana Historical Bureau, Indianapolis, Ind., 1956. (This contains some selections from the 1914 edition.)

28. PUBLICATIONS OF THE INDIANA HISTORICAL SOCIETY (Vol. 1-19)
These are a series of paper-covered pamphlets or books available to members of the Society when published; volumes containing from one to twelve numbers are bound in cloth and sold.

29. SONG OF METAMORIS
Milford E. Anness
The Caxton Printers, 1964
A story of a young Indian and his connection with Indian tribes in the state, especially the Delaware Tribe.

30. THE ANGEL AND THE SERPENT
William E. Wilson
Indiana University Press, 1964
This is the story of the New Harmony settlement in southwestern Indiana.

31. INDIANA HISTORY
    William E. Wilson
        Indiana University Press, 1966
            This is a general history of the development
            of the state.
32. INDIANAPOLIS IN THE "GAY NINETIES"
    High school diaries of Claude G. Bowers
        Indiana Historical Society, 1964
33. INDIANA IN THE CIVIL WAR ERA, 1850-1880
    Emma Lou Thornbrough
        Indiana Historical Bureau and the Indiana
        Historical Society, Indianapolis, Ind., 1965
34. INDIANA HOUSES OF THE NINETEENTH
    CENTURY
        Wilbur D. Peat
            Indiana Historical Society, 1962
35. PORTRAITS AND PAINTINGS OF THE GOV-
    ERNORS OF INDIANA, 1800-1943
        Wilbur D. Peat
            Indiana Historical Society, 1944
36. THE HOUSE OF THE SINGING WINDS, the
    Life and Work of T. C. Steele
        By Selma N. Steele, Theodore L. Steele, Wilbur
        D. Peat
            Indiana Historical Society, Indianapolis, Ind.,
            1966
37. JUST US HOOSIERS, and How We Got That Way
    Dale W. Burgess
        Unified Press, Inc., Indianapolis, Ind., 1966
            A delightful book of sketches dealing with
            the lives and works of Hoosiers.
38. SKETCHES OF LAKE WAWASEE
    Scott A. Egdell
        Indiana Historical Society, 1967

39. THE HEARTLAND, Illinois, Indiana, Michigan,
    Ohio, Wisconsin
        By Robert McLaughlin and the editors of
        TIME-LIFE BOOKS
            Time Inc., New York, 1967
                This is a beautifully written and profusely
                illustrated book dealing with the different
                aspects in the lives of the people living
                within the Heartland of America — the five
                states which were fashioned from the origi-
                nal Northwest Territory.
40. ILLUSTRATED HISTORICAL ATLAS OF THE
    STATE OF INDIANA
        Published by Baskin, Forster and Co., Lakeside
        Building, Chicago, Ill.
        Maps of Indiana Counties in 1876
        Reprinted, 1968 by the Indiana Historical So-
        ciety
            The maps and pictures in this atlas are
            quite interesting and instructive for stu-
            dents of Indiana History.
            This 1968 edition is a limited edition.
41. ANGEL SITE (2 vol.)
    By Glenn Black
        Published by Indiana Historical Society, 1967
            These two volumes narrate the work done
            in excavating Angel Mounds under the di-
            rection of Glenn Black. A very excellent
            reference
42. ENCYCLOPEDIC FACTS ABOUT INDIANA
        Published yearly by
        Public Information Division
        Indiana State Chamber of Commerce
        336 State House
        Indianapolis, Indiana 46204

SPECIAL REFERENCES

There are three publications of special interest to those who are studying Indiana History Each of these contains many articles of value dealing with all phases of the state's life and growth. Specific references to articles in these publications are given at the end of each Unit when available

These three publications are as follows:

Indiana History Bulletin—This is published monthly by the Indiana Historical Bureau with the co-operation of the Indiana Historical Society. It is sent without charge to members of the Indiana Historical Society and to public libraries in the state. Any other person may receive the *Bulletin* for fifty cents per year. Communications concerning this should be addressed to the Indiana Historical Bureau, 408 State Library and Historical Bldg., Indianapolis, Ind.

Indiana Magazine of History — This magazine furnishes some of the best available material for the study of Indiana History. It was started in 1905, and its purpose, as stated in the first issue, was that it should be "a magazine devoted to the preservation of matter that is of real value to the history student." At first it was a private undertaking. Then it was published for a while under the direction of the Indiana Historical Society. In 1913, it became a publication of the Department of History of Indiana University, and is now issued by that department in co-operation with the Indiana Historical Society.

Most public libraries and some school libraries in the state have either a complete or a partial file of the issues of this magazine. It is an excellent source of material for students who are using the *Indiana History Text-Workbook*. The magazine is published quarterly and is sent without charge to each member of the Indiana Historical Society. All communications concerning it should be addressed to the Indiana Magazine of History, Indiana University, Bloomington, Ind.

Indiana Historical Society Publications—These publications are a series of paper-covered pamphlets or books available to the members of the Indiana Historical Society as issued. Volumes containing from one to twelve numbers are bound in cloth and sold. These bound volumes are found in most public libraries and in many school libraries. They are available from the Indiana Historical Society.

UNIT 1
The Setting for Indiana History

HISTORICAL SURVEY OF THE UNIT

History is a record of things that have happened in the past. Usually this record is a written one although sometimes pictures can take the place of writing in a limited way. The history in what is now the state of Indiana goes back about three hundred years. Our small knowledge of Indiana before that time has been obtained by studying the rough pictures which some of the inhabitants made and from an inspection of a few household utensils which these people left.

The history of Indiana before it became a state in the year 1816, is the history of that part of central North America which has been called "The Northwest Territory". Therefore, in order for us to study the earliest Indiana history it is necessary for us to begin with a study of the history of the whole Northwest Territory which included more than the present state of Indiana. In order for us to get the proper understanding of what happened here in the days of the first settlers, we must get a clear picture of ten important things.

These ten things are as follows: (1) The location of the Northwest Territory and especially that part of it which later became Indiana, (2) The nature of this country and a study of the principal physical features of it. (By "physical features" we mean the kind of surface which it has; the rivers, lakes, swamps, hills, rocks, mountains, prairies, etc.) (3) The people who lived here before and at the time the white men came, (4) The reasons for the white men wanting to come here, (5) The reasons for the delay in the settlement by the white men, (6) The white men's life-and-death struggle with the Indians for the permanent possession of this region, (7) The contest between the English and the French for the possession of this territory, and the effect of those wars upon the settlers in the New World, (8) The efforts of the Americans to win these fertile lands from the English, (9) The way in which the pioneer settlers lived, (10) The remarkable growth and development of Indiana into one of the greatest and most important and most substantial states in the United States.

(The first five of these will be studied in Unit I. The others will be taken up in following Units. Number 10 deals with the history of a more recent time.)

The Northwest Territory

The Northwest Territory was composed of all the land which is now included in the states of Ohio, Indiana, Illinois, Michigan, Wisconsin, and a small portion of Minnesota. It was bounded on the west by the Mississippi River, on the south by the Ohio River, and on the north by the Great Lakes. The upper part of the Ohio River also formed a portion of the eastern boundary of this territory. (See the small map on this page.) Your map exercise at the end of this unit will give you an excellent idea of the location of this large tract of land. Of course, the name, "Northwest Territory," was not applied to this region until long after the first white explorers had come and gone. (This name was not officially adopted until the year 1787.) However, in studying Indiana history it is convenient to use this name, Northwest Territory, when referring to this particular section of the country at any time.

The Northwest Territory has been called "The Heartland of America." This is a very fitting name for it because this region is right in the middle of everything that our country stands for. Much of it is fertile farmland which produces immense quantities of various crops

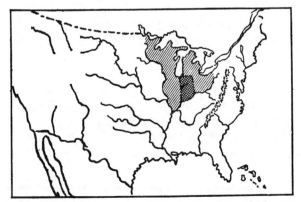

Indiana is in the center of the fertile area which was known as the Northwest Territory.

7

Some of the greatest cities of the world are within its borders. Its huge factories turn out a multitude of different articles which are shipped to all parts of the world. Railroads, highways, lakes, rivers and canals offer the best of transportation. The natural beauty makes the region attractive to people who live there and to tourists, too.

The rivers and lakes were very important to the Indians and to the early white settlers, alike, because water transportation was then much easier than land transportation. Besides the Ohio and Mississippi Rivers mentioned above, there were a number of other rivers of great importance. These were the Wabash, White, (two branches; these join in southern Indiana), Tippecanoe, Eel, Whitewater, Mississinewa, St. Joseph, Elkhart, Salamonie, Iroquois, St. Mary's, Patoka, Blue, Miami, and Kankakee; the Illinois and Kaskaskia, in Illinois; the Wisconsin and the Fox, in Wisconsin; and the St. Joseph of the Lake and Detroit Rivers, in Michigan. Of course the bordering lakes on the north, especially Lakes Michigan, Huron, and Erie, played a very prominent part in the early history of the country which we are studying. There are no very large lakes within the Northwest Territory, but there are many small ones.

The Wabash River is small in comparison with the Mississippi and the Ohio Rivers. However, it is regarded as the most beautiful river in Indiana. Wabash means "pure white" in Indian language and the French called it the Ouibache. It has its beginning near Fort Recovery in Ohio and flows eastward and southward across Indiana for about 475 miles. It then empties into the Ohio River at the southwest corner of Indiana.

The Location of Indiana and Its Physical Features

The name "Indiana" means "Indian's Ground." Indiana is in the very heart of the Northwest Territory. On its northwest corner it touches Lake Michigan and on the south it is bounded by the Ohio River. Its extreme length (on the western side) is 276 miles and its average width is 140 miles. It contains 36,205 square miles of land and 309 square miles of water. The large streams of the state flow across it in a general westward or southwestward direction.

If a person could have flown over Indiana in an airplane at the time the first settlers were coming here, the surface of the state would

have looked like a level green floor criss-crossed by rivers and dotted by small lakes. Actually, there are no mountains in Indiana but its surface is marked into three different sections which are easily noticed when one drives along the fine modern roads, especially if the crossing is from north to south.

Approximately two-thirds of Indiana is level land that can be planted to crops. The other one-third is hilly. The kind of surface which Indiana has is due to great ice sheets or glaciers which came down from the north and northwest many thousands of years ago. Many of these ice sheets were as much as 1,850 feet thick. These glaciers caused the surface of Indiana to be divided into three different regions so far as the physical features are concerned. In the northern part is the *Northern Moraine*

The surface of Indiana is varied. There are many small streams, most of which flow west or southwest.

and Lake Region. This lies north of a line running approximately from Fort Wayne, through Logansport, and then straight westward to the Indiana-Illinois boundary. This division line follows roughly U.S. Highway No. 24 across the state. North of this line the surface is level or gently rolling. There are many small lakes, in this area. Lake Wawasee, Lake Maxinkukee, Lake James, and Cedar Lake are the largest of these. There are several swampy regions, too, in this part of the state. One of these was the great swamp along both sides of the Kankakee River. Most of this has now been drained and the land is used to grow crops. A part of this region is covered by sand dunes. This is especially true along the south shore of Lake Michigan. This dune region is suitable for very little except recreation areas or parks, or possibly for large factories. Other parts of the *Northern Moraine* have a fairly rich soil that is suited for agriculture.

The *Central Till Plain* covers the central part of the state. Its northern boundary is the south edge of the *Northern Moraine,* and its southern boundary is a jagged, irregular line east from Terre Haute to a point about where the Whitewater River crosses the Indiana-Ohio boundary line. The surface of this *Central Till Plain* was ground smooth and flattened out by the ice sheet or glacier. The result was a strip of level prairie land extending entirely across the state. The land in this region is very suitable for agriculture and is very productive for many different kinds of crops.

South of this rich middle section of the state we find the *Southern Uplands and Plains.* The surface of this region is rough and hilly, although there are no mountains. The south central part of it was not touched by the glaciers. As a result, it has the most uneven surface of any portion of the state. Only a thin layer of soil covers the limestone and rock in the *Southern Uplands.* This limits the growing of crops to the more fertile valleys along the streams. In some counties of southern Indiana the limestone is very valuable and is used for building purposes. This part of the state has several large caves, two of which are well-known. These are Marengo Cave and Wyandotte Cave. Lost River is in this region, too. It is a stream which disappears underground and then reappears several miles farther down the valley.

There are three natural divisions of the land in the state, as shown by this map.

Almost all the early settlements made by the white people in Indiana, as well as those in the surrounding states, were made either on a river or on a lake. Quite a number of them were made near portages. (A portage is a strip of land between two rivers or bodies of water, across which boats and supplies had to be carried.) One important portage was near where South Bend is, between the St. Joseph River and the Kankakee River. Another was near the present cities of Fort Wayne and Huntington and was between the Maumee River and Little River, which flows into the Wabash River.

The Inhabitants before the White Man Came

Before going farther, we should make a brief survey of the people who lived here before the white settlers arrived. We do not know a great deal about these people, but historians have called the first ones the "Mound Builders." They got this name from the mounds or small hills which they built. Many of these mounds were in what is now the state of Indiana and traces of them still exist in almost every part of the state. One of the best known locations of these mounds is in Madison County near Anderson where the state has made a park known as Mounds State Park. The mounds here are large and circular in form. Another well-known location is near Evansville in the southwestern part of the state. This is known as Angel Mounds, and the 421 acres in this site are being kept by the state as a State Memorial. Other mounds, evidently made by the Mound Builders, are found near South Bend, Elkhart, Fort Wayne, Vincennes, Terre Haute, Brookville, Connersville, Mount Vernon, New Albany, and near other cities. Perhaps you know of "mounds" near your home.

Several of these mounds have been excavated (opened) and found to contain the remains of these early or prehistoric (prehistoric means before there was any historical record) people and of their belongings. Since there are no written records, these remains furnish us with our only knowledge of the lives and activities of the Mound Builders. One of the largest and most interesting of the excavations has been at Angel Mounds. Here, the site of a prehistoric village has been uncovered. Skeletons of persons, remains of houses, stone axes, cooking utensils, pottery, crude weapons, and many other articles have been found. Such articles which were made by primitive people are called artifacts. There is nothing to show why these people disappeared or what became of them. Perhaps further excavations may give us this information.

The Indians followed the Mound Builders. In fact, it is believed that very early Indian tribes called the Adena and Hopewell Indians constructed some of the mounds. There is nothing to show positively that these Indians were related to mound building, although they might have been. That question is still being studied. Our knowledge of the first Indians in the Northwest Territory is scanty, but we do know enough about them to give us a good idea of what effect they had on the early exploration and settlement of our part of the United States. A more extensive study of these Indians will be made in the next unit in this book.

Reasons for Delay in Settlement

The land of the Northwest Territory is the most fertile of any in the United States and we may wonder why it was not permanently settled by the white man sooner. There are several reasons why it was not. One of these reasons is that it was extremely difficult to reach the Northwest Territory. It is west of the Appalachian Mountains and these highlands proved a "natural barrier" which the white man could not cross for many years. The first entrances into this territory were by way of the Great Lakes, down the Ohio River from w e s t e r n Pennsylvania, and from Kentucky on the south. The people who came from Kentucky had previously come across the mountains through Cumberland Gap.

Another reason for its not being settled sooner — and perhaps this is the most important reason of all — was the opposition of the Indians. The Indians who inhabited the river valleys and the borders of the lakes objected to the white people coming in and taking possession of their native hunting grounds. The Indians resisted so strongly that immigration and permanent settlement were held back for many years.

A third reason was the wildness of the country itself. Most of it was heavily wooded and some of it was swampy. There were no roads, and so travel by land was almost impossible. Travel by boats was limited to the larger streams and this, too, was dangerous enough. Crops could not be grown until the land was cleared. In the prairie country, some of the ground was wet and swampy and it had to be drained before it was fit for agriculture. This clearing and draining was a slow process, especially when the workers were in constant danger from unfriendly Indians and when there were few tools and no machines with which to work.

A fourth reason was the struggle between England and France for possession of this rich land. These two countries were at war with each other in Europe and in the eastern part of North America for more than a century, and the conflict eventually found its way into the Northwest Territory.

STUDY EXERCISES

Write the correct answers in the blanks.

1. In order for us to get a good understanding of Indiana history, we must first get a clear idea of what ten important things?

    (1) _____

    (2) _____

    (3) _____

    (4) _____

    (5) _____

    (6) _____

    (7) _____

    (8) _____

    (9) _____

    (10) _____

2. What is meant by the "physical features" of a country? _____

3. Before it became a state, Indiana was part of what territory? _____

_____

4. The nickname for this territory was _____

5. Lakes Superior, Michigan, Huron, and Erie were in what direction from the territory of which Indiana was a part? _____

6. What formed the southern boundary of this territory? _____

7. What formed the western boundary of this territory? _____

8. What states or parts of states were later made from the land in this territory?

_____   _____

_____   _____

_____   _____

9. Name the three physical regions in Indiana.

   (1) _____
   (2) _____
   (3) _____

10. What does the name "Indiana" mean? _____

11. What two rivers form a part of the boundary of the present state of Indiana?

_____

12. What body of water now forms a part of the northern boundary of Indiana?

_____

13. What is the average width of the present state of Indiana? _____

14. How long is the present state of Indiana on its western side? _____

15. The kind of surface Indiana has is due to _____

16. What are the four largest natural lakes in the state of Indiana?

_____   _____

_____   _____

17. Name eight rivers that are wholly or almost wholly within the state of Indiana.

_____   _____   _____

_____   _____   _____

_____   _____

18. What kind of a surface does southern Indiana have? _____

What is the geographical name for this region? _____

19. Describe the surface of the central part of the state of Indiana. _____

What is the geographical name for this region? _____

20. Describe the surface of the northern part of the state of Indiana. _____

What is the geographical name for this region? _____

21. Which part of Indiana is best suited for agriculture? _____

22. What is a natural resource? _____

    _____

23. What two famous caves are in southern Indiana? _____

24. What is a portage? _____

    _____

25. Where were two important early portages in what is now Indiana?

    _____

    _____

26. Who were the very earliest settlers in Indiana? _____

27. How do we know what these people might have been like and how they lived? _____

    _____

    _____   _____

28. What are the "mounds" that are found in Indiana today? _____

    _____

29. Where in Indiana are the mounds that are best known? _____

    _____

30. What is an artifact? _____

    _____

31. What people inhabited Indiana when the white men came? _____

32. What were the three principal routes by which the white settlers came into the Northwest
    Territory?

    (1) _____

    (2) _____

    (8) _____

THE NORTHWEST
TERRITORY AND INDIANA
IN RELATION TO THE
WHOLE UNITED STATES

Scale 265 miles to 1 inch

ASSIGNMENT FOR MAP EXERCISE

The Northwest Territory and Indiana in Relation to the Whole United States

Show the boundary of the Northwest Territory by drawing a heavy black line around it. With a lighter line, draw in the outlines of the states which were made later from this territory. (You can refer to the small map on the first page of Unit 1 to complete this part of the map exercise.) Then write the name of each state in its proper place.

Locate the following. Do this by putting the corresponding numbers in the right places on the map. (You may use the map on page 165 for reference.)

1. Ohio River	7. Wabash River	13. St. Joseph River	17. Lake Ontario
2. Miami River	8. Mississippi River	14. Maumee River	18. Lake Erie
3. Kankakee River	9. Iroquois River	15. Illinois River	19. Lake Superior
4. Whitewater River	10. Kaskaskia River	16. Appalachian	20. Lake Michigan
5. White River	11. Mississinewa River	Mountains	21. Lake Huron
6. Wisconsin River	12. St. Mary's		

Show Indiana by coloring it red.

Locate Canada by writing the name in the proper place on the map.

Locate the Virginia Colony and the land claimed by it, *not* including the Northwest Territory.

Do this by drawing the boundary line and writing the name of the colony in the right place.

1. Approximately how far is it in a straight line from the eastern boundary of Indiana to the Atlantic Ocean? _____

2. How many square miles are there in the area of the present state of Indiana? _____ sq. mi. This includes how many square miles of water area? _____ sq. mi.

TOPICS FOR DISCUSSION AND REPORT

1. Make a report on the things which have been found in some of the excavations made at Angel Mounds. (See references below for material for this report.)

2. On a separate sheet of paper, draw a map of your own county. Show the physical features such as lakes (if any), rivers, and smaller streams. Describe this to the class, telling whether the surface of the county is level or hilly. Tell about any peculiar physical features which the county has.

3. Make a report on Mounds State Park near Anderson, Indiana. (See references below for material for this report.) What is the latest theory about the mounds?

4. Describe what effect the glaciers had upon the surface of a part of Indiana.

5. Describe the geology and topography of your area.

REFERENCES FOR UNIT 1

GENERAL REFERENCES
No. 5 "Surface and Rivers." (From a New Guide to the West, by J. M. Peck, 1936.)
Barce—The Land of the Miamis—Ch. II.
Black—Angel Mounds—Vol. I & II.
Cottman—Indiana—Map on pg. 9. Taken from the report of the Indiana Bureau of Statistics for 1898. Shows drainage system of the state and the altitudes. Ch. I.—pp. 1-3.
Thompson—Stories of Indiana—pp. 7-20.
Prehistoric Research Series—Indiana Historical Society—"Angel Site, Vanderburgh County, Indiana, an Introduction," By Glenn A. Black
Publication No. 115 of the Indiana Department of Conservation—Mounds State Park in Madison County.
READINGS IN INDIANA HISTORY (1914 edition)
Map on pg. 24—"The Rivers of Indiana." (Taken from a map by Preston H. Miles in the Report of the Commissioner of Fisheries and Game of Indiana for 1911-12.)
READINGS IN INDIANA HISTORY (1956 edition)
pp. 1-5.
Lockridge—The Story of Indiana—Ch. I.
INDIANA HISTORY BULLETIN
"The Angel Mounds and Related Sites in Southwestern Indiana"—Glenn A. Black, IHB, March, 1943.
"Excavation of the Nowlin Mound, Dearborn County Site, with Notes on the Pottery, etc."—IHB, July, 1936.
"Preliterate Cultures in Indiana"—IHB, Feb., 1934.
"Successive Stages of Occupation of a Notable Prehistoric Site, Clarksville Site"—E. Y. Guernsey, IHB, Feb., 1934.
"That Which is Past May Not Be Forever Lost"—Glenn A. Black, IHB, April, 1961.
"Archaelogical Report"—Glenn A. Black, IHB, Vol. 40, No. 11, Nov., 1963.
INDIANA MAGAZINE OF HISTORY
"Prehistoric American Diet"—Glenn A. Black, IMH, June, 1933.
PUBLICATIONS OF INDIANA HISTORICAL SOCIETY
"Archaeology," by E. T. Cox—Vol. 1, No. 8.

UNIT 2

The Indians in the Northwest Territory

HISTORICAL SURVEY OF THE UNIT

When the first white men came to the land which later was known as the Northwest Territory, they found the country inhabited by scattered tribes of Indians. For us to understand properly the events of these early days in this territory, it is necessary for us to know the names of these various Indian tribes and where each lived. Also, it is necessary for us to know how the Indians felt toward the white people who came into this land to trade and to make homes.

These Indians Belonged to the Algonquin Family

All the different Indian tribes in the Northwest Territory were branches of the Algonquin family. The principal tribes were the Wyandot, the Miami, the Shawnee, the Ottawa, the Delaware, the Kickapoo, the Chippewa, and the Potawatomi. Of these tribes, the Miamis and the Shawnees were the most important. The boundary lines between the different Indian

Each Indian tribe is identified with a certain part of the state of Indiana.

tribes never were absolutely fixed. There was a great deal of moving on the part of the Indian. In spite of this, however, each tribe usually is thought of as belonging to a certain general location, as shown on the above map.

Some Jesuit missionaries from France and a few fur traders from the same country were the first white people to come into this region.

When these men made their first appearances here, they found the country just south of the Great lakes inhabited by the Huron Indians. In 1649, these Huron Indians were attacked by the Iroquois Indians from New York and were so completely destroyed that as a tribe they disappeared. The Wyandots were the descendants of the Hurons. They dwelt along the southern shores of Lake Erie until removed by the United States government many years later.

The Miami Tribe Was the Largest

The Miami tribe was the largest Indian tribe in the Northwest Territory. The Miami Confederacy extended throughout Ohio west of the Scioto River, the whole of the present state of Indiana, the southern part of Michigan, and over Illinois southeast of the Fox and the Illinois Rivers. There were at least four divisions of the Miami tribe. One of these was the Twightwees, the Miamis proper. They lived in the region around the headwaters of the Maumee River. This is in the vicinity of the present city of Fort Wayne, Indiana, which was then known as Kekionga (kē kĭ ôn′ gà) and this is where the St. Mary's and the St. Joseph Rivers join to form the Maumee River.

The country near the junction of the Mississinewa and the Wabash Rivers, in the present Miami County, also was a great Miami Indian center. A second division was known as the Wea or the Ouiatenon. They lived along the Wabash River and on the prairie land below the present city of Lafayette, Indiana. The third and fourth divisions were the Piankeshaws and the Shockeys. They inhabited what is now eastern Illinois along the Vermillion River, and western Indiana between Vincennes and the Weas.

The great French explorer, LaSalle, described the Miamis as "The most civilized of all nations of Indians—neat of dress, splendid of bearing, haughty of manner, holding all other tribes as inferiors." It is said that at one time the village of Kekionga was a collection of Indian camps with a total population of ten thousand people. The Miamis could place in the field an army of five thousand painted warriors. They had many great chiefs. The one that is best known in history was Little Turtle. Some people think that Little Turtle was the greatest Indian that ever lived.

Because they belonged to the Algonquin family, the Miamis were bitter enemies of the Iroquois who lived farther east. Wars with the Iroquois and the Shawnees on the south, weakened the Miami nation. Other tribes took part of their land. Among these tribes which moved in were the Potawatomi, the Shawnee, the Kickapoo, the Delaware, the Ottawa, and the Wyandot.

Other Indian Tribes

The Potawatomi Indians originally were in possession of the land extending from southern Wisconsin into northern Illinois, around t h e south end of Lake Michigan, and across northern Indiana. In Indiana their principal camps were along the St. Joseph and Kankakee River valleys. Later, when the Miamis were weakened, they occupied most of the land north of the Wabash River. Many of their camps were along the Tippecanoe River and the prairies west of it.

The Potawatomis were known as fierce, murderous savages. After a large number of white settlers came to the northwest, the Potawatomi culture declined, partially because of alcohol abuse, and sank lower and lower until they finally disappeared as a tribe. The last of these Indians were deported from Indiana and taken to lands west of the Mississippi River in 1837.

The Chippewas and Ottawas never actually had permanent homes on Indiana soil, although they fought with the British against the Americans at many different times. The Chippewas lived in northern Wisconsin and northeastern Michigan and the Ottawas in southern and western Michigan. Pontiac, a famous chieftain about whom you will read later, belonged to the Ottawa tribe. The Delawares were descendants of one of the Indian tribes which was well known in the history of the English colonies east of the Appalachian Mountains. These Indians moved into eastern Ohio and some of them settled farther west in what is now southeastern Indiana. The Delawares kept a pictoral record of their

tribe called the "Walam Olum." It was made up of pictures drawn on sticks and tied in bundles. We have been able to learn much about Indians from these records, which were passed down from generation to generation.

The Indian's Attitude toward the White Man

The Indians resented the white man's coming to the Northwest Territory. For a period of almost two hundred years these Indians fought to keep the white people from making permanent settlements.

Many of the pioneers were killed by the Indians who thought they were fighting to keep from losing their land and their homes. In the end, the Indians were defeated and completely driven from this part of the United States.

Most of the Indians of the Northwest Territory lived along the streams and lakes and did little farming.

The Shawnees were the ones who fought the most bitterly against the westward invasion of the white settlers. This tribe originally had lived in the south but had moved northward through Kentucky, and finally had settled in the western and southern parts of what is now the state of Ohio. Later, the members spread into Indiana and mingled with the Miamis. Tecumseh and his brother, the Prophet, of whom we shall hear later, belonged to the Shawnee tribe. The story of the struggle between the Indians and the pioneers in the Northwest Territory is a long one and we can study only the main events of this bloody conflict. Most of these conflicts were local in nature but they tended to hold back the settlement and development of this terriotory.

How the Indians Lived

The Indians never built any permanent towns because they moved from place to place too often. Their camps usually were along the streams or lakes. Today, it is possible to tell where some of these camps were located because we can find stone arrowheads and stone axes there. The Indians had to depend upon these crude weapons for hunting and for fighting.

The bow and arrow was a dangerous weapon in the hands of the Indian who was skilled in its use. The shaft of the arrow was made of wood. It was then tipped with a sharp pointed head made of flint rock. The peculiar shape of this arrowhead is familiar to all of you. The tomahawk was something like a short handled axe. The handle was of wood and the blade of stone or steel. This stone-tipped arrow and a strong bow, together with the tomahawk, formed the Indians' principal weapons before they were able to get firearms from the white man. Arrowheads, many of them in perfect condition, can be found even today along the streams and in the fields where the Indians hunted. Many people have fine collections of these Indian relics.

The early Indians did not have any horses. Whole settlements of Indians often moved from place to place. When they did move, they usually went on foot. If the warriors of a tribe went

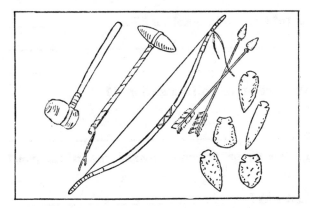

Indian arrowheads were made of flint, and the axes were of heavy stone.

very far while they were on the warpath, they most often used small boats. These boats were made of logs which had been hollowed out. Such boats were called dugouts.

Some of the Indians cultivated small patches of ground and raised some grain and vegetables. Corn was one of the principal crops. The Indians were not thrifty and did not store food or provisions for the future. As a result, they usually went hungry in the winter time. They were superstitious and believed in witch doctors and evil spirits. Disease, especially smallpox,

was common among them and killed great numbers every year. Because of the deaths from disease and from warfare, the population of the Indian tribes did not increase.

The Indian houses were very poor affairs. In fact they were mere shelters. Very few of the Indians had cabins. Most of them lived in rough tent-like structures with the sides made of bark or skins. A few poles would be placed in the ground in a sort of circle and then tied together at the top. The bark or skins were then fastened to these poles. A hole was left in the top to let some of the smoke escape from the fire inside. These houses were called wig-wams or tepees.

The early Indians used skins and furs for clothing. After they began to trade with the white men, they secured blankets and cotton cloth. The Indians were fond of bright colors and they used different colored clays and juices of plants to paint designs on their houses, on their clothing, and even on themselves. They had different symbols or painted signs to mean different things.

Indiana Names

Many places in Indiana and in other states of the Northwest Territory have names which came from the Indians. Also, many rivers and lakes have Indian names. The following is a partial list of these, together with the Indian meanings in English.

Calumet—deep, still water
Cayuga—place of taking out
Chicago—place of wild onions
Escanaba—flat rock
Illinois—men
Indianapolis—place of the Indians
Iroquois—"I have spoken"
Kalamazoo—otter tail
Kankakee—low, swampy country
Kokomo—black walnut
Manitou—supernatural spirit
Maumee—standing rock
Maxinkukee—big stone country
Michigan—lake
Mississinewa—much fall in the river
Mississippi—father of waters
Monon—to tote or carry
Oshkosh—the claw
Ouiatenon—round channel
Patoka—log on the bottom
Saginaw—mouth of river

17

Salamonie—blood root
Shawnee—southern
Tippecanoe—buffalo fish
Vermillion—paint

Wabash—gleaming white
Wawasee—full moon
Wea—abbreviation of Ouiatenon
Winamac—muddy fish

STUDY EXERCISES

Write the correct answers in the blanks.

1. Who were the first white men to come into the Northwest Territory? _____

2. These first white men found what people living in the Northwest Territory at that time?
   _____

3. In order to understand the early history of the Northwest Territory, it is necessary for us to know what three things about the Indians there?

   (1) _____

   (2) _____

   (3) _____

4. The Indian tribes in the Northwest Territory belonged to what Indian family?
   _____

5. The Indian family referred to in question 4 was unfriendly toward what other Indian family?
   _____

6. What was the largest and most powerful Indian tribe in the Northwest Territory?
   _____

7. What description did LaSalle give of the Indians referred to in question 6? _____
   _____
   _____

8. What great Indian chieftain belonged to the tribe referred to in question 6?
   _____

9. Who was a great chieftain of the Ottawa tribe? _____

10. Were the Indians of the Northwest Territory hostile or friendly toward the white men?
    _____

11. What Indian tribe moved into Indiana from Kentucky? _____

12. How would you describe the tribe referred to in question 11? _____
    _____

13. What two Indian chieftains belonged to the tribe referred to in question 11?
    _____   _____

14. There were four main branches of the Miami tribe. Name each of these tribes and give the principal location of each in the Northwest Territory.

Name of Tribe	Location
_____	_____
_____	_____
_____	_____
_____	_____

15. What part of the Northwest Territory did the Potawatomi tribe occupy? _____

16. Characterize the members of the Potawatomi tribe. _____

_____

17. What Indian village was located at the junction of the St. Mary's and St. Joseph Rivers?

_____

18. What effect did the Iroquois Indians have upon the Indians of the Northwest Territory?

_____

19. Where in Indiana did the Delaware Indians live? _____

20. What was the "Walam Olum"? _____

21. In what locations were the Indian camping grounds usually located?

_____

22. How do we know where these camps were? _____

23. What kind of transportation did the Indians who lived in Indiana have? _____

_____

24. Did the Indians live for a long time in one place or did they move often? _____

_____

25. What Indian relics can be found in Indiana yet today? _____

26. What were the principal weapons of the Indians before they had guns?

_____

27. What two ways did the Indians have of getting food for themselves?

_____   _____

28. What disease killed many of the Indians? _____

29. What did the Indians use for clothing? _____

30. What were the Indian boats called? _____

31. What two things kept the population of the Indian tribes from increasing?

_____   _____

32. What was the principal crop that the Indians raised? _____

33. Describe the construction of a typical Indian house.

_____

_____

_____

INDIAN NAMES. THE FOLLOWING NAMES ARE OF INDIAN ORIGIN.

Tell what each is and give its Indian meaning.

Name	What It Is	Indian Meaning
1. Mississippi	_____	_____
2. Chicago	_____	_____
3. Salamonie	_____	_____

19

4. Iroquois _____ _____

5. Calumet _____ _____

6. Wabash _____ _____

7. Saginaw _____ _____

8. Kokomo _____ _____

9. Tippecanoe _____ _____

10. Menominee _____ _____

11. Illinois _____ _____

12. Kalamazoo _____ _____

13. Wawasee _____ _____

14. Oshkosh _____ _____

15. Maxinkukee _____ _____

16. Mississinewa _____ _____

17. Maumee _____ _____

18. Escanaba _____ _____

19. Ouiatenon _____ _____

20. Manitou _____ _____

2. Look at a map of Indiana and make a list of other places in the state which have Indian names. These may be counties, cities, or townships. In your list, identify each place by telling what and where it is.

Place	What And Where It Is
1. _____	_____
2. _____	_____
3. _____	_____
4. _____	_____
5. _____	_____
6. _____	_____
7. _____	_____
8. _____	_____
9. _____	_____
10. _____	_____

In the space below, make a drawing of a typical Indian arrowhead.

LOCATION OF INDIAN
TRIBES IN THE
NORTHWEST TERRITORY

ASSIGNMENT FOR MAP EXERCISE

The Location of Indian Tribes of the Northwest Territory.

Use a heavy black line to mark the boundary of the Northwest Territory.

Locate the following by placing the corresponding numbers in the right places on the map.

1. Lake Erie	9. Tippecanoe River
2. Lake Ontario	10. Wabash River
3. Lake Michigan	11. Maumee River
4. Lake Superior	12. White River
5. Lake Huron	13. Miami River
6. Mississippi River	14. Scioto River
7. Ohio River	15. St. Joseph (of the Lake)
8. Kankakee River	

Locate each of these by a dot in the proper place on the map. At the side of the dot place the letter corresponding to the name of the place.

A. Vincennes	D. Kaskaskia
B. Kekionga	E. Fort Dearborn
C. Ouiatenon	F. Fort Detroit

Show the location of the following Indian tribes in the Northwest Territory by coloring with different colors or by shading with pencil. Place the names of the tribes on the map. Remember that the exact boundaries of each tribe are indefinite, so use your best judgment to show how far the settlements of each tribe extended.

Miami	Shawnee
Wea	Ottawa
Eel River Miami	Delaware
Piankeshaw	Chippewa
Twightwees	Potawatomi
Wyandot	

21

TOPICS FOR DISCUSSION AND REPORT

1. Find out and report to the class what Indian tribe or tribes lived in the region in which you now live. What happened to them?

2. Tell some true Indian stories connected with the region in which you now live.

3. Bring to class some specimens of Indian relics such as arrowheads, stone axes, etc. Display these to the class and, if possible, tell where the relics were found.

4. Describe a collection of Indian relics such as costumes, implements of warfare, things which Indians have made, or the like, which you have seen.

5. Describe the kind of fort which the pioneers built for protection from the Indians.

6. Make a report on some part of Indian life, such as "Indian Clothing," "Indian Homes," "The Food Which the Indians Had." You can find material for this report in your encyclopedia.

7. Make a report on the term "Indian Summer." Tell how it originated, what it means, and what some of the beliefs were concerning it.

8. Make a report on the life of Frances Slocum.

REFERENCES FOR UNIT 2

GENERAL REFERENCES

Esarey—*History of Indiana* (School Edition)—Ch. IV.
Barce—*The Land of the Miamis*—Chs. VI-VII. (This is an especially valuable reference.)
Cottman—*Indiana*—Ch. I.
Thornton, Reade—*Indiana*—Ch. III
Dunn—*True Indian Stories*
Levering—*Historic Indiana*—pp. 10-14.
Roll—*Indiana*—Vol. I, Ch. I.
Barce—*Little Bear*, (fiction).
Thompson—*Stories of Indiana*—pp. 21-30.
Winger, Otho, North Manchester, Ind.—*The Last of the Miamis*.
Compton's Encyclopedia
Encyclopaedia Britannica
Encyclopedia Americana
World Book Encyclopedia
There are many private collections and several excellent museum collections of Indian relics in the United States. The collection in the Museum of Natural History in Chicago is one of the most complete. This includes specimens of dress, implements of warfare and agriculture, and the handiwork of practically all the Indian tribes of North America.
INDIANA HISTORY BULLETIN
"The Historic Mississinewa"—Otho Winger, IHB, Feb., 1939.

READINGS IN INDIANA HISTORY (1956 edition) pp. 116-117, 236-258.
INDIANA MAGAZINE OF HISTORY
"The Red Man of the Wabash"—Elmore Barce, IMH, Dec., 1933.
"History on the Mississinewa"—Ross F. Lockridge, IMH, March, 1934.
"The Potawatomi Reservations in Benton, Fountain, Warren, and Tippecanoe Counties"—J. Wesley Whicker, IMH, March, 1926.
"Indian Captives in Early Indiana"—Logan Esarey, IMH, June, 1913.
Journal of an Emigrating Party of Potawatomi Indians, 1838. Conducted by Wm. Polke, IMH, Dec., 1925.
"An Indian Story"—IMH, Vol. 1. (1905), p. 19.
"The Indians on the Mississinewa"—IMH, Vol. 9 (1913), pp. 187-194.
"Topenebee and the Decline of the Potawatomi Nation"—IMH, Vol. 14 (1918), pp. 3-12.
"The Savage Allies of the Northwest"—IMH, Vol. 16 (1920), pp. 152-171; Vol. 17 (1921), pp. 50-63.
"Pierre Moran, or Chief Parish of the Potawatomi" IMH, Vol. 23 (1927), pp. 229-236.
PUBLICATIONS OF INDIANA HISTORICAL SOCIETY
"The Pokagons"— Mrs. Cecilia B. Buechner, Vol. 10, No. 5.

UNIT 3

French Explorations and Settlements in the Northwest Territory, 1643-1763

HISTORICAL SURVEY OF THE UNIT

Frenchmen were the first white explorers in the Northwest Territory. They came into this region before the English did and, consequently, France had the first claim on it. The English colonies in America were just as close to this territory as the French colonies were and the English wanted it just as badly as the French did. So, one of the questions you probably will want to ask is, "How and why could the French beat the English to this part of North America?" In this Unit you will find the answer and also you will learn what the French tried to do to protect this vast territory from the English.

Jesuit Priests Arrived First

So far as we have any record, some French Jesuit priests from Quebec were the first white explorers in the Northwest Territory. The beginning of their efforts probably was about the

The French wanted to control the rich fur trade with the Indians.

year 1634. This was more than one hundred forty years after Columbus discovered America. This shows how difficult it was for white men to reach the interior of the North American continent. And you must remember, too, that these first explorers were very few in number and that it was not until years later that there was anything like extensive explorations and permanent settlements. These priests came to this region, not from across the Appalachian Mountains which shut out the English, but by a much easier route up the St. Lawrence River and the Great Lakes from Quebec. The first place they located was among the Huron Indians on the southern shores of Lake Erie.

You may now well ask another question as to why these French priests were willing to endure such hardships and even to sacrifice their lives in this perilous work. To this there is only one reply. The priests were missionaries who wanted to convert the Indians to Christianity. They were anxious to establish mission posts so they might bring the Catholic religion to the savages in this wild and unexplored country. They labored in the face of untold dangers and with the greatest zeal without expecting any visible reward for their services.

Needless to say, the Indians did not at all appreciate what the priests were trying to do. The Indians did not want to give up their beliefs, but the priests carried on in spite of dangers. In the early history of the Northwest Territory, these unselfish men played a most important and never-to-be-forgotten part. From place to place they went in their long black robes, mingling with the Indians and at the same time helping to win this territory for their native country of France. Most of these priests are not even known by name to us today, but their work left a lasting impression and the importance of it hardly can be overestimated.

Everything went well until the Huron Indians were attacked by the Iroquois and almost completely wiped out in 1649. Most of the Indians fled from the Northwest Territory at this time and many of them did not return until much later. However, this disaster did not put an end to the priests' work, for other Jesuit fathers continued their explorations and visits to this country. Among these were Fathers Allouez, Dablon, Marquette, and Hennepin, who established important missions around the Great Lakes about 1670-72. Some of these priests probably visited the northern part of what is now the state of Indiana, but there is no record of any mission post being established in Indiana at that time.

Missionaries Were Helped by French Fur Traders

The efforts of the Jesuit priests alone probably would not have been enough to give France a very strong foothold in the Northwest Territory.

A French fur trader and hunter carried a gun and other weapons.

However, the priests were helped immensely by the French fur traders. In 1673, Father Marquette and a French fur trader named Louis Joliet set out in search of the Mississippi River. They started from Lake Michigan by way of Green Bay. From there they proceeded along the Fox and Wisconsin rivers to the Mississippi. They explored this stream as far down as the mouth of the Arkansas River and then returned to their starting point. It is probably true that they did not cross any of the land belonging to the present state of Indiana, but their explorations had a very distinct influence on the history of the Northwest Territory.

Furs were the rich prize which the French hoped to get out of the Northwest Territory. The French traders mingled with the Indians and traded for the furs which were taken during the hunting season. In several places these French traders established small trading posts. These trading posts became little settlements and in this way France was able to lay claim to the whole territory. The first towns in Indiana started in this manner and we shall learn more about these later. The English were not successful in trading with the Indians and so, for many years, it looked as if the French would be so firmly established here that the English could never get them out.

At every trading post there always was a Jesuit priest. The priests circulated among the Indians and tried to do what good they could. This combination of priest and fur trader was a strange one. The priests tried to Christianize the Indians. The traders, almost always were rascals of the first degree. They visited the neighboring tribes and showed them the knives, blankets, cotton cloth, beads, and trinkets that they could get for their furs. The traders' purpose was to get the furs at the lowest possible cost. Many times they gave whiskey to the Indians and cheated them unmercifully. The Indians could not resist the desire to trade their valuable furs for trinkets which were worth only a few cents and for whiskey. However, the work of the missionaries and the fur traders made the Indians firm friends of France.

Robert Cavalier de LaSalle

The report which Marquette and Joliet took back to Quebec inspired Robert Cavalier de LaSalle (or simply LaSalle, as he usually is called), one of the most famous of French explorers, to undertake to establish a claim to the whole Mississippi River Valley for his mother country, France. LaSalle came from a family of wealthy traders. He received a fine education in the Jesuit schools and considered becoming a priest. However, his adventurous spirit led him to give up this idea and it can be said that he did more than any other man to win the land in the interior of North America for the French. The French claims to most of this land were based on LaSalle's explorations. LaSalle made his first trip, from Montreal, Canada, into the valley of the Mississippi in 1679. From that year until his death in 1687, he was engaged in exploring expeditions in the country south of the Great Lakes and down the Mississippi River clear to its mouth. He is believed to be one of the first white men — some historians say that he was the very first white man— to set foot on the soil of the present state of Indiana. This was supposed to have been on December 5, 1679. At any rate, the real exploration of Indiana began with LaSalle, and it is not a misstatement to say that the history of Indiana began with him. Those who may have gone before him were scattered and the results of their explorations were feeble. Between 1679 and 1683 LaSalle made many journeys through Indiana.

The first of these journeys was by the way of Lake Michigan and up the St. Joseph River to a point near the present city of South Bend, Indiana. From there, LaSalle and his party took a portage across several miles of land to the Kankakee River which flowed sluggishly through swamp lands in a westerly direction. Following the Kankakee River to its

LaSalle claimed possession of the whole Mississippi Valley for his native country of France.

mouth they came upon the larger Illinois River and could continue on it to the Mississippi. The influence of the French along this route led to the later establishment of French settlements along the Kankakee River in what afterwards became the state of Illinois. On this trip, LaSalle was accompanied by Father Hennepin, a Catholic priest who wrote a good account of the journey in his *Description of Louisiana.*

Another route which LaSalle followed was from Lake Erie, up the Maumee River to where the city of Fort Wayne now stands, thence by a portage to the Wabash River, and down the Wabash to the Ohio and the Mississippi rivers. This way was one of the best connecting links between the St. Lawrence River and the Mississippi River valley. The fact that the French traveled this route accounts for the fact that they later established trading posts and small settlements at the present site of Fort Wayne, at Ouiatenon, and at Vincennes. It was from these explorations and these trading posts that the French actually came into possession of the land which later became the state of In-

diana before any other foreign nation could get a foothold there.

If LaSalle had been allowed to have his way, he would immediately have built many strong forts in these regions and in that manner would have kept out the English more successfully. However, most of these early Frenchmen did not want to make permanent homes anywhere. France was getting rich from the fur trade and so it was difficult to convince the French governor and the King that the interior of this continent should be fortified. At this very time the English were firmly establishing themselves and their families in good homes along the Atlantic seacoast of North America. But most of these Frenchmen in the Northwest Territory were roving hunters called *coureurs de bois.* They had no families and they roamed the forests trading for or robbing the Indians of their furs. Then they would dispose of these furs at a French trading post and return to the wilderness. They were as wild as the Indians, but they succeeded in getting the support of the Indians for France instead of England.

French Trading Posts

None of the very first trading posts established by the French in the Northwest Territory was on the soil of the present state of Indiana. Some of the most important ones were Fort Michilmackinac between Lakes Huron and Michigan (near the place now known as the Straits of Mackinac), established in 1669; Detroit, founded in 1701; Kaskaskia in lower Illinois, in 1695; Fort St. Joseph in Michigan at the mouth of the St. Joseph River; Cahokia on the east bank of the Mississippi River, opposite the present city of St. Louis. Kaskaskia was an especially important one and was on the east bank of the Mississippi River about one hundred miles above the mouth of the Ohio River. Fort St. Louis was built in 1683 near Starved Rock on the Illinois River.

As the French became better and better acquainted with the richness of this vast region south of the Great Lakes and between the Appalachian Mountains and the Mississippi River, they became anxious to build up a colonial empire there. Father Hennepin had explored the upper Mississippi River as far as the Falls of St. Anthony where the present city of Minneapolis is located. LaSalle had reached the mouth of the Mississippi River and had there set up a large cross and an image of the French King Louis XIV. By this, he claimed for France all the land drained by this great river. He called this Louisiana or the Land of Louis. The French found out the value of the rich fur trade and they had also found out that there were other resources perhaps even more valuable than the furs. So, in order to shut out the English, they planned a chain of forts which would extend like a giant T from Quebec on the east to the farthest limits of Wisconsin on the west, and with the stem of the T extending from the Great Lakes to the Gulf of Mexico by way of the Ohio River, the Wabash River, and the whole Mississippi Valley. The early forts mentioned above, as well as those which were established in Indiana later, were a part of this magnificent scheme.

The First Settlements in Indiana

These first French settlements were three in number and were as follows: Fort Miami, Fort Ouiatenon, and Vincennes. Probably Fort Ouiatenon on the north bank of the Wabash River about six miles below the present city of Lafayette, was the first. The exact date for the founding of this settlement is in dispute. Some records place it as early as the year 1717 and others as late as 1722. Although founded first, Ouiatenon never gained the importance which Vincennes did. No permanent town was ever located there and all traces of the old settlement finally disappeared. In recent years the old blockhouse at Ouiatenon has been rebuilt so that some idea may be had of the looks of the original scene.

Blockhouses, such as this one, had to be built by the settlers for protection against the Indians.

Fort Miami was important in these early days because of its location at the junction of the St. Mary's River and the St. Joseph River.

(This St. Joseph River should not be confused with the St. Joseph of the Lake River which flows into Lake Michigan.) These two rivers join to form the Maumee River which then flows northeastward into Lake Erie at the present city of Toledo. The early traders and settlers could come up the Maumee to Fort Miami and portage across to the Wabash River. Consequently, Fort Miami was known as "The Gateway to the West." This is now the location of the city of Fort Wayne, Indiana.

The probable date for the founding of Vincennes was 1732. The founder of this post was Sieur de Vincennes who was killed by the Chickasaw Indians in 1736. Although it was farther down the Wabash River, Vincennes soon became the center for the activity of the French in the central part of the Northwest Territory and it continued in importance

LaSalle and his men traveled by boats made mostly of birch bark and skins.

throughout the period when Indiana was a territory. In spite of the fact that it was a leading settlement, Vincennes, u n d e r the French, had only a small population. In 1769 there were only sixty-six families there with a total population of two hundred and seventy people. The early "habitants," as they were called, were a mixture of former French soldiers, peasant colonists from Canada, a n d hunters and fur traders. Homes were built and the little settlement was neatly kept. Farming was engaged in on a small scale.

The "habitants" were an easy-going lot and fun-loving. However, they were inclined to do much heavy drinking and sometimes their merrymaking became boisterous. These Frenchmen were very devout Catholics and Vincennes had a small frame church built in 1770, later replaced by the Cathedral of St. Francis Xavier — at which the whole population worshipped. The Catholic priest here, as in all French settlements, was a very important and influential person in the community and was loved and respected by everyone. The good work of these priests can hardly be overestimated. The lives of these French pioneers and adventurers must have been full of romance, but true accounts of their lives and work are very scarce today.

The English Gain Control

A review of the Historical Chart in this Unit shows what events were taking place

France had a chain of forts and trading posts covering the Northwest Territory.

in the eastern part of North America while the French were gaining control of the Northwest Territory. After Montreal was captured by the English in 1760, the French gave up their western lands to the English. Detroit changed hands from the French to the English in the same year. In 1763, the Treaty of Paris was signed and by this treaty France surrendered to England all her possessions in America east of the Mississippi River.

The struggle between the countries had been long and bitter. The principal cause for the contest in the Northwest Territory was the control of the fur trade. Although this territory became an English colony at this time, most of the inhabitants were French, and the English no sooner had taken possession of the French forts than they found themselves in another life-and-death struggle with the Indians who always had been friends of the French and enemies of the English. The history of these struggles is important to us because they form a part of the background of the history of our own state which was then a part of this territory. The outcome of this struggle determined that our surroundings would be English and not French.

STUDY EXERCISES

Write the correct answers in the blanks.

1. What nationality of white men came into the Northwest Territory before the English did?

_____

2. These first white explorers belonged to what group of people? _____
   They were of what religion? _____

3. About what year did these explorers arrive? _____

4. What purpose did these people have in mind? _____

5. Where did they first settle in the Northwest Territory? _____

_____

6. By what route did they come to the Northwest Territory? _____

7. What rewards did the Jesuit priests expect to get for themselves in return for their work?

_____

8. Who were three of the French priests who established missions among the trading posts in the
Northwest Territory? _____

9. What natural barrier kept the English out of the Northwest Territory for a long time?

_____

27

10. What was the one great thing that attracted the French to the Northwest Territory?

_____

11. What was a trading post? _____

_____

12. What were the roving French fur traders called? _____

13. What were the people who lived at the trading posts called? _____

14. What were some of the things which the French traded to the Indians? _____

_____   _____   _____

15. What was the main cause of the struggle between the English and French in the Northwest Territory? _____

16. By what means did the French plan to shut out the English from the whole region west of the Appalachian Mountains? _____

17. Who is supposed to have been the first white man to set foot on the land of what is now Indiana? _____

18. Name the three early settlements that were made by the French in Indiana. Give the location of each and the date of settlement.

Name	Location	Date
_____	_____	_____
_____	_____	_____
_____	_____	_____

19. Name six early important French settlements in the Northwest Territory outside the present state of Indiana. Give the location of each and probable date of settlement.

_____	_____	_____
_____	_____	_____
_____	_____	_____
_____	_____	_____
_____	_____	_____
_____	_____	_____

20. Which of the early French settlements in Indiana was the most important? _____

21. What place was called "Gateway to the West"? _____

22. What man founded the trading post at Vincennes? _____

23. In what year was a Catholic Church built at Vincennes? _____

24. France based its claims to the lands of the Mississippi River Valley principally upon the explorations of what man? _____

25. Trace the route taken by LaSalle from Lake Michigan through Indiana and then to the Gulf of Mexico. _____

_____

_____

_____

26. Trace another route which LaSalle took in going from Lake Erie to the Mississippi River.

_____

_____

_____

27. What two forts did LaSalle establish in Illinois, and where were these located? _____

_____

_____

28. Who was Marquette and why is he considered an important person in the history of this period?

_____

_____

29. Who was Joliet and why is he considered an important character in the history of this period?

_____

_____

30. What change in ownership of the Northwest Territory took place in 1763?

_____

31. Make a list of places or things which were named for characters in this unit.

_____   _____   _____

_____   _____   _____

HISTORICAL CHART EXERCISE

The Northwest Territory	1630 to 1699	The English Colonies	Write these events opposite the correct dates under The English Colonies.
Jesuit missionaries worked among Indians around Great Lakes.	1630		New Amsterdam became New York.
	1636		Fort Frontenac built.
Fur traders and missionaries mingled in this territory.	1643		Bacon's Rebellion.
Iroquois massacred the Huron Indians.	1649		King William's War ended.
	1664		Oldest American College (Harvard) founded.
Marquette established mission at Sault St. Marie.	1668		Massachusetts Bay Colony settled.
	1670		Beginning of conflict between English and French colonies.
Marquette explored Mississippi valley.	1673		First permanent settlement made in South Carolina.
	1676		Pennsylvania Colony settled.
Mississippi River discovered by Father Hennepin.	1680		New England Confederation established.
LaSalle explored Mississippi valley.	1681		Coming of French Huguenots to colonies.
	1689		
	1697		
The Northwest Territory	1700 to 1770	The English Colonies	Write these events opposite the correct dates under The Northwest Territory.
	1701	Queen Anne's War began.	Vincennes founded.
	1713	Queen Anne's War ended.	Mississippi and Ohio valleys came into English possession.
	1717	Governor Spotswood of Virginia explored Shenandoah Valley.	Detroit founded.
	1732	Charter granted for Georgia Colony.	Fort Ouiatenon established.
	1744	King George's War began.	
	1748	King George's War ended.	
	1755	Braddock defeated by French and Indians.	
	1756	Beginning of Seven Years' War.	
	1763	French and Indian War ended. Treaty of Paris.	

ASSIGNMENT FOR MAP EXERCISE

French Forts and Early French Explorations in the Northwest

Outline the Northwest Territory with a heavy black line.

Locate the following by printing the names in the proper places on the map.

Lake Ontario	Lake Michigan	Wisconsin River	Wabash River
Lake Erie	Lake Superior	Mississippi River	St. Lawrence River
Lake Huron	Illinois River	Ohio River	

Show the location of the Appalachian Mountains by placing XXXX's in the proper place on the map.

Locate each of the following by placing a dot and the number corresponding to the name in the proper place on the map. Then, put an X on your town or city.

1. Vincennes	4. Ouiatenon	7. Mackinac	9. Ft. Niagara
2. Ft. Duquesne	5. Cahokia	8. Ft. Miami	10. Crevecouer
3. Kaskaskia	6. Detroit		

Use a blue line to show LaSalle's route from the Great Lakes across northern Indiana and then westward and southward. With a short black line, show the two important portages mentioned in this Unit.

With a broken black line, show the boundary of the present state of Indiana.

With a red line, trace the route of Joliet and Marquette from their starting point to the upper Mississippi River.

Place a large red dot on the map to show the southern-most point reached by Marquette and Joliet.

TOPICS FOR DISCUSSION AND REPORT

1. Prepare a report on LaSalle's exploration of the Mississippi River or Marquette and Joliet's trip down the Mississippi.

2. Make a report on the founding of the trading post at Ouiatenon.

3. If you can, visit the old blockhouse fort at Ouiatenon which is a few miles below Lafayette on the north bank of the Wabash River. Describe it to the class. (This is not the original fort, but it is a restoration of the original.)

4. Make a report on the founding of Vincennes.

5. Read pages 102-112 in *Indiana: a Redemption from Slavery*, by J. P. Dunn, and make a report on French life in early Indiana. Or, from some other source, get information to prepare a report on the home life and conditions in the early French settlement at Vincennes.

6. Prepare a report on the exploration of Father Hennepin.

7. Prepare a report on *Tonty of the Iron Hand*.

8. Prepare a report on the fur trade between the Indians and the French fur traders. Tell what kinds of furs the Indians traded and what the French gave them in return. Find out if you can what quantities of furs might have been traded in one year.

9. Make a report on the history of Ft. St. Louis at Starved Rock.

REFERENCES FOR UNIT 3

GENERAL REFERENCES
Buley—Vol. 1, pp. 403-406.
Esarey (School Edition)—Ch. L
Thornton, Reade—Chs. II, IV.
Cottman—Ch. II.
Roll—Vol. I, Chs. II-V.
Levering—Chs. I-II.
Lockridge—*LaSalle* (World Book Co., 1931).
Lockridge—*The Story of Indiana*—Ch. II.
Thompson—*Stories of Indiana*—pp. 31-40.

INDIANA HISTORY BULLETIN
"LaSalle in the St. Joseph Valley"—Otto M. Knoblock, IHB, May, 1929.
"Indiana in Contention Between France and England"—Theodore C. Pease, IHB, Feb., 1935.

READINGS IN INDIANA HISTORY (1956 edition) pp. 6-13.

INDIANA MAGAZINE OF HISTORY
"Pioneers and Pathfinders of New France"—Jas. A. Woodburn, MH, Dec., 1925.

"Danger on Wabash"—Leonard C. Helderman, Ed., IMH, Dec., 1938.
"The Old Indian Traders of Indiana"—Chas. B. Lasselle, IMH, March, 1906.

PUBLICATIONS OF INDIANA HISTORICAL SOC.
"Documents Relating to the French Settlements on the Wabash"—J. P. Dunn, Vol. 2, No. 11.
"Sieur de Vincennes, the Founder of Indiana's Oldest Town"—Edmund Mallet, Vol. 3, No. 2.
"The Mission to the Ouabache"—J. P. Dunn, Vol. 3, No. 4.
"Sieur de Vincennes Identified"—Pierre-Georges Roy, Vol. 7, No. 1.

"Life in Old Vincennes"—Lee Burns, Vol. 8, No. 9.

"Early Navigation on the St. Joseph River"—Otto M. Knoblock, Vol. 8, No. 4.

"Ouiatenon, a Study in Indiana History"—Oscar J. Craig—Vol. 2, No. 8.

"The Correspondence of John Badollet and Albert Gallatin, 1804-1836"—Edited by Gayle Thornbrough—Vol. 22.

Occupation of the Northwest Territory by the English, 1756-1778

HISTORICAL SURVEY OF THE UNIT

In Unit 3 we saw how the first settlements in what was later called the Northwest Territory were made by the French fur traders and adventurers. We also saw how the control of this territory passed from the hands of the French to the English at the close of the French and Indian Wars in 1763. In fact, as early as 1760—before the end of the wars—the English soldiers had occupied Detroit. A little later, English garrisons were established in all the old French forts except Vincennes.

When these English troops took possession, there were only three white settlements in what is now the state of Indiana. There were eighty or ninety French families living at Vincennes; about fourteen families at Ouiatenon; and probably less than a dozen families at Fort Miami. Only a very, very few of these inhabitants were English. It cannot be said that the change in the ownership of this territory made much difference to the inhabitants of these small settlements at once. But grad-

The early white settlements in Indiana were few in number and were widely scattered.

ually the superior power and numbers of the English began to rob the French of the trade which they had been carrying on with the Indians. The surprising thing about all this, though, is the fact that the English were able to keep control of this hard-won land for only about twenty years.

The Indians Were Unfriendly to the English

When the Indians learned that their lands west of the Appalachian Mountains had been taken by the English, they were very much dissatisfied. These Indians had always been friends of the French and enemies of the English. By this time the Indians were very much confused and were suspicious of the white men, most of whom had treated them badly. So, it was only natural that they should do everything in their power to oppose or drive out the Englishmen. In this emergency an Indian leader arose and his efforts almost resulted in complete disaster to the English in the Northwest Territory. This Indian leader was a chieftain of the Ottawa tribe named Pontiac.

Pontiac was a very shrewd warrior. During the two years between 1760 and 1762, he organized almost all the tribes of the Northwest to drive out the English. This Indian uprising which followed is known in history as Pontiac's Conspiracy. Pontiac's plans were perfected in 1763 and he intended to make attacks on all the English forts and settlements at the same time. Detroit was the most important post, but the commander of that fort had been warned of the danger by a friendly Indian, and so Pontiac was unable to capture this stronghold. Had he been able to do so, it is likely that the English would have been driven out of this entire region.

Other forts did not fare so well as Detroit, however. A number of them suffered surprise attacks and their garrisons were killed. Fort Miami, where Fort Wayne now stands, was captured and its commander slain. Ouiatenon surrendered but no one was killed there. In a short time not an Englishman was left in what is now the state of Indiana. But Pontiac's success was short-lived. English soldiers crushed the rebellion during the next year and the Indians were compelled to give up all the white captives which they had in their possession. Pontiac was murdered by a member of his own race in 1769.

English Government in the Northwest Territory

At the time of Pontiac's War the English had not yet taken possession of Vincennes. There were several reasons, besides the hostility of the Indians, for the slowness of the English in coming into the northwest in any large numbers. One reason was that the King of England, by the Proclamation of 1763, forbade any American to settle west of the Allegheny Mountains. This proclamation was followed by the Quebec Act in 1774 which annexed all lands north of the Ohio River and east of the Mississippi River to the Province of Quebec for purposes of government.

Between 1763 and 1777 there was no official English authority within the boundaries of what is now the state of Indiana. By the Quebec Act of 1774, Vincennes had been placed under the authority of the English governor at Detroit. However, it was not until 1777 that Governor Henry Hamilton sent Lieutenant Governor Abbot to Vincennes to take possession of and to rebuild the fort there. Abbot found the defenses of Vincennes in a very dilapidated condition. He made an attempt to repair the stockade and to mount some cannon. He remained until January, 1778, and then returned to Detroit for a visit. While he was gone, events took place which started a change in the whole history of the Northwest Territory.

The Revolutionary War began in 1775. At the beginning of the war, the English who were in charge of the forts in the Northwest Territory tried to arouse the Indians against the American settlers who had been bold enough to venture west of the Appalachian Mountains. These Englishmen now carried on a profitable fur trade with the Indians. They were also accused of rewarding the red men for bringing in the scalps of American men and women. The fear of being attacked by the Indians caused the Americans from the colonies along the Atlantic coast to hesitate about going into the Northwest Territory.

George Rogers Clark Leads Americans against the English

Virginia was one of the leading eastern English colonies at this time. Quite a number of pioneers had risked their lives by going from there to Kentucky and establishing their homes in the wilderness. These early settlements in Kentucky were constantly being raided by Indian war parties which came from north of the Ohio River. The Indians of the Miami tribe in Indiana were some of the most murderous offenders. The English had three important military posts just north of the Ohio River. One of these was Vincennes on the Wabash River and the others were Kas-

The original St. Xavier Church at Vincennes was a small, crude structure built of logs set on end.

kaskia and Cahokia in what is now southern Illinois. (Locate these places on your map.)

Just at this time there appeared on the scene a soldier and a leader who was destined to become one of the greatest heroes of our country. This man was George Rogers Clark. Clark was born in Virginia but at an early age he migrated to Kentucky which at that time was a territory claimed by Virginia. In many respects Clark was a remarkable man. He was tall, strong, fine-looking, and well able to endure all the hardships of frontier life. In this wilderness region, Clark soon became known as a bold, fearless leader.

The continued Indian raids caused young George Rogers Clark to make a decision to do something to stop them. He believed that the best way to deal with the Indians was to raise an army of Americans and capture the English forts in the Northwest Territory. This would put an end to the encouragement and assistance which the English commanders were giving to the Indians. No one knows whether or not Clark, at first, thought of winning this Northwest Territory for the Americans in the colony of Virginia. However, before the plan had progressed very far, this became one of the objectives of the scheme.

In order to get help for his bold plan, Clark explained it to Patrick Henry, the governor of Virginia. The colony of Virginia already claimed a large part of the Northwest Territory, basing its claim on the original grants of land from the King of England. However, Clark pointed out to the governor of Virginia that mere claims to the Northwest Territory were worthless so long as that country was actually in possession of hostile Indians and British soldiers.

Governor Patrick Henry wanted to help Clark carry out his plan, but if you will look at the Historical Chart in this Unit you will see that in 1776-1778 the colonists were in the very midst of the Revolutionary War. In spite of this, the governor decided to offer all the assistance he possibly could. So he got an appropriation of about twelve hundred pounds in money for expenses and authorized Clark to raise an army of three hundred and fifty men for the expedition.

Clark promptly began recruiting men for his army. In this he was assisted by Captains Leonard Helm and Joseph Bowman. Recruits for his proposed expedition were hard to find and he was not able to raise as large a number as he had hoped to do. He and his little army of backwoodsmen started down the Ohio River from Pittsburgh in May of 1778. There were no regular soldiers in the whole outfit. However, all the men were well-trained and experienced in the kind of fighting which they had ahead of them. They took some families of settlers and the wives of some of the soldiers with them and continued down the Ohio to a place called Corn Island. This island was in the river near the Falls of the Ohio and the present city of Louisville, Kentucky.

Clark Captures Kaskaskia and Vincennes

Clark established his headquarters on Corn Island and proceeded to fortify and cultivate it to some extent. Here he was joined by a few more backwoods fighters from Kentucky. Altogether, there were about two hundred and fifty men. This was a pitifully small army with which to attempt the gigantic task of opposing Great Britain and of establishing American authority over even a portion of the Northwest Territory. The soldiers had no uniforms and they knew very little about military drill. The only weapons they had were their hunting rifles and knives. They were skilled in Indian fighting, though, and in living in this wild country. It is doubtful, considering everything, if anyone less courageous than Colonel Clark would have dared venture ahead.

On June 24, 1778, Colonel Clark and his little army left Corn Island. He had decided to undertake the capture of Kaskaskia first. It was the leading town of the Northwest Territory. The men went by boat down the Ohio River, which was almost at flood stage, to the place where the Tennessee River joins the Ohio. There they disembarked and started overland to Kaskaskia, which was 120 miles north. They chose this overland route instead of going up the Mississippi River because Kaskaskia was strongly defended on the river side. The men reached the outskirts of the settlement on the evening of July 4. Then they slipped quietly into the town and captured the governor who was asleep in bed. The surprise was complete and Clark's strategy had paid off. The British surrendered their strongest fort in the Northwest Territory without a shot being fired or a man being wounded. The French inhabitants of this little settlement were overjoyed when they found out that the Americans meant them no harm. They became very friendly to the Americans and many of them took the oath of allegiance to the American cause. This was the beginning of the downfall of the English in the Northwest Territory.

Colonel Clark now turned his attention to Vincennes, which was still held by the Eng-

One small French settlement was made at a river junction near the present city of Fort Wayne.

lish. He had hesitated to attack that place before moving on Kaskaskia. There was a fort at Vincennes called Fort Sackville and Clark had not known how large a force of English soldiers was stationed there. After the capture of Kaskaskia, Clark did a very wise thing. He cultivated the friendship of Father Gibault. Father Gibault was a French Catholic priest who divided his time between Kaskakia and Vincennes. Father Gibault informed Clark that there was, at that time, no English garrison at Vincennes and that Lieutenant-Governor Abbot, the English commander, was visiting in Detroit.

Father Gibault, a French priest, helped Colonel George Rogers Clark by supplying valuable information.

After considering this information, Colonel Clark decided to send Father Gibault to Vincennes as his representative. The French inhabitants of Vincennes, like those of the other settlements, had never had any love for the English, anyhow. So, they were willing to help the Americans, especially when they were advised to do so by the good Father Gibault. The priest called the inhabitants of the post together and administered to them the oath of allegiance to the United States.

Meanwhile Clark had sent Major Bowman to take charge of Cahokia, which was north of Kaskaskia and almost directly opposite the present city of St. Louis. There was no opposition to the Americans there. Then Captain Helm proceeded up the Wabash to Ouiatenon and surprised the Indian allies of the English at this little post. The audacity, daring, and splendid leadership of Colonel Clark and the courage of his men had resulted in the loss to the English of almost one-half of the Northwest Territory.

The English Retake Vincennes

When the news of all this reached the English governor, Henry Hamilton, at Detroit, he was very angry. He immediately began to take steps to regain what had been lost. It was now necessary for Colonel Clark to return to Virginia so he left a small garrison of Frenchmen under Captain Helm at Vincennes until he should return. Neither Clark nor Captain Helm knew that Governor Hamilton had organized an army of almost six hundred English soldiers and Indians at Detroit and was proceeding down the Wabash. When Governor Hamilton reached Vincennes, he found Captain Helm and one soldier as the only defenders of Fort Sackville. The fort, itself, was in a very bad condition and Captain Helm could not have defended it even if he had had an army. So he surrendered and Vincennes was again occupied by the English. The French inhabitants once more were called together and the oath of allegiance to Great Britain administered to them. Hamilton decided that the weather was too bad to allow him to proceed against Kaskaskia for the time being. His soldiers used their time in remodeling, enlarging, and greatly strengthening Fort Sackville.

Hamilton's spies and agents worked among the Indians to keep them stirred up against the Americans. This was at the end of the year 1778 and it then looked as if most of George Rogers Clark's efforts had been in vain.

Vincennes was defended by a crude wooden stockade and fort. This was known as Fort Sackville.

In the next Unit we shall see how Colonel Clark, with the utmost enthusiasm and courage, undertook to overthrow, forever, the authority of the English in the whole Northwest Territory.

STUDY EXERCISES

Write the correct answers in the blanks.

1. In what year did the French and Indian Wars end? _____

2. After the end of these wars, what country controlled the Northwest Territory?

   _____

3. What city in the Northwest Territory was the seat of government for the territory?

   _____

4. At this time there were what three white settlements in what is now Indiana?

   _____   _____   _____

5. What Indian chieftain organized the Indian tribes in an attempt to drive the English out of

   the Northwest Territory? _____ This chieftain belonged to what tribe?

   _____

6. This uprising was known by what name? _____

7. This uprising took place in what year? _____

8. What finally happened to the leader of this uprising? _____

   _____

9. What two English forts in what is now Indiana fell to the Indians during this uprising?

   _____   _____

10. Why were the English slow in settling the Northwest Territory? _____

    _____

11. What was the Proclamation of 1763? _____

    _____

    _____

    _____

12. What was the Quebec Act? _____

    _____

    _____ In what year was this act passed? _____

13. What effect did the Proclamation of 1763 have upon the Northwest Territory? _____

    _____

    _____

14. What two important forts did the English hold in what is now Illinois?

    _____   _____

15. After the end of the French and Indian Wars, there was no official English authority in

    Indiana until what year? _____

16. In the year mentioned in question No. 14, what did the English do to establish authority in Indiana? _____

_____

_____

_____

17. What part did the Indians play in keeping the American colonists out of what is now Indiana?

_____

_____

_____

18. What is the difference between the "English" and the "Americans" as used in this unit?

_____

_____

_____

_____

19. What territory was called "the dark and bloody ground" during this period?

_____

Complete the following paragraphs by writing the correct words in the blanks.

A. Between the years 1756-1778, the English colony of _____ claimed most of the land which was in the _____ Territory. The English governor of this Territory kept stirring up the _____ against the American settlers in the land which later became the states of _____ and _____. A young Virginian named _____ had a plan for stopping the _____ raids against the _____ settlers in these two _____. He appealed to _____, the governor of _____, for help in raising an _____. At that time the _____ colonies along the _____ coast were engaged in a war with _____, so Governor _____ could offer very little help.

B. George Rogers Clark decided to raise an army of his own. This army was made up of _____ _____, _____, and _____. The army assembled on an island called _____ in the _____ River near the present city of _____. Clark and his men then decided to attack the English fort at _____ first. The only weapons they had were _____ and _____. However, they were skilled in _____ and in _____ in a _____ country. Clark's army completely surprised the _____ at _____ _____ and easily captured the fort. This was on (date) _____

C. George Rogers Clark then decided to attempt to capture Fort _____ at

_____. After the capture of _____, Clark cultivated

the friendship of Father _____, a _____ priest who had

worked among the _____. Father _____ found out that

there were no _____ soldiers at _____. Then the

Americans, led by _____, occupied _____

without opposition. Clark also sent soldiers to occupy the English fort at _____

_____, on the Mississippi River.

D. When the _____ governor, a man named _____,

who had his headquarters at _____, heard how the _____

had captured _____ and _____, he was very

angry. He immediately sent an army down the _____ River to _____

_____ to recapture the fort. In the meantime, the Americans had gone back to

their starting place at _____ Island, leaving only _____ men at

_____. Governor _____ men had no trouble in

retaking _____. As a result, the land which _____

and his band of Americans had taken was again under the control of the _____

This was at the end of the year _____.

TOPICS FOR DISCUSSION AND REPORT

1. Why didn't the King of England want Americans to settle west of the Allegheny Mountains?

2. Why did Pontiac's Conspiracy fail?

3. Which was better for Indiana and the Northwest Territory, English control or French control?
   Give your reasons.

4. Why were the French at Vincennes friendly to Captain Clark and the Americans?

5. How do you account for the fact that the Catholic priests had so much influence with the
   French people in these settlements?

6. Give an account of George Rogers Clark's capture of Kaskaskia.

7. Make a report on Oliver Pollock and tell how he helped furnish George Rogers Clark with
   gunpowder and other supplies.

8. Describe the kind of weapons the men in George Rogers Clark's army carried. Describe the weapons
   that Indians might have used.

REFERENCES FOR UNIT 4

GENERAL REFERENCES

Esarey (School Edition)—Ch. II.
Thornton, Reade—Ch. IV.
Cottman—pp. 14-16.
Roll—Vol. I, Chs. VI-VII of Part I.
Levering—Chs. III-IV.
Thompson—*Stories of Indiana*—pp. 41-46.
Lockridge—*The Story of Indiana*—pp. 57-80.

READINGS IN INDIANA HISTORY (1914 edition)

"Clark Prepares for the Expedition." "Desertion at the Ohio Falls." "Capture of Kaskaskia." "Father Gibaults Mission to Vincennes." "Capture of Ouiatenon." "Vincennes Retaken by the British." (Taken from the George Rogers Clark Papers—pp. 49-59.)

READINGS IN INDIANA HISTORY (1956 edition)
Ch. III.

INDIANA HISTORY BULLETIN

"Captain Leonard Helm"—Bessie Taul Conkwright, IHB, March, 1933.

"George Rogers Clark, Hero of the Northwest"—Ross F. Lockridge, IHB, Jan., 1927.

INDIANA MAGAZINE OF HISTORY

"Francis Bosseron"—Janet P. Shaw, IMH, Sept., 1929.

"The Early Years of Lathrop M. Taylor, the Fur Trader"—Bert Anson, IMH, Dec., 1948.

HISTORICAL CHART EXERCISES

To complete the following chart, write these events opposite the correct dates under The Northwest Territory.

Quebec Act passed.

Clark captured Kaskaskia.

British recaptured Vincennes.

Pontiac's War began.

First English authority established on Indiana soil (Vincennes).

French gave western territory to England.

Clark captured Vincennes.

Write these events opposite the correct dates under The American Colonies.

First Continental Congress.

Declaration of Independence.

Surrender of Burgoyne's army.

Treaty of Paris; end of French and Indian War.

British retreated from Philadelphia.

Beginning of Revolutionary War; Battle of Bunker Hill.

The Boston Massacre.

Treaty of Alliance with France.

Committees of Correspondence organized in New England colonies.

Americans forbidden to settle west of Allegheny Mountains.

The Northwest Territory	1763 to 1778	The American Colonies
	1763	
	1763	
	1770	
	1772	
	1774	
	1775	
	1776	
	1777	
	1778	
	1778	
	1778	

The Conquest of the Northwest Territory by the Americans, and the Immigration to this Territory, 1778-1800

HISTORICAL SURVEY OF THE UNIT

In Unit 4 we studied briefly how Colonel George Rogers Clark made a heroic effort to win at least a part of the Northwest Territory for the Americans and how it appeared that his work had ended in failure. In the present Unit we shall see what further action this determined leader took and also see what some of the important things were which happened in this region during the next few years. In making this study it should be kept clearly in mind that during this period the American colonists were fiercely engaged in The Revolutionary War along the eastern coast to establish their independence from England. Colonel Clark was working for the American colonists against the English government.

George Rogers Clark Decides To Attack Vincennes

George Rogers Clark was at Kaskaskia when he received the news that Vincennes had been recaptured by the English under

Clark's men were backwoodsmen who were experienced as frontier Indian fighters.

Governor Henry Hamilton. Clark learned this from deserters from Vincennes and from Francis Vigo, a Spanish trader who lived in St. Louis. Vigo had been captured and held prisoner for a while by Governor Hamilton. After his release, he gave valuable information to Clark and loaned him money to help equip the French volunteers. Clark learned that Hamilton planned to advance with an army against Kaskaskia in the spring. It was then mid-winter and the land in southern Illinois was considered unfit for travel. In spite of the cold and unfavorable weather conditions, Clark acted with his usual energy and decided to "beat the enemy to it" by marching boldly against Vincennes at once.

The men of the garrison at Kaskaskia constructed a small gunboat which they called the "Willing." This gunboat was equipped with six small cannon and a stock of supplies. It was to be taken down the Mississippi and then up the Ohio and the Wabash Rivers to the vicinity of Vincennes. Clark planned to march overland with his soldiers and to meet the boat at Vincennes. He had but one hundred thirty men, but with these he left Kaskaskia on February 5, 1779, upon a journey which was to be one of the most remarkable expeditions ever undertaken by a military force. It was 160 miles across country to Vincennes. By February 20 the little army had reached the Wabash River. This river, they found, was swollen by rains and the whole country, as far as the eye could see, was a sheet of water. To make matters worse, the supply boat had not yet arrived.

Clark and his men were in a desperate

situation. They had no boats in which to cross the river and they were in constant danger of being discovered by unfriendly Indians. What was worse, though, was the fact that they were out of food. They constructed some crude rafts and with these and two canoes captured from some hunters, the soldiers waded, swam, and ferried themselves across the icy waters. For miles the men struggled in water which came up to their chins. Finally they reached dry land just a few miles below Vincennes. When they secured some food from captured Indian squaws, this put the men in a better humor.

Most of the French inhabitants of Vincennes were friendly to the Americans. The Indians of the surrounding country, however, were friendly to the English. In fact General Hamilton had been accused of giving a reward to every Indian who would bring in the scalp of an American settler. This caused the Americans to hate Hamilton intensely.

When Clark approached Vincennes, he sent a messenger secretly into town telling of the approach of the Americans. He asked the French people to stay indoors until the fort had been captured. All this time the English soldiers within Fort Sackville were completely ignorant of the presence of their enemy. Clark and his small army marched into town, surrounded the fort and then attacked it that evening. The next morning they renewed the attack. The marksmanship of the Americans, many of whom were renowned hunters, was deadly, and whenever a British soldier showed himself he was instantly shot down.

General Hamilton soon asked Clark for a parley. It is told that while this parley was going on, a band of Indians who were friendly to the English, appeared with fresh scalps of American settlers. Clark's men quickly captured these Indians and upon Clark's order tomahawked them within full sight of the English soldiers. You can imagine how this must have frightened Hamilton and his men. In a few hours General Hamilton made an unconditional surrender. The British flag above Fort Sackville was hauled down and the American flag was raised on February 25, 1779.

One historian in writing of this event, said, "The next day, February 25, 1779, at ten o'clock in the morning, Governor Hamilton and his men marched out of Fort Sackville between the lines of American troops, in token of surrender. Col. Clark and two of his captains with their companions marched in, hoisted the American flag and took formal possession, and with that act the soil of Indiana became a permanent American possession. In other words, that climax to a dramatic and heroic chapter may be considered as the starting point of Indiana history, for from the planting of American stock to the development of the state is a succession of steps, one growing out of the other."

The English never made any further effort to recapture Vincennes and this brilliant campaign of Clark and his army firmly established the claims of the Americans to the territory of Indiana.

The Results of Clark's Efforts

After the victories of George Rogers Clark, the region north and northwest of the Ohio River was claimed by the colony of Virginia. They called it the Illinois country. Colonel Clark left Vincennes soon after it was captured by his army and after his departure there was very little organized government in this settlement for several years. Most of the

General Hamilton surrendered Fort Sackville to the Americans under George Rogers Clark, Feb. 25, 1779.

inhabitants were French and they, together with the few Americans who were there, got along the best they could under the authority of the village priest and one or two influential traders.

The capture of Vincennes was one of the most important events of the Revolutionary War, although it was far removed from the principal scene of action in the east. It was important because it determined that the fertile valleys and plains north of the Ohio River and between the Appalachian Mountains and the Mississippi River would belong to America and not to England. It was important, too, because it partially checked the annoying raids of Indians and hence encouraged settlers to come into this region in greater numbers.

A title to this land was not secured without some severe setbacks to the American settlers. The powerful Indian tribes that inhabited this part of the Northwest Territory were still unfriendly to the Americans even after Clark's victory at Vincennes. Clark planned an attack on the English stronghold of Detroit during the Revolutionary War. He was prevented from making this attack, though, because he had difficulty in raising an army, and because several small battles with the Indians turned into disasters for the Americans.

One of these skirmishes was in 1780 near the present site of Michigan City, Indiana.

A beautiful memorial has been erected at Vincennes to the memory of George Rogers Clark.

Here a small band of Americans were routed by the Indians. In another small but bitter battle a little band of men led by Colonel Auguste LaBalme were all killed by Indians led by Little Turtle of the Miami tribe. Little Turtle (Little Turtle's Indian name was Me-she-kin-no-quah) later became a chief and caused the Americans a great deal of trouble.

One of the most disastrous blows that the settlers of Indiana suffered from the Indians at this time took place where a small stream called Laughery (sometimes spelled Lochry) Creek flows into the Ohio River near the present city of Aurora. There, in 1781, Colonel **Laughrey, (sometimes spelled Lochry)** with about one hundred men was surprised by the Indians. Laughery and about one-half of his force were killed. In spite of events such as Laughery's Massacre, General Clark's efforts against the Indians checked their raids and encouraged settlers to come into this region **in greater numbers.**

Clark Rewarded and Honored for His Services

George Rogers Clark was only thirty-one years old when the Revolutionary War ended. Yet, at that early age he had done more than any other one man to win the Northwest Territory for the United States. Money for his soldiers and for his equipment was always scarce. While at Fort Kaskaskia, before his march to Vincennes in 1779, he borrowed money for his army on his own personal security. He expected that the Virginia Colony would pay him back. However, Virginia did not pay this debt and General Clark was stripped of most of his possessions to pay it.

The Virginia Colony did keep its promise to give General Clark and his men a large grant of land in southern Indiana (approximately 150,000 acres) as a reward for their services. The present Clark County in Indiana is a part of that land. The town of Clarksville was founded in 1784, and was the first all-American settlement in the Northwest Territory. George Rogers Clark afterward lived on this land. These years of his life were full of sorrow. His health was failing and he was almost in poverty. Later, he suffered a stroke of paralysis and died February, 1818, at the age of sixty-six, a pauper.

Today, a marker stands near the spot where Clark lived, and bears this inscription which pays tribute to this great hero: "George Rogers Clark, 1752-1818. Near this site stood the home of General George Rogers Clark, Pioneer, Soldier - Patriot - Conqueror of the Northwest Territory, who with dauntless heroism during the Revolutionary War, invaded the enemy territory, captured the posts of Kaskaskia and Vincennes, and won for the United States the Empire Northwest of the Ohio River."

In later years the true value of the work of George Rogers Clark was appreciated more than it was during his lifetime. One hundred fifty years after the capture of Vincennes, provision was made to recognize the importance of Clark's thrilling victory at Vincennes. To do that, the state of Indiana and the government of the United States, together, erected a George Rogers Clark Memorial at Vincennes. This memorial building is located on the site of the old Fort Sackville, overlooking the Wabash River. The memorial grounds are in the form of a park and plaza surrounding and forming the setting for the building. The Congress of the United States appropriated $1,750,000 for this project which has proved to be an imposing memorial to the man who saved the Northwest Territory for the United States. It was formally dedicated in June, 1936.

Government of the Northwest Territory

In 1784, Virginia deeded all her land in the Northwest Territory to the government of the United States. This became known as the public domain. (Recall from your study of American History the land cession of the different states to the Federal government.) Soon after that, a law called the Land Ordinance of 1785 was passed by Congress. This Ordinance provided that the land ceded to the government should be surveyed and divided into townships six miles square (36 square miles). These townships were to be used for surveying and locating land. (See Supplementary Exercise No. 1 in Appendix A, page 164.) These townships were further divided into sections one mile square, each section containing 640 acres. The minimum sale price of this land was set at $1.00 per acre. Section number 16 of each township was set aside for the benefit of the public schools.

Any part of a country which is being newly settled goes through three stages or steps in the development of its government. The land of the Northwest Territory, including that which later became smaller territories and states, went through these three different steps. These steps were as follows:

(1) *Unorganized Territory.* This was the condition of the Northwest Territory (including that part which later became Indiana)

This monument stands on ground which was given to Clark as a reward for his services.

from the time the Americans took charge of it in 1779, until the Ordinance of 1787 was passed by Congress. This Ordinance of 1787 provided for a form of government and the territory then proceeded into the next stage, that of (2) an *Organized Territory.* This was the condition of all the land of the Northwest Territory from 1787 to 1800. (The Unit you are now studying covers this period.) In 1800, Indiana was separated from the remainder of the Northwest Territory and became an Organized Territory (Indiana Territory) of its own. (Unit 6 in this book.) It remained as the Organized Territory of Indiana from 1800 to 1816, and then passed to the third step, that of (3) a *State.* The state government was set up in 1816 and has continued until the present. (Unit 8 in this book.)

In 1787, the famous Ordinance of 1787 was drawn up and adopted by Congress as a sort of Constitution for the governing of the Northwest Territory. This territory, as we have already learned, included what was later to become the states of Ohio, Michigan, Indiana, Illinois, Wisconsin, and a small part of Minnesota. In many ways this Ordinance of 1787 was one of the most remarkable documents of its kind that ever has been written. The people who live in Indiana today are affected by the provisions of this Ordinance. One of the sections of the Ordinance of 1787 declared that slavery should forever be prohibited in the Northwest Territory. At later times, several efforts were made to repeal this provision or to modify it so that slavery could be introduced, but such efforts never were successful. Except for an individual case here and there, there never has been any slavery in the Northwest Territory. Freedom of speech and freedom of religion were guaranteed to all inhabitants and these rights have been maintained to the present day. Education and public schools were encouraged. The section of land which had been set aside in each township for educational purposes was to be held by the state and the income from it used for the schools, or the land was to be sold and the money invested so it would provide an income for the schools. Most of this land was sold many years ago when the price for land was low, and as a result the schools did not benefit as much by it as they would have if the land had been held longer. However, the encouragement given to public education was of far-reaching importance.

Another provision of the Ordinance stated that the lands of the Indians should never be taken away from them without their consent. This accounts for the fact that all later additions of Indian land were acquired by treaty with the tribes that claimed it.

The Ordinance of 1787 provided for a government of the Territory, presided over by a governor, a secretary, and three judges, all to be appointed by Congress. After 1789, these officers were to be appointed by the President. When the population of the Territory had grown to five thousand people, the voters had a right to elect a legislature. There were to be made out of this territory not less than three nor more than five states. Each was to be admitted to the Union as a state as soon as it had sixty thousand inhabitants. General Arthur St. Clair was appointed first governor of the Northwest Territory, and the seat of the first territorial government was at Marietta (Ohio). In June, 1790, the first county in Indiana was created. It was named Knox County and included all the present state of Indiana and parts of the states of Wisconsin, Illinois, Ohio and Michigan.

Trouble with the Indians

After the Revolutionary War, England did not give up all the forts in America as she was supposed to do. Some English soldiers remained at Detroit and at other posts in the vicinity of the Great Lakes, and these English constantly urged the Indians of that region to attack the American settlements. The Indians became increasingly bold and the many raids which the Indians made upon these settlements in Ohio, Indiana, and even in Kentucky made the life there a hazardous one for the pioneers. Finally the Indians organized under a Miami chief named Little Turtle, who has been mentioned before, and decided to make a united effort to drive out or kill all the American settlers. The United States had to send several armies against Little Turtle and his followers before this danger was removed.

The first of these armies was led by General Harmar. In the fall of 1790, he marched with his army from Fort Washington where Cincinnati now stands and soon reached the Indian town of Kekionga at the junction of the St. Mary's and St. Joseph rivers. The army found this town deserted by the Indians, so the soldiers plundered it and destroyed it. A few days later Harmar's army was ambushed and badly beaten by the Indians led by Little Turtle.

The next year. 1791, General Arthur St. Clair, then governor of the Northwest Territory, led another army against the Indians. This army was made up mostly of volunteers and was poorly organized and disciplined. Before daylight on November 4, 1791, the Indians again led by Little Turtle attacked St. Clair's army and utterly routed it. This took place near the present town of Fort Recovery, Ohio. It was the worst defeat that the Indians ever inflicted upon the Americans. General St. Clair, who was old and sick at this time, was not blamed too much for his defeat and he was allowed to continue as Govenor of the Northwest Territory. After these two disasters there was an immediate increase of Indian raids all along the borders. It looked as if the Indians might be entirely successful in driving out the Americans.

They might have been successful if it had not been for General Anthony (Mad Anthony)

Little Turtle was a famous Indian chieftain of the Miami tribe.

Wayne. President Washington sent him to organize an army and crush the Indians in the Northwest Territory. General Wayne chose some very good officers for his army. Among these were William Henry Harrison, William Clark, brother of George Rogers Clark, General James Wilkinson, and General Thomas Posey. Wayne then recruited an army and gave the soldiers thorough drilling in Indian warfare. He brought his army down from the vicinity of Pittsburgh, and in October of 1793 he moved up the same trail that had been so unlucky for Generals Harmar and St. Clair. Through the winter and the next summer there were minor engagements with the Indians. Little Turtle found out, however, that General Wayne knew how to fight.

The real battle came on August 20, 1794,

at Fallen Timbers, a place along the Maumee River not far from the present city of Toledo in northwestern Ohio. The Indians were completely defeated and many of them were killed. The victory was a decisive one for General Wayne. The great Miami Indian confederacy was shattered. The Miami tribe was scattered and the power of these Indians was ended. Acting upon President Washington's orders, General Wayne built a fort near where the business district of Fort Wayne now stands. The present city of Fort Wayne, one of the largest in Indiana, was named for Anthony Wayne. The battle of Fallen Timbers was not fought on Indiana soil but it is very important in Indiana history because of the effect which it had on both the Indians and the white settlers of our state.

In 1795, General Wayne made a very important treaty with the Indians. This is known as the Treaty of Greenville because the meeting was held near the town of Greenville, Ohio. Little Turtle, the Miami chieftain, signed the treaty for the Indians. By the terms of this treaty, all of Ohio and a part of eastern Indiana was opened for settlement by the Americans. The Indians rather faithfully respected this treaty and for several years the dangers from Indian uprisings along the frontier were removed. Little Turtle, himself, never engaged in war again and spent the remaining years of his life trying to improve the conditions of the members of his tribe.

Indiana Separated from the Northwest Territory

Immigration to the Northwest Territory then increased from year to year. Most of the settlers came in by way of the Ohio River and consequently most of the early settlements were stretched out along its length. Marietta, established in 1788, was one of the important places, and Cincinnati was settled a few years later.

The size of the Northwest Territory very soon made it impossible for the judges to hold court at such widely separated places as Marietta, Cincinnati, Kaskaskia, Detroit, and Vincennes, and the result was a government which was not very effective in the scattered settlements. People realized that this vast territory must be divided. In 1799, the territorial legislature elected William Henry Harrison as a delegate to Congress and he was instructed to make every effort to have the territory divided. The result of this was a law, passed on May 7, 1800, which made Indiana a separate territory. This completes our study of the Northwest Territory as a whole and from this time on we will give our attention to the history of that part of it which was designated as "Indiana."

STUDY EXERCISES

Write the correct answers in the blanks.

1. What great war was going on in America in 1778 and why? _____

   _____

2. In 1778 what was the most important town in what is now the state of Indiana?

   _____

3. Fort Sackville was located in what town? _____

4. In 1778, most of the inhabitants of the land which was later called Indiana were of what nationality? _____

5. Who was Henry Hamilton? _____

6. Where was George Rogers Clark when he heard that Vincennes had been recaptured by the enemy? _____

7. Who was Francis Vigo? _____ In what two ways did this man help George Rogers Clark? _____

   _____

47

8. What did Colonel Clark plan to do after he heard the English had recaptured Ft. Sackville? _____

9. What hardships did Clark and his men have to face in getting to Vincennes? _____ _____

10. How far was it from Kaskaskia to Vincennes? _____

11. How many men did Colonel Clark have in his army? _____

12. Why wasn't the Virginia Colony able to give Colonel Clark more help? _____ _____

13. By what means did Colonel Clark attempt to send his supplies to Vincennes? _____

14. What was the name of the gunboat the men built? _____

15. What river formed a barrier for Colonel Clark's army before it reached Vincennes? _____

16. Were the Indians around Vincennes friendly or unfriendly to the Americans? _____

17. Why did the Americans hate the English governor of the Northwest Territory so intensely? _____ _____

18. When Colonel Clark demanded that the English at Ft. Sackville surrender, what did the English general do? _____ What made the English general so afraid of Clark and his men? _____ _____

19. What was the exact date of the happening mentioned in question No. 18? _____ _____

20. What was the main reason for the importance of the surrender of Vincennes by the English to the Americans? _____ _____ _____

21. The region which Clark captured was called what? _____

22. Why didn't Clark attack Detroit as he had planned? _____

23. What was Laughery's Massacre? _____ _____

24. How did the Virginia Colony cause George Rogers Clark great personal financial loss? _____ _____ _____

25. In what way was George Rogers Clark directly rewarded for his military service? _____ _____ _____

26. In what two places have a monument and a memorial been erected in honor of George Rogers Clark? _____ and _____

27. How did the Virginia Colony dispose of its claim to the Northwest Territory in 1784? _____
_____

28. After 1784, this land in the Northwest Territory was referred to by what term? _____
_____

29. What is meant by the term asked for in question No. 28? _____
_____
_____

30. What were the three steps which a new country, such as the Northwest Territory, would go through in organizing its government?

    (1) _____

    (2) _____

    (3) _____

31. What was the first all-American town in the Northwest Territory? _____

32. How many states were later made from the land of the Northwest Territory? _____

33. Why did the settlers in what is now the state of Indiana think that the Northwest Territory should be divided?

    (1) _____

    (2) _____

34. Two important early settlements in the Northwest Territory were _____
and _____.

35. When was Indiana made a separate territory? _____

Complete the following paragraphs by writing the correct words in the blanks.

1. In the year _____, the Congress of the United States passed a very important law concerning the land of the Northwest Territory. This law was called the _____
_____. It provided that this land be surveyed and divided into _____
_____, each of which would be divided into _____, each of which would contain _____ acres and would be _____ mile square. This land of the Northwest Territory was then opened for settlement and the government charged about _____
_____ per acre for it. _____ were set up to take care of the sale of the land. Section number _____ in each _____ was set aside for _____ purposes.

2. The next step which Congress took in regard to this land was to pass a law providing for the government of it. This law was called the _____. It provided for a government for the Territory presided over by a _____, a _____
_____, and three _____, all to be appointed by _____
_____. After 1789, these officers were to be appointed by the _____

3. The Ordinance of ＿＿＿＿＿＿ provided that slavery should be ＿＿＿＿＿＿＿＿＿ in the Northwest Territory. It guaranteed freedom of ＿＿＿＿＿＿＿＿＿ and freedom of ＿＿＿＿＿＿＿＿＿＿＿ to all inhabitants. It also provided that the land of the ＿＿＿＿＿ ＿＿＿＿＿ should never be taken away without their ＿＿＿＿＿＿＿＿. This Ordinance further provided that when the ＿＿＿＿＿＿＿＿＿ of the Territory reached ＿＿＿＿＿ ＿＿＿＿＿＿ people, the voters would have a right to elect a ＿＿＿＿＿＿＿＿＿＿＿.

4. There were to be made of the territory not less than ＿＿＿＿＿ nor more than ＿＿＿＿＿ states. Each of these ＿＿＿＿＿＿＿＿＿ could ask to be admitted to the Union when it had a population of ＿＿＿＿＿＿＿＿ people. General ＿＿＿＿＿＿＿＿＿ was the first governor of the ＿＿＿＿＿＿＿＿＿ Territory. In the year ＿＿＿＿＿＿ the first county in what is now Indiana was created. This was named ＿＿＿＿＿＿＿＿ County. It included all the present state of ＿＿＿＿＿＿＿＿＿ and parts of ＿＿＿＿＿＿＿＿, ＿＿＿＿＿＿＿＿＿＿, ＿＿＿＿＿＿＿＿＿, and ＿＿＿＿＿＿＿＿. The first capital of the government which was established by the Americans in the Northwest Territory was at ＿＿＿＿＿＿＿＿＿＿＿.

Complete the following paragraphs by writing the correct words in the blanks.

1. After the year 1783, ＿＿＿＿＿＿＿＿ did not give up all the forts in America that she was supposed to give up. Also, that country kept stirring up the ＿＿＿＿＿＿＿＿＿ against the American settlers in the ＿＿＿＿＿＿＿＿＿＿＿. The Indians united under their chief, ＿＿＿＿＿＿＿＿＿, who belonged to the ＿＿＿＿＿＿＿＿ tribe, and made an effort to drive out all the Americans. In 1790, a small American army led by ＿＿＿＿＿＿＿＿＿＿ fought a battle with the ＿＿＿＿＿＿＿＿＿ near the present city of ＿＿＿＿＿＿＿＿＿. In this battle, the ＿＿＿＿＿＿＿＿ were badly beaten.

2. In the year 1791, General ＿＿＿＿＿＿＿＿ led another American army against the ＿＿＿＿＿＿＿ and a battle was fought near ＿＿＿＿＿＿＿＿＿＿, Ohio. In this battle the ＿＿＿＿＿＿＿＿＿ were defeated. After this setback, President ＿＿＿＿＿＿＿＿＿ appointed General ＿＿＿＿＿＿＿＿＿＿＿＿ to organize and drill an army to crush the ＿＿＿＿＿＿＿＿＿. A battle was fought at ＿＿＿＿＿ ＿＿＿＿＿＿＿＿＿, and the ＿＿＿＿＿＿＿＿＿＿ were completely victorious. In the year ＿＿＿＿＿＿, General ＿＿＿＿＿＿＿＿ made a treaty with the ＿＿＿＿＿ ＿＿＿＿＿ at ＿＿＿＿＿＿＿＿＿＿. As a result of this treaty, which was called the Treaty of ＿＿＿＿＿＿＿＿＿, all of ＿＿＿＿＿＿＿＿ and the eastern part of ＿＿＿＿＿＿＿＿＿＿＿ were opened for settlement by the Americans. The town of ＿＿＿＿＿＿＿＿＿＿＿ was named for this general.

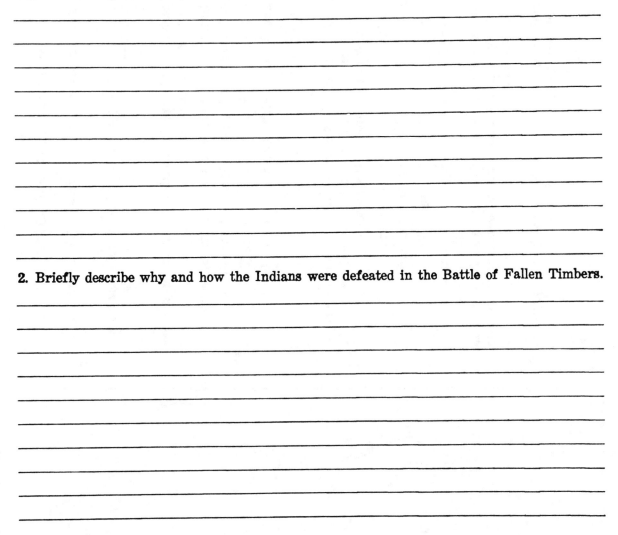

1. In about one hundred words, describe Colonel George Rogers Clark's campaign which ended in the capture of Vincennes.

_____

_____

_____

_____

_____

_____

_____

_____

_____

2. Briefly describe why and how the Indians were defeated in the Battle of Fallen Timbers.

_____

_____

_____

_____

_____

_____

_____

_____

_____

_____

TOPICS FOR DISCUSSION AND REPORT

1. Why did the various colonies give up their claims to the Northwest Territory to the Federal government?

2. Why is the Ordinance of 1787 such an important document?

3. Why is the Treaty of Greenville usually regarded as one of the greatest of Indian treaties?

4. Do you think that George Rogers Clark was such a great man that the state of Indiana and the United States should spend more than a million dollars to erect a memorial to him? Give the reasons for your answer.

5. Read the book, *Alice of Old Vincennes,* and give a report of it to the class.

6. Make a report of the services which were rendered by Francis Vigo to George Rogers Clark and the Americans.

7. If any member of the class has visited the George Rogers Clark Memorial at Vincennes, ask that student to report on his or her experience.

8. Much of the history described in the first units of this text affected the Indians and their lives. Summarize that history from the *Indian's* point of view. Put yourself in the place of an Indian in 1790. Make a diary of the events going on around you.

ASSIGNMENT FOR MAP EXERCISE

The Northwest Territory from 1778 to 1800

Mark with a heavy red line the boundary of the Northwest Territory.

Locate the following by printing the names on the map in the proper locations.

Ohio River	Miami River	Lake Superior
Wabash River	St. Joseph River	Lake Michigan
Illinois River	Wisconsin River	Lake Erie
Kankakee River	White River	Lake Huron
Maumee River		

Locate each of the following by a dot in the proper place on the map. At the side of the dot put the number corresponding to the name of the place.

1. Marietta
2. Detroit
3. Vincennes
4. Ft. Wayne
5. Kaskaskia
6. Fort Recovery
7. Greenville
8. Fallen Timbers

With a broken blue line, trace the route taken from Kaskaskia by General Clark when he made his famous attack on Vincennes.

Color with dark red the land which was given to George Rogers Clark.

THE NORTHWEST TERRITORY FROM 1778 TO 1800

52

HISTORICAL CHART EXERCISES

To complete the following chart, write these events opposite the correct dates under The Northwest Territory.

Law passed for governing of Northwest Territory.

Massacre at Laughery Creek.

Indiana made separate territory.

Wm. H. Harrison elected delegate to Congress.

Treaty of Greenville.

Method of disposing of land set forth by law.

Vincennes recaptured by Clark.

St. Clair's army defeated by Little Turtle.

Indians defeated by General Wayne at Fallen Timbers.

Virginia ceded Northwest Territory to United States.

General Harmar defeated by Indians.

Write these events opposite the correct dates under The American States.

John Adams became President.

Vermont admitted as a state.

Treaty with Spain, opening all Mississippi River to Americans.

Constititutional Convention at Philadelphia.

Treaty ending Revolutionary War signed in Paris.

Naval victory for John Paul Jones.

Thomas Jefferson elected President.

Whiskey Rebellion in Pennsylvania.

Constitution went into effect.

Cornwallis' surrender and end of Revolution.

Kentucky admitted as a state.

Washington became first President.

Tennessee admitted as a state.

The Northwest Territory	1779 to 1800	The American States
	1779	
	1781	
	1783	
	1784	
	1785	
	1787	
	1788	
	1789	
	1790	
	1791	
	1792	
	1794	
	1795	
	1796	
	1797	
	1799	
	1800	

REFERENCES FOR UNIT 5

GENERAL REFERENCES

Buley—Vol. I—pp. 94-104.

Esarey (School Edition)—Chs. IV-V.

Cottman—Chs. III-V.

Thornton, Reade—Chs. V-VI.

Levering—Chs. V-VI.

Roll—pp. 107-219.

Barce—*Land of the Miamis*—Chs. X-XV.

Dunn—*American Commonwealth Series*—Chs. IV-VII.

Dunn—*True Indian Stories*—Ch. II.

Lockridge—*George Rogers Clark*—World Book Co.

Smith—*Indiana History Text-Workbook*—Appendix A, Supplementary Exercise No. 1.

Thompson—*Stories of Indiana*—pp. 47-55.

Thompson—*Alice of Old Vincennes*. This is a book of fiction with an historical background. (Every pupil should read this book while studying this Unit.)

INDIANA HISTORY BULLETIN

"George Rogers Clark, Civilian"—James Alton Jones, IHB, May, 1929.

INDIANA MAGAZINE OF HISTORY

"The First Public Land Surveys in Indiana"—Geo. R. Wilson, IMH, March, 1916.

PUBLICATIONS OF INDIANA HISTORICAL SOC.

"Northwest Territory: Letter of Nathan Dane Concerning the Ordinance of 1787 and Patrick Henry's Secret Letter of Instructions to George Rogers Clark"—Vol. 1, No. 2.

"The Laws and Courts of Northwest Territory and Indiana Territories"—by Daniel Wait Howe—Vol. 2, No. 1.

"Fort Wayne in 1790"—by M. M. Quaife, Vol. 7, No. 7.

"From Greene Ville to Fallen Timbers, a Journal of the Wayne Campaign, 1794" edited by Dwight L. Smith (1952), Vol. 16, No. 8.

Indiana as a Territory, 1800-1816

HISTORICAL SURVEY OF THE UNIT

When the law was passed on May 7, 1800, making Indiana a territory separate from the Northwest Territory, definite boundaries were set for this new territory. The eastern boundary was a line from the mouth of the Kentucky River to Fort Recovery and then due north to Canada. The southern boundary was the Ohio River; the western boundary was the Mississippi River; and the northern boundary was Lake Superior and Canada. This "Indiana Territory" was much larger than the present state of Indiana. In fact, it included what later became the states of Indiana, Illinois, Wisconsin, and a small part of Michigan. (See Map 2, Exercise 1, in Appendix C.) The organization of a government for this large area was going to be a huge task. For this work, President John Adams appointed William Henry Harrison governor of the new Indiana Territory. The old town of Vincennes was chosen as the capital.

Growth of Indiana Territory

When William Henry Harrison became governor of Indiana Territory in 1800, its population was approximately 6,500. There were only a few settlements in the state. Of these, Vincennes was the oldest and also the largest, so naturally it was chosen as the capital. The second largest settlement and the first all-American settlement was at Clarksville near the present city of Jeffersonville. This was on the land which had been granted to General George Rogers Clark and the men in his army for their services in winning the Northwest Territory from the English.

As usual for this time, most of the settlements were on or near the water: the Ohio, the Wabash, the Whitewater, and the White Rivers, and the smaller streams which flowed into these rivers. Nearly all the people lived in the southern part of the state, south of a line drawn between the present cities of Terre Haute and Richmond. The Indians were still in possession of all the part of the state north of this line. Each of these early towns was very little more than a country settlement. Lawrenceburg was established in the extreme southeastern part of the territory. From here the more venturesome families pushed their way up the valley of the Whitewater River.

Vevay and Switzerland County were settled by immigrants whose original home had been Switzerland. Corydon owed its beginning to some pioneers from Kentucky who laid out the town in 1801. From Corydon, settlers proceeded northward toward the present towns of Paoli and Salem. Others from Kentucky crossed the Ohio River and founded Madison. Some ventured farther north to the vicinities of the present towns of Vernon and Columbus. Farther southwest, hun-

Wm. Henry Harrison was only 27 years old when he became governor of Indiana Territory.

ters from Kentucky came to the sites of Boonville and Princeton but towns were not laid out there until after 1812. The most traveled road in the Territory was from New Albany to Vincennes.

Harrison, the First Governor of Indiana Territory

Wm. Henry Harrison was well-fitted for the position of governor of Indiana Territory. He was born in Berkeley, Virginia, in 1773 and belonged to a family which had been prominent in Revolutionary times. At an early age he joined the army and was moved to Ohio. There he saw service with General St. Clair and General Wayne against the Indians. In 1798 he resigned from the army and was appointed Secretary of the Northwest Territory under Governor St. Clair. He had a thorough knowledge of the Indians and although only twenty-seven years old when he became territorial governor, he could deal with the Indians by either war or diplomacy.

Governor Harrison arrived at Vincennes, the capital of Indiana Territory, early in 1801. At the edge of town he built a substantial brick house which still stands. This mansion

The first capitol building for Indiana Territory was a plain dwelling house at Vincennes.

soon became the center of activity for the territorial government. It must be remembered that Indiana Territory at this time included much more than the present state of Indiana. In fact, it took in almost all the original Northwest Territory except Ohio. However, in the territory of Indiana proper, only two counties had been organized by 1800. These were Knox and St. Clair counties. There was a third, called Wayne County, but this included parts of several other states and the county seat was at Detroit. Two new counties were established soon after Indiana became a Territory. One of these was along the Ohio River and was called Clark County. The other was in the southeastern part and was named Dearborn. The county seat of the latter was at Lawrenceburg.

The position of governor of this new Indiana Territory was not an especially attractive one. The country was wild, thinly settled, almost wholly without roads of any kind and constantly threatened by attack from the Indians. Also, there was no proper law enforcement organization. Governor Harrison was confronted immediately with three gigantic tasks. The first of these was to establish a government for the Territory; the second was to deal with the Indians and to secure as much of their land as possible; and the third was to survey this land and grant titles to it to

the white settlers who were now immigrating in large numbers.

As you found out while studying Unit 5, the Ordinance of 1787 provided that the territories of the Northwest Territory must go through two grades of government before they applied for admission as states. The Territory of Indiana was, therefore, organized under Governor Harrison, and three judges were appointed by Congress. The first of Governor Harrison's tasks was the most easily accomplished although the country was wild and lawless at the time. In this work Harrison was greatly aided by an old experienced Indian trader named John Gibson, who had been appointed Secretary of the Territory.

The territorial capitol building was a rudely constructed frame building on the first floor of which were the offices of the government. The assembly room was on the second floor and was reached by an outside stairway. In recent years this old capitol building was moved to Harrison Park in Vincennes and restored as nearly as possible to its original condition.

Treaties with the Indians

As soon as the territorial government was organized and under way, Governor Harrison devoted most of his time to the Indians. In all, he made eight treaties with them by which he secured for the United States the title to most of the land in Indiana south of the present city of Indianapolis. By one of these, signed in 1803, Governor Harrison agreed to purchase from the Indians the land in Indiana bounded by a line which extended from a point twelve miles above Vincennes to the mouth of White River, from there to the north part of Perry County, then to Orleans, and back to the starting point. This is known as the Vincennes Tract.

Gov. Wm. Henry Harrison was very skillful in making important treaties with the Indians.

The second treaty in 1804 opened up all southwestern Indiana. A third treaty in 1805 opened up southeastern Indiana and the north bank of the Ohio River. A fourth treaty in 1809 secured the rights to the land immediately north and northeast of Vincennes. The northern boundary of this last tract was known as the "Ten O'Clock Line" because it was supposed to run in the direction of the sun's rays at ten o'clock in the morning. There are markers in southern Indiana, today, showing the location of this boundary line.

War with the Indians

Some of the Indians were not very well pleased with these treaties because the cessions of the land to the Americans deprived the Indians of some of their best hunting ground. The Indians were becoming unruly, too, because of the enormous amount of whiskey they were getting from the white traders. Governor Harrison did everything in his power to stop this whiskey traffic but he could not succeed. The dissatisfied Indians were led by a Shawnee chief named Tecumseh, and his brother, who was known as the Prophet. They camped along the Wabash with their followers, attacked the outlying settlements, and planned to resist all attempts which the white men would make to permanently settle in those regions. Governor Harrison tried his best to settle the trouble by peaceful means. At least twice Tecumseh frightened the villagers at Vincennes almost out of their wits by appearing there with three or four hundred fully armed Indian warriors to talk to Harrison. However, no amount of parleying could settle the disputes and finally Governor Harrison received orders from the President to take what measures he deemed best to break up the Indian alliance along the Wabash.

Governor Harrison recruited an army of

The Prophet was a Shawnee Indian who stirred up a revolt of the different tribes against the Americans.

about nine hundred men. Approximately two hundred fifty of them were United States soldiers. The remainder were members of the Indiana militia and volunteers. With this small army, Harrison marched northward along the Wabash River. At a spot near the present city of Terre Haute he stopped for a while and built a fort which was named Fort Harrison. From Fort Harrison the army crossed the Wabash River and continued along the west bank because that side offered less opportunity for Indian ambuscades. They proceeded in a few days to a place about eight miles north of Lafayette near the present town of Battle Ground. The route of this march, paralleling the Wabash River, is now designated as "Harrison's Trail" and has been located by markers for at least a part of the way.

Harrison's army was now only about a mile from the main Indian town on the Wabash River. They made camp on a piece of high ground bordered by a small creek and by low ground. Governor Harrison met some of the Indian leaders and they agreed that there would be no fighting until a later conference had been held. However, Harrison was an old Indian fighter and his experience had taught him that the Indians were not to be trusted. He warned his men to keep a sharp watch and to sleep fully prepared to fight. Harrison's precautions were justified, for during the night some of the Indian chiefs, among them the Prophet and another named Winamac, urged the Indians to surprise the Americans and wipe out the little army.

The Indians did attack Harrison's army in the early morning of November 7, 1811. It is said that General Harrison was just putting on his boots in preparation for the giving of orders for his army to stand by when the war cries of the Indians were heard. At any rate, the Americans w e r e partially prepared though some of the Indians were in the camp before the soldiers were fully awake. The battle was fiercely fought for two hours in the early morning light. The Americans were completely victorious. Fifty-two white men were killed or died of their wounds, including several of the officers. It is not known just how many Indians were killed, but the number must have been large. The next day the soldiers proceeded to Prophetstown, the Indian camp on the Wabash River, but it was deserted. The Americans burned the village and destroyed all the Indian property.

The Battle of Tippecanoe was the greatest battle fought on Indiana soil between the white men and the Indians. Also, it was the last large battle between the Americans and the Indians in this state. The Miami tribe did not take part in this battle. The Indians that did were Shawnees, Potawatomi, Winnebagoes, and Chippewas. The scene of this battle has been made into a park and is now maintained by the state as a memorial. A monument, bearing the names of the soldiers killed there, stands in the center of the park in memory of those who were killed. Numerous Indiana counties (Bartholemew, Daviess, Owen, Randolph, Wells) are named for officers of this battle.

Governor Harrison won great fame in this battle and later, when he was a candidate for President of the United States in 1840, he was referred to as "Old Tippecanoe." The reputation which he established at the Battle of Tippecanoe helped him to be elected President.

The defeat of the Prophet at Tippecanoe did not entirely end the danger from the Indians, however. Tecumseh had not taken part in the Battle of Tippecanoe and there was still danger of serious Indian uprisings. In fact, several attacks were made by small roving bands of Indians upon the border settlements. One of these was at Fort Harrison. This place was stoutly defended by Lieutenant Zachary Taylor and a few soldiers, and the Indians were repulsed. On the same day, an attack was made on the Pigeon Roost settlement in Scott County. Here, twenty-two defenseless residents of the community were murdered. The Indians also laid siege to Fort Wayne but quickly dispersed when Governor Harrison appeared with an army. This army, together with another led by General Hopkins, destroyed all the Indian villages along the Wabash. By the end of 1812, there was not an Indian village left south of the Wabash River.

Indiana Territory Divided and the Capital Moved to Corydon

Indiana Territory was so large in area that it was impossible for it to be governed as a whole. We have already seen how the Ohio Territory was separated from Indiana in 1802. In 1805, Indiana Territory was advanced to one of second grade and a territorial legislature and a governor took the place of the old organization which had given the absolute rule to the governor and three judges. In the same year (1805), Michigan Territory was separated from Indiana and was given a government of its own. In 1809, the same thing was done with Illinois. Indiana and Illinois were divided by a line along the middle of the Wabash River from its mouth to a point where a due north line from the town of Vincennes would last touch the shores of the Wabash, from thence due north until the line shall intersect an east and west line drawn through a point at the southern extremity of Lake Michigan. The eastern boundary of the state had previously been set as a line drawn due north from the mouth of the Great Miami River, thence by a meridian line to Canada. The area of Indiana was thus reduced to approximately its present limits. After the Territory was reduced in this manner, the capital at Vincennes was on one side of the Territory instead of near the center as it had been. When the legislature met in 1813, it was decided that the capital should be moved to Corydon, and this was done on May 1, 1813.

The Harrison County courthouse at Corydon served as Indiana's first capitol building.

The state officers were housed in the newly completed Harrison County courthouse and remained there until the capital was moved to Indianapolis. This building was a forty-foot square, thick stone walled, two-story structure with a small tower. The lower floor was of stone flagging and the rooms had high ceilings and large fireplaces. During all the time that the territorial capital, and later the state capital, was at Corydon, the state never owned the building. In 1917, the state legislature appropriated money to purchase this building and it has since been carefully restored.

Soon after the Battle of Tippecanoe, John Gibson became acting governor because all of Harrison's time was taken by his military duties in connection with the War of 1812, and with his duties as Superintendent of Indian Affairs. Gibson acted as governor from July,

1812, to May, 1813. During this time he was not called upon to decide questions of any great importance. However, he was considered a very shrewd and capable man. In his early life he had lived among the Indians and had even married an Indian woman who was later killed. His experience with the Indians had fitted him for dealing with them, and Gibson's services as Secretary of the Territory and as acting governor established for him a place in our early history. Thomas Posey succeeded Gibson and served as Territorial Governor until Indiana became a state in 1816. Posey was in poor health during his term as governor and lived a part of the time at Jeffersonville. However, he was highly regarded and respected.

Indiana Becomes a State

Many settlers poured into Indiana Territory between 1800 and 1816. There was plenty of government land which was sold to the settlers at a very low price, often as little as $1.25 per acre. "Land Offices" were set up at different places by the Federal government, the first one being at Vincennes in 1805. People who wanted land could buy it through a land office. According to the Land Ordinance of 1785 this land had to be surveyed and divided into tracts before it could be sold. However, some of the land had already been claimed by persons who had settled on it before the survey. These people were called "squatters" and the government had to take some recognition of their claims. These problems, together with the question of making further land treaties with the Indians, were ones which Governor Harrison had to solve.

By the year 1815 the population had reached a total of 63,897. In December of that year the territorial legislature petitioned Congress for admission as a state. It was well known that Indiana would enter the Union as a free state and on account of a compromise between the representatives of the slave and the free states in Congress, Indiana could not become a state until there was also a slave state ready for admission. Mississippi was ready to become a state in 1816, so Congress prepared an "Enabling Act" for Indiana. This authorized the people to "form for themselves a constitution and state government." It also provided for certain donations to the state and imposed certain restrictions. In general, these conditions were the same as those included in the famous Ordinance of 1787.

Forty-three delegates from thirteen counties (See Map 3, Exercise 2, Appendix C) met at Corydon on June 10, 1816, for the purpose of framing a constitution for the new state. Their first proceeding was to accept the "Enabling Act" which the national Congress had passed, and thereby become a state. By June 29 they had completed their work and had written a new constitution based largely upon those of the states farther east. It is said that the delegates held many of their sessions under the shade of a large elm tree which was later

The first counties in Indiana were quite large in size. All were in the southern part.

famous in Indiana history as the "Constitutional Elm." This constitution was a statement of what the government was and how the government was to be carried out. It was known as the fundamental law of the state and all laws passed later by the state legislature had to conform to it. This constitution positively forbade slavery in the state forever, and it made provision for a system of public schools which were to serve the people of the state. The state has always provided free public schools for the black citizens of Indiana. The Constitution of 1816 was in effect until 1851 when a new one was drawn up and adopted.

Congress formally admitted Indiana as the 19th state in the Union on December 11, 1816. At this time, the northern boundary of the state was set as a line drawn east and west ten miles north of the southern tip of Lake Michigan. The other boundaries were approximately the same as they are at the present. A state election had already been held in August, and the officers had assumed their positions in November. In 1916 Indiana fittingly celebrated its 100th anniversary as a state. December 11 has officially been made "Indiana Day" by the General Assembly of the state.

STUDY EXERCISES

Complete the paragraphs by writing the correct words in the blanks.

1. Indiana became an organized territory in the year _____. The eastern boundary of it was _____

_____

_____. The southern boundary was _____. The western boundary was _____. The northern boundary was _____. The white population of Indiana at that time was about _____, and most of the land was held by the _____. Most of the white people lived in the _____ part of the territory. Most of the settlements were on the _____, _____, _____ _____, and _____ rivers. The largest town was _____ _____, and the second largest town was _____. At this time, Indiana had no _____ government, the Indians were _____ _____ to the white settlers, and most of the land was _____. However, the population was _____ rapidly.

2. _____ was appointed the first governor of _____ _____ Territory; he was _____ years of age at this time and was well known as an _____ fighter. _____ was appointed Secretary of the Indiana Territory. The new governor was immediately confronted by three large tasks. These were (1) _____ _____, (2) _____ _____, and (3) _____ _____.

3. When Indiana became an organized territory, _____ counties had already been established; these were _____ and _____ counties. Two new counties were established soon after; these were _____ and _____ counties. Most of the towns were only small settlements; six of these were _____ _____, _____, _____, _____ _____, _____, and _____. The main traveled road in the Indiana Territory was from _____ to _____ _____.

Write the correct answers in the blanks.

1. Refer to Map 1, Exercise 3, Appendix C, in this book, and make a list of all the land treaties with the Indians which were made between 1800 and 1816. Tell what land was acquired by each treaty and give the date for each.

(1) _____

_____

_____

_____

_____

(2) _____

(3) _____

_____

_____

(4) _____

_____

2. Where was the "Ten O'Clock Line," and why was it called by that name? _____

_____

_____

_____

_____

3. Who made these treaties with the Indians? _____

4. Why didn't the Indians like these treaties? _____

_____

5. What Indian chief stirred up trouble between the Indians and the Americans during this

period? _____ Who was this chief's brother? _____

To what tribe did they belong? _____

6. What Indian chief, together with a large band of armed warriors, held a long conference

with Governor Harrison? _____ Where did this take place? _____

_____

7. What did Governor Harrison finally decide to do about the Indians who were attacking the

settlements? _____

_____

8. Trace the route of Governor Harrison's army from Vincennes to the place where the Battle

of Tippecanoe was fought. _____

_____

_____

_____

_____

_____

_____

The route which Harrison's army followed is now known by what name? _____

_____

9. Where was the main Indian camp located? _____

_____

_____

10. What was the date of the Battle of Tippecanoe? _____

11. Give a brief description of the Battle of Tippecanoe and state its outcome. _____

_____

_____

_____

_____

_____

12. What was Prophetstown? _____

13. What four Indian tribes took part in this battle? _____

_____

14. What Indian chief led the Indians in the Battle of Tippecanoe? _____

What well-known Indian chief did not take part? _____

15. What is now located where the Battle of Tippecanoe was fought? _____

16. What settlement in Scott County was attacked by the Indians? _____

_____ What did the Indians do here? _____

17. What place near Terre Haute was attacked by the Indians? _____

What was the result of this attack? _____

18. What further action was taken against the Indians along the Wabash River? _____

_____ By the end of

the year 1812, all the Indians had been driven from what part of Indiana Territory? _____

_____

19. "Squatters" were _____

20. What was the Indiana Territory's population in 1815? _____

21. What was the "Constitutional Elm"? _____

_____

22. When is "Indiana Day"? _____
Why is it held on this date? _____
Complete the paragraphs by writing the correct words in the blanks.

1. In the year _____, the capital of Indiana Territory was moved from _____

_____ to _____. This was done because the new location was

thought to be nearer the _____. _____

_____ became acting governor of the Territory. This change was necessary because

_____ was busy with Indian affairs and with the War of

_____. The acting governor served until _____ and was followed by

_____, until the Territory became a _____ in the year _____.

2. Refer to Maps 1, 2, 3, 4, and 5 in Appendix C, in this book, and describe how the Northwest
Territory and Indiana Territory were divided into smaller parts between 1800 and 1816.

(1) In 1800, _____

_____

_____

_____

(2) In 1802, _____

_____

(3) In 1805, _____

_____

_____

(4) In 1809, _____

_____

_____

_____

8. The line for the eastern boundary of Indiana was finally established as one running _____
_____. In 1816,
the northern boundary of Indiana was moved _____.

4. In the year 1815, the legislature of Indiana Territory presented a petition to Congress asking
_____. This petition to Congress was approved by
_____. The Territory then proceeded to call a
_____ Convention. This convention met in the town of _____ and
there were delegates from _____ counties to draw up a _____.
A _____ is a statement of the form of a government and how that
government is to be _____. Indiana then became a _____
on (exact date) _____. It was the _____ state in the Union.

ASSIGNMENT FOR MAP EXERCISE
Indiana Territory from 1800 to 1816.

Locate each of the following early settlements. Do this by placing a dot in the proper place
and then writing the name beside the dot.

Vincennes	Vevay	Vallonia	Pigeon Roost Settlement
Jeffersonville	Boonville	Fort Wayne	Fort Harrison
Lawrenceburg	Princeton	Madison	Lafayette
		Fort Recovery	Prophetstown

Locate by writing the names in the proper locations:

White River	Tippecanoe River	Ohio River
Whitewater River	Lake Michigan	Wabash River

Mark with an X the place where the Battle of Tippecanoe was fought.

Mark with an O the location of Corydon.

Color red the area which was granted to General George Rogers Clark and his soldiers.

Outline with heavy red lines and place the name and date on each of the tracts of land which
Governor Harrison secured by treaties with the Indians. Show the "Ten O'Clock Line" and label it.

Draw a black line across the state to show the northern boundary of Indiana after Michigan
was separated in 1805.

With a black line show the western boundary of the state after Illinois was separated in 1809.

INDIANA TERRITORY
FROM 1800 TO 1816

SCALE OF MILES
0   10   20   30

TOPICS FOR DISCUSSION AND REPORT

1. Make a report on how the government disposed of the land of the Northwest Territory after the eastern states gave up their claims to it. Describe how the land offices carried out their work. What was the meaning of the expression, "land office business"?

2. Make a report on the part which William Henry Harrison took in the War of 1812.

8. What provisions and restrictions did the United States government place upon Indiana when it was admitted as a state?

4. How rapidly did the state grow between 1800 and 1816? What were the reasons for this?

5. If you have visited the Harrison home at Vincennes, the old capitol building at Corydon, or the battlefield of Tippecanoe at Battle Ground, make a report of your visit and what you saw there.

6. The scene of the massacre of white settlers at Pigeon Roost in Scott County is now maintained by the state as a memorial. If any member of the class has visited this spot, ask that student to make a report of it to the class.

7. Where in Indiana are there fine bronze statues of William Henry Harrison and George Rogers Clark? If any member of the class has seen these statues, have him describe their location and appearance.

8. Make a report to the class on the life and activities of Tecumseh and his brother, the Prophet. You can get material for this report from histories and encyclopedias.

9. Make a report to the class of the council held between Governor Harrison and Tecumseh at Vincennes in August of 1810 and again in August of 1811. What happened soon after this last council?

REFERENCES FOR UNIT 6

GENERAL REFERENCES
  Buley—Vol. I, pp. 1-27, 58-78.
  Esarey (School Edition)—Chs. VI-VIII.
  Cottman—pp. 43-73.
  Thornton, Reade—Ch. VII.
  Levering—Chs. VI-VII.
  Roll—Vol. I, Part III, Chs. I-VII; Part IV, Chs. I-II.
  Dunn—*Indiana, Redemption from Slavery*—Chs. VII-XII.
  Barce—*The Land of the Miamis*—Chs. XVI-XXV.
  Governor Leslie—*Indiana*—(Good brief biographies of three governors of the Indiana Territory—Harrison, Gibson, Posey.)
  Thompson—*Stories of Indiana*—pp. 55-128.
  Dillon—*History of Indiana*. This contains one of the best accounts of our territorial periods.
READINGS IN INDIANA HISTORY (1914 edition)
  Selections No. 31 to 41.
READINGS IN INDIANA HISTORY (1956 edition) pp. 100-156.
PUBLICATIONS OF THE INDIANA HISTORICAL SOCIETY
  "Executive Journal of Indiana Territory, 1800-1816," Vol. III, pp. 65-252. This reference is especially valuable for the teacher.)
  "William Henry Harrison's Administration of Indiana Territory" by Homer J. Webster. Vol. IV, pp. 175-294.
  "William Henry Harrison" by Dorothy Burne Goebel, published by the Historical Bureau of the Indiana Library and Historical Department, 1926. Vol. XIV.
  "Fort Wayne, Gateway to the West, 1802-1813," by Bert J. Griswold.
  Published same as above, 1927. (Valuable map of the Northwest Territory given opposite p. 202.) "Laughery's Defeat in Pigeon Roost Massacre," by Charles Martindale. Vol. II, No. 4.
  From Greenville to Fallen Timbers, a journal of the Wayne Campaign, 1794—Vol. XVI, No. 3.
  The Correspondence of John Badollet and Albert Gallatin, 1804-1836—Edited by Gayle Thornbrough—1963.
INDIANA MAGAZINE OF HISTORY
  "Some Letters of John Gibson"—IMH, Vol. 1 (1905), pp. 128-131. (These relate to the attack on Fort Harrison in 1812.)
  Lieutenant Charles Larrabee's Account of the Battle of Tippecanoe, 1811—IMH, Sept., 1961.

Map of Indiana in 1811—IMH, Vol. 2 (1906), p. 164. (This shows General Harrison's line of march to the Battle of Tippecanoe.)
"New Facts About the Corydon Statehouse"—Ethel Cleland, IMH, March, 1918.
"Restoration of the Capitol at Corydon"—Christopher B. Coiman, IMH, Sept., 1934.
"The Battle of Tippecanoe" by Isaac Naylor who fought in this battle—IMH, Vol. 2 (1906), pp. 163-69.
"Governor Harrison and the Treaty of Fort Wayne"—IMH, Vol. II (1915), pp. 352-367.
"Tecumseh's Confederacy"—Elmore Barce, IMH, Vol. 12 (1916), pp. 161-174; Vol. 13 (1917), pp. 67-91.
"Shabonee's Account of the Battle of Tippecanoe" (an account by an Indian)—IMH, Vol. 17 (1921), pp. 353-363.
"Members of the Indiana Constitutional Convention of 1816"—IMH, Vol. 26 (1930), pp. 147-151.
"Sources of Indiana's First Constitution"—John D. Barnhart, IMH, March, 1943.
"The Southern Influence in the Foundation of Indiana"—John D. Barnhart, IMH, Sept., 1937.
"The Discovery and Identification of an Original Copy of the Constitution of 1816—Christopher B. Coleman, IMH, Dec., 1934.
"An Early Crisis in Indiana History"—W. O. Lynch (Financial situation in the new state), IMH, June, 1941.
Members of the Indiana Constitutional Convention of 1816, IMH, June, 1930.
"Admission of Indiana into the Union of States"—James A. Woodburn, IMH, March, 1926.
"Harrison's Councils with Tecumseh"—Rose Schultheis, IMH, March, 1931.
"The Vincennes Days of Zachary Taylor"—Holman Hamilton, IMH, March, 1941.
"Journal of the Convention of the Indiana Territory"—IMH, Vol. LXI, No. 2, June, 1965.
INDIANA HISTORY BULLETIN
"The Contribution of the Southern States to the Settlement of Indiana"—Clarence H. Smith, IHB, April, 1930.
"The Battle of Olde Towne Near Logansport"—James Wilkinson, IHB, Sept., 1928.
"Old Fort Knox Located"—IHB, Vol. 40, No. 8, Aug., 1963.

HISTORICAL CHART EXERCISES

To complete the following chart, write these events opposite the correct dates under Indiana Territory.

Settlement made at Corydon

Indiana reached a population of more than 50,000.

Battle of Tippecanoe.

Capital moved to Corydon.

Harrison appointed as first governor of Indiana Territory.

Illinois Territory separated.

Indiana admitted as a state.

Capital established at Vincennes.

Michigan Territory separated.

Gibson became acting governor.

Ohio Territory separated from Indiana.

"Ten O'Clock Line" Treaty with Indians.

Vincennes Tract obtained from Indians.

Posey became governor of Indiana Territory.

Treaty with Indians, opening up southwestern Indiana.

Write these events opposite the correct dates under The United States.

Burr's conspiracy.

Battle of New Orleans.

James Madison elected President.

War with England began.

End of Madison's administration.

West Point Military Academy organized.

Louisiana Purchase.

Madison became President.

Perry won victory on Lake Erie.

Ohio became a state.

First steamboat on the Ohio.

War with England ended.

Thomas Jefferson elected President.

Surrender of Ft. Dearborn and Ft. Detroit to British and Indians.

Jefferson's Embargo Act passed.

Indiana Territory	Date	The United States
	1800	
	1800	
	1802	
	1803	
	1803	
	1805	
	1805	
	1806	
	1807	
	1808	
	1809	
	1809	
	1811	
	1812	
	1812	
	1813	
	1813	
	1814	
	1815	
	1816	

Pioneer Life in Indiana

HISTORICAL SURVEY OF THE UNIT

The first English and American settlers that came into Indiana Territory settled in the southern part. Most of these people came from Kentucky and, consequently, had to cross the Ohio River before they could reach Indiana. Of course, there were no bridges across the river, so the people had to "ferry" across in small boats or get across the best way they could. Nearly all these people were desperately poor. Whole families moved at one time, taking all their possessions with them. These possessions usually were very few but they were enough to furnish the means for the settlers to make a living from the soil after they located in a new home.

They came on horseback, on foot, and in wagons. Each man had a rifle. This was necessary for protection from the Indians and for hunting game. Some of them brought cows, and pigs, and chickens. Others brought seeds of different kinds for planting. A few brought nothing but themselves and their children and perhaps a dog or two. These depended upon borrowing from their neighbors and upon the food they could get by hunting wild game until they could, perhaps, raise some sort of crop of their own. Occasionally there would be a man without a family. He would be a hunter and a trapper who expected to make a living from the animals which were very plentiful in the woods.

The old Northwest was much damper than today, as it held lots of swamps, licks, salt marshes, lagoons, and ponds. Many flatlands were low and swampy and were called "wet prairies."

The whole southern part of the state was covered by a heavy forest. As soon as the settlers crossed the river they were swallowed up by the forest. There were no r o a d s, n o bridges, no towns and no stores where supplies could be bought. The absence of stores made very little difference to them because none of them had any money, anyhow. With these conditions, it is not strange that the everyday life of the pioneer in Indiana was just about as different from life here in the 20th Century as

anything could be. Even when Indiana became a state in 1816, there were no towns of any size in this territory.

Each family went on its way until it found a place which was considered suitable for a home. Then a small "clearing" was made by cutting down or deadening as many trees as possible and by taking away some of the underbrush. A crude house was hastily built in this clearing and the rest of the cleared ground was used for planting crops. Agriculture was the principal occupation because every family had to grow almost everything that it ate and wore. If they did not do this, they starved or froze to death.

The Home

The favorite location for the house was near a spring which would furnish a supply of water throughout the year. If a spring could not be found, a small running stream would do. Either would insure a supply of fresh water and either could be used to provide a cool place for milk and meats in the summertime.

Of course the pioneer house was built of logs because that was the only building material that was available. Usually there were no saws, so all the logs had to be cut with an axe. This axe, together with an adz, another tool called a frow, and a pick made up the whole tool chest for the pioneer.

First, about twenty logs of as near the

The axe, the frow, the pick, and the adz were the only tools the early pioneers had.

same diameter as possible were cut. The ideal diameter was about one foot. These were cut about twenty to twenty-five feet long for the sides of the house. Then, an equal number of the same diameter were cut ten or twelve feet long for the ends. Other logs were cut shorter for the gables. Each log was notched or flattened at the ends so that one log could rest solidly upon the one underneath it.

The logs were then laid, one upon another, and if the worker used skill, four rather solid walls would be built up. Poles were laid across the top and covered with clapboards to form a roof. The clapboard was a thick flat board which had been hewed from some logs with a straight grain. Each clapboard was about four feet long, at least six inches wide, and an inch or more in thickness. These were laid in an overlapping manner to shed the rain. There were no metal nails in the whole house because there were none to be had. Sometimes wooden pins were used to hold parts of the structure together. The spaces between the logs were filled with clay. This was called "chinking." If all the cracks were well chinked, the rain and wind would be kept out and the house could be kept fairly warm.

On one side or one end the logs were cut to allow an opening. A door was made of split pieces of wood like large clapboards and hung on leather hinges. At the other end, the logs were cut to make a space for the fireplace. A chimney was constructed on the outside of the house and connected with the fireplace inside. The fireplace was lined with stones put together with clay and the chimney also was lined with clay. Windows could be added, although there was no glass available for them. If the settler had time, a puncheon floor was laid in the cabin. This floor was made of split logs with the flat side up. If there was no time

The pioneer settlers had to build their homes of logs cut from the forest.

to lay a wooden floor, hard clay was packed down to form the floor.

Such is a brief description of the homes of the early pioneers, the "log cabins" which you have heard so much about. These cabins, crude as they were, filled one of the first requirements for the pioneer and his family—that of *shelter*. They were the homes of many men and women who later became famous or who founded our great state and worked to make it grow so rapidly.

Sometimes, the settlers built houses with only three walls. These were called "open-faced" houses.

The furniture had to be handmade, too, and it was as crude as the house. The beds were made in the corners by driving posts into the ground and laying poles across to the wall. Sometimes ropes or lengths of buckskin were stretched tightly across instead of poles. The rope bed wasn't quite as hard but these men and women were not used to anything that was very comfortable.

Three-legged stools and rough benches had to serve until better chairs could be made. A long bench did duty as a table. Nearly every family had brought some kind of cooking utensils with it. Usually these consisted of an iron or copper kettle or two, an iron frying pan of some sort, and some assorted pots and pans of iron or earthenware. In the warm weather, the washing and at least part of the cooking was done out of doors. Wood was the only fuel to be had and the ashes were carefully saved for making soap.

Getting the Food

Corn and potatoes were the principal foods that could be grown quickly from the soil. Nearly all bread was made of corn meal. There were three kinds of bread: the "dodger," "pone," and the "johnny cake." Because of the

68

rich and wild nature of the soil, wheat could not be grown for several years and all flour had to be brought from the Whitewater country. It was very expensive and considered a luxury. Hogs were raised and butchered for meat. Wild game was plentiful and could be shot or trapped. Deer, wild turkeys, wild ducks and geese, squirrels, and rabbits were the principal game. Wild pigeons were so plentiful that flocks of them sometimes hid the sun. There were plenty of fish in the streams and lakes, and most of these fish made good food. Catfish, suckers, and bass were the leading kinds. Fishing is still a favorite sport in Indiana.

The garden furnished potatoes, cabbage, radishes, onions, beans, peas, peppers, pickles, pumpkins, turnips, parsnips, and watermelons, as well as other small vegetables. The growing season was rather short and as many vegetables as possible had to be put away for the winter. Some of these, like the beans, peas, and corn, were dried and stored in a safe place. Others, such as the cabbage, onions, turnips, and parsnips, were buried in the ground or stored in caves where they would not freeze.

Berries and different kinds of fruit grew wild in great quantities. There were blackberries, black and red raspberries, dewberries, mulberries, wild grapes, crab apples, wild plums, wild haw, persimmons, and paw paws. Some of these fruits were dried and some were made into preserves and jellies. All these different fruits and berries still grow in Indiana and you probably have picked many of these things, yourself. The paw paw, which has sometimes been called the Hoosier banana, is a native of this state and is not often found growing outside the state.

Besides the wild game, pork was the principal kind of meat. In the winter it could be

The fireplace furnished heat for the cabin and a means for cooking food.

frozen and kept fresh for a long time. In warm weather it would spoil quickly unless it was "cured." To cure the meat, the farmer cut up the carcass of the hog and placed the hams and sides in wooden barrels which were filled with very strong salt water. The meat was allowed to remain in this salt water, or *brine* as it was called, until the brine had penetrated throughout the meat. This was called *pickling* the meat. Sometimes the meat was smoked with hickory smoke and cured in that manner. Smoking the meat took several weeks.

Since there were so many trees, it is not unusual that there were different kinds of nuts which were prized as great delicacies. The hickory trees furnished hickory nuts which sometimes grew as large as hen's eggs. The walnut trees furnished the black walnuts and the butternuts, the beech trees, the sweet triangular shaped beechnuts, and the chestnut trees, the fine-flavored chestnuts. The acorns from the many oak trees were not agreeable for food for human beings, but they were very tasty and fattening for the hogs which roamed through the woods.

Three very important articles of food that were very scarce were sugar, salt, and coffee. Wild honey often took the place of sugar. This honey could frequently be found in hollow trees and a "bee tree' could furnish enough sweets to last for a long time. When the pioneers moved farther north in the state, they came into a region where there were many maple trees. The sap of these trees could be boiled down into maple sugar. About the only substitute for coffee was parched corn or the bark of certain trees. This did not taste much like coffee but it was used anyhow. Salt was so scarce that the pioneers often had to do without it for long periods of time. There were several small salt springs in southern Indiana and these were the main source of supply. One of these was near the present city of French Lick in Orange County. The water from the spring was boiled until it was evaporated. The salt was then left in small crystals. However, this salt had many impurities in it.

Getting the Clothing

The woods of early southern Indiana were full of deer. Deer meat is called venison, and in addition to being eaten as food, the deer furnished the material for much of the pioneer clothing. Deer hides were cleaned and tanned and turned into a leather called buckskin

69

Shoes, skirts, pants, and gloves were made of buckskin. It was tough and yet soft, but it would not turn water. Many a pioneer almost froze to death because his buckskin clothing became soaked with water in cold weather.

Bears were plentiful in Indiana in the early days, and they were also a great nuisance because they killed the pigs and other livestock which they could reach. For this reason the men took great pleasure in bear hunting. Every family had one or more "hound dogs" and these dogs became experts in chasing and cornering the bears on a bear hunt. Bear meat was not a favorite food but the bear grease was used for cooking and for other purposes. The skin made a good robe or overcoat or covering for the bed. Panthers (the settlers called them "painters") were numerous, too.

The spinning wheel was used to make the wool into thread for clothing.

They made a crying noise like a child, especially at night, and this noise was very frightening to hear. Because of this the panthers were hunted and killed whenever possible. Their skins were especially prized for robes and for decoration in the home. Great herds of buffalo roamed over Indiana in the early days. Indians had many ways of hunting them and probably the easiest was to stampede a herd into a river, quicksand, or ravine where they could be easily taken. Stampeding buffalo showed almost no sense when on a dead run and would go right over a steep cliff to their deaths. Many of the first roads through the wilderness were made by following the buffalo trails. The buffalo disappeared from Indiana, almost overnight, about the year 1798. It is thought that they starved on account of an unusually severe winter. Buffalo skins were made into warm coats and robes of all kinds. Other parts of the buffalo were also used for many purposes.

A few sheep were brought in by the very early settlers in Indiana. Sheep were difficult to raise here because they were so easily, and so frequently, killed by wild animals. However, as the country became more thickly settled, more sheep were raised. The heavy wool was sheared from these animals in the early spring. This wool was then washed and combed (this combing process was called "carding") and afterwards spun into threads. Every home had its spinning wheel and every housewife and daughter had to become more or less of an expert in using this old-fashioned machine. Before the mills were built where woolen cloth was made, the women wove the cloth, too. This was done on big wooden looms. This cloth was called "homespun." Later, when woolen mills were built, the cloth was woven there. Even then, all the clothing that was made from the woolen cloth was made by hand by the women in the family. Knitting was done in spare time, and wool socks, underwear, mufflers, and shawls were prepared in this way.

Flax was another source of material for cloth. The flax plant grew tall with long strong fibers which could be turned into thread. Getting these fibers separated from the plant and into condition to use was a long and difficult process. The cloth made from flax was called linen. It was coarse and scratchy but was hard to wear out. Sometimes the linen thread was mixed with the wool threads in the weavings. This cloth was called "linsey-woolsey." Sometimes coloring from vegetables or from the hulls of nuts was used to color the cloth. However, none of the coloring available made the cloth very pretty and the garments were drab and dull looking. This made no difference to the settlers, though. Many people went barefoot all the time, even in winter snows. Their only jewelry was a watch, and both men and women carried them.

Settlers Come in Increasing Numbers

Many of the early pioneers could neither read nor write. In their new home there were no schools, so the children did not have an opportunity to get an education. Getting a bare living from the surroundings was a task for the whole family and the children were kept busy. The women in the family worked as hard as the men did. They not only did the cooking, the housework, and the clothing making for the whole family, but they helped with the crops and the animals and especially with the garden. Drying the vegetables and preserving the fruits for future use required much of their time. The pioneers were strong and active but few of them lived long. The exposure to the weather, the rough life, and the lack of proper medicine for treatment of the diseases usually proved fatal before the age of forty.

Bands of settlers followed one another into Indiana in rapid succession. As new ones came, many of the older ones moved farther north in the territory. These pioneers were restless and they always thought the best land lay a little farther away. Life was still rough but gradual improvements were made as the years passed. Some of the new settlers brought better tools with them. Others brought more livestock. A few had money with which to purchase supplies. Here and there several houses would be built near one another and in this way small settlements would be formed. But the progress was slow. Even in the year 1830, although there had been great advancement, Indiana was still a "backwoods" state.

One of the worst failings of the pioneers was their belief in superstition. The planting of potatoes and other vegetables had to be done in certain "times of the moon." Some crops had to be planted on certain days. The behavior of the animals might foretell the kind of weather approaching. The color of the sky at sunset indicated rain or sunshine. The thickness of the corn husks told how severe the winter would be. In fact, almost every bit of the people's lives was tied up in some way with "signs." If this was not actually harmful, it certainly did not help any.

Disease and Medicine

High birthrate kept mankind going in Hoosier pioneer days. Babies were born at twice the rate they are today, and died off much faster because of disease.

Disease was the pioneer's worse enemy. The rough life and exposure to the weather, the lack of sanitation, the presence of swarms of flies and mosquitoes, the impurity of the drinking water, the general lack of cleanliness in handling food, and the absence of proper medicine and doctors made disease greatly feared. The most common ailment was chills and fever, or the ague (pioneers called it "ager"). Ague was supposed to have been caused by exposure to dampness. There were many different kinds of ague: Dumb, Shaking, and Chill Fever.

Although not often fatal, the victim was

The mortar and pestle were used for grinding herbs and mixing medicines.

prevented from working when he had the attack. Plentiful doses of quinine would have checked or cured this disease, but quinine was not available. So, the person who had the ague had to go on having chills one day and fever the next day until he wore out the disease or the disease wore him out. Hindostan, once county seat of Martin County, had a population of near 2,000 when, in 1826, an epidemic of "fevers" struck and in a few short weeks wiped out the place. It was said that there were more dead than alive to do the burying in the town.

Diseases of the stomach and the digestion were very common. Among these were cholera, morbus, diarrhea, and flux. Cholera spread from Europe to the United States in 1830 and was in Indiana by 1832. First symptoms of cholera were a feeling of queasiness and a craving for water. Severe intestinal spasms came next, then circulation slowed, skin became cold, the eyes became sunken, and collapse followed. Death could come quickly or slowly.

All this was brought on by eating too much fresh meat and too many foods that could not be properly preserved and cared for. Typhoid fever and smallpox were two epidemics which killed whole communities. Measles, whooping cough, scarlet fever, and diphtheria were much more severe than they are now. Another fatal disease was "milk sickness." The cause for this sickness was never definitely known. It was believed to be caused by drinking milk from cows which had eaten a poisonous weed. At any rate, this disease was greatly feared because it, too, resulted in the death of entire families within a few days. There was a danger, also, from pneumonia (then called lung fever), yellow jaundice, blood poisoning, and from the bites of snakes such as rattlesnakes and copperheads.

There were few or no doctors and the knowledge of medicine was not great at this time. Home remedies were used for most diseases. Tea made of sassafras root was one of the favorites. This was drunk in the spring of the year and was supposed to thin the blood which had become too thick during the winter. For a cold and sore throat, goose grease or a piece of fat meat mixed with mustard, onion, and pepper was tied around the neck, or a poultice of flaxseed, licorice, sugar, and vinegar might be used. A drink of rock candy and whiskey was supposed to help. Various herbs such as bloodroot, ginseng, rhubarb, pennyroyal, pokeberry leaves, bitter root, yellow root, and slippery elm were used as medicine in different mixtures. A bottle of "bitters" was supposed to be good for almost anything. One of the favorite recipes for this was a combination of cider, witch hazel, sumac, wild cherry, sarsaparilla, and brandy or whiskey. Goose grease was relied upon to cure many ailments. A bag of camphor or asafoetida hung around the neck was supposed to keep diseases away from a person. Many a child was burdened with such an arrangement during the winter. There were many other recipes and superstitions for curing diseases.

Lack of proper care of the teeth caused these people much suffering. It was generally true that their teeth decayed almost as soon as they acquired a full set. The toothache was very painful, and there were no dentists to treat it. Once in a while some brave individual would try to end his distress by pulling his own tooth. This home dentistry was not often successful. Of course, since there were no dentists, there was no way to replace teeth. So, in addition to the pain, the loss of teeth caused sunken cheeks and distorted features.

Skin diseases were very common among the pioneers. Exposure to the weather reddened and chapped the skin. The harsh, homemade lye soap was the only kind available, and while it would remove the dirt it also had a tendency to remove the outer skin. Two diseases of the skin were quite annoying and were difficult to cure. One was erysipelas and the other was the "itch." The latter was particularly prevalent among the children and was very painful. The erysipelas often resulted in disfigurement of the face.

The women had no cosmetics and no preparations to treat the skin, and it is doubtful if they could have found the time to use cosmetics if such had been available. A naturally clear skin was unusual with both men and women. Most of them had a yellowish tint to their skin caused by eating the wrong kind of food. There were no barber shops and it was much easier for a man to let the hair and beard grow than to attempt to keep either trimmed. All this resulted in the men and women looking much older than they really were. It was common for a woman of twenty-five to look as if she were sixty years of age.

The School and the Church

The famous Ordinance of 1787, which you studied about in Unit 5, stated: "Religion, morality and knowledge being necessary to good government and the happiness of mankind, schools and the means of education shall forever be encouraged." However, the Ordinance did not provide any way for local communities to establish schools. The first wave of settlers in Indiana were not interested in schools. They were interested in only one thing and that was getting enough to live on. With them, it was a tough struggle to keep alive and they did not have time for schools and education. A little later, when the small communities began to grow in population, some thought was given to schools. The people objected to paying tax to support public schools. Also, there were very few persons who were qualified to be teachers, and there were no buildings which could be used for schoolhouses.

In spite of all these obstacles, the demand for schools did grow. The first schools were known as "subscription schools." That meant that the families that had children would agree to pay the teacher a certain amount each month for the schooling of each child in the family. The teacher generally had to "board around"; that is, take turns at living with the different families which sent children to school. The board and room which the teacher got in this way was just about all the pay he received. An early Indiana author, Edward Eggleston, describes the life in one of these early schools very well in *The Hoosier Schoolmaster*. Usually the school term was not more than three months long. All grades were taught in the same room by one teacher. This "one-room school" stayed in the rural communities of Indiana until only a few years ago. Today, there are no one-room schools in the state.

In your study of Indiana history you have already learned that the French, who came

72

The pioneer preachers were called circuit riders because they made their rounds riding horseback.

into Indiana before the English did, had the Catholic priests among them and had established Catholic churches in several places. These Catholic priests, who were really missionaries, performed a service and had an influence which was too great for us to measure.

The early American pioneers in Indiana, on the whole, were not very religious. They didn't have time for religion any more than they had time for education. But, as their numbers increased, and as wealthier and better educated settlers arrived, more attention was given to religion. Several denominations of Protestant churches became firmly established. The principal ones were Presbyterian, Methodist, Baptist, and Christian. Church buildings were erected and the church soon became a strong influence in every community. The early preachers were often peculiar, but they were earnest persons. Few of them had much education. What they lacked in education they made up in willingness to work hard and to face the hardships of the rough country. Many of them would ride h o r s e b a c k f r o m church to church, making a circuit. If they received any pay, it was in the form of meat or vegetables or something that the people had raised. The preachers usually had to engage in some other kind of work on the side in order to make a living. There were many revival meetings and in these the preacher made up for his lack of actual knowledge by his shouting and enthusiasm.

Unusual Pioneer Customs

Whipping posts were erected in towns for use as punishment. A cat o'nine tails was made of 9 knotted thongs. A Russian Knout was made of r a w h i d e with wire barbs woven in. Salt was sometimes poured in wounds after a whipping. The use of tar and feathers as punishment was common. One of the worst insults to a man was to paint his horse or cut off its mane and tail. To poison a man's horse was very insulting.

Marriages of 14 and 15 year-old girls were common. Marriage was extremely important. A woman of 20 years was considered a spinster who would never find a suitable man. Girls went to great extremes in hair-dressing to attract a man, but very seldom used soap and water.

Improvements in Pioneer Living

Indiana grew rapidly from 1800 to 1850 and by the latter date (1850) there were almost one million people in the state. With this increase in population one would expect that the way of living would improve, too, and it did. Agriculture was still the main business but many towns and villages came into existence during this time. A blacksmith shop was one of the necessary things in any community and many of these shops were started at country crossroads. Then, a general store would be added, several houses would be built, after that a schoolhouse and a church, and in this way a new village would be started. Or, the town might grow up around a gristmill. Most of these mills were located on streams. A small dam would be built to back up the water in the stream. Then, the water would be led through a channel or a trough and allowed to fall again-

As the settlers became better established, they built better looking and more substantial homes.

st a mill wheel. This caused the wheel to turn, and the power was transmitted to machinery inside the mill where the corn and wheat were ground into meal and flour. The mill was a necessity and a good one usually operated day and night.

The first settlers ate everything that they raised. Their farming tools were crude and their amount of cleared land was small. They had to rely on oxen to pull the plow and to haul the wagon. The oxen were slow, and the amount that a farmer could raise was limited. The later settlers brought better machinery and used horses to pull the farm implements and the wagons. Thousands of acres of land were cleared and planted in corn, wheat, rye, oats, buckwheat, and barley. Some tobacco was raised in the extreme southeastern part of the state. Hog raising was engaged in extensively.

After larger farms had been laid out and better farming was done, it became necessary for the farmers to build fences around their fields. The favorite kind of fence was the rail fence. The rails were split from logs which had been cut from ten to twelve feet in length. It was necessary for these logs to have a straight grain so they would split straight. The

Fences were made of rails split from logs which had a straight grain.

actual splitting was done with a wedge and a maul and the resulting rails were like long slender poles, yet much more substantial. A good rail splitter could prepare one hundred rails in one day. The rails were used to build a "worm" style rail fence. In this style fence the rails were laid one upon another at the ends and then zigzag fashion around the field. A few of these fences may still be seen in some parts of Indiana.

After the farmers began to produce more than their families could eat, they had the problem of getting the surplus supplies to the market. There were many things to be marketed. The principal ones were wheat, corn, rye, flour, corn meal, pork, wool, furs, and hides. There was a great demand for all these articles in such cities as Cincinnati, New Orleans, and the larger places in the eastern part of the United States. The farm products were loaded on wagons and taken to the river towns like New Albany and Madison. The roads were bad but the trips were always completed, regardless of the obstacles. From the river ports the goods were sent by boat to their destinations.

The farmer's products were sold for cash or traded for other things which could be resold to the folks back home. In this way, a flourishing trade was established and many of the farmers and merchants began to make plenty of money. Some of them built better homes, and many of these new houses were built of brick. The brick had to be brought from long distances. New and better household furnishings were brought, too. These were great improvements at that time, although they would seem somewhat crude and inconvenient to us today.

The period from 1825 to 1850 was one of trade. Indiana grew and expanded at a rapid rate and the Pioneer Era ended with the beginning of the Civil War in 1861. The next era was the Manufacturing Era.

STUDY EXERCISES

Complete the paragraphs by writing the correct words in the blanks.

1. Most of the first American settlers in Indiana Territory came from _____

   In order to reach Indiana, they had to cross the _____, which was a

   natural _____. They crossed this barrier by using _____, and

   this was called _____ across. They traveled on _____,

   by _____, and on _____. Each man carried a _____

   _____ which was used for _____ against the _____

   and for _____ game for _____. The early settlements were

   in the _____ part of Indiana. The whole southern part of the state was covered by _____. There were no _____, no _____

_____, no _____, and no _____. When a family

found a place which they thought would be a good location for a home, they made a _____

_____ there. This was done by _____ and

_____. A crude _____ was then made of

_____ and some ground was prepared for _____.

The principal occupation of the settler was _____ because he had to

_____ all the food for the family.

2. In building a pioneer _____, about twenty _____ of as near the

same diameter as possible were cut. A diameter of _____ inches was con-

sidered best. These _____ were cut approximately _____ to _____

_____ feet long and were for the _____ of the cabin or house. Then an equal

number of _____ of the same _____ were cut ten or twelve

feet long; these were for the _____ of the cabin. Shorter _____ were

cut for the gables. Each _____ was _____ at the end so one could

rest solidly on the one _____ it. The logs were then laid _____ upon

_____. _____ were laid across the top and covered with

_____ to form a roof. The _____ on the roof

were thick, flat boards about _____ feet long and _____ inches wide. These

were laid in an _____ manner to shed the rain. The whole cabin was

put together without using any _____. The _____ was built out-

side the cabin and lined with _____. It was connected with the _____

_____ inside the house. If there was a wooden floor, it was made of _____

_____. This was called a _____ floor. The spaces between the

logs in the walls were filled with _____. This was called _____.

Sometimes, the cabin was built with only _____ walls. This was called an _____

_____ cabin. Usually, the pioneer had but four tools to work with; these were

the _____, the _____, the _____, and the _____. However

crude the cabin might be, it did furnish _____ for the family.

3. The furniture for the house was crude, too. The bed was made by driving _____ into

the ground and laying _____ across to the wall. Sometimes, _____ or

strings of _____ were stretched across instead of _____. Often, a

_____ filled with straw or grass was placed on the bed. Rough _____

or three-legged _____ served for _____. Another rough _____

_____ was used for _____. The principal cooking utensils were _____

_____, _____, and _____. The dishes were made of _____

_____ or _____. The fireplace was used for two things; _____

and _____.

75

4. The _____ in the pioneer family did the housework, made the _____ _____, and helped with the _____. Before making clothes, each woman had to learn the use of the _____ to make the _____ for the cloth. This cloth was called _____. Some articles of clothing, such as _____, _____, and _____, were made by knitting. A certain kind of plant called _____ furnished fibers which could be turned into strong _____ and woven into cloth called _____. Sometimes, coloring from _____ or _____ was used to color the cloth.

Write the correct answers in the blanks.

1. What were "wet prairies"? _____

2. What use was made of the ashes from the wood which was burned in the fireplace? _____
   _____

3. What two things which were the principal food items for the pioneers could be grown quickly from the soil? _____ and _____

4. What animal was raised to supply meat for the family? _____

5. What were the principal kinds of wild game that the pioneer could secure for food?
   _____ _____ _____
   _____ _____ _____
   _____ _____ _____

6. What were the principal vegetables that were grown in the pioneer garden?
   _____ _____ _____
   _____ _____ _____
   _____ _____ _____

7. What two methods did the pioneers have for preparing or keeping vegetables for future use?
   _____ _____

8. What were the principal fruits that the pioneers found growing wild?
   _____ _____ _____
   _____ _____ _____
   _____ _____ _____

9. What were two ways of curing pork? _____ _____

10. What four kinds of nuts were plentiful on the trees of the forest? _____
    _____ _____ _____

11. What three important articles of food were scarce for the pioneers? _____
    _____ _____

12. Why was wheat so expensive? _____

13. What was deer meat called? _____

14. Besides meat, what did the deer furnish? _____

15. How did the pioneers get their principal supply of sugar? _____
_____

16. What was another source of sweetening? _____

17. Where did the pioneers obtain their salt? _____

18. What was sometimes used in the place of real coffee? _____

19. What was the pioneer's worst enemy? _____

20. What was the pioneer's most common disease? _____

21. Where did the pioneers get their medicines? _____

22. Most of the early settlers died before reaching what age? _____

23. What kind of jewelry did the pioneers wear? _____

Do the following things. Use a separate sheet for your drawing.

1. Draw a picture of an ox yoke. Describe how it was used.
_____
_____
_____
_____
_____

2. Draw a picture of a cradle that was used to cut grain. Describe how it was used.
_____
_____
_____
_____

3. Make a drawing showing how rails were laid for a rail fence.

Write the correct answers in the blanks.

1. What five things were the principal ones that caused so much disease among the pioneers?
   (1) _____
   (2) _____
   (3) _____
   (4) _____
   (5) _____

2. What four diseases of the stomach and digestion were very common among the pioneers?
_____ _____ _____ _____

3. What other diseases were also often fatal to the pioneers?
_____ _____ _____
_____ _____ _____

4. What were some of the herbs that were used for medicine?

_____   _____   _____   _____

_____   _____   _____   _____

5. What medicine was supposed to cure any disease? _____

6. What was a favorite treatment for a cold? _____

7. What was a favorite spring tonic that was supposed to thin the blood? _____

_____

8. What were some symptoms of cholera? _____

_____

_____

9. What caused cholera? _____

10. Why did so many of the pioneers have sunken cheeks and distorted features? _____

_____

11. What were two common skin diseases among the pioneers? _____   _____

12. The earliest churches in the Northwest Territory were of what religion? _____

13. What men, in the early churches, performed great service and had much influence with the people? _____

14. What were the three principal denominations of Protestant churches in early Indiana?

_____   _____   _____

15. How were many of the preachers paid? _____

16. Did Indiana grow rapidly or slowly between 1800 and 1850? _____

17. By the year 1850, there were how many people in Indiana? _____

18. Most of the towns grew up around what two things?

_____   _____

19. What was a gristmill? _____

20. What kind of power was used to run a gristmill? _____

21. What was still the principal industry in Indiana in 1850? _____

22. What did the pioneers use to pull the plow and wagon? _____

23. What was the favorite kind of fence used to enclose the farms? _____

24. What tools were used to fashion the material for these fences? _____

25. After the farmers in Indiana produced more than their families could eat, what did they do with what was left? _____

26. What were the principal articles that the farmer marketed?

_____   _____   _____   _____

_____   _____   _____   _____

27. What kinds of transportation were used to get these products to market?

_____   _____

28. What two towns in early Indiana were great shipping points for farm products?

_____   _____

29. These two towns were on what river? _____

80. To what two cities was much of this produce shipped? _____

_____

81. What were some of the things that the settlers bought in exchange for their farm products?

_____   _____   _____

_____   _____   _____

82. When did the Pioneer Era end in Indiana? _____

Complete the paragraphs by writing the correct words in the blanks.

1. Deer hides were cleaned and _____ and made into a leather called _____ . This material was used to make _____ , _____ , _____ , and _____ .

2. Another wild animal which was hunted with much pleasure was the _____ . The meat of this animal was not well liked for food, but the _____ was used for _____ and other purposes. The _____ made a good robe.

8. Another wild animal called a _____ made a crying noise like a child. Because of this frightening noise, these _____ were hunted and killed. In hunting, the pioneers were helped by _____ , which were kept by every family of settlers.

4. Great herds of _____ were found in Indiana in the early days. Many of the _____ through the wilderness were made by these _____ . The _____ disappeared from Indiana about the year _____ , and it is thought that most of them _____ to death because of _____ _____ .

5. Sheep were raised for their _____ . This was _____ from them in the early spring. It was then _____ and combed and _____ into threads. When the country became more thickly settled, this _____ was taken to a _____ and woven into _____ .

6. The Ordinance of _____ stated "Religion, morality, and _____ being necessary to good government and the happiness of mankind, the means of _____ _____ shall forever be encouraged." However, the early settlers were so busy that they did not have _____ for _____ and did not want to pay any _____ to support _____ . The first schools were known as _____ schools because the family that had any _____ _____ to attend the school paid the _____ a certain amount each month. In most cases, the teacher had to get his pay by _____ . The school term was not more than _____ in length. _____ grades were taught in one room, and the school was known as a _____ school.

TOPICS FOR DISCUSSION AND REPORT

1. Picture yourself as a member of a pioneer family just arriving in southern Indiana. Describe how the family proceeded to choose a place for a home and how the land was cleared for a cabin and for crops.

2. Make a list of cooking utensils that were used by the early pioneers. Describe how a meal was prepared. (There are numerous museums in the state where you can see collections of cooking utensils used by the pioneers. The Tippecanoe Historical Society has such a collection in its museum in Lafayette. Perhaps your own County Historical Society has a similar collection.)

3. Describe the furniture in a pioneer home. (Articles of pioneer furniture may also be seen in historical museums in the state.)

4. Describe how the old-fashioned "gourd dipper" was made.

5. Describe how the pioneer got a supply of feathers to make pillows and feather beds.

6. Find out some of the peculiar superstitions of your ancestors or the ancestors of your friends in early Indiana. Make a report of these to the class.

7. Find out some of the peculiar "signs" in which the pioneers believed. Perhaps some of these were about the weather, the time for planting vegetables, the harvesting of crops, or other things of everyday life. Make a report of these to the class.

8. Read *The Hoosier Schoolmaster* and make a report to the class on pioneer school life in southern Indiana.

9. Describe how a mill was built so the water from a stream could turn the wheel to grind the grain. Several old mills are still standing in Indiana. There may be one in your community. Perhaps the best-known one is in the pioneer village in Spring Mill State Park. If you have not visited this pioneer village, you should arrange to do so. In addition to the mill, there is a group of pioneer houses laid out in the typical style of an early village. There is also a museum containing pioneer relics of different kinds.

10. Describe one of the ferry boats such as was used to carry the pioneers and their possessions from Kentucky across the Ohio River to the Indiana shore.

11. Describe how the pioneers got their water from a well when there was no other supply available.

12. Describe a "log rolling."

13. Make a report on how wheat and rye were harvested before the invention of the reaper.

14. Make a report on the games which the pioneers played.

15. Make a report on how the flax plant was handled to prepare it for linen thread.

16. Describe how a "bee trap" was located.

17. What was a "cooper"? Describe how wooden barrels were made. What kinds of wood were used for barrels which were used for various purposes? Make a report to the class.

18. Describe the kind of plow which the early pioneers used to break the soil.

19. What was meant by the expression, "The latch string is out"?

20. Describe how lye soap or "soft soap" was made by the pioneers.

21. Describe how maple sugar was made.

22. Prepare a report on methods of punishment used by the pioneers.

REFERENCES FOR UNIT 7

GENERAL REFERENCES

Buley—Vol. I, Chs. IV-V. Vol. II, pp. 417-513.

Esarey (School Ed.)—Chs. X, XII, XVII.

Cottman—pp. 74-76.

Esarey—*The Indiana Home.* (Limited Ed.)—Complete book.

Eggleston—*The Hoosier Schoolmaster.*

INDIANA HISTORY BULLETIN

"Some Neglected Aspects of Settler Life"—Allan Nevins, IHB, May, 1929.

"The Word Hoosier Again"—Stephen S. Visher, IHB, April, 1949.

"The Pioneer Press in Indiana"—Donald F. Carmony, IHB, Oct., 1954.

"The Conestoga Wagon"—IHB, Jan., 1956.

INDIANA MAGAZINE OF HISTORY

"The American Backwoodsman in Popular Portraiture"—Thos. D. Clark, IMH, March 1946.

"The Pioneer Fourth of July"—Geo. S. Cottman, IMH, June, 1912.

"Building a Pioneer Home"—Louis B. Ewbank, IMH, June, 1944.

READINGS IN INDIANA HISTORY (1956 edition)
Chs. XI, XIV, pp. 479-489.

"Life in Indiana, 1800-1820"—Rolla M. Hogue, IMH, Vol. 9, June, 1913.

"Home Life in Early Indiana"—Wm. Frederick Vogel, IMH, June-Sept., 1914.

"Hoosier Pioneers"—Joseph Wheeler Walker, IMH, March, 1924.

"Local Life and Color in the New Purchase"—James A. Woodburn, IMH, Dec., 1913.

"Pioneer Life"—Benj. S. Parker, IMH, March—Dec., 1907.

"Medical Practices on the Frontier"—Edward E. Dale, IMH, Dec., 1947.

"Pioneer Stories of the Calumet"—IMH, Vol. 18 (1922), pp. 166-176, 347-358.

"My Childhood and Youth in the Early Days of Indiana"—IMH, Vol. 19 (1923), pp. 303-331.

"Early Flour Mills in Indiana"—George Branson, IMH, March, 1926.

"Water Powered Mills of Flat Rock River"—Denzel Doggett, IMH, Dec., 1936.

PUBLICATIONS OF INDIANA HISTORICAL SOC.

"Pioneer Sketches of the Upper Whitewater Valley"—by Bernhard Knollenberg, Vol. 15, No. 1.

"A Home in the Woods; Oliver Johnson's Reminiscences of Early Marion County"—by Howard Johnson, Vol. 16, No. 2.

UNIT 8

Political Development of Indiana, 1816 to the Present

HISTORICAL SURVEY OF THE UNIT

The Territory of Indiana became a state on December 11, 1816. An election of officers had been held before that date and at that election Jonathan Jennings of Charlestown was chosen as the first governor of the State of Indiana. His time was occupied principally in organizing the government for the new state and putting this government to work.

Location of the State Capital

We have already learned that the southern part of Indiana was settled first. If you have passed through southern Indiana you will have noticed the many fine old houses that were built before Indiana became a state. These beautiful old homes, most of which are built of brick, are still standing in such cities as New Albany, Madison, Paoli, Lawrenceburg, Corydon, Vincennes, and Brookville. Many others can be seen on farms and in smaller towns in these vicinities. The first newspaper in the state (the *Indiana Gazette,* founded in 1804), the first county seat, the first library, the first college, the first land office, and the first Masonic Lodge were at Vincennes. The first counties, the first political parties, the first agriculture, and the first trails and roads were in the southern part of the state. As the population of southern Indiana grew, the pioneers gradually began to push into the northern half of the state.

The first capital of the state was at Corydon, which also had been the capital of the Territory since 1813. As the state grew in population and as the settlements spread northward, Corydon was thought to be too far toward the edge of the state, so in 1820 the General Assembly appointed a commission of eight men to select a new location for the capital.

After considering a number of possible locations, these men chose the site where Fall Creek flowed into White River. This was near the center of the state and at this place the present city of Indianapolis was laid out in 1821. The name "Indianapolis" was chosen by the legislature and is a combination of "Indiana" and the Greek word "polis" which means "city." The capital was moved to Indianapolis during 1824 and 1825, the work being completed in January of 1825. The first capitol

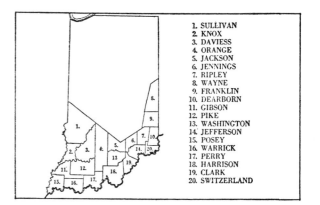

1.	SULLIVAN
2.	KNOX
3.	DAVIESS
4.	ORANGE
5.	JACKSON
6.	JENNINGS
7.	RIPLEY
8.	WAYNE
9.	FRANKLIN
10.	DEARBORN
11.	GIBSON
12.	PIKE
13.	WASHINGTON
14.	JEFFERSON
15.	POSEY
16.	WARRICK
17.	PERRY
18.	HARRISON
19.	CLARK
20.	SWITZERLAND

In 1817, only the southern part of the state had been divided into counties.

building or state house was finished in 1835. This served until the present capitol building, which was begun in 1878 and completed in 1888, was constructed.

The Governors of Indiana

The governor of Indiana has always been elected by the voters in the state. The list of Indiana's governors, together with the dates of their terms and the political parties to which they belonged, is given on the following pages. A survey of the list shows that forty-two different men have served as governor. In addition, one governor — Henry F. Schricker — served two terms. (The terms were not in succession.) Since the year 1861, the control of government in this state has switched back and forth between the Republican party and the Democrat party.

The history of our state is most easily followed by associating the different events with the governors in whose terms these events took place.

Name of Governor	Dates of Term	Political Party
Jonathan Jennings	1816-1822 (Resigned to enter Congress)	Jeffersonian Rep.
Ratliff Boon	1822 (Sept. 12 to Dec. 15)	Jeffersonian Rep.
Wm. Hendricks	1822-1825 (Resigned to enter U. S. Senate)	Jeffersonian Rep.
James B. Ray	1825-1831	Non-Partisan
Noah Noble	1831-1837	Whig
David Wallace	1837-1840	Whig
Samuel Bigger	1840-1843	Whig
James Whitcomb	1843-1848 (Resigned to enter U. S. Senate)	Democrat
Paris C. Dunning	1848-1849 (Served unexpired term of Whitcomb)	Democrat
Joseph A. Wright	1849-1857	Democrat
Ashbel P. Willard	1857-1860 (Died in Office)	Democrat
Abram A. Hammond	1860-1861 (Served unexpired term of Willard)	Democrat
*Oliver P. Morton	1861 (Resigned to enter U. S. Senate)	Republican
Henry S. Lane	1861-1867 (Served unexpired term of Lane. Resigned second term to enter U. S. Senate)	Republican
Conrad Baker	1867-1873	Republican
Thomas A. Hendricks	1873-1877	Democrat
James D. Williams	1877-1880 (Died in office)	Democrat
Isaac P. Gray	1880-1881 (Served 7 weeks)	Democrat
Albert G. Porter	1881-1885	Republican
Isaac P. Gray	1885-1889	Democrat
Alvin P. Hovey	1889-1891 (Died in office)	Republican
Ira J. Chase	1891-1893 (Served unexpired term of Hovey)	Republican
Claude Matthews	1893-1897	Democrat
James A. Mount	1897-1901	Republican
Winfield T. Durbin	1901-1905	Republican
J. Frank Hanly	1905-1909	Republican
Thomas R. Marshall	1909-1913	Democrat
Samuel M. Ralston	1913-1917	Democrat
James P. Goodrich	1917-1921	Republican
Warren T. McCray	1921-1924 (Resigned)	Republican
Emmett F. Branch	1924-1925 (Served unexpired term of McCray)	Republican
Ed Jackson	1925-1929	Republican
Harry G. Leslie	1929-1933	Republican
Paul V. McNutt	1933-1937	Democrat
Clifford Townsend	1937-1941	Democrat
Henry F. Schricker	1941-1945	Democrat
Ralph F. Gates	1945-1949	Republican
Henry F. Schricker	1949-1953	Democrat
George N. Craig	1953-1957	Republican
Harold W. Handley	1957-1961	Republican
Matthew E. Welsh	1961-1965	Democrat
Roger D. Branigin	1965-1969	Democrat
Edgar D. Whitcomb	1969-1973	Republican
Otis R. Bowen, M.D.	1973-1980	Republican
Robert D. Orr	1981-1988	Republican

*The first governor of Indiana born within the boundaries of the state.

The Governors under the First Constitution

Jonathan Jennings is well known because he was the first governor of the state. He was a member of the Jeffersonian Republican political party and had been prominent in politics when Indiana was a territory. Also, he had served as chairman of the constitutional convention in 1816. The business of putting into motion the machinery for the new state government was a very difficult task but it is doubtful whether a more able man could have been selected for the position.

At that time the population of the entire state was just about the same as the population of the city of Terre Haute today. Most of the people depended upon agriculture for a living and there was very little ready money in the

The first state capitol building at Indianapolis was completed in 1835.

state. It was very difficult to collect enough taxes to carry on the government. During the first four years that Jennings served as governor, the total expenses of the state were about $13,000 a year, and even this was more than the state's income. The governor's salary was only $1,000.00 a year, and that of a judge was $700.00 a year.

Jonathan Jennings had been born in New Jersey, and was only thirty-two years old when he was elected governor. He was bitterly opposed to slavery and took a firm stand against it when an attempt was made to introduce slavery into Indiana. It was during Jennings' administration that the Treaty of St. Mary's was made with the Miamis, the Weas, the Potawatomi, and the Delawares. By this treaty, about eight million acres of land composing the whole central part of the state, south of the Wabash River, were bought from the Indians. This vast territory, known as "The New Purchase of 1818," was thrown open for settlement and since it was very choice land,

it was settled rapidly. Governor Jennings resigned from the governorship in 1822, three months before his term expired and was elected to the Congress of the United States. Ratliff Boon, the lieutenant governor, served the remainder of the unexpired term of Jennings. Boon was a true pioneer who had little education. However, his strong common sense partially made up for his lack of learning. Immigrants came to the state in large numbers between 1816 and 1824 because the War of 1812 was over, the Indians were no longer hostile, and land was cheap. The population of the state increased greatly during this time, and in 1820 the census showed 150,000 people in Indiana. Evansville, Terre Haute, Bloomington, and Richmond were founded during this period.

The third governor of Indiana was William Hendricks. He, too, belonged to the Jeffersonian Republican party. He was elected in 1822 without opposition, receiving 18,340 votes, all that were cast. This number of votes gives you an idea of the population of the state at that time. This man, like many of the prominent persons of his day, had only a common school education. However, in his spare time he studied law and later he made the first revision of the state's laws and printed it on his own printing press. During his administration, the capital was moved from Corydon to Indianapolis. All the state records and the money from the state treasury were moved in wagons and the trip took two weeks. Like his predecessor, Hendricks, too, resigned his office as governor when he was elected to Congress.

James B. Ray served as acting governor for the remainder of Hendricks' term and then, in 1825, was elected governor for a full term. Of the early governors, Ray was one of the best known. Personally, he was very fond of display. When he built a large home in Brookville, people said that he was too extravagant and that such a person should not be permitted to handle public money. However, he did make a good governor. He favored the building of good roads, railroads, and canals. During his second term a program of internal improvements was begun, among them the Michigan Road and the Wabash and Erie Canal about which you will study in Unit 9. This work was aided by the fact that the state acquired almost all of the remaining Indian land during this time. Indiana University at Bloomington was organized during his term.

In 1825, the Jeffersonian Republican party split into two groups. One of these was known as the National Republican party which later became the Whig party. The other group was called the Democratic Republicans and it soon became known as the Democrat party.

Noah Noble, who belonged to the Whig party and was Indiana's first Whig governor, was chosen governor in 1831. He has been regarded as one of the most able and popular men to fill that position, and was in office while Andrew Jackson, who was a Democrat, was President of the United States. This was a time of great prosperity in Indiana (1831-1837).

The building of roads and canals was at its height. In January of 1836, Governor Noble signed an Act "to provide for a general system of internal improvements." The chief object of this Act was the building of three huge canals across Indiana and a railroad from Madison to Lafayette by the way of Indianapolis. Everything was on the "boom" and the people were engaged in wild speculation. After President Jackson put the United States Bank out of business, a state bank was chartered in Indiana and much of the credit for its organization and service to the people of the state belongs to Governor Noble. This bank had branches in thirteen of the principal towns of the state and was very successful until it closed in 1856.

David Wallace (the father of Lew Wallace, who wrote *Ben Hur*), who followed Noble, was elected because he favored a strong program of internal improvements which was an important issue throughout the state at that time. During his term in office (1837-1840) the Panic of 1837 caused the collapse of this program of internal improvements and this resulted in great unpopularity for Wallace because of the huge state debt which had been contracted and on account of the high taxes which resulted.

It was during the administration of Governor Wallace that the Potawatomi Indians, the last Indian tribe in Indiana, were removed from the state. These Indians had been living on a large reservation in the central part of northern Indiana, but when trouble arose between the Indians and the white settlers, the governor, in 1838, sent General John Tipton with a force of troops to remove the 900 Indians to land west of the Mississippi River. The preparations for moving the Indians were poorly made. Many hardships were encountered along the way and a large number of the Indians died on the trip.

The Panic of 1837 which swept over the United States affected Indiana, too. The period between 1840 and 1850 was one of "hard times." All construction work on the internal improvements stopped. The state treasury was empty and the state government bankrupt. The state debt had reached $13,000,000. There was a bitter political fight between the Democrats and the Whigs. In the presidential election of 1840, Indiana enthusiastically supported William Henry Harrison, who had been governor of the Territory, for President. Samuel Bigger was elected the seventh governor in Indiana, but he could do little toward reducing the state debt and improving financial conditions.

The Whigs controlled the state government until 1843 and in that year James Whitcomb, a Democrat, was elected. Whitcomb succeeded in reducing the state debt and in restoring the credit of the state. He is also favorably known because he encouraged education, especially for the blind and deaf, and better care for the insane. The Mexican War was fought during his second term. Indiana furnished over five thousand soldiers for the American army in this war. These soldiers took part in many of the principal battles and several of their officers won considerable fame. Governor Whitcomb resigned shortly before the end of his term to become United States Senator from Indiana, and Paris C. Dunning served out the unexpired portion.

The Second Constitution

By the time the Mexican War had closed, there was a feeling in Indiana that the state had outgrown the old Constitution of 1816 and that a new constitution was needed. The question was submitted to the voters and they voted in favor of holding a constitutional convention as soon as possible. In 1850, one hundred and fifty delegates were selected for this convention which met in Indianapolis on October 7, 1850, and remained in session until February 12, 1851. The new state constitution prepared by these delegates was voted on by the people in August of 1851. The vote was 113,230 for the new constitution and 27,638 against it. It went into effect on November 1, 1851, and has been the basic law of the state ever since.

The Constitution of 1851, as it is called, was modeled, in a general way, after the Constitution of the United States. It consists of 16 articles and is much longer than the Constitution of the United States. Article 1 is the Bill of Rights containing 37 different Sections. This Bill of Rights was included to protect the rights of the people of the state. Among these rights are the freedom of religion and worship, and the freedom of speech. Others are the right of a public trial by jury, the right for the people to assemble in a peaceful manner, and the right to be secure against unreasonable search and seizure. Another Section prohibited slavery within the state. The constitution further sets forth many important things and provides for a framework of government for the state. Among these are the following.

1. The state government was to consist of three equal branches or departments. These were, the legislative branch to make the laws, the executive branch to administer the laws or to see that they are carried out, and the judicial branch to interpret or tell what the laws mean.

2. The governor, who is the chief executive and head of that branch of the government, shall hold his office during four years, and shall not be eligible more than eight years in any period of twelve years.

3. The law-making body is called the General Assembly. The legislative meets annually; sessions held in odd-numbered years are limited to 61 session days while those in even-numbered years are limited to 30 session days. The governor may call a special session at any time he desires. The upper house or Senate is limited to 50 members, and the lower house or House of Representatives is limited to 100 members. All members are to be elected by the voters in their respective districts.

4. A state debt is prohibited, except for certain emergencies such as war. This meant that the state cannot borrow money to build roads, canals, public buildings, etc.

5. The General Assembly was given the power to establish a system of free common schools. Article 8 of the constitution also provided for a permanent Common School Fund. This was very important to the earlier schools but it now represents such a small sum that it has lost its importance.

6. Provision was made for state and county officers to carry out the laws. Also, the judges of the various courts were to be elected by the voters. Before this, judges had been appointed by the governor.

7. The qualifications for voting are set forth. One requirement is that a person must be 21 years of age in order to vote at any election.

8. The state constitution can be amended if the amendment is voted on favorably by two successive sessions of the General Assembly and then by a majority of the voters in the state. Numerous amendments have been made since 1851.

Joseph A. Wright was governor while the new constitution was being made and adopted. At the same time, industries were beginning to expand and many of the problems connected with industry had to be faced. Governor Wright was intensely interested in agriculture and the State Fair was started during his administration. Governor Wright takes a place as one of the great governors of our state.

The Period from 1850 to 1860

The period from 1850 to 1860 was one of great prosperity in Indiana. The effects of the depression had worn off and these years are sometimes referred to as the "glorious fifties." The Democrats controlled the state government during the 1850's. Ashbel P. Willard, the "silver-tongued orator," was elected governor in 1856 and was the first governor of the state to die in office. The lieutenant governor, Abram A. Hammond, completed the term. During this time, however, the controversy over the slavery question was being carried on all over the nation and Indiana was involved, too. In 1854, a new political party known as the Peoples' party was organized to take the place of the Whig party which had gone out of favor and which had declined. The Peoples' party soon became known as the Republican party and its members were opposed to the further spread of slavery in the United States. By 1860, the Republicans were strong enough to elect a governor in Indiana. The Republicans also gained control of both houses of the General Assembly for the first time.

It was during this time that the "Underground Railroad" was established. This was actually not a railroad at all but a series of stops along a route in eastern Indiana. Runaway slaves would follow this route in their flight from southern states to Canada. One of the most famous hiding places for the slaves was the home of Mr. and Mrs. Levi Coffin near Fountain City. Here the slaves would be hidden during the daytime and then sent on to another "station" the next night. The Quakers or members of the Friend's Church who had settled in large numbers in eastern Indiana were especially sympathetic to blacks seeking freedom.

Indiana's Part in the Civil War

In 1860, Henry S. Lane was elected governor and Oliver P. Morton was chosen lieutenant governor at the same time. Both men were Republicans and both were strongly opposed to slavery. Two days after he took office,

Governor Oliver P. Morton was known as Indiana's "War Governor."

Governor Lane resigned to become Senator and Oliver P. Morton took his place as governor. Morton is known as Indiana's "War Governor" because of his loyalty to the Union and because upon him fell the burden of directing the state's part in the defense of the Union during the Civil War. Morton was the first governor to be born within the boundaries of the state of Indiana. (His birthplace was Salesbury in Wayne County.) A fine statue of him now stands at the southeast corner of the Soldiers' and Sailors' Monument in Indianapolis.

When war was declared against the South, Indiana was totally unprepared for the conflict. However, Governor Morton immediately called for volunteers and a large number of men responded. The state treasury was empty and its credit was bad, but Morton set about to equip the state's soldiers and to furnish

necessary supplies. In order to do this he had to borrow on his personal credit and on the credit of his friends. Mr. J. F. D. Lanier of Madison, and other wealthy men advanced large sums of money to the state.

Most of the people of the state were in wholehearted sympathy with the North in the war. Indiana furnished a total of 197,649 soldiers for the Union army during this time. Thousands of these soldiers took part in some of the hardest campaigns, especially in the West. They fought in the armies of Generals McClellan, Hooker, Sheridan, Grant, Sherman, Thomas, and others. Several officers, among them Lew Wallace, who later wrote *Ben Hur*, and Benjamin Harrison, who became President of the United States, served with great ability in the war. A military camp, known as Camp Morton, was established in Indianapolis in April of 1861. This was first a training camp for soldiers but later, in 1862, it became a prison camp for captured Confederates. This camp was located in a 36-acre area which is now a residential district north of the present downtown business section of the city. It housed several thousand Confederate prisoners while the war was in progress. Governor Morton appointed Richard Owen of New Harmony to have charge of this camp and Owen was very popular with everyone until he resigned to take up other work.

Although slavery never legally existed in Indiana, and although most of the people were not in favor of slavery, there were a few who sympathized with the South. Some of these people organized secret societies which were formed to aid the South. These organizations took such names as "Knights of the Golden Circle" and "Order of American Knights." The members tried in every way to injure the cause of the North in the war. Governor Morton was also bothered by opponents in the state legislature but in spite of all this, Indiana's record in the Civil War is a glorious one.

The only time that a hostile army ever has invaded Indiana was in July of 1863 when a small force of Confederate cavalry, led by General John Morgan, crossed the Ohio River, marched as far north as Salem, and dashed hurriedly across the southern part of the state. The Confederates were opposed by little bands of militia which were hastily assembled, and from Salem, Morgan's men rode across southern Indiana and into Ohio. "Morgan's Raid," as this is called, accomplished little more than to badly frighten the people of this section and to plunder farms and small villages.

Progress since 1865

Since the Civil War, the history of Indiana has been included, to a very large extent, in the history of the nation as a whole. Many men of national prominence have been governor of Indiana and many famous persons have been natives of this state. (See Unit No. 12.) In the next Units in this history we will take up more in detail such topics as the growth of education, the growth of industry and agriculture, and the development of transportation systems in the state.

Oliver P. Morton, too, resigned from his office of governor before the end of his second term in order to take his place as United States Senator. The lieutenant governor, Conrad Baker, then became governor. Baker made a good record and succeeded in reducing the public debt. When he died, it was said that "Indiana has never had a wiser and better administration of its affairs than while he was governor."

Thomas A. Hendricks, governor from 1873 to 1877, was one of the well-known ones since the Civil War. During his term. there was considerable trouble between laborers and employers. The country was going through a "depression," too, but Indiana was not affected much by that. After serving as governor, Hendricks was elected Vice President of the United States in 1884. James D. Williams, who followed Hendricks as governor, was familiarly known as "Blue Jeans" Williams because he wore clothes made of homespun material. He was a self-educated farmer boy and represented the hard-working agricultural population of the state. He was sometimes referred to as the "farmer governor" of Indiana. During his term, several important amendments to the state constitution were made. One of these provided for holding public elections on the first Tuesday after the first Monday in November. The present state capitol building was begun during Williams' term. He died shortly before the end of his term and was followed by Isaac P. Gray.

Since that time, Indiana has steadily progressed under a long line of such governors as Albert G. Porter, Isaac P. Gray, Alvin P. Hovey,

Ira J. Chase, Claude Matthews, James A. Mount, Winfield T. Durbin, J. Frank Hanly, and Thomas R. Marshall.

The Spanish-American War was fought during Governor Mount's term of office. Indiana was the first state to fill its quota of soldiers. The compulsory school attendance law was passed during his term.

J. Frank Hanly was the 25th governor of Indiana. He had been a poor boy and had struggled hard to get an education. During his term the Indiana Girl's School at Clermont was established. Also, the first coliseum at the State Fair Grounds was built. Governor Hanly was a great believer in temperance reform and succeeded in getting a local option law passed by the legislature. By this law, the people of any county could vote on whether or not liquor could be sold in that county. As a result, more than half the counties abolished the sale of liquor.

Thomas R. Marshall, 1909-1913, was the first Democrat governor since 1897. One of the things for which he is remembered was his attempt to give the state a new constitution. The bill was passed by the legislature, but the Supreme Court of the United States declared it unconstitutional in 1912. He was followed by another Democrat, Samuel M. Ralston. Among the accomplishments of Mr. Ralston's administration were the inheritance tax law, the primary election law, the law in support of vocational training in the schools, the Workman's Compensation law, and the creation of the Public Service Commission. In 1916, the Indiana Centennial Celebration was held. This commemorated the admission of Indiana as a state in 1816. Also in this year, the state purchased the land for Turkey Run State Park, which was the beginning of our present excellent state park system. In 1922, after his term as governor, Mr. Ralston was elected to the United States Senate.

James P. Goodrich, 1917-1921, was governor during World War I. In this war, Indiana furnished its full quota of soldiers and sailors and some of them saw the very hardest of service at the war front. The state also made a splendid record in assisting in other war services. During Governor Goodrich's term, the State Highway Department was organized, a state prohibition law was passed, provision was made to build the Indiana World War Memorial in Indianapolis, and two amendments to the Federal Constitution were ratified. These were the woman suffrage amendment and the prohibition amendment. Also, the governor succeeded in getting several tax-reform laws passed in the state.

Governor Goodrich was followed by Warren T. McCray. At this time, the state of Indiana purchased and equipped a Governor's Mansion and Mr. McCray and his family were the first to occupy it. Governor McCray resigned in 1924 because of financial difficulties and Emmett F. Branch filled out Mr. McCray's unexpired term.

Ed Jackson, a Republican, was governor from 1925 to 1929, and during his term the Ku Klux Klan which had threatened to rule the state went downhill rapidly. Jackson practiced economy in government spending and a large state debt was paid off rapidly.

Harry G. Leslie, also a Republican, held the governor's office from 1929 to 1933. Leslie had been a noted athlete at Purdue University and had been crippled in the train wreck which caused the death of several members of the Purdue football team in 1903. During the great depression, he had many problems to face, including unemployment, low prices for agricultural products, bank failures, and labor troubles.

Paul V. McNutt, a Democrat, was elected governor in 1932 and took office in January of 1933. During his term, many changes were made in the setup of state government in Indiana in which the executive department was completely reorganized. One of the most important accomplishments was the passage of a gross income tax law. This was accompanied by a new law for an intangibles tax and one for an excise tax. M. Clifford Townsend became governor in 1937 and occupied the office until January 15, 1941. Governor McNutt and Governor Townsend's terms extended through the later years of the depression. Both men were capable executives and guided the state through troubled times.

Governor Townsend was succeeded by Henry F. Schricker, who had just completed a term as lieutenant governor of the state. Mr. Schricker was a Democrat, but he was the only Democrat elected on the state ticket in 1940. Since the Republicans controlled the state legislature during the first part of his term, many of the reorganization laws which had been passed during Governor McNutt's term were repealed. Schricker's term extended through the greater part of the World War II period (1941-1945).

Ralph F. Gates followed Mr. Schricker as governor and served from 1945 to 1949. He, in turn, was succeeded by Henry F. Schricker, who thus became the first governor since 1851 to be elected for two terms. Mr. Schricker was followed by George N. Craig. Mr. Craig was a strong supporter of education and worked hard to have the state take better care of the mentally ill. Governor Craig's term expired in 1957, and he was succeeded by Harold W. Handley. Governor Handley's term expired in 1961 and he was followed by Matthew E. Welsh. Welsh, a strong civil rights advocate, created a civil rights commission and appointed many blacks to important state posts.

Indiana's 42nd governor, Roger D. Branigin, a Lafayette lawyer, is known especially for his efforts toward preservation of Indiana's heritage and development of interstate highways.

Edgar D. Whitcomb was elected Indiana's 43rd governor in 1968, moving up from Secretary of State. He was a hero in World War II and author of *Escape From Corregidor*, describing the Japanese occupation of the Philippine Islands. During his administration state services were greatly increased, although he refused to raise taxes.

Otis R. Bowen, M.D., was elected Indiana's 44th governor in 1973. Governor Bowen is Indiana's first Doctor of Medicine to be elected governor. His administration has played an important role in revamping the tax structure and improving the health and penal systems.

In 1980, Robert D. Orr, lieutenant governor during the Bowen administration, became governor. Historians have not yet evaluated his term in office. Perhaps your parents will give you their opinions of one of Indiana's most recent governors.

STUDY EXERCISES

The following items concern the new state constitution of Indiana. Write the correct answers in the blanks.

_____ 1. In what year was a convention held to form a new constitution for Indiana?

_____ 2. This constitution went into effect on what date? (Give day, month, and year.)

_____ 3. Who was governor of Indiana when the constitution went into effect?

_____ 4. This state constitution was modeled after what other document?

_____ 5. What was its general purpose?

_____ 6. How many articles did it contain?

_____ 7. What was Article I called?

_____ 8. What five rights were guaranteed by the constitution?

_____

_____

_____

_____

_____ 9. What three branches of state government were provided for?

_____

_____

_____ 10. The governor was to be head of what branch of the government?

_____ 11. How long a term does the governor serve?

_____ 12. A governor is eligible for how many terms?

_____ 13. What is the name of the state lawmaking body?

_____ 14. Who selects the members of Indiana's state lawmaking body?

_____ 15. What is the upper house of the lawmaking body called?

_____ 16. The upper house consists of how many members?

_____ 17. What is the lower house of the lawmaking body called?

_____ 18. The lower house consists of how many members?

_____ 19. How often does the lawmaking body meet?

_____ 20. How long is each session?

_____ 21. What provision was made about a state debt?

_____ 22. What provision was made for support of public schools?

_____ 23. What requirement for voting was set forth?

_____ 24. How may the constitution be changed?

Complete the paragraphs by writing the correct words in the blanks.

1. Indiana Territory took the _____ step in organizing its government and became the

_____ state in the Union on (give exact date) _____. A man named _____, who was born in the state of _____ _____, was elected by the _____ as the first _____ of the state of Indiana. He belonged to the _____ political party. This man was only _____ years of age when he took office. However, he had great natural ability and proceeded to organize the state _____ _____ according to the provisions of the _____ of 1816. The first capital of the state was set up at _____. The governor's salary was _____ per year, and he was elected for a term of _____ years. In 1819, _____ was elected for a _____ term. Three months before his second term ended, Governor _____ resigned his office and was elected to _____. The lieutenant governor, _____ _____, then became the second man to be governor of _____.

2. Governor _____, the first governor of Indiana, made the treaty of _____ _____ with the _____, the _____, the _____ _____, and the _____ Indian tribes in the year _____. By this treaty, about _____ acres of land in the _____ part of the state, south of the _____ River, were acquired from the _____. This tract of land, known as the _____ _____, was thrown open for _____ and was settled very _____. When Indiana became a state, most of the people lived in the _____ _____ part of it. Three of the most important towns were _____, _____, and _____. The first _____ _____ in the state, the first _____, the first _____ _____, the first _____, and the first _____ were located in the town of _____. In 1820, the population of the state was about _____. The towns of _____, _____, _____, and _____ were started about this time.

3. _____ was the third man to become governor of Indiana. He, too, belonged to the _____ party and began his office in the year _____. He, like Governor Jennings, _____ his office before the end of his term and was elected to _____. As the population of Indiana increased, the people moved _____ in the state and the capital at _____ was thought to be too near the _____ _____. So, a committee of _____ men was appointed to find a new location for the _____. They finally chose a spot where _____ Creek flowed

into the west branch of the _____ River. The new town was called _____ _____. The moving of the capital was completed in the year _____, and the first capitol building was finished in the year _____. Mr. _____ _____ served as acting governor after Governor _____ resigned, and in the year _____ he was elected for a full term of his own. Governor _____ favored the building of _____, _____, and _____. These three things were referred to by the name of _____. During Governor _____ term, two large improvement projects were undertaken in Indiana. These were the _____ _____ and the _____. During this time, the state acquired almost all the remaining _____ land in Indiana.

4. _____ was the first man to be elected governor of Indiana by the Whig party. He served in this office from the year _____ to the year _____. He was in office when _____ was President of the United States. This period was characterized as one of great _____. During this time, Governor _____ signed a law which provided for the building of three _____ across the state and for a _____ from _____ _____ to _____. Also, a state _____ was chartered and this had branches in _____ towns in the state. Governor Noble was followed in office by _____, who was elected on a platform which called for a large program of _____. However, the _____ _____ came during Governor _____ term in office and caused a _____ of this program. The state debt reached the sum of _____ and the state government was _____. The period from 1837 to 1850 is characterized as one of _____ in Indiana. During Governor _____ term, the last of the _____ _____were removed from Indiana in the year _____. These belonged to the _____ tribe.

5. In 1840, there was a hard fight in Indiana between the people who belonged to the _____ party and those who belonged to the _____ party. _____ was elected President of the United States (he belonged to the _____ party) and _____ was elected governor of Indiana (he belonged to the _____ party). _____ was the first Democratic governor of Indiana. He was elected in the year _____. Governor _____ succeeded in _____ the state debt and in restoring the _____ of the state government. The _____ _____ War was fought during his term in office. Indiana furnished more than

92

_____ men for this war. Governor Whitcomb _____ before the end of his term to become _____, and he was succeeded by _____, who filled out the term.

Write the correct answers in the blanks.

_____ 1. The period between 1850 and 1860 in Indiana is characterized by what term?

_____ 2. What political party controlled the Indiana state government during the 1850's?

_____ 3. What governor died in office during this period?

_____ 4. What new political party was organized in 1854?

_____ 5. This party soon became known by what name?

_____ 6. The party mentioned above was strongly opposed to what?

_____ 7. In 1860, the control of Indiana state government passed to what party?

_____ 8. What name was given to the route by which slaves escaped to Canada?

_____ 9. What man resigned as governor of Indiana two days after he was elected?

_____ 10. What man then became governor?

_____ 11. Who was the first governor of Indiana to have been born in the state?

_____ 12. Which did Indiana support, the North or the South, in the Civil War?

_____ 13. What governor of Indiana was known as the "Civil War Governor"?

_____ 14. What prominent citizen loaned the Indiana state government money with which to equip soldiers?

_____ 15-16. What was Camp Morton and where was it located?

_____

_____ 17. How many soldiers did Indiana furnish for the Civil War?

_____ 18. What well-known Indiana author served as a general in the Union army?

_____ 19. What Confederate military move was made in southern Indiana during the Civil War?

_____ 20. What organization of Southern sympathizers was found in Indiana during the Civil War?

_____ 21. Of what governor was it said that, "Indiana has never had a wiser and better administration of its affairs than while he was governor"?

_____ 22-23. What two governors of Indiana later became vice presidents of the United States?

_____

_____ 24. What governor had the nickname of "Blue Jeans"?

_____ 25. Who was the "Silver-Tongued Orator"?

_____ 26-27. What two governors died in office after the Civil War?

_____

_____ 28. In what year was the present Indiana state capitol building begun?

_____ 29. In what year was this capitol building completed?

_____ 30. Who was governor of Indiana from 1893 to 1897?

_____ 31. Who was governor of Indiana when the Spanish-American War was fought?

_____ 32. Who was governor of Indiana from 1901 to 1905?

_____ 33. What governor of Indiana succeeded in getting a local option liquor law passed?

_____ 34. What governor of Indiana attempted to give the state a new constitution?

_____ 35. Who was governor of Indiana during World War I?

_____ 36. What secret organization became quite powerful in Indiana in in the mid-1920's?

_____ 37. Who was governor of Indiana during World War II?

_____ 38. Who was governor of Indiana from 1953 to 1957?

_____ 39. Who are the only men since 1851 to have been elected governor of Indiana twice?

_____ 40. How many different men have been governor of Indiana?

_____ 41. Who was elected governor of Indiana in 1960?

_____ 42. Who was elected governor of Indiana in 1964?

_____ 43. Who was Indiana's 43rd governor?

_____ 44. Who was elected governor in 1973? In 1980?

_____ 45. Who was most recently elected Indiana's governor?

Write the correct answers in the blanks.

1. What effect did the financial condition of Indiana between 1840 and 1850 have upon the building of roads and canals in the state? _____

_____

2. What provision did the Constitution of 1851 make for the government of counties in the state?

_____

3. Beginning with Ed Jackson's term as governor, how many governors of Indiana have belonged to the Republican party? _____ How many to the Democrat? _____

4. What five important laws were passed during Governor Ralston's term?

_____ _____ _____

_____ _____

5. What three important tax laws were passed during Governor Paul McNutt's term?

_____ _____ _____

6. What governor of Indiana completely reorganized the executive branch of the state government during the 1930's? _____ What later action repealed most of this reorganization? _____

7. Who was governor of Indiana from 1945 to 1949? _____

8. From what source does the state of Indiana now get most of its money to operate the state government? _____

9. Select four governors of Indiana that you think were the most outstanding. List them in the left-hand column below. Then, in the right-hand column, opposite each name, list one important event or achievement of that governor's term.

_____   _____

_____   _____

_____   _____

_____   _____

10. You are represented by a number of elected officials. List the names of the people who represent you in each legislative body listed below. Each should be currently in office. A. Mayor _____; B. Governor _____; C. State Representative _____; D. State Senator _____; E. U.S. Representative _____; F. U.S. Senator _____.

ASSIGNMENT FOR MAP EXERCISE
EARLY INDIANA

With a black dot show the location of Corydon. Print the name at the side of it.

With a small red star show the location of Indianapolis. Print the name at the side of it.

Place on the map in the proper locations, the names of the counties which had been formed in the state by the year 1816. Outline each of these counties with red.

With a heavy blue line draw the boundary of "The New Purchase" of 1818. This is the land which was acquired from the Indians by the Treaty of St. Mary's.

With a heavy black line draw the boundary of the land acquired from the Indians in 1828 and 1832.

Locate the west branch of the White River by printing the name in the proper place on the map.

Locate the Wabash River by printing the name in the proper place on the map.

TOPICS FOR DISCUSSION AND REPORT

1. Does or does not Indiana now need a new constitution? Give reasons.
2. Give a report of "Morgan's Raid." Why were the people of Indiana so excited about this?
3. What were the causes for the state being bankrupt between 1840-1850?
4. Where in Indiana is there a fine statue of Governor James Whitcomb? If any member of the class has seen this statue, have him describe its location and appearance.
5. Make a report on the beginning of your own town or city. Include such things as: the date of its first settlement, who founded it, why a settlement was made in this particular location, whether it grew slowly or rapidly, how the first buildings looked, etc. See if you can find some picture of the town in its early years.
6. See if your public library has a file of any newspaper that was published during the Civil War. If so, read some of the news articles about the war. Make a report to the class on something you think is interesting, and which was an important event to the people of Indiana at that time.
7. Do the same thing as was suggested in No. 6, except choose some item concerning an important happening between 1870 and 1900.
8. Do the same thing as was suggested in No. 6, except choose some item concerning an important happening between 1912 and 1925.
9. Write to an elected official listed in No. 10 above. Support or disapprove of legislation that official has recently sponsored.

HISTORICAL CHART EXERCISES

Complete this chart by writing, in the proper places, important events in Indiana which correspond with those listed under the United States heading.

Indiana	1816 to 1960	The United States
	1816	Second Bank of the U.S. chartered
	1819	Florida purchased from Spain.
	1820	Missouri Compromise.
	1823	Monroe Doctrine.
	1836	Van Buren elected President.
	1837	Panic of 1837.
	1840	Wm. H. Harrison elected President.
	1845-48	Mexican War
	1848	California Gold Rush.
	1850	Compromise of 1850.
	1851	Vigilance Committee organized in San Francisco.
	1854	Kansas-Nebraska Act.
	1860	Lincoln elected President.
	1861-65	Civil War.
	1869	First transcontinental railroad.
	1873	Panic of 1873.
	1888	Benj. Harrison elected President
	1893	Panic of 1893.
	1898	Spanish-American War.
	1905	World's Fair in St. Louis
	1917-18	World War I.
	1920	Woman Suffrage Amendment.
	1929	Stock market panic.
	1931	Depression and bank failure.
	1932	F. D. Roosevelt elected President.
	1941	Beginning of World War II.
	1945	End of World War II.
	1950	Korean War.
	1952	Eisenhower elected President.
	1960	Kennedy elected President.

EARLY
INDIANA

SCALE OF MILES

0   10   20   30

REFERENCES FOR UNIT 8

GENERAL REFERENCES

Buley—Vol. I, pp. 74-78, 565-632. Vol. II, pp. 12-42, 160-299.

Esarey (School Edition)—Chs. VII-XV, XVII-XXI, XXIII-XXV, XXVIII-XXXI.

Cottman—Chs. VII, X-XVI, XIX.

Thornton, Read—Chs. VII-XII, XVII-XVIII, XXII.

Levering—Chs. VIII-X, XII-XVI, XXII.

Roll—Vol. I, pp. 344-543. Vol. II, complete volume.

Esarey (2 vol. edition)—Chs. X, XIII-XV, XVII-XXIII, XXVI-XXVII, XXIX, XXXII-XXXIII,

XXVI-XXXVIII.

Lockridge—*The Story of Indiana*—pp. 185-203, Chs.

XIII-XV. pp. 367-380.

Nicholson—The Hoosiers—Ch. IV.

Thompson—*Stories of Indiana*—pp. 128-208, 247-265.

Indiana—Prepared by direction of Governor Harry G. Leslie, 1930. This contains photographs and biographical sketches of all Indiana governors.

INDIANA HISTORY BULLETIN

"Early Financial History of Indiana"—James Edward Hagerty, IHB, Oct., 1941.

"Taxation in Indiana During the Last Forty-Five Years"—Philip Zoercher, IHB, Feb., 1937.

"Our Great War Governor"—William Dudley Foulke, IHB, Apr., 1931.

"Civil War Camps in Indiana"—IHB, Apr., 1960.

"Constitution of the State of Indiana"—Edited by the Legislative Bureau—IHB, Vol. 33, No. 6, June, 1956.

INDIANA MAGAZINE OF HISTORY

"Pioneer Politics in Indiana"—Logan Esarey, IMH, June, 1917.

"The Election of 1852 in Indiana"—A. Dale Beeler, IMH, Dec., 1915; March, 1916.

"The Origin and Rise of the Republican Party in Indiana from 1854 to 1860"—Charles Zimmerman, IMH, Sept.-Dec., 1917.

"Indiana in the Mexican War"—R. C. Buley, IMH, Sept., 1919-March, 1920.

"Morgan's Raid in Indiana"—Margarette Boyer, IMH, Dec., 1912.

"Secret Political Societies in the North During the Civil War. Knights of the Golden Circle; Sons of Liberty"—Mayo Fesler, IMH, Sept., 1918.

"Lambdin P. Milligan—A Knight of the Golden Circle"—Florence L. Grayston, IMH, Dec., 1947.

"Civil War Letters and Dispatches"—Harvey Wish, Ed., IMH, March, 1937.

"The Impact of the Civil War on Indiana"—John D. Barnhart, IMH, Sept., 1961.

"Indian Removal and the Great American Desert"—Francis Paul Prucha, IHM, Dec., 1963.

"Mexican War Journal of Henry S. Lane"—IMH, Dec., 1957.

"The Flow of Colonists to and from Indiana before the Civil War"—IMH, March, 1915.

"Hoosier Cattle Kings"—Paul W. Gates, IMH, March, 1948.

Map of Indiana in 1818—IMH, Vol. 9 (1913), p. 217. "Old Corydon"—IMH, Vol. 13 (1917), pp. 20-41.

"The First Indiana Banks"—Logan Esarey, IMH, Dec., 1910.

"The Removal of the State Capital to Indianapolis"—Mildred C. Stoler (Two accounts of the trip made by the state treasurer and party accompanied by the state printer, 1824), IMH, Sept., 1931.

"Jonathan Jennings"—Dorothy Riker, IMH, Dec., 1932.

READINGS IN INDIANA HISTORY (1914 edition)

Parts III-V. (Selections No. 42-63, 82-103, 107-117, 122-151)

READINGS IN INDIANA HISTORY (1956 edition)
Ch. IX, pp. 501-569.

PUBLICATION OF INDIANA HISTORICAL SOC.

"The National Decline of the Miami Indians"—John B. Dillon, Vol. 1, No. 4.

"Early History of Indianapolis and Central Indiana"—Nathaniel Bolton, Vol. 1, No. 5.

"Making a Capital in the Wilderness"—Daniel Wait Howe, Vol. 4, No. 4.

"Indianapolis and the Civil War"—John H. Holliday, Vol. 4, No. 9.

"Morgan's Raid in Indiana"—Louis B. Ewbank, Vol. 7, No. 2.

"Early Indianapolis"—Mrs. Laura Fletcher Hodges, Vol. 7, No. 5.

"Centennial Handbook, 1830-1930"—Edited by Christopher B. Coleman, Vol. 10, No. 1.

"Camp Morton, Indianapolis, 1861-1865"—Vol. 13, No. 3.

"The Trail of Death, Letters of Benjamin Marie Petit"—Vol. 14, No. 1.

"Diary of William Owen" from Nov. 10, 1824, to April 20, 1825. Edited by Joel Hiatt (1906) Vol. 4, No. 1.

"The Circle; the Center of Our Universe"—Ernestine Bradford Rose (1957), Vol. 18, No. 4.

"The Northern Boundary of Indiana"—Mrs. Frank J. Sheehan (1928), Vol. 8, No. 6.

"Indiana in the War of the Rebellion"—Report of the Adjutant General—W. H. H. Terrell (1869), 1960.

UNIT 9

The Development of Transportation Systems in Indiana

HISTORICAL SURVEY OF THE UNIT

The development of transportation systems in Indiana has been a very important thing in the growth and progress of the state. The first white men who came into Indiana had to travel either by boat on some navigable stream or lake, or on foot or horseback over some wilderness trail. These trails spread like a network over the whole state, but of course some of them were more traveled than others. Many of them had been made in the first place by the herds of buffalo which roamed the country in the earlier days. Then the Indians had followed these well-known paths. Later, the white hunters and the immigrants traveled over these same trails because these were the easiest paths through the wilderness. Quite often the settlers cut patches of bark off the trees along the trail. This was called "blazing" the trail and it served to mark the path which otherwise might have been impossible to find.

Early Trails and Traces

These trails usually were referred to as traces. The difference between a trace and a trail is not clear, so they are generally re-

garded as the same in meaning. One of the best known was the Vincennes Trace or the old "Buffalo Trace" which led from the falls of the Ohio River near where New Albany now stands, to Vincennes. Another important trace, a little less used than the Vincennes Trace, ran from the falls of the Ohio to the Wea Plains just west of Lafayette. This was known as the Wea Trail. A much traveled trail extended from Fort Wayne across northern Indiana to the western shore of Lake Michigan. This was called the Sac Trail because it was followed so much by the Sac Indians. Another followed the Wabash from Fort Wayne to Terre Haute and from there led into central Illinois. Wetzel's Trace was from Brookville to Indianapolis, and Berry's Trace from Indianapolis to Lafayette. The old Chicago Trail was from the Wea Plains through Benton County to Chicago. There were many more less important trails in different parts of the state.

The First Roads

Very few of the first settlers who came to Indiana had wagons. After they got away from the streams they proceeded on foot or on horseback. Gradually it became necessary to have wider roads over which wagons could pass when the grain and livestock had to be taken to market. So, the trails were opened up by cutting down trees and removing the brush, and when they were improved enough to allow vehicles to use them, they were called "wagon roads." The mud was the worst thing that the travelers had to contend with and it seemed bottomless, especially in the winter and spring. The settlers did not have the machinery or the manpower to grade and drain the roads. They didn't have gravel and brick and cement to

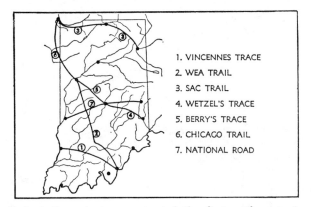

1. VINCENNES TRACE
2. WEA TRAIL
3. SAC TRAIL
4. WETZEL'S TRACE
5. BERRY'S TRACE
6. CHICAGO TRAIL
7. NATIONAL ROAD

Early trails and traces connected the first settlements in Indiana.

pave with, either. Wood was plentiful, though, and so in some places they tried to make a wooden floor for the roads. This was done in one of two ways. One way was simply to fell the trees and place the logs crosswise of the road. This was called a "corduroy" road. It held up the wagons but it was terribly bumpy. The other method was to split logs into boards and make a road surface of these. This was called a "plank" road. It was smooth, but it was constantly in need of repair.

The Michigan Road was the first one built clear across the state from north to south. In 1826, a treaty was made with the Potawatomi Indians, who still claimed the land in the northern part of the state, by which a section of land was given for each mile of road to be built from the Ohio River to Lake Michigan. This was surveyed in 1830. It began at Madison and was laid out through Versailles, Greensburg, Indianapolis, and Logansport to South Bend and from there to Michigan City. This road was made one hundred feet wide, bridges were built over the streams, and some attempts were made to grade it. This was a great improvement but at its best the road was little more than a long mud hole. It was heavily traveled, however, because it was the main north and south highway. The present Federal Highway No. 421 and parts of Interstate 74 follow the general course of the old Michigan Road.

The first east and west road across the state was the National Road. This was a continuation of the Cumberland Road and was surveyed across Indiana in 1827. It extended from Richmond to Terre Haute by way of Indianapolis. Federal Highway No. 40 now follows this route. The old National Road was almost perfectly straight. It was wide and was surfaced with crushed stone for a part of the distance. It was considered for many years to be one of the finest roads in the world.

Both the Michigan Road and the National Road were crowded by steady streams of traffic. Most of the passenger traffic was carried by stage coaches. Freight lines were established, too, and emigrant wagons passed by the hundreds. Many stage lines were operated on other roads, also. The one from Louisville to Vincennes, started in 1820, is supposed to have been the first in the state. Others were put into operation between Madison and Indianapolis by way of Columbus; between Lawrenceburg and Indianapolis; from Cincinnati to Indiana-

The stagecoach was a heavy, wagon-like vehicle which carried passengers from town to town.

polis through Brookville; from Leavenworth on the Ohio River through Paoli, Bedford, and Bloomington to Indianapolis; and from Lafayette to Fort Wayne.

Although the better stage coaches were drawn by four fine horses, and were splendid looking affairs, they could not average more than seven or eight miles per hour. On the National Road, if they did not stop at night, some of the stage coaches could make one hundred fifty miles in twenty-four hours. In 1834, the trip from Madison to Indianapolis could be made in one day.

The stage coaches were well built, but, although they had crude springs, riding very far in one was enough to tire out the strongest person. Inns and taverns along the roads furnished food, drink, and lodging for the coach travelers and for others who traveled in their own wagons. Many of these inns became famous for the quality and quantity of food which they served. Regular stage coach travel was seldom possible the year around because of bad weather and muddy roads.

Some of these early Indiana roads were built by the state government. Some were paid

Many of the early bridges in Indiana were "covered bridges" built entirely of wood.

for by the counties through which they passed, and some were constructed by private companies. In the latter case, "toll gates" were set up and a charge or "toll" was collected from each person who traveled the road. Many of the bridges were "toll bridges," too, and persons who crossed these had to pay the owners for the privilege. Nearly all the first bridges across the Wabash were "toll bridges." They were gradually replaced by free bridges with money raised by taxation. The toll system hindered travel and poorer people could not afford to take trips. Most of the early bridges were "covered bridges." These were built of timber, the whole bridge was enclosed, and the roadway was like a tunnel through the bridge. Some of these old covered bridges are still in use in Indiana.

The Canals

In spite of the improvement of the roads, however, before 1830 the people were clamoring for better means of transportation. Most of the freight to the principal markets was still carried by boat on the rivers or on canals. Many of the eastern states had begun extensive projects of "internal improvements," that is, the building of canals and roads, especially the former. The Erie Canal, from Buffalo, N. Y., to Albany, N. Y., was opened in 1825, and Pennsylvania and Ohio had undertaken the construction of numerous canals to connect the principal lakes and streams in their states.

The first large canal building project which was begun in Indiana was the Wabash and Erie Canal. When completed, this was to join Lake Erie with the Mississippi River by way of the Wabash River valley and the Ohio River. The canal was started by the state in 1832. It was completed to Lafayette by 1842, to Covington by 1846, to Terre Haute by 1849,

During the decade of 1830 to 1840, many canals were begun and some were completed.

and finally to Evansville in 1853. During the first few years that it operated, this canal proved a great boon to the northern part of the state, especially to the Wabash valley. Many towns prospered and grew rapidly in population. Among these were Logansport, Peru, Lafayette, Attica, Williamsport, Covington, and Terre Haute. It had a total length of 380 miles in Indiana and 88 miles in Ohio, and was the longest canal ever built in North America.

Indiana was caught in the wave of agitation for internal improvements which swept over the whole United States. There was a tremendous demand for the building of canals and railroads at the expense of the state. The farmers were especially anxious to have the canals completed so they would have a better and quicker way to get their produce to market. In 1836, the state legislature passed what was known as the Mammoth Internal Improvement Bill, which was one of the most important measures ever passed in Indiana. This Improvement Bill provided for the following things:

1. The Whitewater Canal.
2. The Central Canal.
3. Completion of the Wabash and Erie Canal from Lafayette to the Central Canal.
4. A railroad from Madison, through Columbus and Indianapolis to Lafayette.
5. A turnpike from New Albany to Vincennes.
6. A survey of the route from Jeffersonville to Crawfordsville.
7. A survey for a canal or a railroad from Fort Wayne to Lake Michigan.
8. The setting aside of $50,000 for removing obstructions from the Wabash River.

The total cost of the work was estimated at $13,000,000. However, the scheme proved to be entirely too elaborate to be financed by taxation. Several of the various projects were begun before much progress had been made for financing them. The country was plunged into the Panic of 1837, and by 1839 the work had to stop because no more money could be secured. This really marked the end of the program for internal improvements at state expense. The next ten years were years of "depression" and "hard times" in Indiana. The Wabash and Erie Canal was operated for a while by private individuals, but it was abandoned before it was entirely completed. The Whitewater Canal was begun in 1836 and finished to Brookville. Later, it was extended to Lawrenceburg and Cincinnati. Its length in Indiana was 76 miles, and it cost over $1,000,000. The Central Canal was completed in the 1830's about ten miles each way from Indianapolis. The various other projects were abandoned and altogether the state lost about $10,000,000, which was sufficient to bankrupt it for the time being.

The remains of some of these old canals can be seen in places in Indiana today. The part of the Central Canal which extended from downtown Indianapolis to Broad Ripple is filled with water at the present time. It was sold to the Indianapolis Water Company in 1865, but is not used for traffic now.

Some traces of the Whitewater Canal can be seen in the Whitewater valley, too. That part which extended from Brookville to Metamora, together with a dam near Laurel, Indiana, has been restored and is now a State Memorial. At Metamora, a small town along Highway No. 52, between Indianapolis and Cincinnati, an old aqueduct has been rebuilt. This shows how the water of the canal was carried over the river when it was necessary for the canal to cross the river. Such aqueducts were common along the early canals where they had to cross small streams. These aqueducts were built of wood and it was difficult and expensive to keep them in repair.

At Connersville, Indiana, the route of the old canal can be traced. At this place, the canal was several hundred yards from the river. Sometimes it was necessary for the water level in the canals to be raised to carry the canal boats over the higher ground. In such cases, "locks" were built to contain enough water to raise or lower the boats.

In the northwest part of Lafayette, Indiana, one can see some remains of the Wabash and Erie Canal. One of these spots, which is still partially filled with water, was a turning basin for the canal boats. Actually, it was just a wide place in the canal, providing enough space for the boats to turn around and reverse their journey. Such a turning basin was usually referred to as a "widewater." An 8-mile stretch in Indianapolis also still exists.

The flat bottomed canal boats did not have engines to propel them. They had to be pulled by a horse or a mule. The animal walked along the bank on a well-worn path called the "tow path." The boat was "towed" by the horse or mule which was hitched to it by a rope. Boat operators advertised speeds as much as 9 miles per hour. Large quantities of freight of all kinds could be loaded into one boat. The men who operated the canal boats were rough and often quarrelsome. The canals provided a useful service and their life added to the picturesqueness of the early days in Indiana.

The canals were doomed to failure. They could be used only part of the year. Storms and floods caused much damage. Service was poor and too slow.

The Railroads

By the year 1831, the settlers in Indiana were demanding that the new state government build some railroads with state money. In answer to this, the legislature, in 1831, gave six different companies the right to build railroads in the state. One of these was the Madison and Indianapolis Railroad. At that time, Madison, on the Ohio River, was one of the leading towns in Indiana so it is not surprising that the railroad between Madison and Indianapolis was the first steam road in the state. This railroad was completed to Vernon—20 miles from Madison—in 1839, and to Indianapolis by October 1, 1847. This was a day of great celebration and the arrival of the first train in Indianapolis was greeted by thousands of persons. The first depot was located near the crossing of what are now Pennsylvania and South Streets. The people who predicted that Indianapolis would some day be a great railroad center were correct.

The railroads were chiefly responsible for putting the canals out of business. Transportation by railroads was so much more speedy than by canal boats that the railroads soon got all the traffic. The ten years from 1850 to 1860 were full of railroad building in Indiana. In 1850 there were only 200 miles of track in the state. By 1860 this had increased to 2,000 miles. The railroads played the same important part in the development and growth of Indiana that they did in other parts of the country. Today, there are approximately 6,622 miles of railroad track in Indiana.

The Madison and Indianapolis Railroad had been begun by the state government as a part of the "internal improvement" program. However, the building of railroads proved to be too big an undertaking for the state government and it never engaged in any more railroad building. All the other railroads were constructed by private individuals or by companies which had sold stock in the railroad.

The train took the place of the canal boat and the wagon because it was a quicker form of transportation.

Almost all of them later became parts of the great railroad systems of the nation.

The Bellefontaine and Indianapolis, which later became part of the Penn Central, was begun in 1848 and connected with the east in 1854. The Indianapolis and Peru, later the Norfolk and Western, was completed to Peru about the same time. The Terre Haute and Indianapolis and the Indiana Central, which later became the Penn Central, had been extended across the state by 1853. The Indianapolis and Lafayette and the Indianapolis and Lawrenceburg, which were to become a part of the Penn Central, were completed in 1853. The New Albany and Salem, afterwards known as the Monon, now belongs to the Louisville and Nashville Railroad. It was the first railroad constructed entirely across the state from north to south, joining the Ohio River with Lake Michigan at Michigan City. This line passed through Lafayette, Crawfordsville, and Salem. In 1857, a part of the Ohio and Mississippi Railroad between Mitchell and Vincennes was completed. This was later extended and became the Baltimore and Ohio, which played such an important part in serving southern Indiana. This later became part of the Chessie System. The Toledo, Wabash, and Western later became part of the Norfolk and Western. It paralleled the Wabash and Erie Canal for a long distance and helped to kill the business of the Erie Canal.

Effect upon the Cities

The change from canal and river traffic to rail traffic brought about some curious changes in the location and growth of towns. From this time on the inland towns grew more rapidly. People no longer felt that a town had to be located on navigable water in order to prosper. For example, Madison, which had been dependent upon river trade, lost business rapidly and whole rows of stores were closed at a time. On the other hand, Indianapolis benefited by the change. In some cases, whole towns were gradually moved after a railroad was built. A typical instance of this is found in the history of the town of Williamsport in western Indiana. The site of the original town was in the lowland along the bank of the river. When the Wabash Railroad was built, it ran across the higher land a mile or more from the town as it was then situated. A new Williamsport sprang up along the railroad and the old town was eventually deserted. Remains of old buildings still stand as silent witnesses to progress in the methods of transportation.

River towns and canal towns lost population when the river and canal traffic decreased. For many years the railroads carried most of the passengers and freight. However, within the last fifteen years, things have greatly changed again. Water traffic has begun to increase. The rivers, especially the Ohio River, which forms the south boundary of Indiana, are now carrying great loads of freight. If one looks out across the Ohio River today, it is likely that one will see long strings of barges being pushed up or down the river. These barges are filled with oil, coal, automobiles, and other manufactured articles. On Lake Michigan one can see the boats bringing iron ore and coal to the steel mills and grain to the mills and elevators. Many new factories have been built along the rivers and lakes, and some of these localities have grown into cities.

THE GREAT
PAN-HANDLE ROUTE.

Chicago, St. Louis and Pittsburgh Railway.

Pittsburgh, Cincinnati & St. Louis Railway.
IS THE
SHORTEST, QUICKEST AND BEST
— LINE GOING —
EAST, WEST, NORTHWEST & SOUTH.

Unexcelled Through Car Service. Superior Equipment. Prompt Connections in Union Depot.

NO TRANSFERS.
PULLMAN CARS THROUGH BETWEEN ALL THE GREAT COMMERCIAL CENTERS.

Pittsburgh, Harrisburg, Baltimore, Washington, Philadelphia, New York Columbus, Indianapolis, St. Louis, Chicago, Louisville.

The advantages offered to Passengers via Pan-Handle Route are unequalled. The rates are always as low as by any other line. All modern improvements conduce to speed, comfort and safety. Baggage checked through to destination. Superior service in every respect. Agent of the company will cheerfully furnish information in regard to trains, connections, and rates of fare.
H. R. DERING, Am't Gen'l Pass. Agent, Indianapolis.

JAMES McCREA, General Manager, Pittsburgh, Pa.
JOHN F. MILLER, General Superintendent, Columbus, Ohio.
E. A. FORD, Gen. Pass. Agent, Pittsburgh, Pa.

Local magazines carried advertisements such as this one about the year 1880.

The Electric Lines or Interurbans

Another transportation system which grew up in Indiana and which was very important for a number of years was the electric line or interurban as it was called. The first interurban line was built from Alexandria to Anderson in 1898 and the first line into Indianapolis was in 1900. Other lines were built soon after this. They reached nearly all parts of the state and since most of them entered Indianapolis, this city became the greatest interurban center in the world. The Traction Terminal Station was built there and at one time more than six hundred cars departed from the station each day to three hundred towns in the state. In 1914, there were 2,168 miles of interurban track in the state.

Most of these interurban lines were controlled by three or four large companies. The Union Traction Company operated to Anderson, Muncie, Fort Wayne, Alexandria, Elwood, and Tipton. The Terre Haute, Indianapolis and Eastern System had branches radiating from Indianapolis to Martinsville, Danville, Terre Haute, Crawfordsville, Lebanon, Frankfort, Lafayette, Newcastle, and Richmond. The Interstate Company had a line from Indianapolis to Louisville through Columbus and Jeffersonville. Several other lines operated in other parts of the state. Lafayette was the first city of Indiana to have a completely electrified street railway system (in 1888). By 1914, 67 counties of 92 had electric rails.

A six-week strike in 1937 crippled them and they never recovered, although there's still an electric line operating in Indiana. It is the South Shore in the far northern part of the state.

Railroads Affected by Increased Motor Traffic

The changes which came with time have affected the interurbans in much the same manner that the railroads affected the canals.

After World War I, Indiana began a systematic plan for improvement of the highways of the state. There was an almost immediate effect upon the railroad and upon the electric lines. The interurbans died almost as quickly as they had grown. Most of their business was passenger traffic and the hauling of local freight. Consequently, when the private automobiles, the buses, and the trucks began to swarm over the highways in such large numbers, the loss of business made it unprofitable for most of the interurbans to operate. One by one they

The interurban cars, run by electricity, were used to carry passengers from town to town.

were abandoned and the last interurban car made its final trip early in 1941. Of all the vast network of interurban tracks that was built in the beginning of the century, every mile has now passed into the discard. Large numbers of huge buses enter and depart from bus terminals. Most of the electric street car lines in the cities have been abandoned, too, and their place taken over by buses.

Almost every family now has one or more cars. Mammoth trucks equipped for speedy and efficient service will deliver freight to the customer's door in less time and quite frequently at less cost than the railroads will. Bus lines connect all the principal towns and cities in the state. The Greyhound Bus Line is one of the largest of these companies, although there are other smaller ones offering this service to passengers.

The change in transportation methods has caused much hardship to the railroads, too. In many ways the railroads have been unable to compete with the trucks and buses. The railroads have enormous expenses in keeping up their right of way and paying taxes on it.

The trucks and buses have been using the highways which were built and maintained at public expense and thus have avoided many of the large expenses of operation. Within the last several years, however, larger taxes have been placed on trucks and buses and now they are more nearly bearing their share of road costs than formerly.

The loss of business caused some of the small railroads to fail entirely. An example of this sort of failure was the Midland Railroad which extended in a general east and west direction across the central part of the state and which passed through Noblesville and Lebanon. This road was abandoned and the rails torn up. Another which suffered was the Brazil branch of the C. and E. I., which extended from Momence, Ilinois, to Brazil, Indiana, through Morocco, Attica, Veedersburg, and a number of other towns. This road was later known as the Chicago, Attica, and Southern, but it has been completely abandoned. The small towns on these railroads protested their abandonment but were not successful in keeping the railroads in operation. There are many other cases of the same kind as the ones cited here.

Today, there are few privately owned railroads. Most railroads in the United States have been merged into a national rail system called AMTRAK. Others, particularly freight lines, have been merged into a system known as CONRAIL. Both systems were the direct result of financial difficulties experienced by independent railroads.

In Indiana there are 6,622 miles of track. The state is crossed by almost all main lines east of Chicago and is serviced in part by Amtrak. Indiana's railroads carry more than five million tons of freight per mile each year. The famous *Broadway Limited* goes through Indiana each day. If you live in Gary or a neighboring town, you can watch it pass.

The Improved Highways of the State

In many instances the state highways have not passed through the center of the small towns or have missed them entirely. In almost every case of this sort, this has brought about or is in the process of bringing about a change in the location of that town. Just as the railroad drew the towns away from the canals, so are the state highways drawing the towns away from the railroads. One need not drive many miles today to see examples of this sort. A trip down Highway Number 41 would be sufficient. At Kentland, where Highway No. 41 has been relocated twice, firms have followed the new location each time. At Sterling, where two state highways intersect one mile east of Veedersburg, this intersection gradually became a business center. This instance is very significant because the original town was on the site of the present village of Sterling. When the railroads were built, their tracks crossed at a point farther west and the town of Veedersburg grew up at this crossing. Now, with one of the railroads abandoned and the usefulness of others lessened, the town shows signs of moving back to its original location which is now on the state highways. At Lafayette, a by-pass was built around the city to carry the traffic on Highway No. 52. Within a few years, this by-pass was lined by homes, factories, and businesses. A person could find a long list of similar cases in the state.

Compared to states of a similar size, Indiana has more miles of interstate highways. Seven interstate routes intersect at Indianapolis. Interstates 80, 90, and 94 are in northern Indiana, and I-64 crosses the southern portion of the state. Indiana was one of the first states to complete its interstate system.

The system of state highways now extends to every part of the state. This state highway system consists of more than 11,000 miles of state and interstate roadways. Counties and cities administer 80,000 miles of local roads and streets. This extensive system is made of varying materials. A part of it is cement, brick, or different kinds of blacktop surfaces. The remainder is gravel, stone, or oil-treated surface. More new pavement is being laid each year.

Several bridges have been built in recent years across the Wabash River and the Ohio River to add to the convenience of travelers. Four of these bridges cross the Ohio River at Jeffersonville, at Madison, near Rockport, and at Evansville. Each was formerly a toll bridge. Most recently, two additional bridges were built: one at Cannelton and the other at Maukport. All of the bridges serve to provide better transportation between Indiana and Kentucky.

Since the volume of traffic has greatly increased, the state is confronted with new and serious safety problems. In the early 1970's, oil was in short supply because of embargoes imposed by countries in the Middle East. This led to gas rationing and, during the Carter administration, a new federal law limiting highway speeds to 55 mph. In 1984 the federal government passed another law requiring all states to change laws about seat belt use, or the states would lose federal funding. In recent years, many laws regarding drinking and driving have been passed.

Construction changes in the state's highways also have helped make driving safer. Few major roads now cross rail lines because bridges or overpasses have been built. Major highways have been divided so that two lanes are placed on either side of an "island" or divider. This has significantly reduced the incidence of head-on collisions.

The network of Indiana highways is under the control of the State Highway Commission. It consists of three members and a director appointed by the governor. The roads in the highway system are paid for as they are built using revenue from the tax on gasoline and from automobile licensing fees. This is known as "pay-as-you-build." The state also receives money from the federal government to assist in the construction of certain roads. Most federal funding goes to the interstate highways.

Interstates carry traffic from one state to another. For example, a person from Louisville, Kentucky could drive on Interstate 65 from Louisville to Chicago, Illinois and pass through Indiana on the way. Or a person could travel on Interstate 64 from St.Louis to Cincinnati passing through Indiana on the way.

Interstate Highway 90, located in the northern part of the state, crosses from east to west and is known as the Indiana Toll Road. The original parts of this toll road were built with private funds instead of tax money and completed in 1956. The most recent extension of this interstate now goes to Chicago.

Air and Water Travel

A number of major airlines provide service to the larger cities in Indiana. These trunk airlines join with smaller commuter lines to serve much of the state. Trunk airlines serving Indiana are US Air, American, Delta, Eastern, Ozark, TWA, and United. These lines serve 11 cities: Bloomington, Elkhart, Evansville, Fort Wayne, Indianapolis, Lafayette, Michigan City, Muncie, South Bend, Terre Haute, and Valparaiso. Chicago airports serve the Calumet area, and in the southeastern part of the state, residents use the Cincinnati and Louisville airports.

In Indiana, there are 131 public-use airports and 326 private air and heliports. The largest airport is Indianapolis International Airport.

In recent years, Indiana has built two new ports and has a plan for third one. The first public port is the Burns Waterway Harbor. Located on the southern tip of Lake Michigan, it is about 30 miles from Chicago. Burns Harbor was dedicated in 1970 and by 1980 was handling almost 1.2 million tons of freight. It is surrounded by a large industrial park.

The second port is the Southwind Maritime Centre located near Evansville on the Ohio River. First opened for limited service in 1977, it was completed in June of 1979. It is supported by an 860-acre industrial park.

Plans are under way for a second Ohio River barge port. It is the Clark Maritime Center and located near Jeffersonville. These ports make it easier for goods from all over the world to be shipped to, and through, Indiana. It also means that the Ohio River has become even more important as a means of carrying freight. At times, the Ohio River carries more commercial shipping than the Panama Canal.

STUDY EXERCISES

Write the correct answers in the blanks.

1. The trails used by travelers in early Indiana were also called by what name?

   _____

2. Who, or what, made these trails before the white men came? _____

3. How were trails "blazed" by the settlers? _____

4. The Vincennes Trace was also known by what name? _____

5. By what means did the first Indiana settlers travel? _____

6. Why was it eventually necessary to build roads? _____

   _____

7. How were wagon roads made? _____

   _____

   What was the main drawback to such roads? _____

8. How was a corduroy road constructed? _____
   _____

   What was the "plank" road? _____

   What problems arose in connection with these two types of roads? _____
   _____

9. Define the term "internal improvements." _____
   _____

10. The Mammoth Internal Improvement Bill was passed in what year? _____
    List the eight main provisions of this bill.

    (1) _____
    (2) _____
    (3) _____
    (4) _____
    (5) _____
    (6) _____
    (7) _____
    (8) _____

11. The total cost of these improvements (No. 10, above) was expected to be how much?
    _____

12. For what reasons did the internal improvement plan fail? _____
    _____

13. How much money did the state lose on these projects? _____

14. In 1826, a treaty with what Indian tribe gave Indiana land for a road extending from the
    Ohio River to Lake Michigan? _____

15. What road was built on this land? _____

16. What was the first east and west road across Indiana? _____

17. Complete the following chart on the Michigan Road and the National Road by writing the
    correct information in the blanks.

	Michigan Road	National Road
(1) Year survey was made for road.	_____	_____
(2) Cities at beginning and end of road.	_____	_____
(3) Main cities along road.	_____	_____
	_____	_____
(4) Number of present highway following road.	_____	_____

18. Passenger traffic on the roads was transported by what means? _____
    About how fast did these vehicles travel? _____

19. When was the first stage line in Indiana begun? _____ What two cities did this connect? _____

20. Name the cities connected by other stage lines in Indiana. _____
_____

21. Early Indiana roads were paid for in what three ways (or by what three agencies)?

(1) _____ (2) _____

(3) _____

22. How did the private companies who built roads make money on the roads? _____
_____

23. Why was stage coach travel often interrupted? _____

24. What were covered bridges and of what were they made? _____
_____

Match these items correctly. Do this by choosing the answers from Column II and writing them before the corresponding items in Column I.

	Column I	Column II
_____	1. From Indianapolis to Lafayette	Wea Trail
_____	2. From Brookville to Indianapolis	Chicago Trail
_____	3. From the Ohio River, near New Albany, to Vincennes	Berry's Trace
		Wabash Trail
_____	4. From Fort Wayne to the western shore of Lake Michigan	Sac Trail
_____	5. From the falls of the Ohio River to Wea Plains, near Lafayette	Wetzel's Trace
_____	6. From Wea Plains to Chicago	Vincennes Trace
_____	7. From Fort Wayne to Terre Haute	

Write the correct information in the blanks to complete the following summaries.

I. _____ (Name of first large canal built in Indiana)

A. Two large bodies of water to be connected by this canal. _____
_____

B. Year canal was begun by Indiana. _____

C. Total number of miles canal extended in Indiana. _____

D. Canal was completed to the city of _____ by 1842, to _____
_____ by 1849, and to _____ by 1853.

E. Cities along the route of this canal which developed in size as a result of the canal. _____
_____

F. Main use for canal. _____

G. Part of the state which benefited the most by this canal. _____

H. Reason for which the state halted work on the canal in 1839. _____

I. Progress and final disposition of the canal after 1839. _____

_____

   Where remains can still be seen. _____

II. Whitewater Canal.

   A. Year in which it was begun. _____

   B. Extended from the city of _____, Indiana, to _____

   _____, Indiana, then to _____, Indiana, and

   _____, Ohio.

   C. Total length in Indiana. _____

   D. Part which has been restored as a State Memorial. _____

III. Terms used in description of early Indiana canals and their use. (Define or describe these.)

   A. aqueduct _____

   B. widewater _____

   C. tow path _____

   D. turning basin _____

   E. locks _____

   F. flatboat _____

By 1964, a number of railroads in the eastern part of the United States had joined with other railroads to create new railroad systems. This resulted in changing the old names to new ones. Given below are the old names with the new ones in parentheses.

Match these items correctly. Do this by choosing the answers from Column II and writing them before the corresponding items in Column I.

Column I	Column II
Names of Early Railroads	Present Names of Railroads

_____ 1. Ohio and Mississippi

_____ 2. New Albany and Salem

_____ 3. Bellefontaine and Indianapolis

_____ 4. Indianapolis and Madison

_____ 5. Indianapolis and Peru

_____ 6. Indianapolis and Lafayette, and Indianapolis and Lawrenceburg

_____ 7. Toledo, Wabash and Western

_____ 8. Terre Haute and Indianapolis and Indiana Central

Column II — Present Names of Railroads:

Nickel Plate (Norfolk and Western)

Monon (Louisville and Nashville)

Pennsylvania (Penn-Central)

Baltimore and Ohio (Chessie System)

New York Central-Cinn. Division (Penn Central)

Wabash (Norfolk and Western)

New York Central - Cleveland Div. (Penn Central)

Write the words in the blanks to complete the paragraphs correctly.

1. Railroads were the main reason for causing the use of _____ to decrease as a means of transportation. Of the two means of travel, the _____ was much faster. The ten-year period from _____ to _____ was one of great progress in the building of railroads. In 1850, there were _____ miles of railroad track in Indiana; today there are _____ miles.

2. In the year _____, the Indiana legislature gave six companies the right to build railroads. One of these, the _____, built the first steam road in Indiana, from the city of _____ to _____ by 1839, and to _____ by 1847. This was the only railroad begun by the state as part of the _____ program; the others were built by _____ or by _____.

3. The railroad known as the _____ was the first railroad built from north to south across the state, connecting the _____ River with Lake _____ _____ at _____. A list of cities along this railroad includes _____

4. The _____ Railroad was built along the route of the _____ Canal, taking away much of the business of the canal. Many towns along the waterways of Indiana lost business because of railroads, among them the Ohio River town of _____. Some, such as the town of _____ _____, moved their sites to a location along the railroad. Other towns, however, gained greatly by the development of railroads. One of these was the city of _____ _____, which became the railroad center of the state.

5. Another form of the railroad was the _____, or _____ _____, which connected Indiana cities. The first of such lines connected the cities of _____ and _____ in 1898. The greatest interurban center in the world was the city of _____, with more than _____ cars leaving from the station each day and traveling to _____ (number) towns in the state. In the year 1914, there were _____ miles of interurban track in Indiana. The main companies operating this form of transportation were the (1) _____, (2) _____, and (3) _____ _____. There is still a line operating in northern Indiana called the _____.

110

Choose the correct answers from Column II and write them in the blanks in Column I.

Column I
Name or Route of Highway

Column II
Number of Highway

_____ 1. The National Road

_____ 2. By-pass around Indianapolis

_____ 3. From Louisville, Ky., through Indianapolis to Chicago

_____ 4. Through Vincennes, Shoals, Bedford, Versailles

_____ 5. Through Hammond, Kentland, Terre Haute, Evansville

_____ 6. From Cincinnati, Ohio, through Indianapolis to Danville, Ill.

_____ 7. From Chicago, Ill., through Michigan City, South Bend, and Angola

_____ 8. The "Lincoln Highway"

_____ 9. Through Kentland, Monticello, Logansport, Peru, Ft. Wayne

_____ 10. Michigan Road

_____ 11. From Cincinnati, Ohio, across southern Indiana to St. Louis, Mo.

_____ 12. Through Brookville, Rushville, Indianapolis, Lafayette, to Highway No. 41

_____ 13. From Michigan-Indiana line south through Ft. Wayne, Richmond, to Cincinnati, Ohio

_____ 14. Parallel to U.S. 40, across Indiana from Richmond to Indianapolis.

_____ 15. From South Bend to Louisville through Plymouth, Peru, Indianapolis, Columbus

_____ 16. From Indianapolis to Crawfordsville, Covington, and Illinois state line

Numbers in Column II:

No. 20
No. 70
No. 27
No. 69
No. 41
No. 150
No. 74
No. 40
No. 52
No. 30
No. 421
No. 24
No. 64
No. 65
No. 31
No. 465
No. 50
No. 136

Write the correct answers in the blanks.

1. What kind of transportation has now taken the place of the interurbans? _____
   This has also taken away much of the traffic formerly carried by what means? _____
   _____ What advantages are there to this newer kind of travel and transportation?
   _____

2. What is the name of the large bus company which connects many Indiana cities? _____
   _____ Name some other large bus companies.

3. Why are taxes levied on truck and bus companies operated in the state? _____
   _____

4. Name towns in Indiana which have changed sites in order to be located along highways instead of railroads. _____
   _____

5. What are interstate highways? _____

6. Define the following terms used in description of highways.

    (1) by-pass _____

    (2) toll bridge _____

    (3) overhead crossing _____

    (4) underpass crossing _____

    (5) blacktop surface _____

    (6) clover leaf turns _____

    (7) parkways _____

7. How has the toll road become important once more in Indiana? _____

_____

    Where is one of these roads located in Indiana? _____

    When was it completed? _____

8. Indiana highways are controlled by what agency? _____

9. How does the state pay for our highways? _____

_____

10. Railroads, boat, and motor traffic are now competing with what other form of traffic? _____

_____ For what kind of traffic is this especially important? _____

_____

11. Name airlines which serve Indiana. _____

_____

12. What is the largest airport in Indiana? _____

    Where is it located? _____

13. What kind of economical transportation is again becoming important in Indiana? _____

_____

14. Name two routes or locations of such traffic (No. 13, above) serving Indiana. _____

_____ What kinds of articles are transported in this manner?

_____

15. Many of the smaller railroads were merged into a federal rail system. Name that system.

_____. Why do you think this happened? _____

_____

ASSIGNMENT FOR MAP EXERCISES

Map A. Early Traces and Early Highways

Locate each of the following towns by placing a dot in the proper location on the map and then printing the name beside the dot.

Indianapolis	Lafayette	Brookville
Fort Wayne	Richmond	Corydon
Evansville	New Albany	Lawrenceburg
Michigan City	Madison	South Bend
Terre Haute	Vincennes	Jeffersonville

Locate the following by printing the names in the correct places on the map.

Lake Michigan   Wabash River   Wea Plains

Falls of the Ohio   Ohio River

With a solid red line show the route of each of the following early traces or roads.

The Vincennes Trace

The trace from the falls of the Ohio to the Wea Plains

The trail from Fort Wayne to central Illinois

The Sac Trail across northern Indiana

Wetzel's Trace from Brookville to Indianapolis

Berry's Trace from Indianapolis to the Wabash River

The Chicago Trail from the Wea Plains to Chicago

The Michigan Road

The National Road

Map B. Canals and Railroads

This map exercise calls for the location of a number of towns and cities. The map is too small to allow the writing of so many names on it. Therefore, you may indicate the location of each town with a dot and then write the corresponding number near the dot.

1. Brookville	10. Jeffersonville	19. Peru
2. Connersville	11. Lafayette	20. Plymouth
3. Crawfordsville	12. Lawrenceburg	21. Richmond
4. Evansville	13. Logansport	22. Rushville
5. Fort Wayne	14. Madison	23. Salem
6. Frankfort	15. Michigan City	24. South Bend
7. Gary	16. Monon	25. Terre Haute
8. Hammond	17. Muncie	26. Valparaiso
9. Indianapolis	18. New Albany	27. Vincennes

Locate by printing the names in the right places on the map.

The Wabash River   Lake Michigan   The Whitewater River

With a solid black line show the route of each of the following canals. (Print the name on each.)

The Central Canal   The Wabash and Erie Canal   The Whitewater Canal

With a broken red line show the following railroads of an early date. (Print the name on each.)

Indianapolis and Madison Railroad

The Indianapolis and Bellefontaine

The New Albany and Salem

The Indianapolis and Peru

The Terre Haute and Indianapolis and the Indiana Central

The Indianapolis and Lafayette and the Indianapolis and Lawrenceburg

MAP A.

EARLY TRACES
AND
EARLY HIGHWAYS

SCALE OF MILES

0   10   20   30

114

MAP B.
CANALS AND RAILROADS

SCALE OF MILES
0   10   20   30

MAP C.
STATE HIGHWAYS

SCALE OF MILES
0   10   20   30

With a solid red line, show the main lines these railroads followed.

Penn Central

The Southern

Norfolk and Western

Louisville and Nashville

Illinois Central

Grand Trunk Western

Erie-Lackawanna

Elgin, Joliet and Eastern

Chicago, South Shore and South Bend

Chessie System

Chicago-Milwaukee

Map C. State Highways

Secure an up-to-date road map of Indiana. You can get such a map from almost any filling station.

On the outline map of Indiana on page 114; mark the following highways with red lines:

No. 6, No. 20, No. 24, No. 27, No. 421, No. 30, No. 31, No. 36, No. 40, No. 41, No. 50, No. 52, No. 62, No. 150, No. 136, No. 231.

With a black line show the route of these five interstate highways across Indiana: No. 64, No. 65, No. 69, No. 70, No. 74.

Locate each with a dot and print the names of the principal cities along these highways. Put the number of each highway in the correct place on the map.

Which of these highways mentioned above are main east and west routes across the state?

_____

Which of these highways mentioned above are main north and south routes across the state?

_____

TOPICS FOR DISCUSSION AND REPORT

1. Describe the "keel boat" and the "flat boat." Tell how each of these types of boats was propelled.

2. Do you know where any "toll bridges" or "toll gates" were located in this state in the early days? If so, tell the class about them. Tell where some "toll bridges" are located today.

3. Why were almost all of the early bridges "covered bridges"? Describe the structure of one of the bridges. Do you know where any "covered bridges" are still in use in Indiana?

4. Tell of some cases of which you know where the location of a town has changed or is changing since a state highway was built.

5. Make a report to the class on "The Wabash and Erie Canal in Indiana."

6. Describe some of the recent things which the State Highway Commission or the government has done to increase safety on the highways.

7. Make a report to the class on "The Whitewater Canal in Indiana."

8. If you have seen the parts of the old Whitewater Canal which have been reconstructed near Laurel and Metamora, make a report on these to the class.

9. What was unusual about the track of the Madison and Indianapolis Railroad up the hill from Madison, Indiana? Describe this to the class.

10. Make a report to the class comparing the old National Road to the same road today. Compare the kind of traffic then and now.

REFERENCES FOR UNIT 9

GENERAL REFERENCES
Buley—Vol. I, pp. 395-527. Vol. II, pp. 260-268.
Esarey (School Edition)—Ch. XVI.
Levering—Ch. XI.
Thornton, Reade—Chs. XIII-XVI.
Cottman—Chs. VIII-IX, XVII.
Esarey (2 Vol. Ed.)—pp. 254-272, Chs. XVI, XXV.
Roll—Vol. I, Sec. V, Ch. IV (p. 457). Vol II—pp. 5-14.
Lockridge—*The Story of Indiana*—Ch. XII, pp. 381-384.
Thompson—*Stories of Indiana*—pp. 208-227.
Map of Indiana, showing the railroad and interurban lines. This may be found in any atlas.
Map of the State Highway System of Indiana. A copy of this map may be obtained from any oil company or service station.

INDIANA HISTORY BULLETIN
"Romance of Ohio River Transportation"—William Ross, IHB, Dec., 1925.
"Directory of Covered Bridges in Indiana"—IHB, Feb., 1941.
"The Covered Timber Bridges in Indiana"—R. B. Yule, IHB, Apr., 1931.
"A Hoosier Hostelry a Hundred Years Ago"—Kenneth Loucks, IHB, Apr., 1931.
"The New Albany and Salem Railroad"—Frank F. Hargrove, IHB, Apr., 1928.
"The Whitewater Canal"—Fred W. Eley, IHB, Feb., 1940.
"Whitewater Canal Trip. Historical Visit in 1941"—IHB, Sept., 1941.
"Internal Improvements, 1835-1852."—James Edward Hagerty, IHB, Oct., 1937.
"The Covered Bridges and Indiana"—Eugene R. Bock, IHB, May, 1960.
"Covered Timber Bridges in Indiana (as of Sept. 1, 1959)"—Eugene R. Bock, IHB, May, 1950.
"Indiana-built automobiles." (Indiana's place in automobile history)—Wallace Spencer Huffman, IHB, Sept., 1961. (This gives a list of automobiles that were built in Indiana.)

READINGS IN INDIANA HISTORY (1914 edition)
Chapters XII-XIII (pp. 210-256). This includes articles on Transportation and Travel in early Indiana.
Chapter XXII (pp. 357-362). Four articles dealing with Internal Improvements in Indiana.
Map on p. 356. This shows canals, turnpikes, and railroads in the state in 1836.

READINGS IN INDIANA HISTORY (1916 edition)
Chs. XV-XVI.

PUBLICATIONS OF NORTHERN INDIANA HISTORICAL SOCIETY, South Bend, Indiana.
"The St. Joseph-Kankakee Portage." Publication No. 1, 1899.
Johns Hopkins University Studies in Historical and Political Science. Published by John Hopkins Press, Baltimore.
"The Wabash Trade Route in the Development of the Old Northwest," Series XXI, Nos. 1-2.
"The Buffalo Trace"—Geo. R. Wilson and Gayle Thornbrough, Vol. 15, No. 2.

PUBLICATIONS OF INDIANA HISTORICAL SOC.
"The National Road in Indiana"—Lee Burns, Vol. 7, No. 4.
"Internal Improvements in Early Indiana"—Logan Esarey, Vol. 5, No. 2.
"Early Indiana Trails and Surveys"—George R. Wilson, Vol. 6, No. 3.
"The Village at the End of the Road, A Chapter in Early Railroad History"—Wylie J. Daniels, Vol. 13, No. 1.
To Oregon in 1852—Dr. Thomas White, Vol. 23, No. 1.

INDIANA MAGAZINE OF HISTORY
"The Wabash and Its Valley"—Vol. I (1905), pp. 123-127.
"Internal Improvements in Indiana"—IMH, Vol. 3 (1907).
The First Thoroughfares—pp. 12-25.
The National Road—pp. 58-73.
The Wabash and Erie Canal—pp. 101-107.
"The Michigan Road"—IMH, Vol. 3 (1907), pp. 80-81.
The Whitewater Canal—pp. 108-115.
The Central Canal—pp. 115-116.
Railroads—pp. 149-181.
"The Internal Improvement System of Indiana"—IMH, Vol. 3 (1907), pp. 117-124. (This explains the plan for the system of internal improvements undertaken by the state.)
"Pioneer Transportation on the Ohio River"—IMH, Vol. 4 (1908), pp. 129-133.
"Development of Interurbans in Indiana"—IMH, Vol. 5 (1909), pp. 160-170.
"History of Canals in Indiana"—IMH, Vol. 7, pp. 1-15.
"The Old Chicago Road"—IMH, Vol. 10 (1914), pp. 396-398.
"The Old Chicago Trail and the Old Chicago Road"—IMH, Vol. 15 (1919), pp. 1-14.
"The New Albany-Salem Railroad"—IMH, Vol. 15 (1919), pp. 342-362.
"Interurban Railroads of Indiana"—IMH, Vol. 20 (1924), pp. 221-279.
"The Wabash and Erie Canal in Wabash County"—IMH, Vol. 24 (1928), pp. 295-305.
"The Ohio River, Its Influence in the Development of Indiana"—Lee Burns, IMH, June, 1923.
"Pioneer Transportation on the Ohio River"—Samuel T. Covington, IMH, Sept., 1908.
"Flatboating on the Wabash"—A Diary of 1847, IMH, Dec., 1913.
"The Wabash and Erie Canal at Lafayette"—Wm. M. Reser, IMH, Dec., 1934.
"Post Roads in Southern Indiana"—Geo. E. Amick, IMH, Dec., 1934.
"The Vincennes Bridge over the Wabash River"—Robert B. Yule, IMH, June, 1935.
"The Construction of the Michigan Road, 1830-1840", General Prather, IMH, Sept., 1944.
"The Struggle for the Michigan Road"—IMH, March 1943.
"The Big Four Railroad in Indiana"—Ared M. Murphy, IMH, June-Sept., 1925.
"Railroad Building in Indiana, 1850-1855"—Victor M. Bogle, IMH, Sept., 1962.

UNIT 10

The Growth of Education in Indiana

HISTORICAL SURVEY OF THE UNIT

The State of Indiana is known for its good schools, today. When we see these good schools with which we are surrounded, it is difficult for us to realize that in the early history of our state there were no free public schools. There were several reasons for this situation. One was the fact that each settlement contained only a few children and the settlements were comparatively far apart. Another reason—and this was a very important one—was that there was no money with which to build schoolhouses and pay the teachers. Also, the parents thought that they needed the children to help make the living at home.

The First Provision for Schools in Indiana

The Ordinance of 1785 provided that schools should be encouraged in the Northwest Territory and it set aside one section of land (640 acres) in each congressional township for school purposes. It was expected that this section of land would bring in enough money to support a school in each township. It was soon

Schools of early Indiana were held in crude buildings and had little equipment and short terms.

proved, however, that this land would not furnish nearly enough income to pay the expenses of free public schools. If the land was sold, as much of it was, a whole section would bring only a little over twelve hundred dollars at the most. Since the law stated that nothing

but the interest from this money could be spent, there was practically no revenue at all for school purposes. The governors of the Indiana Territory tried to find ways and means for financing a school system but they were not successful.

The Ordinance of 1787 further encouraged education by stating that education was necessary to free government. When Indiana was admitted as a state in 1816, the constitution called for a general system of education for children from the first grade through the university without cost to those who attended. However, it did not provide any means for raising the money to build and equip schoolhouses and pay teachers. Many people who did not have any children objected to being taxed for the support of schools. Others thought that free schools would do nothing more than encourage people to ask for free homes and free food. Some even said that free schools would cause all the people to become too well educated.

In spite of what was said against public schools and in spite of the lack of public money for education, some schools were established. All the country schools were one-room affairs usually built of logs or rough boards. The benches and desks were very crude; there was no equipment such as we have today; even the books were few in number; and nearly all the teachers were poorly trained and just as poorly paid. Most of the teachers were men. In many backwoods communities the teacher had to prove that he could handle the pupils in the school. The larger boys delighted in "running the teacher out" if they could. The terms were short and there was no such thing as a compulsory attendance law. The children attended school when the weather was unfit for them to work on the farm.

The Fight for Free Public Schools in Indiana

During the first thirty years of Indiana's

existence as a state, there was a gradual increase in the feeling that there should be a better system of public schools. There were several men in the state who kept telling the people that the state should have free public schools. They meant by this that the schools, especially the elementary schools, should be supported by public taxation. One of the men who worked the hardest was Caleb Mills, identified with the early history of Wabash College. His efforts won for him the title of "the father of Indiana's public schools," for he succeeded in getting the people to vote in 1848 on the question, "Shall we have free public schools?" The vote was in favor of this plan. This helped the schools in the state somewhat, but still there was not enough money to expand the educational program very much.

Article VIII of the Constitution of 1851 gave the state legislature the power to pass laws which would provide money for a system of good public schools in Indiana. It stated that: "It shall be the duty of the General Assembly to encourage by all suitable means moral, intellectual, scientific, and agricultural improvement, and to provide by law for a general and uniform system of common schools, wherein tuition shall be without charge and equally open to all."

The constitution also provided for a State Superintendent of Public Instruction who would be head of the school system of the state and was to be elected for a 2-year term. However, the constitution was amended in 1972, and the superintendent of public instruction is to be elected to a four-year term of office beginning January 2, 1977, with elections for the office held every four years thereafter.

In 1852 a law was passed by the General Assembly of the state which was the foundation of the common schools in Indiana. There were three principal features of this law. One was the establishment of a Common School Fund which was made up, chiefly, of the money which had come from the sale of the one section of land which had been set aside for school purposes in each township. This money was to be kept by the state and distributed to the counties according to the number of children in each county. The second feature was the levy of a general tax on property for school purposes. The third was the establishment of a State Board of Education. This board was to have the power to issue teacher's licenses, to select textbooks, and to inspect schools. The actual management of the schools was placed in the hands of the local trustees.

At the first meeting of the General Assembly under the Constitution of 1851, a number of laws were passed to carry out the new provisions for taking care of the schools. Immediately, the schools ran into trouble. In 1853 the Indiana Supreme Court declared that the school tax-raising law was unconstitutional so far as the township schools were concerned. New laws were passed to help the township schools out of the difficulty, but it was not until 1885 that the courts decided that the tax-raising laws did not violate the constitution.

Teaching in the Early Schools

The pioneer schools had no organized course of study and no set rules for classroom instruction. There were practically no textbooks, and there were no reference books and libraries. The schools were not graded and each pupil was supposed to make whatever progress he could in each subject. The variety of subjects was limited to the three R's, "readin'," " 'ritin'," and " 'rithmetic," and these were considered the basis for all study. From that point, the teacher had to use his own resourcefulness and judgment. The first thing taught was the alphabet or a, b, c's. There was

The curriculum of the early schools was limited to a few subjects.

drill on the alphabet until the pupils could say it forward and backward.

After the alphabet, the usual procedure was toward word-making and spelling. The beginning practice in this went something like the following: a, b, ab; e, b, eb; i, b, ib; o, b, ob; u, b, ub; b, a, ba; b, e, be; b, i, bi; b, o, bo; b, u, bu. This same idea was followed through a long list of combinations and the whole thing was recited in a singsong voice. This was thought to be very efficient in the teaching of reading.

The addition combinations were taught first, and woe to the child who couldn't master the combination of 2 plus 2, 3 plus 3, 4 plus 1, and so on. Since every written expression had to be made with handwriting, that subject was considered all-important. Steel pens were not available and everything had to be written with quill pens. Usually these were made from goose quills. Ink was homemade and very watery. The writing was done in crude "copy books" which usually were prepared by the teacher.

Noah Webster's *Elementary Spelling Book* had been first published in 1783. Some of the pioneer teachers in Indiana were familiar with this book and, later, it was used in almost every school. The first real textbook, however, that came into widespread use in Indiana schools was the famous reader first put out by William H. McGuffey in 1836. This book, and the other readers which followed in the same series, became the standard texts for use in Indiana schools, and continued there for many years.

It is interesting to note that the lessons in the McGuffey First Reader resemble some of the lessons found in readers which you may have studied. Also, the method which McGuffey used of teaching new words by associating them with pictures of known objects is a method used today. (See example from a McGuffey Reader shown in the small picture below.)

The lessons from a McGuffey Reader looked surprisingly like some lessons found in the books today.

Spelling matches and ciphering matches were held in the schools and continued as a part of the school activity well into the 20th Century. It was considered great fun and also a great honor to be able to "spell the other fellow down." Each school or community had its champion speller and unusual and little-known words were hunted out to "stump" the champion. Some favorite words for this were sylogism, hyperbole, syzygy, phthisic, and conscientiousness. Ciphering matches dealt with problems in addition, subtraction, multiplication, and division.

As the school system improved, after the Civil War, other subjects were added to the curriculum. Geography was one of these. Instruction in this consisted mostly of teaching the location of rivers, oceans, lakes, countries, capitals, and other large cities. Sometimes curious methods of teaching were used. For example, a favorite topic was the location of the state capitals, and this was put into a sort of song which started like this, "Maine, Augus-ta on the Kenne-bec River; New Hampshire, Concord on the Merri-mac River; etc." When this was repeated in singsong fashion, it was supposed to result in quick learning.

Physiology—the study of the body—was another subject that was introduced. One of the main things required in this was to learn the names of the bones in the body. Many a poor "scholar" flunked this subject because he could not remember that the leg bones were the femur, tibia, and fibula, and the malleus, incus, and stapes were the bones in the ear.

Growth and Support of the Indiana School System

In spite of the unfavorable decisions of the courts, though, the progress of education was steady with the exception of a period during the Civil War when everything was at a standstill. In 1873, a law was passed which provided for a Superintendent of Schools in each county whose duty it would be to have control of and to supervise the schools and teachers of that county.

When the first school laws were passed in Indiana, high schools were not mentioned. The term "common school" was used and this was considered as meaning the elementary school —grades one through eight. The subjects in these grades were referred to as the "common branches." Most children were not expected to carry on their education beyond these elementary subjects.

However, there were a few high schools in Indiana as early as 1850. But it was not until 1873 that the first step was taken toward classifying high schools or issuing a commission to them. The first commissions were given to high schools to show that their graduates were able to enter Indiana University without taking an entrance examination. Later, other standards were set up for high schools and elementary schools, too, and they were classified accordingly.

Much progress in public school education in this state has come since the close of World War I. All the old one-room schools have disappeared from the state. In their place are "consolidated" schools, especially in the country and in the small towns. The pupils are hauled in busses at public expense. Most of these schools were once under the control and management of the township trustee. The incorporated towns and cities in the state have separate schools of their own which have been managed by a Board of Education, usually called a "School Board." In 1959 further consolidation of schools began in the state. As a result of this consolidation program, almost all of the schools in Indiana today are a part of a modern consolidated school district. Statewide, there are 304 such school districts. In these schools emphasis is now being placed on programs for the gifted and talented, and on career and vocational education.

Included in the vocational program are courses in public high schools, the state supported Indiana Vocational Technical College (IVTC), and more than 100 private career schools. The state believes that such education is important in maintaining a steady level of skilled workers.

At the beginning of the 1980s, there were 1,076,200 students in public school (K-12) and slightly fewer than 100,000 in private schools. There were 20.2 students per teacher. It takes a large sum of money to educate these students and to pay their teachers. This money comes from three principal sources: the local government (county, township, and city), the state government, and the federal government. State and local spending for schools costs almost $2 billion a year. Here is how the money is raised:

1. Most of the money furnished by the local government comes from the tax on real estate and personal property, and from the interest from the common school fund.

2. The greater part of the money supplied by the state government comes from the state gross income tax and special sales tax. There are other smaller sources.

3. The Federal government supplies money for some of the vocational training programs and for school lunches.

Every child in Indiana is now compelled by law to attend school when he becomes seven years of age and to continue until he reaches his sixteenth birthday unless he is physically or mentally unable to do so. The various counties and some cities have attendance officers to see that this law is enforced. The regular public school system of Indiana consists of twelve grades. The first eight grades usually are referred to as the elementary school and the upper four grades as the high school. Some of the school systems have six-year high schools and make the high school begin with the seventh grade. Other systems have "junior high schools" and "senior high schools." In this plan, the junior high school usually includes the seventh, eighth, and ninth grades and the senior high school includes the tenth, eleventh, and twelfth grades.

Besides the public schools today, there are numerous elementary schools and several high schools maintained by churches. They are called parochial schools. The Catholic Church supports the largest number of these. There are now 429 elementary and 32 high schools maintained by the Catholic Church in Indiana. There are approximately 75,072 children enrolled in these schools. The children in parochial schools study the same subjects as the children do in public schools. In addition, they have courses dealing with religion and the Bible. Although parochial schools receive no direct support from public finances, the law provides for parochial pupils' transportation on public school busses. Most Catholic schools are taught by Catholic sisters who are well trained, and the quality of the teaching in these schools is very high. Lately, on account of an increased number of pupils, the Catholic schools have been forced to employ lay teachers. (A lay teacher is one who is not a nun.)

Minorities in Indiana Schools

As was mentioned in another unit, the state always has provided elementary and high schools for all people, regardless of race, creed, or color. Until after the close of World War II, however, many schools were segregated so that most blacks attended all black schools. After World War II, a Supreme Court decision made such segregation illegal. Schools were required to accept all people, regardless of color. This is called integration. The famous court decision made it possible for everyone to receive an equal education.

Among outstanding black high schools in Indiana were Crispus Attucks in Indianapolis and George Washington High School in East Chicago. Many superior athletes came from these schools to star in different sports, but especially in basketball, going on to college and professional teams after graduating from high school.

Colleges and Universities in the State

Hanover College was opened near Madison by the Presbyterians in 1827. Franklin College, at Franklin, was founded by the Baptists in 1834. This was first known as the Indiana Baptist Manual Labor Institute, and the name was changed to Franklin College in 1837. In 1842, girls were enrolled in this school, making it the first coeducational college in Indiana. Wabash College, at Crawfordsville, was founded by the Presbyterians in 1832. This was started as a boys' school and has remained so.

Asbury University was founded at Greencastle by the Methodists in 1837. The name of this school was changed to DePauw University in 1884. In 1840, the Catholics started St. Mary-of-the-Woods, a school for young women, near Terre Haute. Two years later, in 1842, the Catholics founded Notre Dame University, a school for boys, now coeducational, at South Bend.

Concordia College was founded by the Lutherans at Fort Wayne in 1839: Earlham College by the Quakers at Richmond in 1847; Moores' Hill College (no longer in existence) at Moores' Hill in 1853; and Valparaiso University at Valparaiso in 1874. Butler University grew out of a meeting of representatives of the Christian Church in 1848. This school was first known as the North Western Christian University and it opened its doors in 1855. This date, 1855, is generally taken as the founding date, although the name Butler University was not applied until 1877.

There are now six schools in the state, above the rank of high school, which are supported by state taxes. These are usually referred to as "state schools."

1. Indiana University has its main campus at Bloomington, with its School of Medicine, its School of Dentistry, and its School of Nursing at Indianapolis. This university was the first state school to be established. It was opened in 1820 as the State Seminary and for a while it was known as Indiana College. In 1838 it was named Indiana University and 1820 is considered its founding date.

2. Purdue University was established at West Lafayette in 1874. Its beginning was made possible by a large grant of land from the Federal government and by a donation of $150,000 from a wealthy landowner named John Purdue. At first, Purdue University was strictly a school for instruction in agriculture. In later years, it has grown to include a School of Home Economics, various engineering schools, a Veterinary School, a School of Pharmacy, and others.

Purdue University now has four Regional Campuses. These are as follows: Calumet in Lake County, Fort Wayne, IUPUI in Indianapolis, and North Central at Michigan City.

3. Indiana State University, first known as the Indiana State Normal School and later as Indiana State Teachers College, was opened to students in 1870. It was located in downtown Terre Haute and was set up especially for the training of teachers. Recently, many other courses have been added, and its name was changed in 1965 to Indiana State University. Indiana State has one regional campus, located at Evansville.

4. Ball State University had its beginning in 1918 at Muncie. It, too, existed first almost wholly for the training of teachers. It now offers many other courses and, in 1965, its name was changed from Ball State Teachers College to Ball State University.

5. Vincennes University is the oldest institution of higher education in the state. It was established by an act of the Territorial Legislature of 1806, when Vincennes University was authorized. It opened as a grammar school in 1810 with Gen. William Henry Har-

rison and Francis Vigo among the first trustees. It is a two-year junior college.

6. Indiana Vocational Technical College was established by an act of the State Legislature in 1963 and further supported by the Legislature in 1965. It is designed to meet the needs of Indiana residents for after-high school, non-high school, and non-degree vocational and technical education. It includes such courses as brick-laying, carpentry, painting and decorating, plumbing, sheet metal, blue print reading, vocational math, computer use, physics, electronics, and many others. The headquarters is in Indianapolis, with regional technical institutes at other locations in the state.

Indiana has created a regional campus system for its main state-run colleges. These regional campuses, or branches, are located throughout the state and include three joint campuses shared by Indiana University (IU) and Purdue. The joint campuses are located at Indianapolis, Fort Wayne, and Columbus. Other branches of IU, Purdue, or Indiana State University are located in the following locations: (Northeast) Fort Wayne, Kokomo; (Northwest) Gary, Calumet, Westville, South Bend (main campus); (Central) Indianapolis; (Southeast) Richmond, New Albany; (Southwest) Terre Haute, Evansville.

The five state universities enrolled 180,000 students in the beginning of the 1980s. There are 53,000 students enrolled in the 35 church-related and private colleges in the state.

The New Harmony Settlement

A discussion of the growth of education in Indiana would not be complete without some mention of the New Harmony settlement which was the beginning of the present town of New Harmony. This settlement was made by a group of people called Harmonists under the leadership of Father George Rapp. They chose a spot on the east bank of the Wabash River about thirty miles above the junction of the Wabash with the Ohio River in what is now Posey County. Here they established a colony in 1814 with about eight hundred men, women, and children and the settlement was known as Harmonie. These people were Germans who had made a temporary home in Pennsylvania and who had then decided to move farther west.

The Harmony Society, the members of which are usually known as Rappites, was an extraordinary religious, social, and economic organization. Religion dominated the everyday life of the members. No individual was allowed to hold property. Everything was held in common. All bound themselves absolutely and only to those interests which would add to the happiness of all. There were to be no marriages in the settlement. Hard work was a principle accepted by all. George Rapp was a tireless worker and a good leader. The Harmony Society prospered from the beginning. General agriculture, wool growing, cotton raising, manufacturing, and cultivation of orchards and vineyards was carried on. An unusual tree, called the raintree, still flourishes here. The Rappites manufactured cotton and woolen goods and produced great quantities of beverages which they sold up and down the river. They built substantial homes and factories, some of which remain today. In the space of ten years it is estimated that they had accumulated a wealth of a million dollars.

In 1824, the Harmony Society decided to sell out, and the land and buildings were purchased by Robert Owen for $190,000. Owen was a wealthy manufacturer from Scotland and his idea was "to introduce an entirely new state of society." He chose Harmonie for the site of this experiment and renamed the place New Harmony. This, too, was to be a "Community of Equality." In a very short time the community was filled with a varied assortment of people who had come from all over the world in response to Robert Owen's invitation. He brought to New Harmony some of the most distinguished educators of the world. He expected to establish here the best and most progressive schools in the world in order to carry out his idea of a perfect state of society. Trade schools were opened, vocational guidance and manual training were provided for, equal educational opportunity for all children was advocated. The world's first kindergarten was established here, and Wm. Maclure set up a library in the town. New Harmony became the "cradle of modern educational ideas." Unfortunately, most of the colonists were dreamers and idealists instead of workers. Also, there were the usual number of loafers, criminals, and selfish persons. The Community of Equality, as it was called, collapsed within three years.

In spite of this collapse, Robert Owen's

The Rappites built many sturdy and useful buildings in New Harmony.

experiment at New Harmony had an undying influence on education and society in Indiana. Robert Owen had four brilliant sons, Robert Dale, William, Donald Dale, and Richard, and the names of these men run through the later history of the state. Many prominent educators had been brought here. Among these were William Maclure, the father of American geology; Thomas Say, the father of American zoology; Joseph Neef; Charles Alexander Lesure; and many others. Jane Dale Owen, daughter of Robert Owen, married Robert Henry Fauntleroy, and the old Fauntleroy home at New Harmony is preserved as a memorial today. So, the New Harmony experiment may be regarded as an educational success even though in other ways it was considered a failure by its founders. On August 21, 1965, New Harmony was dedicated as a National Historical Landmark.

STUDY EXERCISES

Write the correct answers in the blanks and complete the charts correctly.

1. What was the first college in Indiana? _____

   In what year was it started? _____

2. What schools in Indiana, above the rank of high school, are supported by public taxes?

School	Location
_____	_____
_____	_____
_____	_____
_____	_____
_____	_____
_____	_____

3. Which of the schools mentioned in question No. 2 were originally operated principally for the training of teachers? _____ and _____.

4. Tell where each of these schools is located and in what year each was founded.

School	Location	Year Founded
(1) Butler University	_____	_____
(2) DePauw University	_____	_____
(3) Earlham College	_____	_____
(4) Franklin College	_____	_____
(5) Hanover College	_____	_____
(6) Indiana University	_____	_____
(7) Notre Dame University	_____	_____
(8) Purdue University	_____	_____
(9) St. Mary-of-the-Woods	_____	_____
(10) Valparaiso University	_____	_____

(11) Vincennes University   _____   _____

(12) Wabash College   _____   _____

(13) Indiana State University _____   _____

(14) Ball State University   _____   _____

(15) Indiana Vocational

    Technical College   _____   _____

5. Name the church with which each of the following schools was or is now associated or identified.

College	Church
(1) DePauw University	_____
(2) Earlham College	_____
(3) Franklin College	_____
(4) Goshen College	_____
(5) Hanover College	_____
(6) Notre Dame University	_____
(7) St. Joseph's College	_____
(8) St. Mary-of-the-Woods	_____
(9) Valparaiso University	_____

6. By what name was each of the following first known?

Present Name	Original Name
(1) Butler University	_____
(2) Indiana State University	_____
(3) DePauw University	_____
(4) Evansville College	_____
(5) Franklin College	_____
(6) Indiana University	_____

Write the correct answers in the blanks.

1. At what location did the Harmony Society or Harmonists establish a settlement in Indiana?

_____

_____

2. In what year was this settlement made? _____

3. Who was the leader of this society? _____

4. By what name were the members of the society usually known? _____

5. To whom did the property in the settlement belong? _____

_____

6. What two things dominated the everyday life of the people in this settlement?

_____   _____

7. What were some of the things the people of this society produced?

_____   _____   _____   _____

8. What did the people do with their surplus products? _____

_____

9. What did the Harmony Society decide to do in 1824? _____

10. Who purchased the land from the Harmony Society? _____

11. Why did this man want this land with its buildings? _____

_____

12. What did he rename the place? _____

13. What was to be the guiding principle among the people of this settlement? _____

_____

_____

14. What two opposite kinds of people were attracted to New Harmony?

    (1) _____

    (2) _____

15. Name three famous educators who came to New Harmony.

_____   _____   _____

16. What school department which was opened in New Harmony was the first of its kind in the world? _____

17. What did William Maclure do to encourage education and culture?

_____

18. What finally happened to the experiment with the "community of equality"?

_____ Why did this happen? _____

_____

19. What unusual tree is found in great abundance in New Harmony? _____

20. What old home in New Harmony is a state memorial? _____

Write the correct answers in the blanks.

1. What help for schools did the Ordinance of 1785 provide? _____

_____

_____

2. How did the Ordinance of 1787 encourage education in Indiana? _____

_____

3. What did the Indiana Constitution of 1816 call for in regard to education? _____

_____

_____

4. What was it that the Constitution of 1816 did not provide for the schools? _____

_____

5. What is meant by "free public schools"? _____

_____

6. Why did some people object to paying taxes for school purposes? _____

_____

_____

7. What were the **three main reasons** for there being no public schools in the early years of Indiana?

    (1) _____

    (2) _____

    (3) _____

8. What kind of building was used for the early schoolhouse in Indiana? _____

9. Were the early teachers in Indiana men or women? _____

10. What attitude did the larger boys in a school have toward a teacher? _____
_____

11. What kind of training did the early teachers have? _____

12. What kind of equipment did the early schools have? _____
_____

13. What were the three R's of the early school? _____
_____

14. How many grades were taught in the early schools in Indiana? _____

15. What was a "copy book"? _____
_____

_____

What was its purpose? _____

16. What was a "spelling bee"? _____
_____

17. What man, identified with Wabash College, worked hard to get tax-supported schools in

Indiana? _____

What unofficial title was given to this man? _____
_____

18. What was a "ciphering match"? _____
_____

19. What series of readers was popular in the early schools in Indiana? _____
_____

20. What spelling book was popular in the early schools in Indiana? _____
_____

21. The term "common school" was considered to include what grades? _____
_____

22. Upon what school question did the people of Indiana vote in 1848? _____
_____

What was the result of the above vote? _____

23. The State Constitution of 1851 gave the state legislature what general power in regard to the schools in Indiana? _____

24. In what year was a law passed in Indiana which was considered the foundation for the common schools in the state? _____

25. What were the three chief provisions of the law referred to in question 24?

    (1) _____

    _____

    (2) _____

    _____

    (3) _____

    _____

26. What interfered with the carrying out of the school tax-raising law passed by the General Assembly? _____

_____

27. In 1873, a law was passed providing for what school official? _____

What was to be this officer's duty? _____

28. What was the date for the first commissioned high school in the state? _____

29. A commission was issued to the first high schools for what purpose? _____

_____

30. The money furnished by the local government in Indiana for school purposes comes from taxes on what? _____

31. The money furnished by the Indiana state government for school support comes chiefly from what taxes? _____

32. What is a "consolidated school"? _____

_____

_____

33. What name is applied to an elementary school or high school supported by a church?

_____

34. What church supports a large number of elementary schools and high schools in Indiana?

_____

35. What church supports a lesser number of schools in Indiana? _____

_____

36. Do the schools mentioned in questions 34 and 35, above, receive any money from public taxes?

_____

37. Do the church-supported schools have the same courses as the public schools? _____

129

38. Is the number of public high schools in Indiana increasing or decreasing? _____
    Why?_____

39. What officer is the head of the state school system in Indiana? _____
    _____

40. Where do we find the authority for the establishment of the office referred to in question 39?
    _____

41. Who is the head of a city school system? _____

42. Who is the present State Superintendent of Public Instruction in Indiana? _____
    _____

43. Who elects the State Superintendent of Public Instruction in Indiana? _____
    What is the length of the term of office? _____

44. What name is applied to a school made up of grades 9 to 12? _____
    _____

45. In Indiana, every child, unless physically unable to do so, is compelled to attend school between
    what ages? _____

46. What officer is charged with seeing that children of proper age attend school? _____

47. What does "integration" mean?_____
    What judicial body passed a law against segregation?_____
    In what year? _____

48. Why was the law mentioned in #47 necessary? _____

49. What is meant by "equal education"? _____
    _____

50. About how much money did state and local governments in Indiana spend on education in a year?
    _____

ASSIGNMENT FOR MAP EXERCISE

The Location of Colleges and Universities

Locate with an X and write, in its proper place on the map, the number which corresponds to each school listed. Then, print the name of the town or city in which the school is located.

1. Anderson College
2. Ancilli College
3. Ball State University
4. Bethel College
5. Butler University
6. DePauw University
7. Holy Cross Junior College
8. Ft. Wayne Bible College
9. Franklin College
10. Goshen College
11. Grace College
12. Hanover College
13. Huntington College
14. Jordan College of Music
15. Indiana State University
16. Indiana University
17. Indiana Vocational Technical College
18. Manchester College
19. Marian College
20. Marion College
21. Northwood Institute
22. Oakland City College
23. Purdue University
24. Rose-Hulman Institute
25. St. Francis College
26. St. Joseph's College
27. St. Mary's College
28. St. Mary-of-the Woods
29. St. Meinrad Seminary
30. Taylor University
31. Tri-State University
32. University of Evansville
33. University of Notre Dame
34. Valparaiso Technical Institute
35. Valparaiso University
36. Vincennes University
37. Wabash College

LOCATION OF COLLEGES
AND UNIVERSITIES IN
INDIANA

SCALE OF MILES
0   10   20   30

TOPICS FOR DISCUSSION AND REPORT

1. Describe a rural school of the early days in Indiana.

2. Why is it fair for everybody to pay taxes to support the schools whether they have children in school or not?

3. Find out how much training a person must have in order to teach in the elementary school of Indiana today. How much to teach in the high school?

4. What are the advantages of the consolidated school over the one-room school?

5. Give an account of the founding of Harmonie by the Rappites.

6. Make a report on the Quakers in Indiana.

7. Make a report on one of the Normal Colleges which flourished in Indiana about 1880-1895. Tell the purpose of this college, the cost of attending, the courses offered, and the length of the terms.

8. Try to find some old textbooks (those which were used before 1890) and either bring them to class for display or describe them to the class. (Perhaps your public library will have copies of McGuffey Readers, Ray's Arithmetic, or the Webster Blue Back Speller.) In recent years, reprints of the McGuffey Readers have become readily available.

REFERENCES FOR UNIT 10

GENERAL REFERENCES
Buley—Vol. II, pp. 326-416, 597-616.
Cottman—pp. 92-100, Part II, Ch. XXIV.
Esarey (School Edition)—Chs. XII, XXII.
Thornton, Reade—Ch. XIX.
Roll—Vol. I—pp. 402-406, Vol. II—pp. 290-306.
Esarey (2 vol. ed.)—pp. 289-295, Ch. XXIV.
Levering—Ch. XVIII.
Boone—*Education in Indiana.* (This is one of the best accounts of the early history of Indiana's schools. The book is now out of print but copies of it can be found in many public libraries.)
Thompson—*Stories of Indiana*—pp. 228-240.
Hoosier Schoolmaster—Eggleston. (This book of fiction, written by an Indiana author, has a most interesting historical background dealing with pioneer schools.)
READINGS IN INDIANA HISTORY (1914 edition)
Selections No. 104-106 deal with pioneer schools.
INDIANA HISTORY BULLETIN
"Development of Public Education in Southwestern Indiana, 1816-80"—Otis E. Young, IHB, Aug., 1929.
"Catholic Education in Indiana"—Thomas T. McAvoy, IHB, Jan., 1946.
READINGS IN INDIANA HISTORY (1956 edition)
Chs. XII, XX.
INDIANA MAGAZINE OF HISTORY
"The Early Schools of Indiana"—D. D. Banta, IMH, Vol. 2 (1906), pp. 41-48, 81-88, 131-138, 191-194.
"Minutes of the Board of Trustees for Vincennes University"—Edited by Robt. Constantine, IMH, Vol. LX, No. 2, June, 1964.

"Development of the Common Schools of Indiana, 1851"—IMH, Vol. 22 (1926), pp. 229-276.
"James Woodburn, Hoosier Schoolmaster"—James A. Woodburn, IMH, Sept., 1936.
"The Academies of Indiana"—John H. Thomas, IMH, Dec., 1914; March, 1915.
"County Seminaries in Indiana"—Walter J. Wakefield, IMH, June, 1915.
"The Schools of Indianapolis"—A. C. Shortridge, IMH, Jan.-Dec., 1912.
"Catholic Education in Indiana, Past and Present"—Elizabeth Denehie, IMH, Dec., 1916.
"Early History of Vincennes University"—Howard R. Burnett, IMH, June, 1933.
"New Harmony's Golden Years"—Richard E. Banta, IMH, March, 1948.
"The Unique Little Town of New Harmony"—Julia LeClerc Knox, IMH, March, 1936.
"The Founding of Butler University, 1847-1855"—Henry K. Shaw, IMH, Sept., 1962.
"The Owen Family Papers"—Josephine Mirabella Elliott, IMH, Vol. LX, No. 41, Dec., 1964.
PUBLICATIONS OF INDIANA HISTORICAL SOC.
"Caleb Mills and the Indiana School System"—Chas. W. Moore, Vol. 3, No. 6.
"An Indiana Village—New Harmony"—John H. Holliday, Vol. 5, No. 4.
"New Harmony; an Adventure in Happiness"—Papers of Thomas and Sarah Pears, edited by Thomas Pears, Jr. (1933), Vol. 11, No. 1.
"Harmonist Construction"—Don Blair, Vol. 23, No. 2

Population Growth, Agriculture, Natural Resources, and Manu-facturing in the State

HISTORICAL SURVEY OF THE UNIT

The Indiana state motto is "'The Cross-roads of America." This motto aptly describes the very fortunate location of the state. It is literally in the very "center of everything" not only geographically but also so far as its products are concerned. It ranks fourteenth in population among the states. Our state always has been able to depend upon three principal things for its prosperity and growth. These are agriculture, natural resources and manufacturing industries. No other state in the Union has these three things so equally developed as has ours. Agriculture is general over the state while manufacturing plants of different kinds are located in certain areas. Natural resources are the valuable things that were put here by nature; that is, which were not manufactured. Each of the natural resources is also found in certain distinct localities.

Growth and Distribution of Population

The center of population of the United States was in Indiana from 1890 to 1950. In 1890 it was twenty miles east of Columbus, in 1900 it was six miles southeast of Columbus, in 1910 it was in Bloomington, in 1920 it was in the southeastern part of Owen County, and in 1930 it was near Linton. In 1940, it moved a little farther west and was about two miles southeast of Carlisle in Sullivan County. The United States Census Bureau classifies all people who live in towns or cities of over 2500 as urban population. Those living in towns under 2500 and in the country are classified as rural population. In 1950, the urban population was 59.9 percent of the total and the rural population was 40.1 percent of the total. In 1970, the urban population had risen to 64.9 percent of the total and the rural population had fallen to 35.1 percent of the total. In 1980, the urban population dipped slightly to 64.2 percent. The average density of population in 1950, that

is, the average number of people for each square mile of area in Indiana, was 108.7 persons. In 1950 only five cities in the state had a population

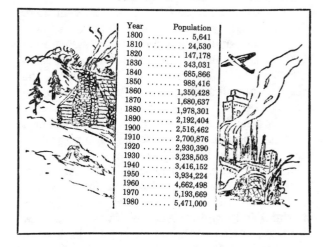

Year	Population
1800	5,641
1810	24,530
1820	147,178
1830	343,031
1840	685,866
1850	988,416
1860	1,350,428
1870	1,680,637
1880	1,978,301
1890	2,192,404
1900	2,516,462
1910	2,700,876
1920	2,930,390
1930	3,238,503
1940	3,416,152
1950	3,934,224
1960	4,662,498
1970	5,193,669
1980	5,471,000

The population of Indiana has steadily increased since the year 1800.

of more than 100,000 each. These were: Indianapolis, Gary, Fort Wayne, Evansville, and South Bend, in the order named. In 1970, there were six with a population of more than 100,000 each. These were Indianapolis, Fort Wayne, Gary, Evansville, South Bend, Hammond, in the order named. By 1980, Hammond had dropped below the 100,000 mark and Fort Wayne had moved ahead of Gary.

Indiana, like the other states, has had a rapid growth in population since 1950. Many of these people have built homes just outside the city limits of the larger cities. The people work in the cities or in nearby factories, and the automobiles and busses make it easy for them to get to their places of employment. However, it has also created a number of problems which are difficult to solve. One of these is the problem of building and equipping enough new schoolhouses in these "fringe" communities. Shopping centers have been built in these outlying communities, too, and almost any article may be purchased there. To make conditions fit for living, new sewers, new gas lines, new electric power lines, new telephone lines, new fire stations, and new police posts have to be built. Money has to be raised for all such purposes and taxes are constantly increasing. All this change and expansion is going on in Indiana today.

Growth of the Black Population in Indiana

There were very few blacks living in Indiana before the Civil War. The ones who were here were those who had been freed by their owners, crossed the Ohio River, and reached river towns such as Madison and New Albany.

The United States Census for the year 1870 gives the black population in Indiana as 24,560. In 1900 this population had risen to 57,505, and in 1930 it was 111,982. In 1970 the black population was 357,464. By the time of the 1980 census, the minority population was more than 500,000, including 414,732 blacks and 87,020 Hispanics.

Historically, the growth of Indiana's minority population is a reflection of a migration many years ago by southern blacks from states such as Alabama, Mississippi, and Tennessee. These people came north looking for jobs and equal opportunity in the years before the passage of the Civil Rights Act. Many of the new Hoosiers settled in the larger cities where work for unskilled laborers was more plentiful. Today, Gary and Indianapolis have the largest percentage of minorities in their populations.

Because of the harsh realities of segration in most parts of the South, the ugliness of prejudice in other regions of the country, and before the passage of anti-discrimination laws, many black people were poorly educated and lacking in specific skills. Denied a proper education, they had to take jobs as unskilled laborers, if they could find jobs at all. Although the change has been slow, many blacks now share equally in the opportunities afforded all Americans.

Although minorities have had the same voting rights as white citizens of Indiana, few exercised these rights until several decades ago. There were two main reasons for this. First, many blacks in the early part of the century were uneducated and unaware of their voting rights. Second, because of incidents all too familiar, particularly in some southern states, many blacks feared to register. They did not want to risk ill will from some segments of the white community.

Of course, that has changed and minorities have, in recent years, used the power of the vote to bring about much needed change. As minorities have moved into the mainstream, more and more of the people in power — from mayors to presidential hopefuls — have come from minority groups. As early as 1967, Richard Hatcher was elected mayor of Gary. He was the first black to be elected to such a high position in any city in the state.

For the purposes of comparison and for the study of different parts of it, the state may be divided into five geographical areas. These are the Northwest, the Northeast, the Central, the Southwest, and the Southeast. The census figures show that the percent of population (percent of population in an area refers to the number of people in that area in relation to the total number of people in Indiana at any given time) has steadily fallen in the Southwest Area, the Southeast Area, and in the Northeast Area since the year 1900. There has been a slight increase in the percent of population in the Central Area and a very large increase in the Northwest Area.

A few cities in the state decreased in population between 1930 and 1980. Several others between 1900 and 1980. Population Tables in Appendix B will show the increase or decrease of population in all the cities in the state. In every case, you will find that there is a direct connection with the kind and amount of industry which the city had or a change in the agriculture or natural resources around it. On the whole, the industrial centers grew more rapidly than any others between 1900 and 1970. The coal-mining centers grew slowly or actually lost population. The steel industry caused the cities of Hammond, East Chicago, and Whiting to expand so quickly that the city limits of these three places touch one another. Just a little farther east is Gary, a city of over one hundred sixty-five thousand population on a site which was a bare sand waste a little more than seventy years ago.

Agriculture in the State

The first permanent settlers in Indiana were farmers. The only way they had of making a living was by tilling the soil. The usual procedure of these pioneers was to clear a small patch of ground of its trees and underbrush, build a cabin of the best logs, and plant crops which would yield enough food for the family to live on throughout the year. Their principal crop was corn, which grew abundantly throughout the state. These early settlers in Indiana, in common with the first settlers of all the state, had little need for many manufactured articles because they produced from the soil or made with their own hands practically everything which they needed. You have already found out from your study of Unit 7 a great deal about how these settlers lived.

The southern part of the state is, on the whole, not as good for agriculture as the northern part. The exception to this is the land in the river valleys. Southern Indiana farms are comparatively small, and farming is diversified. Through the central part there is a strip of level country which is not surpassed for agriculture anywhere in the world. Roughly speaking, this prairie extends from the Kan-

In addition to their crops, Indiana farmers raise hogs, cattle, sheep, and poultry.

kakee River on the north to a line drawn from Fountain County to Shelby County on the south. In the early history of this state much of this prairie land, especially that in the west central part of the state in such counties as Newton, Benton, Jasper, and White, was too wet and swampy for use. At the present time it is well drained by an elaborate system of drainage ditches and is the most productive farm land in the state. As a general rule the farms in the central and northern part of the state are larger than those in the southern part. In 1940, 45% of the population in Indiana were living on farms.

In the amount of crop land used for agriculture, Indiana ranks second of the 26 states east of the Mississippi River. Seventy-four percent of the state's land, or seventeen million acres, is used for farming. There are 88,000 farms, most of them family-owned.

In a recent Department of Agriculture survey prepared by the federal governement, In-

diana ranked tenth in farm sales with crop marketings of almost $2 billion and livestock sales of $1.6 billion. Forty percent of the total farm sales were exports. These exported goods amounted to $1.4 billion worth. The primary exported crops were feed grains, soybeans, and soybean products.

The two largest crops in Indiana are soybeans and corn. In years to come when the final figures are in, Indiana will rank third or fourth in the nation in the production of corn and soybeans.

Wheat, rye, oats, and hay also are important crops in the state. Tobacco is also grown successfully in the southern counties, and that part of the state has extensive peach and apple orchards. Two thirds of the peppermint and spearmint oil produced in the United States comes from northern Indiana. Indiana is the top popcorn producing state in the nation and grows one third of the national total, or about 132 million pounds.

Indiana markets vegetables and fruits for local use and for use in other parts of the country. Some vegetable farms near the larger Indiana cities are called truck farms because the produce is "trucked" into the city for immediate sale.

In recent years, much commercial canning has been done in the state, and in canning tomatoes Indiana ranks third in the nation. Peas and corn are also canned in large quantities.

The dairy industry is an important one in all parts of the state. In some years this industry produces more than two billion pounds of milk and more than three billion eggs. Dairy products include whole milk, cream, butter, and cheese.

Cows and chickens are not the only animals on Indiana farms. Hoosier farmers raised four and half million hogs in 1980 and took them to market for sales of almost seven hundred million dollars. This makes Indiana the third largest hog-producing state in the nation.

Agriculture on Indiana's fertile land is one of the state's principal industries.

135

The larger farms are now operated almost entirely with highpowered machines, including huge combines and tractors. Much of the planning is done with highly-sophisticated computers that help the farmer raise better crops. Farming, for many people in Indiana, is big business.

Agriculture now is carried on much more scientifically than it was a few years ago. Purdue University at Lafayette maintains a School of Agriculture and an Agricultural Experiment Station for the purpose of training leaders and teachers in this field and for finding out new facts and new ways of doing things in farming. Most of the counties have an Agriculture Agent whose business it is to advise the farmers and to acquaint them with the latest methods of carrying on their work. The whole state has benefited, also, by the vocational work in the high schools and by the boys' and girls' club work in the rural districts. More than one-third of the high schools have courses in vocational agriculture and most high schools have courses in home economics.

Natural Resources of Indiana

The natural resources of Indiana are somewhat limited in number but of those which are found, the supply has been plentiful and of a good quality. One of the first to be developed was natural gas. The first gas well to be utilized was at Portland in 1886. Within the next four years, hundreds of gas wells had been drilled. So plentiful was the supply in certain counties that this section became known as the "gas belt." This region included the counties of Delaware, Grant, Madison, Blackford, Howard, Tipton, Hamilton, Hancock, Henry, and Rush. Cities in the "gas belt" grew very rapidly from 1890 to 1900 because many factories of different kinds located there in order to use the gas which was a cheap fuel. Some of these cities were Muncie, Anderson, Kokomo, Hartford City, Gas City, Marion, Fairmount, Alexandria, New Castle, Dunkirk, and many smaller ones. A great many factories, especially those for the manufacture of glassware, were established in these towns. People thought that this supply of gas would last forever and so they wasted it in every conceivable way. Consequently, the supply began to fail about 1900 and gradually faded away almost completely. Many of the cities which had grown so rapidly actually decreased in population for a while because the factories, especially the glass factories, were abandoned after the cheap fuel was gone. Now only 1% of gas Hoosiers use comes from Indiana.

The search for gas brought about discovery of oil in Indiana. One of the first places where this was found was near Terre Haute. Only a few wells ever proved to be paying ones, however. One of the best fields was in the vicinity of Montpelier. Others were near Peru and Alexandria. In 1904, the production of oil in Indiana reached the high point with 11,281,030 barrels for the year. In 1906, there were 16,266 producing wells and from that time the production of oil in this state has declined. Very little oil now comes from the wells in northern and central Indiana. Newer fields have been found in the southwestern part of the state and this region enjoyed a mild "oil boom" in the latter part of the 1930-40 decade. In 1948, oil in considerable quantity was found in Vigo and Sullivan counties, and there are producing wells in Pike, Posey, Gibson, and Vanderburgh counties. Almost every community in the state has bored wells for gas and oil at one time or another. Immense sums of money have been spent by these prospectors with very little return in many areas.

Coal is found in large quantities in almost all the counties in the southwestern part of the state and in paying quantity in as many as twenty-six different counties in the state. It is one of Indiana's most important natural re-

Much of Indiana's coal has been taken from the ground by shaft-mining.

136

sources. This coal has been mined by shaft mining and by strip mining. In the latter, the surface dirt is removed from the layers of coal by huge shovels and piled in adjacent areas. This makes the surface unfit for agriculture. Indiana coal is not considered as valuable as coal from West Virginia and eastern Kentucky, yet there has been a market for it since 1840 and even earlier. Its plentiful supply and its nearness to markets has kept down the cost of it.

The greatest amount of coal in this state has come from Parke, Vermillion, Vigo, Clay, Sullivan, Greene, Knox, Daviess, Pike, Gibson, Warrick, and Vanderburgh counties. Many cities in this region owed their growth to the development of the coal mines. Among these cities were Terre Haute, Clinton, Brazil, Sullivan, Bicknell, Jasonville, Linton, Oakland City, and Boonville. During World War I when there was a great demand for coal these cities reached the peak of their prosperity. Since that time there has been a slump in the market for coal and as a result these cities have suffered a loss of population and wealth. Coal mined in the southwestern counties of Indiana made up 68 percent of the dollar value of Indiana's mineral production. Today, most of this coal is surface mined. Its primary use is for generating electricity over the entire state. According to recent studies, Indiana's supply of coal will last more than 400 years before there is none left to mine.

Clay and shale from which pottery, tile, and brick are made have been found in most places where coal was mined. In many cases the veins of shale alternate with the veins of coal. Some of the earliest potteries were established near Bloomingdale and Annapolis in Parke County in 1840. A stoneware pottery was started at Clay City in 1846. Others were at Shoals, Loogootee, and Worthington. Large brick factories were located at Huntingburg, Brazil, Bloomfield, Veedersburg, and Martinsville, as well as at several other towns. Most of these factories originally made paving brick which were used for paving streets and highways. After cement came into common use for such purposes, the business of these factories fell off and some of them closed. Others began to make building brick and building tile. There were also other factories where glazed drain tile was made. One of these large plants was at Mecca, and another was at Brazil. Large deposits of a mineral called gypsum were discovered near Shoals in Martin County. This is used for making wallboard and other building materials.

Peat from pits in 9 counties north of Indianapolis comes from bogs that were here in Pleistocene times. Every bog bigger than an acre probably contains the bones of at least one mastodon.

Limestone has been one of the most valuable natural resources in the state. About two thirds of all building limestone quarried in the United States come from Lawrence and Monroe Counties in south-central Indiana. For many years, this limestone has been used in a great many of the principal buildings in large cities. Well-known buildings made from Indiana limestone include the Empire State Building, the Pentagon, and Washington Cathedral, the National Archives Building, and the buildings housing the State Department and the departments of Commerce, Labor, and Justice.

In Indiana, the cities of Bedford and Bloomington, and the towns of Oolitic and Ellettsville are centers for quarrying this stone. Most of the stone is shipped by truck and railroad to all parts of the country.

In addition to building stone, there are several deposits of stone which can be crushed and used as a surface for "stone roads." It can also be used for cement work. A deposit of this sort of stone extends from the vicinity of Fort Wayne westward across the state. There are large crushers near Huntington, Peru, Monon, Goodland, Wabash, Logansport, and Rensselaer. Stone from which cement is made is extracted near Greencastle, Mitchell, and Jeffersonville. There are two regions having rock which is suitable for the manufacture of rock or mineral wool. One of these is in the vicinity of Wabash and the other near Alexandria. Indiana ranks first in the United States in the production of this insulating material.

Twenty-five Hoosier counties have produced gold. Brown and Morgan counties have small streams where people can "pan" for gold for the fun of it.

An important pioneer industry which made use of a natural resource was salt making. The early settlers had to depend upon the natural deposits of this mineral for their supply of salt. These natural deposits were limited to certain regions. Some of the best were in Scott, Fountain, Franklin, Monroe, Brown, Orange, and Morgan counties. The salt was taken from the water which flowed from the salt springs in these places. Later some of these springs became health resort centers and large hotels were built at Martinsville, French Lick, West Baden, and other places to get the benefit of these mineral waters.

We have already learned that when the first white people came to Indiana most of the state was covered with trees. The pioneers used the logs from the trees to build houses, furniture, fences, and other things. Mills for making the logs into lumber sprang up all over the state. Most of the wood was what is known as "hard wood," and it came from the oak, the hickory, the maple, the walnut, and the poplar trees. The sawmills worked overtime, and the lumber which could not be used at home was shipped elsewhere. The people were very wasteful in cutting the trees and so the supply of good lumber from Indiana forests is very scarce today. Within the last twenty-five years, the state government has carried out a plan for restoring this natural resource to the state. This has been done by setting aside large tracts of land where timber may be grown under supervision of the State Department of Conservation. One of the best known of these state forests is the Morgan-Monroe County State Forest, located in those two counties.

Woodworking has always been an important industry in Indiana, although not a major one. At the present time there are large furniture factories at Jasper, Huntingburg, Tell City, Evansville and other cities. Most of the hickory, walnut, and poplar trees are gone from Indiana, today. Consequently, the articles which were once manufactured from these woods are no longer made here.

Another natural resource which has been utilized in the state is water power. In the early part of the nineteenth century practically every stream had one or more mills located on its banks. The current of the stream was directed in some way against a water wheel and the power was thus transferred to the machinery inside the mill. Sometimes a dam was constructed in the stream in order to get a greater "fall." The water was then led through an artificial channel called a "mill race" and allowed to run against the mill wheel. Most of these old mills were built for the purpose of grinding grain; they were called gristmills. Other water power mills were built for the purpose of making woolen cloth. The Yountsville Woolen Mills, located on Sugar Creek a few miles below Crawfordsville,

Gristmills and woolen mills were located on streams which furnished power to turn the wheels.

operated for many years. Some of the old gristmills are still standing and a few operated until very recently.

The largest body of water in Indiana is Monroe Reservoir, between Bedford and Bloomington. It has many recreation attractions as well as being a major source of flood prevention and providing water for community supply.

Over the years there has been an attempt to use the water power of some of Indiana's streams in a larger way. Some power companies have built dams and plants for generating electric current at several places. Two of these have been built in the Tippecanoe River, one above and one below Monticello. From these generating plants the electricity is distributed to numerous towns and cities.

Manufacturing Industries

Indiana ranks ninth among the states in the value of manufactured products which amounted to the sum of $52.1 billion. There are more than 8,000 factories in the state and the largest single industry is the making of steel. The beginning of the factories already has been mentioned in the discussion of the gristmills and woolen mills. There were some early attempts to make iron from the ore which was found in several places. However, there never was enough iron ore of good quality found in the state to amount to very much. The first large factories were built for pork packing. Between 1840 and 1850, Madison and Terre Haute were centers for this industry. There were no refrigerators at that time and so all the killing and packing had to be done in freezing weather. Large flour mills grew up at New Albany, Logansport, Lafayette, and Terre Haute. Whiskey was made in large distilleries at Lawenceburg, Vincennes, and Terre Haute.

Factories are now located in many principal cities and make a large number of different things.

Although iron ore is not mined in Indiana, this state is well-known for its iron and steel manufacturing in which Indiana stands second in the nation. Using iron ore shipped to the state by boats on Lake Michigan, Indiana's steel mills have produced 16.8 percent of all the raw steel made in the United States. In 1982, for example, Indiana produced 16,499,000 tons of raw steel.

Steel mills have contributed to the growth and economy of a number of our cities, including Hammond, East Chicago, and Gary. Gary has been the largest of these "steel cities" and was founded more than 70 years ago. Steel production led to the extremely rapid growth of these cities in the northwest corner of the state, usually referred to as the Calumet District.

Steel is an important part of heavy manufacturing and, as a result, Indiana has attracted major manufacturers. Manufacturing employs nearly two thirds of all Hoosier workers and is Indiana's largest employer. In the mid-1980s almost 670,000 people worked in manufacturing. Of this group, 43 percent are employed in three key industries: electrical machinery (electronic components, communications equipment, etc.), primary metals (steel mills and foundaries), and transportation equipment (auto and aircraft parts, recreational vehicles).

Indianapolis, the capital, has had rapid growth and is the largest city in the state, largely due to its long list of varied industries. Along with cities like South Bend, Fort Wayne, Evansville, and Muncie, Indianapolis has been home to nationally-known manufacturers. Famous Indiana companies include the following: General Electric Company, Ball Brothers (canning products), Delco-Remy, Eli Lilly and Co. (pharmaceuticals), Whiting, and National Homes Corporation. These companies and many others manufacture everything from band instruments to prefabricated houses.

The great diversity of Indiana's industry is demonstrated by the state's high ranking in the manufacture of these products: **FIRST** in recreational vehicles, limestone, storage batteries, horsepower motors, magnetic wire, phonograph records and tapes, wood office furniture, rolled steel, truck and bus bodies, and musical instruments.

SECOND in raw steel, pig iron, margarine, gelatine, electric transformers, and whiskey.

THIRD in mobile homes, prefabricated buildings, motor vehicle parts, and parts for internal combustion engines.

The people of Indiana were among the first in the nation to be associated with the invention and the development of automobiles. Elwood Haynes of Kokomo was one of the first men to make a "horseless carriage" which would run up to 6 miles an hour. This was in 1894. This car can still be seen in the Smithsonian Institute in Washington. In 1898 he, together with a man named Apperson, produced the first automobiles for sale in Indiana. Within a few years, 208 different makes of cars and trucks were being built in the state. More than 30 cities in Indiana had automobile factories. Indianapolis, alone, turned out 44 different makes of cars. Many of these factories were ones which had previously made buggies or wagons.

The following is a short list of different makes of cars, and the cities in which they were produced. This activity took place between the years 1900 and 1940.

American—American Motor Car Co.—Indianapolis
Apperson—Apperson Bros. Auto Co.—Kokomo
Auburn—Auburn Auto Co.—Auburn
Cole—Cole Motor Car Co.—Indianapolis
Duesenberg—Duesenberg Motor Co.—Indianapolis
Elcar—Elcar Motor Co.—Elkhart
Haynes—Haynes Auto Co.—Kokomo
Lambert—Buckeye Mfg. Co.—Anderson
Lexington—Lexington Howard Co.—Connersville
Marmon—Nordyke Marmom Co.—Indianapolis
Maxwell—Maxwell Briscoe Co.—New Castle
Overland—Willys-Overland Co.—Indianapolis
Studebaker—Studebaker Corp.—South Bend
Stutz—Stutz Motor Car Co.—Indianapolis
Waverly—Pope Waverly Motor Car Co.—Indianapolis

Today, all of these companies have gone out of business. Other changes are taking place in industry, today, which will, within a few years, make more differences in the kinds of things produced in Indiana and in the further growth and distribution of population in the state.

STUDY EXERCISES

Write the correct answers in the blanks.

1. What is Indiana's state motto? _____

2. This state motto refers to what feature which the state of Indiana possesses? _____
_____

3. The center of population of the United States was in the state of _____ from the
year _____ to the year _____ .

4. In 1820, the population of Indiana was _____ . In 1950, it was _____ ; in
1970 _____ ; in 1980 _____ .

5. In 1970 there were _____ cities in the state with a population of more than 100,000 each and, in
1980 there were only _____ . Why did the figure change? _____ On the lines below, name
the cities that, in 1970, had a population greater than 100,000.
_____
_____

6. Arrange these cities according to size in 1970 and then in 1980. (Use the tables on page 169. Appendix B Table 2.) Start with the Largest.

Kokomo   Indianapolis   Hammond   Gary   Jeffersonville   Goshen   Peru
    Evansville   Fort Wayne   Bloomington   Connersville   Lawrence

	1970	1980
A.	_____	_____
B.	_____	_____
C.	_____	_____
D.	_____	_____
E.	_____	_____
F.	_____	_____
G.	_____	_____
H.	_____	_____
I.	_____	_____
J.	_____	_____
K.	_____	_____
L.	_____	_____
M.	_____	_____

7. How many counties in Indiana lost population between 1950 and 1980? Use the statistical table on
page 170. It is Table 3. _____ Which county gained the most in population between 1970 and
1980? _____ Which lost the most population? _____

Write the correct answers in the blanks.

_____ 1-3. Indiana has always depended upon what three things for its
growth?

_____

_____

_____ 4. What was the main occupation of early settlers in Indiana?

140

_____ 5. What part of Indiana is best for farming?

_____ 6. In 1980, there were how many farms in Indiana?

_____ 7. How many acres of farmland are there in Indiana?

_____ 8. What was the total cash farm income in Indiana?

_____ 9. What is the principal farm crop in Indiana?

_____ 10-12. What are three other important farm crops in the state?

_____

_____

_____ 13-14. What livestock is raised extensively in Indiana?

_____

_____ 15. What crop is grown in a few counties in southern Indiana?

_____ 16-17. A small area in northern Indiana produces most of what two
   things grown in the United States?

_____ 18-19. What two kinds of fruit are raised extensively in Indiana?

_____

_____ 20-22. What three vegetables are canned in great quantities in
   Indiana?

_____

_____

_____ 23. Where does the state of Indiana maintain a School of Agriculture and an Agricultural Experiment Station?

Write the correct answers in the blanks.

1. What natural resource found in Indiana is used extensively for building purposes?

_____

2. Indiana furnishes about what percent of this material? _____

3. Most of this building material is found in what counties? _____

_____   _____

4. What cities and towns are the leading ones in which this material is taken from the ground
   and finished for use? _____   _____

   _____   _____

5. Stone which is later crushed and used for building roads is taken from the ground near what
   places? _____   _____   _____

   _____   _____

6. What was one of the natural resources that the pioneers needed for their food? _____

7. What is the largest body of water in Indiana? _____

8. What natural resource covered much of the land in Indiana when the first white settlers
   arrived? _____

9. What natural resource was furnished by some streams in Indiana? _____

10. The early settlers used this natural resource for what purpose? _____

_____

11. What was a "mill race"? _____

_____

141

12. At what place in Indiana was a well-known woolen mill located? _____

13. In what river in Indiana have two large power dams been built in recent years? _____
_____

14. These dams are near what city? _____

15. The extreme northwest corner of Indiana is known as what area? _____

16. What large city in this area was founded about sixty years ago? _____

17. Why was a need created for "shopping centers"? _____
_____

Complete the paragraphs by writing the correct words in the blanks, or by writing the correct answers to the questions.

1. A natural resource is described as being something that _____
_____. Four of Indiana's most valuable resources have been _____,
_____, _____, and _____. One of these,
namely, _____, was found in great quantities in the east central part of
the state about the year 1886. This region included the counties of _____,
_____, _____, _____,
_____, _____, _____,
_____, and _____
This area was known as the _____. The discovery and use of this
natural resource caused the towns and cities in this region to _____
_____. Some of these cities were _____, _____,
_____, _____, _____, and
_____. One of the main things manufactured here was _____
_____. The supply of this natural resource began to _____ just after the year
_____. This caused many of the factories to _____ and
the cities to _____.

2. Coal was another _____ resource in Indiana and it was found in quantities in the _____ part of the state. Twelve principal counties in which
it was found were _____, _____, _____,
_____, _____, _____,
_____, _____, _____,
_____, _____, and _____
Among the cities that were known as coal-mining towns were _____,
_____, _____, _____,
_____, _____, _____,
_____, and _____. Coal was mined in two ways:
by _____, and by _____.

A. What has been the condition of the coal-mining industry in Indiana since 1920?
_____

B. Most of the coal now mined in the state is used for what purpose? _____

3. The search for natural gas in Indiana brought about the discovery of _____ too. The first discovery of this natural resource in the state was near _____ More recently, _____ was found in the _____ part of the state. The counties of _____, _____, _____, _____, and _____ have been the principal ones to produce this resource.

4. Two other closely related natural resources found in Indiana and known as _____ _____ and _____ are used to make pottery, _____, and _____ _____ Early potteries were located at the towns of _____, _____ _____, and _____. Brick factories were located at _____, _____, _____ _____, and _____. Bricks were used for _____ _____ and for _____. After _____ came into use, the demand for brick _____. Large factories for making tile were at _____ _____ and _____. Large deposits of a mineral called _____ have been found in Martin County, and this is used for making _____.

Write the correct answers in the blanks.

_____ 1. In 1972, Indiana held what rank among the states in the value of manufactured products?

_____ 2. Approximately how many factories were in Indiana in 1974?

_____ 3. What city in Indiana has some of the world's largest oil refineries?

_____ 4. What is Indiana's largest manufacturing industry?

_____ 5. The first large factories in this state were built for what purpose?

_____ 6-7. What two towns were centers for this industry?

_____

_____ 8-10. In what three cities were large flour mills built?

_____

_____

_____ 11-13. What three cities in Indiana have some of the world's largest steel mills?

_____

_____

_____ 14. What city in Indiana is the largest center for the manufacture of pre-fabricated houses?

_____15. What man was the first in Indiana to make an automobile?

_____16. This first automobile was made in what year?

_____17. At one time, how many different makes of trucks and auto-mobiles were being manufactured in the state?

_____18. How many different cities in Indiana had automobile factories?

_____19. What Indiana city had the largest number of different auto-mobile factories?

_____20. How many makes of automobiles are now made in Indiana?

In the blanks before the questions, write the correct answers about Indiana counties.

_____ 1. Which is the largest in area?

_____ 2. Which is the smallest in area?

_____ 3. Which had the largest population in 1970? 1980?

_____ 4. Which had the smallest population in 1970? 1980?

Write the correct answers in the blanks.

1. What is meant by urban population? _____

2. What is meant by rural population? _____

3. The U.S. Census classifies all places as being urban if they have a population of how many?

_____

4. What is meant by a suburban area? _____

5. The large increase in home building since 1950 has taken place in what kind of area?

_____

6. In 1860, how many cities in Indiana had a population of 10,000 or more? _____

7. In 1980, how many cities had a population of 10,000 or more? _____

A. List the ten largest cities in Indiana in order of of their size in 1980 and give the population of each.

	City	Population
(1)	_____	_____
(2)	_____	_____
(3)	_____	_____
(4)	_____	_____
(5)	_____	_____
(6)	_____	_____
(7)	_____	_____
(8)	_____	_____
(9)	_____	_____
(10)	_____	_____

B. What three cities in Indiana had the largest percent of growth in population between 1950 and 1970? (Appendix B)

_____   _____   _____

C. Using a scale of 1/8 inch for each 100,000 of population, construct lines showing the growth of the state by ten-year periods since 1800.

1800
1810
1820
1830
1840
1850
1860
1870
1880
1890
1900
1910
1920
1930
1940
1950
1960
1970
1980

TOPICS FOR DISCUSSION AND REPORT

1. Make a report to the class on which you think is, on the whole, most valuable to the state; agriculture, manufacturing, or natural resources. You may have to back your opinion with statistics.

2. Make a list of all the advantages you can think of that Indiana has for manufacturing.

3. Select some large company such as Chrysler Corporation at Kokomo, United States Steel Corp. at Gary, Perfect Circle Company at Hagerstown, Allison Engine Co. (General Motors) at Indianapolis, National Homes Corp. at Lafayette, or any other large manufacturing company in the state. Give a brief history of its founding and describe its growth to the present time.

4. Select one city, either your own or one with which you are familiar, and make a list of the various industries in it.

5. Make a report to the class on the "shaft mining" of coal.

6. Make a report to the class on "strip mining." Tell how this is done and what the results are to the land which has been mined. (If you live in a strip-mining area, select some other topic.)

7. Make a report to the class on the development of the machinery used to handle the corn crop in Indiana. Begin with the pioneer's crude plow and name each step in the improvement of this machinery.

8. Make a list of the different minerals that are found in Indiana.

9. Make a list of the specific things which have caused the five largest cities in Indiana to be the largest.

10. Make a report to the class on the growing of hybrid seed corn.

11. Describe some of the early models of automobiles that were made in Indiana.

REFERENCES FOR UNIT 11

GENERAL REFERENCES
Buley—Vol. I—pp. 167-228, 519-564.
Esarey (School Edition)—Chs. XXV-XXVII.
Cottman—Chs. XVI, XVIII.
Thornton, Reade—Chs. XX-XXII.
Thompson—*Stories of Indiana*—pp. 279-296.
Roll—Vol. II—pp. 62-109, 251-253, 373-397.
Annual Reports of the State Geologist.
United States Census Reports.
Year Books of State of Indiana.
World Almanac for several recent years.
Indiana State Dept. of Commerce.
Purdue Agricultural Experiment Station.
INDIANA MAGAZINE OF HISTORY

"Natural Gas in Indiana" — Wynn, IMH, March, 1908.
"The Indiana Coal Industry's Part in World War II"—R. C. Freytag, IMH, Sept., 1945.
"Early Commerce in Indiana"—Geo. S. Cottman, IMH. March, 1908.
READINGS IN INDIANA HISTORY (1956 edition) Chs. XVII-XIX.
INDIANA HISTORY BULLETIN
Indiana's Place in Automobile History — Wallace Spencer Huffman, IHB, Sept., 1961.
The Apperson Brothers and their Automobiles—Wallace S. Huffman, IHB, Jan., 1964.

Famous Persons, Places of Interest, and Miscellaneous Facts about Our State

Almost everyone knows that Indiana is called the Hoosier State and the people of Indiana are known as Hoosiers. The origin of this nickname is not known for sure, although there have been various explanations of it. One is that "Hoosier" was a term brought from the south and that it meant an uncouth and ignorant person. Another explanation is that "Hoosier" is a contraction of "Who's yar?" meaning "Who is there?". This might have been used by the early settlers in asking callers to identify themselves at night. Whatever the origin, the term is now in general use. Any citizen of Indiana is likely to hear it in any state into which he might go and any citizen of Indiana is proud to answer to that name.

The State Emblems

Our state has, from time to time, adopted several emblems. The state seal is one of them. The Constitution of Indiana (1851) provides that "there shall be a Seal of State, kept by the Governor for official purposes, which

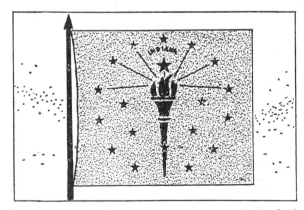

The official state flag shown on the cover of this book has a dark blue background with gold stars.

shall be called the Seal of the State of Indiana." This is the only description of the state seal. It portrays a pioneer scene—a woodsman felling a tree, a buffalo running from the forest, and the sun setting beyond distant hills. The design was used originally on the Seal of Indiana Territory as early as 1801. When Indiana was admitted as a state in 1816, the old design was retained as the state seal. There is no record to show who designed it or when it was first used. The state seal is affixed to all official state documents.

The state banner was adopted by the State Legislature in 1917 as a part of the commemoration of the State's Centennial. A contest for a suitable design was sponsored by the Daughters of the American Revolution and the prize-winning design was submitted by Paul Hadley of Mooresville, Indiana. The flag was used first in a pageant at Indiana University. The torch in the center stands for liberty and enlightenment and the rays represent their far-reaching influence. The outer circle of stars stands for the original thirteen states, and the inner circle of stars for the five states next admitted to the Union. The large star stands for Indiana, which was the nineteenth state. This banner is "regulation in addition to the American flag, with all of the military forces of the State of Indiana, and in all public functions in which the state may or shall officially appear." The banner is five feet six inches fly by four feet four inches hoist. The background of the flag is a deep blue and the design is in gold.

The state tree of Indiana is the tulip tree or yellow poplar. Indiana is its native environment and this tree grows large and straight. It has rich green leaves and a greenish-yellow flower. It was adopted officially as the state tree by the legislature in 1931. Unfortunately, a comparatively small number of these trees are now found in the state. Recently, efforts have been made to plant more tulip trees in Indiana.

The zinnia was adopted as the official state

flower by a law passed by the state legislature in 1931. In 1957, by another act of the state legislature, the state flower was changed from the zinnia to the peony. This was done because the peony was considered a more beautiful flower and also one which was more representative of the state.

In 1933, the redbird or cardinal was designated as the official state bird. Every Hoosier is familiar with this beautiful bird which can be heard in Indiana at almost any time of the year.

The Indiana state song is "On the Banks of the Wabash, Far Away." The words and music of this were written by Paul Dresser, from Terre Haute. It was officially adopted by an act of the state legislature in 1913.

Indiana celebrated its Sesquicentennial (150 years of statehood) in 1966. The seal shown below was designed to help commemorate this event.

This shows the design of the state banner and of the first statehouse.

For 1975 and 1976, many Indiana communities and cities developed special programs in observance of the nation's Bicentennial.

Famous Persons from Indiana

The Hoosier State is noted for the large number of its people who have become famous in the fields of literature, art, education, business, professions, statesmanship, and others. Among its well-known writers are the following: Edward Eggleston, who wrote *The Hoosier Schoolmaster* which was referred to in this book in the Unit on Education; Lew Wallace, author of *Ben Hur*; Meredith Nicholson and Booth Tarkington, authors of many novels and short stories; George Ade of Brook, famous humorist; James Whitcomb Riley, the Hoosier poet, and author of such well-known poems as "When the Frost is on the Punkin' " and "The Old Swimmin' Hole"; Maurice Thompson who wrote *Alice of Old Vincennes*; William Vaughn Moody, playwright and poet;

Charles Major, author of *When Knighthood was in Flower;* Gene Stratton Porter, author of *Girl of the Limberlost* and *Freckles;* Theodore Dreiser; William Herschell; Kin Hubbard, the creator of "Abe Martin"; Margaret Weymouth Jackson; Lloyd Douglas, author of *Magnificent Obsession,* and *The Robe;* George Jean Nathan, playwright and dramatic critic; John T. McCutcheon, who gained fame as a cartoonist on the *Chicago Tribune;* George Barr McCutcheon; Kate Milner Rabb; Edison Marshall, novelist; and John Clark Ridpath and Charles A. Beard, historians. You could add many names to this list.

Among those who have gained a nationwide recognition in other lines, we might mention the following, which is a very incomplete list. Ambrose E. Burnside, general in the

The official state song, "On the Banks of the Wabash," was written by Paul Dresser.

Union army during the Civil War; Walter Q. Gresham, Postmaster-General in President Arthur's cabinet, Secretary of the Treasury, and Secretary of State; Albert J. Beveridge, who served two terms as United States Senator and who was a distinguished orator; Charles Warren Fairbanks, Senator and Vice President of the United States; John Hay, Secretary of State in the President's Cabinet, 1898-1905; Elwood Haynes, automobile inventor; Wilbur Wright, inventor of the early airplane; Will H. Hays, Postmaster General in the President's Cabinet; John W. Kern, United States Senator; Kenesaw Mountain Landis, former Federal Judge and later Commissioner for organized baseball; Thomas R. Marshall, twenty-sixth governor of Indiana and Vice President of the United States under Woodrow Wilson; Harry S. New, United States Senator and Postmaster General of the United States, 1923-1929; Claude G. Bowers, newspaper man and former Ambassador to Spain; Wendell Willkie, candidate for President; Sherman Minton, former Justice of the Supreme Court of the U. S. A.; and Harvey W. Wiley, famous for getting the Federal Pure Food and Drug Act passed.

This list might be extended to include: Hoagland (Hoagy) Carmichael and Cole Porter, modern song writers; Dr. Cleo Blackburn, now the executive director, of Flanner House, a well-known settlement house for social service for Negroes in Indianapolis. Adolph H. Schellschmidt, Elmer Andrew Steffen, Edward Bailey Birge, Paul Dresser, and Nicola A. Montani, musicians and composers; Wes Montgomery, voted Number One jazz guitarist in the United States; T. C. Steele, William Forsythe, J. Ottis Adams, Otto Stark, Eugene Savage, and George Winter, famous painters; Janet Scudder, sculptress; Paul V. McNutt, former governor of Indiana, and former High Commissioner to the Philippines; Edwin C. Hill and Elmer Davis, radio news commentators; Ernie Pyle, newspaper correspondent killed in World War II; Marjorie Main and Carole Lombard, motion picture actresses; Herb Shriner and Red Skeleton, radio and television entertainers; Daniel W. Voorhees, for twenty-five years a U. S. Senator; Benjamin Harrison, President of the United States (not born in Indiana); Schuyler Colfax, Vice President of the United States; Thomas A. Hendricks, governor of Indiana and later Vice President of the United States; Oliver P. Morton, Indiana's Civil War Governor. You could add to this list, too.

The State Parks of Indiana

Indiana's state parks are known throughout the nation for their scenic beauty, their historical background and the opportunities which they afford for varied, year-around, outdoor recreation. The popularity of our state parks among people of our own and of other states has won for Indiana the title of "Vacation Playground of the Middle West." Each year more than a million persons visit these beautiful and well-kept parks.

There are now nineteen state parks, and many additional places of historic interest. In addition, there are state recreation areas on seven flood-control reservoirs.

Admission fees are charged at the entrance of all state parks and state recreation areas. This helps pay the expenses of operating the parks. Hotels are maintained in several but not all the parks. During the 1930s the state had the assistance of labor from the CCC camps to develop the state parks. This made it possible for the state to carry out improvements which made the parks doubly attractive.

STATE PARKS	
1.	Bass Lake
2.	Brown County
3.	Clifty Falls
4.	Indiana Dunes
5.	Harmonie
6.	Lincoln
7.	McCormick's Creek
8.	Mounds
9.	Quabache
10.	Pokagon
11.	Shades
12.	Shakamak
13.	Spring Mill
14.	Tippecanoe River
15.	Turkey Run
16.	Versailles
17.	Whitewater
18.	Lieber
19.	Chain O'Lakes
20.	Raccoon Lake
21.	Potato Creek

The twenty-one state parks are scattered throughout the state and offer many attractions.

Turkey Run State Park was established in 1916 and is the second oldest of the state parks in Indiana. It has an area of 2,382 acres and is in the extreme west central part of the state about forty miles north of Terre Haute and near the small town of Marshall. It is reached by I74 and Highway No. 47 and is just off Highway No. 41. It is named for the great flocks of wild turkeys which once inhabited this region. The park lies on both sides of Sugar Creek and there are, literally, miles of twisting trails through the gorges of solid rock. One of the largest of the state park hotels is located at Turkey Run.

Indiana Dunes State Park, established in 1925, is near Chesterton in Porter County and borders the southern end of Lake Michigan for three miles. It is in the midst of the huge, shifting sand dunes of this region and contains many specimens of plants and wildlife. There is a pavillion and a magnificent beach, camp ground, and other facilities for visitors. This park is only a short distance from Chicago and the cities of Gary, Hammond, East Chicago, Whiting, and Michigan City. Consequently, it has many visitors who flock to its 2,182 acres. It is reached on Route 94.

Clifty Falls State Park is in the southern part of the state near Madison. It has an area of 1,360 acres and consists largely of deep ravines and hills. It is reached on Route 421. The falls in the park is one of the largest in Indiana cascading down a 70 feet drop. Accommodations are available near a 400 feet plateau which provides a spectacular view of miles of the broad Ohio River. The scenery in and around this park is not surpassed anywhere in the state.

Spring Mill State Park is reached on Route 60 and is located just off Route 37 near Mitchell in Lawrence County. It has an area of 1,319 acres and was established in 1927. Once the site of a thriving pioneer village, this park now contains a re-creation of that village. The house and other buildings are grouped around a water-powered gristmill. The mill is operating and shows how the early settlers used the power of small streams to grind their grain, saw timber, and weave cloth. A part of the park is covered by heavy forests and, in other sections, almost every flower, shrub, and tree native to Indiana is found. There is also a large lake in the park and an inn which carries out the style of pioneer architecture. The inn serves meals and takes overnight guests.

Potato Creek State Recreation Area consists of 3,840 acres on Route 4 about four miles west of Route 31. This lovely, tranquil park offers a 300-acre lake and ample trails for hiking and horseback riding. More than 300 campsites afford a chance for a night in the great Indiana woods.

Shakamak State Park is located in Clay, Greene, and Sullivan counties. Its name comes from the old Indian one meaning "the river of long fish." This park is on Route 159. The park is in the midst of the coal-mining region and a large part of it is a former strip mining area. It has two artificial lakes which are well stocked with fish. This park of 1,766 acres was established in 1929.

Brown County State Park is near Nashville in Brown County, which is well-known for its beautiful hill country. The park is the largest of Indiana's state parks in area and contains 15,543 acres. It may be reached over I65. The park was established in 1929. A visit to the park will include a drive over Indiana's oldest covered bridge and, perhaps, a night's stay in the well-known Abe Martin Lodge. This park is particularly famed for its magnificent fall foliage.

Pokagon State Park is in the extreme northeast corner of the state, not far from Angola. It may be reached on the Indiana Toll Road (I90-80); the Angola Interchange is only two miles from the park entrance. The park was established in 1925 and has 1,195 acres. It is located in country which once belonged to the Potawatomi Indians and takes its name from one of the Indian chiefs. This corner of the state has many lakes; two large ones, Lake James and Snow Lake, are in Pokagon Park. Lake James is the third largest lake in Indiana. Potawatomi Inn provides hotel accommodations. It is popular in all seasons. A well-known twin toboggan slide operates from November through mid-March.

McCormick's Creek State Park is on Route 46 near Spencer. With an area of 1,833 acres it became a state park in 1916 and was the first one in Indiana's park system. Once a hunting ground of the Miami Indians, the park borders the White River and a small stream known as McCormick's Creek flows through the park. It features an Olympic-size swimming pool and the Canyon Inn which provides meals and lodgings.

Mounds State Park is near Anderson on high bluffs overlooking White River. The Adena and the Hopewell Indian tribes lived together along the White River more than 2000 years ago. The mounds and earthworks left by these two lost civilizations are a fascinating part of this park. The Great Mound is encircled by an earthen wall twelve hundred feet in circumference and nine feet high. The grounds include 254 acres which can be used for camping, canoeing, swimming, and other outdoor activities.

Lincoln State Park and Lincoln Boyhood National Memorial, which adjoins the park, are in the southern part of the state in Spencer County along Routes 231 and 64. In this region Lincoln spent 14 years of his early life. In the memorial area are the grave of Nancy Hanks Lincoln and the site of the cabin to which Thomas Lincoln brought his family in 1816. Many items connected with the life of Lincoln are found here and, to help give a sense of history, the gardens are planted much as they would have been in Lincoln's boyhood. The state of Indiana has erected a beautiful memorial to Lincoln and his family. The memorial has many interesting exhibits about the Lincoln family and honors, in particular, the pioneer spirit of Nancy Hanks Lincoln.

Versailles State Park was acquired by the state in 1943. It is located in Ripley County just east of the town of Versailles and covers 5,897 acres. It can be reached on Route 421. The center of activity in this park is its 230-acre lake where campers and visitors kayak, pedalboat, fish, and swim.

The Tippecanoe River State Park, also, was acquired by the state in 1943. It is located a short distance north of the town of Winamac. It stretches for six miles along the Tippecanoe River in Pulaski County and contains 2,761 acres. This park can be reached by State Highway No. 35. It is popular for camping and there is excellent fishing there.

Bass Lake State Beach is a twenty-two-acre tract bordering beuatiful Bass Lake in Starke County near Knox. There is a good bathing beach. This park is small and has not been extensively developed.

The Shades State Park is one of the more recent additions to the list of state parks in Indiana. This was taken over by the state from private owners in 1948. It consists of 3,084 acres covered by some of the finest trees still standing in Indiana. More than fifty different kinds of trees are found in the park. It is located along Sugar Creek in Parke and Montgomery counties a few miles above Turkey Run State Park.

The Whitewater State Park is in Union County a short distance south of the town of Liberty. This park is near the East Fork of the Whitewater River and is in a region of great historical interest. This land was donated by the people of Wayne, Union, Franklin, and Fayette counties and is a memorial to those who served in World War II. The park is made up of 1,710 acres. There is a 200-acre lake which furnishes boating, swimming, and fishing.

The Richard H. Lieber Recreation Area was dedicated on July 12, 1958. It was named in honor of Col. Richard H. Lieber, founder of Indiana's

state park system. This park contains 1,400 acres on the northwest side of Cataract Lake in Owen and Putnam counties. It is located about 11 miles southwest of Cloverdale. There is a bathing beach, a bathhouse, a boathouse, boat docks, a shelterhouse, and an excellent picnic area, but no hotel. The park includes state-owned Cataract Falls, the largest in the state.

The Chain-O'Lakes State Park is in Noble County about five miles southeast of the town of Albion. It was purchased by funds provided by Allen, Noble, and Whitley counties and by the state legislature. The principal part consists of a chain of nine connecting lakes.

The park features a bathing beach, modern campground, boat and canoe rentals, fishing and picnicking in its 7,678 acres.

The Raccoon Lake State Recreational Area consists of six hundred acres of land along U.S. Highway No. 36, east of Rockville. It contains a man-made lake of approximately 1,900 acres created by building a dam on Raccoon Creek. There are boat-launching ramps and swimming areas but no hotel. It was dedicated in 1961.

This monument was erected in memory of the soldiers killed on the Tippecanoe Battlefield.

Harmonie State Park is located on the banks of the Wabash River not far from New Harmony, the community founded in 1814 by Father Rapp's Harmony Society. Harmonie's 3,645 acres are noted for the abundance of wildlife, including deer. The park is a popular spot for picnics and a cool summer swin.

Ouabache (say Wabash) State Park was formerly called Wells County State Game Farm. It is located about six miles east of Bluffton on Indiana 124. Facilities include a small lake for boating and fishing, picnic areas, limited camping, and a lodge for one-day use by supervised groups.

In addition to the state parks and recreational areas which we have described, the state maintains several State Memorials, including:

Angel Mounds, near Evansville
Corydon, first state capitol
Indiana Territorial Capitol, at Vincennes
J.F.D. Lanier mansion, at Madison
Limberlost, at Geneva
Gene Stratton Porter Memorial, in Noble County
18th Century Communal Village, at New Harmony
Old State Bank, at Vincennes
Pigeon Roost, near Underwood
Tippecanoe Battlefield, near Lafayette
Whitewater Canal, near Brookville
Wilbur Wright birthplace, near Millville
T. C. Steele studio, near Belmont

Other Interesting Places and Things

The State Soldiers' and Sailors' Monument stands in the center of downtown Indianapolis. It was erected as a memorial to those men of the state who took part in the defense of the Union during the Civil War and to those who fought in previous wars. The monument rises 285 feet above the ground and from its balcony a visitor may get a view of the entire city of Indianapolis. Statues of Governors Morton and Whitcomb and of Generals William Henry Harrison and George Rogers Clark are arranged around the base. The monument was dedicated in 1892. Many persons visit it each year and it has become one of the landmarks of our capital city.

The World War I Memorial is located a few blocks north of the Soldiers' and Sailors' Monument, between Meridian and Pennsylvania Streets in Indianapolis. This was built by public funds raised in the state of Indiana. The main building stands at the south end of the memorial plaza, which is several blocks long. This building is massive and unique in design. The National Headquarters of the

The Soldiers' and Sailors' Monument is in the very center of Indianapolis and is 285 feet high.

American Legion occupies a beautiful building at the north end of the plaza. These memorial buildings were erected in honor of those from this state who served in the American armies during World War I.

In the hills of Orange County, at French Lick, is the magnificent Sheraton French Lick Springs Hotel and vacation resort. This attracts many visitors each year, not a few of whom come to take the mineral baths and to drink the famous "Pluto Water" which comes from the springs there.

Wyandotte and Marengo Caves in the southern part of the state are world famous. Lake Wawasee, near the little town of Syracuse, is Indiana's largest lake and it attracts thousands of summer vacationists. Cedar Lake, in Lake County, is another large lake and is very popular as a summer vacation resort. Shafer Lake, and Lake Freeman, both near Monticello, are artificial lakes which were formed when power dams were built in the Tippecanoe River. The shores of both lakes are now lined with summer homes of people who enjoy being near the water and the good fishing which these lakes provide.

Abraham Lincoln in Indiana

Abraham Lincoln was not born in Indiana. However, the people of our state are especially interested in him because he spent most of his boyhood here. Lincoln was born February 12, 1809, near Hodgenville, Kentucky. His father was Thomas Lincoln and his mother was Nancy Hanks Lincoln. Thomas Lincoln was a farmer and a carpenter and owned a small farm. In 1816, he lost this farm because he had failed to get a clear title to it. So, in that year, when Abraham, was seven years old, the family consisting of Abraham, the mother and father and the sister, Sarah, moved to Indiana. They crossed the Ohio River at Troy and then went about sixteen miles inland. Here, Thomas Lincoln found a site where he thought a home could be made. So, they stayed at this place and decided to build a home and engage in farming. This was in what is now Spencer County, near the present town of Gentryville.

It was wintertime and the weather was cold. The quickest shelter that could be set up was a rough shed called a "half-faced camp." This consisted of three walls and a crude roof with the fourth side open to the weather. A fire, which was kept burning on the open side, furnished the only protection there. Abraham, who was large and strong for his age, helped his father build the house. There was no furniture and the only beds were piles of straw and leaves. The cooking utensils were the same kind of ordinary pots and kettles used by all the early pioneers. By the end of the next summer, a better cabin had been built and some land had been cleared for farming.

In October of 1818, Abraham's mother died. She was a victim of the "milk sickness" which killed whole communities of Indiana pioneers. Mrs. Lincoln was buried on a hill a short distance south of the Lincoln cabin. A few years ago, the state of Indiana erected a beautiful limestone building on this spot in memory of Nancy Hanks Lincoln. The state maintained this memorial until 1962, when the Federal government took it over as a gift from our state.

During the year after Nancy Lincoln's death, Thomas Lincoln went back to Kentucky for a visit. While there, he married Mrs. Sarah Johnston, a widow with three children. Thomas Lincoln returned to Indiana with his new family, bringing a wagon load of house furnishings and other things to make life more comfortable. Abraham's step-mother was very good to him and tried in every way to help him the best she could.

Schools in this state at that time were few and far between. Abraham or "Abe," as he came to be called, attended such schools as were available. Mrs. Lincoln urged him to study and at every opportunity he read all the books that he could borrow. He grew rapidly, and soon reached the height of six feet four inches. He became known as one of the strongest men in southern Indiana. He did all

kinds of farm work and was especially good at handling an axe.

When Lincoln was nineteen years of age, he was hired by a neighbor to help take a flatboat loaded with trade goods down the Ohio and Mississippi rivers to New Orleans. This event was a great one in Lincoln's life because it inspired him to want to take an active part in what was going on in this new country.

In 1830, Thomas Lincoln sold his farm in Indiana and moved to Illinois. Abraham went with him and never returned to Indiana to live. However, the fourteen years which he did spend here helped shape the life of this great American. There are many memorials to Lincoln in Indiana; one of these is Lincoln State Park near his Indiana home.

Among other interesting places in Indiana are: the Lew Wallace Home and Study in Crawfordsville; St. Meinrad's Abbey (Order of St. Benedict) in Spencer County; West Baden University (Jesuit) at West Baden Springs, in Orange County; Culver Military Academy on Lake Maxinkukee; various State Forests; Game Preserves; the famous Speedway at Indianapolis where the 500-mile race is held once each year; and the State Fair Grounds where mammoth Indiana State Fair is held each year.

How the Counties in Indiana Were Named

Do you know how or why the county in which you live got its name? Could you give the origin of many of the 92 counties in Indiana? Probably you have never thought about it, but each county was named for a definite person, for a definite geographical location, or for some specific reason very well known to the people who settled and named the counties. Therefore, by studying the origin of these names, it is possible to learn what people and places were important and meaningful to the citizens of early Indiana, and so to learn a little more about the background of our state.

It is easy to guess the origin of such counties as Adams, Harrison, Jackson, Jefferson, Washington, Hancock, and many others named for famous Americans. It is not difficult to realize the origin of the names of Ohio and Wabash counties, which were named for rivers. However, the reasons for the names of such counties as Howard, Union, and Lagrange counties are not so easily discovered.

If we were to divide the counties into groups according to the origin of their names, we might make three sections: a large one to include those named for famous persons; a smaller section to include the counties named for geographical locations; and a third (and smallest) section for those few counties which would not fit into either of the first two groups.

The first section, the large one including the counties named for famous persons, could be further divided into groups of counties named for men famous for different reasons. For example, some counties were named for men who became President of the United States. Others were named for men who have lived in history because they signed the Declaration of Independence, or because they were members of the Continental Congress. Some were Revolutionary War heroes, soldiers of the War of 1812, Indian fighters, or early explorers of our country. Let us look at the various groups of distinguished men honored by the early citizens of Indiana, who gave their names to our counties.

Seven of our counties were named for men who became President of the United States. These were Adams County (John Adams), Harrison County (William Henry Harrison), Jackson County (Andrew Jackson), Jefferson County (Thomas Jefferson), Madison County (James Madison), Monroe County (James Monroe), and Washington County (George Washington).

Some counties were named for men who are remembered chiefly for signing the Declaration of Independence. These were Carroll County (Charles Carroll of Maryland), Huntington County (Samuel Huntington of Connecticut), Hancock County (John Hancock of Massachusetts), and Rush County (Dr. Benjamin Rush of Pennsylvania). John Adams and Thomas Jefferson also were signers of the Declaration of Independence, but, like several other men for whom Indiana counties were named, they were known for more than one action of historical importance, and so we are listing them according to the one action for which they are best known.

The Continental Congress also is honored by at least one of our counties—Henry County, named for the fiery Patrick Henry of Virginia.

Members of the Supreme Court of the United States for whom Indiana counties have been named were John Jay, first Chief Justice

of the Supreme Court, and Chief Justice John Marshall.

Other famous United States statesmen for whom Indiana counties were named are Alexander Hamilton, first Secretary of the Treasury; Colonel William Crawford, Secretary of the Treasury from 1816 to 1825; Benjamin Franklin, known for many valuable services to the colonies and to the government of the United States; and Tilghman Howard, charge d'affaires to Texas. Howard County was first named Richardville County, in honor of a Miami Indian chief, but it was changed to Howard County in 1846.

Counties named for men who served their respective states and were famous throughout the United States as a whole are Benton County, named in honor of Thomas H. Benton, United States Senator from Missouri; Clinton County, named for DeWitt Clinton, governor of New York and promoter of the Erie Canal; and Clay County, named for the famous Kentucky orator and United States Senator, Henry Clay.

We have one county named for a famous inventor, Robert Fulton, inventor of the steam boat, and one county named for a famous explorer, Major General Zebulon M. Pike, whose name was given to Pikes Peak.

Several statesmen who served Indiana when it was a territory have had counties named in their honor. Vanderburgh County was named for Henry Vander Burgh, territorial judge from 1800 to 1812; Gibson County was named for General John Gibson, secretary and acting governor of Indiana Territory from 1800 to 1813; Randolph County was named for Thomas Randolph, attorney general of Indiana Territory, who was killed in the Battle of Tippecanoe while leading a company of militia; and Parke County was named for Benjamin Parke, first territorial delegate to Congress from Indiana. Posey County was named in honor of Thomas Posey, governor of Indiana Territory from 1813 to 1816.

Statesmen who served Indiana after it reached statehood and for whom counties have been named were William Hendricks and Jonathan Jennings, early governors of Indiana. Noble County was named for James Noble, who was governor of Indiana from 1831 to 1837 and who also served as a United States Senator. Johnson County was named for John Johnson, one of the first judges of the Indiana Supreme

Court, and Blackford County was named for Judge Isaac Blackford, judge of the first Indiana Supreme Court.

War heroes account for many of the names given to counties in Indiana. They include men who found fame and honor in the Revolutionary War, in the War of 1812, and in Indian wars. From heroes of the Revolutionary War come the names of several counties. These include Marion County, named for Brigadier General Francis Marion; Dearborn County, for Major General Henry Dearborn, Secretary of War from 1801 to 1809; Greene County, for General Nathaniel Greene; Jasper County for Sergeant William Jasper of South Carolina; Newton County, for Sergeant John Newton, a friend of Sergeant Jasper; Knox County, for Major General Henry Knox of Massachusetts, who was also the first United States Secretary of War; Montgomery County, for General Richard Montgomery, who was killed at Quebec; Morgan County, for General Daniel Morgan; Putnam County, for General Israel Putnam; Scott County, for General Charles Scott, who fought in both the Revolutionary War and the War of 1812, and who was fourth governor of Kentucky; Shelby County, for Isaac Shelby, who fought in both the Revolutionary War and the War of 1812 and who was the first governor of Kentucky; Starke County for Brigadier General John Stark; Warren County for General Joseph Warren, who was killed at Bunker Hill; and Wayne County for Major General Anthony (Mad Anthony) Wayne, who later led his troops to victory against the Indians at the Battle of Fallen Timbers.

A man who figured prominently in the hisory of Indiana, and from whom one of the first counties formed in Indiana (Clark County, 1801) received its name, was George Rogers Clark. Clark's daring exploits against the British during the period of the Revolutionary War secured the possession of the Northwest Territory for the Americans. He received much valuable aid in this undertaking from a Spanish merchant of Vincennes, Colonel Francis Vigo, for whom Vigo County was named.

Heroes of the United States Navy during the War of 1812 who have had counties in Indiana named for them are: Captain James Lawrence (Lawrence County); Commodore David Porter (Porter County); and Commodore Oliver Hazard Perry (Perry County), who spoke the immortal phrase, "Don't give up the ship." Commodore Stephen Decatur (Decatur County) became famous because of his expedition against Algiers in 1815, although he is regarded as one of the heroes of the War of 1812.

Soldier heroes of the War of 1812 in whose honor counties of Indiana were named are the following: General John Tipton, who was also United States Senator; Colonel William Whitley of Kentucky, who was killed in the Battle of the Thames; General Jacob Brown, who was United States Army commander from 1815 to 1828; Brigadier General Lewis Cass, Secretary of War, 1831-1836; and Major General E. W. Ripley.

Many Indiana counties have honored pioneers and soldiers who fought heroically in Indian wars, and while most of them fought in several of these conflicts, they are usually remembered principally for one or two famous battles in which they participated. Such heroes whose names were given to counties were General Joseph Batholomew, Colonel Abraham Owen of Kentucky, Colonel Isaac White of Kentucky, Captain Spier Spencer, Captain Jacob Warrick, and Major Joseph H. Daviess. All these men were heroes of the Battle of Tippecanoe.

Men who gave their lives in other Indian conflicts, and whose names were given to counties in Indiana, were Major James Fountaine, who was killed near Fort Wayne, in 1790, and for whom Fountain County was named; Captain W. H. Wells, killed in the Fort Dearborn massacre; Samuel and Moses Grant, killed by the Indians in Switzerland County and for whom Grant County is named; and Daniel Sullivan, killed by Indians during the War of 1812.

Other soldier heroes whose names have been the origin of names of Indiana counties were Colonel John Allen and Major Thomas Martin, both of Kentucky, and Colonel John Floyd of Virginia. (Davis Floyd, a soldier and member of the Constitutional Convention, is sometimes given as the man for whom Floyd County was named, but most sources agree that Colonel John Floyd was the man so honored.)

Boone County was, of course, named in honor of the best known of all frontiersmen, Daniel Boone of Kentucky.

The names of several Indiana counties pay homage to men of foreign lands who served our nation in its early struggles. One of them, Toussaint Dubois, a French merchant of Vincennes, had charge of spies under William H. Harrison and played an important part in the Tippecanoe campaign. The following five men were leaders of the American forces in the battles of the Revolution: Baron Johann De-Kalb, a Bavarian nobleman who became a general in the colonial army and who was killed at Camden; Thaddeus Kosciusko and Casimir Pulaski, both of Poland; Major Frederick William de Steuben, a baron of Prussia; and most famous of all, the Marquis de Lafayette, soldier and diplomat of France, for whom Fayette County was named.

As we have stated, not all the counties of Indiana were named for men. A few were named for other locations, such as Switzerland County, named by its early settlers for their homeland, and Orange County, whose early settlers named it for the county in North Carolina from which many of them had come.

Lake County was so named because it lies along Lake Michigan, and the name of La-Porte County was derived from the name given it by the French. Tippecanoe County received its name from either the Tippecanoe River or the Tippecanoe Battleground. The word "Tippecanoe" is a corruption of the Indian name for "place of the buffalo fish."

Several counties named for rivers are Elkhart, Ohio, St. Joseph, Vermillion, and Wabash counties.

Further homage was paid the Marquis de Lafayette with the naming of Lagrange County in honor of Lafayette's home near Paris.

Three counties named for neither men nor locations are Miami, Delaware, and Union counties. The names of the Miami and Delaware Indian tribes were given the first two counties, and Union County was so called because it separated Wayne and Fayette counties, between which there had been conflict before 1821.

STUDY EXERCISES

In the box below are items of information which every citizen of Indiana should be able to state instantly. Complete this summary by writing the correct information in the blanks.

1. The year in which Indiana became a state. _____

2. The capital of Indiana. _____

3. The state flower of Indiana. _____

4. The state tree of Indiana. _____

5. The state bird of Indiana. _____

6. The name of the state song. _____

7. The nickname of the citizens of Indiana. _____

8. The three parts of the pioneer scene pictured on the state seal.
   (1) _____
   (2) _____
   (3) _____

9. The background color of the official state banner. _____
   The color of the design on the state banner. _____

10. The four parts of the design, or emblem, on the state banner.
    (1) a torch and its rays, representing _____
    _____
    (2) an outer circle of 13 stars, representing _____
    (3) an inner circle of 5 stars, representing _____
    (4) a large star, representing _____

11. The number of state parks in Indiana. _____

Match these items correctly. Do this by choosing the answers from Column II and writing them before the corresponding items in Column I.

Column I

Column II

_____ 1. Largest state park in Indiana.

Shakamak

_____ 2. Oldest state park in Indiana.

Wyandotte

_____ 3. State park named for a Potawatomi chief.

Freeman

_____ 4. State park named for people who inhabited Indiana before the Indians came.

Dunes

Wawasee

_____ 5. Newest of the Indiana state parks

Richard H. Lieber

_____ 6.-7. Two famous caves located in Indiana.

McCormick's Creek

Madison

_____ 8. State park which contains a re-created pioneer village.

Brown County

Raccoon Lake

_____ 9. State park which derives its name from Indian word meaning "River of Long Fish."

Spring Mill

Turkey Run

_____ 10. Largest lake in Indiana.

Muscatatuck

_____ 11.-12. Two artificial lakes formed in Indiana by the building of power dams in the Tippecanoe River.

Pokagon

Marengo

James

_____ 13. State park which overlooks the Ohio River.

Shafer

_____ 14. Large state park near Spencer, Indiana.

Mammoth

Mounds

_____ 15. State park bordering southern end of Lake Michigan.

Write the correct answers in the blanks.

1. In what year was the official state banner adopted? _____

What are its dimensions? _____

2. By what other name is the state tree known? _____

Describe this tree. _____

3. In 1931, what flower was made the official flower of Indiana? _____

When was this changed to the present flower? _____

4. By what authority was the state seal of Indiana established? _____

When was the design of the seal originally used? _____

For what is it used? _____

What is the size of the seal? _____

5. It is generally accepted that the nickname of the people of Indiana comes from what expression? _____

6. How many counties are there in Indiana? _____

7. In what county do you live? _____

For what person or thing was your county named? _____

What town or city is the county seat of your county? _____

8. Who is the author of our state song? _____

9. Write the words for the chorus of our state song. _____

_____

_____

_____

_____

_____

_____

10. Abraham Lincoln came to Indiana in what year? _____

Where did his family settle in Indiana? _____

11. What tragedy took place in Lincoln's life while he was living in Indiana?

_____

What memorial to this tragic event exists today in Indiana? _____

_____

12. In what year did Lincoln leave Indiana? _____

Where did he settle after leaving Indiana? _____

13. Name two well-known playwrights who were from Indiana, and name plays which they wrote.

(1) _____

(2) _____

14. What two well-known historians were born in Indiana? _____

_____

15. Make a list of ten well-known Indiana authors and name one thing which each wrote.

(1) _____   _____

(2) _____   _____

(3) _____   _____

(4) _____   _____

(5) _____   _____

(6) _____   _____

(7) _____   _____

(8) _____   _____

(9) _____   _____

(10) _____   _____

16. Make a list of twelve well-known men who have been prominent in politics or government, and who were from Indiana. Tell what position each held or for what he was well-known.

(1) _____   _____
(2) _____   _____
(3) _____   _____
(4) _____   _____
(5) _____   _____
(6) _____   _____
(7) _____   _____
(8) _____   _____
(9) _____   _____
(10) _____   _____
(11) _____   _____
(12) _____   _____

17. Make a list of ten other persons well known as song writers, artists, sculptors, actresses, entertainers, etc., who were from Indiana. Tell for what each is well known.

(1) _____   _____
(2) _____   _____
(3) _____   _____
(4) _____   _____
(5) _____   _____
(6) _____   _____
(7) _____   _____
(8) _____   _____
(9) _____   _____
(10) _____   _____

When completed, the following chart will provide a list of state parks, memorials, and other interesting places in Indiana, together with the location of each place. Complete this chart by writing in the blanks the correct information called for in each of the four parts of this exercise.

I. The names of two memorials which were built in Indianapolis in honor of our soldiers.

(1) _____   _____
(2) _____   _____

II. The memorials maintained by the state, and the location of each.

(1) _____   _____
(2) _____   _____
(3) _____   _____
(4) _____   _____
(5) _____   _____
(6) _____   _____

(7) _____   _____

(8) _____   _____

(9) _____   _____

(10) _____   _____

(11) _____   _____

(12) _____   _____

(13) _____   _____

III.   The nineteen Indiana state parks, and the location of each.

(1) _____   _____

(2) _____   _____

(3) _____   _____

(4) _____   _____

(5) _____   _____

(6) _____   _____

(7) _____   _____

(8) _____   _____

(9) _____   _____

(10) _____   _____

(11) _____   _____

(12) _____   _____

(13) _____   _____

(14) _____   _____

(15) _____   _____

(16) _____   _____

(17) _____   _____

(18) _____   _____

(19) _____   _____

IV. Seven other famous and interesting places in Indiana, and the location of each.

(1) _____   _____

(2) _____   _____

(3) _____   _____

(4) _____   _____

(5) _____   _____

(6) _____   _____

(7) _____   _____

Most of the counties in the state were named for some famous character in the history of our country or for some famous place. In the following list, write opposite the name of the county the origin of its name (the person or thing for which it was named).

Name of County	Origin of Name	Name of County	Origin of Name
Adams		Lawrence	
Allen		Madison	
Bartholomew		Marion	
Benton		Marshall	
Blackford		Martin	
Boone		Miami	
Brown		Monroe	
Carroll		Montgomery	
Cass		Morgan	
Clark		Newton	
Clay		Noble	
Clinton		Ohio	
Crawford		Orange	
Daviess		Owen	
Dearborn		Parke	
Decatur		Pike	
DeKalb		Perry	
Delaware		Porter	
Dubois		Posey	
Elkhart		Pulaski	
Fayette		Putnam	
Floyd		Randolph	
Fountain		Ripley	
Franklin		Rush	
Fulton		St. Joseph	
Gibson		Scott	
Grant		Shelby	
Greene		Spencer	
Hamilton		Starke	
Hancock		Steuben	
Harrison		Sullivan	
Hendricks		Switzerland	
Henry		Tippecanoe	
Howard		Tipton	
Huntington		Union	
Jackson		Vanderburgh	
Jasper		Vermillion	
Jay		Vigo	
Jefferson		Wabash	
Jennings		Warren	
Johnson		Warrick	
Knox		Washington	
Kosciusko		Wayne	
Lagrange		Wells	
Lake		White	
LaPorte		Whitley	

ASSIGNMENT FOR MAP EXERCISES

Map A. Indiana at the Present

Locate the principal rivers of the state by printing the names in the correct places on the map. Print the name of each county in its proper place on the map.

Locate with a dot in the correct place, the county seat of each county. Write or print the names of these places on the map. (See Exercise No. 3, Appendix A.)

Map B. State Parks, State Memorials, and Other Places of Interest

Make a circle (O) to indicate the location of each of the Indiana state parks. Print the name in small letters near the circle.

Make a cross (X) to indicate the location of each of the Indiana state memorials. Print the name in small letters near the cross.

Make a dot (●) to indicate the location of each of the other places of special interest which you think are worthy of being shown on this map. Print the name in small letters near the dot.

TOPICS FOR DISCUSSION AND REPORT

1. Describe the yellow poplar tree. In what parts of Indiana did it grow? What is the present condition of the yellow poplar in Indiana?

2. Give an account of a visit to one of the state parks in Indiana. Name the principal points of general interest about the park. Name the things which appeal to you the most.

3. Make a report to the class on the life of one of the following men: Albert J. Beveridge, Charles Warren Fairbanks, John Hay, Kenesaw Mountain Landis, Walter Q. Gresham.

4. Make a report to the class on one of the following: Ernie Pyle, David Starr Jordan, Kin Hubbard, John T. McCutcheon.

5. Make a list of all books you have read that were written by Indiana authors. Some books are written by non-Indiana authors, but have the state as its setting. Read one book listed below. Tell what it has to do with Indiana. Is the author from Indiana? A. *The Dark Didn't Catch Me* by Crystal Thrasher B. *Search for the Crescent Moon* by Ethel Rosenberg C. *Friendly Persuasion* by Jessamyn West.

6. Give an account of a visit to one of the state memorials in Indiana. Name the principal points of general interest about the memorial. Name the things about it that appealed to you the most.

7. Make a list of all the counties in Indiana that you have been in.

8. Make a drawing of the Indiana State Banner. Color it with the proper colors.

9. In an essay tell why it is important to preserve our natural environment in state parks. Include a discussion of the environmental value of state parks.

10. To find out more about your state and particularly its place names, read these books and prepare a short report on something you think might interest the rest of the class:
    A. *Indiana Place Names* by Ronald Blake (Indiana Univ. Press, 1975).
    B. *The Indiana Experience: An Anthology* by Arnold Lazarus (Indiana Univ. Press, 1977).
    C. *Indiana: A Bicentennial History* by Howard Peckham (Norton, 1978).

REFERENCES FOR UNIT 12

GENERAL REFERENCES

The Hoosiers—Nicholson.

Indiana; an Interpretation—Martin, Chs. 9-12.

INDIANA MAGAZINE OF HISTORY

"The Story of the 'Spring Mill' Water Wheel"—Denzil Doggett, IMH, June, 1932.

"Early Literary Developments in Indiana"—IMH, Dec., 1940.

"The Rise of Albert J. Beveridge to the United States Senate"—IMH, Dec., 1957.

"Early Newspapers of Indiana"—IMH, Sept., 1906.

"Music in Indianapolis, 1821-1900"—IMH, Dec., 1945.

"The Brown County Art Colony"—Josephine Graf, IMH, Dec., 1939.

INDIANA HISTORY BULLETIN

"That word 'Hoosier' Again"—John Vawter—IHB, July, 1958.

"Walter Quintin Gresham,"—Walter Funk,—IHB, Vol. 42, No. 1.

READINGS IN INDIANA HISTORY (1956 edition) pp. 595-605.

PUBLICATIONS OF INDIANA HISTORICAL SOC.

"The Word Hoosier"—Jacob P. Dunn, Vol. 4, No. 2.

"A History of Indiana Literature"—Shumaker, 1962.

SPECIAL REFERENCES

The Indiana State Department of Conservation issues a small leaflet describing each State Park and each State Memorial. These leaflets may be secured without cost from the State Department of Conservation, Indianapolis, Indiana.

MAP A.
INDIANA AT
THE PRESENT

SCALE OF MILES
0   10   20   30

MAP B.

STATE PARKS
STATE MEMORIALS
OTHER PLACES OF INTEREST

SCALE OF MILES
0   10   20   30

Appendix A

SUPPLEMENTARY EXERCISE NO. 1. (To correlate with Unit 5.)

Land Survey in Indiana

HISTORICAL SURVEY OF THE UNIT

After the land of the Northwest Territory had been ceded to the United States government, Congress passed a law, called the Ordinance of 1785, which provided for a complete survey of this land. The location of any piece of land in Indiana today is based upon the system of land survey which was worked out at this early time.

The law stated that, "The surveyors shall proceed to divide the said territory into townships of six miles square, by lines running due north and south and others crossing these at right angles, as near as may be."

The surveyors had to establish north and south and east and west lines which would be starting places for measurements in the different directions. The lines running north and south are called meridians. These meridians are shown in Fig. I. The First Principal Meridian is a line extending due north from the mouth of the Miami River. It is also the boundary line between Ohio and Indiana. The Second Principal Meridian is a line running due north from the mouth of the Little Blue River, eighty-nine miles west of the First Meridian. The Second Meridian is west of the center of the state and passes directly through the court house at Lebanon in Boone County. This meridian extends the entire length of the state.

The line running east and west from which the survey was started was called a Base Line. The only Base Line running through Indiana strikes the Wabash four miles above the mouth of White River and passes six miles south of Paoli.

Almost the whole of the state is divided into "congressional townships" which are six miles square, by lines six miles apart drawn parallel to the Second Principal Meridian and the Base Line. On the east and west sides of

FIGURE I.

the Principal Meridian, the north and south rows of townships (each township six miles square) are called ranges. On the north and south of the Base Line, the east and west rows of squares are called townships. Thus, township number 2 north, range 4 west, means the township in the second row north of the Base Line and the fourth row west of the Principal Meridian. (See Fig. II.)

Each township is divided into 36 equal parts of one square mile each. Each of these squares, consisting of a square mile, is called a "section" and contains 640 acres. These sections are further subdivided. (See Fig. III.)

(In the counties of Switzerland, Dearborn, and parts of Franklin, Union, Wayne, and Randolph, the land was surveyed from a base line 15 miles north of the other and west from the First Principal Meridian. In the Clark grant, the meridians run northwest and southeast.)

ASSIGNMENT FOR MAP EXERCISE

With heavy red lines show the First Principal Meridian and the Second Principal Meridian. With a heavy blue line, show the Base Line which passes across the state (Use map on pg. 165.)

With lighter red lines, show enough of the range lines of the state to include the place where you live. With lighter blue lines show enough of the township lines to include the place where you live. Number the ranges and townships.

LAND SURVEY
IN INDIANA

SCALE OF MILES
0   10   20   30

1. This method of land survey is known as the _____ survey.

2. This method was first used in what territory? _____

3. The First Principal Meridian is the same as what line? _____

4. The range lines are how many miles apart? _____

5. The township lines are how many miles apart? _____

FIGURE II.

Each of the squares contains 36 square miles and is called a "Congressional Township." The north and south lines are range lines and the east and west lines are township lines.

The township marked X is township 3 north, range 4 west.

Describe the location of each of the indicated townships.

A. _____

B. _____

C. _____

D. _____

Give the location of the township in which you live.

Location _____

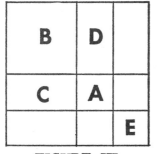

FIGURE III.

Fig. III is an enlarged drawing of one section or 1/36 of a township. Suppose that it is Section 16 of Township 19 north, range 7 west. Give a complete description of the plots of land indicated.

A. _____

B. _____

C. _____

D. _____

E. _____

In Fig. III, tell how many acres each plot contains:

A. _____ acres. D. _____ acres.

B. _____ acres. E. _____ acres.

C. _____ acres. Total number of acres shown in Figure

III is _____ acres.

1. Each congressional township contains how many sections? _____

2. Each section contains how many acres? _____

3. Each township contains how many square miles? _____

4. Each section contains how many square miles? _____

ADDITIONAL ACTIVITIES

1. Each member of the class should examine a deed to some piece of land. What does it say about townships, ranges, and sections? Explain why it is absolutely necessary to have a system of land surveys.

2. Talk to your parents or to a surveyor and find out how the range lines and township lines and the corners of the different sections of land are actually marked. Report to the class.

3. Explain the difference between "congressional township" and "civil township" in Indiana.

4. Locate by congressional township and range, each of the following cities: Bloomington, Fort Wayne, Angola, Terre Haute, South Bend, Crawfordsville.

REFERENCES.

Johnson—*Mathematical Geography*—American Book Co., Ch. XI.

The Indiana Gazeteer, Published 1850, pp. 22-24.

Readings in Indiana History—No. 63, "How the Public Lands Were Surveyed," pp. 206-209, from Niles Register, 1817.

Esarey—*Indiana* (School Edition), pp. 133-134.

Buley—*The Old Northwest*—Vol. 1, pp. 115-123.

SUPPLEMENTARY EXERCISE NO. 2 (To correlate with Unit 12.)

The Organization of Counties in Indiana

An act of 1861 provided a method of forming new counties by directing that a "majority of the legal voters to be affected thereby, in any district embracing an area of not less than 200 square miles" might petition the boards of commissioners of the "several counties to be affected." The commissioners were required to name a committee of three freeholders from each county to establish the boundaries of the proposed new county and then the question was submitted to the voters. If the vote carried, the commissioners entered orders formally creating the new territory, and the governor named three commissioners to locate the county seat and ordered an election held for the purpose of choosing officials for the new unit.

Other acts provide for the relocation of county seats, and for changing county boundaries. Many a bitter dispute has been waged in Indiana over the location of county seats, but in the main the questions not only of county seats, but boundaries as well, have been firmly established.

Following is a list of the 92 counties in Indiana, their county seats, and the year in which each was organized as a county.

County	County Seat	Year	County	County Seat	Year
Adams	Decatur	1836	Lawrence	Bedford	1818
Allen	Ft. Wayne	1824	Madison	Anderson	1823
Bartholomew	Columbus	1821	Marion	Indianapolis	1822
Benton	Fowler	1840	Marshall	Plymouth	1836
Blackford	Hartford City	1839	Martin	Shoals	1820
Boone	Lebanon	1831	Miami	Peru	1834
Brown	Nashville	1836	Monroe	Bloomington	1818
Carroll	Delphi	1828	Montgomery	Crawfordsville	1823
Cass	Logansport	1829	Morgan	Martinsville	1822
Clark	Jeffersonville	1801	Newton	Kentland	1859
Clay	Brazil	1825	Noble	Albion	1836
Clinton	Frankfort	1830	Ohio	Rising Sun	1844
Crawford	English	1818	Orange	Paoli	1816
Daviess	Washington	1817	Owen	Spencer	1819
Dearborn	Lawrenceburg	1803	Parke	Rockville	1821
Decatur	Greensburg	1822	Perry	Cannelton	1814
DeKalb	Auburn	1837	Pike	Petersburg	1817
Delaware	Muncie	1827	Porter	Valparaiso	1836
Dubois	Jasper	1818	Posey	Mt. Vernon	1814
Elkhart	Goshen	1830	Pulaski	Winamac	1840
Fayette	Connersville	1819	Putnam	Greencastle	1822
Floyd	New Albany	1819	Randolph	Winchester	1818
Fountain	Covington	1826	Ripley	Versailles	1818
Franklin	Brookville	1811	Rush	Rushville	1822
Fulton	Rochester	1836	Scott	Scottsburg	1820
Gibson	Princeton	1813	Shelby	Shelbyville	1822
Grant	Marion	1832	Spencer	Rockport	1818
Greene	Bloomfield	1821	Starke	Knox	1850
Hamilton	Noblesville	1823	St. Joseph	South Bend	1830
Hancock	Greenfield	1828	Steuben	Angola	1837
Harrison	Corydon	1808	Sullivan	Sullivan	1817
Hendricks	Danville	1824	Switzerland	Vevay	1814
Henry	New Castle	1822	Tippecanoe	Lafayette	1826
Howard	Kokomo	1844	Tipton	Tipton	1844
Huntington	Huntington	1834	Union	Liberty	1821
Jackson	Brownstown	1816	Vanderburgh	Evansville	1818
Jasper	Rensselaer	1838	Vermillion	Newport	1824
Jay	Portland	1836	Vigo	Terre Haute	1818
Jefferson	Madison	1811	Wabash	Wabash	1835
Jennings	Vernon	1817	Warren	Williamsport	1827
Johnson	Franklin	1823	Warrick	Boonville	1813
Knox	Vincennes	1790	Washington	Salem	1814
Kosciusko	Warsaw	1837	Wayne	Richmond	1811
Lagrange	Lagrange	1832	Wells	Bluffton	1837
Lake	Crown Point	1837	White	Monticello	1834
LaPorte	LaPorte	1832	Whitley	Columbia City	1839

Appendix B

TABLE 1

Population of the State of Indiana by Ten-Year Periods, 1800-1980

Year	Population	Year	Population
1800	5,641	1890	2,192,404
1810	24,530	1900	2,516,462
1820	147,178	1910	2,700,876
1830	343,031	1920	2,930,390
1840	685,866	1930	3,238,503
1850	988,416	1940	3,427,796
1860	1,350,428	1950	3,934,224
1870	1,680,637	1960	4,662,498
1880	1,978,301	1970	5,193,669
		1980	5,490,179

TABLE 2

Populations of Indiana Cities of Over 10,000. Population by 10-Year Periods.

	1860	1870	1880	1890	1900	1910	1920	1930	1940	1950	1960	1970	1980
Indianapolis	8,091	48,244	75,056	105,436	169,164	233,650	314,194	364,161	386,972	427,173	476,258	744,624	700,807
Fort Wayne	4,282	17,718	26,880	35,393	45,115	63,933	86,549	114,946	118,410	133,607	161,776	177,671	172,196
Gary						16,802	55,378	100,426	111,719	133,911	178,320	175,415	151,953
Evansville	3,235	21,830	29,280	50,756	59,007	69,647	85,264	102,249	97,062	128,636	141,543	138,764	130,496
South Bend	1,652	7,206	13,280	21,819	35,999	53,684	70,983	104,193	101,268	115,911	132,445	125,580	109,727
Hammond				5,428	12,376	20,925	36,004	64,560	70,184	87,594	111,698	107,790	93,714
Anderson	383	3,126	4,126	10,741	20,178	22,476	29,767	39,804	41,572	46,820	49,061	70,787	64,695
Terre Haute	4,051	16,103	26,042	30,217	36,673	58,157	66,083	62,810	62,693	64,214	72,500	70,286	61,125
Muncie	666	2,992	5,219	11,345	20,942	24,005	36,524	46,548	49,720	58,479	68,603	69,080	77,216
East Chicago				1,255	3,411	19,098	35,967	54,784	54,784	54,263	57,669	46,982	39,786
Lafayette	8,181	15,396	16,423	21,059	20,628	20,629	22,992	25,819	28,798	35,568	42,330	44,955	43,011
Kokomo		2,177	4,042	8,261	10,609	17,010	30,067	32,843	33,795	38,672	47,197	44,042	47,808
Richmond	1,443	9,445	12,742	16,608	18,226	22,324	26,765	32,493	35,147	39,539	44,149	43,999	41,349
Elkhart		3,265	6,953	11,360	15,184	19,282	24,277	32,949	33,434	35,646	40,274	43,152	41,305
Bloomington	1,305	1,032	2,756	4,018	6,460	8,838	11,595	18,227	20,870	28,163	31,357	42,890	51,646
Marion	703	1,658	3,182	8,769	17,337	19,359	23,747	24,496	26,767	30,081	37,854	39,607	35,874
Michigan City	999	3,985	7,366	10,776	14,850	19,027	19,457	26,735	26,476	28,395	36,653	39,369	36,850
New Albany	6,129	13,506	14,860	16,243	18,116	20,081	22,486	26,240	25,414	29,346	37,812	38,402	37,103
Mishawaka	1,412	2,617	2,640	3,371	5,560	11,886	15,195	28,630	28,298	32,913	33,361	35,517	40,224
Columbus	1,008	3,359	4,813	6,719	8,130	8,813	8,990	9,935	11,738	18,370	20,778	27,141	30,292
La Porte	1,824	6,581	6,195	7,126	7,113	10,525	15,158	15,755	16,180	17,882	21,157	22,140	21,796
Hobart								5,787	7,166	10,244	18,680	21,485	22,987
New Castle	666	1,556	2,299	2,697	3,406	9,446	14,458	14,027	16,620	18,271	20,349	21,215	20,056
Valparaiso										12,028	15,227	20,020	22,247
Jeffersonville	2,122	7,254	9,357	10,666	10,774	10,412	10,098	11,946	11,493	14,685	19,522	20,008	21,220
Vincennes	2,070	5,440	7,680	8,853	10,249	14,895	17,160	17,564	18,228	18,831	18,046	19,867	20,857
Logansport	2,251	8,950	11,198	13,328	16,204	19,050	21,626	18,508	20,177	21,031	21,106	19,255	17,899
West Lafayette									5,095	6,270	11,873	19,157	21,247
Portage											11,822	19,127	27,409
Connersville	1,396	2,496	3,228	4,548	6,836	7,738	9,901	12,795	12,898	15,550	17,698	17,604	17,023
Goshen	780	3,133	4,123	6,033	7,810	8,514	9,525	10,397	11,375	13,003	13,718	17,171	19,665
Lawrence										1,915	10,103	16,646	25,591
Huntington	594	2,925	3,863	7,328	9,491	10,272	14,000	13,420	13,903	15,079	16,185	16,217	16,202
Shelbyville	995	2,731	3,745	5,451	7,169	9,500	9,701	10,618	10,791	11,734	14,317	15,094	14,989
Frankfort	582	1,300	2,803	5,919	7,100	8,634	11,585	12,196	13,706	15,028	15,302	14,956	15,168
Peru	1,266	3,617	5,280	7,028	8,463	10,910	12,410	12,730	12,432	13,308	14,453	14,139	13,764
Crawfordsville	1,513	3,701	5,251	6,089	6,649	9,371	10,139	10,355	11,089	12,851	14,231	13,842	13,325
Beech Grove								3,552	3,907	5,685	10,973	13,468	13,196
Wabash								8,840	9,663	10,621	12,621	13,379	12,985
Seymour								7,508	8,620	9,629	11,629	13,352	15,050
Bedford			2,198	3,351	6,115	8,716	9,076	13,208	12,514	12,562	13,024	13,087	14,410
Madison								6,530	6,923	7,506	10,097	13,081	12,472
Franklin											9,453	11,477	11,563
Greenwood											7,169	11,408	19,327
Washington											10,846	11,358	11,325
Elwood											11,793	11,196	10,867
Crown Point											8,443	10,931	16,455

TABLE 3
Statistical Table

COUNTY	Land Area in sq. mi.	Total pop. in 1950	Total pop. in 1960	Total pop. in 1970	Total pop. in 1980
1. Adams	345	22,393	24,645	26,871	29,619
2. Allen	671	183,722	232,196	280,455	294,335
3. Bartholomew	402	36,108	48,198	57,022	65,088
4. Benton	409	11,462	11,912	11,262	10,218
5. Blackford	167	14,026	14,792	15,888	15,570
6. Boone	427	23,993	27,543	30,870	36,446
7. Brown	319	6,209	7,024	9,057	12,377
8. Carroll	374	16,010	16,934	17,734	19,722
9. Cass	415	38,793	40,931	40,456	40,936
10. Clark	384	48,330	62,795	75,876	88,838
11. Clay	364	23,918	24,207	23,933	24,862
12. Clinton	407	29,734	30,765	30,547	31,545
13. Crawford	312	9,289	8,379	8,033	9,820
14. Daviess	430	26,762	26,636	26,602	27,836
15. Dearborn	306	25,141	28,674	29,430	34,291
16. Decatur	370	18,218	20,019	22,738	23,841
17. DeKalb	366	26,023	28,271	30,837	33,606
18. Delaware	396	90,252	110,938	129,219	128,587
19. Dubois	433	23,785	27,463	30,934	34,238
20. Elkhart	468	84,512	106,790	126,529	137,330
21. Fayette	215	23,391	24,454	26,216	28,272
22. Floyd	149	43,955	51,397	55,622	61,169
23. Fountain	397	17,836	18,706	18,257	19,033
24. Franklin	394	16,034	17,015	16,943	19,612
25. Fulton	368	16,565	16,957	16,984	19,335
26. Gibson	498	30,720	29,949	30,444	33,156
27. Grant	421	62,156	75,741	83,955	80,934
28. Greene	549	27,886	26,327	26,894	30,416
29. Hamilton	401	28,491	40,130	54,532	82,381
30. Hancock	305	20,332	26,665	35,096	43,939
31. Harrison	479	17,858	19,207	20,423	27,276
32. Hendricks	417	24,594	40,896	53,974	60,804
33. Henry	400	45,505	48,899	52,603	53,336
34. Howard	293	54,498	69,509	83,198	86,896
35. Huntington	369	31,400	34,814	34,970	35,596
36. Jackson	520	28,237	30,556	33,187	36,523
37. Jasper	562	17,031	18,842	20,429	26,138
38. Jay	386	23,157	22,572	23,575	23,239
39. Jefferson	366	21,613	24,061	27,006	30,419
40. Jennings	377	15,250	17,267	19,454	22,854
41. Johnson	315	26,183	43,704	61,138	77,240
42. Knox	516	43,415	41,561	41,546	41,838
43. Kosciusko	540	33,002	40,373	48,127	59,555
44. Lagrange	381	15,347	17,380	20,890	25,550
45. Lake	513	368,152	513,269	546,253	522,965
46. LaPorte	607	76,808	95,111	105,342	108,632
47. Lawrence	459	34,346	36,564	38,038	42,472
48. Madison	453	103,911	125,819	138,522	139,336
49. Marion	392	551,777	697,567	793,769	765,233
50. Marshall	443	29,468	32,443	34,986	39,155
51. Martin	345	10,678	10,608	10,969	11,001
52. Miami	377	28,201	38,000	39,246	39,820
53. Monroe	386	50,080	59,225	85,221	98,387
54. Montgomery	507	29,122	32,089	33,930	35,501
55. Morgan	406	23,726	33,875	44,176	51,999
56. Newton	413	11,006	11,502	11,606	14,844
57. Noble	412	25,075	28,162	31,382	35,443
58. Ohio	87	4,223	4,165	4,289	5,114
59. Orange	405	16,879	16,877	16,968	18,677
60. Owen	390	11,763	11,400	12,163	15,840
61. Parke	445	15,674	14,804	14,600	16,372
62. Perry	384	17,367	17,232	19,075	19,346
63. Pike	335	14,995	12,797	12,281	13,465
64. Porter	425	40,076	60,279	87,114	119,816
65. Posey	412	19,818	19,214	21,740	26,414
66. Pulaski	433	12,493	12,837	12,534	13,258
67. Putnam	490	22,950	24,927	26,932	29,163
68. Randolph	457	27,141	28,434	28,915	29,997
69. Ripley	442	18,763	20,641	21,138	24,398
70. Rush	409	19,799	20,393	20,352	19,604
71. St. Joseph	466	205,058	238,614	245,045	241,617
72. Scott	193	11,519	14,643	17,144	20,422

County	Land Area in sq. mi.	Total pop. in 1950	Total pop. in 1960	Total pop. in 1970	Total pop. in 1980
73. Shelby	409	28,026	34,093	37,797	39,887
74. Spencer	396	16,174	16,074	17,134	19,361
75. Starke	310	15,282	17,911	19,280	21,997
76. Steuben	309	17,087	17,184	20,159	24,694
77. Sullivan	457	23,667	21,721	19,889	21,107
78. Switzerland	221	7,599	7,092	6,306	7,153
79. Tippecanoe	500	74,473	89,122	109,378	121,702
80. Tipton	261	15,566	15,856	16,650	16,819
81. Union	168	6,412	6,457	6,582	6,860
82. Vanderburgh	241	160,422	165,794	168,772	167,515
83. Vermillion	263	19,723	17,683	16,793	18,229
84. Vigo	415	150,160	108,458	114,528	112,385
85. Wabash	398	29,047	32,605	35,553	36,640
86. Warren	368	8,535	8,545	8,705	8,976
87. Warrick	391	21,527	23,577	27,972	41,474
88. Washington	516	16,520	17,819	19,278	21,932
89. Wayne	405	68,556	74,039	79,109	76,058
90. Wells	368	19,554	21,220	23,821	25,401
91. White	127	18,042	19,709	20,995	23,867
92. Whitley	337	18,828	20,954	23,395	26,215
Total for state	36,097	3,934,224	4,662,498	5,193,669	5,490,179

TABLE 4

Indiana Population by Geographic Area, Each Census, 1900-1960.

Area	1900	1910	1920	1930	1940	1950	1960
Northwest	377,921	455,630	561,539	735,972	790,618	960,758	1,214,041
Northeast	461,992	467,435	476,343	496,674	521,044	576,169	676,341
Central	867,381	964,115	1,082,712	1,188,157	1,258,435	1,460,179	1,751,669
Southwest	416,523	438,503	444,100	451,421	475,022	497,730	500,773
Southeast	392,645	375,193	365,696	366,279	382,677	439,388	519,674
State Total	2,516,462	2,700,876	2,930,390	3,238,503	3,427,796	3,934,224	4,662,498

TABLE 5

Percent of Indiana Population by Geographic Area, Each Census, 1900-1960.

Area	1900	1910	1920	1930	1940	1950	1960
Northwest	15.0	16.9	19.2	22.7	23.0	24.4	26.0
Northeast	18.4	17.3	16.3	15.3	15.2	14.6	14.5
Central	34.5	35.7	36.9	36.7	36.7	37.1	37.6
Southwest	16.5	16.2	15.1	14.0	13.9	12.7	10.7
Southeast	15.6	13.9	12.5	11.3	11.2	11.2	11.2
State Total	100.0	100.0	100.0	100.0	100.0	100.0	100.0

Supplementary Exercise 3.

1. Obtain a copy of the latest U.S. Census and complete the statistics in Table 4 for the year 1980. Then, prepare a report describing population shifts in each region and try to explain the changes.

APPENDIX C. EXERCISE NO. 1 (To correlate with Units 5 and 6.)

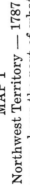

MAP 1
Northwest Territory — 1787

This map shows the part of what is now the United States that was called the Northwest Territory. Much of this land had been claimed by the American colonies along the Atlantic coast. By the year 1787, all these colonies had given up their claims to this land and had ceded it to the national government. In that year—1787—the Northwest Territory was organized by the Continental Congress, which was the head of our national government at that time. The famous Ordinance of 1787 was passed by Congress and became the governing law of the Northwest Territory.

MAP 2
Indiana Territory — 1800

Indiana Territory was separated from the remainder of the Northwest Territory in the year 1800. The Indiana Territory consisted of about four-fifths of the old Northwest Territory. It included what are now the states of Indiana, Illinois, Michigan, Wisconsin, and a small part of Minnesota. The part which later became the state of Ohio was still called the Northwest Territory. Vincennes became the capital of the new Indiana Territory. Notice that the lower end of the eastern boundary of Indiana Territory is bent toward the west.

MAP 3
Ohio Becomes a State — 1803

In the year 1803, Ohio became a state. The boundary line between Ohio and Indiana Territory had already been straightened in 1802. This added a long triangular strip of land known as "The Gore," to Indiana. It ent boundary line of our state.

172

APPENDIX C. EXERCISE NO. 2 (To correlate with Units 5 and 6.)

The Northwest Territory from 1787 to 1816.

MAP 4

Michigan Territory Organized — 1805

Michigan Territory was organized in the year 1805. It was set off from Indiana Territory by a line drawn due east from the extreme southern tip of Lake Michigan. The capital of Indiana Territory remained at Vincennes.

MAP 5

Illinois Territory Organized — 1809

In the year 1809, Illinois Territory was organized and separated from Indiana Territory. The boundary line between the two was the Wabash River north to Vincennes and from there due north to Canada. This left Indiana Territory with the same boundaries as those of the present state, except on the north. The land of the Upper Peninsula, north of Lake Michigan, remained with Indiana Territory until 1816.

MAP 6

Indiana Becomes a State — 1816

Indiana became a state on December 11, 1816. A ten-mile strip was added to the north end of the state by Congress. This was done by making the northern boundary of Indiana an east and west line ten miles north of the southern tip of Lake Michigan. This strip was taken from Michigan Territory. At the same time, Indiana gave up the land of the Upper Peninsula, north of Lake Michigan. In 1818, that land was added to Michigan Territory.

APPENDIX C. EXERCISE NO. 3. (To correlate with Units 5 and 6.)

MAP 1
Land Purchases from Indians

The Americans acquired all the land in Indiana from the Indians who originally claimed it. The Americans did this by a series of treaties shown on the map and listed below.

1. "The Gore," Treaty of Greenville — 1795.
2. Treaty of Ft. Wayne — 1803.
3. Treaty of Vincennes — 1804.
4. Treaty of Grouseland — 1805.
5. Treaty of Ft. Wayne — 10 O'Clock Line — 1809.
6. Treaty of Maumee — 1817.
7. New Purchase — 1818.
8. Treaty of Chicago — 1821.
9. Treaty of Mississinewa — 1826.
10. Treaty of Mississinewa — 1826.
11. Treaty of Carey Mission — 1828.
12. Treaty of Tippecanoe — 1832.
13. Treaty of Tippecanoe — 1832.
14. Treaty of Wabash — 1834.
15. Treaty of Wabash — 1840
16. Clark's Grant — 1783

MAP 2
The First Counties in Indiana

The first counties in Indiana were located, as you might expect, in the southern part of the state. They are Knox County, St. Clair County, and Dearborn County. Knox County is the oldest, having been organized in 1790. These three early counties were quite large compared to the present counties in the state. Although they were large in area, they were very small in population.

MAP 3
Indiana Counties in 1816
(Sending delegates to Constitutional Convention)

Thirteen counties, all from the southern part of the state, sent delegates to the Constitutional Convention in 1816. These were as follows:

Clark	Harrison	Posey
Dearborn	Jefferson	Switzerland
Franklin	Knox	Warrick
Gibson	Perry	Washington
		Wayne

Two more counties, Orange and Jackson, had been organized in 1815, but did not send delegates to the convention.

174

Appendix D   (To correlate with Unit 7.)

Words and Expressions Used by the Pioneers.

The pioneers of Indiana used, in their speech, many expressions which were unusual. They also used many words in a peculiar manner and pronounced other words in a way which was not recommended by the dictionary. Many of these are still heard in Indiana.

The following is a brief list of such words and expressions. You can probably add more.

Pioneer expression	Correct expression	Pioneer expression	Correct expression
1. air	are	21. dauncy	dizzy or lightheaded
2. ary (nary)	none or not any	22. et	ate
3. apt	likely	23. foot-loose	free
4. argyfy	to make argument	24. fetch	bring
5. afeard	afraid	25. fitten	decent or fit for
6. ager	ague	26. fractious	full of life
7. acted like	acted as if	27. go like	imitate
8. b'ar	bear	28. good little piece	quite a distance
9. brash	hasty or brisk	29. guess	think
10. brass	nerve	30. great hand fer	liked
11. bound to	determined to	31. heerd	heard
12. burn down (or up)	burn	32. hern	hers
13. clum	climbed	33. hisn	his
14. crick	creek or small stream	34. houn dog	hound
15. caterwampus	crosswise	35. heap	much — a great deal
16. cheer	chair	36. haft to	have to
17. critter	horse or other domestic animal	37. howdy	how do you do
		38. janders	jaundice
18. caint	can't or cannot	39. jever	did you ever
19. drug	dragged	40. in back of	behind
20. disremember	do not remember	41. ketch (ketched)	catch (caught)

Dictionary of Pronunciations—Proper Nouns

Appalachian — ăp′ á lăch ĭ ăn
Algonquin — ăl gŏn′ kwĭn
Cahokia — ká hō′ kĭ á
Calumet — kăl′ û mĕt
Chippewa — chĭp′ ĕ wä
Corydon — kŏr′ ĭ dŭn
Crevecouer — krĕv kûr′
Duquesne (Ft.) — dōō kān′
Gibault — zhē bō′
Hennepin — hĕn′ ê pĭn
Iroquois — ir′ ō kwoi *or* ir′ ō kwoiz
Jesuit — jĕz′ û ĭt
Joliet — jō′ lĭ ĕt
Kankakee — kăng′ ká kē′
Kaskaskia — kăs kăs′ kĭ á
Kekionga — kē kĭ ôn′ gá
Kickapoo — kĭck′ á pōō
Lanier — lă nēr′
LaSalle — lá sál′
Mackinac — măk′ ĭ nô
Manitou — măn′ ĭ tō
Marietta — mâr′ ĭ ĕt′ á
Marquette — mär kĕt′

Maumee — mô mē′
Menominee — mê nŏm′ ĭ nē
Miami — mĭ ăm′ ĭ
Michilimackinac — mish′) lĭ măk′ ĭ nô
Mississinewa — mĭs ĭs ĭn′ á wä
Ottawa — ŏt′ á wä
Ouiatenon — wē ä′ tá nŏn
Piankeshaw — pē ănk′ ē shaw
Pontiac — pŏn′ tē ăk
Potawatomi — pŏt′ á wŏt′ ô mĭ
Prophet — prŏf ĕt
Scioto — sĭ ō′ tō
Shawnee — shô nē′
Slocum — slō′ cŭm
Tecumseh — tē kŭm′ sĕ
Terre Haute — ter e hŏt
Vevay — vĕ′ vē
Vigo — vē′ gō
Wea — wē′ á
Winamac — wĭn′ á măk
Wyandot — wĭ′ ăn dŏt
Xavier (St. Francis) — zăv′ ĭ ĕr

175

Definitions of Words and Expressions.

abolish — do away with.

adz — a cutting tool having a thin arching blade set at right angles to the handle.

allegiance — devotion or loyalty, as to a country or its flag.

annexed — joined or attached.

aqueduct (ăk′ wê dŭkt) — a trough or other channel for carrying flowing water.

capital — city in which the seat of government (state or national) is located.

capitol — building in which state or national legislature meets.

cede — to give up something.

cholera — a disease which killed many people.

commemorate — celebrate the memory of, or call to remembrance, as with a monument.

constitution — a set of basic rules for a government.

cooper — one who makes or repairs barrels.

county seat — town or city in which county government and courthouse are located.

coureur de bois (kōō′rûr′dê bwả′) — one of the French or half-breed trappers and hunters in North America.

cradle — an attachment of fingerlike rods to a scythe used in cutting grain.

croup — a child's disease affecting the lining of the throat.

delegate — one sent and empowered to act for another; a representative.

eligible — fitted or qualified to be chosen or elected.

erysipelas (ĕr′ĭ sĭp′ĕlăs) — a disease causing intense inflammation of the skin.

ferry — to carry or transport over a river; or, a place of crossing. Also, the vessel used in ferrying.

frow (frō) — a steel wedge for splitting logs.

ginseng — a plant used in the making of some medicines.

gristmill — a mill for grinding grain.

(habitant (ả bē tän′) — a settler of French descent or origin, usually of the farming class.

Indian confederacy — a league of Indian nations or tribes.

interurban — going between or connecting cities or towns, as interurban electrical railways.

linsey-woolsey — a rough, homemade cloth used in making garments for pioneers.

memorial — anything, as a monument, intended to preserve the memory of a person or event.

natural barrier — an obstruction, such as a river or mountain range, which hinders travel or expansion of settlement.

ordinance (ôr′dĭ năns) — a law or governmental decree.

origin — the source or beginning.

pioneer — one who goes forth and explores in advance of others; an early settler.

portage — a narrow strip of land between two bodies of water across which boats could be carried to complete a journey.

prairie (prâr′ĭ) — an extensive tract of level or rolling land, especially in the Mississippi valley.

prehistoric — existing in the period before written history begins.

public domain — public lands.

puncheon (pŭn′chŭn) — a split log or heavy slab with the face smoothed.

ratified — approved.

recruit — to gain more supplies and men for military service.

sassafras — a plant, the root of which is used for tea.

seminary — a school for higher learning; popular in early Indiana.

squatter — a person who settles on a piece of land without having title to it.

stockade — a line of stout posts or timbers set firmly in the earth, close together, to form a defensive fortification.

tract of land — a region or an area of land.

turnpike — a road with tollgates established by law to collect a toll or charge from the traveler to help pay for its construction and repair.

urban — city, not country.

vocational training — guiding or training for the pursuit of some particular business or employment.

Unit Test in Indiana History

UNIT 1. THE SETTING FOR INDIANA HISTORY

A. *Write the correct answers in the blanks.*

1. The territory of which Indiana was a part was called _____

2. Articles made by the primitive people are called _____.

3. A strip of land between 2 bodies of water, across which boats and supplies had to be carried was a _____.

4. _____ is the name of a well-known cave in Indiana.

5. Important and useful things put here by nature and not man are called _____ _____.

6. The _____ time came before there was any written history.

7. The largest natural lake within the present state of Indiana is _____.

8. _____ were the earliest inhabitants of the Northwest Territory.

9. Give the three principal routes by which settlers came to the Northwest Territory. (3 points)

   (A) _____

   (B) _____

   (C) _____

10. In the early history of the Northwest Territory, the white people traveled from place to place by _____.

11. The natural barrier of _____ prevented the Northwest Territory from being settled sooner.

12. The kind of surface a country has, including rivers, lakes, swamps, hills, and kind of soil is called _____.

13. The name "Indiana" means _____.

B. *Choose the correct answers from the answer list and write their letters in the blanks.*

_____ 1. Southern boundary of Northwest Territory.

_____ 2. Physical region in Indiana which is quite hilly.

_____ 3. Region in Indiana north of a line from Ft. Wayne, through Logansport, and west to the Indiana - Illinois boundary.

_____ 4. The region in Indiana which is level and most suited for farming.

_____ 5. Western boundary of Northwest Territory.

_____ 6. Inhabitants of the Northwest Territory when the first white men arrived.

1

_____7-11. Five states which were made from the Northwest Territory.

_____

_____

_____

_____

_____12. The natural location where most of the early settlements in the Northwest Territory were made.

_____13. The average width of the state of Indiana at the present time.

_____14. Things you can find today as proof Indians once lived here.

_____15. Surface of northern Indiana.

Possible Score 30

Name _____ Date _____ Score _____

Unit Test in Indiana History

UNIT 2. THE INDIANS IN THE NORTHWEST TERRITORY

Draw a line under the correct answer to each question. Then write the letter of the correct answer in the blank before the question.

_____ 1. The best known chief of the Miami tribe was:
(a) Kekionga, (b) Little Turtle, (c) Tecumseh, (d) Geronimo.

_____ 2. A famous Indian chief of the Ottawa tribe was:
(a) Little Turtle, (b) Manitou, (c) Pontiac, (d) Kekionga.

_____ 3. The principal crop of the Indians was:
(a) wheat, (b) corn, (c) beans, (d) barley.

_____ 4. An Indian tribe described as tricky, dishonest, and savage was the:
(a) Shawnee, (b) Miami, (c) Algonquin, (d) Potawatomi.

_____ 5. An Indian village located where the St. Mary's and St. Joseph Rivers join was:
(a) Quebec, (b) Manitou, (c) Ouiatenon, (d) Kekionga.

_____ 6. A disease which killed many Indians was:
(a) scarlet fever, (b) smallpox, (c) typhoid, (d) the plague.

_____ 7. This means "gleaming white" in Indian language:
(a) Wabash, (b) Tippecanoe, (c) Iroquois, (d) Ouiatenon.

_____ 8. The first white men in the Northwest Territory were:
(a) Indian traders, (b) slave dealers, (c) Catholic priests, (d) Shawnees.

_____ 9. An Indian tribe which moved to Indiana from Kentucky was:
(a) Miami, (b) Iroquois, (c) Potawatomi, (d) Shawnee.

_____10. An Indian word meaning "supernatural spirit" is:
(a) Manitou, (b) Quebec, (c) Tippecanoe, (d) Kekionga.

_____11. The Indian family to which all the tribes in the Northwest Territory belonged:
(a) Iroquois, (b) Miami, (c) Algonquin, (d) Tippecanoe.

_____12. A Shawnee chief who caused early settlers much trouble was:
(a) Little Turtle, (b) The Prophet, (c) Manitou, (d) Ouiatenon.

_____13. The Indians' attitude toward the settlers was:
(a) friendly, (b) hostile, (c) neutral, (d) none of these.

_____14. The Indians' homes were near:
(a) a buffalo trail, (b) a salt lick, (c) a hunting ground, (d) a lake or a stream.

_____15. A famous fort located near Lafayette was:
(a) Ouiatenon, (b) Kekionga, (c) Cahokia, (d) Maumee.

Write the correct answers in the blanks.

16. What was the largest Indian tribe in the Northwest Territory? _____

17. What Indian name means full moon? _____

18-19. From what two things was most Indian clothing made? _____

and _____

20. What tribe inhabited the southeast part of what is now Indiana? _____

21. What was the most common kind of house for Indians in Indiana? _____

22. Who tended the crops the Indians raised? _____

23-24. By what 2 ways did the Indians move from place to place? _____

and _____

25. What name was given to the Indian boat made from a hollowed out log? _____

26. What Indian tribe living south of the Great Lakes was attacked in 1649 by the Iroquois and almost completely destroyed? _____

27. What Indian word means "round channel"? _____

28. What Indian word means "buffalo fish"? _____

29-30. What were the 2 main weapons the Indians used before they had firearms?

_____ and _____

31, 32, 33, 34. Name the 4 chief branches of the Miami tribe.

_____   _____

_____   _____

Possible score 34

Name _____ Date _____ Score _____

4

Unit Test in Indiana History

UNIT 3. FRENCH EXPLORATIONS AND SETTLEMENTS IN THE NORTHWEST TERRITORY, 1634-1763

Choose the correct answer from column II and write it in the blank in column I.

	I.	II.
_____	1. The first nation to lay claim to the Northwest Territory.	habitants
_____	2. What the people living at French trading posts were called.	Champlain
_____	3. The first white settlement in Indiana.	1693
_____	4. The first white explorers in the Northwest Territory.	Ouiatenon
_____	5. An early French settlement and fort in Southern Illinois.	Kaskaskia
_____	6. The first white man to walk on land that is now Indiana.	LaSalle
_____	7. The probable date for founding Vincennes.	Cumberland Gap
_____	8. In 1763, possession of the Northwest Territory passed to this country.	coureurs de bois
_____	9. The French trader who helped Father Marquette explore the Mississippi.	Hennepin
_____	10. Roving French fur traders.	Vincennes
_____	11. Catholic priest who explored the upper Mississippi.	England
_____	12. Largest early French settlement in Indiana.	Jesuit priests
_____	13. An early settlement at the junction of the St. Mary's River and the St. Joseph River.	1717
_____	14. The first white explorers in the Northwest Territory came by this route.	Father Gibault
_____	15. What kept the English out of the Northwest Territory for a long time?	Ft. Miami

II. (continued)

habitants
Champlain
1693
Ouiatenon
Kaskaskia
LaSalle
Cumberland Gap
coureurs de bois
Hennepin
Vincennes
England
Jesuit priests
1717
Father Gibault
Ft. Miami
St. Lawrence River and Great Lakes
Spain
1732
Indianapolis
France
Ohio River
Appalachian Mts.
Joliet

Write true *in the blanks before true statements and* false *before the false ones.*

_____ 1. The Indians of the Northwest Territory were hostile to the French.

_____ 2. Kaskaskia was called "The Gateway to the West."

_____ 3. Ft. Frontenac was the headquarters of the French on the St. Lawrence River.

_____ 4. The Protestant priests worked among the Indians in the Northwest Territory

_____ 5. The French hoped to get animal skins by trading with the Indians.

_____ 6. The Jesuit priests expected no rewards for themselves in return for their work

_____ 7. Two of the first white settlements in Indiana were on the Ohio River.

_____ 8. France based its claims in the Northwest Territory on the explorations of La Salle.

_____ 9. Ft. Ouiatenon was founded in 1717.

_____10. Father Hennepin explored the lower Mississippi River.

_____11. Cahokia was located across from where St. Louis now stands.

_____12. The French traded blankets and beads to the Indians in return for tomahawks and skins.

_____13. A chain of forts built by the French extended east of the Mississippi River in the shape of an I.

_____14. LaSalle established two large forts in what is now the state of Illinois.

_____15. An important portage, much used by French explorers, was between the St. Joseph River and the Kankakee River.

Possible Score 30

Name _____ Date _____ Score _____

Unit Test in Indiana History

UNIT 4. OCCUPATION OF THE NORTHWEST TERRITORY

BY THE ENGLISH, 1756-1778

Write the correct answers in the blanks.

1. _____ was an important fort and settlement in what is now southern Illinois.

2. The land of the Northwest Territory was given to the English by _____.

3. The Act which forbade Americans to settle west of the Allegheny Mountains was _____ _____.

4. George Rogers Clark assembled a small army at _____.

5. The English governor of the Northwest Territory at this time was _____.

6. _____ was a Spanish trader who was very helpful to George Rogers Clark.

7. _____ was a Catholic priest at Vincennes who helped George Rogers Clark.

8. In 1763, _____ was the most important settlement in what is now Indiana.

9. Colonel George Rogers Clark's army was made up of _____.

10. The first fort George Rogers Clark planned to capture was _____.

11. The next English fort he wanted to take was _____.

12. _____ was the governor of Virginia who helped Clark.

13. An Indian chief who led an uprising against the English during this time was _____ _____.

14. The fort at Vincennes was named _____.

15. Two forts fell to the Indians in a war known as _____.

16. _____ was referred to as "the dark and bloody ground" because the Indians and Americans fought so fiercely there.

17. _____ thought that the Northwest Territory would have to be taken by force and not by peaceful treaties.

18. One cause for the Northwest Territory being so thinly populated before 1778 was _____ _____.

19. The law which put all land north of the Ohio River and east of the Mississippi River under control of the English at Detroit was _____.

20. _____ was the English colony which claimed most of the land of the Northwest Territory.

Identify these terms from the unit.

1. Ft. Sackville _____

2. French and Indian War _____

3. Quebec Act _____

4. Virginia _____

5. Pontiac _____

6. Ouiatenon _____

Possible score 26

Name _____ Date _____ Score _____

8

Unit Test in Indiana History

UNIT 5. THE CONQUEST OF THE NORTHWEST TERRITORY BY THE AMERICANS, AND THE IMMIGRATION TO THIS TERRITORY, 1778-1800

Identify these items from the unit.

1. February 25, 1799 _____
2. Little Turtle _____
3. section of land _____
4. Laughery Massacre _____
5. Knox County _____
6. organized territory _____
7. public domain _____
8. "Willing" _____
9. St. Clair _____
10. Clarksville _____

Essay

Choose one of these topics to write on (about 75-100 words) (10 *points*).

A. Col. George Rogers Clark's campaign ending in the capture of Vincennes.

B. The defeat of the Indians at the Battle of Fallen Timbers.

_____
_____
_____
_____
_____
_____
_____
_____
_____
_____
_____
_____
_____

Write the correct answers in the blanks.

_____ 1. English governor who surrendered at Vincennes.

_____ 2. Southern boundary of Indiana territory.

_____ 3. The law which was the foundation for the new American government in the Northwest Territory.

_____ 4. A piece of land consisting of 640 acres.

_____ 5. The main religion of the Northwest Territory people in 1778.

_____ 6. Spanish trader who helped George Rogers Clark.

_____ 7. First American governor of Northwest Territory.

_____ 8. The fort at Vincennes.

_____ 9. An American who led an army to recapture the most important fort in what is now Indiana.

_____ 10. Law which provided for land survey of the Northwest Territory.

_____ 11. Place in Indiana where a beautiful memorial to George Rogers Clark was built.

_____ 12-14. Three steps which the Northwest Territory had to go through

_____ to organize its government.

_____

_____ 15. What treaty was made with the Indians in 1795?

_____ 16. What American general was responsible for getting the Indians to sign this treaty?

_____ 17. In what year was Indiana made into a separate territory?

_____ 18. The Ordinance of 1787 provides that how many states be made from the Northwest Territory?

_____ 19. The first all-American settlement in the Northwest Territory.

_____ 20.-21. What two things caused the settlers to want the Northwest Territory to be divided?

_____

_____ 22. The Ordinance of 1787 provided that the land of the Indians would never be taken away without what?

_____ 23. The Ordinance of 1787 provided that one section of land in each township be set aside for what?

_____ 24. What was it that the Ordinance of 1787 forever prohibited in the Northwest Territory?

_____ 25. How was George Rogers Clark finally rewarded for his services?

Possible score 45

Name _____ Date _____ Score _____

10

Unit Test in Indiana History

UNIT 6. INDIANA AS A TERRITORY, 1800-1816

Write the correct answers in the blanks.

(1) _____ was appointed first governor of the Indiana Territory; he was well known as an (2) _____ fighter. (3) _____ was appointed Secretary of the Territory. When Indiana became a territory (4) _____ counties had already been established; these were (5) _____ and (6) _____. Two new counties were established soon after; these were (7) _____ and (8) _____. The main traveled road in the Indiana Territory was from (9) _____ to (10) _____.

Write the number of the correct answer in the blank before the question.

_____ 1. Tecumseh and his brother belonged to the
(1) Potawatomi, (2) Miami, (3) Shawnee, (4) Ouiatenon tribe.

_____ 2. The first capital of the Territory was
(1) Vincennes, (2) Knox, (3) Kaskaskia, (4) Clarksville.

_____ 3. Most of the people of the territory lived in the
(1) northern, (2) western, (3) southern, (4) eastern part of the state.

_____ 4. The second largest town in Indiana in 1800 was
(1) Ft. Wayne, (2) Vincennes, (3) Clarksville, (4) Ouiatenon.

_____ 5. The Indiana Territory in 1800 included all the original Northwest Territory except
(1) Michigan, (2) Illinois, (3) Wisconsin, (4) Ohio.

_____ 6. The population of the Indiana Territory in 1800 was
(1) 650, (2) 6500, (3) 7500, (4) 6000.

_____ 7. The date for the Battle of Tippecanoe is
(1) Dec. 11, 1816, (2) Nov. 7, 1811, (3) Nov. 11, 1807, (4) 1815.

_____ 8. A monument for soldiers killed in the Battle of Tippecanoe is located at
(1) Buck Creek, (2) Battle Ground, (3) Lafayette, (4) Ouiatenon.

_____ 9. There was not an Indian village left south of the Wabash River by
(1) 1812, (2) 1811, (3) 1808, (4) 1810.

_____10. The second and last governor of the Indiana Territory was
(1) Clark, (2) Gibson, (3) Posey, (4) Tecumseh.

_____11. The Constitutional Convention was attended by delegates from _____ counties
(1) 12, (2) 10, (3) 9, (4) 13.

_____12. The Constitutional Convention met at
(1) Corydon, (2) Clarksville, (3) Vincennes, (4) Indianapolis.

_____13. How many states were in the Union when Indiana was admitted?
(1) 12, (2) 18, (3) 20, (4) 16.

_____14. The Illinois Territory was organized in
(1) 1816, (2) 1805, (3) 1809, (4) 1807.

_____15. Settlement in Indiana where settlers were killed by Indians:
(1) Cahokia, (2) Angel Mounds, (3) Pigeon Roost, (4) Knox.

Write the correct answers in the blanks before the questions.

_____16. In 1800, a line from the mouth of the Kentucky River to Ft. Recovery and then due north to Canada formed what boundary?

_____17. A statement of the form of government and how it is to be carried out.

_____18. A line due north from the mouth of the Miami River to Canada formed what boundary?

_____19. The second capital of the Indiana Territory.

_____20. Northern boundary of Indiana Territory.

_____21. Decisive battle against the Indians fought during this period.

_____22-24. Three large tasks facing the governor of the Indiana Territory after it was organized.

_____

_____

_____25. The date that Indiana was admitted as a state.

_____26. An Indian town near the junction of the Wabash and Tippecanoe Rivers.

_____27. Route which Governor Harrison's army took from Vincennes to the location of the Battle of Tippecanoe.

_____28. Western boundary of Indiana Territory in 1800.

_____29. Indian chief who tried to organize Indian tribes against the Americans.

_____30. What act of Congress gave Indiana Territory the right to organize a state government and apply for admission as a state?

Possible Score 40

12

Unit Test in Indiana History

UNIT 7. PIONEER LIFE IN INDIANA

Match these items correctly by choosing answers from Column II and writing them in the blanks in Column I.

Column I

—————————— 1. What the pioneer used in place of sugar.

—————————— 2. A kind of nut found in great abundance in Indiana.

—————————— 3. Population of Indiana in 1850.

—————————— 4. When the Pioneer Era ended in Indiana.

—————————— 5. Broad, thick boards used for making a cabin roof.

—————————— 6. Main crop marketed by pioneers.

—————————— 7. Many early towns grew up around one of these.

—————————— 8. A food which pioneers could grow quickly from the soil.

—————————— 9. One of the main causes of sickness among pioneers.

—————————— 10. This food was made from the sap of a tree.

—————————— 11. Wild animal which disappeared from Indiana around 1798.

—————————— 12. Homemade cloth made from flax fibers and wool.

—————————— 13. Wild game that was plentiful.

—————————— 14. These animals were used to pull plows and wagons.

—————————— 15. Machine used to make thread from wool.

—————————— 16. Kind of cabin floor made from split logs.

—————————— 17. Pioneers' worst enemy.

—————————— 18. Material used to make soap.

—————————— 19. Fruit that settlers found growing wild.

—————————— 20. Method used to cure meat.

—————————— 21. Form of punishment used by pioneers.

—————————— 22. One of the few tools pioneers had.

—————————— 23. Name given to tanned deer hide.

—————————— 24. Disease most common to early settlers.

—————————— 25. Place where grain was ground for food.

Column II

ague
hickory
at Civil War
smoking
oxen
1,000,000
acorns
honey
1860
deer
disease
100,000
hammer
blacksmith shop
gristmill
puncheon
potatoes
wood ashes
buckskin
blackberry
wheat
buffalo
maple sugar
dodger
chickens
rayon
clapboard
linsey-woolsey
spinning wheel
axe
water was impure
poisoning man's horse
venison

Fill these blanks to make a complete paragraph.

Many of the settlers in the Indiana Territory came from (1) _____.
In order to reach Indiana, they had to cross (2) _____, which was a
natural (3) _____. They crossed this barrier by using (4) _____
_____, and this was called (5) _____ across. The early
settlements were in the (6) _____ part of Indiana. The whole southern
part of the state was covered by (7) _____. When a family found a place
which they thought would be a good location for a home, they made a (8) _____
there. The principal occupation of the settler was (9) _____, because he
had to (10) _____ all the food for the family.

Write the correct answers in the blanks before the questions.

_____ 1. How were vegetables and fruits prepared for future use?

_____ 2. What did the pioneer sometimes use in place of coffee?

_____ 3. What kind of fuel did the pioneers use for heating and cooking?

_____ 4. Where did the early settlers get food?

_____ 5. What was the main denomination of Protestant church in early Indiana?

_____ 6. What did pioneers use to enclose their fields?

_____ 7. Name given to homemade cloth.

_____ 8. A herb used for medicine.

_____ 9. Jewelry worn by pioneers.

_____10. A disease that often killed whole pioneer families.

_____11. An article of food that was very scarce for pioneers.

_____12. What covered southern Indiana in pioneer days?

_____13. The early mills used what kind of power?

_____14. What did every pioneer have for hunting and protection?

_____15. What part of the cabin was used for cooking and heating?

Possible Score 50

Name _____ Date _____ Score _____

14

Unit Test in Indiana History

UNIT 8. POLITICAL DEVELOPMENT OF INDIANA, 1816 TO THE PRESENT

Write the letter of the correct answer in the blank before the question.

_____ 1. (a) Vincennes, (b) Knox, (c) Corydon, (d) Indianapolis, was the first capital of Indiana.

_____ 2. The first governor of Indiana was elected for a term of
(a) 3 years, (b) 2 years, (c) 4 years, (d) 6 years.

_____ 3. (a) Corydon, (b) Evansville, (c) Terre Haute, (d) Vincennes, had the state's first college.

_____ 4. The Wabash and Erie Canal was begun in the term of Governor
(a) Jennings, (b) Ray, (c) Morton, (d) Gray.

_____ 5. Indiana's second constitution went into effect in
(a) 1861, (b) 1850, (c) 1851, (d) 1950.

_____ 6. The first Indiana governor to be elected by the Democrats was
(a) Whitcomb, (b) Riley, (c) Wallace, (d) Dunning.

_____ 7. The governor of Indiana known for wearing homespun clothes was
(a) McNutt, (b) Jackson, (c) Williams, (d) Lane.

_____ 8. The governor of Indiana during World War I was
(a) Goodrich, (b) McCray, (c) Ralston, (d) Marshall.

_____ 9. Indiana's "Civil War Governor" was
(a) Matthews, (b) Chase, (c) Hovey, (d) Morton.

_____10. Indiana now gets most of its tax money from
(a) alcohol, (b) gross income tax, (c) gas tax, (d) cigarette tax.

_____11. The present state capitol building was completed in
(a) 1898, (b) 1808, (c) 1888, (d) 1800.

_____12. The governor of Indiana during the Spanish-American War was
(a) Baker, (b) Durbin, (c) Mount, (d) Porter.

_____13. The capital of Indiana was moved to its present location in
(a) 1805, (b) 1825, (c) 1855, (d) 1835.

_____14. The governor of the state is head of the
(a) legislative, (b) judicial, (c) executive, (d) none of these branches of the state government.

_____15. The length of the governor's term today is
(a) 4 years, (b) 6 years, (c) 2 years, (d) 3 years.

Write the correct answers in the blanks before the questions.

_____ 1. Who was the first governor of Indiana?

_____ 2. On what date (day, month, year) was Indiana made a state?

15

_____ 3. Why was Indiana's capital moved from its first location?

_____ 4. The site for Indiana's new capital was located on what river?

_____ 5. How often does Indiana's state law-making body meet?

_____ 6. Who was the third governor of Indiana?

_____ 7. What name is applied to Article I of the state constitution?

_____ 8. What was Camp Morton?

_____ 9. Who was the first Whig to be elected governor of Indiana?

_____ 10. Who was governor of Indiana in 1960?

_____ 11. Who is the present governor of Indiana?

_____ 12-13. What two governors of Indiana later became vice presidents of the United States?

_____

_____ 14. What prevented slavery from ever legally existing in Indiana?

_____ 15. Indiana has had how many governors?

_____ 16. The control of Indiana government passed to what party in 1860?

_____ 17. Who was the governor of Indiana during World War II?

_____ 18. The State Fair was started during the term of what governor?

_____ 19. The first newspaper in the state was called what?

_____ 20. What was the last Indian tribe removed from the state, in 1838?

_____ 21. Who selects the members of our state law-making body?

_____ 22. What confederate military expedition crossed Indiana during the Civil War?

_____ 23. What is the name of the state law-making body in Indiana?

_____ 24. What governor was able to get five important tax laws passed?

_____ 25. The building of railroads, canals, and roads at public expense was called what?

_____ 26. Who was governor when the second state constitution went into effect?

_____ 27. The period in Indiana history from 1850-1860 is sometimes referred to by what term?

_____ 28-30. What were the three most important towns in Indiana when it became a state?

_____

_____

Possible score 45

Name _____ Date _____ Score _____

16

Unit Test in Indiana History

UNIT 9. THE DEVELOPMENT OF TRANSPORTATION SYSTEMS IN INDIANA

Name 6 provisions of the Mammoth Internal Improvement Bill.

(1) _____

(2) _____

(3) _____

(4) _____

(5) _____

(6) _____

Write the correct answers in the blanks before the questions.

_____ 1. The name of the interurban line still operating in northern Indiana.

_____ 2. Roads made of logs placed crosswise of the roadbed.

_____ 3. What canal has been partly restored as a state memorial?

_____ 4. Indiana highways are controlled by what agency?

_____ 5. What is the largest airport in Indiana?

_____ 6. Where is the above airport located?

_____ 7. A turning basin in early canals was called what?

_____ 8. Canals were put out of business by what other means of transportation?

_____ 9. The old Chicago Trail began where in Indiana?

_____ 10. In what year was the Mammoth Internal Improvement Bill passed?

_____ 11. What was the first steam railroad in Indiana?

_____ 12. What was the trail from Brookville to Indianapolis?

_____ 13. Early road surfaces made by logs split into boards were called what?

_____ 14. What was the second longest canal built in Indiana?

_____ 15. What 10-year period was the greatest era of railroad building in Indiana?

_____ 16. What was the name given to the charge made for the use of privately owned roads?

_____ 17. The coming of what form of transportation caused the electric lines to fail?

_____ 18. What highway follows the route of the Old National Road?

_____ 19. What name was given the trails used by Indians and buffalo herds in early Indiana?

_____ 20. What trail led from Ft. Wayne to Terre Haute?

_____ 21-22. The canal built across Indiana was to connect what 2 large bodies of water in the United States?

_____

_____ 23-25. From what 3 sources does the state get the money to build

_____ highways?

_____

Write the correct words in the blanks to complete the paragraph.

In the year (1) _____, the Indiana legislature gave 6 companies the right to build railroads. One of these companies, the (2) _____, built the first steam railroad in Indiana, from the city of (3) _____ to (4) _____ by the year 1839, and (5) _____ by 1847. The railroad known as the (6) _____ was the first built from north to south across the state, connecting the (7) _____ River with Lake (8) _____ at (9) _____.

Unit Test in Indiana History

UNIT 10. THE GROWTH OF EDUCATION IN INDIANA

Match these items correctly by choosing answers from Column II and writing them in the blanks in Column I.

	Column I	Column II
_____	1. Name applied to a school made of several schools that have been discontinued.	Grades 1-12
_____	2. Series of readers famous in early Indiana schools.	college
_____	3. First college in Indiana.	Websters
_____	4. Year in which first college was founded.	Indiana Normal
_____	5. Leader of people who settled New Harmony.	1806
_____	6. Head of a city school system in Indiana.	Board of Education
_____	7. "Father of Indiana public schools."	Rappite
_____	8. Had charge of township schools in Indiana.	MacLure
_____	9. Year in which a law was passed which was the foundation for the state's public school system.	trustee
_____	10. Established "Community of Equality."	1804
_____	11. City in which Manchester College is located.	Vincennes
_____	12. The "common school."	McGuffey
_____	13. Member of Harmony Society.	consolidation
_____	14. "Father of American geology."	1852
_____	15. First school of its kind was established at New Harmony.	superintendent

Column II (continued): kindergarten, Owen, North Manchester, Mills, Grades 1-8, George Rapp, Manchester, parochial

Tell where each of these colleges is located.

(1) DePauw University _____

(2) Franklin College _____

(4) Butler University _____

(3) Indiana State University _____

19

(5) Hanover College _____

(6) Notre Dame University _____

(7) Ball State University _____

(8) Indiana University _____

(9) Wabash College _____

(10) Purdue University _____

Write the correct answers in the blanks.

_____ 1. Popular spelling book used in early Indiana schools.

_____ 2. Source of most of the money supplied by the state for school support.

_____ 3. DePauw University was first known by this name.

_____ 4. First law in Indiana which made any provision for supporting free public schools.

_____ 5. Source of most of the money furnished by the city and township for the support of schools in Indiana.

_____ 6. What are the compulsory school attendance ages of children in Indiana?

_____ 7-8. What two schools have changed from teachers colleges to universities?

_____ 9. Who is the present Superintendent of Public Instruction?

_____ 10-11. What 2 churches maintain their own systems of elementary schools in Indiana?

_____ 12. What was the date for the first commissioned high school in the state?

_____ 13. In what year was the first State Superintendent of Public Instruction elected?

_____ 14-16. What were the 3 main subjects taught in early common schools in Indiana?

_____ 17. What name is applied to a school supported by a church (elementary or high school)?

_____ 18-21. What are the 6 schools above the level of high school that are supported by public taxation?

Possible Score 47

Name _____ Date _____ Score _____

20

Unit Test in Indiana History

UNIT 11. POPULATION GROWTH, AGRICULTURE, NATURAL RESOURCES, AND MANUFACTURING IN THE STATE

Write the correct answers in the blanks before the questions.

_____ 1. Largest body of water in the state.

_____ 2-3. The above is located between what two towns?

_____

_____ 4. In 1894 this man made a "horseless carriage" that ran up to 6 miles per hour.

_____ 5. Where the above car can be seen today.

_____ 6. Indiana's state motto.

_____ 7. Largest manufacturing industry in Indiana.

_____ 8. In 1980 what was Indiana's rank in population among the states?

_____ 9. Smallest county in Indiana.

_____ 10. What part of the state is called the "Calumet area"?

_____ 11. City in which first automobiles were manufactured in Indiana.

_____ 12. Main farm crop in Indiana.

_____ 13. Largest county in Indiana.

_____ 14. Clay and shale are used to make what articles?

_____ 15. What city has some of the world's largest oil refineries?

_____ 16. In what Indiana town was a large and well-known woolen mill located?

_____ 17. Where in Indiana has a large resort hotel been built at the site of a mineral spring?

_____ 18. City which was largest center for pork-packing in 1840-50.

_____ 19. What county had the smallest population in 1970?

_____ 20. What natural resource produced here in 1890-1900 has become exhausted?

_____ 21. River in Indiana which furnishes water power to generate electricity.

_____ 22. At what university is Indiana's state school of agriculture located?

_____ 23. In 1980 how many Indiana cities had over 100,000 population?

_____ 24. Has Indiana's urban population increased or decreased since 1860?

_____25-27. Indiana has always depended on what three things for its growth?

_____

_____

_____28. The counties of Vigo, Clay, and Clinton are noted for producing large quantities of what?

_____29. Indiana's largest steel-making center.

_____30. Region composed of Grant, Delaware, Madison, Blackford, and adjoining counties.

Write the correct words in the blanks.

A natural resource is defined as something that (1) _____.
Four of Indiana's most valuable natural resources have been (2) _____, (3) _____,
(4) _____, and (5) _____. Coal was another (6) _____
resource in Indiana and was found in quantities in the (7) _____ part of the
state. Coal was mined in two ways: by (8) _____ and (9) _____.
Most of the coal now mined in the state is used for (10) _____.

List the 10 largest cities in Indiana in order of their size in 1980.

(1) _____

(2) _____

(3) _____

(4) _____

(5) _____

(6) _____

(7) _____

(8) _____

(9) _____

(10) _____

Possible Score 50

Name _____ Date _____ Score _____

Unit Test in Indiana History

UNIT 12. FAMOUS PERSONS, PLACES OF INTEREST, AND MISCELLANEOUS FACTS ABOUT OUR STATE

Write the correct information in the blanks.

1. The year when Indiana became a state. _____

2. The state flower. _____

3. The state bird. _____

4. The capital of Indiana. _____

5. The state tree of Indiana. _____

6. Name of the state song. _____

7. Number of state parks in Indiana. _____

8. State motto. _____

9. Nickname of Indiana citizens. _____

10. Number of counties in the state. _____

Make a list of ten famous persons from Indiana not mentioned elsewhere in the test. Tell for what each is well known.

(1) _____   _____

(2) _____   _____

(3) _____   _____

(4) _____   _____

(5) _____   _____

(6) _____   _____

(7) _____   _____

(8) _____   _____

(9) _____   _____

(10) _____   _____

Write the correct answers in the blanks before the questions.

_____ 1. The author of our state song.

_____ 2. The official state banner was adopted in this year.

_____ 3. The largest state park in Indiana.

_____ 4. Number of stars on the state banner.

_____ 5. The newest state park in Indiana.

_____ 6. Famous cave located in Indiana.

_____ 7. The state park which overlooks the Ohio River near Madison.

_____ 8. Largest natural lake in Indiana.

_____ 9. The "Hoosier Poet."

_____ 10. Culver Military Academy is located here.

_____ 11. Wrote *Alice of Old Vincennes*.

_____ 12. A state park named for a chief of the Potawatomi Indians.

_____ 13. The oldest state park in Indiana.

_____ 14. The author of *Ben Hur*.

_____ 15. What memorial is in downtown Indianapolis?

_____ 16-17. Two colors used on the Indiana state banner.

_____

_____ 18. State park which has a recreated pioneer village.

_____ 19. Brother of Paul Dresser; a famous author.

_____ 20-22. Three parts to the scene shown on the state seal.

_____

_____

_____ 23. Year in which Lincoln came to Indiana to live.

_____ 24. Year in which Lincoln left Indiana.

_____ 25. State memorial created in memory of a settlement of white people massacred by the Indians.

_____ 26. A native of Brook, Indiana, who became a world famous playwright and humorist.

_____ 27. County named for the first governor of Indiana.

_____ 28. What Indiana celebrated in 1966.

_____ 29. Author of *Seventeen* and *Penrod*.

_____ 30. An Indiana man who became famous as a cartoonist for the *Chicago Tribune*.

Possible Score 50

Name _____ Date _____ Score _____

Get Connected.

FEATURES

LearnSmart™

McGraw-Hill LearnSmart is an adaptive learning program that identifies what an individual student knows and doesn't know. LearnSmart's adaptive learning path helps students learn faster, study more efficiently, and retain more knowledge. Reports available for both students and instructors indicate where students need to study more and assess their success rate in retaining knowledge.

Graphing Tool

The graphing tool within Connect Economics provides opportunities for students to draw, interact with, manipulate, and analyze graphs in their online auto-graded assignments, as they would with pencil and paper. The Connect graphs are identical in presentation to the graphs in the book, so students can easily relate their assignments to their reading material.

Get Engaged.

eBook

Connect Plus includes a media-rich eBook that allows you to share your notes with your students. Your students can insert and review their own notes, highlight the text, search for specific information, and interact with media resources. Using an eBook with Connect Plus gives your students a complete digital solution that allows them to access their materials from any computer.

Lecture Capture

Make your classes available anytime, anywhere with simple, one-click recording. Students can search for a word or phrase and be taken to the exact place in your lecture that they need to review.

Essentials *of* Economics

Ninth Edition

Bradley R. Schiller

Professor Emeritus, American University

Essentials of Economics, Ninth Edition

Published by McGraw-Hill Education, 2 Penn Plaza, New York, NY 10121. Copyright © 2014 by McGraw-Hill Education. All rights reserved. Printed in the United States of America. Previous editions © 2011, 2009, and 2007. No part of this publication may be reproduced or distributed in any form or by any means, or stored in a database or retrieval system, without the prior written consent of McGraw-Hill Education, including, but not limited to, in any network or other electronic storage or transmission, or broadcast for distance learning.

Some ancillaries, including electronic and print components, may not be available to customers outside the United States.

This book is printed on acid-free paper.

1 2 3 4 5 6 7 8 9 0 DOW/DOW 1 0 9 8 7 6 5 4 3

ISBN: 978-0-07-802173-2
MHID: 0-07-802173-1

Senior Vice President, Products & Markets: *Kurt L. Strand*
Vice President, Content Production & Technology Services: *Kimberly Meriwether David*
Managing Director: *Douglas Reiner*
Brand Manager: *Scott Smith*
Executive Director of Development: *Ann Torbert*
Development Editor: *Casey Rasch*
Director of Digital Content: *Doug Ruby*
Marketing Manager: *Katie Hoenicke*
Content Project Manager: *Harvey Yep*
Content Project Manager: *Susan Lombardi*
Buyer II: *Debra R. Sylvester*
Design: *Matt Diamond*
Cover Image: *Getty Images*
Content Licensing Specialist: *Joanne Mennemeier*
Typeface: *10/12 New Aster*
Compositor: *Aptara®, Inc.*
Printer: *R. R. Donnelley*

All credits appearing on page or at the end of the book are considered to be an extension of the copyright page.

Library of Congress Cataloging-in-Publication Data

Schiller, Bradley R., 1943—
    Essentials of economics/Bradley R. Schiller, Professor Emeritus American University.—Ninth edition.
        pages cm.—(The McGraw-Hill series economics)
    Includes index.
    ISBN 978-0-07-802173-2 (alk. paper)—ISBN 0-07-802173-1 (alk. paper)
    1. Economics. I. Title.
    HB171.5.S2923 2014
    330—dc23
                            2013026980

The Internet addresses listed in the text were accurate at the time of publication. The inclusion of a website does not indicate an endorsement by the authors or McGraw-Hill Education, and McGraw-Hill Education does not guarantee the accuracy of the information presented at these sites.

www.mhhe.com

The McGraw-Hill Series

Economics

Bradley R. Schiller has over four decades of experience teaching introductory economics at American University, the University of California (Berkeley and Santa Cruz), the University of Maryland, and the University of Nevada (Reno). He has given guest lectures at more than 300 colleges ranging from Fresno, California, to Istanbul, Turkey. Dr. Schiller's unique contribution to teaching is his ability to relate basic principles to current socioeconomic problems, institutions, and public policy decisions. This perspective is evident throughout *Essentials of Economics.*

Dr. Schiller derives this policy focus from his extensive experience as a Washington consultant. He has been a consultant to most major federal agencies, many congressional committees, and political candidates. In addition, he has evaluated scores of government programs and helped design others. His studies of income inequality, poverty, discrimination, training programs, tax reform, pensions, welfare, Social Security, and lifetime wage patterns have appeared in both professional journals and popular media. Dr. Schiller is also a frequent commentator on economic policy for television, radio, and newspapers.

Dr. Schiller received his PhD from Harvard and his BA degree, with great distinction, from the University of California (Berkeley). When not teaching, writing, or consulting, Professor Schiller is typically on a tennis court, schussing down a ski slope, or enjoying the crystal blue waters of Lake Tahoe.

The last few years have been a case study in business cycles. The U.S. economy boomed for a decade, pushing the unemployment rate down to 4.6 percent and adding trillions of dollars to household wealth. Then housing prices collapsed, the financial markets imploded, and 9 million Americans lost their jobs. The Great Recession of 2008–2009 wasn't nearly as bad as the Great Depression of the 1930s, but it evoked similar fears.

The Great Recession officially ended in June 2009, but the subsequent recovery has been agonizingly slow. Four years later over 11 million workers were still jobless and another 6 million were involuntarily working part-time, working for wages below their norm, or simply too discouraged to actively seek employment.

According to what we teach in our economics classes, things shouldn't have worked out so badly. We show students how fiscal and monetary stimulus can shift aggregate demand, restoring full employment. It's just a question of pulling the right policy lever at the right time. Yet despite gargantuan fiscal and monetary interventions, the recession was deeper and the recovery far more tepid than what our theories promised. What accounts for this gap between theory and reality?

As economists themselves pursue this question, the general public has asked similar questions. Even students are expressing unusual interest in how an economy operates (one of the few external benefits of a recession). People want to know how and why an economy gets into trouble—and how it can be set back on track. This has made principles of economics classes more important, more relevant, and more popular.

Essentials of Economics has always had a strong policy focus. The core theme that weaves through the entire text is the need to find the best possible answers to the basic questions of WHAT, HOW, and FOR WHOM to produce. Students are confronted early on with the reality that the economy doesn't always operate optimally at either the macro or micro level. In Chapter 1 they learn that markets sometimes fail to generate optimal outcomes, but also that government interventions can fail to improve economic performance. The policy challenge is to find the mix of market reliance and government regulation that generates the best possible outcomes. Every chapter ends with a Policy Perspectives feature that challenges students to apply the economic concepts they have just encountered to real-world policy issues. In Chapter 1 the policy question is "Is 'Free' Health Care Really Free?"—a question that emphasizes the opportunity costs associated with all economic activity. In Chapter 10 the issue is "Is Another Recession Coming?" which challenges students to think about the causes and advance indicators of economic downturns. And Chapter 16 is devoted to explaining the perennial contrast between theory and reality with a mixture of institutional, political, and theoretical factors. Students love that macro capstone.

FOCUS ON CORE CONCEPTS

It's impossible to squeeze all the content—and the excitement—of both micro and macro economics into a one-semester course, much less an abbreviated intro text. But economics is, after all, the science of choice. Instructors who teach a one-term survey of economics know how hard the content choices can be. There are too many topics, too many economic events, and too little time.

Few textbooks confront this scarcity problem directly. Some one-semester books are nearly as long as full-blown principles texts. The shorter ones tend to condense topics and omit the additional explanations, illustrations, and applications that are especially important in survey courses. Students and teachers alike get frustrated trying to pick out the essentials from abridged principles texts.

Essentials of Economics lives up to its name by making the difficult choices. The standard table of contents has been pruned to the core. The surviving topics are the essence of economic concepts. In microeconomics, for example, the focus is on the polar models of perfect competition and monopoly. These models are represented as the endpoints of a spectrum of market structures (see Figure 6.1 on page 113). Intermediate market structures—oligopoly, monopolistic competition, and the like—are noted but not analyzed. The goal here is simply to convey the sense that market structure is an important determinant of market outcomes. The contrast between the extremes of monopoly and perfect competition is sufficient to convey this essential message. The omission of other market structures from the outline also leaves more space for explaining and illustrating *how* market structure affects market behavior.

The same commitment to essentials is evident in the section on macroeconomics. Rather than attempt to cover all the salient macro models, the focus here is on a straightforward presentation of the aggregate supply–demand framework. The classical, Keynesian, and monetarist perspectives on AD and AS are discussed within that common, consistent framework. There is no discussion of neo-Keynesianism, rational expectations, public choice, or Marxist models. The level of abstraction required for such models is neither necessary nor appropriate in an introductory survey course. Texts that include such models tend to raise more questions than survey instructors can hope to answer. In *Essentials* students are exposed to only the ideas needed for a basic understanding of how macroeconomies function.

CENTRAL THEME

The central goal of this text is to convey a sense of how economic *systems* affect economic *outcomes*. When we look back on the twentieth century, we see how some economies flourished while others languished. Even the "winners" had recurrent episodes of slow, or negative growth. The central analytical issue is how various economic systems influenced those diverse growth records. Was the relatively superior track record of the United States a historical fluke or a by-product of its commitment to market capitalism? Were the long economic expansions of the 1980s and 1990s the result of enlightened macro policy, more efficient markets, or just good luck? What roles did policy, markets, and (bad) luck play in the Great Recession of 2008–2009? What forces deserve credit for the economic recovery that followed?

In the 2012 presidential elections, economic issues were at the forefront (as Yale economist Ray Fair has been telling us for years). Democratic candidates claimed credit for the economic recovery, pointing to their support of President Obama's stimulus program, unemployment assistance, financial regulation, and health care reform. Republican candidates pointed to soaring federal budgets and deficits as harbingers of economic collapse and faulted the Democrats for not giving greater priority to short-term job creation. How are students—and voters—supposed to sort out these conflicting claims? *Essentials* offers an analytical foundation for assessing both economic events and political platforms. Students get an initial bird's-eye view of the macroeconomy (see page 225) that relates macro determinants to macro outcomes. Then they get enough tools to identify cause-and-effect relationships and to sort out competing political claims.

A recurrent theme in *Essentials* is the notion that economic institutions and policies *matter*. Economic prosperity isn't a random occurrence. The right institutions and policies can foster or impede economic progress. The challenge is to know when and how to intervene.

This central theme is the focus of Chapter 1. Our economic accomplishments and insatiable materialism set the stage for a discussion of production possibilities. The role of economic systems and choices is illustrated with the starkly different "guns versus butter" decisions in North and South Korea, Russia, and the United States. The potential for both market failure (or success) and government failure (or success) is highlighted. After reading Chapter 1, students should sense that "the economy" is important to their lives and that our collective choices on how the economy is structured are important.

A GLOBAL PORTRAIT OF THE U.S. ECONOMY

To put some meat on the abstract bones of the economy, *Essentials* offers a unique portrait of the U.S. economy. Few students easily relate to the abstraction of the economy. They hear about specific dimensions of the economy but rarely see all the pieces put together. Chapter 2 fills this void by providing a bird's-eye view of the U.S. economy. This descriptive chapter is organized around the three basic questions of WHAT, HOW, and FOR WHOM to produce. The current answer to the WHAT question is summarized with data on GDP and its components. Historical and global comparisons are provided to underscore the significance of America's $16 trillion economy. Similar perspectives are offered on the structure of production and the U.S. distribution of income. An early look at the role of government in shaping economic outcomes is also provided. This colorful global portrait is a critical tool in acquainting students with the broad dimensions of the U.S. economy and is unique to this text.

REAL-WORLD EMPHASIS

The decision to include a descriptive chapter on the U.S. economy reflects a basic commitment to a real-world context. Students rarely get interested in stories about the mythical widget manufacturers that inhabit so many economics textbooks. But glimmers of interest—even some enthusiasm—surface when real-world illustrations, not fables, are offered.

Every chapter starts out with real-world applications of core concepts. As the chapters unfold, empirical illustrations continue to enliven the text analysis. The chapters end with a **Policy Perspectives** section that challenges the student to apply new concepts to real-world issues. The first Policy Perspective, in Chapter 1, highlights the difficult choices that emerge when we try to offer "free" health care.

POLICY PERSPECTIVES   Is "Free" Health Care Really Free?

Everyone wants more and better health care, and nearly everyone agrees that even the poorest members of society need reliable access to doctors and hospitals. That's why President Obama made health care reform such a high priority in his first presidential year.

Although the political debate over health care reform was intense and multidimensional, the economics of health care are fairly simple. In essence, President Obama wanted to *expand* the health care industry. He wanted to increase access for the millions of Americans who didn't have health insurance and raise the level

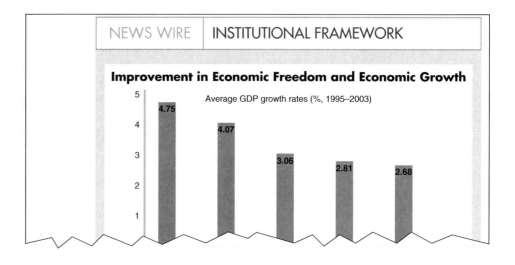

The real-world approach of *Essentials* is reinforced by the boxed **News Wires** that appear in every chapter. The 78 News Wires offer up-to-date domestic and international applications of economic concepts. Some new examples that will particularly interest your students include

- The opportunity cost of North Korea's rocket program (page 11)
- The impact of Hurricane Sandy on used car prices (page 61)
- The diversity in starting pay for various college majors (page 163)
- The incidence of passive smoking deaths (page 184)
- 2012–2013 tuition hikes (page 214)
- The impact of the 2013 payroll tax hike on consumer spending (page 261)
- The impact of Starbucks' mobile payment system on the money supply (page 280)
- The imposition of import tariffs on Chinese solar panels (page 355)

This is just a sampling of the stream of real-world applications that cascades throughout this text. Thirty of the News Wires are new to this edition.

THEORY AND REALITY

In becoming acquainted with the U.S. economy, students will inevitably learn about the woes of the business cycle. As the course progresses, they will not fail to notice a huge gap between the pat solutions of economic theory and the dismal realities of occasional recession. This experience will kindle one of the most persistent and perplexing questions students have. If the theory is so good, why is the economy such a mess?

Economists like to pretend that the theory is perfect but politicians aren't. That's part of the answer, to be sure. But it isn't fair to either politicians or economists. In reality, the design and implementation of economic policy is impeded by incomplete information, changing circumstances, goal trade-offs, and politics. Chapter 16 examines these real-world complications. A News Wire on the "black art" of economic modeling (page 334), together with new examples of the politics of macro policy, enliven the discussion. In this signature chapter, students get a more complete explanation of why the real world doesn't always live up to the promises of economic theory.

NEW IN THIS EDITION

This ninth edition contains an abundance of new material. One of the most exciting new features is the integration of YouTube videos into the learning process—a feature that will certainly enhance student interest and retention. More about this in a moment. As for the text itself, although the structure of the text is unchanged, the content has been extensively refreshed. All of the statistics have been updated. New problems and discussion questions have been added to every chapter. In all, there are 95 (!) new end-of-chapter problems and 30 new questions for discussion. New cartoons and photos have also been added. And new examples, illustrations, and 30 new News Wires appear throughout as well. The chapter-end summaries, questions for discussion, and problems are all keyed to chapter-opening learning objectives, in addition to the supplementary material, which includes the *Test Bank, Instructor's Resource Manual*, and *Student Study Guide*.

The discussion of market versus government failures has been condensed in Chapter 1, with more of the discussion moved to Chapter 9 (Government Intervention). The "guns versus butter" trade-off has been updated with data on the consequences of North Korea's 2012 rocket launch for domestic food shortages.

Chapter 2 updates the U.S. and global statistics so that students can comprehend the relative size and dimensions of the U.S. economy. New data on income distributions both here and abroad also give students an opportunity to assess relative inequalities.

Chapter 3 features four new News Wires, including gas rationing in New Jersey, ticket scalping at a benefit concert, initial iPhone shortages, and the hurricane-induced spike in used car prices across the country.

Chapter 4 offers a view of new expenditure patterns, including differences between young male and female singles.

Chapter 5 has five new questions for discussion and seven new problems, as well as new illustrations of the difference between short-run production decisions (Nissan auto production in Spain) and long-run investment decisions (Fiat's new plant in Russia).

The increasingly competitive and therefore unprofitable catfish industry is the focus of Chapter 6. Emphasis is on the impact of entry and exit on market prices in competitive environments.

Chapter 7 modifies the competitive environment of Chapter 6 to illustrate how the monopolization of an industry can harm consumers. A fresh News Wire on OPEC production coordination drives home the point.

Chapter 8 has a plethora of new issues and policy discussions, including President Obama's latest proposal to raise the national minimum wage and the wage disparities between CEOs and production workers. Data on 2012–2013 starting salaries for college grads with diverse majors is sure to spark some student interest and discussion about marginal productivity.

Chapter 9 features an expanded discussion of both market failure and government failure and new poll data on (dis)trust in government. The four causes of market failure are illustrated with interesting and relevant examples (e.g., secondhand smoke deaths as an externality).

Chapter 10 is enlivened with the experiences of the 2008–2009 Great Recession and some new perspectives on inflation and seasonal unemployment. The chapter-ending Policy Perspectives section looks at the odds of another recession.

In Chapter 11 students get a streamlined view of the aggregate supply–aggregate demand model and how it can illustrate cyclical movements of the economy.

The great fiscal policy debates of the last few years, including the "fiscal cliff" and recurrent debt ceiling crises, bring Chapter 12 to life. A News Wire discussing the 2013 payroll tax hike illustrates the impact of fiscal restraint. There are four new questions and seven new problems.

After covering the basics of money and deposit creation, Chapter 13 examines the impact of new mobile payment systems on the money supply (none) and velocity (some). This helps clarify the unique characteristics of "money."

The Fed's new strategy of tying its monetary policy decisions to the national unemployment rate is examined in Chapter 14, along with an expanded discussion of constraints on monetary policy effectiveness.

Chapter 15 expands the discussion of economic growth to include a new discussion of skill-based immigration visas and more discussion of how financial regulation can restrain bank lending and real investment.

Chapter 16 continues to offer a synopsis of macro theory, an inventory of policy tools, and a track record of economic performance. The 2012–2013 debate on the debt ceiling illustrates some of the political factors that constrain policy decisions.

Chapter 17 not only teaches the core concepts of trade theory but also illustrates how special interests work to restrict trade in ways that benefit few at the expense of many. The sugar quotas and solar panel tariffs are offered as examples.

SCANNING BARCODES

◄ Practice quizzes, student PowerPoints, author podcasts, web activities, and additional materials available at www.mhhe.com/ schilleressentials9e, or scan here. Need a barcode reader? Try ScanLife, available in your app store.

For students using smartphones and tablets, scanning barcodes (or QR codes) located within the chapter guide students to additional chapter resources, including

* Practice quizzes to help students test their knowledge of the material.
* Student PowerPoints to refresh the concepts students have just learned.
* Author podcasts to extend the discussion of the chapter.

Students not using smartphones or tablets can access the same resources by clicking the barcodes when viewing the eBook or by going to www.mhhe.com/ schilleressentials9e.

YOUTUBE INTEGRATION

This book is **YouTube Ready**—over 100 key topics in *Essentials of Economics* are coordinated with interesting and innovative videos on YouTube. Visit the *Online Learning Center* to learn more. This resource is updated every semester to keep your course materials current and on track with events around the world.

SUPPORTIVE PEDAGOGY

The emphasis on real-world applications and online illustrations motivates students to read and learn basic economic concepts. This pedagogical goal is reinforced with several in-text student aids:

* *Chapter learning objectives*   Each chapter opens with a set of chapter-level learning objectives classified according to Bloom's Taxonomy. Students and professors can be confident that each chapter is organized around common themes outlined by the five learning objectives listed on the first page of each chapter.
* *Chapter-opening questions*   Each chapter begins with a short, empirically based introduction to key concepts. Three core questions are posed to motivate and direct student learning.
* *In-margin definitions*   Key concepts are highlighted in the text and defined in the margins. Key definitions are also repeated in subsequent chapters to reinforce proper usage.

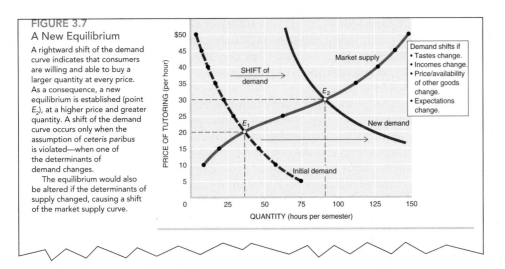

FIGURE 3.7
A New Equilibrium

A rightward shift of the demand curve indicates that consumers are willing and able to buy a larger quantity at every price. As a consequence, a new equilibrium is established (point E_2), at a higher price and greater quantity. A shift of the demand curve occurs only when the assumption of *ceteris paribus* is violated—when one of the determinants of demand changes.

The equilibrium would also be altered if the determinants of supply changed, causing a shift of the market supply curve.

- *Precise graphs*   All the analytical graphs are plotted and labeled with precision. This shouldn't be noteworthy, but other texts are surprisingly deficient in this regard.
- *Synchronized tables and graphs*   The graphs are made more understandable with explicit links to accompanying tables. Notice in Figure 3.2 (page 52), for example, how the lettered rows of the table match the lettered points on the graph.
- *Complete annotations*   All the graphs and tables have self-contained annotations, as do the News Wire boxes, the photos, and the cartoons. These captions facilitate both initial learning and later review.
- *Chapter summaries*   Key points are summarized in bulleted capsules at the end of each chapter.
- *Key term review*   A list of key terms (the ones defined in the margins) is provided at the end of each chapter. This feature facilitates review and self-testing.
- *Questions for discussion*   These are intended to stimulate thought and discussion about the nature of core concepts and their application to real-world settings.
- *Numerical problems*   Numerical problems are set out at the end of each chapter. These problems often require students to use material from earlier tables, graphs, or News Wires. Answers to all problems are provided in the *Instructor's Resource Manual* along with clarifying annotations.
- *End-of-text glossary*   The chapter-specific definitions and key term reviews are supplemented with a comprehensive glossary at the end of the text.
- *Web-based exercises*   Problems on the Online Learning Center for each chapter require students to retrieve and use material from specific websites. Answers and additional suggestions are contained in the *Instructor's Resource Manual*.

CONTENTS: MICROECONOMICS

The micro sequence of the text includes only six chapters. In this brief space students get an introduction to the essentials of consumer demand, producer supply decisions, market structure (competition versus monopoly), and labor market behavior. In each case the objective is to spotlight the essential elements of market behavior—for example, the utility-maximizing behavior of consumers, the profit-maximizing quest of producers, and the interactions of supply and demand in setting both wages and prices. The monopoly chapter (Chapter 7) offers a step-by-step comparison of competitive and monopoly behavior in both the short run and the long run.

The final chapter in the micro core examines the purposes of government intervention. The principal sources of market failure (public goods, externalities, market power, inequity) are explained and illustrated. So, too, is the nature of government intervention and the potential for *government* failure. Students should end the micro core with a basic understanding of how markets work and when and why government intervention is sometimes necessary.

CONTENTS: MACROECONOMICS

The macro sequence begins with a historical and descriptive introduction to the business cycle. The rest of the opening macro chapter explains and illustrates the nature and consequences of unemployment and inflation. This discussion is predicated on the conviction that students have to understand *why* business cycles are feared before they'll show any interest in the policy tools designed to tame the cycle. The standard measures of unemployment and inflation are explained, along with specific numerical goals set by Congress and the president.

The basic analytical framework of aggregate supply and aggregate demand (AS/AD) is introduced in Chapter 11. The focus is on how different shapes and shifts of AS and AD curves affect macro outcomes. The AS/AD framework is also used to illustrate the basic policy options that decision makers confront. The stylized model of the economy illustrated in Figure 11.1 (page 225) is used repeatedly to show how different macro determinants affect macro outcomes (e.g., see the highlighting of fiscal policy in Figure 12.3 on page 251).

The fiscal policy chapter surveys the components of aggregate demand and shows how changes in government spending or taxes can alter macro equilibrium. The multiplier is illustrated in the AS/AD framework, and the potential consequences for price inflation are discussed. The chapter ends with a discussion of budget deficits and surpluses.

The monetary dimensions of the macroeconomy get two chapters. The first introduces students to modern concepts of money and the process of deposit creation. Chapter 14 focuses on how the Federal Reserve regulates interest rates, bank reserves, and lending to influence macro outcomes.

Supply-side concerns are addressed in Chapter 15. The potential of tax cuts, deregulation, and other supply-side policy options to improve both short- and long-term macro performance is explored. The chapter also offers a discussion of why economic growth is desirable, despite mounting evidence of environmental degradation and excessive consumption.

The final chapter in the macro section is every student's favorite. It starts out with a brief review of the nature and potential uses of fiscal, monetary, and supply-side policy options. Then the economic record is examined to highlight the contrast between theory and reality. The rest of the chapter identifies the obstacles that prevent us from eliminating the business cycle in the real world. These obstacles include everything from faulty forecasts to pork-barrel politics.

CONTENTS: INTERNATIONAL PERSPECTIVE

No introduction to economics can omit discussion of the global economy. But how can international topics be included in such a brief survey? *Essentials* resolves this dilemma with a two-pronged approach. The major thrust is to integrate global perspectives throughout the text. Many of the News Wire boxes feature international illustrations of core concepts. In addition, the basic contrast between market and command economies that sets the framework for Chapter 1 is referred to repeatedly in both the micro and macro sections. The U.S. economy is described in a global context (Chapter 2) and analyzed throughout as an open economy with substantial foreign trade and investment sectors. Students will not think of the U.S. economy in insular terms as they work through this text.

The second global dimension to this text is a separate chapter on international trade. Chapter 17 describes U.S. trade patterns and then explains trade on the basis of comparative advantage. Consistent with the real-world focus of the text, a discussion of protectionist pressures and obstacles is also included. Exchange rate determinations are explained, along with the special interests who favor currency appreciations and depreciations. The objective is to convey a sense of not only why trade is beneficial but also why trade issues are so politically sensitive.

TEXT SUPPLEMENTS

Less Managing. More Teaching. Greater Learning.

McGraw-Hill *Connect Economics* is an online assignment and assessment solution that connects students with the tools and resources they'll need to achieve success.

McGraw-Hill *Connect Economics* helps prepare students for their future by enabling faster learning, more efficient studying, and higher retention of knowledge.

McGraw-Hill *Connect Economics* Features

Connect Economics offers a number of powerful tools and features to make managing assignments easier, so faculty can spend more time teaching. With *Connect Economics*, students can engage with their coursework anytime and anywhere, making the learning process more accessible and efficient. *Connect Economics* offers you the features described here.

SIMPLE ASSIGNMENT MANAGEMENT With *Connect Economics*, creating assignments is easier than ever, so you can spend more time teaching and less time managing. The assignment management function enables you to

- Create and deliver assignments easily with selectable end-of-chapter questions and test bank items.
- Streamline lesson planning, student progress reporting, and assignment grading to make classroom management more efficient than ever.
- Go paperless with the eBook and online submission and grading of student assignments.

SMART GRADING When it comes to studying, time is precious. *Connect Economics* helps students learn more efficiently by providing feedback and practice material when they need it, where they need it. When it comes to teaching, your time is precious. The grading function enables you to

- Have assignments scored automatically, giving students immediate feedback on their work and side-by-side comparisons with correct answers.
- Access and review each response; manually change grades or leave comments for students to review.
- Reinforce classroom concepts with practice tests and instant quizzes.

INSTRUCTOR LIBRARY The *Connect Economics* Instructor Library is your repository for instructor ancillaries and additional resources to improve student engagement in and out of class. You can select and use any asset that enhances your lecture. The *Connect Economics* Instructor Library includes

* eBook.
* PowerPoint presentations.
* Test bank.
* Solutions manual.
* Instructor's manual.
* Web activities and answers.
* Digital image library.

STUDENT STUDY CENTER   The *Connect Economics* Student Study Center is the place for students to access additional resources. The Student Study Center

* Offers students quick access to lectures, practice materials, eBooks, and more.
* Provides instant practice material and study questions, easily accessible on the go.

DIAGNOSTIC AND ADAPTIVE LEARNING OF CONCEPTS: LEARNSMART

The LearnSmart adaptive self-study technology within *Connect Economics* provides students with a seamless combination of practice, assessment, and remediation for major concepts in the course. LearnSmart's intelligent software adapts to every student response and automatically delivers concepts that advance the student's understanding while reducing time devoted to the concepts already mastered. LearnSmart

* Applies an intelligent concept engine to identify the relationships between concepts and to serve new concepts to each student only when he or she is ready.
* Adapts automatically to each student, so students spend less time on the topics they understand and more on those they have yet to master.
* Provides continual reinforcement and remediation, but gives only as much guidance as students need.
* Enables you to assess which concepts students have efficiently learned on their own, thus freeing class time for more applications and discussion.

STUDENT PROGRESS TRACKING   *Connect Economics* keeps instructors informed about how each student, section, and class is performing, allowing for more productive use of lecture and office hours. The progress-tracking function enables you to

* View scored work immediately and track individual or group performance with assignment and grade reports.
* Access an instant view of student or class performance relative to learning objectives.
* Collect data and generate reports required by many accreditation organizations, such as AACSB.

LECTURE CAPTURE   Increase the attention paid to lecture discussion by decreasing the attention paid to note taking. For an additional charge, Lecture Capture offers new ways for students to focus on the in-class discussion, knowing they can revisit important topics later. Lecture Capture enables you to

* Record and distribute your lecture with the click of a button.
* Record and index PowerPoint presentations and anything shown on your computer so it is easily searchable, frame by frame.

- Offer access to lectures anytime and anywhere by computer, iPod, or mobile device.
- Increase intent listening and class participation by easing students' concerns about note taking. Lecture Capture makes it more likely you will see students' faces, not the tops of their heads.

McGRAW-HILL CONNECT PLUS ECONOMICS   McGraw-Hill reinvents the textbook learning experience for the modern student with *Connect Plus Economics*. A seamless integration of an eBook and *Connect Economics*, *Connect Plus Economics* provides all of the *Connect Economics* features plus the following:

- An integrated eBook, allowing for anytime, anywhere access to the textbook.
- Dynamic links between the problems or questions you assign to your students and the location in the eBook where that problem or question is covered.
- A powerful search function to pinpoint and connect key concepts in a snap.

In short, *Connect Economics* offers you and your students powerful tools and features that optimize your time and energies, enabling you to focus on course content, teaching, and student learning. *Connect Economics* also offers a wealth of content resources for both instructors and students. This state-of-the-art, thoroughly tested system supports you in preparing students for the world that awaits.

For more information about Connect, go to **www.mcgrawhillconnect.com,** or contact your local McGraw-Hill sales representative.

LearnSmart Advantage

New from McGraw-Hill Education, LearnSmart Advantage is a series of adaptive learning products fueled by LearnSmart, the most widely used and intelligent adaptive learning resource on the market. Developed to deliver demonstrable results in boosting grades, increasing course retention, and strengthening memory recall, the LearnSmart Advantage series spans the entire learning process, from course preparation to the first adaptive reading experience. A smarter learning experience for students coupled with valuable reporting tools for instructors, LearnSmart Advantage is advancing learning like no other products in higher education today. The LearnSmart Advantage suite available with the Schiller product is as follows.

LEARNSMART   LearnSmart is one of the most effective and successful adaptive learning resources in the market today, proven to strengthen memory recall, keep students in class, and boost grades. Distinguishing what students know from what they don't, and honing in on concepts they are most likely to forget, LearnSmart continuously adapts to each student's needs by building an individual learning path so students study smarter and retain more knowledge. Reports provide valuable insight to instructors, so precious class time can be spent on higher-level concepts and discussion.

SMARTBOOK   SmartBook is the first and only adaptive reading experience available today. SmartBook changes reading from a passive and linear experience, to an engaging and dynamic one, in which students are more likely to master and retain important concepts, coming to class better prepared. Valuable reports provide instructors insight as to how students are progressing through textbook content, and are useful for shaping in-class time or assessment.

This revolutionary technology suite is available only from McGraw-Hill Education. To learn more, go to **learnsmart.prod.customer.mcgraw-hill.com** or contact your representative for a demo.

Tegrity Campus: Lectures 24/7

Tegrity Campus is a service that makes class time available 24/7 by automatically capturing every lecture in a searchable format for students to review when they study and complete assignments. With a simple one-click start-and-stop process, you capture all computer screens and corresponding audio. Students can replay any part of any class with easy-to-use browser-based viewing on a PC or Mac.

Educators know that the more students can see, hear, and experience class resources, the better they learn. In fact, studies prove it. With Tegrity Campus, students quickly recall key moments by using Tegrity Campus's unique search feature. This search helps students efficiently find what they need, when they need it, across an entire semester of class recordings. Help turn all your students' study time into learning moments immediately supported by your lecture.

To learn more about Tegrity, watch a two-minute Flash demo at **http://tegrity-campus.mhhe.com.**

ASSURANCE OF LEARNING READY

Many educational institutions today are focused on the notion of *assurance of learning,* an important element of some accreditation standards. *Essentials of Economics* is designed specifically to support your assurance of learning initiatives with a simple yet powerful solution.

Each test bank question for *Essentials of Economics* maps to a specific chapter learning objective listed in the text. You can use our test bank software, EZ Test and EZ Test Online, or in *Connect Economics* to easily query for learning objectives that directly relate to the learning objectives for your course. You can then use the reporting features of EZ Test to aggregate student results in similar fashion, making the collection and presentation of assurance of learning data simple and easy.

AACSB STATEMENT

The McGraw-Hill Companies is a proud corporate member of AACSB International. Understanding the importance and value of AACSB accreditation, *Essentials of Economics, 9e,* recognizes the curricula guidelines detailed in the AACSB standards for business accreditation by connecting selected questions in the text and the test bank to the six general knowledge and skill guidelines in the AACSB standards.

The statements contained in *Essentials of Economics, 9e,* are provided only as a guide for the users of this textbook. The AACSB leaves content coverage and assessment within the purview of individual schools, the mission of the school, and the faculty. While *Essentials of Economics, 9e,* and the teaching package make no claim of any specific AACSB qualification or evaluation, we have within *Essentials of Economics, 9e,* labeled selected questions according to the six general knowledge and skills areas.

McGRAW-HILL CUSTOMER CARE CONTACT INFORMATION

At McGraw-Hill we understand that getting the most from new technology can be challenging. That's why our services don't stop after you purchase our products. You can e-mail our product specialists 24 hours a day to get product training online. Or you can search our knowledge bank of frequently asked questions on our support website. For Customer Support, call **800-331-5094** or visit **www.mhhe.com/support.** One of our technical support analysts will be able to assist you in a timely fashion.

CourseSmart is new way for faculty to find and review eTextbooks. It's also a great option for students who are interested in accessing their course materials digitally. CourseSmart offers thousands of the most commonly adopted textbooks across hundreds of courses from a wide variety of higher education publishers. It is the only place for faculty to review and compare the full text of a textbook online. At CourseSmart, students can save up to 50 percent off the cost of a print book, reduce their impact on the environment, and gain access to powerful web tools for learning, including full text search, notes and highlighting, and e-mail tools for sharing notes between classmates. Complete tech support is also included in each title.

Finding your eBook is easy. Visit www.CourseSmart.com and search by title, author, or ISBN.

Student Study Guide

From the student's perspective, the most important text supplement is the *Study Guide*. The new *Study Guide* has been completely updated by Linda Wilson of the University of Texas at Arlington. The *Study Guide* develops quantitative skills and the use of economic terminology, and it enhances critical thinking capabilities. Each chapter of the *Study Guide* contains these features:

- *Quick review*   Key points in the text chapter are restated at the beginning of each *Study Guide* chapter.
- *Learning objectives*   The salient lessons of the text chapters are noted at the outset of each *Study Guide* chapter.
- *Using key terms*   Definitions of key terms are reviewed using a crossword puzzle format.
- *True–false questions*   Ten true–false questions are included in each chapter. They are similar to the true–false questions in the Test Bank.
- *Multiple-choice questions*   Twenty multiple-choice questions per chapter are provided. Again, the questions are similar to those in the Test Bank.
- *Problems and applications*   These exercises allow students to apply problem-solving skills to current issues and realistic events. Some questions and problems focus on the News Wire articles from the chapter.
- *Common student errors*   The basis for common student errors is explained, along with the correct principles. This unique feature is very effective in helping students discover their own mistakes.
- *Answers*   Answers to *all* problems, exercises, and questions are provided at the end of each chapter.

Instructor's Resource Manual

The *Instructor's Resource Manual* is designed to assist instructors as they cope with the demands of teaching a survey of economics in a single term. The manual has been fully updated for the ninth edition by Larry Olanrewaju of John Tyler Community College. Each chapter of the *Instructor's Resource Manual* contains the following features:

- *What is this chapter all about?*   A brief summary of the chapter.
- *New to this edition*   A list of changes and updates to the chapter since the last edition.
- *Lecture launchers*   Designed to offer suggestions on how to launch specific topics in each chapter.
- *Common student errors*   To integrate the lectures with the student *Study Guide*, this provides instructors with a brief description of some of the most common problems that students have when studying the material in each chapter.
- *News Wires*   A list of News Wires from the text is provided for easy reference.

- *Annotated outline*   An annotated outline for each chapter can be used as lecture notes.
- *Structured controversies*   Chapter-related topics are provided for sparking small group debates that require no additional reading. Also accessible on the website.
- *Mini-Debates*   Additional chapter-related debate topics that require individual students to do outside research in preparation. Also accessible on the website.
- *Mini-debate projects*   Additional projects are provided, cutting across all the chapters. These include several focus questions and outside research. Also accessible on the website.
- *Answers to the chapter questions and problems*   The *Instructor's Resource Manual* provides answers to the end-of-chapter questions and problems in the text, along with explanations of how the answers were derived.
- *Answers to Web activities*   Answers to Web activities from the textbook are provided in the *Instructor's Resource Manual* as well as on the website.
- *Media exercise*   Provides a ready-to-use homework assignment using current newspapers and/or periodicals to find articles that illustrate the specific issues.

Test Bank

The *Test Bank* to accompany *Essentials of Economics* follows the lead of the textbook in its application of economic concepts to worldwide economic issues, current real-world examples, and the role of government in the economy. The *Test Bank* has been prepared by James Roberts of Tidewater Community College. The *Test Bank* contains roughly 2,500 objective, predominantly multiple-choice questions. Each question includes a topic area reference where the underlying concept is discussed. All test bank questions have been tagged with level of difficulty, chapter learning objectives, AACSB learning categories, and Bloom's Taxonomy objectives to provide an assurance of quality learning.

PowerPoints

Mike Cohick of Collin College has prepared a concise set of Instructor and Student PowerPoint presentations to correspond with the ninth edition. The PowerPoints present the text's key content from the chapter.

Web Activities

To keep *Essentials* connected to the real world, **Web activities,** updated by Charles Newton of Houston Community College, appear on the Online Learning Center for each chapter. These require the student to access data or materials on a website and then use, summarize, or explain this external material in the context of the chapter's core economic concepts. The *Instructor's Resource Manual* provides answers to the web-based activities.

Digital Image Library

A digital image library of all figures from the textbook is available on the instructor's side of the Online Learning Center. Professors can insert the exact images from the textbook into their presentation slides or simply post them for student viewing on their course management site.

News Flashes

As up-to-date as *Essentials of Economics* is, it can't foretell the future. As the future becomes the present, however, I will write News Flashes describing major economic events and relate them to specific topics in the text. Four News Flashes are posted on our website each year (www.mhhe.com/schilleressentials9e).

Online Learning Center

The ninth edition website offers students easy access to chapter summaries, key terms, PowerPoints, and the following features that include updated content:

- Self-quizzes—15 multiple-choice questions per chapter, with a self-grading function that allows students to see results and e-mail them to the professor.
- Updated in-class debates.
- Updated extending the debate—for in-class debates, including additional reading.
- Updated debate projects—projects that provide focus questions or require outside research.

Instructors also have online access to the *Instructor's Resource Manual*, PowerPoint slides, and helpful grading resources for the Web activities, structured controversies, mini-debates, and mini-debate projects.

Premium Content

The Online Learning Center now offers students the opportunity to purchase premium content. Like an electronic study guide, the OLC Premium Content enables students to take pre- and post-tests for each chapter, as well as to download Schiller-exclusive iPod content including podcasts by Brad Schiller, practice quizzes, and chapter summaries—all accessible through the student's MP3 device. This icon in the text signifies content that can be used in the student's MP3 device.

ACKNOWLEDGMENTS

Contributing to the revision of the market-leading survey of economics textbook requires a critical eye for detail, innovative thinking, and expertise in economics. The following manuscript reviewers were generous in sharing their teaching experiences and offering suggestions for the revision:

Bob Abadie, *National College*
Vera Adamchik, *University of Houston at Victoria*
Jacqueline Agesa, *Marshall University*
Jeff Ankrom, *Wittenburg University*
J.J. Arias, *Georgia College & State University*
James Q. Aylsworth, *Lakeland Community College*
Mohsen Bahmani-Oskooee, *University of Wisconsin–Milwaukee*
Nina Banks, *Bucknell University*
John S. Banyi, *Central Virginia Community College*
Ruth M. Barney, *Edison State Community College*
Nancy Bertaux, *Xavier University*
John Bockino, *Suffolk County Community College*
T. Homer Bonitsis, *New Jersey Institute of Technology*
Judy Bowman, *Baylor University*
Jeff W. Bruns, *Bacone College*
Douglas N. Bunn, *Western Wyoming Community College*
Ron Burke, *Chadron State College*
Kimberly Burnett, *University of Hawaii–Manoa*
Tim Burson, *Queens University of Charlotte*
Hanas A. Cader, *South Carolina State University*
Raymond E. Chatterton, *Lock Haven University*

Hong-yi Chen, *Soka University of America*
Howard Chernick, *Hunter College*
Porchiung Ben Chou, *New Jersey Institute of Technology*
Jennifer L. Clark, *University of Florida*
Norman R. Cloutier, *University of Wisconsin–Parkside*
Mike Cohick, *Collin County Community College–Plano*
James M. Craven, *Clark College*
Tom Creahan, *Morehead State University*
Kenneth Cross, *Southwest Virginia Community College*
Patrick Cunningham, *Arizona Western College*
Dean Danielson, *San Joaquin Delta College*
Ribhi M. Daoud, *Sinclair Community College*
Amlan Datta, *Cisco College & Texas Tech University*
Susan Doty, *University of Southern Mississippi*
Kevin Dunagan, *Oakton College*
James Dyal, *Indiana University of Pennsylvania*
Angela Dzata, *Alabama State University*
Erick Elder, *University of Arkansas at Little Rock*
Vanessa Enoch, *National College*
Maxwell O. Eseonu, *Virginia State University*
Jose Esteban, *Palomar College*
Bill Everett, *Baton Rouge Community College*
Randall K. Filer, *Hunter College*
John Finley, *Columbus State University*
Daisy Foxx, *Fayetteville Technical Community College*
Scott Freehafer, *The University of Findlay*
Arlene Geiger, *John Jay College*
Lisa George, *Hunter College*
Chris Gingrich, *Eastern Mennonite University*
Yong U. Glasure, *University of Houston–Victoria*
Devra Golbe, *Hunter College*
Emilio Gomez, *Palomar College*
Anthony J. Greco, *University of Louisiana–Lafayette*
Cole Gustafson, *North Dakota State University*
Sheryl Hadley, *Johnson County Community College*
Patrick Hafford, *Wentworth Institute of Technology*
John Heywood, *University of Wisconsin-Milwaukee*
Jim Holcomb, *University of Texas at El Paso*
Philip Holleran, *Radford University*
Ward Hooker, *Orangeburg–Calhoun Technical College*
Yu Hsing, *Southeastern Louisiana University*
Syed Hussain, *University of Wisconsin*
Hans Isakson, *University of Northern Iowa*
Allan Jenkins, *University of Nebraska–Kearney*
Derek M. Johnson, *University of Connecticut*
Bang Nam Jeon, *Drexel University*
Hyojin Jeong, *Lakeland Community College*
Sean LaCroix, *Tidewater Community College*
Willis Lewis, Jr., *Lander University*
Dan Jubinski, *St. Joseph's University*
Judy Kamm, *Lindenwood University*
Jimmy Kelsey, *Whatcom Community College*
R.E. Kingery, *Hawkeye Community College*
Allen Klingenberg, *Ottawa University–Milwaukee*
Shon Kraley, *Lower Columbia College*

Richard Langlois, *University of Connecticut*
Teresa L. C. Laughlin, *Palomar College*
Joshua Long, *Ivy Tech Community College*
B. Tim Lowder, *Florence–Darlington Technical College*
Kjartan T. Magnusson, *Salt Lake Community College*
Tim Mahoney, *University of Southern Indiana*
Michael L. Marlow, *California Polytechnic State University*
Vincent Marra, *University of Delaware*
Mike Mathea, *Saint Charles Community College*
Richard McIntyre, *University of Rhode Island*
Tom Menendez, *Las Positas College*
Amlan Mitra, *Purdue University–Calumet–Hammond*
Robert Moden, *Central Virginia Community College*
Carl Montano, *Lamar University*
Daniel Morvey, *Piedmont Technical College*
John Mundy, *University of North Florida*
Jamal Nahavandi, *Pfeiffer University*
Diane R. Neylan, *Virginia Commonwealth University*
Henry K. Nishimoto, *Fresno City College*
Gerald Nyambane, *Davenport University*
Diana K. Osborne, *Spokane Community College*
Shawn Osell, *Minnesota State University–Mankato*
William M. Penn, *Belhaven College*
Diana Petersdorf, *University of Wisconsin–Stout*
James Peyton, *Highline Community College*
Ron Presley, *Webster University*
Patrick R. Price, *University of Louisiana at Lafayette*
Janet Ratliff, *Morehead State University*
David Reed, *Western Technical College*
Mitchell H. Redlo, *Monroe Community College*
Terry L. Riddle, *Central Virginia Community College*
Jean Rodgers, *Wenatchee Valley College at Omak*
Vicki D. Rostedt, *University of Akron*
Terry Rotschafer, *Minnesota West Community and Technical College–Worthington*
Matthew Rousu, *Susquehanna University*
Sara Saderion, *Houston Community College–Southwest*
George Samuels, *Sam Houston State University*
Mustafa Sawani, *Truman State University*
Joseph A. Schellings, *Wentworth Institute of Technology*
Lee J. Van Scyoc, *University of Wisconsin–Oshkosh*
Dennis D. Shannon, *Southwestern Illinois College*
William L. Sherrill, *Tidewater Community College*
Gail Shipley, *El Paso Community College*
Johnny Shull, *Central Carolina Community College*
James Smyth, *San Diego Mesa College*
John Somers, *Portland Community College–Sylvania*
Rebecca Stein, *University of Pennsylvania*
Carol Ogden Stivender, *University of North Carolina–Charlotte*
Carolyn Stumph, *Indiana University Purdue University–Fort Wayne*
James Tallant, *Cape Fear Community College*
Frank Tenkorang, *University of Nebraska–Kearney*
Audrey Thompson, *Florida State University*
Ryan Umbeck, *Ivy Tech Community College*
Darlene Voeltz, *Rochester Community & Technical College*
Yongqing Wang, *University of Wisconsin–Waukesha*

Dale W. Warnke, *College of Lake County*
Nissan Wasfie, *Columbia College–Chicago*
Luther G. White, *Central Carolina Community College*
Mary Lois White, *Albright College*
Dave Wilderman, *Wabash Valley College*
Amy Wolaver, *Bucknell University*
King Yik, *Idaho State University*
Yongjing Zhang, *Midwestern State University*
Richard Zuber, *University of North Carolina–Charlotte*

At McGraw-Hill, I have been fortunate once again to have Harvey Yep shepherd the manuscript through the many stages of production. His willingness and ability to generate perfect pages from my imperfect manuscript is remarkable. Casey Rasch deserves considerable credit for coordinating the many pieces of the publication package, including the digital supplements. In regards to the digital content I am indebted to Cynthia Hill for her contributions to the Connect homework and LearnSmart content and to Ian Taylor for improving the digital compatibility of the end-of-chapter problems. Scott Smith, my brand manager, deserves ample credit for recruiting and managing the entire production team. Now I place the success of this edition into the capable hands of Katie Hoenicke and Jen Jelinski, whose marvelous marketing efforts have kept this text at the top of the sales charts.

FINAL THOUGHTS

I am deeply grateful for the enormous success *Essentials* has enjoyed. Since its first publication, it has been the dominant text in the one-semester survey course. I hope that its brevity, content, style, and novel features will keep it at the top of the charts for years to come. The ultimate measure of the book's success, however, will be reflected in student motivation and learning. As the author, I would appreciate hearing how well *Essentials* lives up to that standard.

Bradley R. Schiller

CONTENTS IN BRIEF

CONTENTS

Section II MICROECONOMICS

Section IV INTERNATIONAL

Chapter 17
INTERNATIONAL TRADE 342

Essentials *of* Economics

1

The Challenge of Economics

PUBLISHED BY CURRIER & IVES   Copyright 1876 by Currier & Ives, N.Y.   125 NASSAU ST. NEW YORK

THE PROGRESS OF THE CENTURY.
THE LIGHTNING STEAM PRESS.   THE ELECTRIC TELEGRAPH.   THE LOCOMOTIVE.   THE STEAMBOAT.

◀ Practice quizzes, student PowerPoints, author podcasts, web activities, and additional materials available at www.mhhe.com/schilleressentials9e, or scan here. Need a barcode reader? Try ScanLife, available in your app store.

LEARNING OBJECTIVES

After reading this chapter, you should be able to:

1   Explain the meaning of scarcity.
2   Define opportunity cost.
3   Recite society's three core economic questions.
4   Discuss how market and command economies differ.
5   Describe the nature of market and government failure.

The twentieth century was very good to the United States of America. At the beginning of that century, life was hard and short. Life expectancy was only 47 years for whites and a shockingly low 33 years for blacks and other minorities. People who survived infancy faced substantial risk of early death from tuberculosis, influenza, pneumonia, or gastritis. Measles, syphilis, whooping cough, malaria, typhoid, and smallpox were all life-threatening diseases at the turn of the last century.

Work was a lot harder back then, too. In 1900 one-third of all U.S. families lived on farms, where the workday began before sunrise and lasted all day. Those who lived in cities typically worked 60 hours a week for wages of only 22 cents an hour. Hours were long, jobs were physically demanding, and workplaces were often dirty and unsafe.

Library of Congress Prints and Photographs Division
(LC-DIG-nclc-01133)

People didn't have much to show for all that work. By today's standards nearly everyone was poor back then. The average income per person was less than $4,000 per year (in today's dollars). Very few people had telephones, and even fewer had cars. There were no television sets, no home freezers, no microwaves, no dishwashers or central air conditioning, and no computers. Even indoor plumbing was a luxury. Only a small elite went to college; an eighth-grade education was the norm.

All this, of course, sounds like ancient history. Today most of us take new cars, central air and heat, remote-control TVs, flush toilets, smartphones, college attendance, and even long weekends for granted. We seldom imagine what life would be like without the abundance of goods and services we encounter daily. Nor do we often ponder how hard work might still be had factories, offices, and homes not been transformed by technology.

HOW DID WE GET SO RICH?

We ought to ponder, however, how we got so affluent. Billions of people around the world are still as poor as we were in 1900. How did we get so rich? Was it our high moral standards that made us rich? Was it our religious convictions? Did politics have anything to do with it? Did extending suffrage to women, ending prohibition, or repealing the military draft raise our living standards? Did the many wars fought in the twentieth century enhance our material well-being? Was the tremendous expansion of the public sector the catalyst for growth? Were we just lucky?

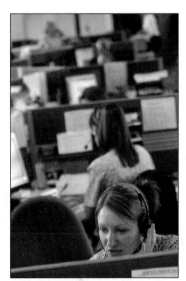

Technology has transformed work.
Ingram Publishing

Some people say America has prospered because our nation was blessed with an abundance of natural resources. But other countries are larger. Many others have more oil, more arable land, more gold, more people, and more math majors. Yet few nations have prospered as much as the United States.

Students of history can't ignore the role that economic *systems* might have played in these developments. Way back in 1776 the English economist Adam Smith asserted that a free market economy would best promote economic growth and raise living standards. As he saw it, people who own a business want to make a profit. To do so, they have to create new products, improve old ones, reduce costs and prices, and advance technology. As this happens, the economy grows, more jobs are created, and living standards rise. *Market capitalism*, Adam Smith reasoned, would foster prosperity.

Karl Marx, a German philosopher, had a very different view of market capitalism. Marx predicted that the *capitalist system* of private ownership would eventually self-destruct. The capitalists who owned the land, the factories, and the machinery would keep wages low and their own lifestyles high. They would continue exploiting the working class until it rose up and overthrew the social order. Long-term prosperity would be possible only if the *state* owned the means of production and managed the economy—a *communist system*.

Subsequent history gave Adam Smith the upper hand. The "working class" that Marx worried so much about now own their own homes, a couple of cars, flat-screen TVs, and smartphones, and they take expensive vacations they locate on the Internet. By contrast, the nations that adopted Marxist systems—Russia, China, North Korea, East Germany, Cuba—fell behind more market-oriented economies. The gap in living standards between communist and capitalist nations got so wide that communism effectively collapsed. People in those countries wanted a different economic system—one that would deliver the goods capitalist consumers were already enjoying. In the last decade of the twentieth century, formerly communist nations scrambled to transform their economies from centrally planned ones to more market-oriented systems. They sought the rules, the mechanisms, the engine that would propel their living standards upward.

Even in the United States the quest for greater prosperity continues. As rich as we are, we always want more. Our materialistic desires, its seems, continue to outpace our ever-rising incomes. We've got to have the newest iPhone, a larger TV, a bigger home, a faster car, and a more exotic vacation. Even multimillionaires say they need much more money to live comfortably (see the accompanying News Wire).

How can any economy keep pace with these ever-rising expectations? Will the economy keep churning out more goods and services every year like some perpetual motion machine? Or will we run out of goods, basic resources, and new technologies?

NEWS WIRE	INSATIABLE WANTS

The Big Picture
How much guarantees a worry-free future? Here's what wealthy individuals said they would need.

CURRENT NET WORTH AND VIEW OF AMOUNT
NEEDED TO LIVE COMFORTABLY
MILLIONS OF DOLLARS

CURRENT NET WORTH	NEEDED TO LIVE COMFORTABLY
$1 million+	$2.4 million
$5 million+	$10.4 million
$10 million+	$18.1 million

Data: PNC Advisors, survey of 792 people during November 2004.

Source: Reprinted from February 28, 2005, issue of Bloomberg *BusinessWeek* by special permission, Copyright © 2005 by Bloomberg L.P.

NOTE: People always want more than they have. Even multimillionaires say they don't have enough to live "comfortably."

THE GREAT RECESSION OF 2008–2009   Anxiety about the ability of the U.S. economy to crank out more goods every year spiked in 2008–2009. Indeed, the economic system screeched to a halt in September 2008, raising widespread fears about another 1930s-style Great Depression. Things didn't turn out nearly that bad, but millions of Americans lost their jobs, their savings, and even their homes in 2008–2009. As the output of the U.S. economy contracted, people's faith in the capitalist *system* plunged. By the end of 2009, only one of four American adults expected their income to increase in the next year. Worse yet, nearly one of four Americans also expected their children to have *fewer* goods and services in the future than people now do (see the News Wire). Could that happen?

People worry not only about the resilience of the economic *system* but also about resource limitations. We now depend on oil, water, and other resources to fuel our factories and irrigate our farms. What happens when we run out of these resources? Do the factories shut down? Do the farms dry up? Does economic growth stop?

An end to world economic growth would devastate people in other nations. Most people in the world have incomes far below American standards. A *billion* of the poorest inhabitants of Earth subsist on less than $3 per day—a tiny fraction of the $75,000 a year the average U.S. family enjoys. Even in China, where incomes have been rising rapidly, daily living standards are below those that U.S. families experienced in the Great Depression of the 1930s. To attain current U.S. standards of affluence, these nations need economic systems that will foster economic growth for decades to come.

Will consumers around the world get the kind of persistent economic growth the United States has enjoyed? Will living standards here and abroad rise, stagnate, or fall in future years? To answer this question, we need to know what makes economies "tick." That is the foremost goal of this course. We want to know what kind of system a "market economy" really is. How does it work? Who determines

NEWS WIRE	ECONOMIC EXPECTATIONS

Will Your Kids Be Better Off?

Question: When your children are at the age you are now, do you think their standard of living will be much better, somewhat better, about the same, somewhat worse, or much worse than yours is now?

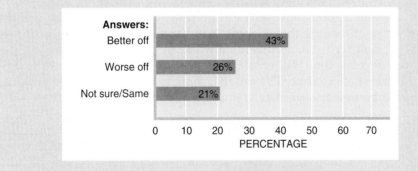

Source: Question 4, Pew Social & Demographic Trends, July 2012 Middle Class Update Survey, http://www.pewsocialtrends.org/filers/2012/08/Middle-Class-Topline-8-2-FINAL.pdf

NOTE: For living standards to keep rising, the economy must continue to grow. Will that happen? How?

the price of a textbook in a market economy? Who decides how many textbooks will be produced? Will everyone who needs a textbook get one? And why are gasoline prices so high? How about jobs? Who decides how many jobs are available or what wages they pay in a market economy? What keeps an economy growing? Or stops it in its tracks?

To understand how an economy works, we have to ask and answer a lot of questions. Among the most important are these:

- What are the basic goals of an economic system?
- How does a market economy address these goals?
- What role should government play in shaping economic outcomes?

We won't answer all of these questions in this first chapter. But we will get a sense of what the study of economics is all about and why the answers to these questions are so important.

THE CENTRAL PROBLEM OF SCARCITY

The land area of the United States stretches over 3.5 million square miles. We have a population of 320 million people, about half of whom work. We also have over $60 trillion worth of buildings and machinery. With so many resources, the United States can produce an enormous volume of output. As we've observed, however, consumers always want more. We want not only faster cars, more clothes, and larger TVs but also more roads, better schools, and more police protection. Why can't we have everything we want?

The answer is fairly simple: *our wants exceed our resources.* As abundant as our resources might appear, they are not capable of producing everything we want. The same kind of problem makes doing homework so painful. You have only 24 hours in a day. You can spend it watching movies, shopping, hanging out with friends, sleeping, tweeting, using Facebook, or doing your homework. With only 24 hours in a day, you can't do everything you want to, however: your time is *scarce.* So you must choose which activities to pursue—and which to forgo.

economics The study of how best to allocate scarce resources among competing uses.

Economics offers a framework for explaining how we make such choices. The goal of economic theory is to figure out how we can use our scarce resources in the *best possible* way.

Consider again your decision to read this chapter right now. Hopefully, you'll get some benefit from finishing it. You'll also incur a *cost,* however. The time you spend reading could be spent doing something else. You're probably missing a good show on TV right now. Giving up that show is the *opportunity cost* of reading this chapter. You have sacrificed the opportunity to watch TV in order to finish this homework. In general, whatever you decide to do with your time will entail an **opportunity cost**—that is, the sacrifice of a next-best alternative. The rational thing to do is to weigh the benefits of doing your homework against the implied opportunity cost and then make a choice.

opportunity cost The most desired goods and services that are forgone in order to obtain something else.

The larger society faces a similar dilemma. For the larger economy, time is also limited. So, too, are the resources needed to produce desired goods and services. To get more houses, more cars, or more movies, we need not only time but also resources to produce these things. These resources—land, labor, capital, and entrepreneurship—are the basic ingredients of production. They are called **factors of production.** The more factors of production we have, the more we can produce in a given period of time.

factors of production Resource inputs used to produce goods and services (land, labor, capital, and entrepreneurship).

As we've already noted, our available resources always fall short of our output desires. The central problem here again is **scarcity,** a situation where our desires for goods and services exceed our capacity to produce them.

scarcity Lack of enough resources to satisfy all desired uses of those resources.

THREE BASIC ECONOMIC QUESTIONS

The central problem of scarcity forces every society to make difficult choices. Specifically, every nation must resolve three critical questions about the use of its scarce resources:

- **WHAT** to produce.
- **HOW** to produce.
- **FOR WHOM** to produce.

We first examine the nature of each question and then look at how different countries answer these three basic questions.

WHAT to Produce

The WHAT question is quite simple. We've already noted that there isn't enough time in the day to do everything you want to. You must decide *what* to do with your time. The economy confronts a similar question: there aren't enough resources in the economy to produce all the goods and services society desires. *Because wants exceed resources, we have to decide WHAT goods and services we want most, sacrificing less desired products.*

PRODUCTION POSSIBILITIES   Figure 1.1 illustrates this basic dilemma. Suppose there are only two kinds of goods, "consumer goods" and "military goods." In this case, the question of WHAT to produce boils down to finding the most desirable combination of these two goods.

To make that selection, we first need to know how much of each good we *could* produce. That will depend on how many resources we have available. The first thing we need to do, then, is count our factors of production.

The factors of production include the following:

- **Land** (including natural resources).
- **Labor** (number and skills of workers).
- **Capital** (machinery, buildings, networks).
- **Entrepreneurship** (skill in creating products, services, and processes).

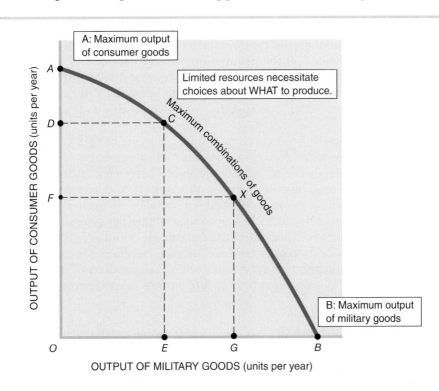

OUTPUT OF CONSUMER GOODS (units per year)

A: Maximum output of consumer goods

Limited resources necessitate choices about WHAT to produce.

Maximum combinations of goods

B: Maximum output of military goods

OUTPUT OF MILITARY GOODS (units per year)

FIGURE 1.1
A Production Possibilities Curve

A production possibilities curve describes the various combinations of final goods or services that could be produced in a given time period with available resources and technology. It represents a menu of output choices.

Point *C* indicates that we could produce a *combination* of *OD* units of consumer goods and the quantity *OE* of military output. To get more military output (e.g., at point *X*), we have to reduce consumer output (from *OD* to *OF*).

We must decide what to produce. Our goal is to select the *best* possible mix of output from the choices on the production possibilities curve.

TABLE 1.1
Specific Production
Possibilities

The choice of WHAT to produce
eventually boils down to specific
goods and services. Here the
choices are defined in terms of
missiles or houses. More missiles
can be produced only if some
resources are diverted from
home construction. Only one of
these output combinations can
be produced in a given time
period. Selecting that mix is a
basic economic issue.

Output	Possible Output Combinations					
	A	B	C	D	E	F
Missiles	0	50	100	150	200	250
Houses	100	90	75	55	30	0

The more we have of these factors, the more output we can produce. Technology
is also critical. The more advanced our technological and managerial abilities, the
more output we will be able to produce with available factors of production. If we
inventoried all our resources and technology, we could figure out what the physical *limits* to production are.

To simplify the computation, suppose we wanted to produce only consumer
goods. How much *could* we produce? Surely not an infinite amount. With *limited*
stocks of land, labor, capital, and technology, output would have a *finite* limit. The
limit is represented by point *A* in Figure 1.1. That is to say, the vertical distance
from the origin (point *O*) to point *A* represents the *maximum* quantity of consumer
goods that could be produced this year. To produce the quantity *A* of consumer
goods, we would have to use *all* available factors of production. At point *A* no resources would be available for producing military goods. The choice of *maximum*
consumer output implies *zero* military output.

We could make other choices about WHAT to produce. Point *B* illustrates another extreme. The horizontal distance from the origin (point *O*) to point *B* represents our *maximum* capacity to produce military goods. To get that much military
output, we would have to devote *all* available resources to that single task. At
point *B*, we wouldn't be producing *any* consumer goods. We would be well protected but ill nourished and poorly clothed (wearing last year's clothes).

Our choices about WHAT to produce are not limited to the extremes of points
A and *B*. We could instead produce a *combination* of consumer and military goods.
Point *C* represents one such combination. To get to point *C*, we have to forsake
maximum consumer goods output (point *A*) and use some of our scarce resources
to produce military goods. At point *C* we are producing only *OD* of consumer
goods and *OE* of military goods.

Point *C* is just one of many combinations we *could* produce. We could produce *any* combination of output represented by points along the curve in Figure
1.1. For this reason we call it the **production possibilities** curve; it represents
the alternative combinations of goods and services that *could* be produced in a
given time period with all available resources and technology. It is, in effect, an
economic menu from which one specific combination of goods and services
must be selected.

The production possibilities curve puts the basic issue of WHAT to produce
in graphic terms. The same choices can be depicted in numerical terms as well.
Table 1.1, for example, illustrates specific trade-offs between missile production
and home construction. The output mix *A* allocates all resources to home construction, leaving nothing to produce missiles. If missiles are desired, the level of
home construction must be cut back. To produce 50 missiles (mix *B*), home construction activity must be cut back to 90. Output mixes *C* through *F* illustrate other
possible choices. Notice that every time we increase missile production (moving
from *A* to *F*), house construction must be reduced. The question of WHAT to produce boils down to choosing one specific mix of output—a specific combination of
missiles and houses.

production possibilities The
alternative combinations of
goods and services that could
be produced in a given time
period with all available
resources and technology.

THE CHOICES NATIONS MAKE   No single point on the production possibilities
curve is best for all nations at all times. In the United States, the share of total output

FIGURE 1.2   Military Share of Total U.S. Output

The share of total output devoted to national defense has risen sharply in war years and fallen in times of peace. The defense buildup of the 1980s increased the military share to more than 6 percent of total output. The end of the Cold War reversed that buildup, releasing resources for other uses (the peace dividend). The September 11, 2001, terrorist attacks on New York City and Washington, DC, altered the WHAT choice again, increasing the military's share of total output.

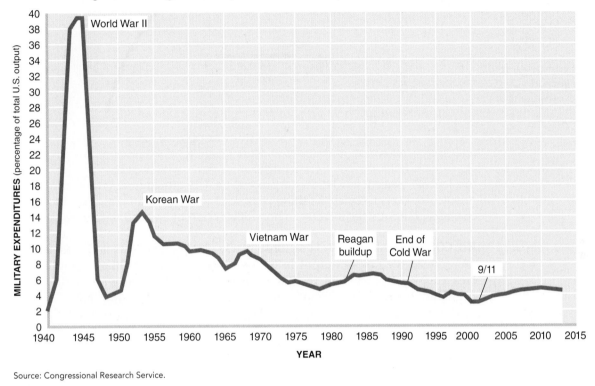

Source: Congressional Research Service.

devoted to "guns" has varied greatly. During World War II, we converted auto plants to produce military vehicles. Clothing manufacturers cut way back on consumer clothing in order to produce more uniforms for the army, navy, and air force. The government also drafted 12 million men to bear arms. By shifting resources from the production of consumer goods to the production of military goods, we were able to move down along the production possibilities curve in Figure 1.1 toward point X. By 1944 fully 40 percent of all our output consisted of military goods. Consumer goods were so scarce that everything from butter to golf balls had to be rationed.

Figure 1.2 illustrates that rapid military buildup during World War II. The figure also illustrates how quickly we reallocated factors of production to consumer goods after the war ended. By 1948 less than 4 percent of U.S. output was military goods. We had moved close to point *A* in Figure 1.1.

PEACE DIVIDENDS   We changed the mix of output dramatically again to fight the Korean War. In 1953 military output absorbed nearly 15 percent of America's total production. That would amount to nearly $2 *trillion* of annual defense spending in today's dollars and output levels. We're not spending anywhere near that kind of military money, however. After the Korean War, the share of U.S. output allocated to the military trended sharply downward. Despite the buildup for the Vietnam War (1966–1968), the share of output devoted to "guns" fell from 15 percent in 1953

FIGURE 1.3
The Cost of War

An increase in military output absorbs factors of production that could be used to produce consumer goods. The military buildup associated with the move from point R to point S reduces consumption output from C_1 to C_2.

The economic cost of war is measured by the implied reduction in nondefense output ("less butter").

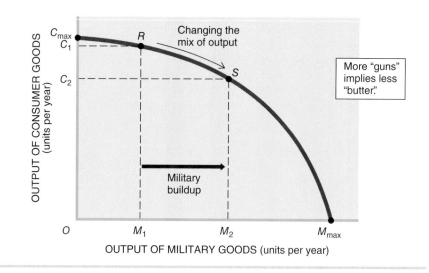

to a low of 3 percent in 2001. In the process, the U.S. armed forces were reduced by nearly 600,000 personnel. As those personnel found civilian jobs, they increased consumer output. That increase in nonmilitary output is called the *peace dividend*.

THE COST OF WAR The 9/11 terrorist attacks on New York City and Washington, DC, moved the mix of output in the opposite direction. Military spending increased by 50 percent in the three years after 9/11. The wars in Iraq and Afghanistan absorbed even more resources. The *economic* cost of those efforts is measured in lost consumer output. The money spent by the government on war might otherwise have been spent on schools, highways, or other nondefense projects. The National Guard personnel called up for the war would otherwise have stayed home and produced consumer goods (including disaster relief). These costs of war are illustrated in Figure 1.3. Notice how consumer goods output declines (from C_1 to C_2) when military output increases (from M_1 to M_2).

In some countries the opportunity cost of military output seems far too high. North Korea, for example, has the fourth largest army in the world. Yet North Korea is a relatively small country. Consequently it must allocate a huge share of its resources to feed, clothe, and arm its military. As Figure 1.4 illustrates,

FIGURE 1.4   The Military Share of Output

The share of output allocated to the military indicates the opportunity cost of maintaining an army. North Korea has the highest cost, using nearly 15 percent of its resources for military purposes. Although China and the United States have much larger armies, their military *share* of output is much smaller.

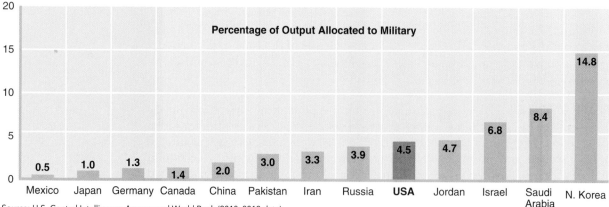

Source: U.S. Central Intelligence Agency and World Bank (2010–2012 data).

NEWS WIRE	OPPORTUNITY COST

North Korea's Rocket Launches Cost $1.3 Billion

Hong Kong (CNN)—While only the highest echelons of North Korea's opaque leadership will know the full financial cost of Wednesday's launch, South Korea's government estimates Pyongyang spent $1.3 billion on its rocket program this year.

The two rockets launched this year—this week's mission and a failed attempt in April—cost $600 million, while the launch site itself is estimated at $400 million. Other related facilities add another $300 million, according to an official from South Korea's Ministry of Unification. "This is equivalent to acquiring 4.6 million tons of corn," the official said. "If this was used for solving the food shortage issue, North Koreans would not have to worry about food for four to five years."

Source: CNN.com, December 12, 2012 © 2012 Cable News Network, Inc. All rights reserved.

NOTE: North Korea's inability to feed itself is due in part to its large army and missile program. Resources used for the military aren't available for producing food.

15 percent of North Korean output consists of military goods and services. That compares with a military share of only 4.5 percent in the United States.

North Korea's military has a high price tag. North Korea is a very poor country, with output per capita in the neighborhood of $1,000 per year. That is substantially less than the American standard of living was in 1900 and a tiny fraction of today's U.S. output per capita (around $50,000). Although one-third of North Korea's population lives on farms, the country cannot grow enough food to feed its population. The farm sector needs more machinery, seeds, and fertilizer; better-trained labor; and improved irrigation systems. So long as the military absorbs one-seventh of total output, however, North Korea can't afford to modernize its farm sector. The implied shortfall in food and other consumer goods is the *opportunity cost* of a large military sector (see News Wire).

Topic Podcast:
Opportunity Cost

THE BEST POSSIBLE MIX   Ultimately the designation of any particular mix of output as "best" rests on the value judgments of a society. A militaristic society would prefer a mix of output closer to point *B* in Figure 1.1. By contrast, Iceland has no military and so produces at point *A*. In general, *one specific mix of output is optimal for a country*—that is, a mix that represents the *best* possible allocation of resources across competing uses. Locating and producing that *optimal* mix of output is the essence of the WHAT challenge.

The same desire for an optimal mix of output drives your decisions on the use of scarce time. There is only one *best* way to use your time on any given day. If you use your time in that way, you will maximize your well-being. Other uses won't necessarily kill you, but they won't do you as much good.

ECONOMIC GROWTH   The selection of an optimal mix depends in part on how future-oriented one is. If you had no concern for future jobs or income, there would be little point in doing homework now. You might as well play all day if you're that present-oriented. On the other hand, if you value future jobs and income, it

What else might these North Korean women be producing?
Associated Press

FIGURE 1.5
Economic Growth

Since 1900 the U.S. population has quadrupled. Investment in machinery and buildings has increased our capital stock even faster. These additional factors of production, together with advancing technology, have expanded (shifted outward) our production possibilities.

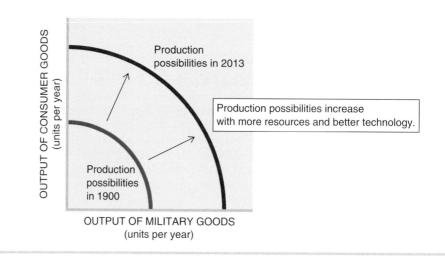

OUTPUT OF CONSUMER GOODS (units per year)

Production possibilities in 2013

Production possibilities increase with more resources and better technology.

Production possibilities in 1900

OUTPUT OF MILITARY GOODS (units per year)

investment Expenditures on (production of) new plant and equipment (capital) in a given time period, plus changes in business inventories.

economic growth An increase in output (real GDP): an expansion of production possibilities.

makes sense to allocate some present time to studying. Then you'll have more human capital (knowledge and skills) later to pursue job opportunities.

The larger society confronts the same choice between present and future consumption. We *could* use all our resources to produce consumer goods this year. If we did, however, there wouldn't be any factors of production available to build machinery, factories, or telecommunications networks. Yet these are the kinds of **investment** that enhance our capacity to produce. If we want the economy to keep growing—and our living standards to rise—we must allocate some of our scarce resources to investment rather than current consumption. The resultant **economic growth** will expand our production possibilities outward, allowing us to produce *more* goods in future years. The phenomenon of economic growth is illustrated in Figure 1.5 by the outward *shift* of the production-possibilities curve. Such shifts occur when we acquire *more* resources (e.g., more machinery) or *better* technology. Our decision about WHAT to produce must take future growth into account.

HOW to Produce

The second basic economic question concerns HOW we produce output. Should this class be taught in an auditorium or in small discussion sections? Should it meet twice a week or only once? Should the instructor make more use of computer aids? Should, heaven forbid, this textbook be replaced with online text files? There are numerous ways of teaching a course. Of these many possibilities, one way is presumably best, given the resources and technology available. That best way is HOW we want the course taught. Educational researchers and a good many instructors spend a lot of time trying to figure out the best way of teaching a course.

Pig farmers do the same thing. They know they can fatten pigs up with a lot of different grains and other food. They can also vary breeding patterns, light exposure, and heat. They can use more labor in the feeder process or more machinery. Faced with so many choices, the pig farmers try to find the *best* way of raising pigs.

Should pig farmers be free to breed pigs and to dispose of waste in any way they desire? Or should the government regulate how pigs are produced?

© Royalty-Free/Corbis/DAL

The HOW question isn't just an issue of getting more output from available inputs. It also encompasses our use of the environment. Should the waste from pig farms be allowed to contaminate the air, groundwater, or local waterways? Or do we want to keep the water clean for other uses? Humanitarian concerns may also come into play. Should live pigs be processed without any concern for their welfare? Or should the processing be designed to minimize trauma? The HOW question encompasses all such issues. Although people may hold different views on these questions, everyone shares a common goal: *to find an optimal method of producing goods and services.* The best possible answer to the HOW question will entail both efficiency in the use of factors of production and adequate safeguards for the environment and other social concerns. Our goal is to find that answer.

FOR WHOM to Produce

The third basic economic question every society must confront is FOR WHOM? The answers to the WHAT and HOW questions determine how large an economic pie we'll bake and how we'll bake it. Then we have to slice it up. Should everyone get an equal slice of the pie? Or can some people have big pieces of the pie while others get only crumbs? In other words, *the FOR WHOM question focuses on how an economy's output is distributed across members of society.*

A pie can be divided up in many ways. Personally, I like a distribution that gives me a big slice even if that leaves less for others. Maybe you feel the same way. Whatever your feelings, however, there is likely to be a lot of disagreement about what distribution is best. Maybe we should just give everyone an equal slice. But should everyone get an equal slice even if some people helped bake the pie while others contributed nothing? The Little Red Hen of the children's fable felt perfectly justified eating all the bread she made herself after her friends and neighbors refused to help sow the seeds, harvest the grain, or bake it. Should such a work-based sense of equity determine how all goods are distributed?

Karl Marx's communist vision of utopia entailed a very different FOR WHOM answer. The communist ideal is "From each according to his ability, to each according to his need." In that vision, all pitch in to bake the pie according to their abilities. Slices of the pie are distributed, however, based on need (hunger, desire) rather than on productive contributions. In a communal utopia there is no direct link between work and consumption.

INCENTIVES   There is a risk entailed in distributing slices of the pie based on need rather than work effort. People who work hard to bake the pie may feel cheated if nonworkers get just as large a slice. Worse still, people may decide to exert less effort if they see no tangible reward to working. If that happens, the size of the pie may shrink, and everyone will be worse off.

This is the kind of problem income transfer programs create. Government-paid income transfers (e.g., welfare, unemployment benefits, Social Security) are intended to provide a slice of the pie to people who don't have enough income to satisfy basic needs. As benefits rise, however, the incentive to work diminishes. If people choose welfare checks over paychecks, total output will decline.

The same problem emerges in the tax system. If Paul is heavily taxed to provide welfare benefits to Peter, Paul may decide that hard work and entrepreneurship don't pay. To the extent that taxes discourage work, production, or investment, they shrink the size of the pie that feeds all of us.

The potential trade-offs between taxes, income transfers, and work don't compel us to dismantle all tax and welfare programs. They do emphasize, however, how difficult it is to select the right answer to the FOR WHOM question. The *optimal* distribution of income must satisfy our sense of fairness as well as our desire for more output.

THE MECHANISMS OF CHOICE

By now, two things should be apparent. First, every society has to make difficult choices about WHAT, HOW, and FOR WHOM to produce. Second, those choices aren't easy. *Every choice involves conflicts and trade-offs.* More of one good implies less of another. A more efficient production process may pollute the environment. Helping the poor may dull work incentives. In every case, society has to weigh the alternatives and try to find the best possible answer to each question.

How does "society" actually make such choices? What are the mechanisms we use to decide WHAT to produce, HOW, and FOR WHOM?

The Political Process

Many of these basic economic decisions are made through the political process. Consider again the decision to increase the military share of output after 9/11. Who made that decision? Not me. Not you. Not the mass of consumers who were streaming through real and virtual malls. No, the decisions on military buildups and builddowns are made in the political arena: the U.S. Congress makes those decisions. Congress also makes decisions about how many interstate highways to build, how many Head Start classes to offer, and how much space exploration to pursue.

Should *all* decisions about WHAT to produce be made in the political arena? Should Congress also decide how much ice cream will be produced and how many DVRs? What about essentials like food and shelter? Should decisions about the production of those goods be made in Washington, DC, or should the mix of output be selected some other way?

The Market Mechanism

The market mechanism offers an alternative decision-making process. In a market-driven economy the process of selecting a mix of output is as familiar as grocery shopping. If you desire ice cream and have sufficient income, you simply buy ice cream. Your purchases signal to producers that ice cream is desired. By expressing the *ability and willingness to pay* for ice cream, you are telling ice cream producers that their efforts are going to be rewarded. If enough consumers feel the same way you do—and are able and willing to pay the price of ice cream—ice cream producers will churn out more ice cream.

The same kind of interaction helps determine which crops we grow. There is only so much good farmland available. Should we grow corn or beans? If consumers prefer corn, they will buy more corn and shun the beans. Farmers will quickly get the market's message and devote more of their land to corn, cutting back on bean production. In the process, the mix of output will change—moving us closer to the choice consumers have made.

market mechanism The use of market prices and sales to signal desired outputs (or resource allocations).

The central actor in this reshuffling of resources and outputs is the **market mechanism.** *Market sales and prices send a signal to producers about what mix of output consumers want.* If you want something and have sufficient income, you buy it. If enough people do the same thing, total sales of that product will rise, and perhaps its price will as well. Producers, seeing sales and prices rise, will want to increase production. To do so, they will acquire more resources and use them to change the mix of output. No direct communication between us and the producer is required; market sales and prices convey the message and direct the market, much like an "invisible hand."

It was this ability of "the market" to select a desirable mix of output that so impressed the eighteenth-century economist Adam Smith. He argued that nations would prosper with less government interference and more reliance on the invisible hand of the marketplace. As he saw it, markets were efficient mechanisms for deciding what goods to produce, how to produce them, and even what wages to pay. Smith's writings (*The Wealth of Nations*, 1776) urged government to pursue a policy of **laissez faire**—leaving the market alone to make basic economic decisions.

laissez faire The doctrine of "leave it alone," of nonintervention by government in the market mechanism.

Central Planning

Karl Marx saw things differently. In his view, a freewheeling marketplace would cater to the whims of the rich and neglect the needs of the poor. Workers would be exploited by industrial barons and great landowners. To "leave it to the market," as Smith had proposed, would encourage exploitation. In the mid-nineteenth century, Karl Marx proposed a radical alternative: overturn the power of the elite and create a communist state in which everyone's needs would be fulfilled. Marx's writings (*Das Kapital*, 1867) encouraged communist revolutions and the development of central planning systems. The (people's) government, not the market, assumed responsibility for deciding what goods were produced, at what prices they were sold, and even who got them.

Central planning is still the principal mechanism of choice in some countries. In North Korea and Cuba, for example, the central planners decide how many cars and how much bread to produce. They then assign workers and other resources to those industries to implement their decisions. They also decide who will get the bread and the cars that are produced. Individuals cannot own factors of production or even employ other workers for wages. The WHAT, HOW, and FOR WHOM outcomes are all directed by the central government.

Mixed Economies

Few countries still depend so fully on central planners (government) to make basic economic decisions. China, Russia, and other formerly communist nations have turned over many decisions to the market mechanism. Likewise, no nation relies exclusively on markets to fashion economic outcomes. In the United States, for example, we let the market decide how much ice cream will be produced and how many cars. We use the political process, however, to decide how many highways to construct, how many schools to build, and how much military output to produce.

Because most nations use a combination of government directives and market mechanisms to determine economic outcomes, they are called **mixed economies.** There is huge variation in that mix, however. The government-dominated economic systems in North Korea, Cuba, Laos, and Libya are starkly different from the free-wheeling economies of Singapore, Bahrain, New Zealand, and the United States.

mixed economy An economy that uses both market and non-market signals to allocate goods and resources.

WHAT ECONOMICS IS ALL ABOUT

The different economic systems employed around the world are all intended to give the right answers to the WHAT, HOW, and FOR WHOM questions. It is apparent, however, that they don't always succeed. We have too much poverty and too much pollution. There are often too few jobs and pitifully small paychecks. A third of the world's population still lives in abject poverty.

Economists try to explain how these various outcomes emerge. Why are some nations so much more prosperous than others? What forces cause economic downturns in both rich and poor nations? What causes prices to go up and down so often? How can economies grow without destroying the environment?

An unregulated market might generate too much pollution. Such a market failure requires government intervention.

© Patrick Clark/Getty Images/DAL

Market Failure

In studying these questions, economists recognize that neither markets nor governments always have the right answers. On the contrary, we know that a completely private market economy can give us the *wrong* answers to the WHAT, HOW, and FOR WHOM questions on occasion. A completely free market economy might produce too many luxury cars and too few hospitals. Unregulated producers might destroy the environment. A freewheeling market economy might neglect the needs of the poor. When the market mechanism gives us these kinds of suboptimal answers, we say the market has *failed*. **Market failure** occurs when the market mechanism does not generate the best possible (optimal) answers to the WHAT, HOW, and FOR WHOM questions.

market failure A situation in which the market mechanism generates suboptimal economic outcomes.

Government Failure

When market failure occurs, there is usually a call for the government to "fix" the failure. This may or may not be a good response. Government intervention doesn't always work out so well. Indeed, economists warn that government intervention can fail as well. **Government failure** occurs when intervention fails to improve—or actually worsens—economic outcomes. The possibility of government failure is sufficient warning that **there is no guarantee that the visible hand of government will be any better than the invisible hand of the marketplace**.

government failure Government intervention that fails to improve economic outcomes.

Economists try to figure out when markets work well and when they are likely to fail. We also try to predict whether specific government interventions will improve economic outcomes—or make them worse.

Macro versus Micro

The study of economics is typically divided into two parts: macroeconomics and microeconomics. Macroeconomics focuses on the behavior of an entire economy— the big picture. In macroeconomics we study such national goals as full employment, control of inflation, and economic growth, without worrying about the well-being or behavior of specific individuals or groups. The essential concern of **macroeconomics** is to understand and improve the performance of the economy as a whole.

macroeconomics The study of aggregate economic behavior, of the economy as a whole.

Microeconomics is concerned with the details of this big picture. In microeconomics we focus on the individuals, firms, and government agencies that actually make up the larger economy. Our interest here is in the behavior of individual economic actors. What are their goals? How can they best achieve these goals with their limited resources? How will they respond to various incentives and opportunities?

microeconomics The study of individual behavior in the economy, of the components of the larger economy.

A primary concern of macroeconomics, for example, is to determine the impact of aggregate consumer spending on total output, employment, and prices. Very little attention is devoted to the actual content of consumer spending or its determinants. Microeconomics, on the other hand, focuses on the specific expenditure decisions of individual consumers and the forces (tastes, prices, incomes) that influence those decisions.

The distinction between macro- and microeconomics is also reflected in discussions of business investment. In macroeconomics we want to know what determines the aggregate rate of business investment and how those expenditures influence the nation's total output, employment, and prices. In microeconomics we focus on the decisions of individual businesses regarding the rate of production, the choice of factors of production, and the pricing of specific goods.

The distinction between macro- and microeconomics is a matter of convenience. In reality, macroeconomic outcomes depend on micro behavior, and micro behavior is affected by macro outcomes. Hence we cannot fully understand how an economy works until we understand how all the participants behave and why they behave as they do. But just as you can drive a car without knowing how its engine is constructed, you can observe how an economy runs without completely disassembling it. In macroeconomics we observe that the car goes faster when the accelerator is depressed and that it slows when the brake is applied. That is all we need to know in most situations. There are times, however, when the car breaks down. When it does, we have to know something more about how the pedals work. This leads us into micro studies. How does each part work? Which ones can or should be fixed?

Theory versus Reality

The distinction between macroeconomics and microeconomics is one of many simplifications we make in studying economic behavior. The economy is much too vast and complex to describe and explain in one course (or one lifetime). Accordingly, we focus on basic relationships, ignoring unnecessary detail. What this means is that we formulate theories, or *models,* of economic behavior and then use those theories to evaluate and design economic policy.

The economic models that economists use to explain market behavior are like maps. To get from New York to Los Angeles, you don't need to know all the details of topography that lie between those two cities. Knowing where the interstate highways are is probably enough. An interstate route map therefore provides enough information to get you to your destination.

The same kind of simplification is used in economic models of consumer behavior. Such models assert that when the price of a good increases, consumers will buy less of it. In reality, however, people *may* buy *more* of a good at increased prices, especially if those high prices create a certain snob appeal or if prices are expected to increase still further. In predicting consumer responses to price increases, we typically ignore such possibilities by *assuming* that the price of the good in question is the *only* thing that changes. This assumption of "other things remaining equal (unchanged)" (in Latin, ***ceteris paribus***) allows us to make straightforward predictions. If instead we described consumer responses to increased prices in any and all circumstances (allowing everything to change at once), every prediction would be accompanied by a book full of exceptions and qualifications. We would look more like lawyers than economists.

ceteris paribus The assumption that nothing else changes.

Although the assumption of *ceteris paribus* makes it easier to formulate economic theory and policy, it also increases the risk of error. Obviously, if other things do change in significant ways, our predictions (and policies) may fail. But like weather forecasters, we continue to make predictions, knowing that occasional failure is inevitable. In so doing, we are motivated by the conviction that it is better to be approximately right than to be dead wrong.

Politics versus Economics

Politicians cannot afford to be quite so complacent about predictions. Policy decisions must be made every day. And a politician's continued tenure in office may depend on being more than approximately right. Economists contribute to those policy decisions by offering measures of economic impact and predictions of economic behavior. But in the real world, those measures and predictions always contain a substantial margin of error.

Even if the future were known, economic policy could not rely completely on economic theory. There are always political choices to be made. The choice of more consumer goods ("butter") or more military hardware ("guns"), for example, is not an economic decision. Rather it is a sociopolitical decision based in part on economic trade-offs (opportunity costs). The "need" for more butter or more guns must be expressed politically—ends versus means again. Political forces are a necessary ingredient in economic policy decisions. That is not to say that all political decisions are right. It does suggest, however, that economic policies may not always conform to economic theory.

Both politics and economics are involved in the continuing debate about laissez faire and government intervention. The pendulum has swung from laissez faire (Adam Smith) to central government control (Karl Marx) and to an ill-defined middle ground where the government assumes major responsibilities for economic stability (John Maynard Keynes) and for answers to the WHAT, HOW, and FOR WHOM questions. In the 1980s the Reagan administration pushed the pendulum a bit closer to laissez faire by cutting taxes, reducing government regulation, and encouraging market incentives.

President Clinton thought the government should play a more active role in resolving basic economic issues. His "Vision for America" spelled out a bigger role for government in ensuring health care, providing skills training, protecting the environment, and regulating working conditions. In this vision, well-intentioned government officials could correct market failures. President George W. Bush favored less government intervention and more reliance on the market mechanism. The debate over market reliance versus government intervention again heated up in the 2012 presidential campaign, especially on issues of health care, job protection, and global warming. President Obama made it clear that he believes *more* government intervention and *less* market reliance are needed to attain the right WHAT, HOW, and FOR WHOM answers.

The debate over markets versus government persists in part because of gaps in our economic understanding. For over 200 years economists have been arguing about what makes the economy tick. None of the competing theories have performed spectacularly well. Indeed, few economists have successfully predicted major economic events with any consistency. Even annual forecasts of inflation, unemployment, and output are regularly in error. Worse still, there are never-ending arguments about what caused a major economic event long after it occurred. In fact, economists are still arguing over the causes of not only the Great Recession of 2008–2009 but even the Great Depression of the 1930s! Did government failure or market failure cause and deepen those economic setbacks?

Modest Expectations

In view of all these debates and uncertainties, you should not expect to learn everything there is to know about the economy in this text or course. Our goals are more modest. We want you to develop some perspective on economic behavior and an understanding of basic principles. With this foundation, you should acquire a better view of how the economy works. Daily news reports on economic events should make more sense. Political debates on tax and budget policies should take on more meaning. You may even develop some insights that you can apply toward running a business or planning a career.

POLICY PERSPECTIVES

Is "Free" Health Care Really Free?

Everyone wants more and better health care, and nearly everyone agrees that even the poorest members of society need reliable access to doctors and hospitals. That's why President Obama made health care reform such a high priority in his first presidential year.

Although the political debate over health care reform was intense and multidimensional, the economics of health care are fairly simple. In essence, President Obama wanted to *expand* the health care industry. He wanted to increase access for the millions of Americans who didn't have health insurance and raise the level of service for people with low incomes and preexisting illnesses. He wasn't proposing to *reduce* health care for those who already had adequate care. Thus his reform proposals entailed a net increase in health care services.

Were health care a free good, everyone would have welcomed President Obama's reforms. But the most fundamental concept in economics is this: *There is no free lunch.* Resources used to prepare and serve even a "free" lunch could be used to produce something else. So it is with health care. The resources used to expand health care services could be used to produce something else. The *opportunity costs* of expanded health care are the other goods we could have produced (and consumed) with the same resources.

© Photodisc/Getty Images/DAL

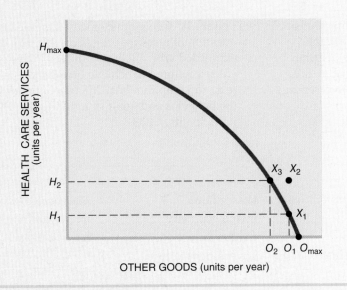

FIGURE 1.6
No Free Health Care

Health care absorbs resources that can be used to produce other goods. Increasing health care services from H_1 to H_2 requires a reduction in other goods from O_1 to O_2.

Figure 1.6 illustrates the basic policy dilemma. In 2013 health care services absorbed about 16 percent of total U.S. output. So the *mix* of output resembled point X_1, where H_1 amount of health care is produced and O_1 of other goods. President Obama's policy goal is to increase health services from H_1 to H_2. If health care were a free good, we could change the mix of output from X_1 to X_2. But X_2 lies *outside* our production possibilities curve. There aren't enough resources to produce all those other goods (O_1) *and* expanded health care. If we want more health care (H_2) we've got to cut back on other goods. That's what opportunity costs are. If we make that sacrifice, we'll end up at X_3, with more health care (H_2) and fewer other goods (O_2) than when we started (at X_1). The real political fight is over who loses those other goods (via increased taxes and fees that reduce consumers' spendable income or by cutbacks in other government services).

SUMMARY

- Every nation confronts the three basic economic questions of WHAT to produce, HOW, and FOR WHOM. **LO3**
- The need to select a single mix of output (WHAT) is necessitated by our limited capacity to produce. Scarcity results when our wants exceed our resources. **LO1**
- The production possibilities curve illustrates the limits to output dictated by available factors of production and technology. Points on the curve represent the different output mixes that we may choose. **LO1**
- All production entails an opportunity cost: we can produce more of output A only if we produce less of output B. The implied reduction in output B is the opportunity cost of output A. **LO2**
- The HOW question focuses on the choice of what inputs to use in production. It also encompasses choices made about environmental protection. **LO3**

- The FOR WHOM question concerns the distribution of output among members of society. **LO3**
- The goal of every society is to select the best possible (optimal) answers to the WHAT, HOW, and FOR WHOM questions. The optimal answers will vary with social values and production capabilities. **LO3**
- The three questions can be answered by the market mechanism, by a system of central planning, or by a mixed system of market signals and government intervention. **LO4**
- Price signals are the key feature of the market mechanism. Consumers signal their desires for specific goods by paying a price for those goods. Producers respond to the price signal by assembling factors of production to produce the desired output. **LO4**

- Market failure occurs when the market mechanism generates the wrong mix of output, undesirable methods of production, or an inequitable distribution of income. Government intervention may fail, too, however, by not improving (or even worsening) economic outcomes. **LO5**

- The study of economics focuses on the broad question of resource allocation. Macroeconomics is concerned with allocating the resources of an entire economy to achieve broad economic goals (e.g., full employment). Microeconomics focuses on the behavior and goals of individual market participants. **LO3**

TERMS TO REMEMBER

Define the following terms:

economics	production possibilities	laissez faire	macroeconomics
opportunity cost	investment	mixed economy	microeconomics
factors of production	economic growth	market failure	*ceteris paribus*
scarcity	market mechanism	government failure	

QUESTIONS FOR DISCUSSION

1. As rich as America is, how can our resources possibly be "scarce"? **LO1**
2. What opportunity costs did you incur in reading this chapter? **LO2**
3. How would you answer the question in the News Wire on page 5? Why? **LO3**
4. Why might it be necessary to reduce consumer spending in order to attain faster economic growth? Would it be worth the sacrifice? **LO2**
5. In a purely private market economy, how is the FOR WHOM question answered? Is that optimal? **LO3**
6. Why doesn't North Korea reduce its military and put more resources into food production (News Wire, page 11)? What is the optimal mix of "guns" and "butter" for a nation? **LO3**
7. If taxes on the rich were raised to provide more housing for the poor, how would the willingness to work be affected? What would happen to total output? **LO3**
8. What kind of knowledge must central planners possess to manage an economy efficiently? **LO4**
9. **POLICY PERSPECTIVES** Why can't we produce at point X_2 in Figure 1.6? Will we ever get there? **LO5**
10. **POLICY PERSPECTIVES** What public sector or private sector output would you cut back to make more resources available for increased health care? **LO2**

PROBLEMS

🔲 connect

1. According to Figure 1.1, what is the peace dividend from reducing military output from OG to OE? **LO2**
2. Draw a production possibilities curve based on Table 1.1, labeling combinations A–F. What is the opportunity cost of increasing missile production **LO2**
   (*a*) From 50 to 100?
   (*b*) From 0 to 150?
3. Assume that it takes six hours of labor time to paint a room and three hours to sand a floor. If all 24 hours were spent painting, (*a*) How many rooms could be painted by one worker? (*b*) If a decision were made to sand two floors, how many painted rooms would have to be given up? (*c*) Illustrate with a production possibilities curve. **LO1**
4. Suppose it takes four hours of labor time to hang sheetrock in a room and two hours to tape and plaster a wall. (*a*) If one person spent an entire eight hour day hanging sheetrock, how many rooms could be hung? (*b*) Illustrate (*a*) with a production possibilities curve. (*c*) If another worker became available for an eight-hour workday, illustrate the resulting change in production possibilities. **LO2**
5. According to Figure 1.3, what is the opportunity cost when military output is increased from M_1 to M_2? **LO2**
6. On a single graph, draw a production possibilities curve for the United States with consumer goods and military goods as the only two output choices. Label the axes from 0 to 100 percent of output. Then identify with Point A the output mix

of 1944 and with Point *B* the output choice of 2013. (See Figures 1.2, 1.4, and the text for data.) **LO3**

7. Assume that the table here describes the production possibilities confronting an economy. Using that information: **LO3**
   (*a*) Draw the production possibilities curve. Be sure to label each alternative output combination (*A* through *E*).
   (*b*) Calculate and illustrate on your graph the opportunity cost of building one hospital.
   (*c*) What is the cost of producing a second hospital?
   (*d*) Why can't more of both outputs be produced?
   (*e*) Which point on the curve is the most desired one?

Potential Output Combinations	Homeless Shelters	Hospitals
A	10	0
B	9	1
C	7	2
D	4	3
E	0	4

8. In 2012 the dollar value of total output was roughly $40 billion in North Korea and $1,100 billion in South Korea. South Korea devotes 2.7 percent of its output to defense. Using the data in Figure 1.4, (*a*) compute how much North Korea spends on its military. (*b*) Which nation spends more, in absolute dollars? **LO3**

9. According to the News Wire on page 11, what is the opportunity cost of North Korea's rocket program in terms of corn? **LO4**

10. **POLICY PERSPECTIVES** In Figure 1.6, (*a*) If as much health care as possible is provided, how many other goods will be provided? (*b*) What is the opportunity cost of producing maximum health care? (*c*) What is the opportunity cost of increasing health care from H_1 to H_2? **LO5**

11. **POLICY PERSPECTIVES** Suppose the following data reflect the production possibilities for providing health care and education:

Units per Year

Health Care	400	370	330	270	190	100	0
Education	0	20	40	50	60	70	80

   (*a*) Graph the production possibilities curve.
   (*b*) If maximum health care is provided, how much education will be provided?
   (*c*) What is the opportunity cast of increasing health care from 270 to 330 units? **LO5**

◄ Practice quizzes, student PowerPoints, author podcasts, web activities, and additional materials available at **www.mhhe.com/schilleressentials9e**, or scan here. Need a barcode reader? Try ScanLife, available in your app store.

APPENDIX

Economists like to draw graphs. In fact, we didn't even make it through the first chapter without a few graphs. The purpose of this appendix is to look more closely at the way graphs are drawn and used.   Using Graphs

The basic purpose of a graph is to illustrate a relationship between two *variables*. Consider, for example, the relationship between grades and studying. In general, you expect that additional hours of study time will result in higher grades. If true, you should be able to see a distinct relationship between hours of study time and grade point average. In other words, there should be some empirical evidence that study time matters.

TABLE A.1
Hypothetical Relationship of Grades to Study Time

These data suggest that grades improve with increased study times.

Study Time (Hours per Week)	Grade Point Average
16	4.0 (A)
14	3.5 (B+)
12	3.0 (B)
10	2.5 (C+)
8	2.0 (C)
6	1.5 (D+)
4	1.0 (D)
2	0.5 (F+)
0	0 (F)

Suppose we actually tracked study times and grades for all the students taking this course. The resulting information might resemble the data in Table A.1.

According to the table, students who don't study at all can expect an F in this course. To get a C, the average student apparently spends eight hours a week studying. All those who study 16 hours a week end up with an A in the course.

These relationships between grades and studying can also be illustrated on a graph. Indeed, the whole purpose of a graph is to summarize numerical relationships in a visual way.

We begin to construct a graph by drawing horizontal and vertical boundaries, as in Figure A.1. These boundaries are called the *axes* of the graph. On the vertical axis we measure one of the variables; the other variable is measured on the horizontal axis.

In this case, we shall measure the grade point average on the vertical axis. We start at the *origin* (the intersection of the two axes) and count upward, letting the distance between horizontal lines represent half (0.5) a grade point. Each horizontal line is numbered, up to the maximum grade point average of 4.0.

The number of hours each week spent doing homework is measured on the horizontal axis. We begin at the origin again, and count to the right. The *scale* (numbering) proceeds in increments of 1 hour, up to 20 hours per week.

When both axes have been labeled and measured, we can begin to illustrate the relationship between study time and grades. Consider the typical student who does eight hours of homework per week and has a 2.0 (C) grade point average. We illustrate this relationship by first locating eight hours on the horizontal axis. We then move up from that point a distance of 2.0 grade points, to point *M*. Point *M* tells us that eight hours of study time per week is typically associated with a 2.0 grade point average.

The rest of the information in Table A.1 is drawn (or *plotted*) on the graph in the same way. To illustrate the average grade for people who study 12 hours per week, we move upward from the number 12 on the horizontal axis until we reach the height of 3.0 on the vertical axis. At that intersection, we draw another point (point *N*).

Once we have plotted the various points describing the relationship of study time to grades, we may connect them with a line or curve. This line (curve) is our summary. In this case, the line slopes upward to the right—that is, it has a *positive*

FIGURE A.1
The Relationship of Grades to Study Time

The upward (positive) slope of the curve indicates that additional studying is associated with higher grades. The average student (2.0, or C grade) studies eight hours per week. This is indicated by point *M* on the graph.

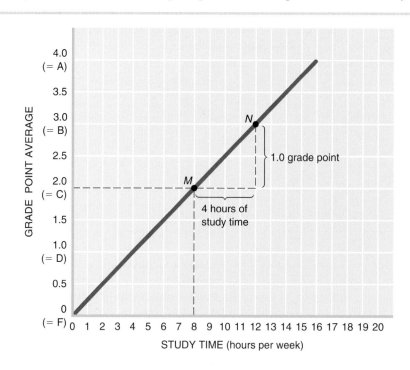

slope. This slope indicates that more hours of study time are associated with *higher* grades. Were higher grades associated with *less* study time, the curve in Figure A.1 would have a *negative* slope (downward from left to right)—a puzzling outcome.

Slopes

The upward slope of Figure A.1 not only tells us that more studying raises your grade, it also tells us *by how much* grades rise with study time. According to point *M* in Figure A.1, the average student studies eight hours per week and earns a C (2.0 grade point average). In order to earn a B (3.0 grade point average), a student apparently needs to study an average of 12 hours per week (point *N*). Hence an increase of four hours of study time per week is associated with a 1-point increase in grade point average. This relationship between *changes* in study time and *changes* in grade point average is expressed by the steepness, or *slope*, of the graph.

The slope of any graph is calculated as

$$\text{Slope} = \frac{\text{vertical distance between two points}}{\text{horizontal distance between two points}}$$

Some people simplify this by saying

$$\text{Slope} = \frac{\text{the rise}}{\text{the run}}$$

In our example, the vertical distance (the "rise") between points *M* and *N* represents a change in grade point average. The horizontal distance (the "run") between these two points represents the change in study time. Hence the slope of the graph between points *M* and *N* is equal to

$$\text{Slope} = \frac{3.0 \text{ grade} - 2.0 \text{ grade}}{12 \text{ hours} - 8 \text{ hours}} = \frac{1 \text{ grade point}}{4 \text{ hours}}$$

In other words, a 4-hour increase in study time (from 8 to 12 hours) is associated with a 1-point increase in grade point average (see Figure A.1).

Shifts

The relationship between grades and studying illustrated in Figure A.1 is not inevitable. It is simply a graphical illustration of student experiences, as revealed in our hypothetical survey. The relationship between study time and grades could be quite different.

Suppose that the university decided to raise grading standards, making it more difficult to achieve good grades. To achieve a C, a student now would need to study 12 hours per week, not just 8 (as in Figure A.1). To get a B, you now have to study 16 hours, not the previous norm of only 12 hours per week.

Figure A.2 illustrates the new grading standards. Notice that the new curve lies to the right of the earlier curve. We say that the curve has *shifted* to reflect a change in the relationship between study time and grades. Point *R* indicates that 12 hours of study time now "produces" a C, not a B (point *N* on the old curve). Students who now study only four hours per week (point *S*) will fail. Under the old grading policy, they could have at least gotten a D. **When a curve shifts, the underlying relationship between the two variables has changed.**

A shift may also change the slope of the curve. In Figure A.2, the new grading curve is parallel to the old one; it therefore has the same slope. Under either the new grading policy or the old one, a four-hour increase in study time leads to a 1-point increase in grades. Therefore, the slope of both curves in Figure A.2 is

$$\text{Slope} - \frac{\text{vertical change}}{\text{horizontal change}} = \frac{1}{4}$$

FIGURE A.2
A Shift

When a relationship between two variables changes, the entire curve *shifts*. In this case a tougher grading policy alters the relationship between study time and grades. To get a C, one must now study 12 hours per week (point *R*), not just 8 hours (point *M*).

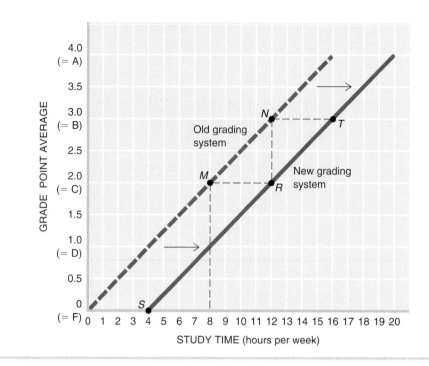

This, too, may change, however. Figure A.3 illustrates such a possibility. In this case, zero study time still results in an F. But now the payoff for additional studying is reduced. Now it takes six hours of study time to get a D (1.0 grade point), not four hours as before. Likewise, another four hours of study time (to a total of 10) raises the grade by only two-thirds of a point.

It takes six hours to raise the grade a full point. The slope of the new line is therefore

$$\text{Slope} = \frac{\text{vertical change}}{\text{horizontal change}} = \frac{1}{6}$$

The new curve in Figure A.3 has a smaller slope than the original curve and so lies below it. What all this means is that it now takes a greater effort to *improve* your grade.

Linear versus Nonlinear Curves

In Figures A.1–A.3, the relationship between grades and studying is represented by a straight line—that is, a *linear* curve. A distinguishing feature of linear curves is that they have the same (constant) slope throughout. In Figure A.1, it appears that *every* four-hour increase in study time is associated with a 1-point increase in average grades. In Figure A.3, it appears that every six-hour increase in study time leads to a 1-point increase in grades.

In reality, the relationship between studying and grades may not be linear. Higher grades may be more difficult to attain. You may be able to raise a C to a B by studying six hours more per week. But it may be harder to raise a B to an A. According to Figure A.4, it takes an additional *eight* hours of studying to raise a B to an A. Thus the relationship between study time and grades is *nonlinear* in Figure A.4; the slope of the curve *changes* as study time increases. In this case, the slope decreases as study time increases. Grades continue to improve, but not so fast, as more and more time is devoted to homework. You may know the feeling.

Causation

Figure A.4 does not itself guarantee that your grade point average will rise if you study four more hours per week. In fact, the graph drawn in Figure A.4 does not

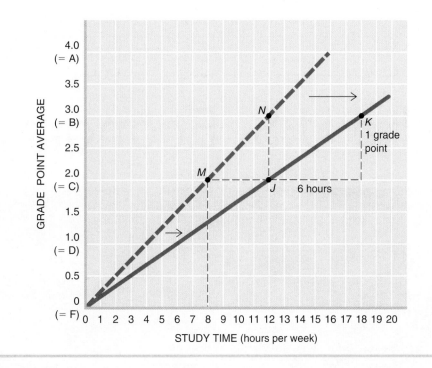

FIGURE A.3
A Change in Slope

When a curve shifts, it may change its slope as well. In this case, a new grading policy makes each higher grade more difficult to achieve. To raise a C to a B, for example, one must study six additional hours (compare points *J* and *K*). Earlier it took only four hours to move up the grade scale a full point. The slope of the line has declined from 0.25 (= 1 ÷ 4) to 0.17 (= 1 ÷ 6).

prove that additional study ever results in higher grades. The graph is only a summary of empirical observations. It says nothing about cause and effect. It could be that students who study a lot are smarter to begin with. If so, then less able students might not get higher grades if they studied harder. In other words, the *cause* of higher grades is debatable. At best, the empirical relationship summarized in the graph may be used to support a particular theory (e.g., that it pays to study more). Graphs, like tables, charts, and other statistical media, rarely tell their own stories; rather, they must be *interpreted* in terms of some underlying theory or expectation. That's when the real fun starts.

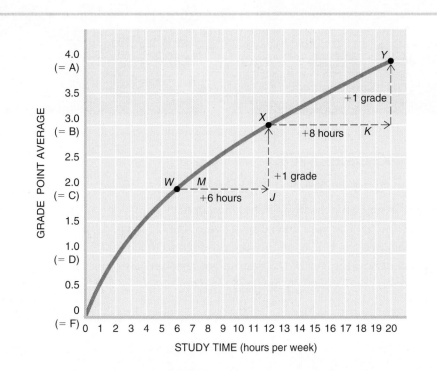

FIGURE A.4
A Nonlinear Relationship

Straight lines have a constant slope, implying a constant relationship between the two variables. But the relationship (and slope) may vary. In this case it takes six extra hours of study to raise a C (point *W*) to a B (point *X*) but eight extra hours to raise a B to an A (point *Y*). The slope is decreasing as we move up the curve.

2 The U.S. Economy

◄ Practice quizzes, student PowerPoints, author podcasts, web activities, and additional materials available at www.mhhe.com/ schilleressentials9e, or scan here. Need a barcode reader? Try ScanLife, available in your app store.

LEARNING OBJECTIVES

After reading this chapter, you should be able to:

1 Explain how an economy's size is measured.
2 Describe the absolute and relative size of the U.S. economy.
3 Explain why the U.S. economy can produce so much.
4 Recount how the mix of U.S. output has changed over time.
5 Describe how (un)equally incomes are distributed.

Wte are surrounded by the economy but never really see it. We see only fragments, never the entirety. We see boutiques at the mall, never total retail sales. We visit virtual stores in cyberspace but can't begin to describe the dimensions of e-commerce. We pump gas at the service station but have no notion of how many millions of barrels of oil are consumed each day. We know every detail on our paychecks but don't have a clue about how much income the entire workforce earns. Nor can many of us tell how our own income stacks up against that of the average U.S. household, much less that of earlier generations or other nations. Such details simply aren't a part of our daily agendas. For most people, the "economy" is just a vague reference to a mass of meaningless statistics.

The intent of this chapter is to provide a more user-friendly picture of the U.S. economy. This profile of the economy is organized around the three core questions of WHAT, HOW, and FOR WHOM. Our interest here is to see how these questions are answered at present in the United States—that is,

- WHAT goods and services does the United States produce?
- HOW is that output produced?
- FOR WHOM is the output produced?

We focus on the big picture without going into too much statistical detail. Along the way, we'll see how the U.S. economy stacks up against other nations.

WHAT AMERICA PRODUCES

In Chapter 1 we used the two-dimensional production possibilities curve to describe WHAT output combinations can be produced. In reality, the mix of output includes so many different products that we could never fit them on a graph. We can, however, sketch what the U.S. mix of output looks like and how it has changed over the years.

How Much Output

The first challenge in describing the actual output of an economy is to somehow add up the millions of different products produced each year into a meaningful summary. The production possibilities curve did this in *physical* terms for only two products. We ended up at a specific mix of output with precise quantities of two goods. In principle we could list all of the millions of products produced each year. But such a list would be longer than this textbook and a lot less useful. We need a summary measure of how much is produced.

The top panel of Table 2.1 illustrates the problem of obtaining a summary measure of output. Even if we produced only three products—oranges, disposable razors, and video games—there is no obvious way of summarizing total output in *physical* terms. Should we count *units* of output? In that case oranges would appear to be the most important good produced. Should we count the *weight* of different products? In that case video game software would not count at all. Should we tally their *sizes?* Clearly *physical* measures of output aren't easy to aggregate.

If we use monetary *value* instead of physical units to compute total output, the accounting chore is much easier. In a market economy, every product commands a specific price. Hence the value of each product can be observed easily. ***By multiplying the physical output of each good by its price, we can determine the total value of each good produced.*** Notice in the bottom panel of Table 2.1 how easily the separate values for the output of oranges, razors, and video games can be added up. The resultant sum ($4.2 billion, in this case) is a measure of the *value of* total output.

TABLE 2.1
Measuring Output

It is impossible to add up all output when it is counted in *physical terms*. Accordingly, total output is measured in *monetary terms*, with each good or service valued at its market price.

GDP refers to the total market value of all goods and services produced in a given time period. According to the numbers in this table, the total *value* of the oranges, razors, and video games produced is $4.2 billion.

Output	Amount
Measuring output	
. . . in physical terms	
Oranges	6 billion
Disposable razors	3 billion
Video games	70 million
Total	?
. . . in monetary terms	
6 billion oranges @ 20¢ each	$1.2 billion
3 billion razors @ 30¢ each	0.9 billion
70 million games @ $30 each	2.1 billion
Total	$4.2 billion

gross domestic product (GDP) The total value of final goods and services produced within a nation's borders in a given time period.

nominal GDP The value of output measured in current prices.

real GDP The inflation-adjusted value of GDP: the value of output measured in constant prices.

GROSS DOMESTIC PRODUCT   The summary measure of output most frequently used is called **gross domestic product (GDP).** *GDP refers to the total value of all final goods and services produced in a country during a given time period: it is a summary measure of a nation's output.* GDP enables us to add oranges and razors and even video games into a meaningful summary of economic activity (see Table 2.1). The U.S. Department of Commerce actually does this kind of accounting every calendar quarter. Those quarterly GDP reports tell us how much output the economy is producing.

REAL GDP   Although GDP is a convenient summary of how much output is being produced, it can be misleading. GDP is based on both physical output and prices. Accordingly, from one year to the next either rising prices or an increase in physical output could cause **nominal GDP** to increase.

Notice in Table 2.2 what happens when all prices double. The measured value of total output also doubles—from $4.2 to $8.4 billion. That sounds like an impressive jump in output. In reality, however, no more goods are being produced; *physical quantities* are unchanged. So the apparent jump in *nominal* GDP is an illusion caused by rising prices (inflation).

To provide a clearer picture of how much output we are producing, GDP numbers must be adjusted for inflation. These inflation adjustments delete the effects of rising prices by valuing output in *constant* prices. The end result of this effort is referred to as **real GDP,** an inflation-adjusted measure of total output.

TABLE 2.2
Inflation Adjustments

If prices rise, so does the *value* of output. In this example, the *nominal* value of output doubles from Year 1 to Year 2 solely as a result of price increases; physical output remains unchanged. *Real* GDP corrects for such changing price levels. In this case *real* GDP in Year 2, measured in Year 1 prices, is unchanged at $4.2 billion.

Product	Physical Output Year 1	Year 2	Unit Prices Year 1	Year 2	Year 1 (@Year 1 Prices)	Year 2 (@Year 2 Prices)	Year 2 (@Year 1 Prices)
Oranges	6 billion	6 billion	$0.20	$0.40	$1.2	$2.4	$1.2
Razors	3 billion	3 billion	0.30	0.60	0.9	1.8	0.9
Video games	70 million	70 million	30.00	60.00	2.1	4.2	2.1
					$4.2	$8.4	$4.2
						Nominal value	Real value

In 2012 the U.S. economy produced over $15 *trillion* of output. That was a lot of oranges, razors, and video games—not to mention the tens of thousands of other goods and services produced.

INTERNATIONAL COMPARISONS   The $15 trillion of output that the United States produced in 2012 looks particularly impressive in a global context. The output of the entire world in that year was only $80 trillion. Hence the U.S. economy produces roughly 20 percent of the entire planet's output. With less than 5 percent of the world's population, that's a remarkable feat. It clearly establishes the United States as the world's economic giant.

Figure 2.1 provides some specific country comparisons for a recent year. The U.S. economy is three times larger than Japan's, the world's third largest. It is nine times larger than Mexico's. In fact, the U.S. economy is so large that its output exceeds by a wide margin the *combined* production of *all* the countries in Africa and South America.

PER CAPITA GDP   Another way of putting these trillion-dollar figures into perspective is to relate them to individuals. This can be done by dividing a nation's total GDP by its population, a calculation that yields **per capita GDP.** Per capita GDP tells us how much output is potentially available to the average person. It doesn't tell us how much any specific person gets. *Per capita GDP is an indicator of how much output each person would get if all output were divided evenly among the population.*

per capita GDP Total GDP divided by total population: average GDP.

In 2012 per capita GDP in the United States was approximately $49,000—more than four times the world average. Individual country comparisons are even more startling. In Ethiopia and Haiti, per capita incomes are less than $2,000—less than $6 per day. *Homeless* people in the United States fare better than that—typically

FIGURE 2.1   How Much Output Nations Produce

The United States is by far the world's largest economy. America's annual output of goods and services is three times that of Japan and equal to all of Western Europe. The output of Third World countries is only a tiny fraction of U.S. output.

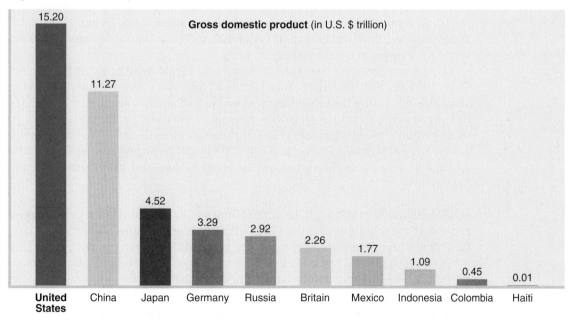

Source: World Bank, *World Development Indicators 2013.*

TABLE 2.3
Per Capita Incomes around the World

The American standard of living is four times higher than the world average. People in the poorest nations of the world (e.g., Haiti, Ethiopia) barely survive on per capita incomes that are a tiny fraction of U.S. standards.

United States	$48,820
France	35,910
Japan	35,330
Spain	31,400
Greece	25,100
Mexico	15,390
World average	**11,549**
China	8,390
Jordan	5,930
Indonesia	4,500
India	3,590
Haiti	1,180
Ethiopia	1,110

Source: World Bank, *World Development Indicatiors 2012.* World Bank data based on purchasing power parity.

© 2009 Jupiterimages Corporation/DAL

© The McGraw-Hill Companies, Inc./Berry Barker, photographer/DAL

economic growth An increase in output (real GDP); an expansion of production possibilities.

Topic Podcast:
America's Wealth

much better. Americans classified as poor have more food, more shelter, and more amenities than most people in the less developed nations even hope for. That is the reality depicted in the statistics of Table 2.3 and the accompanying photos.

HISTORICAL COMPARISONS   Still another way of digesting the dimensions of the American economy is to compare today's living standards with those of earlier times. Some of your favorite consumer gadgets (e.g., smartphones, 3D TVs, iPods, wifi, Wii consoles) didn't even exist a generation ago. People worked harder and got fewer goods and services. The living standards Americans now call "poor" resemble the lifestyle of the middle class in the 1930s. Since 1900 the per capita output of the U.S. economy has risen 500 percent. That means you're now enjoying six times as many goods and services (and much better quality) than people did back then. We're so rich that we now spend over a billion dollars a year on closet organizers alone! And we spend over $50 billion on pet food and supplies—about twice as much as the *total* output of Congo's 70 million people. Although many of us still complain that we don't have enough, we enjoy an array of goods and services that other nations and earlier generations only dreamed about.

What's even more amazing is that our abundance keeps growing. America's real GDP increases by about 3 percent a year. That may not sound like much, but it adds up. With the U.S. population growing by only 1 percent a year, continued **economic growth** implies more output per person. Like interest accumulating in the bank, economic growth keeps adding to our standard of living. If real GDP keeps growing 2 percentage points faster than our population, per capita incomes will double again in approximately 35 years.

There is no certainty that the economy will continue to grow at that speed. From 1929 to 1939, real GDP didn't grow at all. As a consequence, U.S. living standards *fell* during the Great Depression. We had another setback in 2008–2009. But those are exceptions from the American norm of persistent growth. In other nations, the struggle between population growth and economic growth is a persistent source of anxiety. From 2008 to 2012, output per capita actually *declined* in Venezuela, Madagascar, the Ivory Coast, and many other already poor nations.

SOCIAL WELFARE   Although the United States is indisputably the world's largest economy, we must not confuse GDP with broader measures of social welfare. GDP is simply a measure of the volume of goods and services produced. That material production is just one element of our collective well-being. Environmental health and beauty, family harmony, charitable activity, personal security, friendship networks, social justice, good health, and religious convictions all affect our sense of well-being. Material possessions don't substitute for any of those other dimensions. In fact, production of material goods can occasionally *detract* from our social welfare by increasing pollution, congestion, or social anxiety levels. With more love, fewer crimes, and less pollution our social welfare might increase even if GDP declined.

Although GDP is an incomplete measure of social welfare, it is still the single best measure of a nation's *economic* well-being. Way back in 1776 Adam Smith recognized that the wealth of nations was best measured by output produced rather than by the amount of gold possessed or resources owned. More output in poor nations will improve health, education, living standards, and even life expectancies. More output in the United States will not only increase our creature comforts but also enable us to eliminate more diseases and even to clean up the environment.

The Mix of Output

In addition to the *amount* of total output, we care about its *content.* As the production possibilities curve illustrated in Chapter 1, there are many possible output combinations for any given level of GDP. In Chapter 1 we examined the different mixes of military and civilian output nations choose. We could also compare the number of cars produced to the number of homes, schools, or hospitals produced. Clearly the *content* of total output is important.

In the broadest terms, the content of output is usually described in terms of its major end uses rather than by specific products. ***The major uses of total output include***

- *Household consumption.*
- *Business investment.*
- *Government services.*
- *Exports.*

CONSUMER GOODS   Consumer goods dominate the U.S. mix of output, accounting for more than two-thirds of total output. Consumer goods include everything from breakfast cereals and textbooks to music downloads and beach vacations— anything and everything consumers buy.

The vast array of products consumers purchase is classified into three categories: *durable goods, nondurable goods,* and *services.* Consumer durables are products that are expected to last at least three years. They tend to be big-ticket items like cars, appliances, TVs, and furniture. They are generally expensive and often are purchased on credit. Because of this, consumers tend to postpone buying durables when they are worried about their incomes. Conversely, consumers tend to go on durables spending sprees when times are good. This spending pattern makes durable goods output highly *cyclical*—that is, very sensitive to economic trends.

Nondurables and services are not as cyclical. Nondurables include clothes, food, gasoline, and other staples that consumers buy frequently. Services are the largest and fastest-growing component of consumption. At present, over half of all consumer output consists of medical care, entertainment, utilities, education, and other services.

INVESTMENT GOODS   Investment goods are a completely different type of output. **Investment** goods include the plant, machinery, and equipment that are produced for use in the business sector. These investment goods are used

investment Expenditures on (production of) new plant and equipment (capital) in a given time period, plus changes in business inventories.

1. To replace worn-out equipment and factories, thus *maintaining* our production possibilities.
2. To increase and improve our stock of capital, thereby *expanding* our production possibilities.

FIGURE 2.2
The Uses of GDP

Total GDP amounted to more than $15 trillion in 2012. Over two-thirds of this output consisted of private consumer goods and services. The next largest share (20 percent) of output consisted of public sector goods and services. Investment absorbed 13 percent of GDP in 2012. Finally, because imports exceeded exports, we ended up consuming 4 percent more than we produced.

Source: U.S. Department of Commerce.

We also count as investment goods those products that businesses hold as inventory for later sale to consumers.

The economic growth that has lifted our living standards so high was fueled by past investments—the factories, telecommunications networks, and transportation systems built in the past. To keep raising our living standards, we have to keep churning out new plant and equipment. This requires us to limit our production of consumer goods (i.e., save) so scarce resources can be used for investment. This is not a great sacrifice in the United States since our consumption levels are already so high. In poor nations, however, reducing consumer goods production entails great sacrifices in the short run. Less than 15 percent of America's GDP today consists of investment goods (see Figure 2.2).

Note that the term *investment* here refers to real output—plant and equipment produced for the business sector. This is not the way most people use the term. People often speak, for example, of "investing" in the stock market. Purchases of corporate stock, however, do not create goods and services. Such *financial* investments merely transfer ownership of a corporation from one individual to another. Such financial investments may enable a corporation to purchase real plant and equipment. Tangible (economic) investment does not occur, however, until the plant and machinery are actually produced. Only tangible investment is counted in the mix of output.

GOVERNMENT SERVICES   A third component of GDP is government services. Federal, state, and local governments purchase resources to police the streets, teach classes, write laws, and build highways. The resources used by the government for these purchases are unavailable for either consumption or investment. The production of government services currently absorbs one-fifth of total output (Figure 2.2).

Notice the emphasis again on the production of real goods and services. The federal government *spends* nearly $4 trillion a year. Much of that spending, however, is in the form of income transfers, not resource purchases. **Income transfers** are payments to individuals for which no direct service is provided. Social Security benefits, welfare checks, food stamps, and unemployment benefits are examples of income transfers. Such transfer payments account for half of all federal spending (see Figure 2.3). This spending is *not* part of our output of goods and services. *Only that part of federal spending used to acquire resources and produce*

income transfers Payments to individuals for which no current goods or services are exchanged, such as Social Security, welfare, and unemployment benefits.

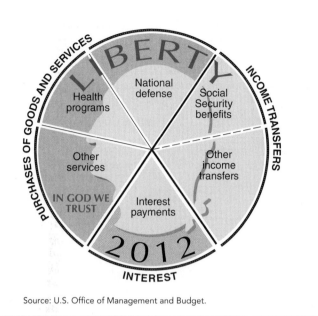

Source: U.S. Office of Management and Budget.

FIGURE 2.3
Federal Outlays,
by Type
The federal government spent nearly $4 trillion in 2012. Only half of all this spending was for goods and services (including national defense, health programs, and all other services). The rest was spent on income transfers (Social Security benefits, government pensions, welfare, unemployment benefits, etc.) and interest payments. Transfer payments are not counted in GDP.

services is counted in GDP. In 2012 federal purchases (production) of goods and services accounted for only 8 percent of total output.

State and local governments use far more of our scarce resources than does the federal government. These are the governments that build roads; provide schools, police, and firefighters; administer hospitals; and provide social services. The output of all these state and local governments accounts for roughly 13 percent of total GDP. In producing this output, they employ four times as many people (16 million) as does the federal government (4 million).

NET EXPORTS   Finally, we should note that some of the goods and services we produce each year are shipped abroad rather than consumed at home. That is to say, we **export** some of our output to other countries, for whatever use they care to make of it. Thus GDP—the value of output *produced* within the United States—can be larger than the sum of our own consumption, investment, and government purchases if we export some of our output.

exports Goods and services sold to foreign buyers.

International trade is not a one-way street. While we export some of our own output, we also **import** goods and services from other countries. These imports may be used for consumption (Scotch whiskey, Samsung smartphones), investment (German ball bearings), or government (French radar screens). Whatever their use, imports represent goods and services that are used by Americans but are not produced in the United States.

imports Goods and services purchased from foreign sources.

The GDP accounts subtract imports from exports. The difference represents *net* exports. In 2012 the value of exports was less than the value of imports. **When imports exceed exports, we are *using* more goods and services than we are *producing.*** Hence we have to subtract net imports from consumption, investment, and government services to figure out how much we actually *produced.* That is why net exports appear as a negative item in Figure 2.2.

Changing Industry Structure

As we noted earlier, many of the products we consume today did not exist 10 or even 2 years ago. We have also observed how much the volume of output has grown over time. **As the economy has grown, the mix of output has changed dramatically.**

FIGURE 2.4 The Changing Mix of Output

In the twentieth century the total output of the U.S. economy increased thirteenfold. As the economy grew, the farm sector shrank and the manufacturing *share* of total output declined. Since 1930 the American economy has been predominantly a service economy, with output and job growth increasingly concentrated in retail trade, education, health care, entertainment, personal and business services, and government.

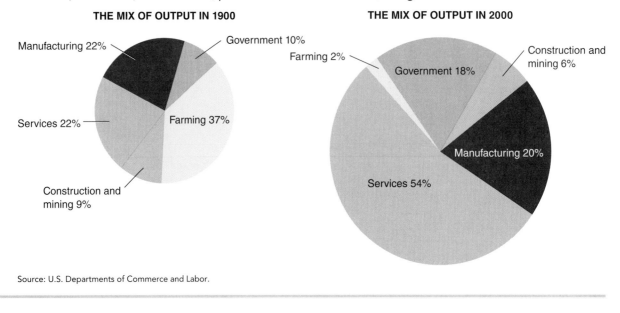

Source: U.S. Departments of Commerce and Labor.

DECLINE IN FARMING   The most dramatic change in the mix of output has been the decline in the relative size of the farm sector. In 1900 farming was the most common occupation in the American economy. As Figure 2.4 illustrates, nearly 4 out of 10 workers were employed in agriculture back then.

Today the mix of output is radically different. Between 1900 and 2000 over 25 *million* people left farms and sought jobs in the cities. As a result, less than 2 percent of the workforce is now employed in agriculture. And their number keeps shrinking a bit further every year as new technology makes it possible to grow *more* food with *fewer* workers.

DECLINE OF MANUFACTURING SHARE   Most of the farmers displaced by technological advances in the early 1900s found jobs in the expanding manufacturing sector. The industrial revolution that flourished in the late 1800s led to a massive increase in manufacturing activity (e.g., steel, transportation systems, automobiles, airplanes). Between 1860 and 1920, the manufactured share of GDP doubled, reaching a peak at 27 percent. World War II also created a huge demand for ships, airplanes, trucks, and armaments, requiring an enlarged manufacturing sector. After World War II, the manufactured share of output declined; it now accounts for less than 20 percent of total output.

The *relative* decline in manufacturing does not mean that the manufacturing sector has actually shrunk. ***As in farming, technological advances have made it possible to increase manufacturing output tremendously, even though employment in this sector has grown only modestly.*** Just in the last 50 years, manufactured *output* has increased fourfold even though manufacturing *employment* has increased only 20 percent. The same thing is happening in China and other countries (see News Wire).

NEWS WIRE	MANUFACTURING

The factory-based economy is nearly over because of technological improvements. Fifteen years ago, Boeing took 22 days to build a 737 airliner; today it takes 12 days. Such changes mean fewer factory jobs even as production rises. China is losing factory jobs much faster than the United States as efficiency improves. Soon there won't be any nation with a factory-based economy, and that would have happened regardless of whether there was trade liberalization. Higher productivity, in turn, generates the social wealth that creates more jobs for teachers, health care providers, and other essential needs. The world is actually better off with declining factory employment, which is no consolation if you lost a job.

Source: Gregg Easterbrook: "The Boom Is Nigh," *Newsweek*, February 22, 2010, Vol. 155, No. 8, p. 48. Used with permission.

NOTE: As more output can be produced with fewer workers, manufacturing *employment* declines even while *output* increases.

GROWTH OF SERVICES   The *relative* decline in manufacturing is due primarily to the rapid expansion of the service sector. ***America has become largely a service economy.*** A hundred years ago less than 25 percent of the labor force was employed in the service sector; today service industries (including government) generate over 70 percent of total output. Among the fastest-growing service industries are health care, computer science and software, financial services, retail trade, business services, and law. According to the U.S. Department of Labor, this trend will continue; 98 percent of net job growth over the next 10 years will be in service industries.

GROWTH OF TRADE   International trade also plays an increasingly important role in how goods are produced. Roughly one-eighth of the output Americans produce is exported. As noted earlier, an even larger share of output is imported (hence the negative "net exports" in Figure 2.2).

What is remarkable about these international transactions is how fast they have grown. Advances in communications and transportation technologies make international trade and investment easier. You can click on a British clothier's website just as easily as on the site of a U.S. merchant. And consumers in other nations can easily purchase goods from American cybermerchants. Then FedEx or another overnight delivery service can move the goods across national borders. As a result, the volume of both imports and exports keeps growing rapidly. The growth of trade is also fueled by the increased consumption of *services* (e.g., travel, finance, movies, computer software) rather than goods. With trade in services, you don't even need overnight delivery.

HOW AMERICA PRODUCES

International trade has also affected HOW goods and services are produced. Hundreds of foreign-owned firms (e.g., Toyota, BMW, Shell, Air France) produce goods or services in the United States. Any output they produce within U.S. borders is counted in America's GDP. By contrast, U.S.-owned **factors of production** employed elsewhere (e.g., a Nike shoe factory in Malaysia, an Apple factory in China) don't contribute directly to U.S. output.

factors of production Resource inputs used to produce goods and services, such as land, labor, capital, and entrepreneurship.

Factors of Production

Even without foreign investments, the United States would have ample resources to produce goods and services. The United States has the third largest population in the world (behind China and India). The United States also has the world's fourth largest land area (behind Russia, China, and by a hair, Canada) and profuse natural resources (e.g., oil, fertile soil, hydropower).

Abundant labor and natural resources give the United States a decided advantage. But superior resources alone don't explain America's economic dominance. After all, China has five times as many people as the United States and equally abundant natural resources. Yet China's annual output is less than two-thirds of America's output.

CAPITAL STOCK   In part, America's greater economic strength is explained by the abundance of capital. America has accumulated a massive stock of capital—over $60 *trillion* worth of machinery, factories, and buildings. As a result, American production tends to be very **capital intensive.** The contrast with *labor-intensive* production in poorer countries is striking. A Chinese farmer mostly works with his or her hands and crude implements, whereas an American farmer works with computers, automated irrigation systems, and mechanized equipment. Ethiopian business managers don't have the computer networks or telecommunications systems that make American business so efficient.

capital intensive Production processes that use a high ratio of capital to labor inputs.

FACTOR QUALITY   The greater **productivity**—output per worker—of American workers reflects not only the capital intensity of the production process but also the *quality* of both capital and labor. America invests each year not just in *more* plant and equipment but in *better* plant and equipment. Today's new computer is faster and more powerful than yesterday's. Today's laser surgery makes yesterday's surgical procedures look primitive. Even textbooks get better each year. Such improvements in the quality of capital expand production possibilities.

productivity Output per unit of input, such as output per labor hour.

Labor quality also improves with education and skill training. Indeed, one can invest in human capital much as one invests in physical capital. **Human capital** refers to the productive capabilities of labor. In the Stone Age, one's productive capacity was largely determined by physical strength and endurance. In today's economy, human capital is largely a product of education, training, and experience. Hence a country can acquire more human capital even without more bodies.

human capital The knowledge and skills possessed by the workforce.

Over time, the United States has invested heavily in human capital. In 1940 only 1 out of 20 young Americans graduated from college; today over 35 percent of young people are college graduates. High school graduation rates have jumped from 38 percent to over 85 percent in the same time period. In some poor countries only one out of two youths ever *attends* high school, much less graduates (see the News Wire on the next page). In certain nations girls are virtually prohibited from

America's enormous output is made possible by huge investments in physical and human capital. In poorer countries, production is constrained by low levels of education and a scarcity of plant, equipment, and technology.

© Scott Bauer/USDA Agricultural Research Services/DAL

© The McGraw-Hill Companies, Inc., Barry Barker, photographer/DAL

NEWS WIRE | HUMAN CAPITAL

The Education Gap between Rich and Poor Nations
Virtually all Americans attend high school, and roughly 85 percent graduate. In poor countries relatively few workers attend high school, and even fewer graduate. Half of the workers in the world's poorest nations are illiterate. This education gap limits their productivity.

Enrollment in Secondary Schools
(Percentage of School-Age Youth Attending Secondary Schools)

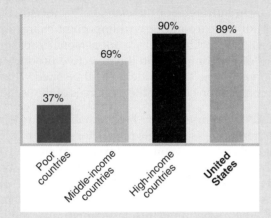

Source: World Bank, *World Development Indicators 2012.*

NOTE: The high productivity of the American economy is explained in part by the quality of its labor resources. Workers in poorer, less developed countries get much less education or training.

getting an education. As a consequence, over 1 billion people—one-sixth of the world's population—are unable to read or even write their own names.

America's tremendous output is thus explained not only by a wealth of resources but by the quality of these resources as well. ***The high productivity of the U.S. economy results from using highly educated workers in capital-intensive production processes.***

FACTOR MOBILITY   Our continuing ability to produce the goods and services that consumers demand also depends on our agility in *reallocating* resources from one industry to another. Every year some industries expand and others contract. Thousands of new firms are created each year, and almost as many others disappear. In the process, land, labor, capital, and entrepreneurship move from one industry to another in response to changing demands and technology. In 1975 Federal Express, Compaq Computer, Microsoft, America Online, Amgen, and Oracle didn't exist. In 1995 Google and Yahoo hadn't yet been founded. In 2003 Facebook was still a concept, not an operational networking site. Yet these companies collectively employ over 300,000 people today. These workers came from other firms and industries that weren't growing as fast.

The Private Sector: Business Types
The factors of production released from some industries and acquired by others are organized into productive entities we call *businesses*. A business is an organization that uses factors of production to produce specific goods or services. Actual

production activity takes place in the 30 million business firms that participate in the U.S. product markets.

Business firms come in all shapes and sizes. A basic distinction is made, however, among three different legal organizations:

- Corporations
- Partnerships
- Proprietorships

The primary distinction among these three business forms lies in their ownership characteristics. A single proprietorship is a firm owned by one individual. A partnership is owned by a small number of individuals. A corporation is typically owned by many—even hundreds of thousands of—individuals, each of whom owns shares (stock) of the corporation. An important characteristic of corporations is that their owners (stockholders) are not personally responsible (liable) for the debts or actions of the company. So if a defective product injures someone, only the corporation—not the stockholders—will be sued. This limited liability makes it easier for corporations to pool the resources of thousands of individuals.

CORPORATE AMERICA   Because of their limited liability, corporations tend to be much larger than other businesses. Single proprietorships are typically quite small because few individuals have vast sources of wealth or credit. The typical proprietorship has less than $20,000 in assets, whereas the average corporation has assets in excess of $4 million. As a result of their size, corporate America dominates market transactions, accounting for more than 80 percent of all business sales.

We can describe who's who in the business community, then, in two very different ways. In terms of numbers, the single proprietorship is the most common type of business firm in America. Proprietorships are particularly dominant in agriculture (the family farm), retail trade (the corner grocery store), and services (your dentist). In terms of size, however, the corporation is the dominant force in the U.S. economy (see Figure 2.5). The four largest nonfinancial corporations in the country (ExxonMobil, Walmart, Chevron, and Apple) alone have more assets than *all* the 25 million proprietorships doing business in the United States. Even in agriculture, where corporate entities are still comparatively rare, the few agribusiness corporations are so large as to dominate many thousands of small farms.

FIGURE 2.5   U.S. Business Firms: Numbers versus Size

Proprietorships (individually owned companies) are the most common form of American business firm. Corporations are so large, however, that they account for most business sales and assets. Although only 18 percent of all firms are incorporated, corporations control 81 percent of all sales and 84 percent of all assets.

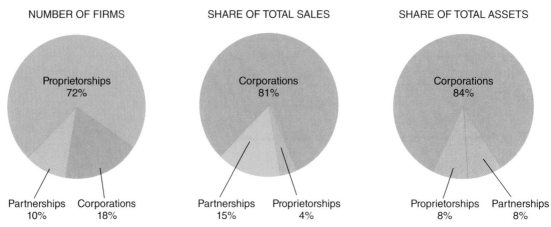

Source: U.S. Department of Commerce, *Statistical Abstract of the United States, 2012.*

The Government's Role

Although corporate America dominates the U.S. economy, it does not have the last word on WHAT, HOW, or FOR WHOM goods are produced. In our mixed economy, the government has a significant voice in all of these decisions. Even before America became an independent nation, royal charters bestowed the right to produce and trade specific goods. Even the European discovery of America was dependent on government financing and the establishment of exclusive rights to whatever treasures were found. Today over 50 federal agencies and thousands of state and local government entities regulate the production of goods. In the process, they profoundly affect HOW goods are produced.

PROVIDING A LEGAL FRAMEWORK   One of the most basic functions of government is to establish and enforce the rules of the game. In some bygone era maybe a person's word was sufficient to guarantee delivery or payment. Businesses today, however, rely more on written contracts. The government gives legitimacy to contracts by establishing the rules for such pacts and by enforcing their provisions. In the absence of contractual rights, few companies would be willing to ship goods without prepayment (in cash). Without legally protected ownership rights, few individuals would buy or build factories. Even the incentive to write textbooks would disappear if government copyright laws didn't forbid unauthorized downloading or photocopying. *By establishing ownership rights, contract rights, and other rules of the game, the government lays the foundation for market transactions.*

PROTECTING CONSUMERS   Much government regulation is intended to protect the interests of consumers. One way to do this is to prevent individual business firms from becoming too powerful. In the extreme case, a single firm might have a **monopoly** on the production of a specific good. As the sole producer of that good, a monopolist could dictate the price, the quality, and the quantity of the product. In such a situation, consumers would likely end up with the short end of the stick—paying too much for too little.

monopoly A firm that produces the entire market supply of a particular good or service.

To protect consumers from monopoly exploitation, the government tries to prevent individual firms from dominating specific markets. Antitrust laws prohibit mergers or acquisitions that threaten competition. The U.S. Department of Justice and the Federal Trade Commission also regulate pricing practices, advertising claims, and other behavior that might put consumers at an unfair disadvantage in product markets.

Government also regulates the safety of many products. Consumers don't have enough expertise to assess the safety of various medicines, for example. If they relied on trial and error to determine drug safety, they might not get a second chance. To avoid this calamity, the government requires rigorous testing of new drugs, food additives, and other products.

PROTECTING LABOR   The government also regulates how our labor resources are used in the production process. As recently as 1920, children between the ages of 10 and 15 were employed in mines, factories, farms, and private homes. They picked cotton and cleaned shrimp in the South, cut sugar beets and pulled onions in the Northwest, processed coal in Appalachia, and pressed tobacco leaves in the mid-Atlantic states. They often worked six days a week in abusive conditions for a pittance in wages. Private employers got cheap labor, but society lost valuable resources when so much human capital remained uneducated and physically abused. First the state legislatures and then the U.S. Congress intervened to protect children from such abuse by limiting or forbidding the use of child labor and making school attendance mandatory. In poor nations, governments do much less to limit use of child labor. In Africa, for example, 40 percent of children under age 14 work to survive or to help support their families.

Government regulations further change HOW goods are produced by setting standards for workplace safety and even minimum pay, fringe benefits, and overtime provisions. After decades of bloody confrontations, the government also established the right of workers to organize and set rules for union–management relations. Unemployment insurance, Social Security benefits, disability insurance, and guarantees for private pension benefits also protect labor from the vagaries of the marketplace. They have had a profound effect on how much people work, when they retire, and even how long they live.

PROTECTING THE ENVIRONMENT   In earlier times, producers didn't have to concern themselves with the impact of their production activities on the environment. The steel mills around Pittsburgh blocked out the sun with clouds of sulfurous gases that spewed out of their furnaces. Timber companies laid waste to broad swaths of forestland without regard to animal habitats or ecological balance. Paper mills used adjacent rivers as disposal sites, and ships at sea routinely dumped their waste overboard. Neither cars nor airplanes were equipped with controls for noise or air pollution.

In the absence of government intervention, such side effects would be common. Decisions on how to produce would be based on private costs alone, not on how the environment is affected. However, such **externalities**—spillover costs imposed on the broader community—affect our collective well-being. To reduce the external costs of production, the government limits air, water, and noise pollution and regulates environmental use.

externalities Costs (or benefits) of a market activity borne by a third party.

Striking a Balance

All of these government interventions are designed to change HOW goods and services are produced. Such interventions reflect the conviction that the market alone would not always select the best possible way of producing goods and services. The market's answer to the HOW question would be based on narrow profit-and-loss calculations, not on broader measures of societal well-being. To redress this market failure, the government regulates production behavior.

As noted in Chapter 1, there is no guarantee that government regulation of HOW goods are produced always makes us better off. Excessive regulation may inhibit production, raise product prices, and limit consumer choices. In other words, *government* failure might replace *market* failure, leaving us no better off and possibly even worse off.

FOR WHOM AMERICA PRODUCES

However imperfect our answers to the WHAT and HOW questions might be, they cannot obscure how rich America is. As we have observed, the American economy produces a $15 trillion economic pie. The final question we have to address is how that pie will be sliced. Will everyone get an equal slice, or will some Americans be served gluttonous slices while others get only crumbs?

Were the slices of the pie carved by the market mechanism, the slices surely would not be equal. Markets reward individuals on the basis of their contribution to output. *In a market economy, an individual's income depends on*

- *The quantity and quality of resources owned.*
- *The price that those resources command in the market.*

That's what concerned Karl Marx so much. As Marx saw it, the capitalists (owners of capital) had a decided advantage in this market-driven distribution. By owning the means of production, capitalists would continue to accumulate wealth, power, and income. Members of the proletariat would get only enough output to ensure their survival. Differences in income within the capitalist

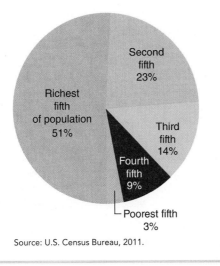

Source: U.S. Census Bureau, 2011.

FIGURE 2.6
Slices of the U.S. Income Pie

The richest fifth of U.S. households gets half of all the income—a huge slice of the income pie. By contrast, the poorest fifth gets only a sliver. Should the government do more to equalize the slices or let the market serve up the pie?

class or within the working class were of no consequence in the face of these class divisions. All capitalists were rich, all workers poor.

Marx's predictions of how output would be distributed turned out to be wrong in two ways. First, labor's share of total output has risen greatly over time. Second, differences *within* the labor and capitalist classes have become more important than differences between the classes. Many workers are rich, and a good many capitalists are poor. Moreover, the distinction between workers and capitalists has been blurred by profit-sharing plans, employee ownership, and widespread ownership of corporate stock. Accordingly, in today's economy it is more useful to examine how the economic pie is distributed across *individuals* rather than across labor and capitalist *classes.*

The Distribution of Income

Figure 2.6 illustrates how uneven the individual slices of the income pie are. Imagine dividing up the population into five subgroups of equal size, but sorted by income. Thus the top fifth (or quintile) would include that 20 percent of all households with the most income. The bottom fifth would include the 20 percent of households with the least income. The rest of the population would be spread across the other three quintiles.

Figure 2.6 shows that the richest fifth of the population gets *half* of the income pie. By contrast, the poorest fifth gets a tiny sliver. The dimensions of this inequality are spelled out in Table 2.4. Both the figure and the table underscore how unequally the FOR WHOM question is settled in the United States.

As shocking as U.S. income inequalities might appear, incomes are distributed even less equally in many other countries. The following News Wire displays the share of total income received by the top decile (tenth) of households in various

Income Group	2011 Income (Dollars)	Average Income	Share of Total Income (Percent)
Highest fifth	Above $100,000	178,020	51.1%
Second fifth	60,000–100,000	80,080	23.0
Third fifth	40,000–60,000	49,842	14.3
Fourth fifth	20,000–40,000	29,204	8.4
Lowest fifth	0–20,000	11,239	3.2

Source: U.S. Department of Commerce, Bureau of the Census.

TABLE 2.4
Unequal Incomes

The size distribution of income indicates how total income is distributed among income classes. That fifth of our population with the lowest incomes gets only 3.2 percent of total income while the highest income class (fifth) gets half of total income.

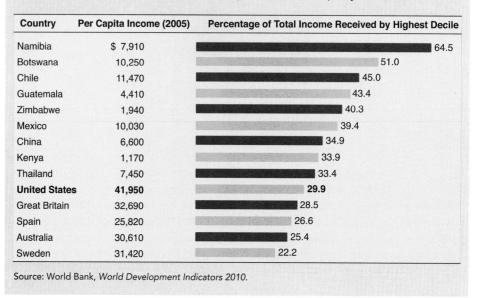

NEWS WIRE | **INEQUALITY**

Income Share of the Rich

Incomes are distributed much less equally in poor countries than in rich ones. In most developing countries the top tenth of all households receives 30–50 percent of all income. In the United States and other developed countries inequality is much less severe.

Country	Per Capita Income (2005)	Percentage of Total Income Received by Highest Decile
Namibia	$ 7,910	64.5
Botswana	10,250	51.0
Chile	11,470	45.0
Guatemala	4,410	43.4
Zimbabwe	1,940	40.3
Mexico	10,030	39.4
China	6,600	34.9
Kenya	1,170	33.9
Thailand	7,450	33.4
United States	**41,950**	**29.9**
Great Britain	32,690	28.5
Spain	25,820	26.6
Australia	30,610	25.4
Sweden	31,420	22.2

Source: World Bank, *World Development Indicators 2010*.

---

personal distribution of income The way total personal income is divided up among households or income classes.

countries. In general, inequalities tend to be larger in poorer countries. As countries develop, the **personal distribution of income** tends to become more equal.

Income Mobility

Another important feature of any income distribution is how long people stay in any one position. Being poor isn't such a hardship if your poverty lasts only a week or even a month. Likewise, unequal slices of the economic pie aren't so unfair if the slices are redistributed frequently. In that case, everyone would have a chance to be rich or poor on occasion.

In reality, the slices of the pie are not distributed randomly every year. Some people get large slices every year, and other people always seem to end up with crumbs. Nevertheless, such *permanent* inequality is more the exception than the rule in the U.S. economy. One of the most distinctive features of the U.S. income distribution is how often people move up and down the income ladder. This kind of income *mobility* makes lifelong incomes much less unequal than annual incomes. In many nations, income inequalities are much more permanent.

Government Redistribution: Taxes and Transfers

Even if income inequality is more severe or more permanent elsewhere, U.S. citizens may feel that the market fails to generate a "fair" enough distribution in this country. If so, another role for the government is to *redistribute* incomes. The mechanisms for reslicing the income pie are taxes and income transfers.

progressive tax A tax system in which tax rates rise as incomes rise.

TAXES Taxes are also a critical mechanism for redistributing market incomes. A **progressive tax** does this by imposing higher tax *rates* on people with larger incomes. Under such a system a rich person pays not only more taxes but also a larger *portion* of his or her income. Thus *a progressive tax makes after-tax incomes more equal than before-tax incomes.*

The federal income tax is designed to be progressive. Individuals with less than $7,500 of income paid no income tax in 2012 and might even have received a spendable tax credit from Uncle Sam. Middle-income households confronted an average tax rate of 20 percent, and rich households faced a top federal income tax rate of 35 percent. In 2013 Congress raised that top tax rate to 39.6, making the tax system even more progressive (redistributive).

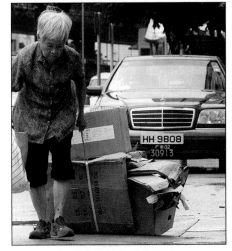

INCOME TRANSFERS   Taxes are only half the redistribution story. Equally important is who gets the income the government collects. The government completes the redistribution process by transferring income to consumers and providing services. The largest *income transfer* program is Social Security, which pays over $700 billion a year to 50 million older or disabled persons. Although rich and poor alike get Social Security benefits, low-wage workers get more retirement benefits for every dollar of earnings. Hence the benefits of the Social Security program are distributed in a *progressive* fashion. Income transfers reserved exclusively for poor people—welfare benefits, food stamps, Medicaid, and the like—are even more progressive. As a result, ***the income transfer system gives lower-income households more output than the market itself would provide.*** In the absence of transfer payments and taxes, the lowest income quintile would get only 1 percent of total income. The tax transfer system raises their share to 3.2 percent (see Table 2.4). That's still not much of a slice, but it's more of the income pie than they got in the marketplace. To get a still larger slice, they need more market income or more government-led income redistribution.

Income inequalities are more vivid in poor nations than in rich ones.

© Mike Clarke/Getty Images

POLICY PERSPECTIVES

Can We End Global Poverty?

The United States is the economic powerhouse of the world. As we've seen, the 5 percent of the world's population that lives within our nation's borders consumes over 20 percent of the world's output. The three richest Americans—Bill Gates, Warren Buffet, and Paul Allen—have more wealth than the combined total output of the world's 40 poorest countries (roughly 600 million people!). Even the 40 million officially classified "poor" people in the United States enjoy living standards that *3 billion* inhabitants of Earth can only dream of. According to the World Bank, 3 billion people scrape by on less than $3 per day. In the poorest nations—where half the world's population lives—only three of every four people have access to safe water, and less than one of two have sanitation facilities. One-fourth of these people are undernourished; malnutrition is even higher among children. Not surprisingly, 12 percent of live births end in a child's death before age five (versus 0.8 percent in the United States). Illiteracy is the norm for those who survive beyond childhood.

In September 2000 the United Nations adopted a "Millennium Declaration" to reduce global poverty. Given the enormity of the task, the United Nations didn't vow to *eliminate* poverty, but instead just to *reduce* poverty, illiteracy, child mortality, and HIV/AIDS over a period of 15 years. We haven't come close to achieving these goals. If the rich nations of the world gave more assistance than the 0.23 percent of GDP they now offer, that would help. Even doubling aid wouldn't do the job, however. Ultimately the well-being of the world's poor hinges on the development of strong national economies. Only persistent economic growth can end global poverty. The real millennium challenge is fostering that growth. That's where economic theory can help.

Even America's "poor" look affluent by comparison to impoverished residents of some other countries.

Marcus Lindstrom

SUMMARY

- The answers to the WHAT, HOW, and FOR WHOM questions are reflected in the dimensions of the economy. These answers are the product of market forces and government intervention. **LO1**
- Gross domestic product (GDP) is the basic measure of how much an economy produces. It is the *value* of total output.
- *Real* GDP measures the inflation-adjusted value of output; *nominal* GDP, the current dollar value. **LO1**
- The United States produces roughly $15 trillion of output, one-fifth of the world's total. American GDP per capita is four times the world average. **LO2**
- The high level of U.S. per capita GDP reflects the high productivity of American workers. Abundant capital, education, technology, training, and management all contribute to high productivity. **LO3**
- Over 70 percent of U.S. output consists of services. The service industries continue to grow faster than goods-producing industries. **LO4**

- Most of America's output consists of consumer goods and services. Investment goods account for less than 15 percent of total output. **LO4**
- Proprietorships and partnerships outnumber corporations nearly five to one. Nevertheless, corporate America produces 80 percent of total output. **LO3**
- Government intervenes in the economy to establish the rules of the (market) game and to correct the market's answers to the WHAT, HOW, and FOR WHOM questions. The risk of government failure spurs the search for the right mix of market reliance and government regulation. **LO4**
- Incomes are distributed very unequally among households, with households in the highest income class (quintile) receiving 15 times more income than the average low-income (quintile) household. **LO5**
- The progressive income tax system is designed to make after-tax incomes more equal. Tax-financed transfer payments such as Social Security and welfare also redistribute a significant amount of income. **LO5**

TERMS TO REMEMBER

Define the following terms:

gross domestic product	investment	capital intensive	personal distribution of
nominal GDP	income transfers	productivity	income
real GDP	exports	human capital	progressive tax
per capita GDP	imports	monopoly	
economic growth	factors of production	externality	

QUESTIONS FOR DISCUSSION

1. Americans already enjoy living standards that far exceed world averages. Do we have enough? Should we even try to produce more? **LO2**
2. Why do we measure output in value terms rather than in physical terms? For that matter, why do we bother to measure output at all? **LO1**
3. Why do people suggest that the United States needs to devote more resources to investment goods? Why not produce just consumption goods? **LO3**
4. The U.S. farm population has shrunk by over 25 million people since 1900. Where did they all go? Why did they move? **LO4**

5. Rich people have over 15 times as much income as poor people. Is that fair? How should output be distributed? **LO5**
6. If taxes were more progressive, would total output be affected? **LO5**
7. Why might income inequalities diminish as an economy develops? **LO5**
8. Why is per capita GDP so much higher in the United States than in Mexico? **LO3**
9. Do we need more or less government intervention to decide WHAT, HOW, and FOR WHOM? Give specific examples. **LO4**
10. **POLICY PERSPECTIVES** What can poor nations do to raise their living standards? **LO3**

PROBLEMS

■ connect

1. Draw a production possibilities curve with consumer goods on one axis and investment goods on the other axis.   **LO1**
   (a) Identify the opportunity cost of increasing investment from I_1 to I_2.
   (b) What will happen to future production possibilities if investment increases now?
   (c) What will happen to future production possibilities if only consumer goods are produced now?

2. Suppose the following data describe output in two different years: **LO1**
   (a) Compute *nominal* GDP in each year.
   (b) By what percentage did nominal GDP increase between Year 1 and Year 2?
   (c) Now compute *real* GDP in Year 2 by using the prices of Year 1.
   (d) By what percentage did real GDP increase between Year 1 and Year 2?

Item	Year 1	Year 2
Apples	20,000 @ 25¢ each	30,000 @ 30¢ each
Bicycles	700 @ $800 each	650 @ $900 each
Movie rentals	10,000 @ $1.00 each	12,000 @ $1.50 each

3. GDP per capita in the United States was approximately $50,000 in 2013. What will it be in the year 2016 if GDP per capita grows each year by   **LO1**
   (a) 0 percent?
   (b) 2 percent?

4. According to Figure 2.4,   **LO4**
   (a) Did the *quantity* of manufactured output increase or decrease between 1900 and 2000?
   (b) By how much (in percentage terms)?
   (c) Did the manufacturing *share* of GDP rise or fall during that time?

5. Assume that total output is determined by this formula: **LO3**

   number of workers × productivity = total output
   (output per worker)

   (a) If the workforce is growing by 1 percent but productivity doesn't improve, how fast can output increase?
   (b) If productivity increases by 3 percent *and* the number of workers increases by 1 percent a year, how fast will output grow?

6. According to the News Wire on page 35, by what percentage did productivity increase at Boeing between 1995 and 2010?   **LO3**

7. According to Table 2.4,   **LO5**
   (a) What is the *average* income in the United States?
   (b) What percentage of the income of people in the highest fifth would have to be taxed away to bring them down to that average?

8. According to the News Wire on page 42, what percentage of their income would the highest-decile households in Namibia have to give up to end up with an *average* income?   **LO5**

9. Complete the following table:

	Before-Tax Income	Tax Rate	Tax Paid	After-Tax Income
Rich Family	$500,000	30%	____	____
Middle-Class Family	50,000	20%	____	____
Poor Family	20,000	2%	____	____

What is the ratio of a rich family's income to a poor family's income (a) before taxes and (b) after taxes? (c) Is this tax progressive?   **LO5**

10. **POLICY PERSPECTIVES** The United States devotes 0.20 percent of its GDP to development assistance.   **LO2**
   (a) How much money is that? (See Figure 2.1.)
   (b) If the aid share doubled, how much more (than the value determined in part (a)) would that be for each of the 3 billion "extremely poor" people in developing nations?

◄ Practice quizzes, student PowerPoints, author podcasts, web activities, and additional materials available at **www.mhhe.com/schileressentials9e**, or scan here. Need a barcode reader? Try ScanLife, available in your app store.

3

Supply and Demand

◄ Practice quizzes, student PowerPoints, author podcasts, web activities, and additional materials available at www.mhhe.com/ schilleressentials9e, or scan here. Need a barcode reader? Try ScanLife, available in your app store.

LEARNING OBJECTIVES

After reading this chapter, you should be able to:

1   Explain why people participate in markets.
2   Describe what market demand and supply measure.
3   Depict how and why a market equilibrium is found.
4   Illustrate how and why demand and supply curves sometimes shift.
5   Explain how market shortages and surpluses occur.

A few years ago a Florida man tried to sell one of his kidneys on eBay. As his offer explained, he could supply only one kidney because he needed the other to survive. He wanted the bidding to start out at $25,000, plus expenses for the surgical removal and shipment of his kidney. He felt confident he could get at least that much money since thousands of people have potentially fatal kidney diseases.

He was right. The bids for his kidney quickly surpassed $100,000. Clearly there were lots of people with kidney disease who were willing and able to pay high prices to get a lifesaving transplant.

The seller never got the chance to sell his kidney to the highest bidder. Although organ transplants are perfectly legal in the United States, the purchase or sale of human organs is not. When eBay learned the pending sale was illegal, it shut down the man's advertisement.

Despite its illegality, there is clearly a market for human kidneys. That is to say, there are people who are willing to *sell* kidneys and others who are willing to *buy* kidneys. Those are sufficient conditions for the existence of a market. The market in kidneys happens to be illegal in the United States, but it is still a market, although illegal. The markets for drugs, prostitution, and nuclear warheads are also illegal, but still reflect the intentions of potential buyers and sellers.

Fortunately we don't have to venture into the underworld to see how markets work. You can watch markets work by visiting eBay or other electronic auction sites. Or you can simply go to the mall and watch people shop. In either location you will observe people deciding whether to buy or sell goods at various prices. That's the essence of market activity.

The goal in this chapter is to assess how markets actually function. How does the invisible hand of the market resolve the competing interests of buyers (who want low prices) and sellers (who want high prices)? Specifically,

- What determines the price of a good or service?
- How does the price of a product affect its production or consumption?
- Why do prices and production levels often change?

MARKET PARTICIPANTS

More than 300 million individual consumers, about 30 million business firms, and thousands of government agencies participate directly in the U.S. economy. Millions of foreigners also participate by buying and selling goods in American markets.

Goals

All these economic actors participate in the market to achieve specific goals. Consumers strive to maximize their own happiness; businesses try to maximize profits; government agencies attempt to maximize social welfare. Foreigners pursue the same goals as consumers, producers, or government agencies. In every case, they strive to achieve those goals by buying or selling the best possible mix of goods, services, or factors of production.

Constraints

The desire of all market participants to maximize something—profits, private satisfaction, or social welfare—is not their only common trait. Another element common to all participants is their *limited resources*. You and I cannot buy everything we desire; we simply don't have enough income. As a consequence, we must make *choices* among available products. We're always hoping to get as much satisfaction as possible for the few dollars we have to spend. Likewise, business firms and government agencies must decide how *best* to use their limited resources to maximize profits or public welfare. This is the scarcity problem we examined in Chapter 1. It is central to all economic decisions.

Specialization and Exchange

To maximize the returns on our limited resources, we participate in the **market,** buying and selling various goods and services. Our decision to participate in these exchanges is prompted by two considerations. First, most of us are incapable of producing everything we desire to consume. Second, even if we *could* produce all our own goods and services, it would still make sense to *specialize,* producing only one product and trading it for other desired goods and services.

Suppose you were capable of growing your own food, stitching your own clothes, building your own shelter, and even writing your own economics text. Even in this little utopia, it would still make sense to decide how *best* to expend your limited time and energy and to rely on others to fill in the gaps. If you were *most* proficient at growing food, you would be best off spending your time farming. You could then exchange some of your food output for the clothes, shelter, and books you desired. In the end, you'd be able to consume more goods than if you had tried to make everything yourself.

Our economic interactions with others are thus necessitated by two constraints:

- Our inability as individuals to produce all the things we desire.
- The limited amount of time, energy, and resources we possess for producing those things we could make for ourselves.

Together these constraints lead us to specialize and interact. Most of the interactions that result take place in the market.

> **market** Any place where goods are bought and sold.

MARKET INTERACTIONS

Figure 3.1 summarizes the kinds of interactions that occur among market participants. Note, first of all, that we have identified *four separate groups of market participants:*

- *Consumers.*
- *Business firms.*
- *Governments.*
- *Foreigners.*

Domestically, the "consumers" rectangle includes all 320 million consumers in the United States. In the "business firms" box we have grouped all the domestic business enterprises that buy and sell goods and services. The third participant, "governments," includes the many separate agencies of the federal government, as well as state and local governments. Figure 3.1 also illustrates the role of foreigners.

The Two Markets

The easiest way to keep track of all this market activity is to distinguish two basic markets. Figure 3.1 does this by depicting separate circles for product markets and factor markets. In **factor markets,** factors of production are exchanged. Market participants buy or sell land, labor, or capital that can be used in the production process. When you go looking for work, for example, you are making a factor of production—your labor—available to producers. You are offering

> **factor market** Any place where factors of production (e.g., land, labor, capital, entrepreneurship) are bought and sold.

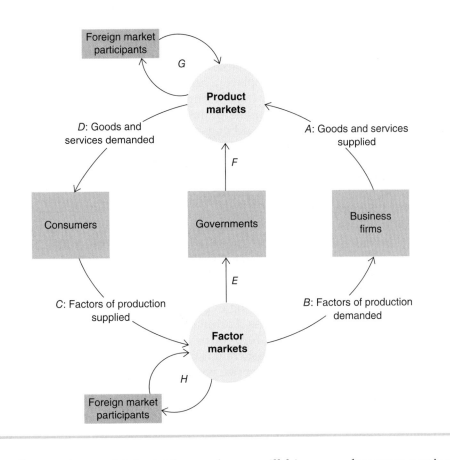

FIGURE 3.1
Market Interactions

Business firms participate in markets by supplying goods and services to product markets (point *A*) and purchasing factors of production in factor markets (*B*).

Individual consumers participate in the marketplace by supplying factors of production such as their own labor (*C*) and purchasing final goods and services (*D*).

Federal, state, and local governments also participate in both factor (*E*) and product markets (*F*).

Foreigners participate by supplying imports, purchasing exports (*G*), and buying and selling resources (*H*).

to *sell* your time and talent. The producers will hire you—*buy* your services in the factor market—if you are offering the skills they need at a price they are willing to pay.

The activity in factor markets is only half the story. At the end of a hard day's work, consumers go to the grocery store, the mall, or the movies to purchase desired goods and services—that is, to buy *products.* In this context, consumers again interact with business firms. This time, however, their roles are reversed: consumers are doing the *buying,* and businesses are doing the *selling.* This exchange of goods and services occurs in **product markets.**

Governments also supply goods and services to product markets. The consumer rarely buys national defense, schools, or highways directly; instead such purchases are made indirectly through taxes and government expenditure. In Figure 3.1, the arrows running from governments through product markets to consumers remind us, however, that all government output is intended "for the people." In this sense, the government acts as an intermediary, buying factors of production (e.g., government employees) and providing certain goods and services consumers desire (e.g., police protection).

In Figure 3.1, the arrow connecting product markets to consumers (point *D*) emphasizes the fact that consumers, by definition, do not supply products. When individuals produce goods and services, they do so within the government or business sector. An individual who is a doctor, a dentist, or an economic consultant functions in two sectors. When selling services in the market, this person is regarded as a "business"; when away from the office, he or she is regarded as a "consumer." This distinction is helpful in emphasizing that *the consumer is the final recipient of all goods and services produced.*

product market Any place where finished goods and services (products) are bought and sold.

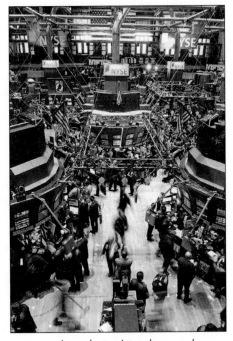

A market exists wherever buyers and sellers interact.

© Stephen Chernin/Getty Images

LOCATING MARKETS   Although we refer repeatedly to two kinds of markets, it would be a little foolish to go off in search of the product and factor markets. Neither a factor market nor a product market is a single, identifiable structure. The term *market* simply refers to any place where an economic exchange occurs—where a buyer and seller interact. The exchange may take place on the street, in a taxicab, over the phone, by mail, online, or through the classified ads of the newspaper. In some cases, the market used may in fact be quite distinguishable, as in the case of a retail store, the Chicago Commodity Exchange, or a state employment office. But whatever it looks like, *a market exists wherever and whenever an exchange takes place.*

Dollars and Exchange

Sometimes people exchange one good for another directly. On eBay, for example, you might persuade a seller to accept some old DVDs in payment for the Xbox 360 she is selling. Or you might offer to paint someone's house in exchange for "free" rent. Such two-way exchanges are called **barter.**

> **barter** The direct exchange of one good for another, without the use of money.

The problem with bartered exchanges is that you have to find a seller who wants whatever good you are offering in payment. This can make shopping an extremely time-consuming process. Fortunately, most market transactions are facilitated by using money as a form of payment. If you go shopping for an Xbox, you don't have to find a seller craving old DVDs; all you have to do is find a seller willing to accept the dollar price you are willing to pay. Because money facilitates exchanges, *nearly every market transaction involves an exchange of dollars for goods (in product markets) or resources (in factor markets).* Money thus plays a critical role in facilitating market exchanges and the specialization they permit.

Supply and Demand

The two sides of each market transaction are called **supply** and **demand.** As noted earlier, we are *supplying* resources to the market when we look for a job—that is, when we offer our labor in exchange for income. But we are *demanding* goods when we shop in a supermarket—that is, when we are prepared to offer dollars in exchange for something to eat. Business firms may *supply* goods and services in product markets at the same time that they are *demanding* factors of production in factor markets.

> **supply** The ability and willingness to sell (produce) specific quantities of a good at alternative prices in a given time period, *ceteris paribus*.

> **demand** The ability and willingness to buy specific quantities of a good at alternative prices in a given time period, *ceteris paribus*.

Whether one is on the supply side or the demand side of any particular market transaction depends on the nature of the exchange, not on the people or institutions involved.

DEMAND

Although the concepts of supply and demand help explain what's happening in the marketplace, we are not yet ready to summarize the countless transactions that occur daily in both factor and product markets. Recall that *every market transaction involves an exchange and thus some element of both supply and demand.* Then just consider how many exchanges you alone undertake in a single week, not to mention the transactions of the other 320 million or so consumers among us. To keep track of so much action, we need to summarize the activities of a great many individuals.

Individual Demand

We can begin to understand how market forces work by looking more closely at the behavior of a single market participant. Let us start with Tom, a senior at Clearview College. Tom has majored in everything from art history to government in his five years at Clearview. He didn't connect with any of those fields and is on the brink of academic dismissal. To make matters worse, his parents have threatened to cut him off financially unless he graduates sometime soon. They want him to take courses that will lead to a job after graduation so they don't have to keep supporting him.

Tom thinks he has found the perfect solution: web design. Everything associated with the Internet pays big bucks. Plus, girls seem to think webbies are "cool." Or at least so Tom thinks. And his parents would definitely approve. So Tom has enrolled in web design courses.

Unfortunately for Tom, he never developed computer skills. Until he got to Clearview College, he thought mastering Sony's latest alien attack video game was the pinnacle of electronic wizardry. His parents gave him an iMac with a Mountain Lion operating system but he used it only for surfing hot video sites. The concept of using his computer for coursework, much less developing some web content, was completely foreign to him. To compound his problems, Tom didn't have a clue about streaming, interfacing, animation, or the other concepts the web design instructor outlined in the first lecture.

Given his circumstances, Tom was desperate to find someone who could tutor him in web design. But desperation is not enough to secure the services of a web architect. In a market-based economy, you must also be willing to *pay* for the things you want. Specifically, ***a demand exists only if someone is willing and able to pay for the good***—that is, exchange dollars for a good or service in the marketplace. Is Tom willing and able to pay for the web design tutoring he so obviously needs?

Let us assume that Tom has some income and is willing to spend some of it to get a tutor. Under these assumptions, we can claim that Tom is a participant in the *market* for web design services.

But how much is Tom willing to pay? Surely Tom is not prepared to exchange *all* his income for help in mastering web design. After all, Tom could use his income to buy more desirable goods and services. If he spent all his income on a web tutor, that help would have an extremely high **opportunity cost.** He would be giving up the opportunity to spend that income on other goods and services. He might pass his web design class but have little else. That doesn't sound like a good idea to Tom. Even though he says he would be willing to pay *anything* to pass the web design course, he probably has lower prices in mind. Indeed, there are *limits* to the amount Tom is willing to pay for any given quantity of web design tutoring. These limits will be determined by how much income Tom has to spend and how many other goods and services he must forsake to pay for a tutor.

Tom also knows that his grade in web design will depend in part on how much tutoring service he buys. He can pass the course with only a few hours of design help. If he wants a better grade, however, the cost is going to escalate quickly.

Naturally Tom wants it all—an A in web design and a ticket to higher-paying jobs. But here again the distinction between *desire* and *demand* is relevant. He may *desire* to master web design, but his actual proficiency will depend on how many hours of tutoring he is willing to *pay* for.

We assume, then, that when Tom starts looking for a web design tutor he has in mind some sort of **demand schedule,** like that described in Figure 3.2. According to row *A* of this schedule, Tom is willing and able to buy only one hour of tutoring service per semester if he must pay $50 an hour. At such an "outrageous" price he will learn minimal skills and just pass the course. But that's all Tom is willing to buy at that price.

At lower prices, Tom would behave differently. According to Figure 3.2, Tom would purchase *more* tutoring services if the price per hour were *less*. At lower

opportunity cost The most desired goods or services that are forgone in order to obtain something else.

demand schedule A table showing the quantities of a good a consumer is willing and able to buy at alternative prices in a given time period, *ceteris paribus.*

FIGURE 3.2
A Demand Schedule and Curve

A **demand schedule** indicates the quantities of a good a consumer is able and willing to buy at alternative prices (*ceteris paribus*). The demand schedule indicates that Tom would buy five hours of web design tutoring per semester if the price were $35 per hour (row *D*). If tutoring were less expensive (rows *E–I*), Tom would purchase a larger quantity.

A **demand curve** is a graphical illustration of a demand schedule. Each point on the curve refers to a specific quantity that will be demanded at a given price. If the price of tutoring were $35 per hour, this curve tells us that the consumer would purchase five hours per semester (point *D*). Each point on the curve corresponds to a row in the above schedule.

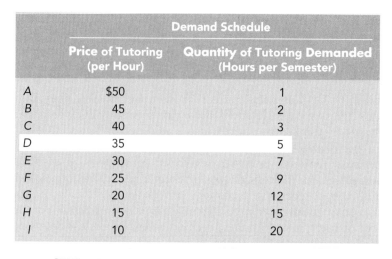

	Demand Schedule	
	Price of Tutoring (per Hour)	**Quantity of Tutoring Demanded (Hours per Semester)**
A	$50	1
B	45	2
C	40	3
D	35	5
E	30	7
F	25	9
G	20	12
H	15	15
I	10	20

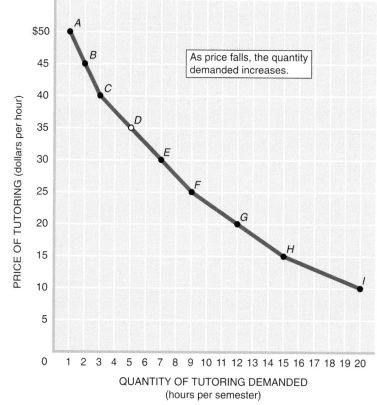

prices, he would not have to give up so many other goods and services for each hour of technical help. The reduced opportunity costs implied by lower service prices increase the attractiveness of professional help. Indeed, we see from row *I* of the demand schedule that Tom is willing to purchase 20 hours per semester—the whole bag of design tricks—if the price of tutoring is as low as $10 per hour.

Notice that the demand schedule doesn't tell us *why* Tom is willing to pay these specific prices for various amounts of tutoring. Tom's expressed willingness to pay for web design tutoring may reflect a desperate need to finish a web design course, a lot of income to spend, or a relatively small desire for other goods and services. All the demand schedule tells us is what this consumer is *willing and able* to buy, for whatever reasons.

Also observe that the demand schedule doesn't tell us how many hours of design help the consumer will *actually* buy. Figure 3.2 simply states that Tom is *willing and able* to pay for one hour of tutoring at $50 per hour, for two hours at $45 each, and so on. How much service he purchases will depend on the actual price of web services in the market. Until we know that price, we cannot tell how much service will be purchased. Hence **demand is an expression of consumer buying intentions, of a willingness to buy, not a statement of actual purchases.**

A convenient summary of buying intentions is the **demand curve,** a graphical illustration of the demand schedule. The demand curve in Figure 3.2 tells us again that this consumer is willing to pay for only one hour of web design tutoring if the price is $50 per hour (point *A*), for two if the price is $45 (point *B*), for three at $40 a hour (point *C*), and so on. Once we know what the market price of web tutoring actually is, a glance at the demand curve tells us how much service this consumer will buy.

demand curve A curve describing the quantities of a good a consumer is willing and able to buy at alternative prices in a given time period, *ceteris paribus.*

What the notion of *demand* emphasizes is that the amount we buy of a good depends on its price. We seldom if ever decide to buy a certain quantity of a good at whatever price is charged. Instead we enter markets with a set of desires and a limited amount of money to spend. *How much we actually buy of any good will depend on its price.*

A common feature of demand curves is their downward slope. As the price of a good falls, people tend to purchase more of it. In Figure 3.2 the quantity of web tutorial services demanded increases (moves rightward along the horizontal axis) as the price per hour decreases (moves down the vertical axis). This inverse relationship between price and quantity is so common that we refer to it as the **law of demand.**

law of demand The quantity of a good demanded in a given time period increases as its price falls, *ceteris paribus.*

College administrators think the law of demand could be used to curb student drinking. Low retail prices and bar promotions encourage students to drink more alcohol. As the accompanying News Wire explains, higher prices would reduce the quantity of alcohol demanded.

Determinants of Demand

The demand curve in Figure 3.2 has only two dimensions—quantity demanded (on the horizontal axis) and price (on the vertical axis). This seems to imply that the amount of tutorial services demanded depends only on the price of that

---

NEWS WIRE	LAW OF DEMAND

Higher Alcohol Prices and Student Drinking

Raise the price of alcohol substantially, and some college students will not drink or will drink less. That's the conclusion from a Harvard survey of 22,831 students at 158 colleges. Students faced with a $1 increase above the average drink price of $2.17 will be 33 percent less likely to drink at all or as much. So raising the price of alcohol in college communities could significantly lessen student drinking and its associated problems (alcohol-related deaths, property damage, unwanted sexual encounters, arrests). This could be done by raising local excise taxes, eliminating bar promotions, and forbidding all-you-can-drink events.

Source: Jenny Williams, Frank Chaloupka, and Henry Wechsler, "Are There Differential Effects of Price and Policy on College Students' Drinking Intensity?" Copyright Blackwell Publishing. Used with permission by the author, Jenny Williams.

NOTE: The law of demand predicts that the quantity demanded of any good—even beer and liquor—declines as its price increases.

service. This is surely not the case. A consumer's willingness and ability to buy a product at various prices depend on a variety of forces. We call those forces *determinants of demand*. **The determinants of market demand include**

- *Tastes* (desire for this and other goods).
- *Income* (of the consumer).
- *Other goods* (their availability and price).
- *Expectations* (for income, prices, tastes).
- *Number of buyers.*

If Tom didn't have to pass a web design course, he would have no taste (desire) for web page tutoring and thus no demand. If he had no income, he would not have the ability to pay and thus would still be out of the web design market. The price and availability of other goods affect the opportunity cost of tutoring services—that is, what Tom must give up. Expectations for income, grades, graduation prospects, and parental support also influence his willingness to buy such services.

Ceteris Paribus

ceteris paribus The assumption of nothing else changing.

If demand is in fact such a multidimensional decision, how can we reduce it to only the two dimensions of price and quantity? This is the **ceteris paribus** trick we encountered earlier. To simplify their models of the world, economists focus on only one or two forces at a time and *assume* nothing else changes. We know a consumer's tastes, income, other goods, and expectations all affect the decision to buy web design services. But **we focus on the relationship between quantity demanded and price.** That is to say, we want to know what *independent* influence price has on consumption decisions. To find out, we must isolate that one influence, price, and assume that the determinants of demand remain unchanged.

The *ceteris paribus* assumption is not as far-fetched as it may seem. People's tastes (desires) don't change very quickly. Income tends to be fairly stable from week to week. Even expectations for the future are slow to change. Accordingly, the price of a good may be the only thing that changes on any given day. In that case, a change in price may be the only thing that prompts a change in consumer behavior.

Shifts in Demand

The determinants of demand do change, of course, particularly over time. Accordingly, **the demand schedule and curve remain unchanged only so long as the underlying determinants of demand remain constant.** If the *ceteris paribus* assumption is violated—if tastes, income, other goods, or expectations change—the ability or willingness to buy will change. When this happens, the demand curve will **shift** to a new position.

shift in demand A change in the quantity demanded at any (every) given price.

Suppose, for example, that Tom wins $1,000 in the state lottery. This increase in his income would increase his ability to pay for tutoring services. Figure 3.3 shows the effect of this windfall on Tom's demand. The old demand curve, D_1, is no longer relevant. Tom's lottery winnings enable him to buy more tutoring services at any price. This is illustrated by the new demand curve, D_2. According to this new curve, lucky Tom is now willing and able to buy 11 hours per semester at the price of $35 per hour (point d_2). This is a large increase in demand, as previously (before winning the lottery) he demanded only five hours at that price (point d_1).

With his higher income, Tom can buy more tutoring services at *every* price. Thus **the entire demand curve shifts to the right when income goes up.** Both the old (pre-lottery) and the new (postlottery) demand curves are illustrated in Figure 3.3.

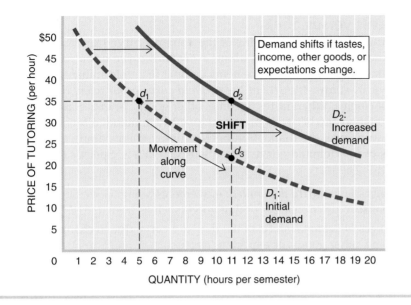

Demand shifts if tastes, income, other goods, or expectations change.

SHIFT

Movement along curve

D_2: Increased demand

D_1: Initial demand

d_1 d_2 d_3

PRICE OF TUTORING (per hour)

QUANTITY (hours per semester)

FIGURE 3.3
A Shift in Demand
A demand curve shows how the quantity demanded changes in response to a change in price, *if* all else remains constant. But the determinants of demand may themselves change, causing the demand curve to *shift*.

In this case, an increase in income increases demand from D_1 to D_2. After this shift, Tom demands 11 hours (d_2), rather than 5 (d_1), at the price of \$35. The quantity demanded at all other prices increases as well.

Income is only one of four basic determinants of demand. Changes in any of the other determinants of demand would also cause the demand curve to shift. Tom's taste for web design tutoring might increase dramatically, for example, if his other professors made the quality of personal web pages a critical determinant of course grades. His taste (desire) for web design services might increase even more if his parents promised to buy him a new car if he got an A in the course. Whatever its origins, *an increase in taste (desire) or expectations also shifts the demand curve to the right.*

Other goods can also shift the demand curve. Hybrid vehicles became more popular when gasoline prices rose. The demand for gas-saving hybrids increased, while demand for gas guzzlers declined. A change in expectations can also shift demand. This was clearly the case in early 2010, when Toyota revealed that sudden-acceleration failures in its cars had caused fatal accidents. This abruptly changed consumer expectations about the safety of Toyotas, shifting the demand curve to the left: consumers demanded fewer Toyotas at every price (see the News Wire).

NEWS WIRE	SHIFTS OF DEMAND

Toyota's February Sales Suffer over Safety Concerns
Toyota Motor's (TM) recall woes have put a dent in sales. The Japanese automaker reported that sales fell 8.7% in February as production and sales halts combined with consumer concerns about safety recalls took a toll on demand. Several of those recalls involve popular Camry sedans, which recorded a 20% drop in sales during February, the first full sales month following the latest recall of vehicles for unintended acceleration in late January.

Source: Daily Finance, March 2, 2010 © 2010 AOL Inc. All rights reserved.

NOTE: Demand decreases (shifts left) when tastes diminish, the price of substitute goods declines, or income or expectations worsen. What happened here?

Movements versus Shifts

It is important to distinguish shifts of the demand curve from movements along the demand curve. *Movements along a demand curve are a response to price changes for that good.* Such movements assume that determinants of demand are unchanged. By contrast, *shifts of the demand curve occur when the determinants of demand change.* When tastes, income, other goods, or expectations are altered, the basic relationship between price and quantity demanded is changed (shifts).

For convenience, the distinction between movements along a demand curve and shifts of the demand curve have their own labels. Specifically, take care to distinguish

- *Changes in quantity demanded:* movements along a given demand curve in response to price changes of that good (such as from d_1 to d_2 in Figure 3.3).
- *Changes in demand:* shifts of the demand curve due to changes in tastes, income, other goods, or expectations (such as from D_1 to D_2 in Figure 3.3).

The News Wire on page 53 told how higher alcohol prices could reduce college drinking—pushing students up the demand curve to a smaller quantity demanded. College officials might also try to *shift* the entire demand curve leftward: if the penalties for campus drinking were increased, altered expectations might shift the demand curve to the left, causing students to buy less booze at any given price.

Tom's behavior in the web tutoring market is subject to similar influences. A change in the *price* of tutoring will move Tom up or down his demand curve. By contrast, a change in an underlying determinant of demand will shift his entire demand curve to the left or right.

Market Demand

The same forces that change an individual's consumption behavior also move entire markets. Suppose you wanted to assess the *market demand* for web tutoring services at Clearview College. To do that, you'd want to identify every student's demand for that service. Some students, of course, have no need or desire for professional web design services and are not willing to pay anything for such tutoring; they do not participate in the web design market. Other students have a desire for such services but not enough income to pay for them; they, too, are excluded from the web design market. A large number of students, however, not only have a need (or desire) for tutoring but also are willing and able to purchase such services.

market demand The total quantities of a good or service people are willing and able to buy at alternative prices in a given time period; the sum of individual demands.

What we start with in product markets, then, is many individual demand curves. Then we combine all those individual demand curves into a single **market demand.** Suppose you would be willing to buy one hour of tutoring at a price of $80 per hour. George, who is also desperate to learn web design, would buy two at that price; and I would buy none, since my publisher (McGraw-Hill) creates a web page for me (try http://www.mhhe.com/schileressentials9e). What would our combined (market) demand for hours of design services be at that price? Our individual inclinations indicate that we would be willing to buy a total of three hours of tutoring if the price were $80 per hour. Our combined willingness to buy—our collective market demand—is nothing more than the sum of our individual demands. The same kind of aggregation can be performed for all the consumers in a particular market. The resulting *market demand is determined by the number of potential buyers and their respective tastes, incomes, other goods, and expectations.*

The Market Demand Curve

Figure 3.4 provides a market demand schedule and curve for a situation in which only three consumers participate in the market. The three individuals

FIGURE 3.4   The Market Demand Schedule and Construction of the Market Demand Curve

Market demand represents the combined demands of all market participants. To determine the total quantity of tutoring demanded at any given price, we add up the separate demands of the individual consumers. Row *G* of this demand schedule indicates that a *total* quantity of 39 hours of service per semester will be demanded at a price of $20 per hour.

The market demand curve illustrates the same information. At a price of $20 per hour, the total quantity of web design services demanded would be 39 hours per semester (point *G*): 12 hours demanded by Tom, 22 by George, and 5 by Lisa. As price declines, the quantity demanded increases (the law of demand).

	Market Demand Schedule					
	Quantity of Tutoring Demanded (Hours per Semester)					
	Price per Hour	**Tom**	**+** **George**	**+**	**Lisa**	**=** **Total Quantity Demanded**
A	$50	1	4		0	5
B	45	2	6		0	8
C	40	3	8		0	11
D	35	5	11		0	16
E	30	7	14		1	22
F	25	9	18		3	30
G	20	12	22		5	39
H	15	15	26		6	47
I	10	20	30		7	57

(a) Tom's demand curve   + (b) George's demand curve   + (c) Lisa's demand curve   = (d) **The market demand curve**

PRICE (per hour)

QUANTITY DEMANDED (hours per semester)

who participate in this market obviously differ greatly, as suggested by their respective demand schedules. Tom *has* to pass his web design classes or confront college and parental rejection. He also has a nice allowance (income), so he can afford to buy a lot of tutorial help. His demand schedule is portrayed in the first column of the table in Figure 3.4 (and is identical to the one we examined in Figure 3.2). George, as we already noted, is also desperate to acquire some job skills and is willing to pay relatively high prices for web design tutoring. His demand is summarized in the second column under "Quantity of Tutoring Demanded."

Would this many fans show up if concert prices were higher?
© Frank Micelotta/Getty Images

The third consumer in this market is Lisa. Lisa already knows the nuts and bolts of web design, so she doesn't have much need for tutorial services. She would like to upgrade her skills, however, especially in animation and e-commerce applications. But her limited budget precludes paying a lot for help. She will buy some technical support only if the price falls to $30 per hour. Should tutors cost less, she'd even buy quite a few hours of design services.

The differing personalities and consumption habits of Tom, George, and Lisa are expressed in their individual demand schedules and associated curves, as depicted in Figure 3.4. To determine the *market* demand for tutoring services from this information, we simply add up these three separate demands. The end result of this aggregation is, first, a *market* demand schedule (the last column in the table) and, second, the resultant *market* demand curve (the curve in Figure 3.4d). These market summaries describe the various quantities of tutoring services that Clearview College students are *willing and able* to purchase each semester at various prices.

The Use of Demand Curves

So why does anybody care what the market demand curve looks like? What's the point of doing all this arithmetic and drawing so many graphs?

If you were a web designer at Clearview College, you'd certainly like to have the information depicted in Figure 3.4. What the market demand curve tells us is how much tutoring service could be sold at various prices. Suppose you hoped to sell 30 hours at a price of $30 per hour. According to Figure 3.4d (point E), students will buy only 22 hours at that price. Hence, you won't attain your sales goal. You could find that out by posting ads on campus and waiting for a response. It would be a lot easier, however, if you knew in advance what the market demand curve looked like.

People who promote music concerts need the same kind of information. They want to fill the stadium with screaming fans. But fans have limited income and desires for other goods. Accordingly, the number of fans who will buy concert tickets depends on the price. If the promoter sets the price too high, there will be lots of empty seats at the concert. If the price is set too low, the promoter may lose potential sales revenue. What the promoter wants to know is what price will induce the desired quantity demanded. If the promoter could consult a demand curve, the correct price would be evident.

SUPPLY

Even if we knew what the demand for every good looked like, we couldn't predict what quantities would be bought. The demand curve tells us only how much consumers are willing and able to buy at specific prices. We don't know the price yet, however. To find out what price will be charged, we've got to know something about the behavior of people who *sell* goods and services. That is to say, we need to examine the *supply* side of the marketplace. The **market supply** of a good reflects the collective behavior of all firms that are willing and able to sell that good at various prices.

market supply The total quantities of a good that sellers are willing and able to sell at alternative prices in a given time period, *ceteris paribus*.

Determinants of Supply

Let's return to the Clearview campus for a moment. What we need to know now is how much web tutorial services people are willing and able to provide.

Web page design can be fun, but it can also be drudge work, especially when you're doing it for someone else. Software programs like PhotoShop, Flash, and Fireworks have made web page design easier and more creative. But teaching someone else to design web pages is still work. So few people offer to supply web services just for the fun of it. Web designers do it for money. Specifically, they do it to earn income that they, in turn, can spend on goods and services they desire.

How much income must be offered to induce web designers to do a job depends on a variety of things. The *determinants of market supply include*

- *Technology.*
- *Factor costs.*
- *Other goods.*
- *Taxes and subsidies.*
- *Expectations.*
- *Number of sellers.*

The technology of web design, for example, is always getting easier and more creative. With a program like PageOut, for example, it's very easy to create a basic web page. A continuous stream of new software programs (e.g., Fireworks, Dreamweaver) keeps stretching the possibilities for graphics, animation, interactivity, and content. These technological advances mean that web design services can be supplied more quickly and cheaply. They also make *teaching* web design easier. As a result, they induce people to supply more web design services at every price.

How much tutoring is offered at any given price also depends on the cost of factors of production. If the software programs needed to create web pages are cheap (or, better yet, free!), web designers can afford to charge lower prices. If the required software inputs are expensive, however, they will have to charge more money per hour for their services.

Other goods can also affect the willingness to supply web design services. If you can make more income waiting tables than you can designing web pages, why would you even boot up the computer? As the prices paid for other goods and services change, they will influence people's decisions about whether to offer web services.

In the real world, the decision to supply goods and services is also influenced by the long arm of Uncle Sam. Federal, state, and local governments impose taxes on income earned in the marketplace. When tax rates are high, people get to keep less of the income they earn. Some people may conclude that tutoring is no longer worth the hassle and withdraw from the market.

Expectations are also important on the supply side of the market. If web designers expect higher prices, lower costs, or reduced taxes, they may be more willing to learn new software programs. On the other hand, if they have poor expectations about the future, they may just find something else to do.

Finally, the *number* of available web designers will affect the quantity of service offered for sale at various prices. If there are lots of willing web designers on campus, a large quantity of tutoring services will be available.

The Market Supply Curve

Figure 3.5 illustrates the market supply curve of web services at Clearview College. Like market demand, the market supply curve is the sum of all the individual supplier decisions about how much output to produce at any given price. The market supply curve slopes upward to the right, indicating that *larger quantities will be offered at higher prices.* This basic **law of supply** reflects the fact that increased output typically entails higher costs and so will be forthcoming only at higher prices. Higher prices may also increase profits and so entice producers to supply greater quantities.

Note that Figure 3.5 illustrates the *market* supply. We have not bothered to construct separate supply curves for each person who is able and willing to supply web services on the Clearview campus. We have skipped that first step and

law of supply The quantity of a good supplied in a given time period increases as its price increases, *ceteris paribus.*

FIGURE 3.5
The Market Supply
Curve

The market supply curve indicates the *combined* sales intentions of all market participants. If the price of tutoring were $25 per hour (point *e*), the *total* quantity of tutoring service supplied would be 62 hours per semester. This quantity is determined by adding together the supply decisions of all individual producers.

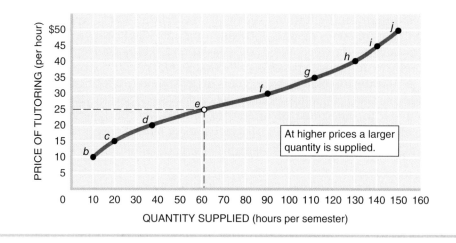

gone right to the *market* supply curve. Like the market demand curve, however, the market supply curve is based on the supply decisions of individual producers. The curve itself is computed by adding up the quantities each producer is willing and able to supply at every given price. Point *f* in Figure 3.5 tells us that those individuals are collectively willing and able to produce 90 hours of tutoring per semester at a price of $30 per hour. The rest of the points on the supply curve tell us how many hours of tutoring will be offered at other prices.

None of the points on the market supply curve (Figure 3.5) tell us how much tutoring service is actually being sold. *Market supply is an expression of sellers' intentions, of the ability and willingness to sell, not a statement of actual sales.* My next-door neighbor may be *willing* to sell his 1996 Honda Civic for $6,000, but it is most unlikely that he will ever find a buyer at that price. Nevertheless, his *willingness* to sell his car at that price is part of the *market supply* of used cars.

Shifts in Supply

As with demand, there is nothing sacred about any given set of supply intentions. Supply curves *shift* when the underlying determinants of supply change. Thus we again distinguish

- *Changes in quantity supplied:* movements along a given supply curve.
- *Changes in supply:* shifts of the supply curve.

Our Latin friend *ceteris paribus* is once again the decisive factor. If the price of tutoring services is the only thing changing, then we can **track changes in quantity supplied along the supply curve** in Figure 3.5. But if *ceteris paribus* is violated—if technology, factor costs, other goods, taxes, or expectations change—then **changes in supply are illustrated by shifts of the supply curve.** The following News Wire illustrates how a hurricane caused a leftward shift in the supply of used cars, raising their prices.

EQUILIBRIUM

We now have the tools to determine the price and quantity of web tutoring services being sold at Clearview College. The market supply curve expresses the *ability and willingness* of producers to *sell* web services at various prices. The market demand curve illustrates the *ability and willingness* of Tom, George, and Lisa to *buy* web services at those same prices. When we put the two curves together, we see that *only one price and quantity are compatible with the existing intentions of both buyers and sellers.* This **equilibrium price** occurs at the intersection of the two curves in

equilibrium price The price at which the quantity of a good demanded in a given time period equals the quantity supplied.

NEWS WIRE | SUPPLY SHIFT

Hurricane Sandy to Raise Prices on Used Cars

The immediate impact of Hurricane Sandy was devastating, and the storm's ripple effects will continue to be felt in the weeks and months ahead as communities work to recover. One side effect becoming apparent is Sandy's influence on the used car market.

Andrea Boother/FEMA

According to the *Detroit Free Press*, the destruction of some 250,000 vehicles has led to a shortage that could affect late-model used vehicle prices nationwide. The National Auto Dealers Association estimates that prices could increase 0.5% to 1.5%. That may not seem like much ($50–$175 per vehicle), but Edmunds.com suggests that in the short term, prices could jump $700 to $1,000.

Source: George Kennedy, Autoblog, November 10, 2012. © 2012 AOL Inc. All rights reserved.

NOTE: If an underlying determinant of supply changes, the entire supply curve shifts. A hurricane reduced the available supply of used cars, causing their prices to spike.

Figure 3.6. Once it is established, web tutoring services will cost $20 per hour. At that price, campus web designers will sell a total of 39 hours of tutoring service per semester—exactly the same amount that students wish to buy at that price.

Market Clearing

An equilibrium doesn't imply that everyone is happy with the prevailing price or quantity. Notice in Figure 3.6, for example, that some students who want to buy web tutoring don't get any. These would-be buyers are arrayed along the demand curve *below* the equilibrium. Because the price they are *willing* to pay is less than the equilibrium price, they don't get any tutoring.

Likewise, there are would-be sellers in the market who don't sell as much tutoring services as they might like. These people are arrayed along the supply curve *above* the equilibrium. Because they insist on being paid a price that is higher than the equilibrium price, they don't actually sell anything.

FIGURE 3.6
Market Equilibrium

Only at equilibrium is the quantity demanded equal to the quantity supplied. In this case, the **equilibrium price** is $20 per hour, and 39 hours is the **equilibrium quantity.**

At above-equilibrium prices, a market surplus exists—the quantity supplied exceeds the quantity demanded. At prices below equilibrium, a market shortage exists.

The intersection of the demand and supply curves determines the equilibrium price and output in this market.

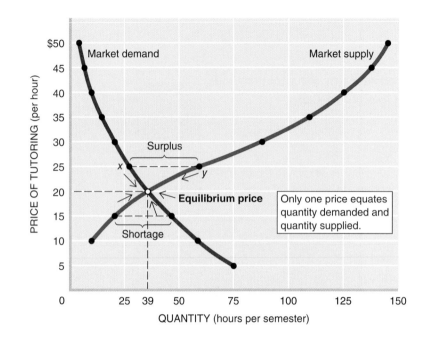

Price per Hour	Quantity Supplied (Hours per Semester)		Quantity Demanded (Hours per Semester)
$50	148		5
45	140		8
40	130	Market	11
35	114	surplus	16
30	90		22
25	62		30
20	39	**Equilibrium**	39
15	20	Market	47
10	10	shortage	57

Although not everyone gets full satisfaction from the market equilibrium, that unique outcome is efficient. *The equilibrium price and quantity reflect a compromise between buyers and sellers. No other compromise yields a quantity demanded that is exactly equal to the quantity supplied.*

THE INVISIBLE HAND   The equilibrium price is not determined by any single individual. Rather it is determined by the collective behavior of many buyers and sellers, each acting out his or her own demand or supply schedule. It is this kind of impersonal price determination that gave rise to Adam Smith's characterization of the market mechanism as the "invisible hand." In attempting to explain how the market mechanism works, the famed eighteenth-century economist noted a certain feature of market prices. The market behaves as if some unseen force (the invisible hand) were examining each individual's supply or demand schedule, then selecting a price that ensured an equilibrium. In practice, the process of price determination is not so mysterious; rather, it is a simple one of trial and error.

Market Shortage

Suppose for the moment that someone were to spread the word on the Clearview campus that tutors were available at only $15 per hour. At that price Tom, George, and Lisa would be standing in line to get help with their web classes, but campus web designers would not be willing to supply the quantity desired at that price. As Figure 3.6 confirms, at $15 per hour, the quantity demanded (47 hours per semester) would exceed the quantity supplied (20 hours per semester). In this situation, we speak of a **market shortage**—that is, an excess of quantity demanded over quantity supplied. At a price of $15 an hour, the shortage amounts to 27 hours of web service.

When a market shortage exists, not all consumer demands can be satisfied. Some people who are *willing* to buy tutoring services at the going price ($15) will not be able to do so. To assure themselves of good grades, Tom, George, Lisa, or some other consumer may offer to pay a *higher* price, thus initiating a move up the demand curve of Figure 3.6. The higher prices offered will in turn induce other enterprising students to offer more web tutoring, thus ensuring an upward movement along the market supply curve. Thus a higher price tends to call forth a greater quantity supplied, as reflected in the upward-sloping supply curve. Notice, again, that the *desire* to tutor web design has not changed: only the quantity supplied has responded to a change in price.

The accompanying News Wire illustrates what happens at music concerts when tickets are priced below equilibrium. On December 12, 2012, a benefit concert for survivors of Hurricane Sandy was held at New York City's Madison Square Garden. The lineup of superstars included the Rolling Stones, Bruce Springsteen, and other megastars. The 20,000 seats were priced at $150 to $2,500. Those seemingly high prices, however, were far below the market equilibrium. As the accompanying News Wire recounts, tickets were resold for as much as $10,400! Had the concert promoters priced tickets closer to the market equilibrium, they would have pulled in a lot more money for Sandy survivors. As it turned out, scalpers got a big chunk of that money. Such "scalping" would not be possible if the initial price of the tickets had been set by supply and demand.

A similar but less dramatic situation occurred when the iPhone 5 was released in September 2012. At the initial list price of $199 for the 16 GB model, the quantity

market shortage The amount by which the quantity demanded exceeds the quantity supplied at a given price; excess demand.

| NEWS WIRE | MARKET SHORTAGE |

Ticket Scalpers Making Big Bucks Off 12/12/12 Concert to Benefit Hurricane Sandy Victims

The 12/12/12 concert to benefit survivors of Superstorm Sandy has become a scalper's bonanza.

A pair of tickets to the star-studded charity event Wednesday evening were going for a laughable $808,500 each on StubHub—though the listing was hastily removed after *The Daily News* called the website about it.

So as of 12:30 p.m. Wednesday, the most expensive seat is selling for $10,400 on the resale site—a more believable, yet still outrageous price.

Tickets have face value from $150 to $2,500, with all proceeds going to the Robin Hood Relief Fund charity organization. But many ticketholders are using online sites such as StubHub to resell coveted tickets to a megashow featuring Bruce Springsteen, Billy Joel, the Who, Paul McCartney and the Rolling Stones—and pocket the profits.

Source: December 12, 2012 © Daily News, L.P. (New York)

NOTE: A below-equilibrium price creates a market shortage. When that happens, another method of distributing tickets—like scalping or time in line—must be used to determine who gets the available tickets.

| NEWS WIRE | MARKET SHORTAGE |

iPhone 5 Sales: Many U.S. Stores Reportedly Sold Out of the Device Already

It was possible to walk into a store Saturday and buy an iPhone 5, but it took some hunting.

Some stores reported having Apple's newest phone available for walk-up customers, though not all versions of it. A random check of about a dozen stores indicated that most were sold out.

A Verizon store in New York City said the 32 and 64 gigabyte models, but not the 16 GB version, were available. A Sprint store in a suburb of St. Paul, Minnesota, said all but the most expensive 64 GB iPhone 5s were sold out.

"Before we were even scheduled to open, we were pretty much out," said Eric Rayburn, a worker at a Sprint store in Phoenix.

There were long lines Friday at Apple's stores in Asia, Europe and North America as customers pursued the new smartphone.

Source: Associated Press, September 22, 2012. Used with permission of the Associated Press. Copyright © 2012. All rights reserved.

NOTE: If price is below equilibrium, the quantity demanded exceeds the quantity supplied. The willingness to pay the advertised (list) price of $199 for an iPhone 5 didn't ensure its purchase.

demanded greatly exceeded the quantity supplied (see the accompanying News Wire). To get an iPhone 5, people had to spend hours in line or pay a premium price in resale markets like eBay.

Market Surplus

A very different sequence of events occurs when a market surplus exists. Suppose for the moment that the web designers at Clearview College believed tutoring services could be sold for $25 per hour rather than the equilibrium price of $20. From the demand and supply schedules depicted in Figure 3.6, we can foresee the consequences. At $25 per hour, campus web designers would be offering more web tutoring services (point y) than Tom, George, and Lisa were willing to buy (point x) at that price. A **market surplus** of web services would exist, in that more tutoring was being offered for sale (supplied) than students cared to purchase at the available price.

As Figure 3.6 indicates, at a price of $25 per hour, a market surplus of 32 hours per semester exists. Under these circumstances, campus web designers would be spending many idle hours at their computers, waiting for customers to appear. Their waiting will be in vain because the quantity of tutoring demanded will not increase until the price of tutoring falls. That is the clear message of the demand curve. The tendency of quantity demanded to increase as price falls is illustrated in Figure 3.6 by a movement along the demand curve from point x to lower prices and greater quantity demanded. As we move down the market demand curve, the desire for tutoring does not change, but the quantity people are able and willing to buy increases. Web designers at Clearview would have to reduce their price from $25 (point y) to $20 per hour in order to attract enough buyers.

U2 learned the difference between market shortage and surplus the hard way. Cheap tickets ($28.50) for their 1992 concerts not only filled up every concert venue but left thousands of fans clamoring for entry. The group began another tour in April 1997, with scheduled concerts in 80 cities over a period of 14 months.

market surplus The amount by which the quantity supplied exceeds the quantity demanded at a given price; excess supply.

NEWS WIRE	LOCATING EQUILIBRIUM

U2's 360° Tour Named Top North American Trek of 2009

U2's massive 360° Tour wasn't just the biggest trek this year in terms of sheer size: the band's latest jaunt supporting No Line on the Horizon has also been named the year's most successful show by concert tracker Pollstar. Their research also revealed that despite the recession, concert ticket sales for the top 50 tours were up this year across the board compared to 2008's final numbers. That's thanks largely to U2, who easily surpassed all other acts by selling 1.3 million tickets during the first leg of their 360° Tour, grossing $123 million along the way.

Source: Copyright © Rolling Stone LLC 2009. All Rights Reserved. Reprinted by Permission.

NOTE: Lower prices increased the quantity demanded. At a minimum price of $30, U2 sold out every 2009 concert.

This time around, however, U2 was charging as much as $52.50 a ticket—nearly double the 1992 price. By the time they got to the second city, they were playing in stadiums with lots of empty seats. The apparent market surplus led critics to label the 1997 PopMart tour a disaster. For their 2009, 360° Tour, U2 offered festival seating for only $30 and sold out every performance (see the accompanying News Wire). By this process of trial and error, U2 ultimately located the equilibrium price for their concerts.

What we observe, then, is that *whenever the market price is set above or below the equilibrium price, either a market surplus or a market shortage will emerge.* To overcome a surplus or shortage, buyers and sellers will change their behavior. Only at the *equilibrium* price will no further adjustments be required.

Business firms can discover equilibrium market prices by trial and error. If they find that consumer purchases are not keeping up with production, they may conclude that price is above the equilibrium. To get rid of their accumulated inventory, they will have to lower their prices (by a grand end-of-year sale, perhaps). In the happy situation where consumer purchases are outpacing production, a firm might conclude that its price was a trifle too low and give it a nudge upward. In either case, the equilibrium price can be established after a few trials in the marketplace.

Changes in Equilibrium

The collective actions of buyers and sellers will quickly establish an equilibrium price for any product. **No equilibrium price is permanent,** however. The equilibrium price established in the Clearview College web services market, for example, was the unique outcome of specific demand and supply schedules. Those schedules are valid for only a certain time and place. They will rule the market only so long as the assumption of *ceteris paribus* holds.

In reality, tastes, incomes, the price and availability of other goods, or expectations could change at any time. When this happens, *ceteris paribus* will be violated, and the demand curve will have to be redrawn. Such a shift of the demand curve will lead to a new equilibrium price and quantity. Indeed, *the equilibrium price will change whenever the supply or demand curve shifts.*

DEMAND SHIFTS   We can illustrate how equilibrium prices change by taking one last look at the Clearview College web services market. Our original supply

FIGURE 3.7
A New Equilibrium

A rightward shift of the demand curve indicates that consumers are willing and able to buy a larger quantity at every price. As a consequence, a new equilibrium is established (point E_2), at a higher price and greater quantity. A shift of the demand curve occurs only when the assumption of *ceteris paribus* is violated—when one of the determinants of demand changes.

The equilibrium would also be altered if the determinants of supply changed, causing a shift of the market supply curve.

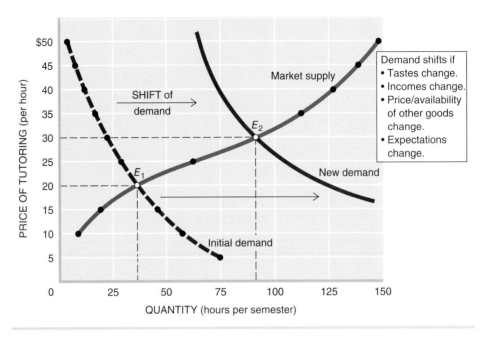

and demand curves, together with the resulting equilibrium (point E_1), are depicted in Figure 3.7. Now suppose that the professors at Clearview begin requiring more technical expertise in their web design courses. These increased course requirements will affect market demand. Tom, George, and Lisa will suddenly be willing to buy more web tutoring at every price than they were before. That is to say, the *demand* for web services will increase. We represent this increased demand by a rightward *shift* of the market demand curve, as illustrated in Figure 3.7.

Note that the new demand curve intersects the (unchanged) market supply curve at a new price (point E_2); the equilibrium price is now $30 per hour. This new equilibrium price will persist until either the demand curve or the supply curve shifts again.

SUPPLY AND DEMAND SHIFTS   Even more dramatic price changes may occur when *both* demand and supply shift. Suppose the demand for tutoring increased at the same time supply decreased. With demand shifting right and supply shifting left, the price of tutoring would jump.

The kinds of price changes described here are quite common. A few moments in a stockbroker's office or a glance through the stock pages of the daily newspaper should be testimony enough to the fluid character of market prices. If thousands of stockholders decide to sell Google shares tomorrow, you can be sure that the market price of that stock will drop. Notice how often other prices—in the grocery store, in the music store, or at the gas station—change. Then determine whether it was supply, demand, or both curves that shifted.

DISEQUILIBRIUM PRICING

The ability of the market to achieve an equilibrium price and quantity is evident. Nevertheless, people are often unhappy with those outcomes. At Clearview College, the students buying tutoring services feel that the price of such services is too high. On the other hand, campus web designers may feel that they are getting paid too little for their tutorial services.

Price Ceilings

Sometimes consumers are able to convince the government to intervene on their behalf by setting a limit on prices. In many cities, for example, poor people and their advocates have convinced local governments that rents are too high. High rents, they argue, make housing prohibitively expensive for the poor, leaving them homeless or living in crowded, unsafe quarters. They ask government to impose a *limit* on rents in order to make housing affordable for everyone. Two hundred local governments—including New York City, Boston, Washington, DC, and San Francisco—have responded with rent controls. In all cases, rent controls are a **price ceiling**—an upper limit imposed on the price of a good or service.

Rent controls have a very visible effect in making housing more affordable. But such controls are *disequilibrium* prices and will change housing decisions in less visible and unintended ways. Figure 3.8 illustrates the problem. In the absence of government intervention, the quantity of housing consumed (q_e) and the prevailing rent (p_e) would be established by the intersection of market supply and demand curves (point E). Not everyone would be housed to his or her satisfaction in this equilibrium. Some of those people on the low end of the demand curve (below p_e) simply do not have enough income to pay the equilibrium rent p_e. They may be living with relatives or roommates they would rather not know. Or in extreme cases, they may even be homeless.

To remedy this situation, the city government imposes a rent ceiling of p_c. This lower price seemingly makes housing more affordable for everyone, including the poor. At the controlled rent p_c, people are willing and able to consume a lot more housing: the quantity *demanded* increases from q_e to q_d at point A.

But what about the quantity of housing *supplied*? Rent controls do not increase the number of housing units available. On the contrary, price controls tend to have the opposite effect. Notice in Figure 3.8 how the quantity *supplied* falls from q_e to q_s when the rent ceiling is enacted. When the quantity supplied slides down the supply curve from point E to point B, less housing is available than there was before. Thus *price ceilings have three predictable effects; they*

- *Increase the quantity demanded.*
- *Decrease the quantity supplied.*
- *Create a market shortage.*

price ceiling Upper limit imposed on the price of a good or service.

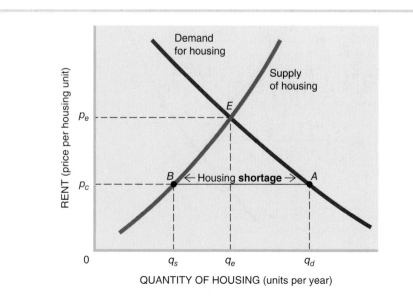

QUANTITY OF HOUSING (units per year)

FIGURE 3.8
Price Ceilings Create Shortages

Many cities impose rent controls to keep housing affordable. Consumers respond to the below-equilibrium price ceiling (p_c) by demanding more housing (q_d vs. q_e). But the quantity of housing supplied diminishes as landlords convert buildings to other uses (e.g., condos) or simply let rental units deteriorate. New construction also slows. The result is a housing shortage ($q_d - q_s$) and an actual reduction in available housing ($q_e - q_s$).

You may well wonder where the "lost" housing went. The houses did not disappear. Some landlords simply decided that renting their units was no longer worth the effort. They chose, instead, to sell the units, convert them to condominiums, or even live in them themselves. Other landlords stopped maintaining their buildings, letting the units deteriorate. The rate of new construction slowed too, as builders decided that rent control made new construction less profitable. Slowly but surely the quantity of housing declines from q_e to q_s. Hence *there will be less housing for everyone when rent controls are imposed to make housing more affordable for some.*

Figure 3.8 illustrates another problem. The rent ceiling p_c has created a housing shortage—a gap between the quantity demanded (q_d) and the quantity supplied (q_s). Who will get the increasingly scarce housing? The market would have settled this FOR WHOM question by permitting rents to rise and allocating available units to those consumers willing and able to pay the rent p_e. Now, however, rents cannot rise, and we have lots of people clamoring for housing that is not available. A different method of distributing goods must be found. Vacant units will go to those who learn of them first, patiently wait on waiting lists, or offer a gratuity to the landlord or renting agent. In New York City, where rent control has been the law for 70 years, people "sell" their rent-controlled apartments when they move elsewhere.

Price Floors

price floor Lower limit imposed on the price of a good.

Artificially high (above-equilibrium) prices create similar problems in the marketplace. A **price floor** is a minimum price imposed by the government for a good or service. The objective is to raise the price of the good and create more income for the seller. Federal minimum wage laws, for example, forbid most employers from paying less than $7.25 an hour for labor.

Price floors are also common in the farm sector. To stabilize farmers' incomes, the government offers price guarantees for certain crops. The government sets a price guarantee of 18.75 cents per pound for domestically grown cane sugar. If the market price of sugar falls below 18.75 cents, the government promises to buy at the guaranteed price. Hence farmers know they can sell their sugar for 18.75 cents per pound, regardless of market demand.

Figure 3.9 illustrates the consequences of this price floor. The price guarantee (18.75¢) lies above the equilibrium price p_e (otherwise it would have no effect). At

FIGURE 3.9
Price Floors Create Surplus

The U.S. Department of Agriculture sets a minimum price for sugar at 18.75 cents. If the market price drops below 18.75 cents, the government will buy the resulting surplus.

Farmers respond by producing the quantity q_s. Consumers would purchase the quantity q_s, however, only if the market price dropped to p_m (point a on the demand curve). The government thus has to purchase and store the surplus ($q_s - q_d$).

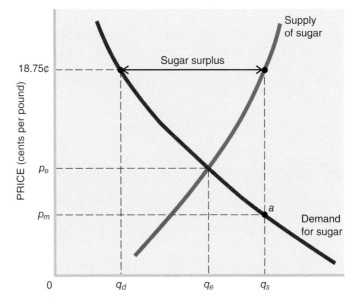

that higher price, farmers supply more sugar (q_s versus q_e). However, consumers are not willing to buy that much sugar: at that price they demand only the quantity q_d. Hence the *price floor has three predictable effects: it*

- *Increases the quantity supplied.*
- *Reduces the quantity demanded.*
- *Creates a market surplus.*

In 2008 the government-guaranteed price (18.75¢) was nearly double the world price. At that price U.S. cane and beet sugar growers were willing to supply far more sugar than consumers demanded. To prevent such a market surplus, the federal government sets limits on sugar production—and decides who gets to grow it. This is a classic case of **government failure**: society ends up with the wrong mix of output (too much sugar), an increased tax burden (to pay for the surplus), an altered distribution of income (enriched sugar growers)—and a lot of political favoritism.

government failure Government intervention that fails to improve economic outcomes.

Laissez Faire

The apparent inefficiencies of price ceilings and floors imply that market outcomes are best left alone. This is a conclusion reached long ago by Adam Smith, the founder of modern economic theory. In 1776 he advocated a policy of **laissez faire**—literally, "leave it alone." As he saw it, the market mechanism was an efficient procedure for allocating resources and distributing incomes. The government should set and enforce the rules of the marketplace, but otherwise not interfere. Interference with the market—through price ceilings, floors, or other regulation—was likely to cause more problems than it could hope to solve.

laissez faire The doctrine of "leave it alone," of nonintervention by government in the market mechanism.

The policy of laissez faire is motivated not only by the potential pitfalls of government intervention but also by the recognition of how well the market mechanism can work. Recall our visit to Clearview College, where the price and quantity of tutoring services had to be established. There was no central agency that set the price of tutoring service or determined how much tutoring service would be done at Clearview College. Instead both the price of web services and its quantity were determined by the **market mechanism**—the interactions of many independent (decentralized) buyers and sellers.

market mechanism The use of market prices and sales to signal desired outputs (or resource allocations).

WHAT, HOW, FOR WHOM   Notice how the market mechanism resolved the basic economic questions of WHAT, HOW, and FOR WHOM. The WHAT question refers to how much web tutoring to include in society's mix of output. The answer at Clearview College was 39 hours per semester. This decision was not reached in a referendum but instead in the market equilibrium (see Figure 3.6). In the same way but on a larger scale, millions of consumers and a handful of auto producers decide to include 12 million cars and trucks in each year's mix of output.

The market mechanism will also determine HOW these goods are produced. Profit-seeking producers will strive to produce web services and automobiles in the most efficient way. They will use market prices to decide not only WHAT to produce but also what resources to use in the production process.

Finally, the invisible hand of the market will determine who gets the goods produced. At Clearview College, who got tutorial help in web design? Only those students who were willing and able to pay $20 per hour for that service. FOR WHOM are all those automobiles produced each year? The answer is the same: consumers who are willing and able to pay the market price for a new car.

OPTIMAL, NOT PERFECT   Not everyone is happy with these answers, of course. Tom would like to pay only $10 an hour for web tutoring. And some of the Clearview students do not have enough income to buy any assistance. They think it is unfair that they have to master web design on their own while richer students can have someone tutor them. Students who cannot afford cars are even less happy with the market's answer to the FOR WHOM question.

Although the outcomes of the marketplace are not perfect, they are often *optimal*. Optimal outcomes are the best possible given the level and distribution of incomes and scarce resources. In other words, we expect the choices made in the marketplace to be the best possible choices for each participant. Why do we draw such a conclusion? Because Tom and George and everybody in our little Clearview College drama had (and continue to have) absolute freedom to make their own purchase and consumption decisions. And also because we assume that sooner or later they will make the choices they find most satisfying. The results are thus *optimal* in the sense that everyone has done as well as can be expected, given his or her income and talents.

The optimality of market outcomes provides a powerful argument for *laissez faire*. In essence, the laissez faire doctrine recognizes that decentralized markets not only work but also give individuals the opportunity to maximize their satisfaction. In this context, government interference is seen as a threat to the attainment of the "right" mix of output and other economic goals. Since its development by Adam Smith in 1776, the laissez faire doctrine has had a profound impact on the way the economy functions and what government does (or doesn't do).

POLICY PERSPECTIVES

Did Gas Rationing Help or Hurt New Jersey Motorists?

Hurricane Sandy was the largest Atlantic storm on record. When it slammed into New Jersey on October 29, 2012, it destroyed thousands of homes, knocked out electricity for 2 million homes, flooded highways, damaged port facilities, and killed 37 people.

The gasoline market in New Jersey was particularly hard hit by Superstorm Sandy. One-third of the fuel terminals in New Jersey were closed down due to storm damage, cutting off wholesale gasoline supplies. Damage to oceanside ports, highways, and bridges cut off the tankers and trucks that normally brought

---

NEWS WIRE	PRICE CONTROLS

Gov. Christie Signs Order to Ration Gas in 12 NJ Counties
New Jersey's gas crunch in the wake of Hurricane Sandy has become so severe that state officials are implementing gas rationing for passenger vehicles in the counties hardest hit by the storm.

Gov. Chris Christie signed an executive order today announcing a state of energy emergency and instituting gas rationing for the purchase of fuel by motorists in 12 counties, starting Saturday at noon.

Calling the fuel supply in the state a "shortage" that could endanger public health, safety, and welfare, the rationing will take place in Bergen, Essex, Hudson, Hunterdon, Middlesex, Morris, Monmouth, Passaic, Somerset, Sussex Union, and Warren counties.

Source: *The Star-Ledger*, November 2, 2012. © 2012 *The Star-Ledger*. All rights reserved.

NOTE: The intent of price controls is to distribute scarce supplies fairly. But price controls create market shortages and delay market adjustments.

in gasoline. Worse yet, retail gas stations that had gasoline in their storage tanks couldn't pump it out because they had no electricity. Over 60 percent of the gas stations in New Jersey were inoperable in the wake of Sandy. At stations that were open, motorists lined up for miles to fill their gas tanks and gas cans.

Governor Christie responded to this crisis by imposing gas rationing in northern New Jersey (see News Wire). He also declared that gas stations could not charge a price that was more than 10 percent above prehurricane levels. Those who did would be charged with price gouging and subjected to both civil and criminal penalties.

Brenden Smialowski/AFP/Getty Images

Although the price controls introduced by the governor seemed like a fair way to ration available gasoline, we have to consider how an unregulated (free) market would have responded to Sandy. The damage inflicted by Sandy caused a leftward shift of the market supply curve. Such a shift would normally cause a significant price increase. While no consumer wants to pay more for gasoline, we have to ask how that higher price would have affected market behavior.

On the demand side, the higher price would have reduced the quantity demanded. Higher prices cause consumers to reevaluate their consumption decisions. Do they really have to get to the grocery store today? Or can they wait a day or two? Higher prices induce consumers to forgo less important trips, reducing the quantity demanded. The market price allocates available gasoline to its highest-valued uses.

On the supply side, there would be even more visible effects. Price controls reduce the incentive for truckers in other states to bring more gasoline to New Jersey. At higher prices, the quantity supplied would increase, moving us up the market supply curve. That increase in the quantity of gasoline supplied would have brought relief to New Jersey motorists faster. Price controls slow the market adjustment process.

SUMMARY

- Consumers, business firms, government agencies, and foreigners participate in the marketplace by offering to buy or sell goods and services, or factors of production. Participation is motivated by the desire to maximize utility (consumers), profits (business firms), or the general welfare (government agencies).   **LO1**

- All interactions in the marketplace involve the exchange of either factors of production or finished products. Although the actual exchanges can take place anywhere, we say that they take place in product markets or factor markets, depending on what is being exchanged.   **LO1**

- People who are willing and able to buy a particular good at some price are part of the market demand for that product. All those who are willing and able to sell that good at some price are part of the market supply. Total market demand or supply is the sum of individual demands or supplies.   **LO2**

- Supply and demand curves illustrate how the quantity demanded or supplied changes in response to a

change in the price of that good. Demand curves slope downward; supply curves slope upward.   **LO2**

- The determinants of market demand include the number of potential buyers and their respective tastes (desires), incomes, other goods, and expectations. If any of these determinants change, the demand curve shifts. Movements along a demand curve are induced only by a change in the price of that good.   **LO4**

- The determinants of market supply include technology, factor costs, other goods, taxes, expectations, and the number of sellers. Supply shifts when these underlying determinants change.   **LO4**

- The quantity of goods or resources actually exchanged in each market depends on the behavior of all buyers and sellers, as summarized in market supply and demand curves. At the point where the two curves intersect, an equilibrium price—the price at which the quantity demanded equals the quantity supplied—will be established.   **LO3**

- A distinctive feature of the market equilibrium is that it is the only price–quantity combination that is acceptable to buyers and sellers alike. At higher prices, sellers supply more than buyers are willing to purchase (a market surplus); at lower prices, the amount demanded exceeds the quantity supplied (a market shortage). Only the equilibrium price clears the market. **LO3**

- Price ceilings and floors are disequilibrium prices imposed on the marketplace. Such price controls create an imbalance between quantities demanded and supplied. **LO5**

- The market mechanism is a device for establishing prices and product and resource flows. As such, it may be used to answer the basic economic questions of WHAT to produce, HOW to produce it, and FOR WHOM. Its apparent efficiency prompts the call for laissez faire—a policy of government nonintervention in the marketplace. **LO3**

TERMS TO REMEMBER

Define the following terms:

market	opportunity cost	market demand	price ceiling
factor market	demand schedule	market supply	price floor
product market	demand curve	law of supply	government failure
barter	law of demand	equilibrium price	laissez faire
supply	*ceteris paribus*	market shortage	market mechanism
demand	shift in demand	market surplus	

QUESTIONS FOR DISCUSSION

1. What does the supply and demand for human kidneys look like? If a market in kidneys were legal, who would get them? How does a law prohibiting kidney sales affect the quantity of kidney transplants or their distribution? **LO2**

2. In the web tutoring market, what forces might cause **LO4**
   (*a*) A rightward shift of demand?
   (*b*) A leftward shift of demand?
   (*c*) A rightward shift of supply?
   (*d*) A leftward shift of supply?
   (*e*) An increase in the equilibrium price?

3. Did the price of tuition at your school change this year? What might have caused that? **LO3**

4. Illustrate the market shortage for tickets to the 2012 Sandy benefit concert (News Wire, page 63). Why were the tickets priced so low initially? **LO5**

5. When concert tickets are priced below equilibrium, who gets them? Is this distribution of tickets fairer than a pure market distribution? Is it more efficient? Who gains or loses if all the tickets are resold (scalped) at the market-clearing price? **LO5**

6. Is there a shortage of on-campus parking at your school? How might the shortage be resolved? **LO5**

7. If departing tenants sell access to rent-controlled apartments, who is likely to end up with the apartments? How else might scarce rent-controlled apartments be distributed? **LO5**

8. If rent controls are so counterproductive, why do cities impose them? How else might the housing problems of poor people be solved? **LO5**

9. Why did Apple set the initial price of the iPhone 5 below equilibrium (see the News Wire, page 64). Should Apple have immediately raised the price? **LO5**

10. **POLICY PERSPECTIVES** Was the gas rationing in New Jersey the *fairest* response to the gasoline crisis? The most efficient? **LO5**

PROBLEMS   ▦ connect

1. Using the "new demand" in Figure 3.7 as a guide, determine the size of the market surplus or shortage that would exist at a price of (*a*) $40 and (*b*) $20. **LO5**

2. (*a*) Illustrate the different market situations for the 1992 and 1997 U2 concerts, assuming constant supply and demand curves. (*b*) What is the equilibrium price? (See the discussion and News Wire on page 65.) **LO5**

3. Given the following data, (*a*) complete the following table; (*b*) construct market supply and demand curves; (*c*) identify the equilibrium price; and (*d*) identify the amount of shortage or surplus that would exist at a price of $5.   **LO2**

Participant	Quantity Demanded (per Week)				
Price	$5	$4	$3	$2	$1
Demand side					
Al	1	2	3	4	5
Betsy	1	2	2	2	3
Casey	2	2	3	3	4
Daisy	2	3	4	4	6
Eddie	2	2	2	3	5
Market total	—	—	—	—	—

Participant	Quantity Supplied (per Week)				
Price	$5	$4	$3	$2	$1
Supply side					
Firm A	3	3	3	3	3
Firm B	7	5	4	4	2
Firm C	6	4	3	3	1
Firm D	6	5	4	3	0
Firm E	4	3	3	3	2
Market total	—	—	—	—	—

4. If a product becomes more popular,
   (*a*) Which curve will shift?
   (*b*) Along which curve will price and quantity move?
   At the new equilibrium price, will
   (*c*) price
   (*d*) quantity
   be higher or lower?   **LO4**

5. Which curve shifts, and in what direction, when the following events occur in the domestic car market?   **LO4**
   (*a*) The U.S. economy falls into a recession.
   (*b*) U.S. autoworkers go on strike.

   (*c*) Imported cars become more expensive.
   (*d*) The price of gasoline increases.

6. Show graphically the market situation for the iPhone 5 in September 2012 (see News Wire on page 64).   **LO4**

7. Assume the following data describe the gasoline market: **LO3**

Price per gallon	$2.00	2.25	2.50	2.75	3.00	3.25	3.50
Quantity demanded	36	35	34	33	32	31	30
Quantity supplied	24	26	28	30	32	34	36

   (*a*) Graph the demand and supply curves.
   (*b*) What is the equilibrium price?
   (*c*) If supply at every price is reduced by 6 gallons, what will the new equilibrium price be?
   (*d*) If the government freezes the price of gasoline at its initial equilibrium price, how much of a surplus or shortage will exist when supply is reduced as described in part (*c*)?

8. Graph the response of students to higher alcohol prices, as discussed in the News Wire on page 53.   **LO2**

9. (*a*) Graph the outcomes in the used car market (News Wire, page 61) if the government had put a ceiling of $20,000 on used-car prices after Hurricane Sandy.
   (*b*) How large would the resulting market shortage be?   **LO5**

10. **POLICY PERSPECTIVES** Illustrate on a graph the impact on the New Jersey gasoline market of   **LO4**
    (*a*) Hurricane Sandy.
    (*b*) The governor's price controls.

11. If the average face value of tickets for the Hurricane Sandy benefit concert (see the News Wire on page 63) was $600 and the equilibrium price was $1,000, how much ticket revenue was lost due to disequilibrium pricing?   **LO1**

◀ Practice quizzes, student PowerPoints, author podcasts, web activities, and additional materials available at **www.mhhe.com/schilleressentials9e**, or scan here. Need a barcode reader? Try ScanLife, available in your app store.

4

Consumer Demand

◄ Practice quizzes, student PowerPoints, author podcasts, web activities, and additional materials available at www.mhhe.com/ schilleressentials9e, or scan here. Need a barcode reader? Try ScanLife, available in your app store.

LEARNING OBJECTIVES

After reading this chapter, you should be able to:

1 Explain why demand curves slope downward.
2 Describe what the price elasticity of demand measures.
3 Depict the relationship of price elasticity, price, and total revenue.
4 Recite the factors that influence the degree of price elasticity.
5 Discuss how advertising affects consumer demand.

"**S**hop until you drop" is apparently a way of life for many Americans. The *average* American (man, woman, or child) spends a whopping $35,000 per year on consumer goods and services. This adds up at the cash register to a consumption bill of over $11 *trillion* a year.

A major concern of microeconomics is to explain this shopping frenzy. What drives us to department stores, grocery stores, and every big sale in town? More specifically,

- How do we decide how much of any good to buy?
- How does a change in a product's price affect the quantity we purchase or the amount of money we spend on it?
- What factors other than price affect our consumption decisions?

The law of demand, first encountered in Chapter 3, gives us some clues for answering these questions. But we need to look beyond that law to fashion more complete answers. Knowing that demand curves are downward-sloping is important, but that knowledge won't get us far in the real world. In the real world, producers need to know the exact quantities demanded at various prices. Producers also need to know what forces will shift consumer demand.

The specifics of consumer demand are also important to public policy decisions. Suppose a city wants to relieve highway congestion and encourage more people to use public transit. Will public appeals be effective in changing commuter behavior? Probably not. But a change in relative prices might do the trick. Experience shows that raising the *price* of private auto use (e.g., higher parking fees, bridge tolls) and lowering transit fares *are* effective in changing commuters' behavior. Economists try to predict just how much prices should be altered to elicit the desired response.

Your school worries about the details of consumer demand as well. If tuition goes up again, some students will go elsewhere. Other students may take fewer courses. As enrollment begins to drop, school administrators may ask economics professors for some advice on tuition pricing. Their advice will be based on studies of consumer demand.

PATTERNS OF CONSUMPTION

A good way to start a study of consumer demand is to observe how consumers spend their incomes. Figure 4.1 provides a quick summary. Note that close to half of all consumer spending is for food and shelter. Out of the typical consumer dollar, 34 cents is devoted to housing—everything from rent and repairs to utility bills

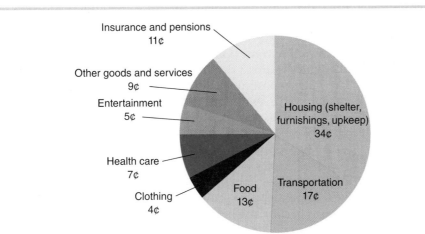

Source: U.S. Department of Labor, 2011. Consumer Expenditure Survey.

FIGURE 4.1
How the Consumer Dollar is Spent

Consumers spend their incomes on a vast array of goods and services. This figure summarizes those consumption decisions by showing how the average consumer dollar is spent. The goal of economic theory is to explain and predict these consumption choices.

and grass seed. Another 13 cents is spent on food, including groceries and trips to McDonald's. We also spend a lot on cars: transportation expenditures (car payments, maintenance, gasoline, insurance) eat up 17 cents of the typical consumer dollar.

Taken together, housing, transportation, food, and health expenditures account for 70 percent of the typical household budget. Most people regard these items as the "basic essentials." However, there is no rule that says 13 cents of every consumer dollar must be spent on food or that 34 percent of one's budget is "needed" for shelter. What Figure 4.1 depicts is how the average consumer has *chosen* to spend his or her income. We could choose to spend our incomes in other ways.

A closer examination of consumer patterns reveals that we do in fact change our habits on occasion. In the last 10 years, our annual consumption of red meat has declined from 125 pounds per person to 115 pounds. In the same time, our consumption of chicken has increased from 47 pounds to 70 pounds. We now consume less coffee, whiskey, beer, and eggs but more wine, asparagus, and ice cream compared to 10 years ago. Smartphones and computer tablets are regarded as essentials today, even though no one had these products 15 years ago. What prompted these changes in consumption patterns?

Some changes in consumption are more sudden. In the recession of 2008–2009, Americans abruptly stopped buying new cars. Does that mean that cars were no longer essential? When oil prices rose sharply in 2011, people *drove* their cars less. Does that mean they *liked* driving less? Or did changes in income and prices alter consumer behavior?

DETERMINANTS OF DEMAND

In seeking explanations for consumer behavior, we have to recognize that economics doesn't have all the answers. But it does offer a unique perspective that sets it apart from other fields of study.

The Sociopsychiatric Explanation

Consider first the explanations of consumer behavior offered by other fields of study. Psychiatrists and psychologists have had a virtual field day formulating such explanations. The Austrian psychiatrist Sigmund Freud (1856–1939) was among the first to describe us as bundles of subconscious (and unconscious) fears, complexes, and anxieties. From a Freudian perspective, we strive for ever-higher levels of consumption to satisfy basic drives for security, sex, and ego gratification. Like the most primitive of people, we clothe and adorn ourselves in ways that assert our identity and worth. We eat and smoke too much because we need the oral gratification and security associated with the mother's breast. Self-indulgence, in general, creates in our minds the safety and satisfactions of childhood. Oversized homes and cars provide us with a source of warmth and security remembered from the womb. On the other hand, we often buy and consume some things we expressly don't desire, just to assert our rebellious feelings against our parents (or parent substitutes). In Freud's view, it is the constant interplay of id, ego, and superego drives that motivates us to buy, buy, buy.

Sociologists offer additional explanations for our consumption behavior. They emphasize our yearning to stand above the crowd, to receive recognition from the masses. For people with exceptional talents, such recognition may come easily. But for the ordinary person, recognition may depend on conspicuous consumption. A larger car, a newer fashion, a more exotic vacation become expressions of identity that provoke recognition, even social envy. Thus we strive for higher levels of consumption—so as to *surpass* the Joneses, not just to keep up with them.

Not *all* consumption is motivated by ego or status concerns, of course. Some food is consumed for the sake of self-preservation, some clothing for warmth, and some housing for shelter. The typical American consumer has more than enough

NEWS WIRE	CONSUMPTION PATTERNS

Men versus Women: How They Spend

Are men really different from women? If spending habits are any clue, males do differ from females. That's the conclusion one would draw from the latest Bureau of Labor Statistics (BLS) survey of consumer expenditures. Here's what BLS found out about the spending habits of young (under age 25) men and women who are living on their own.

Common Traits

- Young men have a bit more income to spend ($14,672) than do young women ($13,258). Both sexes go deep into debt, however, by spending $4,000–$6,000 more than their incomes.
- Neither sex spends much on charity, reading, or health care.

Distinctive Traits

- Young men spend 15 percent more at fast-food outlets, restaurants, and carryouts.
- Men spend nearly twice as much on alcoholic beverages and smoking.
- Men spend nearly twice as much as women do on television, cars, and stereo equipment.
- Young women spend twice as much money on clothing, pets, and personal care items.

Source: U.S. Bureau of Labor Statistics, 2011 Consumer Expenditure Survey.

NOTE: Consumer patterns vary by gender, age, and other characteristics. Economists try to isolate the common influences on consumer behavior.

income to satisfy these basic needs, however. In today's economy, consumers have a lot of *discretionary* income that can be used to satisfy psychological or sociological longings. As a result, single women are able to spend a lot of money on clothing and pets, while men spend freely on entertainment, food, and drink (see the accompanying News Wire). As for teenagers, they show off their affluence in purchases of electronic goods, cars, and clothes (see Figure 4.2).

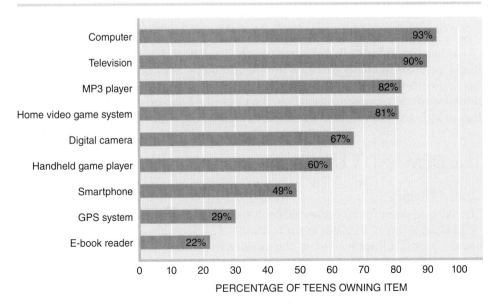

FIGURE 4.2
Affluent Teenagers

Teenagers spend over $300 billion a year. Much of this spending is for cars, stereos, and other durables. The percentage of U.S. teenagers owning certain items is shown here.

Source: © 2009 TRU, www.tru-insight.com. Used with permission.

You may desire this car, but are you able and willing to buy it?

© Car Culture/Corbis

demand The ability and willingness to buy specific quantities of a good at alternative prices in a given time period, *ceteris paribus*.

market demand The total quantities of a good or service people are willing and able to buy at alternative prices in a given time period; the sum of individual demands.

The Economic Explanation

Although psychiatrists and sociologists offer many reasons for these various consumption patterns, their explanations all fall a bit short. At best, sociopsychiatric theories tell us why teenagers, men, and women *desire* certain goods and services. They don't explain which goods will actually be *purchased*. Desire is only the first step in the consumption process. To acquire goods and services, one must be willing and able to *pay* for one's wants. Producers won't give you their goods just because you want to satisfy your Freudian desires. They want money in exchange for their goods. Hence *prices and income are just as relevant to consumption decisions as are more basic desires and preferences.*

In explaining consumer behavior, then, economists focus on the demand for goods and services. To say that someone **demands** a particular good means that he or she is able and willing to buy it at some price(s). In the marketplace, money talks: *the willingness and ability to pay* are critical. Many people with a strong desire for a Maserati (see photo) have neither the ability nor the willingness to actually buy it; they do not *demand* Maseratis. Similarly, there are many rich people who are willing and able to buy goods they only remotely desire; they *demand* all kinds of goods and services.

What determines a person's willingness and ability to buy specific goods? As we saw in Chapter 3, economists have identified four different influences on consumer demand: tastes, income, expectations, and the prices of other goods. Note again that desire (tastes) is only one determinant of demand. Other determinants of demand (income, expectations, and other goods) also influence whether a person will be willing and able to buy a certain good at a specific price.

As we observed in Chapter 3, the **market demand** for a good is simply the sum of all individual consumer demands. Hence *the market demand for a specific product is determined by*

* *Tastes* (desire for this and other goods).
* *Income* (of consumers).
* *Expectations* (for income, prices, tastes).
* *Other goods* (their availability and price).
* *The number of consumers in the market.*

In the remainder of this chapter we shall see how these determinants of demand give the demand curve its downward slope. Our objective is not only to explain consumer behavior but also to see (and predict) how consumption patterns *change* in response to *changes* in the price of a good or service or to *changes* in the underlying determinants of demand.

THE DEMAND CURVE

Utility Theory

The starting point for an economic analysis of demand is straightforward. Economists accept consumer tastes as the outcome of sociopsychiatric and cultural influences. They don't look beneath the surface to see how those tastes originated. Economists simply note the existence of certain tastes (desires) and then look to see how those tastes affect consumption decisions. We assume that the more pleasure a product gives us, the higher the price we would be willing to pay for it. If gobbling buttered popcorn at the movies really pleases you, you're likely to be willing to pay dearly for it. If you have no great taste or desire for popcorn, the theater might have to give it away before you'd eat it.

TOTAL VERSUS MARGINAL UTILITY   Economists use the term **utility** to refer to the expected pleasure, or satisfaction, obtained from goods and services. **Total utility** refers to the amount of satisfaction obtained from your *entire* consumption of a product. By contrast, **marginal utility** refers to the amount of satisfaction you get from consuming the *last* (i.e., marginal) unit of a product.

utility The pleasure or satisfaction obtained from a good or service.

total utility The amount of satisfaction obtained from entire consumption of a product.

DIMINISHING MARGINAL UTILITY   The concepts of total and marginal utility explain not only why we buy popcorn at the movies but also why we stop eating it at some point. Even people who love popcorn (i.e., derive great total utility from it), and can afford it, don't eat endless quantities of popcorn. Why not? Presumably because the thrill diminishes with each mouthful. The first box of popcorn may bring gratification, but the second or third box is likely to bring a stomachache. We express this change in perceptions by noting that the *marginal* utility of the first box of popcorn is higher than the additional or *marginal* utility derived from the second box.

marginal utility The satisfaction obtained by consuming one additional (marginal) unit of a good or service.

The behavior of popcorn connoisseurs is not that unusual. Generally speaking, the amount of additional utility we obtain from a product declines as we continue to consume larger quantities of it. The third slice of pizza is not as desirable as the first, the sixth soda not so satisfying as the fifth, and so forth. Indeed, this phenomenon of diminishing marginal utility is so commonplace that economists have fashioned a law around it. This **law of diminishing marginal utility** states that each successive unit of a good consumed yields less *additional* utility.

law of diminishing marginal utility The marginal utility of a good declines as more of it is consumed in a given time period.

The law of diminishing marginal utility does *not* say that we won't like the third box of popcorn, the second pizza, or the sixth soda; it just says we won't like them as much as the ones we've already consumed. Note also that time is important here: if the first pizza was eaten last year, the second pizza, eaten now, may taste just as good. The law of diminishing marginal utility applies to short time periods.

The expectation of diminishing marginal utility is illustrated in Figure 4.3. The graph on the left depicts the *total* utility obtained from eating popcorn.

FIGURE 4.3   Total versus Marginal Utility

The *total* utility (a) derived from consuming a product comes from the *marginal* utilities of each successive unit. The total utility curve shows how each of the first five boxes of popcorn contributes to total utility. Note that each successive step is smaller. This reflects the law of diminishing marginal utility.

The sixth box of popcorn causes the total utility steps to descend; the sixth box actually *reduces* total utility. This means that the sixth box has *negative* marginal utility.

The marginal utility curve (b) shows the change in total utility with each additional unit. It is derived from the total utility curve. Marginal utility here is positive but diminishing for the first five boxes. For the sixth box, marginal utility is negative.

I ate my first slice of this pizza, and it was fantastic. The next two slices were pretty good. My fourth slice was alright, and the fifth was okay. But I don't think I want another bite.

You can have too much of a good thing. No matter how much we like a product, marginal utility is likely to diminish as we consume more of it.

Source: Lillian Dougherty.

Notice that total utility continues to rise as we consume the first five boxes of popcorn. But total utility increases by smaller and smaller increments. Each successive step of the total utility curve in Figure 4.3 is a little shorter.

The height of each step of the total utility curve in Figure 4.3 represents *marginal* utility—the increments to total utility. The graph on the right in Figure 4.3 illustrates these marginal increments—the height of each step of the total utility curve (left graph). This graph shows more clearly how *marginal* utility diminishes.

Do not confuse *diminishing* marginal utility with dislike. Figure 4.3 doesn't imply that the second box of popcorn isn't desirable. It only says that the second box isn't as satisfying as the first. It still tastes good, however. How do we know? Because its *marginal* utility is positive (right graph), and therefore *total* utility (left graph) rises when the second box is consumed. *So long as marginal utility is positive, total utility must be increasing.*

The situation changes abruptly with the sixth box of popcorn. According to Figure 4.3, the good sensations associated with popcorn consumption are completely forgotten by the time the sixth box arrives. Nausea and stomach cramps dominate. Indeed, the sixth box is absolutely *distasteful,* as reflected in the downturn of total utility and the *negative* value for marginal utility. We were happier—in possession of more total utility—with only five boxes of popcorn. The sixth box—yielding *negative* marginal utility—has reduced total satisfaction. This is the kind of sensation you'd also experience if you ate too much pizza (see the accompanying cartoon).

Marginal utility explains not only why we stop eating before we explode but also why we pay so little for drinking water. Water has a high *total* utility: we would die without it. But its *marginal* utility is low, so we're not willing to pay much for another glass of it.

Not all goods approach zero (much less negative) marginal utility. Yet the more general principle of diminishing marginal utility is experienced daily. That is to say, *additional quantities of a good eventually yield increasingly smaller increments of satisfaction.* Total utility continues to rise, but at an ever slower rate as more of a good is consumed. There are exceptions to the law of diminishing marginal utility, but not many. (Can you think of any?)

Price and Quantity

Marginal utility is essentially a measure of how much we *desire* particular goods. But which ones will we *buy?* Clearly, we don't always buy the products we most desire. *Price* is often a problem. All too often we have to settle for goods that yield less marginal utility simply because they are less expensive. This explains why most people don't drive Porsches. Our desire ("taste") for a Porsche may be great, but its price is even greater. The challenge for most people is to somehow reconcile our tastes with our bank balances.

In deciding whether to buy something, our immediate focus is typically on a single variable—namely *price.* Assume that a person's tastes, income, and expectations are set in stone and that the prices of other goods are fixed as well. This is the *ceteris paribus* assumption we first encountered in Chapter 1. It doesn't mean that other influences on consumer behavior are unimportant. Rather, **the *ceteris paribus* simply allows us to focus on one variable at a time.** In this case, we are focusing on *price.* What we want to know is how high a price a consumer is willing to pay for another unit of a product.

ceteris paribus The assumption of nothing else changing.

The concepts of marginal utility and *ceteris paribus* enable us to answer this question. The more marginal utility a good delivers, the more you're willing to pay for it. But marginal utility *diminishes* as increasing quantities of a product are consumed. Hence you won't be willing to pay so much for additional quantities of the same good. The moviegoer who is willing to pay 50 cents for that first mouth-watering ounce of buttered popcorn may not be willing to pay so much for a second or third ounce. The same is true for the second pizza, the sixth soda, and so forth. *With given income, taste, expectations, and prices of other goods and services, people are willing to buy additional quantities of a good only if its price falls.* In other words, as the marginal utility of a good diminishes, so does our willingness to pay.

This inverse relationship between the quantity demanded of a good and its price is referred to as the **law of demand.** Figure 4.4 illustrates this relationship again for the case of popcorn. Notice that the **demand curve** slopes downward: more popcorn is purchased at lower prices.

The law of demand and the law of diminishing marginal utility tell us nothing about why we crave popcorn or why our cravings subside. That's the job of psychiatrists, sociologists, and physiologists. The laws of economics simply describe our market behavior.

law of demand The quantity of a good demanded in a given time period increases as its price falls, *ceteris paribus.*

demand curve A curve describing the quantities of a good a consumer is willing and able to buy at alternative prices in a given time period, *ceteris paribus.*

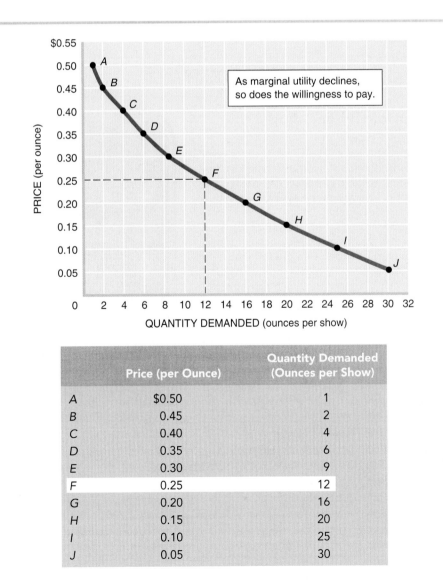

As marginal utility declines, so does the willingness to pay.

FIGURE 4.4
A Demand Schedule and Curve

Because marginal utility diminishes, consumers are willing to buy larger quantities of a good only at lower prices. This demand schedule and curve illustrate the specific quantities demanded at alternative prices.

Notice that points A through J on the curve correspond to the rows of the demand schedule. If popcorn sold for 25 cents per ounce, this consumer would buy 12 ounces per show (point F). More popcorn would be demanded only if the price were reduced (points G–J).

	Price (per Ounce)	Quantity Demanded (Ounces per Show)
A	$0.50	1
B	0.45	2
C	0.40	4
D	0.35	6
E	0.30	9
F	0.25	12
G	0.20	16
H	0.15	20
I	0.10	25
J	0.05	30

PRICE ELASTICITY

The theory of demand helps explain consumer behavior. Often, however, much more specific information is desired. Imagine you owned a theater and were actually worried about popcorn sales. Knowing that the demand curve is downward-sloping wouldn't tell you a whole lot about what price to charge. What you'd really want to know is *how much* popcorn sales would change if you raised or lowered the price.

Airlines want the same kind of hard data. Airlines know that around Christmas they can charge full fares and still fill all their planes. After the holidays, however, people have less desire to travel. To fill planes in February, the airlines must offer discount fares. But how far should they lower ticket prices? That depends on *how much* passenger traffic *changes* in response to reduced fares.

Apple Computer confronted a similar problem in 2007. Apple was launching its new iPhone at a price of $599. The product was an instant hit. But Apple wanted even greater sales. So it cut the price to $399, and unit sales skyrocketed from 9,000 iPhones a day to 27,000 a day. In 2009 Apple again reduced the price of its entry-level iPhone—to $99!—setting off another sales surge (see the accompanying News Wire).

The central question in all these decisions is the response of quantity demanded to a change in price. ***The response of consumers to a change in price is measured by the***

NEWS WIRE	PRICE ELASTICITY

To Sustain iPhone, Apple Halves Price

Apple Inc. halved the price of its entry-level iPhone to $99 and rolled out a next-generation model, looking to sustain the momentum for its popular smartphone amid the recession and fresh competition.

Toni Sacconaghi, an analyst at Sanford Bernstein & Co., said Apple's price cut shows the company is making an aggressive move to "enhance its first-mover advantage" by getting as many iPhone users as it can now despite the cost. He said the $99 price could increase iPhone demand by as much as 50 percent.

At Monday's event, Apple said it was cutting the price of its entry-level iPhone 3G, which has eight gigabytes of storage space, to $99, down from $199, effective immediately.

—Yukari Iwatani Kane

Source: *The Wall Street Journal*, June 9, 2009. Used with permission of Dow Jones & Company, Inc., via Copyright Clearance Center, Inc.

Apple

Courtesy of Apple

NOTE: According to the law of demand, quantity demanded increases when price falls. The price elasticity of demand measures how price sensitive consumers are.

price elasticity of demand. Specifically, the **price elasticity of demand** refers to the *percentage* change in quantity demanded divided by the *percentage* change in price:

price elasticity of demand The percentage change in quantity demanded divided by the percentage change in price.

$$\text{Price elasticity } (E) = \frac{\text{percentage change in quantity demanded}}{\text{percentage change in price}}$$

Suppose we increased the price of popcorn by 20 percent. We know from the law of demand that the quantity of popcorn demanded will fall. But we need to observe market behavior to see *how far* sales drop. Suppose that unit sales (quantity demanded) fall by 10 percent. We could then compute the price elasticity of demand as

$$E = \frac{\text{percentage change in quantity demanded}}{\text{percentage change in price}} = \frac{-10\%}{+20\%} = -0.5$$

Since price and quantity demanded always move in opposite directions (the law of demand), E is a negative value (-0.5 in this case). For convenience, however, we use the absolute value of E (without the minus sign). What we learn here is that popcorn sales decline at half (0.5) the rate of price increases. Moviegoers cut back grudgingly on popcorn consumption when popcorn prices rise.

Elastic versus Inelastic Demand

We characterize the demand for various goods in one of three ways: *elastic, inelastic,* or *unitary elastic.* If E is larger than 1, we say demand is elastic: consumer response is large relative to the change in price.

If E is less than 1, we say demand is inelastic. This is the case with popcorn, where E is only 0.5. *If demand is inelastic, consumers aren't very responsive to price changes.*

If E is equal to 1, demand is unitary elastic. In this case, the percentage change in quantity demanded is exactly equal to the percentage change in price.

Consider the case of smoking. Many smokers claim they'd "pay anything" for a cigarette after they've run out. But would they? Would they continue to smoke just as many cigarettes if prices doubled or tripled? Research suggests not: higher cigarette prices *do* curb smoking. There is at least *some* elasticity in the demand for cigarettes. But the elasticity of demand is low; Table 4.1 indicates

Degree of Elasticity	Estimate
Relatively elastic ($E > 1$)	
Airline travel, long run	2.4
Fresh fish	2.2
New cars, short run	1.2–1.5
Unitary elastic ($E = 1$)	
Private education	1.1
Radios and televisions	1.2
Shoes	0.9
Relatively inelastic ($E < 1$)	
Cigarettes	0.4
Coffee	0.3
Gasoline, short run	0.2
Long-distance telephone calls	0.1

Sources: Compiled from Hendrick S. Houthakker and Lester D. Taylor, *Consumer Demand in the United States, 1929–1970* (Cambridge, MA: Harvard University Press, 1966); F. W. Bell, "The Pope and Price of Fish," *American Economic Review*, December 1968; and Michael Ward, "Product Substitutability and Competition in Long-Distance Telecommunications," *Economic Inquiry*, October 1999.

TABLE 4.1
Elasticity Estimates
Price elasticities vary greatly. When the price of gasoline increases, consumers reduce their consumption only slightly: demand for gasoline is *in*elastic. When the price of fish increases, however, consumers cut back their consumption substantially: demand for fish is elastic. These differences reflect the availability of immediate substitutes, the prices of the goods, and the amount of time available for changing behavior.

NEWS WIRE | **PRICE ELASTICITY OF DEMAND**

Biggest U.S. Tax Hike on Tobacco Takes Effect

Smokers are gasping at higher cigarette and cigar prices as the largest federal tobacco tax increase in history takes effect. . . .

The increases, which raise the federal cigarette tax from 39 cents a pack to $1.01, applies to all tobacco products. It comes as more than two dozen states, desperate for revenue in a sunken economy, consider boosting their own tobacco taxes this year.

"This is very historic," said Mathew McKenna, director of the Office of Smoking and Health at the Centers for Disease Control and Prevention.

Before the tax hike, cigarette prices averaged about $5 a pack. Now tobacco companies are raising prices by different amounts. Some are absorbing part of the increase; others are raising prices more.

In the past, a 10 percent price increase reduced cigarette consumption about 4 percent, McKenna said. He expects the federal tax hike to prompt at least 1 million of the 45 million adult smokers to kick the habit.

—Wendy Koch

Source: USA TODAY. March 31, 2009. Reprinted with permission.

NOTE: Higher prices reduce quantity demanded. How much? It depends on the price elasticity of demand.

that the elasticity of cigarette demand is only 0.4. As a result, the *tripling* of the federal tax on cigarettes in 2009 had only a modest effect on adult smoking, as the News Wire explains.

Although the average adult smoker is not very responsive to changes in cigarette prices, teen smokers apparently are: teen smoking drops by almost 7 percent when cigarette prices increase by 10 percent. Thus the price elasticity of *teen* demand for smoking is

$$E = \frac{\text{percent drop in quantity demanded}}{\text{percent increase in price}} = \frac{-7\%}{+10\%} = -0.7$$

Hence higher cigarette prices can be an effective policy tool for curbing teen smoking. The decline in teen smoking after the 2009 tax increase confirms this expectation.

According to Table 4.1, the demand for airline travel is even more price elastic. Whenever a fare cut is announced, the airlines get swamped with telephone inquiries. If fares are discounted by 25 percent, the number of passengers may increase by as much as 60 percent. As Table 4.1 shows, the elasticity of airline demand is 2.4, meaning that the percentage change in quantity demanded (60 percent) will be 2.4 times larger than the price cut (25 percent). The price elasticity of demand for iPhones wasn't that large in 2009, according to News Wire on page 82. But iPhone sales still increased a lot in response to Apple's price cut.

Price Elasticity and Total Revenue

The concept of price elasticity refutes the popular misconception that producers charge the highest price possible. Except in the rare case of completely inelastic demand ($E = 0$), this notion makes no sense. Indeed, higher prices may actually *reduce* total sales revenue.

Price cuts *increase* total revenue if E > I.

	Price	×	Quantity Demanded	=	Total Revenue
A	$0.50		1		$0.50
B	0.45		2		0.90
C	0.40		4		1.60
D	0.35		6		2.10
E	0.30		8		2.40
F	0.25		12		3.00
G	0.20		16		3.20
H	0.15		20		3.00
I	0.10		25		2.50
J	0.05		30		1.50

FIGURE 4.5
Elasticity and Total Revenue

Total revenue is equal to the price of the product times the quantity sold. It is illustrated by the area of the rectangle formed by $p \times q$. The shaded rectangle illustrates total revenue ($3.00) at a price of 25 cents and a quantity demanded of 12 ounces.

When price is reduced to 20 cents, the rectangle and total revenue expand (see the dashed lines connected to point G) because demand is elastic (E > 1) in that price range.

Price cuts reduce total revenue only if demand is inelastic (E < 1), as it is here for prices below 20 cents (compare the total revenue at points G and H).

The **total revenue** of a seller is the amount of money received from product sales. It is determined by the quantity of the product sold and the price at which it is sold. Specifically,

$$\frac{\text{Total}}{\text{revenue}} = \text{price} \times \frac{\text{quantity}}{\text{sold}}$$

total revenue The price of a product multiplied by the quantity sold in a given time period: $p \times q$.

If the price of popcorn is 25 cents per ounce and 12 ounces are sold (point *F* in Figure 4.5), total revenue equals $3.00 per show. This total revenue is illustrated by the shaded rectangle in Figure 4.5. (Recall that the area of a rectangle is equal to its height, *p*, times its width, *q*.)

EFFECT OF A PRICE CUT   Now consider what happens to total revenue when the price of popcorn is reduced. Will total revenue decline along with the price? Maybe not. Remember the law of demand: as price falls, the quantity demanded *increases*. Hence total revenue *might* actually *increase* when the price of popcorn is reduced. Whether it does or not depends on *how much* quantity demanded goes up when price goes down. This brings us back to the concept of elasticity.

TABLE 4.2
Price Elasticity of
Demand and Total
Revenue

The impact of higher prices on
total revenue depends on the
price elasticity of demand.
Higher prices result in higher
total revenue only if demand is
inelastic. If demand is elastic,
lower prices result in *higher*
revenues.

If Demand Is:	When Price Increases, Total Revenue Will:	When Price Decreases, Total Revenue Will:
Elastic ($E > 1$)	Decrease	Increase
Inelastic ($E < 1$)	Increase	Decrease
Unitary elastic ($E = 1$)	Not change	Not change

Suppose we reduce popcorn prices from 25 cents to only 20 cents per ounce. What happens to total revenue? We know from Figure 4.5 that total revenue at point *F* was $3.00. When the price drops to 20 cents, unit sales increase significantly (to 16 ounces). In fact, they increase so much that total revenue actually increases as well. Total revenue at point *G* ($3.20) is larger than at point *F* ($3.00). Because total revenue *rose* when price *fell*, demand must be *elastic* in this price range. (See the last column in Table 4.2.)

Total revenue can't continue rising as price falls. At the extreme, price would fall to zero, and there would be no revenue. So somewhere along the demand curve falling prices will begin to pinch total revenue. In Figure 4.5 this happens when the price of popcorn drops from 20 cents to 15 cents. Unit sales again increase (from 16 to 20 ounces) but not enough to compensate for the price decline. As a result, total revenue at point *H* ($3.00) is less than at point *G* ($3.20). Total revenue falls in this case because the consumer response to a price reduction is small compared to the size of the price cut. In other words, demand is price *inelastic*. Thus we can conclude that

- *A price cut reduces total revenue if demand is inelastic (E < 1).*
- *A price cut increases total revenue if demand is elastic (E > 1).*
- *A price cut does not change total revenue if demand is unitary elastic (E = 1).*

Table 4.2 summarizes these responses as well as responses to price increases.

Once we know the price elasticity of demand, we can predict how consumers will respond to changing prices. We can also predict what will happen to total revenue when a seller raises or lowers the price. Presumably Starbucks performed these calculations before increasing coffee prices in 2010 (see the following News Wire).

Determinants of Price Elasticity

Table 4.1 (p. 83) indicates the actual price elasticity for a variety of familiar goods and services. These large differences in elasticity are explained by several factors.

NECESSITIES VERSUS LUXURIES   Some goods are so critical to our everyday life that we regard them as necessities. A hairbrush, toothpaste, and perhaps textbooks might fall into this category. Our taste for such goods is so strong that we can't imagine getting along without them. As a result, we don't change our consumption of necessities much when the price increases; *demand for necessities is relatively inelastic.*

A luxury good, by contrast, is something we'd *like* to have but aren't likely to buy unless our income jumps or the price declines sharply; vacation travel, new cars, and 3D television sets are examples. We want them, but we can get by without them. Thus *demand for luxury goods is relatively elastic.*

AVAILABILITY OF SUBSTITUTES   Our notion of what goods are necessities is also influenced by the availability of substitute goods. The high elasticity of demand for fish recorded in Table 4.1 reflects the fact that consumers can always eat tofu,

NEWS WIRE	PRICE, SALES, AND TOTAL REVENUE

Starbucks Customers Feel Burned by Surprise Price Hikes

Starbucks customers in New York this week could no longer pay for their venti mochas with a five-dollar bill after a 20-cent price hike brought the cost with tax to $5.06. In Seattle, the company's home, a grande mocha is now $3.91, up 10 percent. In Washington, DC, an upgrade to new loose-leaf tea bags also meant an upgrade in prices: a 50-cent hike to more than $2.00 for a mug. What's more, the company

© The McGraw-Hill Companies, Inc./John Flournoy, photographer/DAL

ended its 10 percent discount for "Black Gold Card" rewards members on the day after Christmas, leading many loyal customers to complain that demand for Starbucks coffee "is not inelastic."

Elasticity, though, is such a hard thing to measure. Certainly New York customers on Twitter are (sporadically) complaining they'll stop shopping there "once my Christmas Starbucks cards are done," decamping for Dunkin Donuts. . . .

This limited-edition price hike looks for all the world like a test of whether customers will reduce their visits once prices go up. A 10 percent increase in prices could certainly erase those same-store declines if only 5 percent of customers drop out. The latest same-store sales were only a 1 percent decline from the year-earlier quarter, making this a relatively easy hump to overcome.

—Sarah Gilbert

Source: Daily Finance, January 14, 2010 © 2010 AOL Inc. All rights reserved.

NOTE: The impact of a price increase on unit sales and total revenue depends on the price elasticity of demand. Starbucks was counting on *in*elastic demand.

---

chicken, beef, or pork if fish prices rise. On the other hand, most coffee drinkers cannot imagine anything substituting for a cup of coffee. As a consequence, when coffee prices rise, consumers do not reduce their purchases very much at all. Likewise, the low elasticity of demand for gasoline reflects the fact that most cars can't run on alternative fuels. In general, *the greater the availability of substitutes, the higher the price elasticity of demand.* This is a principle that San Francisco learned when it introduced a "butt tax" of 20 cents per pack in 2009 (see the accompanying News Wire). In-city sales declined as smokers turned to adjoining states and cities, Indian reservations, and the Internet for their cigarette purchases.

PRICE RELATIVE TO INCOME   Another important determinant of elasticity is the price of the good itself. If the price of a product is very high in relation to the consumer's income, then price *changes* will be important. Airline travel and new cars, for example, are quite expensive, so even a small percentage change in their prices can have a big impact on a consumer's budget (and consumption decisions). The demand for such big-ticket items tends to be elastic. By contrast, coffee is so cheap for most people that even a large *percentage* change in price doesn't affect consumer behavior much.

Topic Podcast:
Price Elasticity

NEWS WIRE | SUBSTITUTE GOODS

San Francisco: The Butts Stop Here
San Francisco mayor Gavin Newsom says there are far too many butts in the City by the Bay. Not human butts, of course, but cigarette butts. Picking up the discarded butts costs the city $6 million a year. To make careless smokers pay these cleanup costs, he levied a tax of 20 cents on every pack of cigarettes sold in the city, effective October 2009. With 30 million packs being sold in the city annually, the 20 cent "fee" looked high enough to cover the costs of the butt cleanup ($6 million).

Mayor Gavin shouldn't count those chickens before they hatch. The only way the new 20 cent fee can generate $6 million a year is if San Franciscans continue to purchase 30 million packs per year. That just isn't going to happen. The law of demand is more powerful than the laws of San Francisco, and the **law of demand** clearly states that the quantity demanded goes down when price goes up. Finding substitute goods for San Francisco cigarettes is easy. Buy a carton of cigarettes in the neighboring communities of Daly City, Oakland, or Sausalito and you save $2.00. Buy cigarettes online from an Indian reservation (which does not pay federal or state taxes) and save even more. As a quick search on Google or Yahoo will confirm, over 2,000 websites offer to facilitate those untaxed shipments. So untaxed substitutes for San Francisco cigarettes are literally only a click away. Mayor Gavin should have consulted New York City Mayor Michael Bloomberg, who saw in-city cigarette sales plunge by 50 percent when he raised that city's tax in 2002.

—Bradley Schiller

Source: "San Francisco: The Butts Stop Here" by Bradley Schiller. McGraw-Hill News Flash, August 2009.

NOTE: Demand for cigarettes in general is inelastic. However, demand for San Francisco's cigarettes is elastic because smokers can purchase cigarettes elsewhere.

Other Changes in Consumer Behavior

We stated at the outset of this discussion that we were going to focus on the *price* of a product and its quantity demanded. So we ignored everything else. It's time, however, to consider other influences on consumer behavior.

SUBSTITUTE GOODS When Hurricane Sandy sent gasoline prices higher in November 2012, consumers cut back on their driving. So how did they get around? In part, they simply traveled less, but they also made more use of public transportation like buses, subways, and trains. Thus public transportation became a *substitute* for higher gas prices and private transportation. The demand for *substitute goods* increases (shifts to the right) when the price of a product goes up. When movie theater prices go up, the demand for streaming movies (e.g., Netflix) and DVDs increases. When airfares go down, the demand for bus and rail travel decreases. When Starbucks raised its prices in 2010, demand for Dunkin Donuts coffee increased.

COMPLEMENTARY GOODS A 2005 spike in gasoline prices had the opposite effect on SUV sales. As the accompanying News Wire reports, the demand for trucks and SUVs *declined* when gasoline prices *rose*. Gas guzzlers and gasoline are *complementary goods*, not substitute goods. If the demand for another good moves in the opposite direction (up or down) of the price of a product, the two goods are *complements* (e.g., gas price *up*, SUV demand *down*). If they move in the same direction, the goods are substitutes (e.g., gas prices *up*, subway demand *up*).

NEWS WIRE	SUBSTITUTE AND COMPLEMENTARY GOODS

Truck and SUV Sales Plunge as Gas Prices Rise

Sales of Detroit trucks stalled in September as spiking gas prices sped up a consumer shift toward more fuel-efficient vehicles.

In the first look at sales since Hurricane Katrina drove gasoline pump prices to $3 a gallon and beyond, sales of passenger cars grew last month while large, fuel-thirsty sport utility vehicles languished. Overall, industry sales in September slid 7.6 percent from a year ago.

General Motors Corp. reported a sales drop of 24 percent compared with the same month a year ago. Ford Motor Co.'s sales declined 20 percent.

At Honda, sales of the Civic, one of the industry's most popular small cars, grew 37 percent from a year ago. Honda reported a 25 percent sales increase in the gasoline-electric hybrid version of the Civic. Sales of the hybrid Toyota Prius nearly doubled to 8,193 for the month.

—Sholnn Freeman

Source: *The Washington Post,* © October 4, 2005, The Washington Post. All rights reserved.

NOTE: Changes in the price of one good will affect the demand for other goods. Higher gasoline prices reduce the demand for SUVs (a complementary good) and increase the demand for hybrids (a substitute good).

The important thing to notice here is that *a change in the price of one product will affect not only the quantity of that product demanded (as measured by price elasticity) but also the demand for other goods* (substitute goods and complementary goods). This is why auto manufacturers worry a lot about gasoline prices and record companies worry about the price of music downloads.

Changes in Income

Auto manufacturers and record companies would worry less if consumers had more money to spend. As we observed earlier, income is a *determinant* of demand. Our analysis of the demand curve was based on the *ceteris paribus* assumption that only *one* thing was changing—namely price. This assumption allowed us to observe how price changes propel consumers up and down the demand curve, altering both unit sales and total revenue.

The picture would look different if *incomes* were to change. If our incomes increased, we could buy *more* products at every price. **We illustrate income changes with shifts of the demand curve** rather than movements along it (due to changes in price). When the economy falls into a recession and people are losing jobs and income, demand for most products—especially big-ticket items like cars, vacations, and new homes—declines (shifts left). In more prosperous times, cash registers keep humming.

POLICY PERSPECTIVES

Does Advertising Change Our Behavior?

Marketing people have been quick to recognize the importance of demand curve *shifts*. Producers can't change consumer incomes, but what about the other determinants of demand? Wasn't *tastes* one of those determinants?

A whole new range of profit opportunities suddenly appears. If producers can change consumers' tastes, they can *shift* the demand curve and sell *more* output at *higher* prices. How will they do this? By advertising. As noted earlier, psychiatrists see us as complex bundles of basic drives, anxieties, and layers of consciousness. They presume that we enter the market with confused senses of guilt, insecurity, and ambition. Economists, on the other hand, regard the consumer as the rational *Homo economicus,* aware of his or her wants and knowledgeable about how to satisfy them. In reality, however, we do not always know what we want or which products will satisfy us. This uncertainty creates a vacuum into which the advertising industry has eagerly stepped.

The efforts of producers to persuade us to buy, buy, buy are as close as the nearest television, radio, magazine, web page, or billboard. American producers now spend over $200 *billion* per year to change our tastes. This spending works out to over $400 per consumer, the highest per capita advertising rates in the world. Much of this advertising (including product labeling) is intended to provide information about existing products or to bring new products to our attention. A great deal of advertising, however, is also designed to exploit our senses and lack of knowledge. Recognizing that we are guilt-ridden, insecure, and sex-hungry, advertisers offer us pictures and promises of exoneration, recognition, and love: all we have to do is buy the right product.

One of the favorite targets of advertisers is our sense of insecurity. Brand images are developed to give consumers a sense of identity. Smoke a Marlboro cigarette, and you're a virile cowboy. Drink the right beer or vodka, and you'll be a social success. Use the right perfume, and you'll be irresistibly sexy. Wear Brand X jeans, and you'll be way cool. Or at least that's what advertisers want you to believe.

ARE WANTS CREATED?   Advertising cannot be blamed for all of our "foolish" consumption. Even members of the most primitive tribes, uncontaminated by the seductions of advertising, adorned themselves with rings, bracelets, and pendants. Furthermore, advertising has grown to massive proportions only in the last fifty years, but consumption spending has been increasing throughout recorded history.

Although advertising cannot be charged with creating our needs, it does encourage specific outlets for satisfying those needs. The objective of all advertising is to alter the choices we make. Advertising seeks to increase our desire (taste) for particular products and therewith our willingness to pay. *A successful advertising campaign is one that shifts the demand curve for a product to the right,* inducing consumers to increase their purchases of a product at every price (see Figure 4.6). Advertising may also increase brand loyalty, making the demand curve less elastic, thereby reducing consumer responses to price increases.

FIGURE 4.6
The Impact of Advertising on a Demand Curve

Advertising seeks to increase our taste for a particular product. If our taste (the product's perceived marginal utility) increases, so will our willingness to buy. The resulting change in demand is reflected in a rightward shift of the demand curve, often accompanied by a diminished price elasticity of demand.

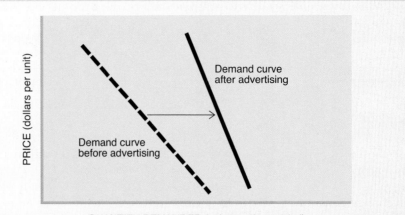

SUMMARY

- Our desires for goods and services originate in the structure of personality and social dynamics and are not explained by economic theory. Economic theory focuses on *demand*—that is, our ability and willingness to buy specific quantities of a good or service at various prices.   **LO1**
- *Utility* refers to the satisfaction we get from consumer goods and services. *Total utility* refers to the amount of satisfaction associated with all consumption of a product. *Marginal utility* refers to the satisfaction obtained from the last unit of a product.   **LO1**
- The law of diminishing marginal utility says that the more of a product we consume, the smaller the increments of pleasure we get from each additional unit. This is the foundation for the law of demand.   **LO1**
- The price elasticity of demand (*E*) is a numerical measure of consumer response to a change in price (*ceteris paribus*). It equals the percentage change in

quantity demanded divided by the percentage change in price.   **LO2**
- If demand is elastic ($E > 1$), a small change in price induces a large change in quantity demanded. "Elastic" demand indicates that consumers are very price sensitive.   **LO2**
- If demand is *elastic*, a price increase will reduce total revenue. Price and total revenue move in the *same* direction only if demand is *inelastic*.   **LO3**
- The shape and position of any particular demand curve depend on a consumer's income, tastes, expectations, and the price and availability of other goods. Should any of these things change, the assumption of *ceteris paribus* will no longer hold, and the demand curve will *shift*.   **LO4**
- Advertising seeks to change consumer tastes and thus the willingness to buy. If tastes do change, the demand curve will shift.   **LO5**

TERMS TO REMEMBER

Define the following terms:

demand	marginal utility	law of demand	price elasticity of demand
market demand	law of diminishing	demand curve	total revenue
utility	marginal utility		
total utility	*ceteris paribus*		

QUESTIONS FOR DISCUSSION

1. Why do people routinely stuff themselves at all-you-can-eat buffets? Explain in terms of both utility and demand theories.   **LO1**
2. What does the demand for education at your college look like? What is on each axis? Is the demand elastic or inelastic? How could you find out?   **LO1**
3. What would happen to unit sales and total revenue for this textbook if the publisher reduced its price?   **LO3**
4. Should Starbucks have increased its prices in 2010? What was the substitute good cited in the News Wire on page 87?   **LO4**
5. Identify three goods each for which your demand is (*a*) elastic or (*b*) inelastic. What accounts for the differences in elasticity?   **LO2**
6. Utility companies routinely ask state commissions for permission to raise utility rates. What does this

suggest about the price elasticity of demand? Why is demand so (in)elastic?   **LO3**
7. Why is the demand for San Francisco cigarettes so much more price elastic than the overall market demand for cigarettes (see News Wire, page 88)?   **LO4**
8. When gasoline prices go up, how is demand for the following products affected: (*a*) SUVs; (*b*) hybrid cars; (*c*) beach hotels; (*d*) iPads?   **LO4**
9. What goods do people buy a lot more of when their incomes go up? What goods are unaffected by income changes?   **LO4**
10. **POLICY PERSPECTIVES** If *all* soda advertisements were banned, how would Pepsi sales be affected? How about total soda consumption?   **LO5**

PROBLEMS

1. (a) In Figure 4.3, which box of popcorn first has diminished marginal utility?
   (b) In the cartoon on page 80 , which pizza slice first yields negative marginal utility? **LO1**

2. The following is a demand schedule for shoes: **LO3**

Price (per pair)	$120	$100	$80	$60	$40
Quantity demanded (in pairs per year)	6	10	15	20	26

   (a) Illustrate the demand curve on the following graph.
   (b) How much will consumers spend on shoes at the price of (i) $100 and (ii) $80?
   (c) As the price drops from $100 to $80 a pair, is demand elastic or inelastic?
   (d) Between what two prices is demand unitary elastic?
   (e) Between what two prices is demand inelastic?

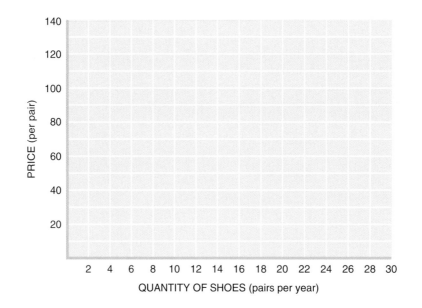

QUANTITY OF SHOES (pairs per year)

3. According to the elasticity computation on page 83, (a) by how much would popcorn sales fall if the price increased by 20 percent? (b) By 50 percent? **LO2**

4. According to Table 4.1, if price increases by 10 percent, how much will unit sales decline for (a) coffee, (b) shoes, and (c) airline travel? Will total revenue increase or decrease for (d) coffee, (e) shoes, (f) airline travel? **LO3**

5. According to the News Wire on page 53, what is the price elasticity of demand for alcohol among college students? **LO2**

6. (a) According to Table 4.1, by how much would coffee sales decline if the price of coffee increased 20 percent? (b) If Starbucks raised *its* coffee prices by the same amount, would sales decline by more, less, or the same amount? **LO4**

7. According to the News Wire on page 84, the average cigarette price rose by 12 percent on April 1, 2009. (a) According to the story, by what percentage might smoking be expected to decline? (b) By how much would *teen* smoking decline (see the text on page 84)? **LO2**

8. Suppose the following table reflects the total satisfaction (utility) derived from eating pizza: **LO1**

Quantity consumed	1	2	3	4	5	6	7
Total utility	47	92	122	135	137	120	70

   (a) What is the marginal utility of each pizza?
   (b) When does marginal utility first diminish?
   (c) When does marginal utility first turn negative?

9. What was the price elasticity of demand for iPhones in June 2009 (News Wire, page 82)?   **LO2**

10. Economists estimate price elasticities more precisely by using *average* price and quantity to compute percentage changes. Thus,

$$E = \frac{Q_1 - Q_2}{\dfrac{Q_1 + Q_2}{2}} \div \frac{P_1 - P_2}{\dfrac{P_1 + P_2}{2}}$$

Using this formula, compute E for a popcorn price increase from 15 cents to 25 cents per ounce (Figure 4.5).   **LO3**

11. **POLICY PERSPECTIVES** Suppose the following demand exists for iPhone apps:

Price	$10	9	8	7	6	5	4	3
Quantity demanded (millions)	2	3	4	5	6	7	8	9

(a) At $9, what quantity is demanded?

(b) If the price drops to $6, what quantity is demanded?

(c) Is demand elastic or inelastic in that price range?

(d) If advertising convinces people to demand three more apps at every price, how many apps will be demanded at $9?

(e) Graph the above answers, using point A for (a), point B for (b), and point C for (d).   **LO5**

◄ Practice quizzes, student PowerPoints, author podcasts, web activities, and additional materials available at **www.mhhe.com/schileressentials9e**, or scan here. Need a barcode reader? Try ScanLife, available in your app store.

5

Supply
Decisions

◄ Practice quizzes, student PowerPoints, author podcasts, web activities, and additional materials available at www.mhhe.com/ schilleressentials9e, or scan here. Need a barcode reader? Try ScanLife, available in your app store.

LEARNING OBJECTIVES

After reading this chapter, you should be able to:

1 Explain what the production function reveals.
2 Explain why the law of diminishing returns applies.
3 Describe the nature of fixed, variable, and marginal costs.
4 Illustrate the difference between production and investment decisions.
5 Discuss how accounting costs and economic costs differ.

Most consumers think that producers reap huge profits from every market sale. Most producers wish that were true. The average producer earns a profit of only four to six cents on every sales dollar. And those profits don't come easily. Producers earn a profit only if they make the correct supply decisions. They have to keep a close eye on prices and costs and produce the right quantity at the right time. If they do all the right things, they *might* make a profit. Even when a producer does everything right, however, profits are not assured. Over 50,000 U.S. businesses fail every year despite their owners' best efforts to make a profit.

In this chapter we look at markets from the supply side, examining two distinct concerns. First, how much output *can* a firm produce? Second, how much output will it *want* to produce? As we'll see, the answers to these two questions are rarely the same.

The question of how much *can* be produced is largely an engineering and managerial problem. The question of how much *should* be produced is an *economic* issue. If costs escalate as capacity is approached, it might make sense to produce less than capacity output. In some situations, the costs of production might even be so high that it doesn't make sense to produce *any* output from available facilities. The end result will be a **supply** decision—that is, an expressed *ability* and *willingness* to produce a good at various prices.

A producer's supply decision is similar to your homework decision. The amount of homework you *could* do in the next two hours is determined by available resources (e.g., brain power, computer access, tutorial help, space). How much homework you *actually* do ("produce") will be determined by how you *choose* to use your time. You rarely produce at capacity, and neither do business firms: they *choose* how much of their capacity to utilize.

This chapter focuses on those *supply* decisions. We look first at the capacity to produce and then at how choices are made about how much of that capacity to utilize. The discussion revolves around three questions:

- What limits a firm's ability to produce?
- What costs are incurred in producing a good?
- How do costs affect supply decisions?

Once we have answered these questions, we should be able to understand how supply-side forces affect the price and availability of the goods and services we demand in product markets.

CAPACITY CONSTRAINTS: THE PRODUCTION FUNCTION

No matter how large a business is or who owns it, all businesses confront one central fact: you need resources to produce goods. To produce corn, a farmer needs land, water, seed, equipment, and labor. To produce fillings, a dentist needs a chair, a drill, some space, and labor. Even the "production" of educational services (e.g., this economics class) requires the use of labor (your teacher), land (on which the school is built), and some capital (bricks and mortar or electronic classrooms). In short, unless you are producing unrefined, unpackaged air, you need **factors of production**—that is, resources that can be used to produce a good or service.

The factors of production used to produce a good or service provide the basic measure of economic cost. If someone asked you what the cost of your econ class was, you'd probably quote the tuition you paid for it. But tuition is the *price of consuming* the course, not the *cost of producing* it. The cost of producing your economics class is measured by the amounts of land, labor, and capital it requires. These are *resource* costs of production.

supply The ability and willingness to sell (produce) specific quantities of a good at alternative prices in a given time period, *ceteris paribus*.

factors of production Resource inputs used to produce goods and services (land, labor, capital, entrepreneurship).

An essential question for production is, How many resources are actually needed to produce a given product? You could use a lot of resources to produce a product or use just a few. What we really want to know is how *best* to produce. What is the *smallest* amount of resources needed to produce a specific product? Or we could ask the same question from a different perspective: What is the *maximum* amount of output attainable from a given quantity of input resources?

These aren't easy questions to answer. But if we knew the technology of the production process, we could come up with an answer. The answer would tell us the *maximum* amount of output attainable from a given quantity of resources. These limits to the production of any good are reflected in the **production function.** The production function tells us the maximum amount of good *X* producible from various combinations of factor inputs. With one chair and one drill, a dentist can fill a maximum of 32 cavities per day. With two chairs, a drill, and an assistant, a dentist can fill up to 55 cavities per day.

A production function is a technological summary of our ability to produce a particular good. Figure 5.1 provides a partial glimpse of one such function. In this case, the desired output is designer jeans, as produced by Tight Jeans Corporation. The essential inputs in the production of jeans are land, labor (garment workers), and capital (a factory and sewing machines). With these inputs, Tight Jeans can produce and sell fancy jeans to status-conscious consumers.

As in all production endeavors, we want to know how many pairs of jeans we can produce with available resources. To make things easy, we will assume that the factory is already built. We will also assume that only one leased sewing machine is available. Thus both land and capital inputs are fixed. Under these circumstances, only the quantity of labor can be varied. In this case, the quantity of jeans we can produce depends directly on the amount of labor we employ. ***The purpose of a production function is to tell us just how much output we can produce with varying amounts of factor inputs.*** Figure 5.1 provides such information for jeans production.

production function A technological relationship expressing the maximum quantity of a good attainable from different combinations of factor inputs.

FIGURE 5.1
A Production Function

A production function tells us the *maximum* amount of output attainable from alternative combinations of factor inputs. This particular function tells us how many pairs of jeans we can produce in a factory that has only one sewing machine and varying quantities of labor.

With only one operator, we can produce a maximum of 15 pairs of jeans per day, as indicated in column B of the table and point *B* on the graph. To produce more jeans, we need more labor. The short-run production function shows how output changes when more labor is used.

	Short-Run Production Function								
	A	B	C	D	E	F	G	H	I
Labor input (workers per day)	0	1	2	3	4	5	6	7	8
Output (pairs of jeans per day)	0	15	34	44	48	50	51	51	47

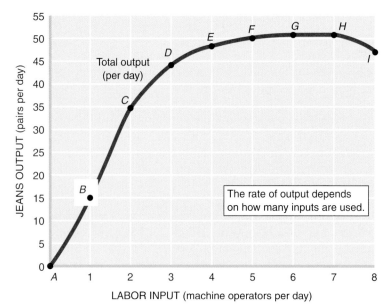

The rate of output depends on how many inputs are used.

LABOR INPUT (machine operators per day)
JEANS OUTPUT (pairs per day)
Total output (per day)

Column A of the table in Figure 5.1 confirms the obvious: you can't manufacture jeans without any workers. Even though land, capital (an empty factory and an idle machine), and denim are available, essential labor inputs are missing, and jeans production is impossible. Maybe advances in robotics will change that reality. For now, however, the factory depicted in Figure 5.1 isn't nearly that advanced. It still needs live bodies in the production process.

Column B in the table shows what happens to jeans output when just one worker is employed. With only one machine and one worker, the jeans start rolling out the front door. Maximum output under these circumstances (row 2, column B) is 15 pairs of jeans per day. Now we're in business!

The remaining columns of the table tell us how many additional jeans we can produce if we hire still more workers, still leasing only one sewing machine. With one machine and two workers, maximum output rises to 34 pairs per day (column C). If a third worker is hired, output could increase to 44 pairs.

This information on our production capabilities is also illustrated graphically in Figure 5.1. Point A illustrates the fact that we can't produce any jeans without some labor. Points B through I show how production increases as additional labor is employed.

*Labor is a vital but **variable** input in production.*

© Marsaili McGrath/Stringer/Getty Images

Efficiency

Every point on the production function in Figure 5.1 represents the *most* output we could produce with a specific number of workers. Point D, for example, tells us we could produce as many as 44 pairs of jeans with three workers. We recognize, however, that we might also produce less. If the workers goof off or the sewing machine isn't maintained well, total output might be less than 44 pairs per day. In that case, we wouldn't be making the best possible use of scarce resources: we would be producing *inefficiently*. In Figure 5.1 this would imply a rate of output *below* point D. Only if we produce with maximum *efficiency* will we end up at point D or some other point on the production function.

Capacity

Although the production function emphasizes how output increases with more workers, the progression can't go on forever. Labor isn't the only factor of production needed to produce jeans. We also need capital. In this case, we have only a small factory and one sewing machine. If we keep hiring workers, we will quickly run out of space and available equipment. ***Land and capital constraints place a ceiling on potential output.***

Notice in Figure 5.1 how total output peaks at point G. We can produce a total of 51 pairs of jeans at that point by employing six workers. What happens if we hire still more workers? According to Figure 5.1, if we employed a seventh worker, total output would not increase further. At point H, total output is still 51 pairs, just as it was at point G, when we hired only six workers.

Were we to hire an *eighth* worker, total jeans output would actually *decline,* as illustrated by point I. An eighth worker *reduces* total output by increasing congestion on the factory floor, delaying access to the sewing machine, and just plain getting in the way. Given the size of the factory and the availability of only one sewing machine, no more than six workers can be productively employed. Hence the *capacity* production of this factory is 51 pairs of jeans per day. We could hire more workers, but output would not go up.

Marginal Physical Product

The land and capital constraints that limit output have some interesting effects on the productivity of individual workers. Consider that seventh worker at the jeans factory. If she were hired, total output would not increase: total output is 51 pairs of jeans when either six or seven workers are employed. Accordingly, that seventh worker contributes nothing to total output.

The contribution of each worker to production is measured by the change in *total* output that occurs when the worker is employed. This is **marginal physical product (MPP)** and is measured as

marginal physical product (MPP) The change in total output associated with one additional unit of input.

$$\text{Marginal physical product (MPP)} = \frac{\text{change in total output}}{\text{change in input quantity}}$$

In this case, total output doesn't change when the seventh worker is hired, so her MPP equals zero. She contributes nothing to production.

Contrast that experience with that of the *first* worker hired. When the first worker is employed at the jeans factory, total output jumps from zero (point *A* in Figure 5.1) to 15 pairs of jeans per day (point *B*). This *increase* in output reflects the marginal physical product (MPP) of that first worker—that is, the *change* in total output that results from employment of one more unit of (labor) input.

If we employ a second operator, jeans output more than doubles to 34 pairs per day (point *C*). Whereas the marginal physical product of the first worker was only 15 pairs, a second worker increases total output by 19 pairs.

The higher MPP of the second worker raises a question about the first. Why was the first's MPP lower? Laziness? Is the second worker faster, less distracted, or harder working?

The higher MPP of the second worker is not explained by superior talents or effort. We assume in this exercise that all units of labor are equal—that is, one worker is just as good as another. Their different marginal products are explained by the structure of the production process, not by their respective abilities. The first garment worker had to not only sew jeans but also unfold bolts of denim, measure the jeans, sketch out the patterns, and cut them to approximate size. A lot of time was spent going from one task to another. Despite the worker's best efforts, this person simply could not do everything at once.

A second worker alleviates this situation. With two workers, less time is spent running from one task to another. Now there is an opportunity for each worker to specialize a bit. While one is measuring and cutting, the other can continue sewing. This improved *ratio* of labor to other factors of production results in the large jump in total output. The superior MPP of the second worker is not unique to this person: it would have occurred even if we had hired the workers in the reverse order. What matters is the amount of capital or land each unit of labor can work with. In other words, *a worker's productivity (MPP) depends in part on the amount of other resources in the production process.*

Law of Diminishing Returns

Unfortunately, output cannot keep increasing at this rate. Look what happens when a third worker is hired. Total jeans production continues to increase. But the increase from point *C* to point *D* in Figure 5.1 is only 10 pairs per day. Hence the MPP of the third worker (10 pairs) is *less* than that of the second (19 pairs). Marginal physical product is *diminishing*.

RESOURCE CONSTRAINTS   What accounts for this decline in MPP? The answer again lies in the ratio of labor to other factors of production. A third worker begins to crowd our facilities. We still have only one sewing machine. Two people cannot sew at the same time. As a result, some time is wasted as the operators wait for their turns at the machine. Even if they split up the various jobs, there will still be some downtime, since measuring and cutting are not as

Topic Podcast:
Diminishing Returns

time-consuming as sewing. In this sense, we cannot make full use of a third worker. *The relative scarcity of other inputs (capital and land) constrains the marginal physical product of labor.*

Resource constraints are even more evident when a fourth worker is hired. Total output increases again, but the increase this time is very small. With three workers, we got 44 pairs of jeans per day (point *D*); with four workers, we get a maximum of 48 pairs (point *E*). Thus the marginal physical product of the fourth worker is only four pairs of jeans. A fourth worker really begins to strain our productive capacity. There simply aren't enough machines to make productive use of so much labor.

NEGATIVE MPP If a seventh worker is hired, the operators get in each other's way, argue, and waste denim. As we observed earlier, total output does not increase at all when a seventh worker is hired. The MPP of the seventh worker is zero. The seventh worker is being wasted in the sense that she contributes nothing to total output. This waste of scarce resources (labor) was commonplace in communist countries, where everyone was guaranteed a job (see the News Wire below). At Tight Jeans, however, they do not want to hire someone who doesn't contribute to output. And they certainly wouldn't want to hire an *eighth* worker because total output actually *declines* from 51 pairs of jeans (point *H* in Figure 5.1) to 47 pairs (point *I*) when an eighth worker is hired. In other words, the eighth worker has a *negative* MPP.

The problem of crowded facilities applies to most production processes. In the short run, a production process is characterized by a fixed amount of available land and capital. Typically the only factor that can be varied in the short run is labor. Yet *as more labor is hired, each unit of labor has less capital and land to work with.* This is simple division: the available facilities are being shared by more and more workers. At some point, this constraint begins to pinch. When it does, marginal physical product starts to decline. This situation is so common that it is the basis for an economic principle: the **law of diminishing returns.** This law says that the marginal physical product of any factor of production (e.g., labor) will begin to diminish at some point as more of it is used in a given production setting.

law of diminishing returns
The marginal physical product of a variable input declines as more of it is employed with a given quantity of other (fixed) inputs.

NEWS WIRE	MARGINAL PHYSICAL PRODUCT

"We Pretend to Work, They Pretend to Pay Us"
One of the attractions of communist nations was their promise of employment. Passing through the factory gate was not proof of productive employment, however. Ordered to hire all comers, state-run enterprises became bloated with surplus workers. Although payrolls climbed, output stagnated.

As it turned out, the paychecks handed out to the workers weren't very good anyway. Runaway inflation and a scarcity of consumer goods rendered the paychecks almost worthless. The futility of the situation was summed up by one worker who explained that "we pretend to work and they pretend to pay us."

When communism collapsed, the factory gates were no longer open to all. New profit-oriented owners were unwilling to pay workers whose marginal physical product was zero. In East Germany alone, over 400,000 workers lost their jobs when 126 state-owned enterprises were sold to private investors—without any decline in output.

NOTE: As more workers are hired in a given plant, marginal physical product declines. It may even fall to zero or less.

You could put the law of diminishing returns to an easy test. Start a lawn-mowing service. Assuming you have only one electric mower and a few rakes, what will happen to total output (lawns mowed per day) as you hire more workers? How soon before marginal physical product reaches zero? Then visit a Starbucks outlet. How much would output (drinks per day) increase if they hired more baristas? What keeps output from increasing faster in the short run? Would marginal physical product decline as more baristas competed for access to the espresso machines?

Short Run versus Long Run

The limited availability of space or equipment is the cause of diminishing returns. Once we have purchased or leased a specific factory, it sets a limit to current jeans production. When such commitments to fixed inputs (e.g., the factory and machinery) exist, we are dealing with a **short-run** production problem. If no land or capital were in place—if we could build or lease any size factory—we would be dealing with a *long-run* decision. In the **long run** we might also learn new and better ways of making jeans and so increase our production capabilities. For the time being, however, we must accept the fact that the production function in Figure 5.1 defines the *short-run* limits to jeans production. Our short-run objective is to make the best possible use of the factory we have acquired. This is the challenge producers face every day.

short run The period in which the quantity (and quality) of some inputs cannot be changed.

long run A period of time long enough for all inputs to be varied (no fixed costs).

COSTS OF PRODUCTION

A production function tells us how much output a firm *could* produce with its existing plant and equipment. It doesn't tell us how much the firm will *want* to produce. The level of desired output depends on prices and costs. A firm *might* want to produce at capacity if the profit picture were bright enough. On the other hand, a firm might not produce *any* output if costs always exceeded sales revenue. *A firm's goal is to maximize profits, not production.* The most desirable rate of output is the one that maximizes total **profit**—the difference between total revenue and total costs.

profit The difference between total revenue and total cost.

The production function, then, is just a starting point for supply decisions. To decide how much output to produce with that function, a firm must next examine the dollar costs of production.

Total Cost

The economic cost of producing a good is ultimately gauged by the amount of scarce resources used to produce it. In a market economy, however, we want a more convenient measure of cost. Instead of listing all the input quantities used, we want a single dollar figure. To get that dollar amount, we must identify all the resources used in production, compute their value, and then add everything up. The end result will be a dollar figure for the **total cost** of production.

total cost The market value of all resources used to produce a good or service.

In the production of jeans, the resources used include land, labor, and capital. Table 5.1 identifies these resources, their unit values, and the total costs associated with their use. This table is based on an assumed output of 15 pairs of jeans per day, with the use of one machine operator and one sewing machine (point *B* in Figure 5.1). The rent on the factory is $100 per day, a sewing machine costs $20 per day, and the wages of a garment worker are $80 per day. We will assume Tight Jeans Corporation can purchase bolts of denim for $30 apiece, each of which provides enough denim for 10 pairs of jeans. In other words, one-tenth of a bolt ($3 worth of material) is required for one pair of jeans. We will ignore any other potential expenses. With these assumptions, the total cost of producing 15 pairs of jeans per day amounts to $245, as shown in Table 5.1.

Cost of Producing Jeans (15 Pairs per Day)				
Resource Used	×	**Unit Price**	=	**Total Cost**
1 factory		$100 per day		$100
1 sewing machine		20 per day		20
1 operator		80 per day		80
1.5 bolts of denim		30 per bolt		45
Total cost				$245

TABLE 5.1
The Total Costs of Production

The total cost of producing a good equals the market value of all the resources used in its production. In this case, we have assumed that the production of 15 pairs of jeans per day requires resources worth $245.

FIXED COSTS Total costs will change, of course, as we alter the rate of production. But not all costs increase. In the short run, some costs don't increase at all when output is increased. These are **fixed costs** in the sense that they do not vary with the rate of output. The factory lease is an example. Once you lease a factory, you are obligated to pay for it whether you use it or not. The person who owns the factory wants $100 per day. Even if you produce no jeans, you still have to pay that rent. That is the essence of fixed costs.

The leased sewing machine is another fixed cost. When you rent a sewing machine, you must pay the rental charge. It doesn't matter whether you use it for a few minutes or all day long—the rental charge is fixed at $20 per day.

fixed costs Costs of production that do not change when the rate of output is altered, such as the cost of basic plant and equipment.

VARIABLE COSTS Labor costs are another story altogether. The amount of labor employed in jeans production can be varied easily. If we decide not to open the factory tomorrow, we can just tell our only worker to take the day off. We will still have to pay rent and the sewing machine lease, but we can cut back on wages. Alternatively, if we want to increase daily output, we can also hire workers easily and quickly. Labor is regarded as a **variable cost** in this line of work—that is, a cost that *varies* with the rate of output.

The denim itself is another variable cost. Denim not used today can be saved for tomorrow. Hence how much we "spend" on denim today is directly related to how many pairs of jeans we produce. In this sense, the cost of denim input varies with the rate of jeans output.

variable costs Costs of production that change when the rate of output is altered, such as labor and material costs.

Figure 5.2 illustrates how these various costs are affected by the rate of production. On the vertical axis are the costs of production in dollars per day. Notice that the total cost of producing 15 pairs per day is still $245, as indicated by point *B*. This figure consists of $120 of fixed costs (factory and sewing machine rents) and $125 of variable costs ($80 in wages and $45 for denim). If we increase the rate of output, total costs will rise. *How fast total costs rise depends on variable costs only,* however, since fixed costs remain at $120 per day. (Notice the horizontal fixed cost curve in Figure 5.2.)

With one sewing machine and one factory, there is an absolute limit to daily jeans production. As we observed in the production function (Figure 5.1), the capacity of a factory with one machine is 51 pairs of jeans per day. If we try to produce more jeans than this by hiring additional workers, total *costs* will rise, but total *output* will not. In fact, we could fill the factory with garment workers and drive total costs sky-high. But the limits of space and one sewing machine do not permit output in excess of 51 pairs per day. This limit to productive capacity is represented by point *G* on the total cost curve. Further expenditure on inputs will increase production costs but not output.

Although there is no upper limit to costs, there is a lower limit. If output is reduced to zero, total costs fall only to $120 per day, the level of fixed costs. This is illustrated by point *A* in Figure 5.2. As before, *there is no way to avoid fixed costs in the short run.* If you have leased a factory or machinery, you must pay the rent whether or not you produce any jeans.

FIGURE 5.2
The Costs of Jeans Production

Total cost includes both fixed and variable costs. Fixed costs must be paid even if no output is produced (point *A*). Variable costs start at zero and increase with the rate of output. The total cost of producing 15 pairs of jeans (point *B*) includes $120 in fixed costs (rent on the factory and sewing machines) and $125 in variable costs (denim and wages). Total cost rises as output increases.

In this example, the short-run capacity is equal to 51 pairs (point *G*). If still more inputs are employed, costs will rise but not total output.

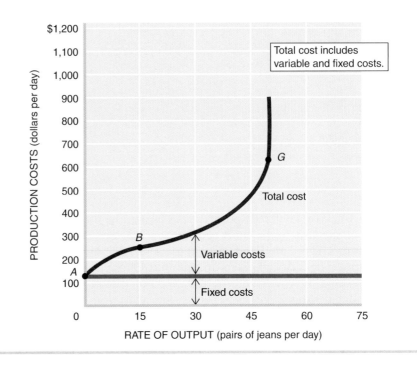

Which Costs Matter?

The different nature of fixed and variable costs raises some intriguing questions about how to measure the cost of producing a pair of jeans. In figuring how much it costs to produce one pair, should we look only at the denim and labor time used to produce that pair? Or should we also take into account the factory rent and lease payments on the sewing machines?

A similar problem arises when you try to figure out whether a restaurant overcharges you for a steak dinner. What did it cost the restaurant to supply the dinner? Should only the meat and the chef's time be counted? Or should the cost include some portion of the rent, the electricity, and the insurance?

The restaurant owner, too, needs to figure out which measure of cost to use. She has to decide what price to charge for the steak. She wants to earn a profit. Can she do so by charging a price just above the cost of meat and wages? Or must she charge a price high enough to cover some portion of her fixed costs as well?

To answer these questions, we need to introduce two distinct measures of cost: *average* cost and *marginal* cost.

Average Cost

average total cost (ATC)
Total cost divided by the quantity produced in a given time period.

Average total cost (ATC) is simply total cost divided by the rate of output:

$$\text{Average total cost (ATC)} = \frac{\text{total cost}}{\text{total output}}$$

If the total cost (including both fixed and variable costs) of supplying 10 steaks is $62, then the *average* cost of the steaks is $6.20.

As we observed in Figure 5.2, total costs change as the rate of output increases. Hence both the numerator and the denominator in the ATC formula change with the rate of output. This complicates the arithmetic a bit, as Figure 5.3 illustrates.

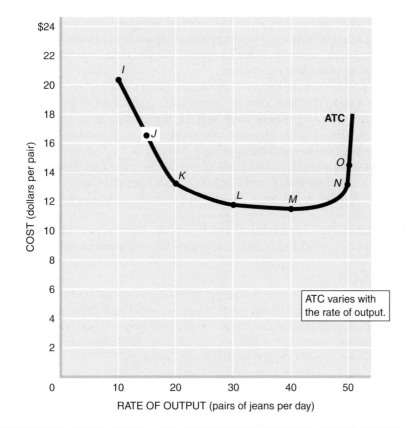

FIGURE 5.3
Average Total Cost

Average total cost (ATC) in column 5 of the accompanying table equals total cost (column 4) divided by the rate of output (column 1). Notice how ATC falls initially as output increases and then later rises. This gives the ATC curve a distinctive U shape, as illustrated in the graph.

	(1) Rate of Output	(2) Fixed Costs	+	(3) Variable Costs	=	(4) Total Cost	(5) Average Total Cost
H	0	$120		$ 0		$120	—
I	10	120		85		205	$20.50
J	15	120		125		245	16.33
K	20	120		150		270	13.50
L	30	120		240		360	12.00
M	40	120		350		470	11.75
N	50	120		550		670	13.40
O	51	120		633		753	14.76

Figure 5.3 shows how average total cost changes as the rate of output varies. Row *J* of the cost schedule, for example, again indicates the fixed, variable, and total costs of producing 15 pairs of jeans per day. Fixed costs are still $120 (for factory and machine rentals); variable costs (denim and labor) are $125. Thus the total cost of producing 15 pairs per day is $245. The *average* cost for this rate of output is simply total cost ($245) divided by quantity (15), or $16.33 per day. This ATC is indicated in column 5 of the table and by point *J* on the graph.

U-SHAPED ATC CURVE   An important feature of the ATC curve is its shape. *Average costs start high, fall, then rise once again, giving the ATC curve a distinctive U shape.*

The initial decline in ATC is largely due to fixed costs. At low rates of output, fixed costs are a high proportion of total costs. Quite simply, it's very expensive to lease (or buy) an entire factory to produce only a few pairs of jeans. The entire cost of the factory must be averaged out over a small quantity of output. This results in a high average cost of production. To reduce *average* costs, we must make fuller use of our leased plant and equipment.

The same problem of cost spreading would affect a restaurant that served only two dinners a day. The *total* cost of operating a restaurant might easily exceed $500 a day. If only two dinners were served, the *average* total cost of each meal would exceed $250. That's why restaurants need a high volume of business to keep average total costs—and meal prices—low.

As output increases, the fixed costs of production are distributed over an increasing quantity of output. Fixed costs no longer dominate total costs as production increases (compare columns 2 and 3 in Figure 5.3). As a result, average total costs tend to decline.

Average total costs don't fall forever, however. They bottom out at point *M* in Figure 5.3 and then start rising. What accounts for this turnaround?

Marginal Cost

marginal cost (MC) The increase in total cost associated with a one-unit increase in production.

The upturn of the ATC curve is caused by rising *marginal* costs. **Marginal cost (MC)** *refers to the change in total costs when one more unit of output is produced.* In practice, marginal cost is easy to measure; just observe how much total costs increase when one more unit of output is produced. For larger increases in output, marginal cost can also be approximated by the formula

$$\text{Marginal cost} = \frac{\text{change in total cost}}{\text{change in total output}}$$

Using this formula and Figure 5.3, we could confirm how marginal costs rise in jeans production. Take this slowly. Notice that as jeans production increases from 20 pairs (row *K*) to 30 pairs (row *L*) per day, total costs rise from $270 to $360. Hence the *change* in total cost ($90) divided by the *change* in total output (10) equals $9. This is the *marginal* cost of jeans in that range of output (20 to 30 pairs).

Figure 5.4 shows how marginal costs change as jeans output increases. As output continues to increase further from 30 to 40 pairs per day, marginal costs rise. *Total* cost rises from $360 (row *L*) to $470 (row *M*), a *change* of $110. Dividing this by the *change* in output (10) reveals that *marginal* cost is now $11. Marginal costs are rising as output increases.

Rising marginal cost implies that each additional unit of output becomes more expensive to produce. Why is this? Why would a third pair of jeans cost more to produce than a second pair did? Why would it cost a restaurant more to serve the twelfth dinner than the eleventh dinner?

The explanation for this puzzle of rising marginal cost lies in the production function. As we observed earlier, output increases at an ever-slower pace as capacity is approached. The law of diminishing marginal product tells us that we need an increasing amount of labor to eke out each additional pair of jeans. The same law applies to restaurants. As more dinners are served, the waiters and cooks get pressed for space and equipment. It takes a little longer (and hence more wages) to prepare and serve each meal. So the *marginal* costs of each meal increase as the number of patrons rises.

SUPPLY HORIZONS

All these cost calculations can give you a real headache. They can also give you second thoughts about jumping into Tight Jeans, restaurant management, or any other business. There are tough choices to be made. Any firm can produce many

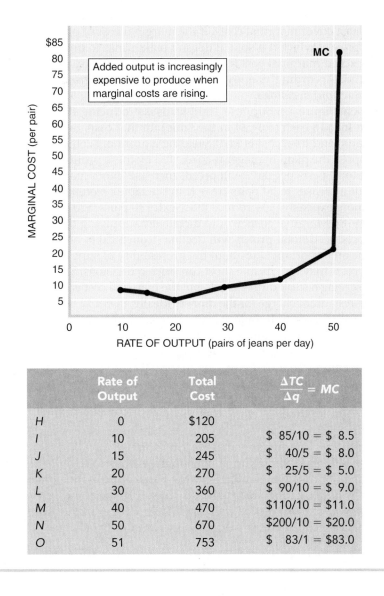

FIGURE 5.4
Marginal Cost

Marginal cost is the change in total cost that occurs when more output is produced. *MC* equals $\Delta TC/\Delta q$.

Marginal costs rise as more workers have to share limited space and equipment (fixed costs) in the short run. This "crowding" reduces marginal physical product and increases marginal costs.

Chart: Added output is increasingly expensive to produce when marginal costs are rising.

Y-axis: MARGINAL COST (per pair), values $85, 80, 75, 70, 65, 60, 55, 50, 45, 40, 35, 30, 25, 20, 15, 10, 5

X-axis: RATE OF OUTPUT (pairs of jeans per day), values 0, 10, 20, 30, 40, 50

	Rate of Output	Total Cost	$\frac{\Delta TC}{\Delta q} = MC$
H	0	$120	
I	10	205	$ 85/10 = $ 8.5
J	15	245	$ 40/5 = $ 8.0
K	20	270	$ 25/5 = $ 5.0
L	30	360	$ 90/10 = $ 9.0
M	40	470	$110/10 = $11.0
N	50	670	$200/10 = $20.0
O	51	753	$ 83/1 = $83.0

different rates of output, each of which entails a distinct level of costs. Someone has to choose which level of output to produce and thus how many goods to supply to the market. That decision has to be based not only on the *capacity* to produce (the production function) but also on the *costs* of production (the cost functions). Only those who make the right decisions will succeed in business.

The Short-Run Production Decision

The nature of supply decisions also varies with the relevant time frame. In this regard, we must distinguish *short*-run decisions from *long*-run decisions.

THE SHORT RUN The *short run* is characterized by the existence of fixed costs. A commitment has been made: a factory has been built, an office leased, or machinery purchased. The only decision to make is how much output to produce with these existing facilities. This is the **production decision,** the choice of how intensively to use available plant and equipment. This choice is typically made daily (e.g., jeans production), weekly (e.g., auto production), or seasonally (e.g., farming).

FOCUS ON MARGINAL COST The most important factor in the short-run production decision is marginal costs. Producers will be willing to supply output only if

production decision The selection of the short-run rate of output (with existing plant and equipment).

they can at least cover marginal costs. If the marginal cost of producing a product exceeds the price at which it is sold, it doesn't make sense to produce that last unit. Price must exceed marginal cost for the producer to reap any profit from the last unit produced. Accordingly, *marginal cost is a basic determinant of short-run supply (production) decisions.*

Look back at Figure 5.4. Suppose Tight Jeans is producing 40 pairs per day and selling them for $18 each (row *M* in the table). In that case, total revenue is $720 ($18 × 40 pairs) and total cost is $470, yielding a profit of $250 per day.

Now suppose the plant manager is so excited by these profits that she increases total output to 50 pairs per day. Will profits increase? Not according to Figure 5.4. When output increases to 50 pairs (row *N* in the table), *marginal* cost rises to $20. Hence it is more expensive to produce those extra 10 pairs ($20 each) than they can be sold for ($18). Marginal costs would dictate *not* supplying the additional jeans. If they are produced, total profits will decline (from $250 to only $230). Marginal costs provide an important clue about the profitability of supplying more output.

Marginal costs may also dictate short-run pricing decisions. Suppose the average total cost of serving a steak dinner is $12, but the marginal cost is only $7. How low a price can the restaurant charge for the dinner? Ideally, it would like to charge at least $12 and cover all of its costs. It could at least cover *marginal* costs, however, if it charged only $7. At that price the restaurant would be no worse or better off for having served an extra dinner. The additional cost of serving that one meal would be covered.

It must be emphasized that covering marginal cost is a *minimal* condition for supplying additional output. A restaurant that covers only marginal costs but not average total cost will lose money. It may even go out of business. This is a lesson lots of now-defunct Internet companies learned. They spent millions of dollars building telecommunications networks to produce Internet services. The *marginal* costs of producing Internet service was low, so they sold their services at low prices. Those low prices didn't bring in enough revenue to cover *fixed* costs, however, so legions of dot.com companies went bankrupt. As they quickly learned, you can get by just covering marginal costs. To stay in the game, however, you've got to cover average *total* costs as well. In Chapter 6 we examine more closely just how marginal cost considerations affect short-run supply behavior.

The Long-Run Investment Decision

The long run opens up a whole new range of options. In the *long run,* we have no lease or purchase commitments. We are free to start all over again, with whatever scale of plant and equipment we desire. *There are no fixed costs in the long run.* Accordingly, long-run supply decisions are more complicated. If no commitments to production facilities have been made, a producer must decide how large a facility to build, buy, or lease. Hence the size (scale) of plant and equipment becomes an additional option for long-term supply decisions. In a long-run (no fixed costs) situation, a firm can make the **investment decision.**

investment decision The decision to build, buy, or lease plant and equipment; to enter or exit an industry.

NO FIXED COSTS   Note that the distinction between short- and long-run supply decisions is not based on time. The distinction instead depends on whether commitments have been made. If no leases have been signed, no construction contracts awarded, no acquisitions made, a producer still has a free hand. With no fixed costs, the producer can walk away from the potential business at a moment's notice.

Once fixed costs are incurred, the options narrow. Then the issue becomes one of making the best possible use of the assets (e.g., factory, office space, equipment) that have been acquired. Once fixed costs have been incurred, it's hard to walk away from the business. The goal then becomes to make as much profit as possible from the investments already made. The accompanying News Wire illustrates the distinction between these production and investment decisions. The decision by Nissan to produce more vehicles at its Madrid plant is a short-run production

NEWS WIRE	PRODUCTION AND INVESTMENT DECISIONS

Nissan to Boost Spanish Output, Hire Workers

MADRID—Nissan Motor Co. said it will expand production in Spain and hire an additional 1,000 workers.

The Japanese manufacturer will produce a new compact car at its Barcelona plant starting next year and increase output of a pickup truck already manufactured there, a company spokeswoman said Monday.

Source: *The Wall Street Journal* online, February 4, 2013. Used with permission of Dow Jones & Company, Inc. via Copyright Clearance Center, Inc.

Fiat Looks for New Plant Site in Russia

DETROIT—Fiat SpA is considering a new location to build Jeeps in Russia as a deal to construct a factory near St. Petersburg hits roadblocks, a Russian newspaper reported Monday.

The Italian automaker, which owns U.S.-based Chrysler Group LLC, has been searching for a place to manufacture the brand's sport-utility vehicles in Russia as it tries to expand Jeep's global reach.

Source: *The Wall Street Journal* online, March 18, 2013. Used with permission of Dow Jones & Company, Inc. via Copyright Clearance Center, Inc.

NOTE: Production decisions focus on the (short-run) use of existing facilities. Investment decisions relate to the (long-run) acquisition of productive facilities.

decision. They are deciding how fully to utilize their production capacity. By contrast, Fiat decided to create new production *capacity* by building a Jeep factory in Russia; that was an investment decision.

ECONOMIC VERSUS ACCOUNTING COSTS

The cost concepts we have discussed here are based on *real* production relationships. The dollar costs we compute reflect underlying resource costs—the land, labor, and capital used in the production process. Not everyone counts this way. On the contrary, accountants and businesspeople often count dollar costs only and ignore any resource use that doesn't result in an explicit dollar cost. This kind of tunnel vision can cause serious mistakes.

Return to Tight Jeans for a moment to see the difference. When we computed the dollar cost of producing 15 pairs of jeans per day, we noted the following resource inputs:

Inputs	Cost
1 factory rent	@ $100
1 machine rent	@ 20
1 machine operator	@ 80
1.5 bolts of denim	@ 45
Total cost	$245

The total value of the resources used in the production of 15 pairs of jeans was thus $245 per day. But this economic cost need not conform to *actual* dollar costs. Suppose the owners of Tight Jeans decided to sew jeans. Then they would not have to hire a worker or pay $80 per day in wages. *Dollar* costs would drop to $165 per day. The producers and their accountant would consider this to be a remarkable achievement. They would assert that the costs of producing jeans had fallen.

Economic Cost

An economist would draw no such conclusions. ***The essential economic question is how many resources are used in production.*** This has not changed. One unit of labor is still being employed at the factory; now it's simply the owner, not a hired worker. In either case, one unit of labor is not available for the production of other goods and services. Hence society is still incurring an opportunity cost of $245 for jeans, whether the owners of Tight Jeans write checks in that amount or not. We really don't care who sews jeans—the essential point is that someone (i.e., a unit of labor) does.

The same would be true if Tight Jeans owned its factory rather than rented it. If the factory was owned rather than rented, the owners probably would not write any rent checks. Accounting costs would drop by $100 per day. But society would not be saving any resources. The factory would still be in use for jeans production and therefore unavailable for the production of other goods and services. Hence the *opportunity cost* of the factory would still be $100 per day. As a result, the economic (resource) cost of producing 15 pairs of jeans would still be $245.

The distinction between an economic cost and an accounting cost is essentially one between resource and dollar costs. *Dollar cost* refers to the explicit dollar outlays made by a producer; it is the lifeblood of accountants. **Economic cost,** in contrast, refers to the dollar *value* of all resources used in the production process: it is the lifeblood of economists. The accountant's dollar costs are usually *explicit* in the sense that someone writes a check. The economist takes into consideration *implicit* costs as well—that is, even those costs for which no direct payment is made. In other words, economists count costs as

> **economic cost** The value of all resources used to produce a good or service; opportunity cost.

$$\text{Economic cost} = \text{explicit costs} + \text{implicit costs}$$

As this formula suggests, ***economic and accounting costs will diverge whenever any factor of production is not paid an explicit wage (or rent, etc.).***

THE COST OF HOMEWORK   These distinctions between economic and accounting costs apply also to the "production" of homework. You can pay people to write term papers for you or even buy them off the Internet. At large schools you can often buy lecture notes as well. But most students end up doing their own homework so that they will learn something and not just turn in required assignments.

Doing homework is expensive, however, even if you don't pay someone to do it. The time you spend reading this chapter is valuable. You could be doing something else if you weren't reading right now. What would you be doing? The forgone activity—the best alternative use of your time—represents the opportunity cost of doing homework. Even if you don't pay yourself for reading this chapter, you'll still incur that *economic* cost.

Economic Profit

The distinction between economic cost and accounting cost directly affects profit computations. People who supply goods and services want to make a profit from their efforts. But what exactly *is* "profit"? In economic terms, profit is the difference between total revenues and *total* economic costs:

$$\text{Profit} = \text{total revenue} - \text{total cost}$$

Economists don't rely on accountants to compute profits. Instead they factor in not just the explicit costs that accountants keep track of but also the implicit costs that arise when resources are used but not explicitly paid (e.g., an owner's time and capital investment). Suppose total revenue at Tight Jeans was $300 per day. With total costs of $245 per day (see the foregoing cost computation), profit would be $55 per day. If the owner did her own stitching, *accounting* costs would drop by $80 and *accounting* profits would increase by the same amount. *Economic* profits would *not* change, however. By keeping track of *all* costs (implicit and explicit), economists can keep a consistent eye on profits. In the next chapter we'll see how business firms use supply decisions to maximize those profits.

Can We Outrun Diminishing Returns?

The U.S. labor force continues to grow by more than a million workers per year. If capital investments don't keep pace, these added workers will strain production facilities. The law of diminishing marginal product would push wages lower and reduce living standards. This is hardly a cheerful prospect.

To beat the law of diminishing marginal productivity, we have to *increase* the productivity of all workers. This means that we have to *shift* production functions upward, as shown graphically in Figure 5.5a.

How can we achieve such across-the-board productivity gains? There are several possibilities. One possibility is to invest in labor by increasing education and training. Better-educated workers are apt to squeeze more output from any production facility. In the world's poorest nations, one out of every two workers is illiterate (see the News Wire on page 37). In those nations, even basic literacy training can boost labor productivity substantially. In the United States, most workers have at least some college education. That isn't the end of skill training, however. Skill training in classrooms and on the job continues to boost U.S. labor productivity. The government encourages such training with student loans, school subsidies, and training programs. In 2013, the federal government spent over $100 billion on education, and state and local governments spent 10 times that much.

Spending on *capital* investment also boosts productivity. As we observed in Chapter 2, American workers have the productivity advantage of not just more education but also far more capital resources in the workplace. Additional investment in capital not only adds to the stock (quantity) of resources but increases its *quality* as well. New machines, factories, and networks almost always embody the latest technology. Hence more capital investment typically results in improved technology as well, giving a double boost to production possibilities. The government can encourage such investments with targeted tax incentives.

(a) When the production function shifts up...

(b) Cost curves shift down.

TOTAL OUTPUT (units per time period)

RESOURCE INPUTS (units per time period)

COST (dollars per unit)

RATE OF OUTPUT (units per time period)

ATC₁ ATC₂ MC₁ MC₂

FIGURE 5.5

Improvements in Productivity Reduce Costs

Advances in technological or managerial knowledge increase our productive capability. This is reflected in upward shifts of the production function (a) and downward shifts of production cost curves (b). Investments in either labor (educating and training) or capital (new plant and equipment) propel such shifts.

Investments in either human or nonhuman capital shift the production function upward, as in Figure 5.5*a*. In either case, the marginal physical product of labor rises and marginal costs fall (Figure 5.5*b*). This not only increases worker productivity but also expands (shifts) society's production possibilities outward, potentially making everyone better off.

SUMMARY

- Supply decisions are constrained by the *capacity* to produce and the *costs* of using that capacity.   **LO1**
- In the short run, some inputs (e.g., land and capital) are fixed in quantity. Increases in (short-run) output result from more use of variable inputs (e.g., labor).   **LO1**
- A production function indicates how much output can be produced from available facilities using different amounts of variable inputs. Every point on the production function represents efficient production. Capacity output refers to the maximum quantity that can be produced from a given facility.   **LO1**
- Output tends to increase at a diminishing rate when more labor is employed in a given facility. Additional workers crowd existing facilities, leaving each worker with less space and machinery to work with.   **LO2**
- The costs of production include both fixed and variable costs. Fixed costs (e.g., space and equipment leases) are incurred even if no output is produced. Variable costs (e.g., labor and material) are incurred when plant and equipment are put to use.   **LO3**

- Average cost is total cost divided by the quantity produced. The ATC curve is typically U-shaped.   **LO3**
- Marginal cost is the increase in total cost that results when one more unit of output is produced. Marginal costs increase because of diminishing returns in production.   **LO3**
- The production decision is the short-run choice of how much output to produce with existing facilities. A producer will be willing to supply output only if price at least covers marginal cost.   **LO4**
- The long run is characterized by an absence of fixed costs. The investment decision entails the choice of whether to acquire fixed costs—that is, whether to build, buy, or lease plant and equipment.   **LO4**
- The economic costs of production include the value of *all* resources used. Accounting costs typically include only those dollar costs actually paid (explicit costs).   **LO5**
- Historically, advances in technology and the quality of our inputs have been the major source of productivity growth. These advances have shifted production functions up and pushed cost curves down.   **LO1**

TERMS TO REMEMBER

Define the following terms:

supply	law of diminishing returns	total cost	production decision
factors of production		fixed costs	investment decision
production function	short run	variable costs	economic cost
marginal physical product (MPP)	long run	average total cost (ATC)	
	profit	marginal cost (MC)	

QUESTIONS FOR DISCUSSION

1. Is your school currently producing at capacity (i.e., teaching as many students as possible)? What considerations might inhibit full capacity utilization?   **LO1**
2. What are the production costs of your economics class? What are the fixed costs? The variable costs? What is the marginal cost of enrolling more students?   **LO3**
3. Suppose you set up a lawn-mowing service and recruit friends to help you. Would the law of diminishing returns apply? Explain.   **LO2**
4. What are the fixed and variable costs of (*a*) a pizza shop, (*b*) an Internet service provider, (*c*) a corn farm, (*d*) a movie theater? Which needs the highest sales volume to earn a profit?   **LO3**

5. Owner-operators of small gas stations rarely pay themselves an hourly wage. How does this practice affect the economic cost of dispensing gasoline? **LO5**

6. In the News Wire on page 99, why did MPP fall to zero? What was the opportunity cost of those surplus workers? **LO2**

7. What role do expectations play in the production and investment decisions described in the News Wire on page 107? **LO3**

8. Why does marginal physical product decline at a fast-food outlet (e.g., McDonald's) when more employees are hired? What are the fixed input constraints that limit worker productivity? **LO2**

9. Why doesn't maximum output generate maximum profits? **LO3**

10. **POLICY PERSPECTIVES** If capital investment ceased, what would happen over time to worker productivity and living standards? **LO1**

PROBLEMS

connect

1. (*a*) What is the marginal physical product of each successive worker in Figure 5.1? For which worker is marginal physical product (*b*) first diminishing? (*c*) zero? **LO2**

2. (*a*) Compute *average* fixed costs and *average* variable costs in Figure 5.3 for all rates of output. At what rate of output **LO3**
   (*b*) are average fixed costs the lowest?
   (*c*) are average variable costs the lowest?
   (*d*) is average total cost the lowest?

3. (*a*) Complete the following table; (*b*) then plot the marginal cost and average total cost curves on the same graph. (*c*) What output has the lowest per-unit cost. (*d*) What is the value of fixed costs? **LO3**

Rate of Output	Total Cost	Marginal Cost	Average Total Cost
0	$130	_____	_____
1	140	_____	_____
2	160	_____	_____
3	190	_____	_____
4	240	_____	_____
5	310	_____	_____

4. Suppose the mythical Tight Jeans Corporation leased a *second* sewing machine, giving it the following production function: **LO1**

Number of workers:	0	1	2	3	4	5	6	7	8
Quantity of output:	0	10	36	56	68	74	76	76	74

(*a*) Graph the production function.
(*b*) On a separate graph, illustrate marginal physical product.
At what level of employment does
(*c*) the law of diminishing returns become apparent?
(*d*) MPP hit zero?
(*e*) MPP become negative?

5. Using the data in problem 4 and a price of $20 per pair of jeans, compute the value of the MPP of (*a*) the third worker, (*b*) the seventh worker. **LO3**

6. Using Figure 5.3 as a guide, compute total profits at a price of $15 per pair of jeans and output of (*a*) 40 pairs, (*b*) 50 pairs. **LO3**

7. Suppose a company incurs the following costs:

Labor	$700
Equipment	$400
Materials	$300

It owns the building, so it doesn't have to pay the usual $800 in rent. **LO5**
(*a*) What is the total accounting cost?
(*b*) What is the total economic cost?
(*c*) How would accounting and economic costs change if the company sold the building and then leased it back?

8. **POLICY PERSPECTIVES** If investment in new machinery doubles the productivity of every worker, what will be the MPP of the fifth worker in Figure 5.1? **LO4**

◄ Practice quizzes, student PowerPoints, author podcasts, web activities, and additional materials available at **www.mhhe.com/schilleressentials9e**, or scan here. Need a barcode reader? Try ScanLife, available in your app store.

6 Competition

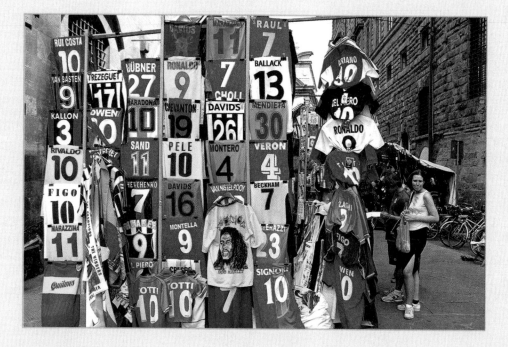

◄ Practice quizzes, student PowerPoints, author podcasts, web activities, and additional materials available at www.mhhe.com/schilleressentials9e, or scan here. Need a barcode reader? Try ScanLife, available in your app store.

LEARNING OBJECTIVES

After reading this chapter, you should be able to:

1 Identify the unique characteristics of perfectly competitive firms and markets.
2 Illustrate how total profits change as output expands.
3 Describe how the profit-maximizing rate of output is found.
4 Recite the determinants of competitive market supply.
5 Explain why profits get eliminated in competitive markets.

Catfish farmers in the South are upset. During the last two decades they have invested millions of dollars in converting cotton farms into breeding ponds for catfish. They now have over 100,000 acres of ponds and supply over 90 percent of the nation's catfish. From January 2010 to January 2012, catfish prices rose dramatically, from 76 cents a pound to $1.25 a pound. That made catfish farming look pretty good. But then prices started slipping again, falling as low as 75 cents a pound by January 2013. This abrupt price decline killed any hopes the farmers had of making huge profits. Indeed, catfish prices got so low that many farmers started draining their ponds and planting crops again.

The dilemma the catfish farmers find themselves in is a familiar occurrence in competitive markets. When the profit prospects look good, everybody wants to get in on the act. As more and more firms start producing the good, however, prices and profits tumble. This helps explain why over 200,000 new firms are formed each year as well as why 50,000 others fail.

In this chapter we examine how supply decisions are made in competitive markets—markets in which all producers are relatively small. Our focus on competition centers on the following questions:

- What are the unique characteristics of competitive markets?
- How do competitive firms make supply decisions?
- How are production levels, prices, and profits determined in competitive markets?

By answering these questions, we will develop more insight into supply decisions and thus the core issues of WHAT, HOW, and FOR WHOM goods and services are produced.

MARKET STRUCTURE

The quest for profits is the common denominator of business enterprises. But not all businesses have the same opportunity to pursue profits. Millions of firms, like the southern catfish farms, are very small and entirely at the mercy of the marketplace. A small decline in the market price of their product often spells financial ruin. Even when such firms make a profit, they must always be on the lookout for new competition, new products, or changes in technology.

Larger firms don't have to work quite so hard to maintain their standing. Huge corporations often have the power to raise prices, change consumer tastes (through advertising), or even prevent competitors from taking a slice of the profit pie. Such powerful firms can protect and perpetuate their profits. They are more likely to dominate markets than to be at their mercy.

Business firms aren't always either giants or dwarfs. Those are extremes of **market structure** that illustrate the range of power a firm might possess. Most real-world firms fall along a spectrum that stretches from the powerless to the powerful. At one end of the spectrum (Figure 6.1) we place perfectly

market structure The number and relative size of firms in an industry.

FIGURE 6.1
Market Structures

The number and relative size of firms producing a good vary across industries. Market structures range from perfect competition (a great many firms producing the same goods) to monopoly (only one firm). Most real-world firms are along the continuum of *imperfect* competition.

competitive firm A firm without market power, with no ability to alter the market price of the goods it produces.

competitive market A market in which no buyer or seller has market power.

monopoly A firm that produces the entire market supply of a particular good or service.

competitive firms—firms that have no power over the price of goods they produce. Like the catfish farmers in the South, a perfectly competitive firm must take whatever price for its wares the market offers; it is a *price taker*. A market composed entirely of competitive firms—and without anyone dominating the demand side either—is referred to as a (perfectly) **competitive market.** *In a perfectly competitive market, no single producer or consumer has any control over the price or quantity of the product.*

At the other end of the spectrum of market structures are monopolies. A **monopoly** is a single firm that produces the entire supply of a particular good. Despite repeated legal and technological attacks, Microsoft still has a near monopoly on computer operating systems. That position gives Microsoft the power to *set* market prices rather than simply respond to them. With nearly 75 percent of the soft drink market between them, Coke and Pepsi are a virtual duopoly (two-firm market). Together they have the power to set prices for their beverages. All firms with such power are price *setters*, not price *takers*.

Monopolies are the extreme case of market power. In Figure 6.1 they are at the far right end of the spectrum, easily distinguished from the small, competitive firms that reside at the low (left) end of the power spectrum.

Among the 26 million or so business enterprises in the United States, there are relatively few monopolies. Local phone companies, cable TV companies, and utility firms often have a monopoly in specific geographic areas. The National Football League also has a monopoly on professional football. The NFL owners know that if they raise ticket prices, fans won't go elsewhere to watch a football game. These situations are the exception to the rule, however. Typically more than one firm supplies a particular product.

Consider the case of IBM. IBM is a megacorporation with over $100 billion in annual sales revenue and more than 400,000 employees. It is not a monopoly, however. Other firms produce computers that are virtually identical to IBM products. These IBM clones limit IBM's ability to set prices for its own output. In other words, other firms in the same market limit IBM's **market power.** IBM is not completely *powerless*, however; it is still large enough to have some direct influence on computer prices and output. Because it has some market power over computer prices, IBM is not a *perfectly* competitive firm.

market power The ability to alter the market price of a good or service.

Economists have created categories to distinguish the degrees of competition in product markets. These various market structures are illustrated in Figure 6.1. At one end of the spectrum is perfect competition, where lots of small firms vie for consumer purchases. At the other extreme is monopoly, where only one firm supplies a particular product.

In between the extremes of monopoly (no competition) and perfect competition lie various forms of imperfect competition:

- *Duopoly:* Only two firms supply a particular product.
- *Oligopoly:* A few large firms supply all or most of a particular product.
- *Monopolistic competition:* Many firms supply essentially the same product, but each enjoys significant brand loyalty.

How a firm is classified across this spectrum depends not only on its size but also on how many other firms produce identical or similar products. IBM, for example, would be classified in the oligopoly category for large business computers. IBM supplies nearly 70 percent of all business computers and confronts only a few rival producers. In the personal computer market, however, IBM has a small market share (under 10 percent) and faces dozens of rivals. In that market IBM would fit into the category of monopolistic competition. Gasoline stations, fast-food outlets, and even colleges are other examples of monopolistic competition: many firms are trying to rise above the crowd and to get the consumer's attention (and purchases).

Market structure has important effects on the supply of goods. How much you pay for a product depends partly on how many firms offer it for sale. This textbook would be even more expensive if other publishers weren't offering substitute goods. And long-distance telephone service didn't become inexpensive until competing firms broke AT&T's monopoly control of that market. The number of firms in the market has had a significant effect on price.

The quality of the product also depends on the degree of competition in the marketplace. Why did the look, the feel, and the features of an iPod change so fast? Largely because dozens of firms were nipping at Apple's heels, trying to get a piece of the digital music player market that Apple created. Apple wasn't a perfectly competitive firm, but it still felt the heat of competitive pressure. The same kind of competitive pressure is evident in the smartphone market. By contrast, the U.S. Department of Justice contended that the lack of effective competition allowed Microsoft to sell operating systems that were too complex and unwieldy for the typical computer user. With more firms in the market, consumers would have gotten a *better* product at a *lower* price.

With other firms producing iPod look-alikes, Apple had to keep improving its product.

© PR NewsFoto/Apple, Peter Belanger

In this chapter we focus on only one market structure—namely perfect competition. Our goal is to see how perfectly competitive firms make supply decisions. In the next chapter we contrast *monopoly* behavior with this model of perfect competition.

PERFECT COMPETITION

It's not easy to visualize a perfectly competitive firm. None of the corporations you could name are likely to fit the model of perfect competition. Perfectly competitive firms are pretty much faceless. They have no brand image, no real market recognition.

No Market Power

The critical factor in perfect competition is the total absence of market power for individual firms. *A perfectly competitive firm is one whose output is so small in relation to market volume that its output decisions have no perceptible impact on price.* A competitive firm can sell all its output at the prevailing market price. If it tries to charge a higher price, it will not sell anything because consumers will shop elsewhere. In this sense, a perfectly competitive firm has no *market power*—no ability to control the market price for the good it sells.

At first glance, it might appear that all firms have market power. After all, who is to stop a producer from raising prices? The critical concept here, however, is *market* price—that is, the price at which goods are actually sold. You might want to resell this textbook for $80. But you will discover that the bookstore will not buy it at that price. Anyone can change the *asking* price of a good, but actual sales will occur only at the market price. With so many other students offering to sell their books, the bookstore knows it does not have to pay the $80 you are asking. Because you do not have any market power, you have to accept the "going price" for used texts if you want to sell this book.

The same kind of powerlessness is characteristic of the small catfish farmer. Like any producer, the lone catfish farmer can increase or reduce his rate of output. But this production decision will not affect the market price of catfish.

Even a larger farmer who can alter a harvest by as much as 100,000 pounds of fish per year will not influence the market price of catfish. Why not? Because over 600 *million* pounds of catfish are brought to market every year, and another 100,000 pounds simply won't be noticed. In other words, *the output of the lone farmer is so small relative to the market supply that it has no significant effect on the total quantity or price in the market.*

NEWS WIRE	COMPETITIVE MARKETS

Catfish Farmers Feel Forced Out of Business

Also feeling the pinch from foreign imports and rising grain costs, Jerry Seamans is cutting back his 1,200 acres of catfish ponds by 20 percent and returning the acreage to soybeans and rice. . . .

"I really don't know of a fish operation that's not changing," said Seamans, whose farm is just outside of Lake Village. "Some people are going out of business, several people are doing the same thing I'm doing. Most everybody in the business is trying to make major adjustments."

At its peak in 2002, Arkansas' catfish industry numbered 195 operations covering 38,000 acres of ponds. The latest numbers from the U.S. Department of Agriculture show 128 catfish farms with 29,900 acres of ponds. Production has dropped from 106,821 pounds two years ago to the current 90,400 pounds.

Source: TheFishSite.com, May 26, 2008. Used with permission of 5M Publishing.

NOTE: In competitive markets, new firms enter quickly when profitable opportunities exist. As a result of such entry, profits often don't last long, forcing some firms to quit the business.

One can visualize the difference between competitive firms and firms with market power by considering what happened in 2008 to U.S. catfish supplies and prices when Farmer Seamans drained some of his catfish ponds (see News Wire). No one really noticed: total U.S. catfish production and market prices were unaffected. Contrast that scenario with the likely consequences for U.S. auto supplies and prices if the Ford Motor Company were to close down suddenly. Farmer Seamans's cutbacks had no impact on market outcomes; the impact of a Ford shutdown would be dramatic.

The same contrast is evident when a firm's output is increased. Were Farmer Seamans to double his production capacity (build another 10 ponds), the added catfish output would not show up in commerce statistics. U.S. catfish production is calibrated in the hundreds of millions of pounds, and no one is going to notice another 100,000 pounds of fish. Were Ford, on the other hand, to double its production, the added output would depress automobile prices as Ford tried to unload its heavy inventories.

Price Takers

The critical distinction between Ford and Farmer Seamans is not in their motivation but in their ability to alter market outcomes. Both are out to make a profit. What makes Farmer Seamans's situation different is the fact that his output decisions do not influence catfish prices. All catfish look alike, so Farmer Seamans's catfish will fetch the same price as everyone else's catfish. Were he to attempt to enlarge his profits by raising his catfish prices above market levels, he would find himself without customers because consumers would go elsewhere to buy their catfish. To maximize his profits, Farmer Seamans can only strive to run an efficient operation and to make the right supply decisions. He is a *price taker*, taking the market price of catfish as a fact of life and doing the best he can within that constraint.

Ford Motor Company, on the other hand, can behave like a *price setter*. Instead of waiting to find out what the market price is and making appropriate output adjustments, Ford has the discretion to announce prices at the beginning of every model year. Fords are not exactly like Chevrolets or Toyotas in the minds of consumers. Because Fords are *differentiated*, Ford knows that sales will not fall to zero if its car prices are set a little higher than those of other car manufacturers. Ford confronts a downward-sloping rather than a perfectly horizontal demand curve for its output.

Market Demand versus Firm Demand

To appreciate the unique nature of perfect competition, *you must distinguish between the market demand curve and the demand curve confronting a particular firm.* Farmer Seamans's small operation does not contradict the law of demand. The quantity of catfish purchased in the supermarket still depends on catfish prices. That is to say, the *market* demand curve for catfish is downward-sloping, just as the market demand for cars is downward-sloping.

THE FIRM'S HORIZONTAL DEMAND CURVE   But the demand curve facing Farmer Seamans has a unique shape: it is *horizontal.* Remember, if he charges a price above the prevailing market, he will lose *all* his customers. So a higher price results in quantity demanded falling to zero. On the other hand, he can double or triple his output and still sell every fish he produces at the prevailing market price. As a result, *the demand curve facing a perfectly competitive firm is horizontal.* Farmer Seamans himself faces a horizontal demand curve because his share of the market is so infinitesimal that changes in his output do not disturb the market equilibrium.

Collectively, though, individual farmers do count. If 10,000 small, competitive farmers expand their catfish production at the same time, the market equilibrium will be disturbed. That is to say, a competitive market composed of 10,000 individually powerless producers still sees a lot of action. The power here resides in the collective action of all the producers, however, not in the individual action of any one. Were catfish production to increase abruptly, the catfish could be sold only at lower prices, in accordance with the downward-sloping nature of the *market* demand curve.

The distinction between the actions of a single producer and those of the market are illustrated in Figure 6.2. Notice that

- *The market demand curve for a product is always downward-sloping.*
- *The demand curve facing a perfectly competitive firm is horizontal.*

FIGURE 6.2   Market Demand versus Firm Demand

The *market* demand for any product is downward-sloping. The equilibrium price (p_e) of catfish is established by the intersection of *market demand* and *market supply* in the graph on the left.

This market-established price is the only one at which an individual farmer can sell catfish. If the farmer asks a higher price (e.g., p_1), no one will buy the catfish since people can buy identical catfish from other farmers at p_e. But a farmer can sell all of his catfish at the equilibrium price. The lone farmer thus confronts a horizontal demand curve for his own output. (Notice the difference in quantities on the horizontal axes of the two graphs.)

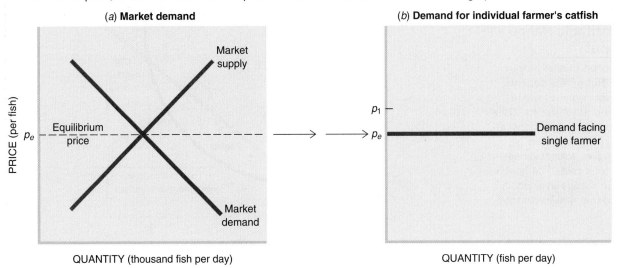

(*a*) **Market demand**

(*b*) **Demand for individual farmer's catfish**

That horizontal demand curve is the distinguishing feature of *perfectly* competitive firms. If a firm can raise its price without losing *all* its customers, it is not a perfectly competitive firm. (Does McDonald's meet this condition? United Airlines? Apple? Your college?)

THE FIRM'S PRODUCTION DECISION

Because a competitive firm is a price taker, it doesn't have to worry about what price to charge: everything it produces will be sold at the prevailing *market* price. It still has an important decision to make, however. The competitive firm must decide *how much* output to sell at the going price.

Choosing a rate of output is a firm's **production decision.** Should it produce all the output it can? Or should it produce at less than its capacity output?

Output and Revenues

If a competitive firm produces more output, its sales revenue will definitely increase. **Total revenue** is the price of the good multiplied by the quantity sold:

$$\text{Total revenue} = \text{price} \times \text{quantity}$$

Since a competitive firm can sell all of its output at the market price, total revenue is a simple multiple of that price. That is why the total revenue line in Figure 6.3 keeps rising.

Revenues versus Profits

If a competitive firm wanted to maximize total *revenue,* its strategy would be obvious: it would simply produce as much output as possible. But maximizing total revenue isn't the goal. Business firms try to maximize total *profits,* not total *revenue.*

As we saw in Chapter 5, total **profit** is the *difference* between total revenues and total costs. Hence a profit-maximizing firm must look not only at revenues but at costs as well. As output increases, total revenues go up, but total costs do as well. If costs rise too fast, profits may actually decline as output increases.

production decision The selection of the short-run rate of output (with existing plant and equipment).

total revenue The price of a product multiplied by the quantity sold in a given time period, $p \times q$.

profit The difference between total revenue and total cost.

FIGURE 6.3
The Profitable Range of Output

Total revenue rises as output expands. But profits depend on how fast revenues rise in comparison to total costs. Only in the range of output between q_1 and q_2 is this business profitable (i.e., total revenue exceeds total cost). The goal is to find the output level within this range that *maximizes* total profits.

We may embark on the search for maximizing profits with two clues:

* *Maximizing output or revenue is not the way to maximize profits.*
* *Total profits depend on how both revenues and costs increase as output expands.*

Notice in Figure 6.3 how total costs start out above total revenue. Do you remember why this is the case? Because of fixed costs—costs that are incurred even when no output is produced. At low levels of output, costs exceed revenues, and losses are incurred. As production increases, however, revenues increase faster than costs (at q_1), making production profitable. But profits don't keep growing. At some point (q_2) escalating costs may overtake revenues, creating economic losses again. Hence *a business is profitable only within a certain range of output* (q_1 to q_2 in Figure 6.3).

The goal of the firm is to find the single rate of output that *maximizes* total profit. That output rate must lie somewhere between q_1 and q_2 in Figure 6.3. But how can we locate it?

PROFIT MAXIMIZATION

We can advance still further toward the goal of maximum profits by employing a simple rule of thumb: Produce an additional unit of output only if that unit brings in more revenue than it costs. A producer who follows this rule will move steadily closer to maximum profits. We will explain this rule by looking first at the revenue side of production (what it brings in) and then at the cost side (what it costs).

Price

For a perfectly competitive firm, it is easy to determine how much revenue a unit of output will bring in. All we have to look at is price. *Since competitive firms are price takers, they must take whatever price the market has put on their products.* Thus a catfish farmer can readily determine the value of the fish by looking at the market price of catfish.

Marginal Cost

Once we know what one more unit brings in (its price), all we need to know for profit maximization is the cost of producing an additional unit.

The production process for catfish farming is fairly straightforward. The "factory" in this case is a pond; the rate of production is the number of fish harvested from the pond per hour. A farmer can alter the rate of production at will, up to the breeding capacity of the pond.

Assume that the *fixed* cost of the pond is $10 per hour. The fixed costs include the rental value of the pond and the cost of electricity for keeping the pond oxygenated so the fish can breathe. These fixed costs must be paid no matter how many fish the farmer harvests.

To harvest catfish from the pond, the farmer must incur additional costs. Labor is needed to net and sort the fish. The cost of labor is *variable*, depending on how much output the farmer decides to produce. If no fish are harvested, no variable costs are incurred.

The **marginal costs (MC)** of harvesting refer to the additional costs incurred to harvest *one* more basket of fish. Generally, marginal costs rise as the rate of production increases. The law of diminishing returns we encountered in Chapter 5 applies to catfish farming as well. As more labor is hired, each worker has less space (pond area) and capital (access to nets, sorting trays) to work with. Accordingly, it takes a little more labor time (marginal cost) to harvest each additional fish.

marginal cost (MC) The increase in total costs associated with a one-unit increase in production.

© Bill Barksdale/AgStock Images/Corbis

FIGURE 6.4
Increasing Marginal Cost

Marginal cost is the cost of producing one more unit. When production expands from two to three units per hour, total costs increase by $9 (from $22 to $31 per hour). The marginal cost of the third basket is therefore $9, as seen in row *D* of the table and point *D* in the graph. Marginal costs increase as output expands.

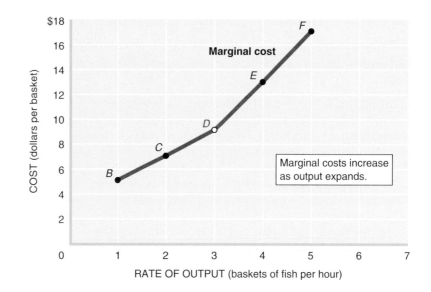

Marginal costs increase as output expands.

	Rate of Output (Baskets per Hour)	Total Cost (per Hour)	Marginal Cost (per Unit)	Average Total Cost (per Unit)
A	0	$10	—	—
B	1	15	$ 5	$15.00
C	2	22	7	11.00
D	3	31	9	10.33
E	4	44	13	11.00
F	5	61	17	12.20

Fish production is most profitable when MC = p.

competitive profit maximization rule Produce at that rate of output where price equals marginal cost.

Figure 6.4 illustrates these marginal costs. The unit of production used here is baskets of fish per hour. Notice how the MC rises as the rate of output increases. At the output rate of four baskets per hour (point *E*), marginal cost is $13: the fourth basket increases total costs by $13. The fifth basket is even more expensive with a marginal cost of $17.

Profit-Maximizing Rate of Output

We are now in a position to make a production decision. All we have to know is the price of the product and its marginal cost. We do not want to produce an additional unit of output if its MC exceeds its price. If MC exceeds price, we are spending more to produce that extra unit than we are getting back: total profits will decline if we produce it.

The opposite is true when price exceeds MC. If an extra unit brings in more revenue than it costs to produce, it is adding to total profit. Total profits must increase in this case. Hence *a competitive firm wants to expand the rate of production whenever price exceeds MC.*

Since we want to expand output when price exceeds MC and contract output if price is less than MC, the profit-maximizing rate of output is easily found. *Short-run profits are maximized at the rate of output where price equals marginal cost.* The **competitive profit maximization rule** is summarized in Table 6.1.

Figure 6.5 illustrates the application of our profit maximization rule. The market price of catfish is $13 a basket. At this price we can sell all the fish we produce, up to our short-run capacity. The fish cannot be sold at a higher price because lots of farmers grow fish and sell them for $13. If we try to charge a

FIGURE 6.5
Maximizing Profits for
a Competitive Firm

A competitive firm maximizes
total profits at the output rate
where MC = p. If MC is less
than price, the firm can increase
profits by producing more.
If MC exceeds price, the firm
should reduce output. In this
case, profit maximization occurs
at an output of four baskets of
fish per hour.

	(1) Number of Baskets (per Hour)	(2) Price	(3) Total Revenue	(4) Total Cost	(5) Total Profit	(6) Price	(7) Marginal Cost
A	0	—	0	$10.00	−$10.00	—	—
B	1	$13.00	$13.00	15.00	− 2.00	$13.00	$ 5.00
C	2	13.00	26.00	22.00	+ 4.00	13.00	7.00
D	3	13.00	39.00	31.00	+ 8.00	13.00	9.00
E	4	13.00	52.00	44.00	+ 8.00	13.00	13.00
F	5	13.00	65.00	61.00	+ 4.00	13.00	17.00

higher price, consumers will buy their fish from these other producers. Hence
the demand curve facing this one firm is horizontal at the price of $13 a basket.

The costs of harvesting catfish were already examined in Figure 6.4. The key
concept illustrated here is marginal cost. The MC curve slopes upward.

Also depicted in Figure 6.5 are the total revenues, costs, and profits of alternative production rates. Study the table in Figure 6.5 first. Notice that the firm loses
$10 per hour if it produces no fish (row *A*). At zero output, total revenue is zero
($p \times q = 0$). However, the firm must still contend with fixed costs of $10 per hour.
Total profit—total revenue minus total cost—is therefore *minus* $10; the firm
incurs a loss.

Row *B* of the table shows how this loss is reduced when one basket of fish is
produced per hour. The production and sale of just one basket per hour brings in
$13 of total revenue (column 3). The total cost of producing that one basket is $15
(column 4). Hence the total loss associated with an output rate of one basket per
hour is $2 (column 5). This $2 loss may not be what we hoped for, but it is certainly
better than the $10 loss incurred at zero output.

If a firm had a complete table of revenues and costs, it could identify the
profit-maximizing rate of output. But it would be nice to have a shortcut to that
conclusion. Fortunately there is an easier way to make production decisions.

DECISION WHEN *p* > MC   The superior profitability of producing one basket per
hour rather than none is evident in columns 6 and 7 of row *B*. The first basket produced fetches a price of $13. Its *marginal cost* is only $5. Hence it brings in more

TABLE 6.1
Short-Run Decision
Rules for a
Competitive Firm
The relationship between price
and marginal cost dictates short-
run production decisions. For
competitive firms, profits are
maximized at that rate of output
where price = MC.

Price Level	Production Decision
Price > MC	Increase output rate.
Price = MC	Maintain output rate (profits maximized).
Price < MC	Decrease output rate.

added revenue ($13) than it costs to produce ($5). Under these circumstances—whenever price exceeds MC—output should definitely be expanded. That is one of the decision rules summarized in Table 6.1.

The excess of price over MC for the first unit of output is also illustrated by the graph in Figure 6.5. Point B ($13) lies above MC_B ($5); the *difference* between these two points measures the contribution that the first basket of fish makes to the total profits of the firm. In this case, that contribution equals $13 − $5 = $8, and production losses are reduced by that amount when the rate of output is increased from zero to one basket per hour.

So long as price exceeds MC, further increases in the rate of output are desirable. Notice what happens to profits when the rate of output is increased from one to two baskets per hour (row C). The price of the second basket is $13; its MC is $7. Therefore, it *adds* $6 to total profits. Instead of losing $2 per hour, the firm is now making a profit of $4 per hour.

The firm can make even more profits by expanding the rate of output further. Look what happens when the rate of output reaches three baskets per hour (row D of the table). The price of the third basket is $13; its marginal cost is $9. Therefore, the third basket makes a $4 contribution to profits. By increasing its rate of output to three baskets per hour, the firm doubles its total profits.

This firm will never make huge profits. The fourth unit of output has a price of $13 and an MC of $13 as well. It does not contribute to total profits, nor does it subtract from them. The fourth unit of output represents the highest rate of output the firm desires. *At the rate of output where price = MC, total profits of the firm are maximized.*

DECISION WHEN p < MC   Notice what happens if we expand output beyond four baskets per hour. The price of the fifth basket is still $13, but its MC is $17. The fifth basket costs more than it brings in. If we produce that fifth basket, total profit will decline by $4. The fifth unit of output makes us worse off. This is evident in the graph in Figure 6.5: at the output rate of five baskets per hour, the MC curve lies above the price curve. The lesson here is clear: *output should not be increased if MC exceeds price.*

MAXIMUM PROFIT AT p = MC   The outcome of the production decision is illustrated in Figure 6.5 by the intersection of the price and MC curves. At this intersection, price equals MC and profits are maximized. If we produced less, we would be giving up potential profits. If we produced more, total profits would also fall. Hence the point where MC = p is the limit to profit maximization.

Total Profit

So what have we learned here? The message is simple: To reach the right production decision, we need only compare price and marginal costs. Having found the desired rate of output, however, we may want to take a closer look at the profits we are accumulating. We could, of course, content ourselves with the statistics in the table of Figure 6.5. But a picture would be nice, too, especially if it reflected our success in production. Figure 6.6 provides such a picture.

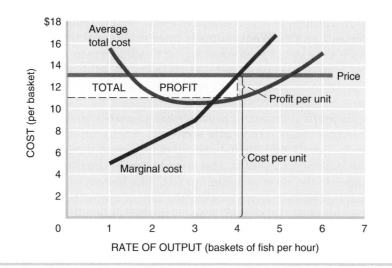

FIGURE 6.6
Illustrating Total Profit
Total profits can be computed as profit *per unit* ($p -$ ATC) multiplied by the quantity sold. This is illustrated by the shaded rectangle. To find the profit-maximizing rate of output, we could use this graph or just the MC and price curves of Figure 6.5.

Figure 6.6 takes advantage of the fact that total profit can be computed in one of two ways:

$$\text{Total profit} = \text{total revenue} - \text{total cost}$$

or

$$\text{Total profit} = \text{average profit} \times \text{quantity sold}$$
$$(\text{profit per unit})$$

In Figure 6.6 the focus is on the second formula. To use it, we compute profit per unit as price *minus* average total cost—that is,

$$\text{profit per unit} = p - \text{ATC}$$

Figure 6.6 adds an *average* total cost curve to the graphs of Figure 6.4. This curve allows us to see how *profit per unit* changes as the rate of output increases. Like the ATC curve we first encountered in Chapter 5 (Figure 5.3, page 103), this ATC curve has the distinctive U shape.

We compute profit per unit as price minus ATC. As before, the market price of catfish is assumed to be $13 per basket, as illustrated by the horizontal price line at that level. Therefore, the *difference* between price and average cost—profit per unit—is illustrated by the vertical distance between the price and ATC curves. At four baskets of fish per hour, for example, profit per unit equals $13 - $11 = $2.

To compute *total* profits at the output rate of four baskets, we note that

$$\text{Total profit} = \text{profit per unit} \times \text{quantity}$$
$$= (p - \text{ATC}) \times q$$
$$= (\$13 - \$11) \times 4$$

In this case, the *total* profit would be $8 per hour. *Total* profits are illustrated in Figure 6.6 by the shaded rectangle. (Recall that the area of a rectangle is equal to its height [profit per unit] multiplied by its width [quantity sold].)

Profit per unit not only is used to compute total profits but is often of interest in its own right. Businesspeople like to cite statistics on markups, which are a crude index to per-unit profits. However, *the profit-maximizing producer never seeks to maximize per-unit profits.* **What counts is *total* profits,** not the amount of profit per unit. This is the age-old problem of trying to sell ice cream for $5 a cone. You might be able to maximize profit per unit if you could sell 1 cone for $5, but you would make a lot more money if you sold 100 cones at a per-unit profit of only 50 cents each.

Similarly, *the profit-maximizing producer has no particular desire to produce at that rate of output where ATC is at a minimum.* Minimum ATC does represent least-cost production. But additional units of output, even though they raise average costs, will increase total profits. This is evident in Figure 6.6: price exceeds MC for some output to the right of minimum ATC (the bottom of the U). Therefore, total profits are increasing as we increase the rate of output beyond the point of minimum average costs. *Total profits are maximized only where p = MC.*

SUPPLY BEHAVIOR

Right about now you may be wondering why we're memorizing formulas for profit maximization. Who cares about MC, ATC, and all these other cost concepts? Maybe we all do. If we don't know how firms make production decisions, we'll never figure out how the market establishes prices and quantities for the products we desire. Knowledge of supply decisions can also be valuable if you are purchasing a car, a vacation package, or even something in an electronic auction. What we're learning here is how much of a good sellers are *willing* to offer at any given price.

A Firm's Supply

The most distinctive feature of perfectly competitive firms is the lack of pricing decisions. As price takers, the only decision competitive firms make is how much output to produce at the prevailing market price. Their **supply** behavior is determined by the rules for profit maximization. Specifically, *competitive firms adjust the quantity supplied until MC = price.*

supply The ability and willingness to sell (produce) specific quantities of a good at alternative prices in a given time period, *ceteris paribus.*

Suppose the price of catfish was only $9 per basket instead of $13. Would it still make sense to harvest four baskets per hour? No. Four baskets is the profit-maximizing rate of output only when the price of catfish is $13. At a price of $9 a basket, it would not make sense to produce four baskets because the MC of the fourth basket ($13) would exceed its price. The decision rule (Table 6.1) in this case requires a cutback in output. At a market price of $9, the most profitable rate of output would be only three baskets of fish per hour (see Figure 6.5).

The marginal cost curve thus tells us how much output a firm will supply at different prices. Once we know the price of catfish, we can look at the MC curve to determine exactly how many fish Farmer Seamans will harvest. In other words, *the marginal cost curve is the short-run supply curve for a competitive firm.*

SUPPLY SHIFTS   Since marginal costs determine the supply decisions of a firm, *anything that alters marginal cost will change supply behavior.* The most important influences on marginal cost (and supply behavior) are

- *The price of factor inputs.*
- *Technology.*
- *Expectations.*

A catfish farmer will supply more fish at any given price if the price of feed declines. If fish can be bred faster because of advances in genetic engineering, productivity will increase and the farmer's MC curve will shift downward. With lower marginal costs, the firm will supply more output at any given price.

Conversely, if wages increased, the marginal cost of producing fish would rise as well. This upward shift of the MC curve would cause the firm to supply fewer fish at any prevailing price. Finally, if producers expect factor prices to rise or demand to diminish, they may be more willing to supply output now.

You can put the concept of marginal cost pricing to use the next time you buy a car. The car dealer wants to get a price that covers all costs, including a share of the rent, electricity, and insurance (fixed costs). The dealer might, however, be willing to sell the car for only its *marginal* cost—that is, the wholesale price paid for the car plus a little labor time (variable costs). So long as the price exceeds marginal cost, the dealer is better off selling the car than not selling it.

Market Supply

Up until now we have focused on the supply behavior of a single competitive firm. But what about the **market supply** of catfish? We need a *market* supply curve to determine the *market* price the individual farmer will confront. In the previous discussion, we simply picked a price arbitrarily at $13 per basket. Now our objective is to find out where that market price comes from.

Like the market supply curves we first encountered in Chapter 3, the market supply of catfish is obtained by simple addition. All we have to do is add up the quantities each farmer stands ready to supply at each and every price. Then we will know the total number of fish to be supplied to the market at that price. Figure 6.7 illustrates

market supply The total quantities of a good that sellers are willing and able to sell at alternative prices in a given time period, *ceteris paribus*.

FIGURE 6.7   Competitive Market Supply

The MC curve is a competitive firm's short-run supply curve. The curve MC$_A$ tells us that Farmer A will produce 40 pounds of catfish per day if the market price is $3 per pound.

To determine the *market supply*, we add up the quantities supplied by each farmer. The total quantity supplied to the market here is 150 pounds per day ($= a + b + c$). Market supply depends on the number of firms in an industry and their respective marginal costs.

this summation. Notice that *the market supply curve is the sum of the marginal cost curves of all the firms.* Hence whatever determines the marginal cost of a typical firm will also determine industry supply. Specifically, the *market supply of a competitive industry is determined by*

- *The price of factor inputs.*
- *Technology.*
- *Expectations.*
- *The number of firms in the industry.*

INDUSTRY ENTRY AND EXIT

equilibrium price The price at which the quantity of a good demanded in a given time period equals the quantity supplied.

With a market supply curve and a market demand curve, we can identify the **equilibrium price**—the price that matches the quantity demanded to the quantity supplied. This equilibrium is shown as E_1 in Figure 6.8.

If truth be told, locating a market's equilibrium is neither difficult nor terribly interesting—certainly not in competitive markets. In *competitive markets, the real action is in changes to market equilibrium.* In competitive markets, new firms are always beating down the door, trying to get a share of industry profits. Entrepreneurs are always looking for ways to improve products or the production process. Nothing stays in equilibrium very long. Hence, to understand how competitive markets really work, we have to focus on *changes* in equilibrium rather than on the identification of a static equilibrium. One of the forces driving those changes is the entry of new firms into an industry.

Entry

Suppose that the equilibrium price in the catfish industry is $13. This short-run equilibrium is illustrated in Figure 6.8 by the point E_1 at the intersection of market demand and the market supply curve S_1. At that price, the typical catfish farmer would harvest four baskets of fish per hour and earn a profit of $8 per hour (as seen earlier in Figure 6.6). All the farmers together would be producing the quantity q_1 in Figure 6.8.

The profitable equilibrium at E_1 is not likely to last, however. Farmers still growing cotton or other crops will see the profits being made by catfish farmers and lust after them. They, too, will want to dig up their crops and replace them with catfish ponds.

FIGURE 6.8
Market Entry Pushes Prices Down

If there are profits at the initial equilibrium (E_1), more firms will enter the industry. As they do, the market supply curve (S_1) shifts to the right (S_2). This creates a new equilibrium (E_2), where output is higher (q_2) and price is lower (p_2).

NEWS WIRE	ENTRY AND PRICE

Flat Panels, Thin Margins
Rugged Competition from Smaller Brands

Has Made the TV Sets Cheaper Than Ever

Like just about everyone else checking out the flat-panel TVs at Best Buy in Manhattan, graphic designer Roy Gantt came in coveting a Philips, Sony, or Panasonic. But after seeing the price tags, he figured a Westinghouse might be a better buy. . . .

It is just one of more than 100 flat-panel brands jamming the aisles of retailers such as Best Buy, Target, and Costco. The names on the sets range from the obscure (Sceptre, Maxent) to the recycled (Polaroid).

The free-for-all is a boon to the millions of Americans who want to trade in their bulky analog sets. . . .

For many in the industry, though, the competition is brutal. Prices for LCD sets are falling so rapidly that retailers who place orders too far in advance risk getting stuck with expensive inventory.

—Pete Engardio

THE STAT

102

LCD television brands available in the United.States., up from 26 in 2002

Data: Pacific Media Associates.

Source: *BusinessWeek*, February 26, 2007, p. 50. Used with permission of Bloomberg L.P. Copyright © 2011. All rights reserved.

NOTE: When more firms enter an industry, the market supply increases (shifts right) and price declines.

This is a serious problem for the catfish farmers in the South. It is fairly inexpensive to get into the catfish business. You can start with a pond, some breeding stock, and relatively little capital equipment. Accordingly, when catfish prices are high, lots of cotton farmers are ready and willing to bulldoze a couple of ponds and get into the catfish business. The entry of more farmers into the catfish industry increases the market supply and drives down catfish prices.

The impact of market entry on market outcomes is illustrated in Figure 6.8. The initial equilibrium at E_1 was determined by the supply behavior of existing producers. If those producers are earning a profit, however, other firms will want to enter the industry. When they do, the industry supply curve shifts to the right (S_2). This entry-induced shift of the market supply curve changes market equilibrium. A new equilibrium is established at E_2. At E_2, the quantity supplied is larger and the price is lower than at the initial equilibrium E_1. Hence *industry output increases and price falls when firms enter an industry.* This is the kind of competitive behavior that has made flat-panel TVs so cheap (see the accompanying News Wire).

Tendency toward Zero Economic Profits
Whether more cotton farmers enter the catfish industry depends on their expectations for profit. If catfish farming looks more profitable than cotton, more farmers will flood their cotton fields. As they do, the market supply curve will continue shifting to the right, driving catfish prices down.

How far can catfish prices fall? *The force that drives catfish prices down is market entry.* **New firms continue to enter a competitive industry so long as profits exist.** Hence the price of catfish will continue to fall until all economic profits disappear.

Notice in Figure 6.9 where this occurs. When price drops from p_1 to p_2, the typical firm reduces its output from q_1 to q_2. At the price p_2, however, the firm is still making a profit because price exceeds average cost at the output q_2. This profit is illustrated by the shaded rectangle that appears in Figure 6.9*b*.

The persistence of profits lures still more firms into the industry. As they enter the industry, the market price of fish will be pushed ever lower (Figure 6.9*a*). When the price falls to p_3, the most profitable rate of output will be q_3 (where MC = p). But at that level, price no longer exceeds average cost. **Once price falls to the level of minimum average cost, all economic profits disappear.** This zero-profit outcome occurs at the bottom of the U-shaped ATC curve.

When economic profits vanish, market entry ceases. No more cotton farmers will switch to catfish farming once the price of catfish falls to the level of minimum average total cost.

Exit

In the short run, catfish prices might actually fall *below* average total cost. This is what happened in 2012 when Vietnamese and Chinese catfish farmers increased exports to the United States, hoping to take advantage of high prices. The resultant shift of market supply pushed prices so low (from $1.25 to 75 cents a pound) that many U.S. catfish farmers incurred an economic *loss* ($p <$ ATC).

Suddenly fields of rice looked a lot more enticing than ponds full of fish. Before long, some catfish farmers started filling in their ponds and planting rice. As they

---

FIGURE 6.9   The Lure of Profits

If economic profits exist in an industry, more firms will want to enter it. As they do, the market supply curve will shift to the right and cause a drop in the market price (*left graph*). The lower market price, in turn, will reduce the output and profits of the typical firm (*right graph*). Once the market price is driven down to p_3, all profits disappear and entry ceases.

(*a*) **Market entry pushes price down and . . .**

(*b*) **Reduces profits of competitive firms.**

| NEWS WIRE | ENTRY AND EXIT |

U.S. Catfish Growers Struggle Against High Feed Prices, Foreign Competition

LITTLE ROCK, Ark.—The catfish industry in the state continued its downward spiral in 2011, with declines in acreage, production, and sales . . .

Catfish farms shed about 3,500 water surface acres in the state in 2011, a 26.5 percent decrease to 9,700 acres, the lowest in a decade, according to USDA figures.

Nationwide, surface acres fell a little more than 10 percent in 2011, to 89,390 . . .

With fewer fish available, the price paid by processors to farmers was up in 2011, averaging $1.05 a pound—an increase from an average of 77 cents in 2010.

Ted McNulty, head of the Aquaculture Division of the Arkansas Department of Agriculture, said he expects food inventory and acreage to stabilize but that it is unlikely for at least a few years.

Source: Associated Press, February 11, 2012. Used with permission of The Associated Press Copyright © 2012. All rights reserved.

exited the catfish industry, the market supply curve shifted to the left and catfish prices rose (see the accompanying News Wire). Eventually price rose to the level of average total costs, at which point further exits ceased. Once entry and exit cease, the market price stabilizes.

Equilibrium

The lesson to be learned from catfish farming is straightforward:

- *The existence of profits in a competitive industry induces entry.*
- *The existence of losses in a competitive industry induces exits.*

Accordingly, we can anticipate that prices in a competitive market will continue to adjust until all entry and exit cease. At that point, the market will be in equilibrium. *In long-run competitive market equilibrium,*

- *Price equals minimum average total cost.*
- *Economic profit is eliminated.*

Catfish farmers would be happier, of course, if the price of catfish did not decline to the point where economic profits disappeared. But how are they going to prevent it? Farmer Seamans knows all about the law of demand and would like to get his fellow farmers to slow production a little before all the profits disappear. But Farmer Seamans is powerless to stop the forces of a competitive market. He cannot afford to reduce his own catfish production. Nobody would notice the resulting drop in market supplies, and catfish prices would continue to slide. The only one affected would be Farmer Seamans, who would be denying himself the opportunity to share in the good fortunes of the catfish market while they last. As long as others are willing and able to enter the industry and increase output, Farmer Seamans must do the same or deny himself even a small share of the available profits. Others will be willing to expand catfish production so long as catfish breed economic profits—that is, so long as the rate of return in catfish production is superior to that available elsewhere. They will be able to do so as long as it is easy to get into catfish production.

Farmer Seamans's dilemma goes a long way toward explaining why catfish farming is not highly profitable. Every time the profit picture looks good, everybody tries to get in on the action. This kind of pressure on prices and profits is a fundamental characteristic of competitive markets. *As long as it is easy for existing producers to expand production or for new firms to enter an industry, economic profits will not last long.* Industry output will expand, market prices will fall, and rates of profit will diminish. Thus the rate of profits in catfish farming is kept down by the fact that anyone with a pond and a couple of catfish can get into the business fairly easily.

Low Barriers to Entry

barriers to entry Obstacles, such as patents, that make it difficult or impossible for would-be producers to enter a particular market.

New producers will be able to enter a profitable industry and help drive down prices and profits as long as there are no significant **barriers to entry.** Such barriers may include patents, control of essential factors of production, brand loyalty, and various forms of price control. All such barriers make it expensive, risky, or impossible for new firms to enter into production. In the absence of such barriers, new firms can enter an industry more readily and at less risk.

Not surprisingly, firms already entrenched in a profitable industry do their best to keep newcomers out by erecting barriers to entry. As we saw, there are few barriers to entering the catfish business. When catfish imports from Vietnam first soared in 2002–2003, domestic farmers sought to stem the inflow with new entry barriers, including country-of-origin labeling, tougher health inspections, and outright import quotas. Such entry barriers would have impeded rightward shifts of the market supply curve and kept catfish prices higher. Without such protection, domestic farmers who couldn't keep up with falling prices and increased productivity exited the industry. Owners of T-shirt shops also fret over the low entry barriers that keep their prices and profits low (see the accompanying News Wire).

NEWS WIRE	COMPETITIVE PRESSURE

T-Shirt Shop Owner's Lament: Too Many T-Shirt Shops

The small Texas beach resort of South Padre Island boasts white sand, blue skies (much of the time), the buoyant waters of the Gulf of Mexico and, at last count, more than 40 T-shirt shops.

And that's a problem for Shy Oogav, who owns one of those shops. "Every day you have to compete with other shops," he says. "And if you invent something new, they will copy you."

Padre Island illustrates a common condition in the T-shirt industry—unbridled, ill-advised growth. Many people believe T-shirts are the ticket to a permanent vacation—far too many people. "In the past years, everything that closed opened up again as a T-shirt shop," says Maria C. Hall, executive director of the South Padre Island Chamber of Commerce.

Mr. Oogav, a 29-year-old immigrant from Israel, came to South Padre Island on vacation six years ago, thought he had found paradise and stayed on. He subsequently got a job with one of the town's T-shirt shops, which then numbered fewer than a dozen. Now that he owns his own shop, and the competition has quadrupled, his paradise is lost. "I don't sleep at night," he says, morosely.

—Mark Pawlosky

Source: *The Wall Street Journal*, July 31, 1995. Used with permission of Dow Jones & Company, Inc., via Copyright Clearance Center Inc.

NOTE: The ability of a single firm to increase the price of its product depends on how many other firms offer identical products. A perfectly competitive firm has no market power.

Market Characteristics

This brief review of catfish economics illustrates a few general observations about the structure, behavior, and outcomes of a competitive market:

- *Many firms.* A competitive market will include a great many firms, none of which has a significant share of total output.
- *Horizontal firm demand.* Perfectly competitive firms confront horizontal demand curves; they don't have the power to raise their price above the prevailing market price.
- *Identical products.* Products are homogeneous. One firm's product is virtually indistinguishable from any other firm's product.
- *MC = p.* All competitive firms will seek to expand output until marginal cost equals price.
- *Low entry barriers.* Barriers to enter the industry are low. If economic profits are available, more firms will enter the industry.
- *Zero economic profit.* The tendency of production and market supplies to expand when profit is high puts heavy pressure on prices and profits in competitive industries. Economic profit will approach zero in the long run as prices are driven down to the level of average production costs.
- *Perfect information.* All buyers and sellers are fully informed of market opportunities.

POLICY PERSPECTIVES

Does Competition Help Us or Hurt Us?

This profile of competitive markets has important implications for public policy. As we noted in Chapter 3, a strong case can be made for the market mechanism. In particular, we observed that the market mechanism permits individual consumers and producers to express their views about WHAT to produce, HOW to produce, and FOR WHOM to produce by "voting" for particular goods and services with market purchases and sales. How well this market mechanism works depends in part on how competitive markets are.

THE RELENTLESS PROFIT SQUEEZE   The unrelenting squeeze on prices and profits that we have observed in this chapter is a fundamental characteristic of the competitive process. Indeed, the **market mechanism** works best under such circumstances. The existence of economic profits implies that consumers place a high value on a particular product and are willing to pay a comparatively high price to get it. The high price and profits signal this information to profit-hungry entrepreneurs, who eagerly come forward to satisfy consumer demands. Thus *high profits in a particular industry indicate that consumers want a different mix of output* (more of that industry's goods). They get that desired mix when more firms enter the industry, increasing its total output (and reducing output in the industries they left). Low entry barriers and the competitive quest for profits enable consumers to get more of the goods they desire, and at a lower price. We get a good answer to the WHAT question.

market mechanism The use of market prices and sales to signal desired outputs (or resource allocations).

MAXIMUM EFFICIENCY   When the competitive pressure on prices is carried to the limit, the products in question are also produced at the least possible cost. This is *how* we want goods produced—at minimum cost. This was illustrated by the tendency of catfish prices to be driven down to the level of minimum average costs (Figure 6.9). Once the market equilibrium has been established, society is getting the most it can from its available (scarce) resources.

Topic Podcast:
Competitive Behavior

ZERO ECONOMIC PROFITS At the limit of the process, all economic profit is eliminated. This doesn't mean that producers are left empty-handed, however. To begin with, the zero profit limit is rarely, if ever, reached. New products are continually being introduced, consumer demands change, and more efficient production processes are discovered. In fact, *the competitive process creates strong pressures to pursue product and technological innovation.* In a competitive market, the adage about the early bird getting the worm is particularly apt. As we observed in the catfish market, the first ones to take up catfish farming were the ones who made the greatest profits.

The sequence of events common to a competitive market situation includes the following:

- High prices and profits signal consumers' demand for more output.
- Economic profit attracts new suppliers.
- The market supply curve shifts to the right.
- Prices slide down the market demand curve.
- A new equilibrium is reached at which increased quantities of the desired product are produced and its price is lowered. Average costs of production are at or near a minimum, more of the product is supplied and consumed, and economic profit approaches zero.
- Throughout the process producers experience great pressure to keep ahead of the profit squeeze by reducing costs, a pressure that frequently results in product and technological innovation.

What is essential to note about the competitive process is that the potential threat of other firms to expand production or new firms to enter the industry keeps existing firms on their toes. Even the most successful firm cannot rest on its laurels for long. To stay in the game, competitive firms must continually improve technology, improve their products, and reduce costs.

THE SOCIAL VALUE OF LOSSES Not all firms can maintain a competitive pace. Throughout the competitive process, many firms incur economic losses, shut down production, and exit the industry. These losses are a critical part of the market mechanism. *Economic losses are a signal to producers that they are not using society's scarce resources in the best way.* Consumers want those resources reallocated to other firms or industries that can better satisfy consumer demands. In a competitive market, money-losing firms are sent packing, making scarce resources available to more efficient firms.

The dog-eat-dog character of competitive markets troubles many observers. Critics say competitive markets are "all about money," with no redeeming social attributes. But such criticism is ill founded. The economic goals of society are to produce the best possible mix of output, in the most efficient way, and then to distribute the output fairly. In other words, society seeks optimal answers to the basic WHAT, HOW, and FOR WHOM questions. What makes competitive markets so desirable is that they are most likely to deliver those outcomes.

SUMMARY

- Market structures range from perfect competition (many small firms in an industry) to monopoly (one firm). **LO1**
- A perfectly competitive firm has no power to alter the market price of the goods it sells: it is a *price taker*. The firm confronts a horizontal demand curve for its own output even though the relevant *market* demand curve is negatively sloped. **LO1**
- The competitive firm maximizes profit at that rate of output where marginal cost equals price. This represents the short-term equilibrium of the firm. **LO3**
- A competitive firm's supply curve is identical to its marginal cost curve. In the short run, the quantity supplied will rise or fall with price. **LO3**
- The determinants of supply include the price of inputs, technology, and expectations. If any of these determinants change, the *firm's* supply curve will shift. *Market* supply will shift if costs or the number of firms in the industry changes. **LO4**
- If short-term profits exist in a competitive industry, new firms will enter the market. The resulting shift
- of supply will drive market prices down the market demand curve. As prices fall, the profit of the industry and its constituent firms will be squeezed. **LO5**
- The limit to the competitive price and profit squeeze is reached when price is driven down to the level of minimum average total cost. Additional output and profit will be attained only if technology is improved (lowering costs) or if demand increases. **LO5**
- If the market price falls below ATC, firms will exit an industry. Price will stabilize only when entry and exit cease (and zero profit prevails). **LO5**
- The most distinctive thing about competitive markets is the persistent pressure they exert on prices and profits. The threat of competition is a tremendous incentive for producers to respond quickly to consumer demands and to seek more efficient means of production. In this sense, competitive markets do best what markets are supposed to do—efficiently allocate resources. **LO1**

TERMS TO REMEMBER

Define the following terms:

market structure	market power	marginal cost (MC)	market supply
competitive firm	production decision	competitive profit maximization rule	equilibrium price
competitive market	total revenue		barriers to entry
monopoly	profit	supply	market mechanism

QUESTIONS FOR DISCUSSION

1. What industries do you regard as being highly competitive? Can you identify any barriers to entry in those industries? **LO1**
2. According to the News Wire on page 116, how many catfish farms exited the industry in 2002–2008? What did they then do? Was this socially desirable? **LO5**
3. If there were more bookstores around your campus, would textbook prices rise or fall? Why aren't there more bookstores? **LO5**
4. Why doesn't Coke lose all its customers when it raises its price? Why would a catfish farmer lose all her customers if she raised her price? **LO1**
5. How many fish should a commercial fisherman try to catch in a day? Should he catch as many as possible or return to dock before filling the boat with fish? Under what economic circumstances should he not even take the boat out? **LO3**

6. Why would anyone want to enter a profitable industry knowing that profits would eventually be eliminated by competition? **LO5**

7. What rate of output is appropriate for a nonprofit corporation (e.g., a university or hospital)? **LO3**

8. **POLICY PERSPECTIVES** If Apple had no competitors, would it be improving iPhone features as fast? **LO5**

9. **POLICY PERSPECTIVES** Who gained or lost when money-losing catfish farmers left the industry (see the News Wire on page 129)? **LO4**

10. **POLICY PERSPECTIVES** Adam Smith in *The Wealth of Nations* asserted that the pursuit of self-interest by competitive firms promoted the interests of society. What did he mean by this? **LO1**

PROBLEMS

■ connect

1. Use Figure 6.5 to determine the following: **LO3**
   (a) How many baskets of fish should be harvested at market prices of
      i. $7?
      ii. $13?
      iii. $17?
   (b) How much total revenue is collected at each price?
   (c) How much profit does the farmer make at each of these prices?

2. In Figure 6.5, what rate of output **LO2**
   (a) Maximizes total revenue?
   (b) Maximizes profit per unit?
   (c) Maximizes total profit? (Choose the higher level of output.)

3. Graph a situation where the typical catfish farmer is incurring a loss at the prevailing market price p_1.
   (a) What is MC equal to at the best possible rate of output?
   (b) Is ATC above or below p_1?
   (c) Which of the following would raise the market price?
      i. A reduction in the firm's output.
      ii. An increase in the firm's input costs.
      iii. Exits from the industry.
      iv. An improvement in technology.
   (d) What price would prevail in long-term equilibrium? **LO4**

4. Suppose a firm has the following costs: **LO3**

Output (units):	10	11	12	13	14	15	16	17	18	19
Total cost:	$50	$52	$56	$62	$70	$80	$92	$106	$122	$140

   (a) If the prevailing market price is $14 per unit, how much should the firm produce?
   (b) How much profit will it earn at that output rate?

5. Graph the market behavior described in the News Wire on page 127. **LO5**

6. (a) According to the News Wire on p.127, how many LCD television brands entered the market between 2002 and 2007?
   (b) What happened to the market price? **LO1**

   (c) If the market price dropped to $8, how much output should the firm produce?
   (d) How much profit will it make at that lower price?

7. Under perfectly competitive scenarios firms exit the business when economic losses are incurred. According to the News Wire on p.116, how many Arkansas catfish farms quit the business due to economic losses? **LO4**

8. **POLICY PERSPECTIVES** What are expected profits for a perfectly competitive firm in the long run? **LO5**

9. **POLICY PERSPECTIVES** Suppose that the monthly market demand schedule for Frisbees is

Price	$8	$7	$6	$5	$4	$3	$2	$1
Quantity demanded	1,000	2,000	4,000	8,000	16,000	32,000	64,000	150,000

Suppose further that the marginal and average costs of Frisbee production for every competitive firm are

Rate of output	100	200	300	400	500	600
Marginal cost	$2.00	$3.00	$4.00	$5.00	$6.00	$7.00
Average total cost	$2.00	$2.50	$3.00	$3.50	$4.00	$4.50

Finally, assume that the equilibrium market price is $6 per Frisbee.   **LO5**

(a) Draw the cost curves of the typical firm.

(b) Draw the market demand curve and identify market equilibrium.

(c) How many Frisbees are being sold in equilibrium?

(d) How many (identical) firms are initially producing Frisbees?

(e) How much profit is the typical firm making?

(f) In view of the profits being made, more firms will want to get into Frisbee production. In the long run, these new firms will shift the market supply curve to the right and push the price down to minimum average total cost, thereby eliminating profits. At what equilibrium price are all profits eliminated?

(g) How many firms will be producing Frisbees at this price?

◄ Practice quizzes, student PowerPoints, author podcasts, web activities, and additional materials available at **www.mhhe.com/schilleressentials9e**, or scan here. Need a barcode reader? Try ScanLife, available in your app store.

7

Monopoly

◄ Practice quizzes, student PowerPoints, author podcasts, web activities, and additional materials available at www.mhhe.com/schilleressentials9e, or scan here. Need a barcode reader? Try ScanLife, available in your app store.

LEARNING OBJECTIVES

After reading this chapter, you should be able to:

1   Define what a monopoly is.
2   Explain why price exceeds marginal revenue in monopoly.
3   Describe how a monopoly sets output and price.
4   Illustrate how monopoly and competitive outcomes differ.
5   Discuss the pros and cons of monopoly structures.

▌n 1908 Ford produced the Model T, the car "designed for the common man." It was cheap, reliable, and as easy to drive as the horse and buggy it was replacing. Ford sold 10,000 Model Ts in its first full year of production (1909). After that, sales more than doubled every year. In 1913 nearly 200,000 Model Ts were sold, and Ford was fast changing American patterns of consumption, travel, and living standards.

During this early development of the U.S. auto industry, Henry Ford dominated the field. There were other producers, but the Ford Motor Company was the only producer of an inexpensive "motorcar for the multitudes." In this situation, Henry Ford could dictate the price and the features of his cars. When he opened his new assembly line factory at Highland Park, he abruptly raised the Model T's price by $100—an increase of 12 percent—to help pay for the new plant. Then he decided to paint all Model Ts black. When told of consumer complaints about the lack of colors, Ford advised one of his executives in 1913, "Give them any color they want so long as it's black."[1]

Henry Ford had market power. He could dictate what color car Americans would buy. And he could raise the price of Model Ts without fear of losing all his customers. Such power is alien to competitive firms. Competitive firms are always under pressure to reduce costs, improve quality, and cater to consumer preferences.

In this chapter we will continue to examine how market structure influences market outcomes. Specifically, we examine how a market controlled by a single producer—a monopoly—behaves. We are particularly interested in the following questions:

- What price will a monopolist charge for its output?
- How does a monopolist keep potential competitors at bay?
- Are consumers better or worse off when only one firm controls an entire market?

MONOPOLY STRUCTURE

The essence of **market power** is the ability to alter the price of a product. The catfish farmers of Chapter 6 had no such power. Because many other farms were producing and selling the same good, each catfish producer had to act as a *price taker*. Each farm could sell all the fish it harvested at the prevailing market price. If a farmer tried to charge a higher price for his catfish, that individual farmer would lose all his customers. This inability to set the price of their output is the most distinguishing characteristic of perfectly competitive firms.

Catfish don't, of course, violate the law of demand. As tasty as catfish are, people are not willing to buy unlimited quantities of them at $13 per basket. The marginal utility of extra fish, in fact, diminishes rapidly. To induce consumers to buy more fish, the price of fish must be reduced.

This seeming contradiction between the law of demand and the situation of the competitive firm was explained by the existence of two distinct demand curves. The demand for catfish refers to the **market demand** for that good: like all other consumer demand curves, this market demand curve is downward-sloping. A second demand curve was constructed to represent the situation confronting a *single firm* in the competitive catfish market; that demand curve was horizontal.

market power The ability to alter the market price of a good or service.

market demand The total quantities of a good or service people are willing and able to buy at alternative prices in a given time period; the sum of individual demands.

---

[1]Charles E. Sorensen. *My Forty Years with Ford* (New York: W. W. Norton & Co., 1956), p. 127.

Monopoly = Industry

We now confront an entirely different market structure. Suppose that the entire output of catfish could be produced by a single large producer. Assume that Universal Fish had a patent on the oxygenating equipment needed to maintain commercial-size fish ponds. A **patent** gives a firm the exclusive right to produce or license a product. With its patent, Universal Fish can deny other farmers access to oxygenating equipment and thus establish itself as the sole supplier of catfish. Such a firm is a **monopoly**—that is, a single firm that produces the entire market supply of a good.

In view of the fact that a monopoly has no direct competition, you'd hardly expect it to behave like a competitive firm. Competitive firms are always under pressure from other firms in the industry to hold down costs and improve product quality. Competitive firms also have to worry about new entrants into their industry and the resultant downward pressure on prices. A monopolist, however, owns the ballpark and can set the rules of the game. Is a monopoly going to charge the same price for fish as a competitive industry would? Not likely. As we'll see, a monopolist can use its market power to charge higher prices and retain larger profits.

The emergence of a monopoly obliterates the distinction between industry demand and the demand curve facing the firm. A monopolistic firm *is* the industry. Hence there is only *one* demand curve to worry about, and that is the market (industry) demand curve. ***In monopoly situations the demand curve facing the firm is identical to the market demand curve for the product.***

Price versus Marginal Revenue

Although monopolies simplify the geometry of the firm, they complicate the arithmetic of supply decisions. Competitive firms maximize profits by producing at that rate of output where *price* equals marginal cost. Monopolies do not maximize profits in the same way. They still heed the advice about never producing anything that costs more than it brings in. But as strange as it may seem, what is brought in from an additional sale is not the price in this case.

The contribution to total revenue of an additional unit of output is called **marginal revenue (MR).** To calculate marginal revenue, we compare the total revenues received before and after a one-unit increase in the rate of production; the difference between the two totals equals *marginal* revenue.

If every unit of output could be sold at the same price, marginal revenue would equal price. But what would the demand curve look like in such a case? It would have to be *horizontal,* indicating that consumers were prepared to buy everything produced at the existing price. As we have observed, however, a horizontal demand curve applies only to small competitive firms—firms that produce only a tiny fraction of total market output. ***Only for perfectly competitive firms does price equal marginal revenue.***

The situation in a monopoly is different. The firm is so big that its output decisions affect market prices. Keep in mind that a monopolist confronts the *market* demand curve, which is always downward-sloping. As a consequence, a monopolist can sell additional output only if it *reduces* prices.

Suppose Universal Fish could sell one ton of fish for $6,000. If it wants to sell two tons, however, it has to heed the law of demand and reduce the price per ton. Suppose it has to reduce the price to $5,000 in order to get the additional sales. In that case, we would observe

Total revenue   = 1 ton × $6,000 = $6,000
before price reduction   per ton

Total revenue   = 2 tons × $5,000 = $10,000
after price reduction   per ton

---

patent Government grant of exclusive ownership of an innovation.

monopoly A firm that produces the entire market supply of a particular good or service.

marginal revenue (MR) The change in total revenue that results from a one-unit increase in quantity sold.

To compute marginal revenue, we observe that

$$\text{Marginal revenue} = \text{total revenue} - \text{total revenue}$$
$$\phantom{\text{Marginal revenue} = }\text{@ 2 tons} \text{@ 1 ton}$$
$$\phantom{\text{Marginal revenue} } = \$10,000 - \$6,000 = \$4,000$$

Notice how the quantity demanded in the marketplace increases as the unit price is reduced (the law of demand again). Notice, also, however, what happens to total revenue when unit sales increase: total revenue here *increases* by $4,000. This *change* in total revenue represents the *marginal* revenue of the second ton.

Notice in the calculation that marginal revenue ($4,000) is less than price ($5,000). This will always be the case when the demand curve facing the firm is downward-sloping. To get added sales, price must be reduced. The additional quantity sold is a plus for total revenue, but the reduced price per unit is a negative. The net result of these offsetting effects represents *marginal* revenue. Since the demand curve facing a monopolist is always downward-sloping, ***marginal revenue is always less than price for a monopolist,*** as shown in Figure 7.1.

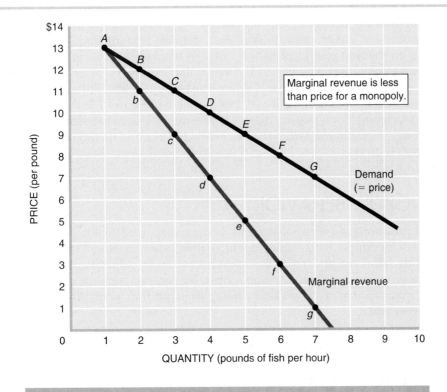

FIGURE 7.1
Price Exceeds Marginal Revenue in Monopoly

If a firm must lower its price to sell additional output, marginal revenue is less than price. If this firm wants to increase its sales from one to two pounds per hour, for example, price must be reduced from $13 to $12. The marginal revenue of the second pound is therefore only $11 (= $24 of total revenue at $p = \$12$ *minus* $13 of total revenue at $p = \$13$). This is indicated in row *B* of the table and by point *b* on the graph.

	(1) Quantity	×	(2) Price	=	(3) Total Revenue	(4) Marginal Revenue
A	1		$13		$13	
						$11
B	2		12		24	
						9
C	3		11		33	
						7
D	4		10		40	
						5
E	5		9		45	
						3
F	6		8		48	
						1
G	7		7		49	

Figure 7.1 provides more detail on how marginal revenue is calculated. The demand curve and schedule represent the market demand for catfish and thus the sales opportunities for the Universal Fish monopoly. According to this information, Universal Fish can sell one pound of fish per hour at a price of $13. If the company wants to sell a larger quantity of fish, it has to reduce its price. According to the market demand curve shown here, the price must be lowered to $12 to sell two pounds per hour. This reduction in price is shown by a movement along the demand curve from point *A* to point *B*.

Our primary focus here is on marginal revenue. We want to show what happens to total revenue when unit sales increase by one pound per hour. To do this, we must compute the total revenue associated with each rate of output, then observe the changes that occur.

The calculations necessary for computing MR are summarized in Figure 7.1. Row *A* of the table indicates that the total revenue resulting from one sale per hour is $13. To increase unit sales, price must be reduced. Row *B* indicates that total revenues rise to only $24 per hour when catfish sales double. The *increase* in total revenues resulting from the added sale is thus $11. The marginal revenue of the second pound is therefore $11. This is illustrated in the last column of the table and by point *b* on the marginal revenue curve.

Notice that the MR of the second pound of fish ($11) is *less* than its price ($12). This is because both pounds are being sold for $12 apiece. In effect, the firm is giving up the opportunity to sell only one pound per hour at $13 in order to sell a *larger* quantity at a *lower* price. In this sense, the firm is sacrificing $1 of potential revenue on the first pound of fish in order to increase *total* revenue. Marginal revenue measures the change in total revenue that results.

So long as the demand curve is downward-sloping, MR will always be less than price. Compare columns 2 and 4 of the table in Figure 7.1. At each rate of output in excess of one pound, marginal revenue is less than price. This is also evident in the graph: *the MR curve lies below the demand (price) curve at every point but the first.*

MONOPOLY BEHAVIOR

Like all producers, a monopolist wants to maximize total profits. A monopolist does this a bit differently than a competitive firm, however. Recall that a perfectly competitive firm is a *price taker*. It maximizes profits by adjusting its rate of output to a *given* market price. A monopolist, by contrast, *sets* the market price. Hence *a monopolist must make a pricing decision that perfectly competitive firms never make.*

Profit Maximization
In setting its price, the monopolist first identifies the profit-maximizing rate of output (the production decision) and then determines what price is compatible with that much output.

profit maximization rule
Produce at that rate of output where marginal revenue equals marginal cost.

To find the best rate of output, a monopolist will follow the general **profit maximization rule** about equating marginal cost (what an additional unit costs to produce) and marginal revenue (how much more revenue an additional unit brings in). Hence *a monopolist maximizes profits at the rate of output where MR = MC.*

Note that competitive firms actually do the same thing. In their case, MR and price are identical. Hence a competitive firm maximizes profits where $MC = MR = p$. Thus the general profit maximization rule (MR = MC) applies to *all* firms; only those firms that are perfectly competitive use the special case of $MC = p = MR$.

FIGURE 7.2
Profit Maximization

The most profitable rate of output is indicated by the intersection of marginal revenue and marginal cost (point *d*). In this case, marginal revenue and marginal cost intersect at an output of four pounds per hour.

Point *D* indicates that consumers will pay $10 per pound for this much output. Total profits equal price ($10) minus average total cost ($8), multiplied by the quantity sold (4).

The Production Decision

Figure 7.2 shows how a monopolist applies the profit maximization rule to the **production decision.** The demand curve represents the market demand for catfish; the marginal revenue curve is derived from it, as shown in Figure 7.1. The marginal cost curve in Figure 7.2 represents the costs incurred by Universal Fish in supplying the market. As we've seen before, the MC curve slopes upward. Universal's goal is to use these curves to find the one rate of output that maximizes total profit.

Competitive firms make the production decision by locating the intersection of marginal cost and price. A monopolist, however, looks for the rate of output at which marginal cost equals marginal revenue. This is illustrated in Figure 7.2 by the intersection of the MR and MC curves (point *d*). Looking down from that intersection, we see that the associated rate of output is four pounds per hour. Thus four pounds is the profit-maximizing rate of output for this monopoly: the only rate of output where MC=MR.

production decision The selection of the short-run rate of output (with existing plant and equipment).

The Monopoly Price

How much should Universal Fish charge for these four pounds of fish? Naturally, the monopolist would like to charge a very high price. But its ability to charge a high price is limited by the demand curve. The demand curve always tells us the *most* consumers are willing to pay for any given quantity. Once we have determined the quantity that is going to be supplied (four pounds per hour), we can look at the demand curve to determine the price ($10 at point *D*) that consumers will pay for these catfish. That is to say,

- *The intersection of the marginal revenue and marginal cost curves (point d) establishes the profit-maximizing rate of output.*
- *The demand curve tells us the highest price consumers are willing to pay for that specific quantity of output (point D).*

If Universal Fish ignored these principles and tried to charge $13 per pound, consumers would buy only one pound, leaving it with three unsold pounds of fish. As the monopolist will soon learn, *only one price is compatible with the profit-maximizing rate of output.* In this case the price is $10. This price is found in Figure 7.2 by moving up from the intersection of MR = MC until reaching the demand curve at point D. Point D tells us that consumers are able and willing to buy exactly four pounds of fish per hour at the price of $10 each. A monopolist that tries to charge more than $10 will not be able to sell all four pounds of fish. That could turn out to be a smelly and unprofitable situation.

Monopoly Profits

Also illustrated in Figure 7.2 are the total profits of the Universal Fish monopoly. To compute total profits, we again take advantage of the average total cost (ATC) curve. The distance between the price (point D) and ATC at the output rate of 4 represents profit *per unit*. In this case, profit per unit is $2 (price of $10 minus ATC of $8). Multiplying profit per unit ($2) by the quantity sold (4) gives us total profits of $8 per hour, as illustrated by the shaded rectangle.

We could also compute total profit by comparing *total* revenue and *total* cost. Total revenue at $q = 4$ is price ($10) times quantity (4), or $40. Total cost is quantity (4) times average total cost ($8), or $32. Subtracting total cost ($32) from total revenue ($40) gives us the total profit of $8 per hour already illustrated in Figure 7.2.

BARRIERS TO ENTRY

The profits attained by Universal Fish as a result of its monopoly position are not the end of the story. As we observed earlier, the existence of economic profit tends to bring profit-hungry entrepreneurs swarming. Indeed, in the competitive catfish industry of Chapter 6, the lure of high profits brought about an enormous expansion in domestic catfish farming, a flood of imported fish, and a steep decline in catfish prices. What, then, can we expect to happen in the catfish industry now that Universal has a monopoly position and is enjoying economic profits?

The consequences of monopoly on prices and output can be seen in Figure 7.3. In this case, we must compare monopoly behavior to that of a competitive *industry*. Remember that a monopoly is a single firm that constitutes the entire industry. What we want to depict, then, is how a different market structure (perfect competition) would alter industry prices and the quantity supplied.

If a *competitive* industry were producing at point D it too would be generating an economic profit with the costs shown in Figure 7.3. A competitive industry would not stay at that rate of output, however. All the firms in a competitive industry try to maximize profits by equating price and marginal cost. But at point D, price exceeds marginal cost. Hence a competitive industry would quickly move from point D (the monopolist's equilibrium) to point E, where marginal cost and price are equal. At point E (the short-run competitive equilibrium), more fish are supplied, their price is lower, and industry profits are smaller.

Threat of Entry

At point E, catfish farming is still profitable, since price ($9) exceeds average cost ($8) at that rate of production. Although total profits at the competitive point E

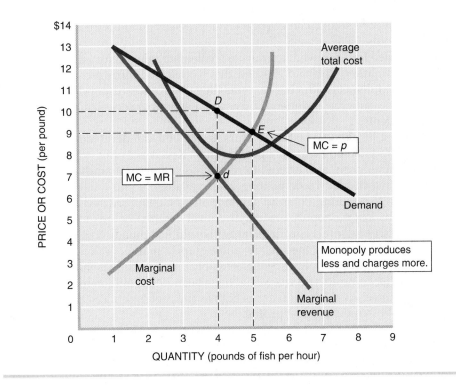

FIGURE 7.3
Monopoly versus
Competitive Outcomes

A monopoly will produce at the rate of output where MR = MC. A competitive industry will produce where MC = p. Hence a monopolist produces less (q = 4) than a competitive industry (q = 5). It also charges a higher price ($10 versus $9).

($5 per hour) are less than at the monopolist's point *D* ($8 per hour), they are still attractive. These remaining profits will lure more entrepreneurs into a competitive industry. As more firms enter, the market supply curve will shift to the right, driving prices down further. As we observed in Chapter 6, output will increase and prices will decline until all economic profit is eliminated and entry ceases (long-run competitive equilibrium).

Will this sequence of events occur in a monopoly? Absolutely not. Remember that Universal Fish is now assumed to have an exclusive patent on oxygenating equipment and can use this patent as an impassable barrier to entry. Consequently, would-be competitors can swarm around Universal's profits until their wings drop off; Universal is not about to let them in on the spoils. Universal Fish has the power to maintain production and price at point *D* in Figure 7.3. In the absence of competition, monopoly outcomes won't budge. We conclude, therefore, that *a monopoly attains higher prices and profits by restricting output.*

The secret to a monopoly's success lies in its **barriers to entry.** So long as entry barriers exist, a monopoly can control (restrict) the quantity of goods supplied. The barrier to entry in this catfish saga is the patent on oxygenating equipment. Without access to that technology, would-be catfish farmers must continue to farm cotton or other crops.

barriers to entry Obstacles that make it difficult or impossible for would-be producers to enter a particular market, e.g., patents.

Patent Protection: Polaroid versus Kodak

A patent was also the source of monopoly power in the historic battle between Polaroid and Eastman Kodak. Edwin Land invented the instant development camera in 1947 and got a patent on his invention. Over the subsequent 29 years, the company he founded was the sole supplier of instant photography cameras and racked up billions of dollars in profits.

Polaroid's huge profits were too great a prize to ignore. In 1976 the Eastman Kodak Company decided to enter the market with an instant camera of its own.

The availability of a second camera quickly depressed camera prices and squeezed Polaroid's profits.

Polaroid cried foul and went to court to challenge Kodak's entry into the instant photography market. Polaroid claimed that Kodak had infringed on Polaroid's patent rights and was producing cameras illegally. Kodak responded that it had developed its cameras independently and used no processes protected by Polaroid's patents.

The ensuing legal battle lasted 14 years. In the end, a federal judge concluded that Kodak had violated Polaroid's patent rights. Kodak not only stopped producing instant cameras but also offered to repurchase all of the 16 million cameras it had sold (for which film would no longer be available).

In addition to restoring Polaroid's monopoly, the court ordered Kodak to pay Polaroid for its lost monopoly profits. The court essentially looked at Figure 7.3 and figured out how much profit Polaroid would have made had it enjoyed an undisturbed monopoly in the instant photography market. Prices would have been higher, output lower, and profits greater. Using such reasoning, the judge determined that Polaroid's profits would have been $909.5 million higher if Kodak had never entered the market—*twice* as high as the profits actually earned. Kodak had to repay Polaroid these lost profits.

Although Polaroid won the legal battle, consumers ended up losing. What the Kodak entry demonstrated was how just a little competition (a second firm) can push consumer prices down, broaden consumer options, and improve product quality. Once its monopoly was restored, Polaroid didn't have to try as hard to satisfy consumer desires.

Other Entry Barriers

Patents are a highly visible and effective barrier. There are numerous other ways of keeping potential competitors at bay, however.

LEGAL HARASSMENT An increasingly effective way of suppressing competition is to sue new entrants. Even if a new competitor hasn't infringed on a monopolist's patents or trademarks, it is still fair game for legal challenges. Recall that Kodak spent 14 years battling Polaroid in court. Small firms can't afford all that legal skirmishing. When Napster, one of the first companies to offer free music downloads, got sued for copyright infringement in 2000, its fate was sealed. It simply didn't have the revenues needed to wage an extended legal battle. Even before the court ruled against it, Napster chose to compromise rather than fight. Because lengthy legal battles are so expensive, even the *threat* of legal action may dissuade entrepreneurs from entering a monopolized market. Kazaa customers were scared away from using its music file-sharing network when the record companies filed suit against 261 download users in 2003. Linux sales were also slowed by legal threats, as the following News Wire explains.

EXCLUSIVE LICENSING Nintendo allegedly used another tactic to control the video game market in the early 1990s. Nintendo forbade game creators from writing software for competing firms. Such exclusive licensing made it difficult for potential competitors to acquire the factors of production (game developers) they needed to compete against Nintendo. Only after the giant electronics company Sony entered the market in 1995 with new technology (PlayStation) did Nintendo have to share its monopoly profits.

| NEWS WIRE | BARRIERS TO ENTRY |

SCO Suit May Blunt the Potential of Linux

SCO Group Inc., the software firm that has accused industry giant IBM Corp. of stealing its trade secrets and incorporating them into the Linux operating system, has begun showing the allegedly pilfered code to analysts in an attempt to convince the industry that it has a strong case.

While the facts of the SCO-IBM case may be impenetrable to most who don't write programs, the possible ramifications are undeniable: The free Linux system might not be free anymore and, as a result, might not live up to its hoped-for potential as a formidable threat to Microsoft.

Some in the Linux camp accuse Microsoft of trying to scare potential users away from Linux by sowing doubt about its future as a free operating system.

SCO's aggressive stance is having at least some effect on companies considering making the switch to Linux, software writers and buyers said. It "puts fear" into the minds of chief information officers, said Chris Yeun, a systems administrator at Silicon Valley firm Electronics for Imaging, which is shifting from software from Sun and Silicon Graphics Inc. to Linux.

—Joseph Menn

Source: *Los Angeles Times*, June 6, 2003, used with permission.

NOTE: Legal action—or even the *threat* of legal action—may dissuade a firm from entering an industry or its customers from buying its product.

BUNDLED PRODUCTS   Another way to thwart competition is to force consumers to purchase complementary products. The U.S. Justice Department repeatedly accused Microsoft Corporation of "bundling" its applications software (e.g., Internet Explorer) with its Windows operating software. With a near monopoly on operating systems, Microsoft could charge a high price for Windows and then give "free" applications software with each system. Such bundling makes it almost impossible for potential competitors in the *applications* market to sell their products at a profitable price. The following News Wire cites this practice as one of the many "oppressive" tactics that Microsoft used to protect and exploit its monopoly position. Bundling helped Microsoft gain 96 percent of the Internet browser market (displacing Netscape), 94 percent of the office suites markets (displacing Word Perfect), and an increased share of money management applications (gaining on Intuit). The federal courts concluded that consumers would have enjoyed better products and lower prices had the market for computer operating systems been more competitive. In 2009 European Union regulators required Microsoft to give consumers a choice of web browsers.

When Microsoft started bundling its Media Player with its Windows operating system, the same concern over entry barriers came to the fore again. This time the European Union really cracked down. It fined Microsoft $600 million and required the company to offer both bundled and unbundled versions of Windows. In 2005 Microsoft started doing exactly that. But it continued to offer *free* downloads of Media Player via the Internet.

GOVERNMENT FRANCHISES   In many cases, a monopoly persists just because the government gave a single firm the exclusive right to produce a particular good in a specific market. The entry barrier here is not a patent on a product but instead an

---

NEWS WIRE	BARRIERS TO ENTRY

Judge Says Microsoft Broke Antitrust Law

A federal judge yesterday found Microsoft Corp. guilty of violating antitrust law by waging a campaign to crush threats to its Windows monopoly, a severe verdict that opens the door for the government to seek a breakup of one of the most successful companies in history.

Saying that Microsoft put an "oppressive thumb on the scale of competitive fortune," U.S. District Judge Thomas Penfield Jackson gave the Justice Department and 19 states near-total victory in their lawsuit. His ruling puts a black mark on the reputation of a software giant that has been the starter engine of the "new economy."

"Microsoft mounted a deliberate assault upon entrepreneurial efforts that, left to rise or fall on their own merits, could well have enabled the introduction of competition into the market for Intel-compatible PC operating systems," Jackson said.

In blunt language, Jackson depicted a powerful and predatory company that employed a wide array of tactics to destroy any innovation that posed a danger to the dominance of Windows. Among the victims were corporate stars of the multibillion-dollar computer industry: Intel Corp., Apple Computer Inc., International Business Machines Corp., and RealNetworks Inc.

To crush the competitive threat posed by the Internet browser, Jackson ruled, Microsoft integrated its own Internet browser into its Windows operating system "to quell incipient competition," bullied computer makers into carrying Microsoft's browser by threatening to withhold price discounts, and demanded that computer makers not feature rival Netscape's browser in the PC desktop as a condition of licensing the Windows operating system.

"Only when the separate categories of conduct are viewed, as they should be, as a single, well-coordinated course of action does the full extent of the violence that Microsoft has done to the competitive process reveal itself," Jackson wrote in the 43-page ruling. . . .

—James V. Grimaldi

Source: *The Washington Post*, April 4, 2000, © 2000 Washington Post Company. All rights reserved.

NOTE: Microsoft tried to keep competitors out of its operating system and applications software markets by erecting various barriers to entry. This behavior slowed innovation, restricted consumer choices, and kept prices too high.

---

exclusive franchise to sell that product. Local cable and telephone companies are often franchised monopolies. So is the U.S. Postal Service in the provision of first-class mail. Your campus bookstore might also have exclusive rights to sell textbooks on campus.

COMPARATIVE OUTCOMES

These and other entry barriers are the ultimate sources of monopoly power. With that power, monopolies can change the way the market responds to consumer demands.

Competition versus Monopoly

By way of summary, we recount the different ways in which perfectly competitive and monopolized markets behave. The likely sequence of events that occurs in each type of market structure is as follows:

Topic Podcast:
Monopoly Behavior

Competitive Industry	Monopoly Industry
• High prices and profits signal consumers' demand for more output.	• High prices and profits signal consumers' demand for more output.
• The high profits attract new suppliers.	• Barriers to entry are erected to exclude potential competition.
• Production and supplies expand.	• Production and supplies are constrained.
• Prices slide down the market demand curve.	• Prices don't move down the market demand curve.
• A new equilibrium is established in which more of the desired product is produced, its price falls, average costs of production approach their minimum, and economic profits approach zero.	• No new equilibrium is established, average costs are not necessarily at or near a minimum, and economic profits are at a maximum.
• Price equals marginal cost throughout the process.	• Price exceeds marginal cost at all times.
• Throughout the process, there is great pressure to keep ahead of the profit squeeze by reducing costs or improving product quality.	• There is no squeeze on profits and thus no pressure to reduce costs or improve product quality.

Near Monopolies

These comparative sequences aren't always followed exactly. Nor is the monopoly sequence available only to a single firm. In reality, two or more firms may rig the market to replicate monopoly outcomes and profits.

DUOPOLY   In a duopoly there are two firms rather than only one. They may literally be the only two firms in the market, or two firms may so dominate the market that they can still control price and output even if other firms are present.

How would you expect duopolists to behave? Will they slug it out, driving prices and profits down to competitive levels? Or will they recognize that less intense competition will preserve industry profits? If they behave like true competitors, they risk losing economic profits. If they work together, they assure themselves a continuing share of monopoly-like profits.

The two giant auction houses, Sotheby's and Christie's, figured out which strategy made more sense. Together the two companies control 90 percent of the $4 billion auction market. Rather than compete for sales by offering lower prices to potential sellers, Sotheby's and Christie's agreed to fix commission prices at a high level. When they got caught in 2000, the two firms agreed to pay a $512 million fine to auction customers.

OLIGOPOLY   In an oligopoly, *several* firms (rather than one or two) control the market. Here, too, the strategic choice is whether to compete feverishly or

NEWS WIRE	MIMICKING MONOPOLY

OPEC Keeps Output Target on Hold amid Weak Economy

VIENNA—OPEC ministers agreed to keep their daily crude production target unchanged at a meeting Wednesday. . . .

The agreement to leave the production ceiling at 30 million barrels a day was expected. . . .

The decision to keep to the present production target reflected most OPEC nations' belief that prices remain high enough to keep sales profitable, despite the weak global economy.

Benchmark crude for January delivery was up 70 cents to $86.49 a barrel in electronic trading on the New York Mercantile Exchange, gaining for the second day after falling for five straight sessions.

—George Jahn

Source: Associated Press, December 12, 2012. Used with permission of The Associated Press Copyright © 2012. All rights reserved.

NOTE: The 12 member-nations of OPEC collectively set their combined rate of output. In doing so, they are trying to duplicate monopoly outcomes.

live somewhat more comfortably. To the extent that the dominant firms recognize their mutual interest in higher prices and profits, they may avoid the kind of price competition common in perfectly competitive industries. Coca-Cola and Pepsi, for example, much prefer to use clever advertising rather than lower prices to lure customers away from each other. With 75 percent of industry sales between them, Coke and Pepsi realize that price competition is a no-win strategy.

In some instances, an oligopoly may have explicit limits on production and price. The 12 nations that constitute the Organization of Petroleum Exporting Countries (OPEC), for example, meet every six months or so to limit output (quantity supplied) and maintain a high price for oil (see the accompanying News Wire). OPEC operates outside U.S. borders and is therefore immune to U.S. laws against price fixing. The record industry doesn't enjoy such immunity, however. In October 2002 eight music companies agreed to refund $67.4 million to consumers for inflating CD prices at Tower Records, Musicland Stores, and Trans World Entertainment (see the News Wire on the next page).

MONOPOLISTIC COMPETITION   Starbucks, too, has the power to set prices for its products even though many other firms sell coffee. But it has much less power than Coca-Cola or OPEC because many firms sell coffee. A market made up of many firms, each of which has some distinct brand image, is called *monopolistic competition*. Each company has a monopoly on its brand image but still must contend with competing brands. This is still very different from *perfect* competition, in which no firm has a distinct brand image or price-setting power. As a result, any industry dominated by relatively few firms is likely to behave more like a monopoly than like perfect competition.

WHAT Gets Produced

To the extent that dominating firms behave as we have discussed, they alter the output of goods and services in two specific ways. You remember that competitive industries tend, in the long run, to produce at minimum average total costs. Competitive industries also pursue cost reductions and product improvements relentlessly. These pressures tend to expand our production possibilities and

NEWS WIRE	PRICE FIXING

Music Firms Settle Lawsuit
Refund Pact Ends CD Price-Fixing Case

Five of the nation's largest music companies and three of the biggest music retailers agreed to refund $67.4 million to consumers some time next year to settle a multi-state price-fixing lawsuit involving the sale of music on compact discs.

The lawsuit, filed in August 2000, alleges that for five years the music companies and the retailers had an illegal marketing agreement that stifled competition and inflated prices for CDs sold at Tower Records, Musicland Stores, and Trans World Entertainment.

Under the arrangement, the record companies would subsidize the cost of advertisements, in-store displays, and other promotions if retailers advertised CDs at the minimum prices set by the companies, which they did, the lawsuit alleged.

Source: *The Washington Post*, October 1, 2002, © 2002 Washington Post Company. All rights reserved.

NOTE: When a handful of companies dominate an industry, they may conspire to fix prices at monopoly levels.

---

enrich our consumption choices. No such forces are at work in the monopoly we have discussed here. Hence there is a basic tendency for monopolies to inhibit economic growth and limit consumption choices.

Another important feature of competitive markets is their tendency toward **marginal cost pricing.** Marginal cost pricing is important to consumers because it informs consumers of the true opportunity costs of various goods. This allows us to choose the mix of output that delivers the most utility with available resources. In our monopoly example, however, consumers end up getting fewer catfish than they would like, while the economy continues to produce cotton and other goods that are less desired. Thus the mix of output shifted away from catfish when Universal took over the industry. The presence of a monopoly therefore alters society's answer to the question of WHAT to produce.

marginal cost pricing The offer (supply) of goods at prices equal to their marginal cost.

FOR WHOM

Monopoly also changes the answer to the FOR WHOM question. The reduced supply and higher price of catfish imply that some people will have to eat canned tuna instead of breaded catfish. The monopolist's restricted output will also reduce job opportunities in the South, leaving some families with less income. The monopolist will end up with fat profits and thus greater access to all goods and services.

HOW

Finally, monopoly may also alter the HOW response. Competitive firms are likely to seek out new ways of breeding, harvesting, and distributing catfish. A monopoly, however, can continue to make profits from existing equipment and technology. Accordingly, monopolies tend to inhibit technology—how things are produced—by keeping potential competition out of the market.

ANY REDEEMING QUALITIES?

Despite the strong case to be made against monopoly, it is conceivable that monopolies could also benefit society. One of the arguments made for concentrations of market power is that monopolies have greater ability to pursue research and development. Another is that the lure of monopoly power creates a tremendous incentive for invention and innovation. A third argument in defense of monopoly is that large companies can produce goods more efficiently than smaller firms. Finally, it is argued that even monopolies have to worry about *potential* competition and will behave accordingly. We must pause to reflect, then, on whether and how market power might be of some benefit to society.

Research and Development

In principle, monopolies are well positioned to undertake valuable research and development. First, such firms are sheltered from the constant pressure of competition. Second, they have the resources (monopoly profits) with which to carry out expensive R&D functions. The manager of a perfectly competitive firm, by contrast, has to worry about day-to-day production decisions and profit margins. As a result, she is unable to take the longer view necessary for significant research and development and could not afford to pursue such a view even if she could see it.

The basic problem with the R&D argument is that it says nothing about *incentives.* Although monopolists have a clear financial advantage in pursuing research and development, they have no clear incentive to do so. They can continue to make substantial profits just by maintaining market power. Research and development are not necessarily required for profitable survival. In fact, research and development that make existing products or plant and equipment obsolete run counter to a monopolist's vested interest and so may actually be suppressed.

In 2003 two drug companies admitted to paying a third company $100 million a year to suppress its new competing product. As the News Wire on the next page notes, consumers were paying $73 a month for medication that the third company could produce and sell for only $32 a month. In a truly competitive market, there would be too many firms to conspire in this way. Everyone would be scrambling to bring improved products to market.

Entrepreneurial Incentives

The second defense of market power tries to use the incentive argument in a novel way. As we observed in Chapter 6, every business is out to make a profit, and it is the quest for profits that keeps industries running. Thus, it is argued, even greater profit prizes will stimulate more entrepreneurial activity. Little Horatio Algers will work harder and longer if they can dream of one day possessing a whole monopoly.

The incentive argument for market power is enticing but not entirely convincing. After all, an innovator can make substantial profits in a competitive market, as it typically takes a considerable amount of time for the competition to catch up. Recall that the early birds did get the worm in the catfish industry in Chapter 6 even though profit margins were later squeezed. Hence it is not evident that the profit incentives available in a competitive industry are inadequate.

Economies of Scale

A third defense of market power is the most convincing. A large firm, it is argued, can produce goods at a lower unit (average) cost than a small firm. That is, there are **economies of scale** in production. Thus if we desire to produce goods in the most efficient way—with the least amount of resources per unit of output—we should encourage and maintain large firms.

Consider once again the comparison we made earlier between Universal Fish and the competitive catfish industry. We explicitly assumed that Universal confronted the same production costs as the competitive industry. Thus Universal

economies of scale Reductions in minimum average costs that come about through increases in the size (scale) of plant and equipment.

NEWS WIRE	R&D INCENTIVES

Two Drug Firms Agree to Settle Pricing Suit

ALBANY, NY, Jan. 27—Two drug companies have agreed to pay $80 million to settle allegations that they conspired to keep a cheaper, generic version of a blood pressure medication off the market.

Under the settlement announced today, Aventis Pharmaceuticals Inc. and Andrx Corp. will pay that amount to states, insurance companies, and consumers nationwide.

Consumers paid too much for the drugs Cardizem CD and its generic equivalents because the companies conspired to delay the marketing of cheaper competitors, said New York state Attorney General Eliot L. Spitzer.

Spitzer said that in 1998, the German pharmaceutical giant Hoechst—which merged with Rhone-Poulenc in 1999 to form Aventis—paid Andrx just under $100 million to not market a generic form of Cardizem CD for 11 months. The agreement was to be renewed annually, he said.

This "most craven form of anticompetitive behavior" kept the drug financially out of the reach of countless people, Spitzer said.

Consumer groups have said that Cardizem sales total about $700 million a year domestically. Users of Cardizem were paying about $73 a month for the drug when a generic cost about $32 a month.

—Michael Gormley

Source: Associated Press, January 28, 2003. Used with permission of The Associated Press Copyright © 2003. All rights reserved.

NOTE: A firm that dominates a market may not have sufficient incentive to improve its product or reduce costs. It may even try to suppress product improvements that weaken its monopoly hold.

was not able to produce catfish any more cheaply than the competitive counterpart, and we concerned ourselves only with the different production decisions made by competitive and monopolistic firms.

It is conceivable, however, that Universal Fish might use its size to achieve greater efficiency. Perhaps the firm could build one enormous pond and centralize all breeding, harvesting, and distributing activities. If successful, this centralization might reduce production costs, making Universal more efficient than a competitive industry composed of thousands of small farms (ponds).

Even though large firms *may* be able to achieve greater efficiencies than smaller firms, there is no assurance that they actually will. Increasing the size (scale) of a plant may actually *reduce* operating efficiency. Workers may feel alienated in a massive firm and perform below their potential. Centralization might also increase managerial red tape and increase costs. In evaluating the economies-of-scale argument for market power, then, we must recognize that *efficiency and size do not necessarily go hand in hand.* In fact, monopolies may generate *dis*economies of scale, producing at higher cost than a competitive industry.

Even where economies of scale do exist, there is no guarantee that consumers will benefit. Consider the case of multiplex theaters that offer multiple movie screens. Multiplex theaters have significant economies of scale (e.g., consolidated box office, advertising, snack bar, restrooms, projection) compared to single-screen theaters. Once they drive smaller theaters out of business, however, they rarely lower ticket prices.

natural monopoly An industry in which one firm can achieve economies of scale over the entire range of market supply.

Natural Monopolies

There is a special case where the economies-of-scale argument is potentially more persuasive. In this case—called **natural monopoly**—a single firm can produce the entire market supply more efficiently than any larger number of (smaller) firms. As the size (scale) of the one firm increases, its average total costs continue to fall. These economies of scale give the one large producer a decided advantage over would-be rivals. Hence economies of scale act as a "natural" barrier to entry.

Local telephone, cable, and utility services are classic examples of natural monopoly. They have extraordinarily high fixed costs (e.g., transmission lines and switches) and exceptionally small marginal costs. Hence average total costs keep declining as output expands. As a result, it is much cheaper to install one system of cable or phone lines than a maze of competing ones. Accordingly, a single telephone or power company can supply the market more efficiently than a large number of competing firms.

Although natural monopolies are economically desirable, they may be abused. We must ask whether and to what extent consumers are reaping some benefit from the efficiency a natural monopoly makes possible. Do consumers end up with lower prices, expanded output, and better service? Or does the monopoly tend to keep the benefits for itself in the form of higher profits, better wages, and more comfortable offices? Typically federal, state, and local governments are responsible for regulating natural monopolies to ensure that the benefits of increased efficiency are shared with consumers.

Contestable Markets

Governmental regulators are not necessarily the only force keeping monopolists in line. Even though a firm may produce the entire supply of a particular product at present, it may face *potential* competition from other firms. Potential rivals may be sitting on the sidelines, watching how well the monopoly fares. If it does too well, these rivals may enter the industry, undermining the monopoly structure and profits. In such **contestable markets,** monopoly behavior may be restrained by potential competition.

contestable market An imperfectly competitive industry subject to potential entry if prices or profits increase.

How contestable a market is depends not so much on its structure as on entry barriers. If entry barriers are insurmountable, would-be competitors are locked out of the market. But if entry barriers are modest, they will be surmounted when the lure of monopoly profits is irresistible. Foreign rivals already producing the same goods are particularly likely to enter domestic markets when monopoly prices and profits are high.

Structure versus Behavior

From the perspective of contestable markets, the whole case against monopoly is misconceived. Market *structure* per se is not a problem; what counts is market *behavior*. If potential rivals force a monopolist to behave like a competitive firm, then monopoly imposes no cost on consumers or on society at large.

The experience with the Model T Ford illustrates the basic notion of contestable markets. At the time Henry Ford decided to increase the price of the Model T and paint all Model Ts black, the Ford Motor Company enjoyed a virtual monopoly on mass-produced cars. But potential rivals saw the profitability of offering additional colors and features (e.g., self-starter, left-hand drive). When they began producing cars in volume, Ford's market power was greatly reduced. In 1926 the Ford Motor Company tried to regain its dominant position by again supplying cars in colors other than black. By that time, however, consumers had more choices. Ford ceased production of the Model T in May 1927.

The experience with the Model T suggests that potential competition can force a monopoly to change its ways. Critics point out, however, that even contestable markets don't force a monopolist to act exactly like a competitive firm. There will always be a gap between competitive outcomes and those monopoly outcomes likely to entice new entry. That gap can cost consumers a lot. The absence of *existing* rivals is also likely to inhibit product and productivity improvements. From 1913 to 1926, all Model Ts were black, and consumers had few alternatives. Ford changed its behavior only after *potential* competition became *actual* competition. Even after 1927, when the Ford Motor Company could no longer act like a monopolist, it still didn't price its cars at marginal cost.

POLICY PERSPECTIVES

Why Is Flying Monopoly Air Routes So Expensive?

Ever wonder why it's so cheap to fly to one place yet so expensive to fly somewhere else of equal distance? The answer is likely to be market structure. As we've observed in this and the previous chapter, the greater the number of firms in a market, the lower prices are likely to be. More competition also increases the quantity supplied.

INDUSTRY STRUCTURE   From a national perspective, the airline industry looks pretty competitive. Over 90 domestic airline companies offer scheduled passenger service, and at least 150 foreign carriers serve U.S. cities. So there are a lot of firms competing for the $100 billion that Americans spend annually on airline travel.

All those airlines don't fly to the places you want to go, however. If you're looking for a nonstop flight from Los Angeles to Palm Springs, don't bother calling US Airways, Northwest, or Delta, much less Air France. None of those firms fly that route. In fact, only one airline (United) was flying that route in 2013. Hence travelers in the Los Angeles–Palm Springs market end up paying monopoly fares.

How much it costs to fly depends on how many airlines compete.
Christopher Herwig

"We make money the old-fashioned way . . . first we undercut the competition into bankruptcy, and then we jack up the prices!"

NOTE: Predatory pricing—or even the threat of it—can be used to eliminate competition.

© Roy Delgado/Artizans.com

predatory pricing Temporary price reductions designed to drive out competition.

Travelers between Huntsville, Alabama, and Houston Intercontinental confront outright monopoly fares since only Continental flies that route. When other carriers entered the US Airways' monopoly Pittsburgh–Philadelphia route in 2005, the round-trip fare fell from $680 to $186.

When assessing market structure, it is essential to specify the relevant market. In this case the relevant market is best defined by specific intercity routes. The number of airlines serving a particular route is a far better measure of market power than the number of airlines flying anywhere. By this yardstick, the airline industry is beset with market power. In two-thirds of U.S. air routes, a single carrier accounts for at least half of all service. In "hub" airports the dominance of a single carrier is even greater. As a result of such high local concentrations, 1 out of 10 domestic routes is monopolized.

INDUSTRY BEHAVIOR If market structure really matters, airline fares should vary with the number of firms serving a particular route. And so they do. A study by the U.S. General Accounting Office (GAO) found that fares from airports dominated by one or two carriers were 45–85 percent higher than at more competitive airports.

ENTRY EFFECTS Another way to assess the impact of market structure on prices is to observe how airline fares *change* when airlines enter or exit a specific market. According to an antitrust suit filed by the U.S. Justice Department, American Airlines slashed fares whenever a new carrier entered a market it dominated. As soon as the new carrier was forced out of the market, American raised fares to monopoly levels again. The accompanying News Wire offers some examples of this **predatory pricing.**

NEWS WIRE	PREDATORY PRICING

Following the Fares

The Justice Department says American Airlines cut its fares when low-cost carriers arrived—then raised them when they left. Fares* shown are for 1995–1996 from the Dallas–Fort Worth airport to

	Colorado Springs	Wichita	Kansas City
Before low-cost	$180	$110	$113
Low-cost in the market	$88	$57	$83
After low-cost exit	$133	$96	$125

*Average for all local carriers, nonstop.
Source: The United States Department of Justice; U.S. v. AMR Corporation, American Airlines, Inc., and AMR Eagle Holding; www.justice.gov/atr/cases/f8100/8134.htm.

NOTE: A monopoly carrier may use a sharp but temporary cut in fares to drive a new entrant out of the market—or to discourage others from entering.

BARRIERS TO ENTRY For the largest carriers to maintain high profits on specific routes, they must be able to keep new firms from entering those markets. One of the most formidable entry barriers is their ownership of slots (landing rights) and gates. At Washington, DC's Reagan Airport, for example, the six largest carriers owned 97 percent of available takeoff/landing slots in 2000. To offer service from that airport, a new entrant would have to buy or lease a slot from one of them. It would also have to secure a gate so passengers could access the plane. Would-be competitors complain that the dominant carriers unfairly withhold access to slots and gates, thereby thwarting competition.

The U.S. Department of Transportation has examined options for giving would-be entrants more access to airline markets. One proposal envisions a lottery system for redistributing some slots. In a prior lottery, however, almost all the new entrants that were awarded slots simply resold them to the largest carriers, choosing quick, sure cash over uncertain competition. That left travelers with the all-too-familiar choice of either staying home or flying Monopoly Air.

SUMMARY

- Market power is the ability to influence the market price of goods and services. The extreme case of market power is monopoly, where only one firm produces the entire supply of a particular product. A monopolist selects the quantity to be supplied to the market and sets the market price.   **LO1**

- The distinguishing feature of any firm with market power is that the demand curve it faces is downward-sloping. In a monopoly, the demand curve facing the firm and the market demand curve are identical.   **LO1**

- The downward-sloping demand curve facing a monopolist creates a divergence between marginal revenue and price. To sell larger quantities of output, the monopolist must lower product prices. Marginal revenue is the *change* in total revenue divided by the *change* in output.   **LO2**

- A monopolist maximizes total profit at the rate of output at which marginal revenue equals marginal cost.   **LO3**

- A monopolist will produce less output than will a competitive industry confronting the same market demand and cost opportunities. That reduced rate of output will be sold at higher prices, in accordance with the (downward-sloping) market demand curve.   **LO4**

- A monopoly will attain a higher level of profit than a competitive industry because of its ability to equate industry (i.e., its own) marginal revenues and costs. By contrast, a competitive industry ends up equating marginal costs and *price* because its individual firms have no control over the market supply curve.   **LO4**

- Because the higher profits attained by a monopoly attract envious entrepreneurs, barriers to entry are needed to prohibit other firms from expanding market supplies. Patents are one such barrier to entry. Other barriers are legal harassment, exclusive licensing, product bundling, and government franchises.   **LO4**

- The defense of market power rests on (1) the ability of large firms to pursue research and development, (2) the incentives implicit in the chance to attain market power, (3) the efficiency that larger firms may attain, and (4) the contestability of even monopolized markets. The first two arguments are weakened by the fact that competitive firms are under much greater pressure to innovate and can stay ahead of the profit game only if they do so. The contestability defense at best concedes some amount of monopoly exploitation.   **LO5**

- A natural monopoly exists when one firm can produce the output of the entire industry more efficiently than can a number of smaller firms. This advantage is attained from economies of scale. Large firms are not necessarily more efficient, however.   **LO5**

TERMS TO REMEMBER

Define the following terms:

market power	marginal revenue (MR)	barriers to entry	contestable market
market demand	profit maximization	marginal cost pricing	predatory pricing
patent	rule	economies of scale	
monopoly	production decision	natural monopoly	

QUESTIONS FOR DISCUSSION

1. If you owned the only bookstore on or near campus, what would you charge for this textbook? How much would you pay students for their used books? **LO3**

2. Why don't competitive industries produce at the rate of output that maximizes industry profits, as a monopolist does? **LO4**

3. Is single ownership of a whole industry necessary to exercise monopoly power? How might an industry with several firms achieve the same result? Can you think of any examples? **LO1**

4. Despite its reaffirmed monopoly position (page 143–144), Polaroid went bankrupt in 2001 and stopped making instant development cameras in 2007. What happened? **LO4**

5. Why don't monopolists try to establish the highest price possible, as many people allege? What would happen to sales? To profits? **LO3**

6. What circumstances might cause a monopolist to charge less than the profit-maximizing price? **LO3**

7. How could free Media Player software (either bundled or downloaded with Windows) possibly harm consumers? **LO4**

8. What entry barriers exist in (a) the fast-food industry; (b) cable TV; (c) the auto industry; (d) illegal drug trade? **LO1**

9. Why would any firm pay another firm to *not* produce? (See the News Wire on page 151.) **LO4**

10. **POLICY PERSPECTIVES** What are the economies of scale in multiplex theaters? Why aren't their prices less than those of single-screen theaters? **LO5**

PROBLEMS

■ connect

1. In Figure 7.1, **LO2**
   (a) What is the highest price the monopolist could charge and still sell fish?
   (b) What is total revenue at that highest price?
   (c) What happens to total revenue as price is reduced from A to G?
   (d) What is the value of marginal revenue as price is reduced from F to G?

2. In Figure 7.1's graph, **LO3**
   (a) At what output rate is total revenue maximized?
   (b) What is MR at that output rate?

3. Use Figure 7.2 to answer the following questions: **LO2**
   (a) What rate of output maximizes total profit?
   (b) What is the MR at that rate of output?

   (c) What is the price?
   (d) If output is increased by 1 pound beyond that point, what is the relationship of MC to MR?
   (e) What happens to total profits?

4. Compute marginal revenues from the following data on market demand: **LO2**

Price per unit	$38	36	34	32	30	28	26
Units demanded	10	11	12	13	14	15	16
Marginal revenue	—	—	—	—	—	—	—

   (a) At what price does MR = 0?
   (b) At what price is MR < 0?
   (c) At what price is MR < p?

5. Suppose the following data represent the market demand for catfish: **LO2**

Price (per unit)	$20	19	18	17	16	15	14	13	12	11
Quantity demanded (units per day)	12	13	14	15	16	17	18	19	20	21
Total revenue	—	—	—	—	—	—	—	—	—	—
Marginal revenue	—	—	—	—	—	—	—	—	—	—

(a) Compute total and marginal revenue to complete the table above.

(b) At what rate of output is total revenue maximized?

(c) At what rate of output is MR less than price?

(d) At what rate of output does MR first become negative?

(e) Graph the demand and MR curves.

6. Assume that the following marginal costs exist in catfish production: **LO4**

Quantity produced (units per day)	10	11	12	13	14	15	16	17
Marginal cost (per unit)	$4	6	8	10	12	14	16	18

(a) Graph the MC curve.

(b) Use the data on market demand below and graph the demand and MR curves on the same graph.

Price (per unit)	$25	24	23	22	21	20	19	18
Quantity demanded (units per day)	10	11	12	13	14	15	16	17

(c) At what rate of output is MR = MC?

(d) What price will a monopolist charge for that much output?

(e) If the market were perfectly competitive, what price would prevail?

(f) How much output would be produced?

7. (a) According to the News Wire on p. 148, OPEC ministers agreed to keep their daily crude production target at what level?

(b) This explicit limit on production lead to how much of an immediate increase in price?   **LO3**

8. According to the News Wire on p. 151, how much profit per year per user might the producers of Cardizem have been making if their average total costs were equal to that of the generic substitute?   **LO4**

9. **POLICY PERSPECTIVES** If the on-campus demand for soda is as follows: **LO4**

Price (per can)	$0.25	0.50	0.75	1.00	1.25	1.50	1.75	2.00
Quantity demanded (per day)	100	90	80	70	60	50	40	30

and marginal cost of supplying a soda is 50 cents, what price will students end up paying in

(a) A perfectly competitive market?

(b) A monopolized market?

◄ Practice quizzes, student PowerPoints, author podcasts, and web activities, and additional materials available at **www.mhhe.com/schilleressentials9e**, or scan here. Need a barcode reader? Try ScanLife, available in your app store.

8

The Labor Market

◄ Practice quizzes, student PowerPoints, author podcasts, and web activities, additional materials available at www.mhhe.com/schilleressentials9e, or scan here. Need a barcode reader? Try ScanLife, available in your app store.

LEARNING OBJECTIVES

After reading this chapter, you should be able to:

1   Cite the forces that influence the supply of labor.
2   Explain why the labor demand curve slopes downward.
3   Describe how the equilibrium wage and employment level are determined.
4   Depict how a legal minimum wage alters market outcomes.
5   Explain why wages are so unequal.

D ale Earnhardt Jr. rakes in around $4.5 million a year from winning NASCAR races. But that's chump change for Dale Jr.: he gets another $25–30 million a year from product endorsements—everything from the National Guard (his primary sponsor at $20 million per year) to Barrel O'Fun potato chips and Dale Jr. "88" stogies. Yet the president of the United States gets paid only $400,000. And the secretary who typed the manuscript of this book was paid just $19,000. What accounts for these tremendous disparities in earnings?

And why is it that the average college graduate earns over $55,000 a year, while the average high school graduate earns just $32,000? Are such disparities simply a reward for enduring four years of college, or do they reflect real differences in talent? Are you really learning anything that makes you that much more valuable than a high school graduate? For that matter, what are you worth—not in metaphysical terms but in terms of the wages you would be paid in the marketplace?

If we are to explain why some people earn a great deal of income while others earn very little, we will have to consider both the *supply* and the *demand* for labor. In this regard, the following questions arise:

- How do people decide how much time to spend working?
- What determines the wage rate an employer is willing to pay?
- Why are some workers paid so much and others so little?

To answer these questions, we need to examine the behavior of labor *markets*.

LABOR SUPPLY

The following two ads appeared in the campus newspaper of a well-known university:

Will do ANYTHING for money: able-bodied liberal-minded male needs money, will work to get it. Have car. Call Tom 555-0244.

Web Architect: Computer sciences graduate, strong programming skills and software knowledge (e.g., Flash, DreamWeaver). Please call Margaret 555-3247, 9–5.

Although placed by individuals with very different talents, the ads clearly expressed Tom's and Margaret's willingness to work. We don't know how much money they were asking for their respective talents or whether they ever found jobs, but we can be sure that they were prepared to take a job at some wage rate. Otherwise they would not have paid for the ads in the "Jobs Wanted" column of their campus newspaper.

The advertised willingness to work expressed by Tom and Margaret represents a **labor supply.** They are offering to sell their time and talents to anyone who is willing to pay the right price. Their explicit offers are similar to those of anyone who looks for a job. Job seekers who check the current job openings at the student employment office or send résumés to potential employers are demonstrating a willingness to accept employment—that is, to *supply* labor. The 10,000 people who showed up at the Dodger Stadium job fair (see the following News Wire) were also offering to supply labor.

Our first concern in this chapter is to explain these labor supply decisions. As Figure 8.1 illustrates, we expect the quantity of labor supplied—the number of hours people are willing to work—to increase as wage rates rise.

But how do people decide how many hours to supply at any given wage rate? Do people try to maximize their income? If they did, we would all be holding three jobs and sleeping on the commuter bus. Few of us actually live this way. Hence we must have other goals than simply maximizing our incomes.

labor supply The willingness and ability to work specific amounts of time at alternative wage rates in a given time period, *ceteris paribus.*

NEWS WIRE	LABOR SUPPLY

Thousands of Hopeful Job Seekers Attend Career Fair at Rutgers

An estimated 3,000 job seekers attended the state's largest career fair Thursday, as economic indicators suggested that the employment picture might be brightening somewhat . . .

The fair, held at Rutgers University, drew mostly young, soon-to-be college graduates. But older workers armed with resumes also visited some of the 174 employers who attended on the university's College Avenue campus in New Brunswick.

—Patricia Alex

Source: © 2012 Patricia Alex/northjersey.com

NOTE: People supply labor by demonstrating a willingness to work. The quantity of labor supplied increases as the wage rate rises.

Income versus Leisure

The most visible benefit obtained from working is a paycheck. In general, the fatter the paycheck—the greater the wage rate offered—the more willing a person is to go to work.

As important as paychecks are, however, people recognize that working entails real sacrifices. Every hour we spend working implies one less hour available for other pursuits. If we go to work, we have less time to watch TV, go to a soccer game, or simply enjoy a nice day. In other words, there is a real **opportunity cost** associated with working. Generally, we say that *the opportunity cost of working is the amount of leisure time that must be given up in the process.*

Because both leisure and income are valued, we confront a trade-off when deciding whether to go to work. Going to work implies more income but less leisure. Staying home has the opposite consequences.

The inevitable trade-off between labor and leisure explains the shape of individual labor supply curves. As we work more hours, our leisure time becomes more scarce and thus more valuable. We become increasingly reluctant to give up any remaining leisure time as it gets scarcer. People who work all week long are reluctant to go to work on Saturday. It's not that they are physically exhausted. It's just

opportunity cost The most desired goods and services that are forgone in order to obtain something else.

FIGURE 8.1
The Supply of Labor

The quantity of any good or service offered for sale typically increases as its price rises. Labor supply responds in the same way. At the wage rate w_1, the quantity of labor supplied is q_1 (point A). At the higher wage w_2, workers are willing to work more hours per week—that is, to supply a larger quantity of labor (q_2).

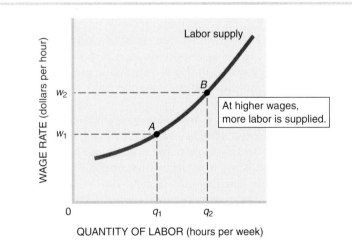

At higher wages, more labor is supplied.

that they want some time to enjoy the fruits of their labor. In other words, *as the opportunity cost of job time increases, we require correspondingly higher rates of pay.* We will supply additional labor—work more hours—only if higher wage rates are offered: this is the message conveyed by the upward-sloping labor supply curve.

The upward slope of the labor supply curve is reinforced with the changing value of income. Our primary motive for working is the income a job provides. Those first few dollars are really precious, especially if you have bills to pay. As you work and earn more, however, you discover that your most urgent needs have been satisfied. You may still want more things, but your consumption desires aren't so urgent. In other words, *the marginal utility of income declines as you earn more.* Accordingly, the wages offered for more work lose some of their allure. You may not be willing to work more hours unless offered a higher wage rate.

The upward slope of an individual's labor supply curve is thus a reflection of two phenomena:

* The increasing opportunity cost of labor.
* The decreasing marginal utility of income as a person works more hours.

Nearly one of every two U.S. workers now says he or she would be willing to give up some pay for more leisure. As wages and living standards have risen, the urge for more money has abated. What people want is more leisure time to *spend* their incomes. As a result, ever-higher wages are needed to lure people into working longer hours.

Money isn't necessarily the only thing that motivates people to work, of course. People *do* turn down higher-paying jobs in favor of lower-wage jobs that they like. Many parents forgo high-wage "career" jobs in order to have more flexible hours and time at home. Volunteers offer their services just for the sense of contributing to their communities; no paycheck is required. Even MBA graduates say they are motivated more by the challenge of high-paying jobs than by the money. When push comes to shove, however, money almost always makes a difference: people *do* supply more labor when offered higher wages.

Market Supply

The **market supply of labor** refers to all the hours people are willing to work at various wages. It, too, is upward-sloping. As wage rates rise, not only do existing workers offer to work longer hours but other workers are drawn into the labor market as well. If jobs are plentiful and wages high, many students leave school and start working. Likewise, many homemakers decide that work outside the home is too hard to resist. The flow of immigrants into the labor market also increases when wages are high. As these various flows of labor market entrants increase, the total quantity of labor supplied to the market goes up.

market supply of labor The total quantity of labor that workers are willing and able to supply at alternative wage rates in a given time period, *ceteris paribus.*

LABOR DEMAND

Regardless of how many people are *willing* to work, it is up to employers to decide how many people will *actually* work. Employers must be willing and able to hire workers if people are going to find the jobs they seek. That is to say, there must be a **demand for labor.**

The demand for labor is readily visible in the help wanted section of the newspaper or the listings at Monster.com, CareerBuilder.com, and other online job sites. Employers who pay for these ads are willing and able to hire a certain number of workers at specific wage rates. How do they decide what to pay or how many people to hire?

demand for labor The quantities of labor employers are willing and able to hire at alternative wage rates in a given time period, *ceteris paribus.*

Derived Demand

In earlier chapters we emphasized that employers are profit maximizers. In their quest for maximum profits, firms seek the rate of output at which marginal revenue equals marginal cost. Once they have identified the profit-maximizing rate of output, firms enter factor markets to purchase the required amounts of labor, equipment, and

---

NEWS WIRE | DERIVED DEMAND

HP to Cut 27,000 Jobs

Hewlett-Packard Co., battered by declining profits and tech rivals with flashier handheld devices, is slashing 27,000 jobs, or 8 percent of its workforce.

The Silicon Valley tech firm, one of the world's largest computer makers with nearly 325,000 employees, said the job reductions—through layoffs and a voluntary early retirement program—would occur by the end of fiscal 2014. The cuts are expected to save the company $3 billion to $3.5 billion annually. . . .

The company has seen customer demand for its PCs plummet in favor of tablets and smartphones made by Apple Inc. and other competitors. Analysts have criticized the company for its lack of direction and for developing products too late. Profits and employee morale have eroded, and instability at the top has added to HP's woes; last fall Whitman became the firm's fourth CEO in little more than a year.

The McGraw-Hill Companies, Inc./
Christopher Kerrigan, photographer

— W.J. Hennigan and Andrea Chang

Source: Los Angeles Times, November 2, 2008. Used with permission.

NOTE: A firm's demand for labor depends on the demand for the products the firm produces.

---

derived demand The demand for labor and other factors of production results from (depends on) the demand for final goods and services produced by these factors.

other resources. Thus *the quantity of resources purchased by a business depends on the firm's expected sales and output.* In this sense, we say that the demand for factors of production, including labor, is a **derived demand;** it is derived from the demand for goods and services. As 27,000 employees of Hewlett-Packard learned in 2012–2014, when the demand for personal computers declines, so does the demand for the workers who manufacture those machines (see above News Wire).

Consider also the plight of strawberry pickers. Strawberry farming is a $2 billion industry. Yet the thousands of pickers who toil in the fields earn only $8 an hour. The United Farm Workers union blames greedy growers for the low wages. They say if the farmers would only raise the price of strawberries by a nickel a pint, they could raise wages by 50 percent.

Unfortunately, employer greed is not the only force at work here. Strawberry growers, like most producers, would love to sell more strawberries at higher prices. If they did, there is a strong possibility that the growers would hire more pickers and even pay them a higher wage rate. But the growers must contend with the market demand for strawberries. If they increase the price of strawberries—even by only 5 cents a pint—the quantity of berries demanded will decline. They'd end up hiring fewer workers. If profits declined, wage rates might suffer as well.

The link between the product market and the labor market also explains why graduates with engineering or computer science degrees are paid so much (see the following News Wire). Demand for related products is growing so fast that employers are desperate to hire individuals with the necessary skills. By contrast, the wages of philosophy majors suffer from the fact that the search for meaning is no longer a growth industry.

The principle of derived demand suggests that if consumers really want to improve the lot of strawberry pickers, they should eat more strawberries. An increase in consumer demand for strawberries will motivate growers to plant more berries and hire more labor to pick them. Until then, the plight of the pickers is not likely to improve.

| NEWS WIRE | UNEQUAL WAGES |

Most Lucrative College Degrees

NEW YORK—Math majors don't always get much respect on college campuses, but fat postgrad wallets should be enough to give them a boost.

The top 15 highest-earning college degrees all have one thing in common—math skills. That's according to a recent survey from the National Association of Colleges and Employers, which tracks college graduates' job offers.

What happened to well-rounded? There are far fewer people graduating with math-based majors, compared to their liberal arts counterparts, which is why they are paid at such a premium. The fields of engineering and computer science each make up about 4 percent of all college graduates, while social science and history each comprise 16 percent. . . .

"It's a supply and demand issue," he added. "So few grads offer math skills, and those who can are rewarded."

—Julianne Pepitone

Source: CNNMoney.com, July 24, 2009 © 2009 Time Inc. Used under license.

What Does Your Major Pay? 2012–2013 Survey

Major	Median Starting Salary
Petroleum engineering	$98,000
Chemical engineering	67,500
Computer science	58,400
Civil engineering	53,800
Management info systems	51,600
Economics	**48,500**
Finance	47,700
Accounting	44,300
Business	41,400
Political science	40,300
Marketing	39,000
History	39,000
Philosophy	38,300
English	38,100
Sociology	36,000

Source: "PayScale College Salary Report," www.PayScale.com, 2013. Used with permission of PayScale, Inc.

NOTE: The pay of college graduates depends in part on what major they studied. Graduates who can produce goods and services in great demand get the highest pay.

THE WAGE RATE   The number of strawberry pickers hired by the growers is not completely determined by consumer demand for strawberries. A farmer with tons of strawberries to harvest might still be reluctant to hire many workers at $30 an hour. At $8 per hour, however, the same farmer would hire a lot of help. That is to say, *the quantity of labor demanded will depend on its price (the wage rate).* In general, we expect that strawberry growers will be *willing to hire* more pickers at low wages than at high wages. Hence the demand for labor is not a fixed quantity; instead there is a varying relationship between quantity demanded and price (wage rate). Like virtually all other demand curves, the labor demand curve is downward-sloping (see Figure 8.2).

FIGURE 8.2

The Demand for Labor

The higher the wage rate, the smaller the quantity of labor demanded (*ceteris paribus*). At the wage rate W_1, only L_1 of labor is demanded (point *A*). If the wage rate falls to W_2, a larger quantity of labor (L_2) will be demanded. The labor demand curve obeys the law of demand.

Marginal Physical Product

The downward slope of the labor demand curve reflects the changing productivity of workers as more are hired. Each worker isn't as valuable as the last. On the contrary, each additional worker tends to be *less* valuable as more workers are hired. In the strawberry fields, a worker's value is measured by the number of boxes he or she can pick in an hour. More generally, we measure a worker's value to the firm by his or her **marginal physical product (MPP)**—that is, the *change* in total output that occurs when an additional worker is hired. In most situations, *marginal physical product declines as more workers are hired.*

Suppose for the moment that Marvin, a college dropout with three summers of experience as a canoe instructor, can pick five boxes of strawberries per hour. These five boxes represent Marvin's marginal physical product (MPP)—in other words, the *addition* to total output that occurs when the grower hires Marvin:

marginal physical product (MPP) The change in total output associated with one additional unit of input.

$$\text{Marginal physical product} = \frac{\text{change in total output}}{\text{change in quantity of labor}}$$

Marginal physical product establishes an *upper limit* to the grower's willingness to pay. Clearly the grower can't afford to pay Marvin more than five boxes of strawberries for an hour's work; the grower will not pay Marvin more than he produces.

Marginal Revenue Product

Most strawberry pickers don't want to be paid in strawberries, of course. At the end of a day in the fields, the last thing a picker wants to see is another strawberry. Marvin, like the rest of the pickers, wants to be paid in cash. To find out how much cash he might be paid, all we need to know is what a box of strawberries is worth. This is easy to determine. The market value of a box of strawberries is simply the price at which the grower can sell it. Thus Marvin's contribution to output can be measured in either marginal *physical* product (five boxes per hour) or the dollar *value* of that product.

The dollar value of a worker's contribution to output is called **marginal revenue product (MRP).** Marginal revenue product is the change in total revenue that occurs when more labor is hired:

marginal revenue product (MRP) The change in total revenue associated with one additional unit of input.

$$\text{Marginal revenue product} = \frac{\text{change in total revenue}}{\text{change in quantity of labor}}$$

If the grower can sell strawberries for $2 a box, Marvin's marginal revenue product is five boxes per hour × $2 per box, or $10 per hour. This is Marvin's value to the grower. Accordingly, the grower can afford to pay Marvin up to $10 per hour. Thus *marginal revenue product sets an upper limit to the wage rate an employer will pay.*

But what about a lower limit? Suppose that the pickers aren't organized and that Marvin is desperate for money. Under such circumstances, he might be willing to work—to supply labor—for only $6 an hour.

Should the grower hire Marvin for such a low wage? The profit-maximizing answer is obvious. If Marvin's marginal revenue product is $10 an hour and his wages are only $6 an hour, the grower will be eager to hire him. The difference between Marvin's marginal revenue product ($10) and his wage ($6) implies additional profits of $4 an hour. In fact, the grower will be so elated by the economics of this situation that he will want to hire everybody he can find who is willing to work for $6 an hour. After all, if the grower can make $4 an hour by hiring Marvin, why not hire 1,000 pickers and accumulate profits at an even faster rate?

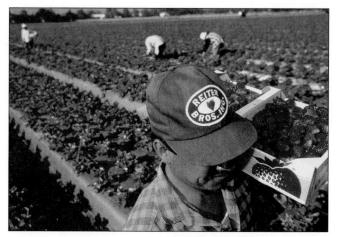

The 25,000 pickers who harvest America's $2 billion strawberry crop are paid only $8 an hour. Why is their pay so low?

© David Butow/Corbis/SABA

The Law of Diminishing Returns

The exploitive possibilities suggested by Marvin's picking are too good to be true. For starters, how could the grower squeeze 1,000 workers onto one acre of land and still have any room left over for strawberry plants? You don't need two years of business school to recognize a potential problem here. Sooner or later the farmer will run out of space. Even before that limit is reached, the rate of strawberry picking may slow. Indeed, the grower's eagerness to hire additional pickers will begin to fade long before 1,000 workers are hired. The critical concept here is *marginal productivity.*

DIMINISHING MPP   The decision to hire Marvin originated in his marginal physical product—that is, the five boxes of strawberries he can pick in an hour's time. To assess the wisdom of hiring additional pickers, we have to consider what happens to total output as more workers are employed. To do so, we need to keep track of marginal physical product.

Figure 8.3 shows how strawberry output changes as additional pickers are hired. We start with Marvin, who picks five boxes of strawberries per hour. Total output and his marginal physical product are identical because he is initially the only picker employed. When the grower hires George, Marvin's old college roommate, we observe that the total output increases to 10 boxes per hour (point *B* in Figure 8.3). This figure represents another increase of five boxes per hour. Accordingly, we may conclude that George's *marginal physical product* is five boxes per hour, the same as Marvin's. Naturally, the grower will want to hire George and continue looking for more pickers.

As more workers are hired, total strawberry output continues to increase, but not nearly as fast. Although the later hires work just as hard, the limited availability of land and capital constrains their marginal physical product. One problem is the number of boxes. There are only a dozen boxes, and the additional pickers often have to wait for an empty box. The time spent waiting depresses marginal physical product. The worst problem is space: as additional workers are crowded onto the one-acre patch, they begin to get in one another's way. The picking process is slowed, and marginal physical product is further depressed. Note that the MPP of the fifth picker is two boxes per hour, while the MPP of the sixth picker is only one box per hour. By the time we get to the seventh picker, marginal physical product actually falls to zero—no further increases in total strawberry output take place.

FIGURE 8.3
Diminishing Marginal Physical Product

The marginal physical product of labor is the increase in total production that results when one additional worker is hired. Marginal physical product tends to fall as additional workers are hired. This decline occurs because each worker has increasingly less of other factors (e.g., land) with which to work.

When the second worker (George) is hired, total output increases from 5 to 10 boxes per hour. Hence the second worker's MPP equals five boxes per hour. Thereafter, capital and land constraints diminish marginal physical product.

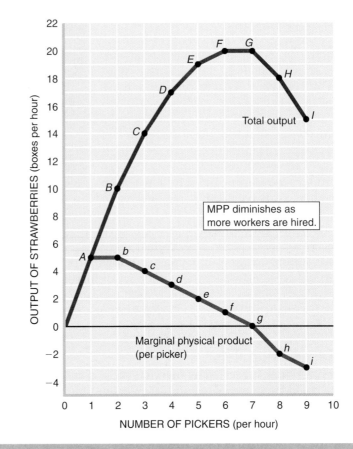

	Number of Pickers (per Hour)	Total Strawberry Output (Boxes per Hour)	Marginal Physical Product (Boxes per Hour)
A	1 (Marvin)	5	5
B	2 (George)	10	5
C	3	14	4
D	4	17	3
E	5	19	2
F	6	20	1
G	7	20	0
H	8	18	-2
I	9	15	-3

Things get even worse if the grower hires still more pickers. If eight pickers are employed, total output actually *declines*. The pickers can no longer work efficiently under such crowded conditions. Hence the MPP of the eighth worker is *negative*, no matter how ambitious or hardworking this person may be. Points *H* and *h* in Figure 8.3 illustrate this negative marginal physical product.

Our observations on strawberry production apply to most industries. Indeed, diminishing returns are evident in even the simplest production processes. Suppose you ask a friend to help you with your homework. A little help may go a long way toward improving your grade. Does that mean that your grade improvement will *double* if you get *two* friends to help? What if you get five friends to help? Suddenly everyone's chatting, and your homework performance deteriorates. In general, **the marginal physical product of labor eventually declines as the quantity of labor employed increases.**

Number of Pickers (per Hour)	Total Strawberry Output (Boxes × per Hour)	Price of Strawberries = (per Box)	Total Strawberry Revenue (per Hour)	Marginal Revenue Product
0	0	$2	0	
1 (Marvin)	5	$2	$10	$ 10
2 (George)	10	$2	$20	$ 10
3	14	$2	$28	$ 8
4	17	$2	$34	$ 6
5	19	$2	$38	$ 4
6	20	$2	$40	$ 2
7	20	$2	$40	$ 0
8	18	$2	$36	$ -4
9	15	$2	$30	$ -6

TABLE 8.1
Diminishing Marginal Revenue Product

Marginal revenue product measures the change in total revenue that occurs when one additional worker is hired. At constant product prices, MRP equals MPP × price. Hence MRP declines along with MPP.

You may recognize the **law of diminishing returns** at work here. *Marginal productivity declines as more people must share limited facilities.* Typically, diminishing returns result from the fact that an increasing number of workers leaves each worker with less land and capital to work with.

law of diminishing returns The marginal physical product of a variable input declines as more of it is employed with a given quantity of other (fixed) inputs.

DIMINISHING MRP   As marginal *physical* product diminishes, so does marginal *revenue* product (MRP). As noted earlier, marginal revenue product is the increase in the *value* of total output associated with an added unit of labor (or other input). In our example, it refers to the increase in strawberry revenues associated with one additional picker.

The decline in marginal revenue product mirrors the drop in marginal physical product. Recall that a box of strawberries sells for $2. With this price and the output statistics of Figure 8.3, we can readily calculate marginal revenue product, as summarized in Table 8.1. As the growth of output diminishes, so does marginal revenue product. Marvin's marginal revenue product of $10 an hour has fallen to $6 an hour by the time four pickers are employed and reaches zero when seven pickers are employed.

THE HIRING DECISION

The tendency of marginal revenue product to diminish will clearly cool the strawberry grower's eagerness to hire 1,000 pickers. We still don't know, however, how many pickers will be hired.

The Firm's Demand for Labor

Figure 8.4 provides the answer. We already know that the grower is eager to hire pickers whose marginal revenue product exceeds their wage. Suppose the going wage for strawberry pickers is $6 an hour. At that wage, the grower will certainly want to hire at least one picker because the MRP of the first picker is $10 an hour (point *A* in Figure 8.4). A second worker will be hired as well because that picker's MRP (point *B* in Figure 8.4) also exceeds the going wage rate. In fact, *the grower will continue hiring pickers until the MRP has declined to the level of the market wage rate.* Figure 8.4 indicates that this intersection of MRP and the market wage rate (point *C*) occurs after four pickers are employed. Hence we can conclude that the grower will be willing to hire—will *demand*—four pickers if wages are $6 an hour.

The folly of hiring more than four pickers is also apparent in Figure 8.4. The marginal revenue product of the fifth worker is only $4 an hour (point *D*). Hiring a fifth

FIGURE 8.4
The Marginal Revenue Product Curve Is the Firm's Labor Demand Curve

An employer is willing to pay a worker no more than his or her marginal revenue product. In this case, a grower would gladly hire a second worker because that worker's MRP (point *B*) exceeds the wage rate ($6). The fifth worker will not be hired at that wage rate, however, since that worker's MRP (at point *D*) is less than $6. The MRP curve is the firm's labor demand curve.

picker will cost more in wages than the picker brings in as revenue. The *maximum* number of pickers the grower will employ at prevailing wages is four (point *C*).

The law of diminishing returns also implies that all of the four pickers will be paid the same wage. Once four pickers are employed, we cannot say that any single picker is responsible for the observed decline in marginal revenue product. Marginal revenue product diminishes because each worker has less capital and land to work with, not because the last worker hired is less able than the others. Accordingly, the fourth picker cannot be identified as any particular individual. Once four pickers are hired, Marvin's MRP is no higher than any other picker's. *Each (identical) worker is worth no more than the marginal revenue product of the last worker hired, and all workers are paid the same wage rate.*

The principles of marginal revenue product apply to football coaches as well as strawberry pickers. Nick Saban, Alabama's football coach, earns $4 million a year (see the accompanying News Wire). Why does he get paid 10 times more than the university's president? Because a winning football team brings in tens of thousands of paying fans per game, lots of media exposure, and grateful alumni. The university thinks his MRP easily justifies the high salary.

If we accept the notion that marginal revenue product sets the wages of both football coaches and strawberry pickers, must we give up all hope for low-paid workers? Can anything be done to create more jobs or higher wages for pickers? To answer this, we need to see how market demand and supply interact to establish employment and wage levels.

MARKET EQUILIBRIUM

The principles that guide the hiring decisions of a single strawberry grower can be extended to the entire labor market. This suggests that the *market* demand for labor depends on

- The number of employers.
- The marginal revenue product of labor in each firm and industry.

On the supply side of the labor market we have already observed that the market supply of labor depends on

- The number of available workers.
- Each worker's willingness to work at alternative wage rates.

NEWS WIRE | MARGINAL REVENUE PRODUCT

Saban returns Tide to prominence

Under Saban's watch, Alabama has won 47 of its 53 games over the past four seasons going into Monday's BCS National Championship Game against LSU. The coach has transformed a program that was coming out of ravages of NCAA sanctions into a national powerhouse, ringing in a new era of success for an Alabama program that claims 13 national titles.

Saban didn't come cheap. His Alabama salary turned heads and made national headlines when he was hired for $32 million over eight years.

For Alabama's part, Saban's salary was an investment. Alabama didn't rank in the top 10 in college athletic department revenue in the 2006–2007 academic year, before Saban's first season as coach, bringing in $70.5 million. For the 2010–2011 school year, Alabama ranked behind only Texas and Ohio State at $123.9 million.

Aside from the increased television revenue, Alabama was able to add more than 9,000 seats to Bryant-Denny Stadium to take capacity above 101,000 while also adding more high-dollar luxury boxes.

—Tommy Deas

Source: Tommy Deas, *Tuscaloosa News*, January 4, 2012

NOTE: Colleges are willing to pay more for football coaches than professors. Successful coaches bring in much more revenue.

The supply decisions of each worker are in turn a reflection of tastes, income, wealth, expectations, other prices, and taxes.

Equilibrium Wage

Figure 8.5 brings these market forces together. *The intersection of the market supply and demand curves establishes the* **equilibrium wage.** In our previous example we assumed that the prevailing wage was $6 an hour. In reality, the market wage will be w_e, as illustrated in Figure 8.5. *The equilibrium wage is the only wage at which the quantity of labor supplied equals the quantity of labor demanded.* Everyone who is willing and able to work for this wage will find a job.

Many people will be unhappy with the equilibrium wage. Employers may grumble that wages are too high. Workers may complain that wages are too low. Nevertheless, the equilibrium wage is the only one that clears the market.

equilibrium wage The wage at which the quantity of labor supplied in a given time period equals the quantity of labor demanded.

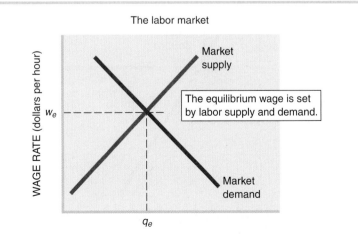

The labor market

QUANTITY OF LABOR (workers per time period)

FIGURE 8.5
Equilibrium Wage

The intersection of *market supply* and *demand* determines the equilibrium wage in a competitive labor market. All of the firms in the industry can then hire as much labor as they want at that equilibrium wage. Likewise, anyone who is willing and able to work for the wage w_e will be able to find a job.

Equilibrium Employment

The intersection of labor supply and demand determines not just the prevailing wage rate but the level of employment as well. In Figure 8.5 this equilibrium level of employment occurs at q_e. That is the only sustainable level of employment in that market, given prevailing supply and demand conditions.

CHANGING MARKET OUTCOMES

The equilibrium established in any market is subject to change. If Alabama's football team started losing too many games, ticket and ad revenues would fall. Then the coach's salary might shrink. Likewise, if someone discovered that strawberries cure cancer, those strawberry pickers might be in great demand. In this section we examine how changing market conditions alter wages and employment levels.

Changes in Productivity

The law of diminishing returns is responsible for the trade-off between wage and employment levels. The downward slope of the labor demand curve does not mean wages *and* employment can never rise together, however. *If labor productivity (MPP) rises, wages can increase without sacrificing jobs.*

Suppose that Marvin and his friends enroll in a local agricultural extension course and learn new methods of strawberry picking. With these new methods, the marginal physical product of each picker increases by one box per hour. With the price of strawberries still at $2 a box, this productivity improvement implies an increase in marginal *revenue* product of $2 per worker. Now farmers will be more eager to hire pickers. This increased demand for pickers is illustrated by the upward *shift* of the labor demand curve in Figure 8.6.

Notice how the improvement in productivity has altered the value of strawberry pickers. The MRP of the fourth picker is now $7 an hour (point S) rather than $6 (point C). Hence the grower can now afford to pay higher wages. Or the grower could employ more pickers than before, moving from point C to point E. *Increased productivity implies that workers can get higher wages without sacrificing jobs or more employment without lowering wages.* Historically, increased productivity has been the most important source of rising wages and living standards.

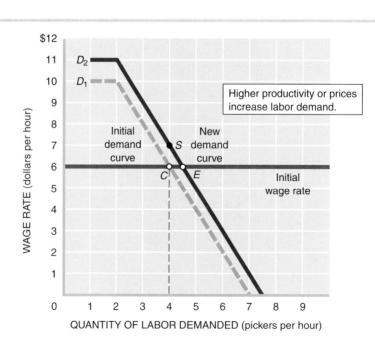

FIGURE 8.6
Increased Productivity

Wage and employment decisions depend on marginal revenue product. If productivity improves, the labor demand curve shifts upward (e.g., from D_1 to D_2), raising the MRP of all workers. The grower can now afford to pay higher wages (point S) or hire more workers (point E).

NEWS WIRE | MINIMUM WAGE EFFECTS

Obama Proposes to Increase Federal Minimum Wage

During Tuesday's State of the Union address, President Barack Obama proposed increasing the federal minimum wage from $7.25 an hour to $9 in stages by the end of 2015.

The minimum wage in Florida is currently $7.79 an hour, and the proposed increase to $9 an hour is receiving split responses in Southwest Florida. On the one hand, it would assist those receiving minimum wages and improve their standard of living. But it could also impact local businesses by increasing their costs.

"If you raise the minimum wage and don't let markets determine the wage, then there's going to be some winners and some losers," said Gary Jackson, an economist and director of the Regional Economic Research Institute at FGCU.

Minimum Wage History

Oct. '38	$0.25	Jan. '78	$2.65
Oct. '39	0.30	Jan. '79	2.90
Oct. '45	0.40	Jan. '80	3.10
Jan. '50	0.75	Jan. '81	3.35
Mar. '56	1.00	Apr. '90	3.80
Sept. '61	1.15	Apr. '91	4.25
Sept. '63	1.25	Oct. '96	4.75
Feb. '67	1.40	Sept. '97	5.15
Feb. '68	1.60	July '07	5.85
May. '74	2.00	July '08	6.55
Jan. '75	2.10	July '09	7.25
Jan. '76	2.30		

Source: *News-Press*, Ft. Meyers, FL, February 13, 2013.

NOTE: An increase in the minimum wage raises wages for some workers but eliminates jobs for others.

Changes in Price

An increase in the price of strawberries would also help the pickers. Marginal revenue product reflects the interaction of productivity and product prices. If strawberry prices were to double, strawberry pickers would become twice as valuable, even without an increase in *physical* productivity. Such a change in product prices depends, however, on changes in the market supply and demand for strawberries.

Legal Minimum Wages

Rather than waiting for *market* forces to raise their wages, the strawberry pickers might seek *government* intervention. The U.S. government decreed in 1938 that no worker could be paid less than 25 cents per hour. Since then the U.S. Congress has repeatedly raised the legal minimum wage, bringing it to $7.25 in 2009 (see the accompanying News Wire).

Figure 8.7 illustrates the consequences of such minimum wage legislation. In the absence of government intervention, the labor supply and labor demand curves would establish the wage w_e. At that equilibrium q_e workers would be employed.

DEMAND-SIDE EFFECTS   When a legislated minimum wage of w_m is set, things change. Suddenly the quantity of labor *demanded* declines. In the prior equilibrium

FIGURE 8.7
Minimum Wage Effects

A minimum wage increases the quantity of labor supplied but reduces the quantity demanded. Some workers (q_d) end up with higher wages, but others ($q_s - q_d$) remain or become jobless.

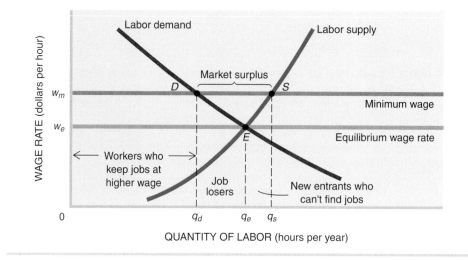

employers kept hiring workers until their marginal revenue product fell to w_e. If a minimum wage of w_m must be paid, it no longer makes sense to hire that many workers. So employers back up on the labor demand curve from point E to point D. At D, marginal revenue product is high enough to justify paying the legal minimum wage. As a result of these retrenchments, however, some workers ($q_e - q_d$) lose their jobs.

SUPPLY-SIDE EFFECTS   Note in Figure 8.7 what happens on the *supply* side as well. The higher minimum wage attracts more people into the labor market. The number of workers willing to work jumps from q_e (point E) to q_s (point S). Everybody wants one of those better-paying jobs.

There aren't enough jobs to go around, however. The number of jobs available at the minimum wage is only q_d; the number of job seekers at that wage is q_s. With more job seekers than jobs, unemployment results. We now have a market surplus (equal to q_s minus q_d). Those workers are unemployed.

Government-imposed wage floors thus have two distinct effects. *A minimum wage*

* *Reduces the quantity of labor demanded.*
* *Increases the quantity of labor supplied.*

Thus it

* *Creates a market surplus.*

The market surplus creates inefficiency and frustration, especially for workers who are ready and willing to work but can't find a job. Not everyone suffers, however. Those workers who keep their jobs (at q_d in Figure 8.7) end up with higher wages than they had before. Accordingly, *a legal minimum wage entails a trade-off: some workers end up better off, while others end up worse off.* That's why the News Wire refers to "winners" and "losers" from President Obama's proposed $9 minimum wage. Those most likely to end up worse off are teenagers and other inexperienced workers whose marginal revenue product is below the legal minimum wage. They will have the hardest time finding jobs when the legal wage floor is raised.

How many potential jobs are lost to minimum wage hikes depends on how far the legal minimum is raised. The elasticity of labor demand is also important. Democrats argue that labor demand is inelastic, so few jobs will be lost. Republicans argue that labor demand is elastic, so more jobs are lost. The state of the economy is also critical. If the economy is growing rapidly, increases (shifts) in labor demand will help offset job losses resulting from a minimum wage hike.

Topic Podcast:
Minimum Wage Debates

Labor Unions

Labor unions are another force that attempts to set aside equilibrium wages. The workers in a particular industry may not be satisfied with the equilibrium wage. They may decide to take *collective* action to get a higher wage. To do so, they form a labor union and bargain collectively with employers. This is what the United Farm Workers has tried to do in California's strawberry fields.

The formation of a labor union does not set aside the principles of supply and demand. The equilibrium wage remains at w_e, the intersection of the labor supply and demand curves (see Figure 8.8a). If the union were successful in negotiating a higher wage (w_u in the figure), a labor market surplus would appear ($l_3 - l_2$ in Figure 8.8a). These jobless workers would compete for the union jobs, putting downward pressure on the union-negotiated wage. Hence **to get and maintain an above-equilibrium wage, a union must exclude some workers from the market.** Effective forms of exclusion include union membership, required apprenticeship programs, and employment agreements negotiated with employers.

What happens to the excluded workers? In the case of a national minimum wage (Figure 8.7), the surplus workers remain unemployed. A union, however, sets above-equilibrium wages in only one industry or craft. Accordingly, there are lots of other potential jobs for the excluded nonunion workers. Their wages will suffer, however. As workers excluded from the unionized market (Figure 8.8a) stream into the nonunionized market (Figure 8.8b), they shift the nonunionized labor supply to the right. This influx of workers depresses nonunion wages, dropping them from w_e to w_n.

Although the theoretical impact of union exclusionism on relative wages is clear, empirical estimates of that impact are fairly rare. We do know that union wages in general are significantly higher than nonunion wages ($943 versus $742 per week in 2012). But part of this differential is due to the fact that unions are more common in industries that have always been more capital-intensive and have paid relatively high wages. When comparisons are made within particular industries or sectors, the differential narrows considerably. Nevertheless, there is a consensus that unions have managed to increase their relative wages from 15 to 20 percent above the competitive equilibrium wage.

FIGURE 8.8   The Effect of Unions on Relative Wages

In the absence of unions, the average wage rate would be equal to w_e. As unions take control of the market, however, they seek to raise wage rates to w_u. The higher wage reduces the amount of employment in the unionized market from l_1 to l_2. The workers displaced from the nonunionized market will seek work in the nonunionized market, thereby shifting the nonunion supply curve to the right. The result will be a reduction of wage rates (to w_n) in the nonunionized market. Thus union wages (w_u) end up higher than nonunion wages (w_n).

(a) **Unionized labor market**

(b) **Nonunionized labor market**

POLICY PERSPECTIVES

Should CEO Pay Be Capped?

The chairman of the Walt Disney Company signed a 5-year contract in 2011 that will pay him an astronomical $200 million. If Disney could pay that much to its chairman, surely it could afford to pay more than the legal minimum wage to its least skilled workers. But Disney says such a comparison is irrelevant. When challenged to defend his pay, Disney's Board of Directors insisted that Bob Iger had earned every penny of it by enhancing the value of the company's stock.

Critics of CEO pay don't accept this explanation. They make three points. First, the rise in the price of Disney's *stock* is not a measure of marginal revenue product. Stock prices rise in response to both company performance and general changes in financial markets. Hence only part of the stock increase could be credited to the CEO. Second, the revenues of the Walt Disney Company probably wouldn't be $200 million less in the absence of CEO Bob Iger. Hence his marginal revenue product was less than $200 million. Finally, Iger probably would have worked just as hard for, say, just $100 million or so. Therefore, his actual pay was more than required to elicit the desired supply response.

Critics conclude that many CEO paychecks are out of line with the realities of supply and demand. President Obama was particularly outraged by the multimillion-dollar salaries and bonuses paid to Wall Street executives during the 2008–2009 recession. He wanted corporations to reduce CEO pay and revise the process used for setting CEO pay levels (see the following News Wire). And he was willing to pass laws that would force them to do so.

NEWS WIRE	CAPPING CEO PAY

Obama Lays Out Limits on Executive Pay

WASHINGTON—President Barack Obama laid out strict new regulations on executive compensation Wednesday, strafing Wall Street with tough talk as Washington asserts increasing control over a financial sector seeking more government funds.

The plan, which represents the most aggressive assault on executive pay by federal officials, includes salary caps of $500,000 for top executives at firms that accept "extraordinary assistance" from the government. . . .

The compensation initiative risks crossing a line into the kind of government intervention that unnerves some voters. "I understand the mood of the country right now," says S. Phillip Collins, president and chief executive of Sound Banking Co., Morehead City, NC, which received $3 million in bailout funds. But if executives are making money for shareholders, "they should be rewarded for it."

Some compensation experts and bank executives worry the new moves may backfire by discouraging firms from seeking federal assistance and making it harder for them to recruit top talent.

—Jonathan Weisman and Joann Lublin

Source: *The Wall Street Journal*, February 5, 2009. Used with permission of Dow Jones & Company, Inc., via Copyright Clearance Center, Inc.

NOTE: Critics of "excessive" CEO pay want limits on executive compensation. Defenders of CEO pay warn that arbitrary limits will discourage talented people from assuming CEO responsibilities.

UNMEASURED MRP   One of the difficulties in determining the appropriate level of CEO pay is the elusiveness of marginal revenue product. It is easy to measure the MRP of a strawberry picker or even a sales clerk who sells Disney toys. But a corporate CEO's contributions are less well defined. A CEO is supposed to provide strategic leadership and a sense of mission. These are critical to a corporation's success but hard to quantify.

Congress confronts the same problem in setting the president's pay. We noted earlier that President Obama himself is paid $400,000 a year. Can we argue that this salary represents his marginal revenue product? The wage we actually pay the president of the United States is less a reflection of his contribution to total output than a matter of custom. His salary also reflects the price voters believe is required to induce competent individuals to forsake private sector jobs and assume the responsibilities of the presidency. In this sense, the wage paid to the president and other public officials is set by their **opportunity wage**—that is, the wage they could earn in private industry.

The same kinds of considerations influence the wages of college professors. The marginal revenue product of a college professor is not easy to measure. Is it the number of students he or she teaches, the amount of knowledge conveyed, or something else? Confronted with such problems, most universities tend to pay college professors according to their *opportunity wage*—that is, the amount the professors could earn elsewhere.

Opportunity wages also help explain the difference between the wage of the chairman of Disney and that of the workers who peddle its products. The lower wage of sales clerks reflects not only their marginal revenue product at Disney stores but also the fact that they are not trained for many other jobs. That is to say, their opportunity wages are low. By contrast, Disney's CEO has impressive managerial skills that are in demand by many corporations; his opportunity wages are high.

Opportunity wages help explain CEO pay but don't fully justify such high pay levels. If Disney's CEO pay is justified by opportunity wages, that means that another company would be willing to pay him that much. But what would justify such high pay at another company? Would his MRP be any easier to measure? Maybe *all* CEO paychecks have been inflated.

Critics of CEO pay conclude that the process of setting CEO pay levels should be changed. All too often, executive pay scales are set by self-serving committees composed of executives of the same or similar corporations (see the accompanying cartoon). Critics want a more independent assessment of pay scales, with nonaffiliated experts and stockholder representatives. Some critics want to go a step further and set mandatory caps on CEO pay. President Clinton rejected legislated caps but convinced Congress to limit the tax deductibility of CEO pay. Any "unjustified" CEO pay in excess of $1 million a year cannot be treated as a business expense but must instead be paid out of after-tax profits. This change puts more pressure on corporations to examine the rationale for multimillion-dollar paychecks.

If markets work efficiently, such government intervention should not be necessary. Corporations that pay their CEOs excessively will end up with smaller profits than companies that pay market-based wages. Over time, lean companies will be more competitive than fat companies, and excessive pay scales will be eliminated. Legislated CEO pay caps imply that CEO labor markets aren't efficient or that the adjustment process is too slow.

"O.K. guys, now lets go and __earn__ that four hundred times our workers' salaries."

The wages of top corporate officers may not be fully justified by their marginal revenue product.

© William Hamilton/The New Yorker Collection/www.cartoonbank.com.

opportunity wage The highest wage an individual would earn in his or her best alternative job.

SUMMARY

- The economic motivation to work arises from the fact that people need income to buy the goods and services they desire. As a consequence, people are willing to work—to supply labor. **LO1**
- There is an opportunity cost involved in working—namely, the amount of leisure time one sacrifices. People willingly give up additional leisure only if offered higher wages. Hence the labor supply curve is upward-sloping. **LO1**
- A firm's demand for labor reflects labor's marginal revenue product. A profit-maximizing employer will not pay a worker more than the value of what the worker produces. **LO2**
- The marginal revenue product of labor diminishes as additional workers are employed in a particular job (the law of diminishing returns). This decline occurs because additional workers have to share existing land and capital, leaving each worker with less land and capital to work with.

The decline in MRP gives labor demand curves their downward slope. **LO2**
- The equilibrium wage is determined by the intersection of labor supply and labor demand curves. Attempts to set above-equilibrium wages cause labor surpluses by reducing the jobs available and increasing the number of job seekers. **LO3**
- Labor unions attain above-equilibrium wages by excluding some workers from a particular industry or craft. The excluded workers increase the labor supply in the nonunion market, depressing wages there. **LO4**
- Differences in marginal revenue product are an important explanation of wage inequalities. But the difficulty of measuring MRP in many instances leaves many wage rates to be determined by custom, power, discrimination, or opportunity wages. **LO5**

TERMS TO REMEMBER

Define the following terms:

labor supply	demand for labor	marginal revenue product (MRP)	equilibrium wage
opportunity cost	derived demand		opportunity wage
market supply of labor	marginal physical product (MPP)	law of diminishing returns	

QUESTIONS FOR DISCUSSION

1. Why are you doing this homework? What are you giving up? What do you expect to gain? If homework performance determined course grades, would you spend more time doing it? **LO1**
2. Why does the opportunity cost of doing homework increase as you spend more time doing it? **LO1**
3. How do "supply and demand" explain the wage gap between petroleum engineering and sociology majors (News Wire, p. 163)? **LO3**
4. Explain why marginal physical product would diminish as **LO2**
   (a) More secretaries are hired in an office.
   (b) More professors are hired in the economics department.
   (c) More construction workers are hired to build a school.
5. Under what conditions might an increase in the minimum wage *not* reduce the number of low-wage jobs? How much of a job loss is acceptable? **LO4**
6. The United Farm Workers wants strawberry pickers to join their union. They hope then to convince consumers to buy only union-picked strawberries. Will such activities raise picker wages? Increase employment? **LO3**
7. Why did Hewlett-Packard eliminate so many jobs (News Wire, p. 162)? **LO1**
8. Why are engineering professors paid more than English professors? **LO5**
9. **POLICY PERSPECTIVES**   How might you measure the marginal revenue product of (a) a quarterback, (b) the team's coach, and (c) the team's owner? **LO5**

PROBLEMS

connect

1. (*a*) If each of the companies at the Rutgers Job Fair was hiring two people, what was the quantity of labor demanded?
   (*b*) What was the quantity supplied? (News Wire, p. 160) **LO3**

2. According to Figure 8.4, how many workers would be hired if the prevailing wage were **LO3**
   (*a*) $8 an hour?
   (*b*) $2 an hour?

3. The following table depicts the number of grapes that can be picked in an hour with varying amounts of labor: **LO2**

Number of pickers (per hour)	1	2	3	4	5	6	7	8
Output of grapes (in flats)	10	28	43	54	61	64	65	61

   Use this information to graph the total and marginal physical product of grape pickers.

4. (*a*) Assuming that the price of grapes is $2 per flat, use the data in Problem 3 to graph the marginal revenue product of grape pickers.
   (*b*) How many pickers will be hired if the going wage rate is $14 per hour? **LO2**

5. In Figure 8.7, **LO4**
   (*a*) How many workers lose their jobs when the minimum wage is enacted?
   (*b*) How many workers are unemployed at the minimum wage?

6. What is the MRP of Alabama's football coach according to the News Wire on p. 169? **LO5**

7. In November 2007 the New York Yankees agreed to pay Alex Rodriguez at least $275 million over 10 years. If this salary were to be covered by ticket sales only, how many more tickets per game would the Yankees have to sell to cover Rodriguez's salary in the 81 home games per year if the average ticket price is $50? **LO4, LO5**

8. Assuming that a college graduate on average earns their MRP, what is the MRP for a newly hired Economics major? (See the News Wire on p. 163.) **LO4**

9. **POLICY PERSPECTIVES**   If Nick Saban (News Wire, p. 169) were offered a CEO position at a sporting goods company,
   (*a*) What would his opportunity cost be?
   (*b*) By how much would his income decline if the company were subject to President Obama's proposed CEO salary cap (News Wire, p. 174)? **LO4**

◄ Practice quizzes, student PowerPoints, author podcasts, web activities, and additional materials available at **www.mhhe.com/schilleressentials9e**, or scan here. Need a barcode reader? Try ScanLife, available in your app store.

9

Government Intervention

◄ Practice quizzes, student PowerPoints, author podcasts, web activities, and additional materials available at www.mhhe.com/ schilleressentials9e, or scan here. Need a barcode reader? Try ScanLife, available in your app store.

LEARNING OBJECTIVES

After reading this chapter, you should be able to:

1   Define what "market failure" means.
2   Explain why the market underproduces "public goods."
3   Tell how externalities distort market outcomes.
4   Describe how market power prevents optimal outcomes.
5   Define what "government failure" is.

The market has a keen ear for private wants, but a deaf ear for public needs.

—Robert Heilbroner

Adam Smith was the eighteenth-century economist who coined the phrase **laissez faire.** He wanted the government to "leave it [the market] alone" so as not to impede the efficiency of the marketplace. But even Adam Smith felt the government had to intervene on occasion. He warned in *The Wealth of Nations* (1776), for example, that firms with market power might meet together and conspire to fix prices or restrain competition. He also recognized that the government might have to give aid and comfort to the poor. So he didn't really believe that the government should leave the market *entirely* alone. He just wanted to establish a *presumption* of market efficiency.

laissez faire The doctrine of "leave it alone," of nonintervention by government in the market mechanism.

Economists, government officials, and political scientists have been debating the role of government ever since. So has the general public. Although people are quick to assert that government is too big, they are just as quick to demand more schools, more police, and more income transfers.

The purpose of this chapter is to help define the appropriate scope of government intervention in the marketplace. To this end, we try to answer the following questions:

- Under what circumstances do markets fail?
- How can government intervention help?
- How much government intervention is desirable?

As we'll see, there is substantial agreement about how and when markets fail to give us the best WHAT, HOW, and FOR WHOM answers. There is much less agreement about whether government intervention improves the situation. Indeed, an overwhelming majority of Americans are ambivalent about government intervention. They want the government to fix the mix of output, protect the environment, and ensure an adequate level of income for everyone. But voters are equally quick to blame government meddling for many of our economic woes.

MARKET FAILURE

We can visualize the potential for government intervention by focusing on the WHAT question. Our goal here is to produce the best possible mix of output with existing resources. We illustrated this goal earlier with production possibilities curves. Figure 9.1 assumes that of all the possible combinations of output we could produce, the unique combination at point *X* represents the most

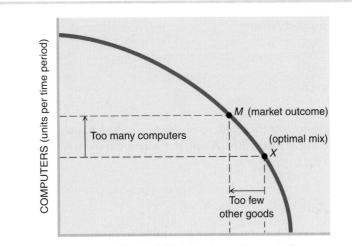

ALL OTHER GOODS (units per time period)

FIGURE 9.1
Market Failure

We can produce any mix of output on the production possibilities curve. Our goal is to produce the optimal (best possible) mix of output, as represented by point *X*. Market forces, however, may produce another combination, such as point *M*. In that case, the market fails—it produces a *sub*optimal mix of output.

optimal mix of output The most desirable combination of output attainable with existing resources, technology, and social values.

desirable—that is, the **optimal mix of output.** The exact location of X in the graph is arbitrary—we're just using that point to remind us that some specific mix of output must be better than all other combinations. Thus point X is *assumed* to be *optimal*—the mix of output society would choose after examining all other options, their opportunity costs, and social preferences.

The Nature of Market Failure

We have observed how the market mechanism can help us find this desired mix of output. The **market mechanism** moves resources from one industry to another in response to consumer demands. If we demand more computers—offer to buy more at a given price—more resources (labor) will be allocated to computer manufacturing. Similarly, a fall in demand will encourage producers to stop making computers and offer their services in another industry. Changes in market prices direct resources from one industry to another, moving us along the perimeter of the production possibilities curve.

market mechanism The use of market prices and sales to signal desired outputs (or resource allocations).

The big question is whether the mix of output the market mechanism selects is the one society most desires. If so, we don't need government intervention to change the mix of output. If not, we may need government intervention to guide the invisible hand of the market.

We use the term **market failure** to refer to less than perfect (suboptimal) outcomes. If the invisible hand of the marketplace produces a mix of output that is different from the one society most desires, then it has failed. *Market failure implies that the forces of supply and demand have not led us to the best point on the production possibilities curve.* Such a failure is illustrated by point M in Figure 9.1.

market failure An imperfection in the market mechanism that prevents optimal outcomes.

Point M is assumed to be the mix of output generated by market forces. Notice that the market mix (point M) is not identical to the optimal mix (point X). The market in this case *fails;* we get the wrong answer to the WHAT question. Specifically, too many computers are produced at point M and too few of other goods. It's not that we have no use for more computers—additional computers are still desired. But we'd *rather* have more of other goods. In other words, we'd be better off with a slightly different mix of output, such as that at point X.

Market failure opens the door for government intervention. If the market can't do the job, we need some form of *nonmarket* force to get the right answers. In terms of Figure 9.1, we need something to change the mix of output—to move us from point M (the market mix of output) to point X (the optimal mix of output). Accordingly, *market failure establishes a basis for government intervention.*

Sources of Market Failure

Because market failure is the justification for government intervention, we need to know how and when market failure occurs. *There are four specific sources of microeconomic market failure:*

- *Public goods.*
- *Externalities.*
- *Market power.*
- *Inequity.*

We examine the nature of these micro problems in this chapter. We also take note of failures due to *macro* instability. Along the way we'll see why government intervention is called for in each case.

PUBLIC GOODS

The market mechanism has the unique capability to signal consumer demands for various goods and services. By offering to pay higher or lower prices for specific products, we express our collective answer to the question of WHAT to produce.

However, the market mechanism works efficiently only if the benefits of consuming a particular good or service are available only to the individuals who purchase that product.

Consider doughnuts, for example. When you eat a doughnut, you alone enjoy its greasy, sweet taste—that is, you derive a *private* benefit. No one else reaps any significant benefit from your consumption of a doughnut: the doughnut you purchase in the market is yours alone to consume. Accordingly, your decision to purchase the doughnut will be determined only by your anticipated satisfaction, your income, and your opportunity costs.

Joint Consumption

Many of the goods and services produced in the public sector are different from doughnuts—and not just because doughnuts look, taste, and smell different from nuclear submarines. When you buy a doughnut, you exclude others from consumption of that product. If Dunkin' Donuts sells a particular pastry to you, it cannot supply the same pastry to someone else. If you devour it, no one else can. In this sense, the transaction and product are completely private.

The same exclusiveness is not characteristic of public goods such as national defense. If you buy a nuclear submarine to patrol the Pacific Ocean, there is no way you can exclude your neighbors from the protection your submarine provides. Either the submarine deters would-be attackers or it doesn't. In the former case, both you and your neighbors survive happily ever after; in the latter case, we are all blown away together. In that sense, you and your neighbors either consume or don't consume the benefits of nuclear submarine defenses *jointly*. There is no such thing as exclusive consumption here. The consumption of nuclear defenses is a communal feat, no matter who pays for them. For this reason, national defense is regarded as a **public good** in the sense that *consumption of a public good by one person does not preclude consumption of the same good by another person.* By contrast, a doughnut is a **private good** because if I eat it, nobody else can consume it.

public good A good or service whose consumption by one person does not exclude consumption by others.

private good A good or service whose consumption by one person excludes consumption by others.

The Free-Rider Dilemma

The communal nature of public goods leads to a real dilemma. If you and I will *both* benefit from nuclear defenses, which one of us should buy the nuclear submarine? I would prefer, of course, that *you* buy it, thereby providing me with protection at no direct cost. Hence I may profess no desire for nuclear subs, secretly hoping to take a **free ride** on your market purchase. Unfortunately, you, too, have an incentive to conceal your desire for national defense. As a consequence, neither one of us may step forward to demand nuclear subs in the marketplace. We will both end up defenseless.

free rider An individual who reaps direct benefits from someone else's purchase (consumption) of a public good.

Flood control is also a public good. No one in the valley wants to be flooded out. But each landowner knows that a flood control dam will protect *all* the landowners, regardless of who pays. Either the entire valley is protected or no one is. Accordingly, individual farmers and landowners may say they don't *want* a dam and aren't willing to *pay* for it. Everyone is waiting and hoping that someone else will pay for flood control. In other words, everyone wants a *free ride*. Thus, if we leave it to market forces, no one will *demand* flood control and everyone in the valley will be washed away.

EXCLUSION   The difference between public goods and private goods rests on *technical* considerations, not political philosophy. ***The central question is whether we have the technical capability to exclude nonpayers.*** In the case of national defense or flood control, we simply don't have that capability. Even city streets have the characteristics of public goods. Although we could theoretically restrict the use of streets to those who pay to use them, a toll gate on every corner

Flood protection is a public good: downriver nonpayers can't be excluded from flood protection.

© Akira Kaede/Getty Images/DAL

NEWS WIRE	PUBLIC GOODS

Napster Gets Napped

Shawn Fanning had a brilliant idea for getting more music—download it from friends' computers to the Internet. So he wrote software that enables online sharing of audio files. This peer-to-peer (P2P) online distribution system became an overnight sensation: within a year's time, 38 million consumers were using Napster's software to acquire recorded music.

At first blush, Napster's service looked like a classic public good. The service was free, and one person's consumption did not impede another person from consuming the same service. Moreover, the distribution system was configured in such a way that nonpayers could not be excluded from the service.

The definition of *public good* relies, however, on whether nonpayers *could* be excluded, not whether they are excluded. In other words, technology is critical in classifying goods as public or private. In Napster's case, encryption technology that could exclude nonpayers was available, but the company had *chosen* not to use it. After being sued by major recording companies for copyright infringement, Napster sold out. In 2001 the company joined up with Bertelsmann (BMG Records) and reconfigured its software to exclude nonpayers. Now consumers have to pay for that private good. In response, Apple Computer and a dozen other companies started selling music downloads.

NOTE: A product is a public good only if nonpayers *cannot* be excluded from its consumption.

would be exceedingly expensive and impractical. Here, again, joint or public consumption appears to be the only feasible alternative. As the News Wire about Napster emphasizes, the technical capability to exclude nonpayers is the key factor in identifying public goods.

To the list of public goods we could add the administration of justice, the regulation of commerce, and the conduct of foreign relations. These services—which cost tens of *billions* of dollars and employ thousands of workers—provide benefits to everyone, no matter who pays for them. More important, there is no evident way to exclude *nonpayers* from the benefits of these services.

The free rides associated with public goods upset the customary practice of paying for what you get. If I can get all the streets, defenses, and laws I desire without paying for them, I am not about to complain. I am perfectly happy to let you pay for the services while all of us consume them. Of course, you may feel the same way. Why should you pay for these services if you can consume just as much of them when your neighbors foot the whole bill? It might seem selfish not to pay your share of the cost of providing public goods. But you would be better off in a material sense if you spent your income on doughnuts, letting others pick up the tab for public services.

UNDERPRODUCTION   Because the familiar link between paying and consuming is broken, public goods cannot be peddled in the supermarket. People are reluctant to buy what they can get free. This is a perfectly rational response for a consumer who has only a limited amount of income to spend. Hence *if public goods were marketed like private goods, everyone would wait for someone else to pay.* The end result might be a total lack of public services. This is the kind of dilemma Robert Heilbroner had in mind when he spoke of the market's "deaf ear" (see the quote at the beginning of this chapter).

The production possibilities curve in Figure 9.2 illustrates the dilemma created by public goods. Suppose that point X again represents the optimal mix of private and

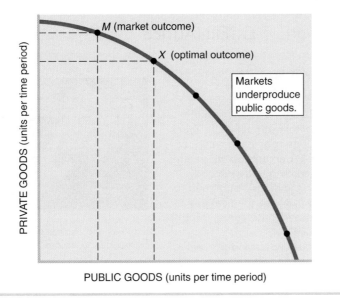

FIGURE 9.2
Underproduction of Public Goods

Suppose point *X* represents the optimal mix of output—the mix of private and public goods that maximizes society's welfare. Because consumers will not demand purely public goods in the marketplace, the price mechanism will not allocate enough resources to the production of public goods. Instead the market will tend to produce a mix of output like point *M*, which includes fewer public goods and more private goods than is *optimal*.

public goods. It is the mix of goods and services we would select if everyone's preferences were known and reflected in production decisions. The market mechanism will not lead us to point *X*, however, because the demand for public goods will be hidden. If we rely on the market, nearly everyone will withhold demand for public goods, waiting for a *free ride* to point *X*. As a result, **the market tends to underproduce public goods and overproduce private goods.** The market mechanism will leave us at a mix of output like that at point *M*, with few, if any, public goods. Since point *X* is assumed to be optimal, point *M* must be *suboptimal* (inferior to point *X*).

Figure 9.2 illustrates how the market fails: we cannot rely on the market mechanism to allocate resources to the production of public goods, no matter how much they might be desired. If we want more public goods, we need a *nonmarket* force—government intervention—to get them. The government will have to force people to pay taxes and then use the tax revenues to pay for the production of defense, flood control, and other public goods.

Note that we are using *public good* in a different way than most people use it. To most people, the term *public good* refers to any good or service the government produces. In economics, however, the meaning is much more restrictive. **The distinction between public goods and private goods is based on the nature of the goods, not who produces them.** The term "public good" refers only to those goods and services that are consumed jointly, both by those who pay for them and by those who don't. Public goods can be produced by either the government or the private sector. Private goods can be produced in either sector as well.

EXTERNALITIES

The free-rider problem associated with public goods provides an important justification for government intervention into the market's decision about WHAT to produce. It is not the only justification, however. Further grounds for intervention arise from the tendency of the costs or benefits of some market activities to "spill over" onto third parties.

Your demand for a good reflects the amount of satisfaction you expect from its consumption. Often, however, your consumption may affect others. The purchase of cigarettes, for example, expresses a smoker's demand for that good. But others may suffer from that consumption. In this case, smoke literally spills over onto other consumers, causing them discomfort, ill health, and even death

NEWS WIRE	EXTERNALITIES

Secondhand Smoke Kills 600,000 People a Year: Study

Secondhand smoke globally kills more than 600,000 people each year, accounting for 1 percent of all deaths worldwide, according to a new study.

The alarming findings—published on Thursday in the British medical journal *Lancet*—are based on a survey of 192 countries in 2004. . . .

"This helps us understand the real toll of tobacco," said Armando Peruga, of the World Health Organization, who led the study. He said the estimated 603,000 deaths from passive smoking should be added to the 5.1 million that smoking claims annually.

—James Fanelli

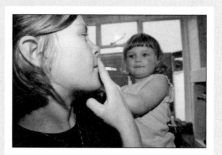

Secondhand smoke has deadly effects for nonsmokers too, according to a recent study.
Image Source/Corbis

Source: November 26, 2010 © Daily News, L.P. (New York).

NOTE: People who smoke feel the pleasures of smoking justify the cost (price). But nonsmokers end up bearing an external cost—secondhand smoke—that they don't voluntarily assume.

---

externalities Costs (or benefits) of a market activity borne by a third party; the difference between the social and private costs (or benefits) of a market activity.

(see the accompanying News Wire). Yet their loss is not reflected in the market—the harm caused to nonsmokers is *external* to the market price of cigarettes.

The term **externalities** refers to all costs or benefits of a market activity borne by a third party—that is, by someone other than the immediate producer or consumer. Whenever externalities are present, the preferences expressed in the marketplace will not be a complete measure of a good's value to society. As a consequence, the market will fail to produce the right mix of output. Specifically, *the market will underproduce goods that yield external benefits and overproduce those that generate external costs.* Government intervention may be needed to move the mix of output closer to society's optimal point.

Consumption Decisions

Externalities often originate on the demand side of markets. Consumers are always trying to maximize their personal well-being by buying products that deliver the most satisfaction (marginal utility) per dollar spent. In the process, they aren't likely to consider how the well-being of others is affected by their consumption behavior.

EXTERNAL COSTS   Automobile driving illustrates the problem. The amount of driving one does is influenced by the price of a car and the marginal costs of driving it. But automobile use involves not only *private costs* but *external costs* as well. When you cruise down the highway, you are adding to the congestion that slows other drivers down. You're also fouling the air with the emissions (carbon monoxide, hydrocarbons, etc.) your car spits out. The quality of the air other people breathe gets worse. You may even be accelerating climate change. Hence other people are made *worse* off at the same time as your auto consumption is making you *better* off.

Do you take account of such *external* costs when you buy a car? Not likely. Your willingness to buy a car is more likely to reflect only *your* expected satisfaction.

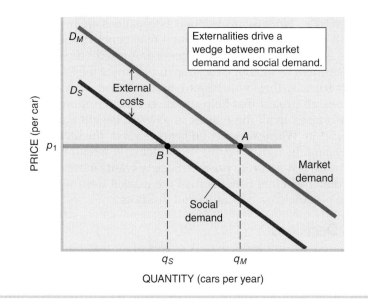

External costs

Externalities drive a wedge between market demand and social demand.

FIGURE 9.3
Social versus Market Demand

Whenever external costs exist, market demand overstates (lies above) social demand. At p_1 the market would demand q_M cars. Because of external costs, however, society wants only q_S cars at that price. Hence the market *overproduces* goods with external costs.

Hence the *market* demand for cars doesn't fully represent the interests of society. Instead market demand reflects only *private* benefits.

To account more fully for our *collective* well-being, we must distinguish the *social* demand for a product from the *market* demand whenever externalities exist. This isn't that difficult. We simply recognize that

> Social demand = market demand + externalities

In the case of autos, the externality is *negative*—that is, an external *cost*. Hence the social demand for cars is less than the (private) market demand. Put simply, this means we'd own and drive fewer cars if we took into account the external costs (pollution, congestion) that our cars caused. We don't, of course, since we're always trying to maximize our personal well-being. Market failure results.

Figure 9.3 illustrates the divergence of the *social* demand for automobiles and the *market* demand. The market demand expresses the anticipated *private* benefits of driving. Because of the *external* costs (congestion, pollution) associated with driving, the market demand *overstates* the social benefits of auto consumption. ***To represent the social demand for cars, we must subtract external costs from the private benefits.*** This leaves us with the *social demand* curve in Figure 9.3. Notice that the social demand curve lies below the market demand curve by the amount of external cost. Also notice that the market alone would produce *more* cars at any price than is socially optimal. At the price p_1, for example, the market demands q_M cars (point *A*), but society really wants only the quantity q_S (at point *B*).

A divergence between social and private costs can be observed even in the simplest consumer activities, such as throwing an empty soda can out the window of your car. To hang on to the soda can and later dispose of it in a trash barrel involves personal effort and thus private marginal costs. Throwing it out the window transfers the burden of disposal costs to someone else. Thus private costs can be distinguished from social costs. The resulting externality ends up as roadside litter.

The same kind of divergence between private and social costs helps explain why people abandon old cars in the street rather than haul them to scrap yards. It also explains why people use vacant lots as open dumps. In all these cases, ***the polluter benefits by substituting external costs for private costs.*** In other words, market incentives encourage environmental damage.

EXTERNAL BENEFITS   Not all consumption externalities are negative. Completing this course will benefit you personally, but it may benefit society as well. If more knowledge of economics makes you a better-informed voter, your community will reap some benefit from your education. If you share the lessons of supply and demand with friends, they will benefit without ever attending class. If you complete a research project that helps markets function more efficiently, others will sing your praises. In all these cases, an *external* benefit augments the private benefit of education. ***Whenever external benefits exist, the social demand exceeds the market demand.*** In Figure 9.3, the social demand would lie *above* the market demand if external *benefits* were present. Society wants more of those goods and services generating external benefits than the market itself will demand. This is why governments subsidize education and flu shots.

Production Decisions

Externalities also exist in production. A power plant that burns high-sulfur coal damages the surrounding environment. Yet the damage inflicted on neighboring people, vegetation, and buildings is external to the cost calculations of the firm. Because the cost of such pollution is not reflected in the price of electricity, the firm will tend to produce more electricity (and pollution) than is socially desirable. To reduce this imbalance, the government has to step in and change market outcomes.

Suppose you're operating an electric power plant. Power plants are major sources of air pollution and are responsible for nearly all thermal water pollution. Hence your position immediately puts you on the most-wanted list of pollution offenders. But suppose you bear society no grudges and would truly like to help eliminate pollution. Let's consider the alternatives.

PROFIT MAXIMIZATION   Figure 9.4*a* depicts the marginal and average total costs (MC and ATC) associated with the production of electricity. By equating marginal cost (MC) to price (= marginal revenue, MR), we observe (point *A*) that profit maximization occurs at an output of 1,000 kilowatt-hours per day. Total profits are illustrated by the shaded rectangle between the price line and the average total cost (ATC) curve.

The profits illustrated in Figure 9.4*a* are achieved in part by use of the cheapest available fuel under the boilers (which create the steam that rotates the generators). Unfortunately, the cheapest fuel is high-sulfur coal, a major source of air pollution. Other fuels (e.g., low-sulfur coal, fuel oil, natural gas) pollute less but cost more. Were you to switch to one of them, the ATC and MC curves would both shift upward, as shown in Figure 9.4*b*. Under these conditions, the most profitable rate of output (point *B*) would be less than before (point *A*), and total profits would decline (note the smaller profit rectangle in Figure 9.4*b*). Thus pollution abatement can be achieved, but only by sacrificing some profit. If you owned this power plant, would you sacrifice profits for the sake of cleaner air? Would your competitors?

The same kinds of cost considerations lead the plant to engage in thermal pollution. Cool water must be run through an electric utility plant to keep the turbines from overheating. And once the water runs through the plant, it is too hot to recirculate. Hence it must be either dumped back into the adjacent river or cooled off by being circulated through cooling towers. As you might expect, it is cheaper simply to dump the hot water in the river. The fish don't like it, but they don't have to pay the construction costs of cooling towers. Were you to get on the environmental bandwagon and build those towers, your production costs would rise, just as they did in Figure 9.4*b*. The fish would benefit, but at your expense.

EXTERNAL COST   The big question here is whether you and your fellow stockholders would be willing to incur higher costs in order to cut down on pollution. Eliminating either the air pollution or the water pollution emanating from the

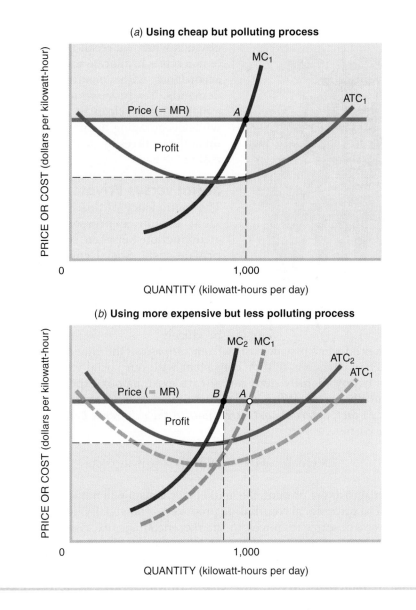

(a) **Using cheap but polluting process**

MC₁

Price (= MR)   A   ATC₁

Profit

0   1,000

QUANTITY (kilowatt-hours per day)

(b) **Using more expensive but less polluting process**

MC₂ MC₁   ATC₂ ATC₁

Price (= MR)   B A

Profit

0   1,000

QUANTITY (kilowatt-hours per day)

FIGURE 9.4
Profit Maximization versus Pollution Control
Production processes that control pollution may be more expensive than those that do not. If they are, the MC and ATC curves will shift upward (to MC₂ and ATC₂). These higher internal costs will reduce output and profits. In this case, environmental protection moves the profit-maximizing point to point B from point A and total profit shrinks. Hence a producer has an incentive to continue polluting, using cheaper technology and external costs.

electric plant will cost a lot of money; eliminating both will cost much more. And to whose benefit? To the people who live downstream and downwind? We don't expect profit-maximizing producers to take such concerns into account. The behavior of profit maximizers is guided by comparisons of revenues and costs, not by philanthropy, aesthetic concerns, or the welfare of fish.

The moral of this story—and the critical factor in pollution behavior—is that *people tend to maximize their personal welfare, balancing* **private** *benefits against* **private** *costs.* For the electric power plant, this means making production decisions on the basis of revenues received and costs incurred. The fact that the power plant imposes costs on others, in the form of air and water pollution, is irrelevant to its profit-maximizing decision. Those costs are *external* to the firm and do not appear on its profit-and-loss statement. Those external costs are no less real, but they are incurred by society at large rather than by the firm.

Whenever external costs exist, a private firm will not allocate its resources and operate its plant in such a way as to maximize social welfare. In effect, society is permitting the power plant the free use of valued resources—clean air and clean water. Thus the power plant has a tremendous incentive to substitute those resources for others (such as high-priced fuel or cooling towers) in the production process.

"Where there's smoke, there's money."

© Joseph Mirachi/The New Yorker
Collection/www.cartoonbank.com.

social costs The full resource
costs of an economic activity,
including externalities.

private costs The costs of an
economic activity directly borne
by the immediate producer or
consumer (excluding externalities).

The inefficiency of such an arrangement is obvious when we recall that the function of markets is to allocate scarce resources in accordance with consumers' expressed demands. Yet here we are, proclaiming a high value for clean air and clean water while encouraging the power plant to use up both resources by offering them at zero cost to the firm.

Social versus Private Costs

The inefficiency of this market arrangement can be expressed in terms of a distinction between social costs and private costs. **Social costs** are the total costs of all the resources that are used in a particular production activity. On the other hand, **private costs** are the resource costs that are incurred by the specific producer.

Ideally, a producer's private costs will encompass all the attendant social costs, and production decisions will be consistent with our social welfare. Unfortunately, this happy identity does not always exist, as our experience with the power plant illustrates. *When social costs differ from private costs, external costs exist. In fact, external costs are equal to the difference between the social and private costs:*

$$\text{External costs} = \text{social costs} - \text{private costs}$$

When external costs are present, the market mechanism will not allocate resources efficiently. The price signal confronting producers is flawed. By not conveying the full (social) cost of scarce resources, the market encourages excessive pollution. We end up with a suboptimal mix of output, the wrong production processes, and a polluted environment. This is another case of market failure.

The nature and consequences of this market failure are illustrated in Figure 9.5, which again depicts the cost situation confronting the electric power plant. Notice that we use two different marginal cost curves this time. The lower one, the *private*

FIGURE 9.5
Market Failure

Social costs exceed private costs by the amount of external costs. Production decisions based on private costs alone will lead us to point *B*, where private MC = MR. At point *B*, the rate of output is q_p.

To maximize social welfare, we equate *social* MC and MR, as at point *A*. Only q_s of output is socially desirable. The failure of the market to convey the full costs of production keeps us from attaining this outcome.

MC curve, reflects the private costs incurred by the power plant when it uses the cheapest production process, including high-sulfur coal and no cooling towers. It is identical to the MC curve of Figure 9.4*a*. We now know, however, that such operations impose *external* costs on others in the form of air and water pollution. Hence social costs are higher than private costs, as reflected in the *social* MC curve. To maximize *social* welfare, we would equate *social* marginal costs with marginal revenue (point *A* in Figure 9.5) and thus produce at the output level q_s. The private profit maximizer, however, equates *private* marginal costs and marginal revenue (point *B*) and thus ends up producing at q_p, making more profit but also causing more pollution. As a general rule, ***if pollution costs are external, firms will produce too much of a polluting good.*** Fear of such external costs was the driving force behind the opposition to President Obama's decision to allow more oil drilling in coastal waters (see News Wire). The BP oil spill of April 2010 illustrated how high those external costs could be.

Policy Options

What should the government do to remedy market failures caused by externalities?

Our goal is to discourage production and consumption activities that impose external costs on society. We can do this in one of two ways:

- *Alter market incentives.*
- *Bypass market incentives.*

EMISSION FEES   Consider our pollution problem. The key to market-based environmental protection is to eliminate the gap between private costs and social costs. The opportunity to shift some costs onto others lies at the heart of the pollution problem. If we could somehow compel producers to *internalize* all costs—pay for both private and previously external costs—the gap would disappear, along with the incentive to pollute.

One possibility is to establish a system of **emission charges,** direct costs attached to the act of polluting. Suppose that we let you keep your power plant and permit you to operate it according to profit-maximizing principles. The only difference is that we no longer agree to supply you with clean air and cool water at zero cost. Instead we will charge you for these scarce resources. We might, say, charge you 2 cents for every gram of noxious emission you discharge into the air. In addition we might charge you 3 cents for every gallon of water you use, heat, and discharge back into the river.

emission charge   A fee imposed on polluters, based on the quantity of pollution.

NEWS WIRE	EXTERNAL COSTS

Environmentalists File Lawsuit to Block Offshore Drilling

GULF OF MEXICO—The Mississippi Sierra Club and the Gulf Restoration Network have asked a Hinds County Judge to block the state from enacting new regulations on offshore drilling.

Dan Turner, spokesman for the Mississippi Development Authority, said he has not seen the lawsuit and cannot comment.

The groups contend the process is moving too fast and hasn't been properly studied, and they have filed a lawsuit in Hinds County Chancery Court seeking to block the drilling regulations MDA has drafted.

Source: Associated Press, March 15, 2012. Used with permission of The Associated Press Copyright © 2012. All rights reserved.

NOTE: Oil drilling in coastal waters is profitable, based on market prices and *private* costs. Opponents argue that the *external* costs are too high, however.

FIGURE 9.6
Emission Fees

Emission charges can be used to close the gap between social costs and private costs. Faced with an emission charge of t, a private producer will reduce output from q_0 to q_1.

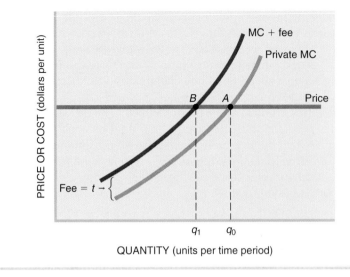

Confronted with such emission charges, a producer would have to rethink the production decision. *An emission charge increases private marginal cost and thus encourages lower output.* Figure 9.6 illustrates this effect.

Once an emission fee is in place, a producer may also reevaluate the production process. Consider again the choice of fuels to be used in our fictional power plant. We earlier chose high-sulfur coal because it was the cheapest fuel available. Now, however, there is an added cost to burning such fuel, in the form of an emission charge on noxious pollutants. This higher marginal cost might prompt a switch to less polluting fuels. The actual response of producers will depend on the relative costs involved. If emission charges are too low, it may be more profitable to continue burning and polluting with high-sulfur coal and pay a nominal fee. This is a simple pricing problem. The government can set the emission price higher, prompting the desired behavioral responses.

What works on producers will also sway consumers. Surely you've heard of deposits on returnable bottles. At one time the deposits were imposed by beverage producers to encourage you to bring the bottle back for reuse. Thirty years ago, virtually all soft drinks and most beer came in returnable bottles. But producers discovered that such deposits discouraged sales and yielded little cost savings. The economics of returnable bottles were further undermined by the advent of metal cans and, later, plastic bottles. Today returnable bottles are rarely used. One result is the inclusion of over 30 billion bottles and 60 billion cans in our solid waste disposal problem.

We could reduce this solid waste problem by imposing a deposit on all beverage containers. This would internalize pollution costs for the consumer and render the throwing of a soda can out the window equivalent to throwing away money. Some people would still find the thrill worthwhile, but they would be followed around by others who attached more value to money. When Oregon imposed a 5-cent deposit on beverage containers, related litter in that state declined by 81 percent!

REGULATION Although emission fees can be used to alter market incentives, direct regulation is another option for altering market outcomes. The federal government began regulating auto emissions in 1968 and got tough under the provisions of the Clean Air Act of 1970. The act required auto manufacturers to reduce hydrocarbon, carbon monoxide, and nitrogen oxide emissions by 90 percent within six years of the act's passage. Although the timetable for reducing pollutants was later extended, the act forced auto manufacturers to reduce auto emissions dramatically: by 1990 new cars were emitting only 4 percent as much pollution as 1970

| NEWS WIRE | CHANGING MARKET BEHAVIOR |

Breathing Easier

America's air has become a great deal cleaner over the last generation. Since measurement began in 1970, U.S. emissions have fallen dramatically, even while GDP and travel have more than doubled. America, in other words, is producing much more while polluting less.

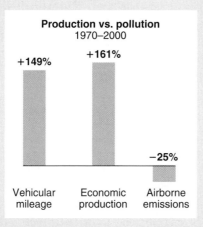

Production vs. pollution
1970–2000

+149% +161%

−25%

Vehicular mileage   Economic production   Airborne emissions

Source: *The American Enterprise*, July/August 2003, p. 17. www.aei.org.

NOTE: A combination of market incentives and government mandates has enabled output to increase even while the volume of pollution has diminished. The market alone would not have done as well.

models. This dramatic reduction in per-vehicle emissions enabled auto production to increase even while pollution declined (see the accompanying News Wire).

Regulatory standards may specify not only the required reduction in emissions but also the *process* by which those reductions are to be achieved. Clean air legislation mandated not only fewer auto emissions but also specific processes (e.g., catalytic converters, lead-free gasoline) for attaining them. Specific processes and technologies are also required for toxic waste disposal and water treatment. Laws requiring the sorting and recycling of trash are also examples of process regulation.

Although such hands-on regulation can be effective, this policy option also entails risks. By requiring market participants to follow specific rules, the regulations may impose excessive costs on some activities and too low a constraint on others. Some communities may not need the level of sewage treatment the federal government prescribes. Individual households may not generate enough trash to make sorting and separate pickups economically sound. Some producers may have better or cheaper ways of attaining environmental standards. *Excessive process regulation may raise the costs of environmental protection* and discourage cost-saving innovation. There is also the risk of regulated processes becoming entrenched long after they are obsolete.

Regulation also entails compliance and enforcement costs. Government agencies must monitor market behavior to ensure that regulations are enforced. Market participants must learn about the regulations, implement them, and usually complete some compliance paperwork. All these activities require scarce resources (labor) that could be used to produce other goods and services. Accordingly, regulations must not only be well designed but also be beneficial enough to justify their opportunity costs. New York City Mayor Michael Bloomberg concluded forced recycling didn't pass this test (see the following News Wire).

NEWS WIRE | OPPORTUNITY COSTS

Forced Recycling Is a Waste

As New York City faces the possibility of painful cuts to its police and fire department budgets, environmentalists are bellyaching over garbage. Mayor Michael Bloomberg's proposed budget for 2003 would temporarily suspend the city's recycling of metal, glass, and plastic, saving New Yorkers $57 million.

The city's recycling program—like many others around the country—has long hemorrhaged tax dollars. Every mayor has tried to stop the waste since the program began in 1989, when local law 19 mandated the city to recycle 25 percent of its waste by 1994.

The city spends about $240 per ton to "recycle" plastic, glass, and metal, while the cost of simply sending waste to landfills is about $130 per ton.

You don't need a degree in economics to see that something is wrong here. Isn't recycling supposed to save money and resources? Some recycling does—when driven by market forces. Private parties don't voluntarily recycle unless they know it will save money and resources. But forced recycling can be a waste of both because recycling itself entails using energy, water, and labor to collect, sort, clean, and process the materials. There are also air emissions, traffic, and wear on streets from the second set of trucks prowling for recyclables. The bottom line is that most mandated recycling hurts, not helps, the environment.

"You could do a lot better things in the world with $57 million," says Mayor Bloomberg. Like rebuilding from the greatest catastrophe ever to befall New York. But first Mayor Bloomberg is going to have to battle the green lobby to eliminate his city's wasteful recycling program.

—Angela Logomasini

Source: *The Wall Street Journal*, March 19, 2002, p. A22. Used with permission of Dow Jones & Company, Inc., via Copyright Clearance Center, Inc.

NOTE: Recycling programs reduce pollution but also use resources that could be employed for other purposes. The benefits of recycling should exceed its opportunity costs.

MARKET POWER

When either public goods or externalities exist, the market's price signal is flawed. The price consumers are willing and able to pay for a specific good does not reflect all the benefits or costs of producing that good. As a result, the market fails to produce the socially desired mix of output.

Even when the price signals emitted in the market are accurate, however, we may still get a suboptimal mix of output. The *response* to price signals, rather than the signals themselves, may be flawed.

Restricted Supply

Market power is often the cause of a flawed response. Suppose there were only one airline company in the world. As a monopolist, the airline could charge extremely high prices without worrying that travelers would flock to a competing airline. Ideally, such high prices would act as a signal to producers to build and fly more planes—to change the mix of output. But a monopolist does not have to cater to every consumer whim. It can limit airline travel and thus obstruct our efforts to achieve an optimal mix of output.

Monopoly is the most severe form of **market power.** More generally, market power refers to any situation where a single producer or consumer has the ability to alter the market price of a specific product. If the publisher (McGraw-Hill) charges a high price for this book, you will have to pay the tab. McGraw-Hill has market power because there are relatively few economics textbooks and your professor has required you to use this one. You don't have power in the textbook market because your purchase decision will not alter the market price of this text. You are only one of the million students who are taking an introductory economics course this year.

market power The ability to alter the market price of a good or service.

The market power McGraw-Hill possesses is derived from the copyright on this text. No matter how profitable textbook sales might be, no one else is permitted to produce or sell this particular text. Patents are another source of market power because they also preclude others from making or selling a specific product. Market power may also result from control of resources, restrictive production agreements, or efficiencies of large-scale production.

Whatever the source of market power, *the direct consequence of market power is that one or more producers attain discretionary power over the market's response to price signals.* They may use that discretion to enrich themselves rather than to move the economy toward the optimal mix of output. In this case, the market will again fail to deliver the most desired goods and services. As we observed in Chapter 7, the government concluded that Microsoft used its virtual monopoly in computer operating systems to limit consumer choice and enrich itself.

Antitrust Policy

A primary goal of government intervention in such cases is to prevent or dismantle concentrations of market power. That is the essential purpose of **antitrust** policy. The legal foundations of federal antitrust activity are contained in three laws:

antitrust Government intervention to alter market structure or prevent abuse of market power.

- **The Sherman Act (1890).** The Sherman Act prohibits "conspiracies in restraint of trade," including mergers, contracts, or acquisitions that threaten to monopolize an industry. Firms that violate the Sherman Act are subject to fines of up to $1 million, and their executives may be subject to imprisonment. In addition, consumers who are damaged—for example, via high prices—by a conspiracy in restraint of trade may recover treble damages. The U.S. Department of Justice has used this trust-busting authority to block attempted mergers and acquisitions, force changes in price or output behavior, require companies to sell some of their assets, and even send corporate executives to jail for conspiracies in restraint of trade.
- **The Clayton Act (1914).** The Clayton Act of 1914 was passed to outlaw specific antitrust behavior not covered by the Sherman Act. The principal aim of the act was to prevent the development of monopolies. To this end the Clayton Act prohibits price discrimination, exclusive dealing agreements, certain types of mergers, and interlocking boards of directors among competing firms.
- **The Federal Trade Commission Act (1914).** The increased antitrust responsibilities of the federal government created the need for an agency that could study industry structures and behavior so as to identify anticompetitive practices. The Federal Trade Commission was created for this purpose in 1914.

In the early 1900s this antitrust legislation was used to break up the monopolies that dominated the steel and tobacco industries. In the 1980s the same legislation was used to dismantle AT&T's near monopoly of telephone service. The court forced AT&T to sell off its local telephone service companies (the Baby

Bells) and allow competitors more access to long-distance service. The resulting competition pushed prices down and spawned a new wave of telephone technology and services.

Although antitrust policy has produced some impressive results, its potential is limited. There are over 28 million businesses in the United States, and the trustbusters can watch only so many. Even when they decide to take action, antitrust policy entails difficult decisions. What, for example, constitutes a monopoly in the real world? Must a company produce 100 percent of a particular good to be a threat to consumer welfare? How about 99 percent? Or even 75 percent?

And what specific monopolistic practices should be prohibited? Should we be looking for specific evidence of price gouging? Or should we focus on barriers to entry and unfair market practices? In the antitrust case against Microsoft (see the News Wire on page 146, Chapter 7) the Justice Department asserted that bundling its Internet Explorer with Windows was an anticompetitive practice. Microsoft chairman Bill Gates responded that the attorney general didn't understand how the fiercely competitive software market worked. Who was right?

These kinds of questions determine how and when antitrust laws will be enforced. Just the threat of enforcement, however, may help push market outcomes in the desired direction. In the Microsoft case, for example, the company changed some of its exclusionary licensing practices soon after the government filed its antitrust case. Presumably, other powerful companies also became more cautious about abusing market power when they saw the guilty verdict against Microsoft.

INEQUITY

Public goods, externalities, and market power all cause resource misallocations. Where these phenomena exist, the market mechanism will fail to produce the optimal mix of output.

Beyond the question of WHAT to produce, we are also concerned about FOR WHOM output is to be produced. Is the distribution of goods and services generated by the marketplace fair? If not, government intervention may be needed to redistribute income.

In general, the market mechanism tends to answer the basic question of FOR WHOM to produce by distributing a larger share of total output to those with the most income. Although this result may be efficient, it is not necessarily equitable. Individuals who are aged or disabled, for example, may be unable to earn much income yet may still be regarded as worthy recipients of goods and services. In such cases, we may want to change the market's answer to the basic question of FOR WHOM goods are produced.

The government alters the distribution of income with taxes and transfers. The federal income tax takes as much as 39.6 percent of income from rich individuals.

FIGURE 9.7
Moderating Inequity

The market alone would distribute only 1.1 percent of total income to the poor. Government taxes and transfers raise that share to 4.4 percent.

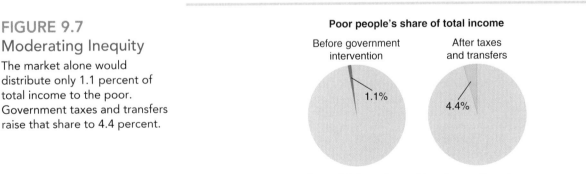

Poor people's share of total income

Before government intervention

After taxes and transfers

1.1%

4.4%

Source: U.S. Census Bureau data on income of lowest quintile (2010).

TABLE 9.1
Income Transfers
The market mechanism might leave some people with too little income and others with too much. The government uses taxes and transfers to redistribute income more fairly.

Program	Recipient Group	Number of Recipients	Value of Transfers
Social Security	Retired and disabled workers	58 million	$700 billion
Medicare	Individuals over age 65	53 million	$600 billion
Medicaid	Medically needy individuals	72 million	$250 billion
Unemployment compensation	Unemployed workers	15 million	$ 68 billion
Food stamps	Low-income households	48 million	$ 76 billion
Earned Income Tax Credit	Low-wage workers	24 million	$ 50 billion
Temporary Aid to Needy Families	Poor families	4 million	$ 17 billion

Source: Congressional Budget Office (2013 data).

A big chunk of this tax revenue is then used to provide **income transfers** for poor people.

income transfers Payments to individuals for which no current goods or services are exchanged, such as Social Security, welfare, unemployment benefits.

As Figure 9.7 illustrates, poor people would get only a tiny sliver of the economic pie—about 1 percent—without government intervention. The tax and transfer system more than quadruples the amount of income they end up with. Although poor people still don't have enough income, government intervention clearly remedies some of the inequities the market alone creates.

Table 9.1 indicates some of the larger income transfer programs. The largest transfer program is Social Security. Although Social Security benefits are paid to virtually all retirees, they are particularly important to the aged poor. In the absence of those monthly Social Security checks, almost half of this country's aged population would be poor. For younger families, food stamps, welfare checks, and Medicaid are all important income transfers for reducing poverty.

MACRO INSTABILITY

The micro failures of the marketplace imply that we are at the wrong point on the production possibilities curve or inequitably distributing the output produced. There is another basic question we have swept under the rug, however. How do we get to the production possibilities curve in the first place? To reach the curve, we must utilize all available resources and technology. Can we be confident that the invisible hand of the marketplace will use all of our resources? Or will some people remain unemployed—that is, willing to work but unable to find a job?

And what about prices? Price signals are a critical feature of the market mechanism. But the validity of those signals depends on some stable measure of value. What good is a doubling of salary when the price of everything you buy doubles as well? Generally, rising prices enrich people who own property and impoverish people who rent. That is why we strive to avoid inflation—a situation where the *average* price level is increasing.

Historically, the marketplace has been wracked with bouts of both unemployment and inflation. These experiences have prompted calls for government intervention at the macro level. *The goal of macro intervention is to foster economic growth—to get us on the production possibilities curve (full employment), maintain a stable price level (price stability), and increase our capacity to produce (growth).* The means for achieving this goal are examined in the macro section of this course.

POLICY PERSPECTIVES

Topic Podcast:
Market Failure

Will the Government Get It Right?

The potential micro and macro failures of the marketplace provide specific justifications for government intervention. The question then turns to how well the activities of the public sector correspond to these implied mandates. Can we trust the government to fix the shortcomings of the market?

INFORMATION   If the government is going to fix things, it must not only confirm market failure but identify the social optimum. This is no easy task. Back in Figure 9.1 we arbitrarily designated point X as the social optimum. In the real world, however, only the *market* outcome is visible. The social optimum isn't visible; it must be inferred. To locate it, we need to know the preferences of the community as well as the dimensions of any externalities. Likewise, if we want the government to change the market distribution of income, we need to know what society regards as fair. No one really has all the required information. Consequently, government intervention typically entails a lot of groping in the dark for *better,* if not *optimal,* outcomes.

VESTED INTERESTS   Vested interests often try to steer the search away from the social optimum. Cigarette manufacturers don't want people to stop smoking. Car companies don't want consumers to reject the fuel technology they have developed. So they try to keep the government from altering market outcomes. To do so, they may generate studies that minimize the size of external costs. They may try to sway public opinion with public interest advertising. And they may use their wealth to finance the campaigns of sympathetic politicians. Government officials, too, may have personal agendas that don't reflect society's interests. In these circumstances it becomes more difficult to figure out where the social optimum is, much less how to get there.

GOVERNMENT FAILURE   These are just a couple of reasons why government intervention won't always improve market outcomes. Yes, an unregulated market might produce the wrong mix of output, generate too much pollution, or leave too many people in poverty. However, government intervention might *worsen,* rather than improve, market outcomes. In that case, we would have to conclude that government intervention *failed.*

The possibility of government failure is illustrated in Figure 9.8. We start with the recognition of market failure: the market *under*produces military goods at point M, relative to society's optimal mix at point X. Because national defense is a *public good,* private consumers don't demand it directly. So the government

FIGURE 9.8
Government Failure

The goal of government intervention is to correct market failuer (e.g., by chaning the mix of output from M to X). It is possible, however, that government policy might move the economy beyond the optimal mix (to point G₁), in the wrong direction (G₂), or even inside the production possibilities curve (point G₃).

Survey Question: How much trust and confidence do you have in our federal government in Washington when it comes to handling domestic problems?

Answers:

Great deal — 12%

Fair amount — 39%

Not very much — 36%

Not at all — 11%

No opinion — 1%

Source: Copyright © (2012) Gallup, Inc. All rights reserved. The content is used with permission; however, Gallup retains all rights of republication.

FIGURE 9.9
Low Expectations
The public has substantial doubts about the ability of government to fix market failures.

intervenes. Will the government move us to point X? Maybe. But it might also move us to point G_1, where *too many* resources are being allocated to the military. Or pacifists might move us to point G_2, where *too little* military output is produced. Maybe government procurement will be so inefficient that we end up at G_3, producing *less* output than possible. Any of these outcomes (G_1, G_2, G_3) fall short of our goal; they may even be worse than the initial market outcome (point M).

Government failure refers to any intervention that fails to improve market outcomes. Perhaps the mix of output or the income distribution got worse when the government intervened. Or the regulatory/administrative cost of intervention outweighed its benefits. Clearly, *there is no guarantee that the visible hand of government will be any cleaner than the invisible hand of the marketplace.*

The average citizen clearly understands that government intervention does not always succeed as hoped. A 2012 opinion poll revealed considerable doubt about the government's ability to improve market outcomes. As Figure 9.9 illustrates, only one out of eight Americans has a "great deal" of confidence that the federal government will do the right thing when it intervenes. One out of nine believes this never happens. Confidence levels are higher for state and local governments, but still far short of comfort levels.

Neither market failure nor government failure is inevitable. The challenge for public policy is to decide when *any* government intervention is justified, then intervene in a way that improves outcomes in the least costly way.

government failure Government intervention that fails to improve economic outcomes.

SUMMARY

- Government intervention in the marketplace is justified by market failure—that is, suboptimal market outcomes.   **LO1**

- The micro failures of the market originate in public goods, externalities, market power, and inequity. These flaws deter the market from achieving the optimal mix of output or distribution of income.   **LO1**

- Public goods are those that cannot be consumed exclusively; they are jointly consumed regardless of who pays. Because everyone seeks a free ride,

no one demands public goods in the marketplace. Hence the market underproduces public goods.   **LO2**

- Externalities are costs (or benefits) of a market transaction borne by a third party. Externalities create a divergence of social and private costs (or benefits), causing suboptimal market outcomes. The market overproduces goods with external costs and underproduces goods with external benefits.   **LO3**

- Market power enables a producer to thwart market signals and maintain a suboptimal mix of output. Antitrust policy seeks to prevent or restrict market power. **LO4**
- The market-generated distribution of income may be regarded as unfair. This equity concern may prompt the government to intervene with taxes and transfer payments that redistribute incomes. **LO5**

- The macro failures of the marketplace are reflected in unemployment and inflation. Government intervention at the macro level is intended to achieve full employment and price stability. **LO5**
- Government failure occurs when intervention fails to improve, or even worsens, economic outcomes. **LO5**

TERMS TO REMEMBER

Define the following terms:

laissez faire	public good	social costs	antitrust
optimal mix of output	private good	private costs	income transfers
market mechanism	free rider	emission charge	government failure
market failure	externalities	market power	

QUESTIONS FOR DISCUSSION

1. Why should taxpayers subsidize public colleges and universities? What external benefits are generated by higher education? **LO3**
2. If everyone seeks a free ride, what mix of output will be produced in Figure 9.2? Why would anyone voluntarily contribute to the purchase of public goods like flood control or snow removal? **LO2**
3. Could local fire departments be privately operated, with services sold directly to customers? What problems would be involved in such a system? **LO3**
4. Identify a specific government activity that is justified by each source of market failure. **LO1**
5. What are the external costs of coastal oil drilling (see News Wire on p. 189)? How would you put

dollar values on them? Do they foreclose all oil drilling? **LO3**
6. Does anyone have an incentive to maintain auto exhaust control devices in good working order? How can we ensure that they will be maintained? **LO5**
7. What are the costs of New York City's recycling program (see News Wire on p. 192)? Are these costs justified? **LO5**
8. Most cities are served by only one cable company. How might this monopoly power affect prices and service? What should the government do, if anything? **LO4, LO5**
9. **POLICY PERSPECTIVES** Why might the market underproduce military output and the government overproduce it? **LO1**

PROBLEMS

■ connect

1. In Figure 9.3, by how much is the market overproducing cars? **LO3**
2. If life expectancy among nonsmokers is reduced by two years due to secondhand smoke and each life-year is worth $20,000, what is the implied annual external cost of worldwide smoking (see News Wire on p. 184)? **LO3**

3. (a) Draw a production possibilities curve (PPC) with cars on the horizontal axis and other goods on the vertical axis.
   (b) Illustrate on your PPC the market failure that occurs in Figure 9.3. **LO3**
4. Draw market demand and social demand curves for flu shots. **LO3**

5. Suppose the following data represent the market demand for college education: **LO3**

Tuition (per year)	$1,000	2,000	3,000	4,000	5,000	6,000	7,000	8,000
Enrollment demanded (in millions)	10	9	8	7	6	5	4	3

(a) If tuition is set at $3,000, how many students will enroll?

(b) Draw the social and market demand curves for this situation.

Now suppose that society gets an external benefit of $1,000 for every enrolled student (for, say, more informed voting).

(c) What is the socially optimal level of enrollments at the tuition price of $3,000?

(d) What amount of tax or subsidy would bring about the socially optimal level?

6. Assume the market demand for cigarettes is as follows: **LO3**

Price per pack	$1.00	1.50	2.00	2.50	3.00	3.50	4.00	4.50	5.00
Quantity (packs per day)	100	90	80	70	60	50	40	30	20

Suppose further that smoking creates external costs valued at 50 cents per pack.

(a) Draw the social and market demand curves.

(b) At $3.50 per pack, what quantity is demanded in the market?

(c) What is the socially optimal quantity at that price?

(d) How large would a tax need to be in order to bring about this socially optimal level?

7. Suppose in the previous problem that a tax of $1 per pack is imposed.   **LO5**

(a) How many packs will be consumed?

(b) Is this rate too high, too low, or the socially optimal rate of consumption?

8. Redraw Figure 9.4b and indicate the amount of profit that would be sacrificed if the firm adopted less polluting technology.   **LO3**

9. Suppose a product can be produced with the following marginal costs: **LO3**

Quantity (units)	1	2	3	4	5	6	7	8	9	10
Marginal cost	$2	3	4	5	6	7	8	9	10	11

If the market price of the product is $9,

(a) How much output will a competitive firm produce?

(b) If each unit produced causes $2 of pollution, what is the socially desired rate of production?

(c) Graph your answers.

10. (a) Graph the following data on social and market demand:

Price	$10	9	8	7	6	5	4	3	2	1
Social quantity demanded	4	8	12	16	20	24	28	32	36	40
Market quantity demanded	2	6	10	14	18	22	26	30	34	38

(b) Does this product have A: external benefits or B: external costs?

(c) How large ($) is that externality?   **LO3**

11. **POLICY PERSPECTIVES** (a) Graph a market outcome wherein 40 units of a polluting good are being produced at the price of $40. Assume the market is overproducing the product at that price because of external costs of $5 per unit.

(b) Illustrate the above market failure on a production possibilities curve.

(c) If the government imposes a pollution fee of $10 per unit, what happens?

A. production ceases

B. government failure occurs

C. production increases

D. market failure is eliminated

(d) Graph the impact of the pollution fee on (i) market outcomes and (ii) the production possibilities curve.   **LO5**

◄ Practice quizzes, student PowerPoints, author podcasts, web activities, and additional materials available at **www.mhhe.com/schilleressentials9e**, or scan here. Need a barcode reader? Try ScanLife, available in your app store.

10

The Business Cycle

◄ Practice quizzes, student PowerPoints, author podcasts, web activities, and additional materials available at www.mhhe.com/schilleressentials9e, or scan here. Need a barcode reader? Try ScanLife, available in your app store.

LEARNING OBJECTIVES

After reading this chapter, you should be able to:

1. Explain how growth of the economy is measured.
2. Tell how unemployment is measured and affects us.
3. Discuss why inflation is a problem and how it is measured.
4. Define "full employment" and "price stability."
5. Recite the U.S. track record on growth, unemployment, and inflation.

n 1929 it looked as though the sun would never set on the American economy. For eight years in a row, the U.S. economy had been expanding rapidly. During the Roaring Twenties the typical American family drove its first car, bought its first radio, and went to the movies for the first time. With factories running at capacity, virtually anyone who wanted to work readily found a job.

Under these circumstances everyone was optimistic. In his acceptance address in November 1928, President-elect Herbert Hoover echoed this optimism by declaring, "We in America today are nearer to the final triumph over poverty than ever before in the history of any land. . . . We shall soon with the help of God be in sight of the day when poverty will be banished from this nation."

The booming stock market seemed to confirm this optimistic outlook. Between 1921 and 1927, the stock market's value more than doubled, adding billions of dollars to the wealth of American households and businesses. The stock market boom accelerated in 1927, causing stock prices to double again in less than two years. The roaring stock market made it look easy to get rich in America.

The party ended abruptly on October 24, 1929. On what came to be known as Black Thursday, the stock market crashed. In a few hours, the market value of U.S. corporations fell abruptly in the most frenzied selling ever seen (see News Wire). The next day President Hoover tried to assure America's stockholders that the economy was "on a sound and prosperous basis." But despite his assurances and the efforts of leading bankers to stem the decline, the stock market continued to plummet. The following Tuesday (October 29) the pace of selling quickened. By the end of the year, over $40 billion of wealth had vanished in the Great Crash. Rich men became paupers overnight; ordinary families lost their savings, their homes, and even their lives.

The devastation was not confined to Wall Street. The financial flames engulfed farms, banks, and industries. Between 1930 and 1935, millions of rural families lost

---

NEWS WIRE	THE CRASH OF 1929

Market in Panic as Stocks Are Dumped in 12,894,600 Share Day; Bankers Halt It

Effect Is Felt on the Curb and throughout Nation—Financial District Goes Wild

The stock markets of the country tottered on the brink of panic yesterday as a prosperous people, gone suddenly hysterical with fear, attempted simultaneously to sell a record-breaking volume of securities for whatever they would bring.

The result was a financial nightmare, comparable to nothing ever before experienced in Wall Street. It rocked the financial district to its foundations, hopelessly overwhelmed its mechanical facilities, chilled its blood with terror.

In a society built largely on confidence, with real wealth expressed more or less inaccurately by pieces of paper, the entire fabric of economic stability threatened to come toppling down.

Into the frantic hands of a thousand brokers on the floor of the New York Stock Exchange poured the selling orders of the world. It was sell, sell, sell—hour after desperate hour until 1:30 p.m.

—Laurence Stern

Source: *The World*, October 25, 1929.

NOTE: The stock market is often a barometer of business cycles. The 1929 crash both anticipated and worsened the Great Depression.

their farms. Automobile production fell from 4.5 million cars in 1929 to only 1.1 million in 1932. So many banks were forced to close that newly elected President Roosevelt had to declare a "bank holiday" in March 1933, closing all the nation's banks for four days. It was a desparate move to stem the outflow of cash to anxious depositors.

Throughout those years, the ranks of the unemployed continued to swell. In October 1929 only 3 percent of the workforce was unemployed. A year later over 9 percent of the workforce was unemployed. Still, things got worse. By 1933 over one-fourth of the labor force was unable to find work. People slept in the streets, scavenged for food, and sold apples on Wall Street.

The Great Depression seemed to last forever. In 1933 President Roosevelt lamented that one-third of the nation was ill clothed, ill housed, and ill fed. Thousands of unemployed workers marched to the Capitol to demand jobs and aid. In 1938, nine years after the Great Crash, nearly 20 percent of the workforce was still unemployed.

The Great Depression shook not only the foundations of the world economy but also the self-confidence of the economics profession. No one had predicted the depression, and few could explain it. How could the economy perform so poorly for so long? What could the government do to prevent such a catastrophe? Suddenly there were more questions than answers.

macroeconomics The study of aggregate economic behavior, of the economy as a whole.

The scramble for answers became the springboard for modern **macroeconomics,** the study of aggregate economic behavior. A basic purpose of macroeconomic theory is to *explain* the **business cycle**—to identify the forces that cause the overall economy to expand or contract. Macro *policy* tries to *control* the business cycle, using the insights of macro theory.

business cycle Alternating periods of economic growth and contraction.

In this chapter we focus on the nature of the business cycle and the related problems of unemployment and inflation. Our goal is to acquire a sense of why the business cycle is so feared. To address these concerns, we need to know

- What are business cycles?
- What damage does unemployment cause?
- Who is hurt by inflation?

As we answer these questions, we will get a sense of why people worry so much about the macro economy and why they demand that Washington do something about it. We'll also see why President Obama was determined not to let the 2008–2009 recession turn into another Great Depression.

ASSESSING MACRO PERFORMANCE

Doctors gauge a person's health with a few simple measurements such as body temperature, blood pressure, and blood content. These tests don't tell doctors everything they need to know about a patient, but they convey some important clues about a patient's general health. In macroeconomics, the economic doctors need comparable measures of the patient's health. The macro economy is a complex construction, encompassing all kinds of economic activity. To get a quick reading of how well it is doing, economists rely on three gauges. *The three basic measures of macro performance are*

- *Output (GDP) growth.*
- *Unemployment.*
- *Inflation.*

The macro economy is in trouble when output growth slows down—or worse, turns negative, as it did during the Great Depression. Economic doctors also worry about the macro economy when they see either unemployment or inflation rising. Any one of these symptoms is painful and may be the precursor to a more serious ailment. Someone has to decide whether to intervene or instead wait to see if the economy can overcome such symptoms by itself.

GDP GROWTH

The first test of the economy's macro health is the rate of output growth. As we first saw in Chapter 1, an economy's *potential* output is reflected in its **production possibilities** curve. That curve tells us how much output the economy *could* produce with available resources and technology. The relevant performance test is whether we are living up to that potential. Are we fully using available resources—or producing at less than capacity? If we are producing *inside* the production possibilities curve, some resources (e.g., workers) are unnecessarily idle. If we are inside the production possibilities curve, the macro economy isn't doing well.

production possibilities The alternative combinations of goods and services that could be produced in a given time period with all available resources and technology.

In reality, output has to *keep* increasing if an economy is to stay healthy. The population increases, and technology advances every year. So the production possibilities curve keeps shifting outward. This means *output* has to keep expanding at a healthy clip just to keep from falling further behind that expanding capacity.

Business Cycles

The central concern in macroeconomics is that the rate of output won't always keep up with ever-expanding production possibilities. Indeed, when macro doctors study the patient's charts, they often discern a pattern of fits, starts, and stops in the growth of output. Sometimes the volume of output grows at a healthy clip. At other times, the growth rate slips. And in some cases total output actually contracts, as it did in 2008–2009 (see News Wire).

Figure 10.1 illustrates this typical business cycle chart. During an economic expansion total output grows rapidly. Then a peak is reached, and output starts dropping. Once a trough is reached, the economy prospers again. This roller-coaster pattern begins to look like a recurring cycle.

NEWS WIRE	DECLINING OUTPUT

Economy: Sharpest Decline in 26 Years

Economic Activity Shrank by 3.8 percent in Last Three Months of 2008, According to the Government's Gross Domestic Product Report

NEW YORK (CNNMoney.com)—The U.S. economy suffered its biggest slowdown in 26 years in the last three months of 2008, according to the government's first reading about the fourth quarter released Friday.

Gross domestic product, the broadcast measure of the nation's economic activity, fell at an annual rate of 3.8 percent in the fourth quarter, adjusted for inflation.

That's the largest drop in GDP since the first quarter of 1982, when the economy suffered a 6.4 percent decline.

—Chris Isidore

Source: CNNMoney.com, January 30, 2009, © 2009 Time Inc. Used under license.

NOTE: A contraction in output indicates that the economy has moved to a point inside its production possibilities curve. Such contractions lower living standards and create more joblessness.

FIGURE 10.1
The Business Cycle

The model business cycle resembles a roller coaster. Output first climbs to a peak and then decreases. After hitting a trough, the economy recovers, with real GDP again increasing.

A central concern of macroeconomic theory is to determine whether a recurring business cycle exists and, if so, what forces cause it.

gross domestic product (GDP) The total value of goods and services produced within a nation's borders in a given time period.

nominal GDP The total value of goods and services produced within a nation's borders, measured in current prices.

real GDP The inflation-adjusted value of GDP; the value of output measured in constant prices.

Real GDP

When we talk about output expanding or contracting, we envision changes in the physical quantity of goods and services produced. But the physical volume of output is virtually impossible to measure. Millions of different goods and services are produced every year, and no one has figured out how to add up their physical quantities (e.g., 30 million grapefruits + 128 million music downloads = ?). So *we measure the volume of output by its market value*, not by its physical volume (e.g., the dollar *value* of grapefruits + the dollar *value* of electronic commerce = a dollar value total). We refer to the dollar value of all the output produced in a year as **gross domestic product (GDP)**.

Because prices vary from one year to the next, GDP yardsticks must be adjusted for inflation. Suppose that from one year to the next all prices doubled. Such a general price increase would double the *value* of output even if the *quantity* of output were totally unchanged. So an unadjusted measure of **nominal GDP** would give us a false reading: we might think output was racing ahead when in fact it was standing still.

To avoid such false readings, we adjust our measure of output for changing price levels. The yardstick of **real GDP** does this by valuing output at constant prices. Thus changes in real GDP are a proxy for changes in the number of grapefruits, houses, cars, items of clothing, movies, and everything else we produce in a year.

Economic activity in 2008 illustrates the distinction between real and nominal GDP. Nominal GDP increased from $14.498 trillion in the second quarter of 2008 to $14.547 trillion in the third quarter, a rise of $49 billion. But that increase in *nominal* GDP growth was due solely to rising prices. *Real* GDP *fell* by more than $90 billion: the *quantity* of output was falling. This decline in *real* GDP was what made people anxious about their livelihoods (see the previous News Wire).

Erratic Growth

Fortunately, declines in real GDP are more the exception than the rule. As Figure 10.2 illustrates, the annual rate of real GDP growth between 1992 and 2000 was never less than 2.4 percent and got as high as 5.0 percent. Those may not sound like big numbers. In a $16 *trillion* economy, however, even small growth rates imply a *lot* of added output. Moreover, the GDP growth of those years exceeded the rate of expansion in production possibilities. Hence the economy kept moving closer to the limits of its (expanding) production possibilities. In the process, living standards rose, and nearly every job seeker could find work.

FIGURE 10.2   The Business Cycle in U.S. History

From 1929 to 2013, real GDP increased at an average rate of 3 percent a year. But annual growth rates have departed widely from that average. Years of above-average growth seem to alternate with years of sluggish growth and years in which total output actually *declines*. Such *recessions* occurred in 1980, 1981–1982, 1990–1991, 2001, and again in 2008–2009.

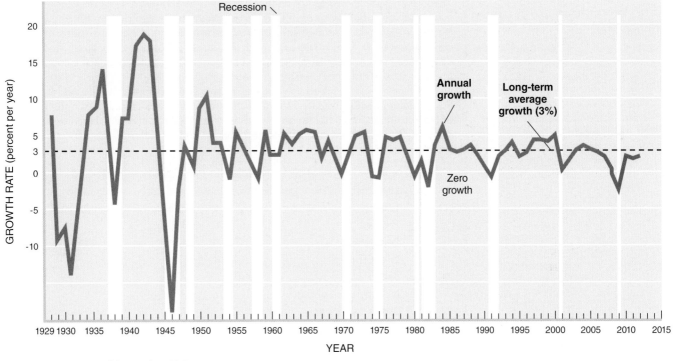

Source: *Economic Report of the President, 2013.*

The economy doesn't always perform so well. Take a closer look at Figure 10.2. The dashed horizontal line across the middle of the chart illustrates the long-term *average* real GDP growth rate, at 3.0 percent a year. Then notice how often the economy grew more slowly than that. Notice also the periodic economic busts when the growth rate fell below zero and total output actually *decreased* from one year to the next, as in 2009. This experience confirms that *real GDP increases not in consistent, smooth increments but in a pattern of steps, stumbles, and setbacks.*

THE GREAT DEPRESSION   The most prolonged setback occurred during the Great Depression. Between 1929 and 1933, total U.S. output steadily declined. Real GDP fell by nearly 30 percent in those four years. Industrial output declined even further, as investments in new plants and equipment virtually ceased. Economies around the world came to a grinding halt (see the following News Wire).

The U.S. economy started to grow again in 1934, but the rate of expansion was modest. Millions of people remained out of work. In 1936–1937 the situation worsened again, and total output once more declined. As a consequence, the rate of total output in 1939 was virtually identical to that in 1929. Because of continuing population growth, **GDP per capita was actually *lower* in 1939 than it had been in 1929.** American families had a *lower* standard of living in 1939 than they had enjoyed 10 years earlier. That had never happened before.

Topic Podcast:
Business Cycles

NEWS WIRE | **WORLDWIDE LOSSES**

Depression Slams World Economies

The Great Depression was not confined to the U.S. economy. Most other countries suffered substantial losses of output and employment over a period of many years. Between 1929 and 1932, industrial production around the world fell 37 percent. The United States and Germany suffered the largest losses, while Spain and the Scandinavian countries lost only modest amounts of output. For specific countries, the decline in output is shown in the accompanying table.

Some countries escaped the ravages of the Great Depression altogether. The Soviet Union, largely insulated from Western economic structures, was in the midst of Stalin's forced industrialization drive during the 1930s. China and Japan were also relatively isolated from world trade and finance and so suffered less damage from the depression.

Country	Percentage Decline in Industrial Output
Chile	−22%
France	−31
Germany	−47
Great Britain	−17
Japan	−2
Norway	−7
Spain	−12
United States	−46

NOTE: Trade and financial links make countries interdependent. When one economy falls into a recession, other economies may suffer as well.

recession A decline in total output (real GDP) for two or more consecutive quarters.

Recessions vary in length and magnitude. A deep and prolonged recession is called a depression.

Rogers © 1990 Pittsburgh Post–Gazette. Reprinted by permission of Universal Uclick for UFS. All rights reserved.

WORLD WAR II   World War II greatly increased the demand for goods and services and ended the Great Depression. During the war years, output grew at unprecedented rates—almost 19 percent in a single year (1942). Virtually everyone was employed, either in the armed forces or in the factories. Throughout the war, our productive capacity was strained to the limit.

RECENT RECESSIONS   After World War II the U.S. economy resumed a pattern of alternating growth and contraction. The contracting periods are called recessions. Specifically, the term **recession** refers to a decline in real GDP that continues for at least two successive calendar quarters. As Table 10.1 indicates, there have been 12 recessions since 1944. The most severe recession occurred immediately after World War II ended, when sudden cutbacks in defense production caused sharp declines in output (−24 percent). That first postwar recession lasted only eight months, however, and raised the rate of unemployment to just 4.3 percent. By contrast, the recession of 1981–1982 was much longer (16 months) and pushed the national unemployment

Dates	Duration (Months)	Percentage Decline in Output	Peak Unemployment Rate
Aug. 1929–Mar. 1933	43	−26.7%	24.9%
May 1937–June 1938	13	−18.2	19.0
Feb. 1945–Oct. 1945	8	−12.7	5.2
Nov. 1948–Oct. 1949	11	−1.7	7.9
July 1953–May 1954	10	−2.6	6.1
Aug. 1957–Apr. 1958	8	−3.7	7.5
Apr. 1960–Feb. 1961	10	−1.6	7.1
Dec. 1969–Nov. 1970	11	−0.6	6.1
Nov. 1973–Mar. 1975	16	−3.2	9.0
Jan. 1980–July 1980	6	−2.2	7.8
July 1981–Nov. 1982	16	−2.7	10.8
July 1990–Feb. 1991	8	−1.4	7.8
Mar. 2001–Nov. 2001	8	−0.3	6.3
Dec. 2007–June 2009	18	−5.1	10.0

TABLE 10.1
Business Slumps, 1929–2009
The U.S. economy has experienced 14 business slumps since 1929. None of the post–World War II recessions came close to the severity of the Great Depression of the 1930s. Recent slumps have averaged 10 months in length (versus 10 *years* for the 1930s depression).

rate to 10.8 percent. That was the highest unemployment rate since the Great Depression of the 1930s. The recession of 2008–2009 again pushed the unemployment rate up to 10 percent.

UNEMPLOYMENT

Although the primary measure of the economy's health is the real GDP growth rate, that measure is a bit impersonal. *People,* not just output, suffer in recessions. When output declines, *jobs* are eliminated. In the 2008–2009 recession over 8 million American workers lost their jobs. Other would-be workers—including graduating students—had great difficulty finding jobs. These are the human dimensions of a recession.

The Labor Force

Our concern about the human side of recession doesn't mean that we believe *everyone* should have a job. We do, however, strive to ensure that jobs are available for all individuals who *want* to work. This requires us to distinguish the general population from the smaller number of individuals who are ready and willing to work—that is, those who are in the **labor force**. The *labor force consists of everyone over the age of 16 who is actually working plus all those who are not working but are actively seeking employment.* As Figure 10.3 shows, only about half of the population participates in the labor market. The rest of the population (nonparticipants) are too young, in school, retired, sick or disabled, institutionalized, or taking care of household needs.

labor force All people over age 16 who are either working for pay or actively seeking paid employment.

Note that our definition of labor force participation excludes most household and volunteer activities. A woman who chooses to devote her energies to household responsibilities or to unpaid charity work is not counted as part of the labor force, no matter how hard she works. Because she is neither in paid employment nor seeking such employment in the marketplace, she is regarded as outside the labor market (a nonparticipant). But if she decides to seek a paid job outside the home and engages in an active job search, we would say that she is "entering the labor force." Students, too, are typically out of the labor force until they leave school and actively look for work, either during summer vacations or after graduation.

FIGURE 10.3
The U.S. Labor Force

Only half of the total U.S. population participates in the civilian labor force. The rest of the population is too young, in school, at home, retired, or otherwise unavailable.

Unemployment statistics count only those participants who are not currently working *and* actively seeking paid employment. Nonparticipants are neither employed nor actively seeking employment.

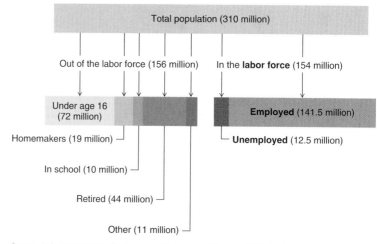

Source: U.S. Department of Labor and U.S. Bureau of Census (2012 data).

The Unemployment Rate

To assess how well labor force participants are faring in the macro economy, we compute the **unemployment rate** as follows:

unemployment rate The proportion of the labor force that is unemployed.

$$\text{Unemployment rate} = \frac{\text{number of unemployed people}}{\text{size of the labor force}}$$

To be counted as *unemployed,* a person must not only be jobless but also be actively looking for work. A full-time student, for example, may be jobless but would not be counted as unemployed. Likewise, a full-time homemaker who is not looking for paid employment outside the home would not be included in our measure of **unemployment.**

unemployment The inability of labor force participants to find jobs.

Figure 10.3 indicates that 12.5 million Americans were counted as unemployed in 2012. The civilian labor force (excluding the armed forces) at that time included 154 million individuals. Accordingly, the civilian unemployment *rate* was

$$\text{Civilian unemployment rate in 2012} = \frac{12.5 \text{ million unemployed}}{154 \text{ million in labor force}} = 8.1\%$$

As Figure 10.4 illustrates, the unemployment rate in 2012 was just below the recession experience of 1990–1991 and had been exceptionally high for four years (2009–2012).

As noted earlier, the unemployment rate is our second measure of the economy's health. It is often regarded as an index of human misery. The people who lose their jobs in a recession experience not only a sudden loss of income but also losses of security and self-confidence. Extended periods of unemployment may undermine families as well as finances. One study showed that every percentage increase in the unemployment rate causes an additional 10,000 divorces. An unemployed person's health may suffer too. Thomas Cottle, a lecturer at Harvard Medical School, stated the case more bluntly: "I'm now convinced that unemployment is *the* killer disease in this country—responsible for wife beating, infertility, and even tooth decay." The following News Wire documents some of the symptoms on which such diagnoses are based.

The Full Employment Goal

In view of the human misery caused by high unemployment rates, it might seem desirable to guarantee every labor force participant a job. But things are never that simple. The macroeconomic doctors never propose to *eliminate* unemployment.

FIGURE 10.4   The Unemployment Record

Unemployment rates reached record heights during the Great Depression. The postwar record is much better than the prewar record, even though full employment has been infrequent.

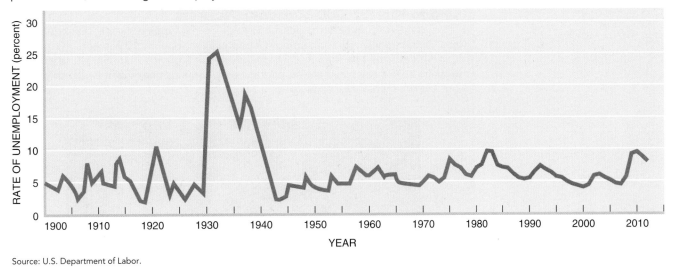

Source: U.S. Department of Labor.

They instead prescribe a *low,* but not a *zero,* unemployment rate. They come to this conclusion for several reasons.

SEASONAL UNEMPLOYMENT   Seasonal variations in employment conditions are a persistent source of unemployment. Some joblessness is inevitable as long as we

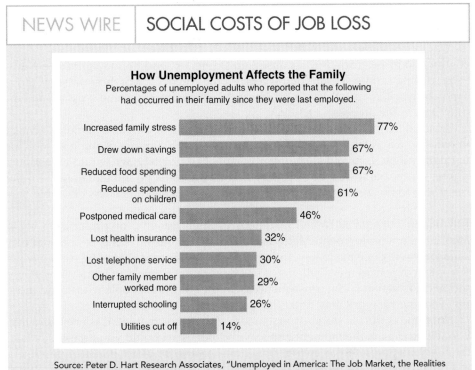

NEWS WIRE | SOCIAL COSTS OF JOB LOSS

How Unemployment Affects the Family
Percentages of unemployed adults who reported that the following had occurred in their family since they were last employed.

Increased family stress	77%
Drew down savings	67%
Reduced food spending	67%
Reduced spending on children	61%
Postponed medical care	46%
Lost health insurance	32%
Lost telephone service	30%
Other family member worked more	29%
Interrupted schooling	26%
Utilities cut off	14%

Source: Peter D. Hart Research Associates, "Unemployed in America: The Job Market, the Realities of Unemployment, and the Impact of Unemployment Benefits," Survey among 413 unemployed adults, conducted April 17–28, 2003, commissioned by National Employment Law Project.

NOTE: The cost of unemployment goes beyond the implied loss of output. Unemployment may breed despair, crime, ill health, and other social problems.

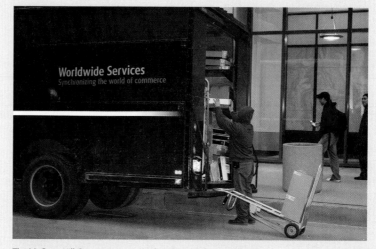

| NEWS WIRE | SEASONAL UNEMPLOYMENT |

UPS to Hire 55,000 Seasonal Workers

NEW YORK–UPS expects to deliver 527 million packages between Thanksgiving and Christmas this year, surpassing last year's record high by 10 percent. . . .

To handle the big jump in package volume, UPS plans to hire 55,000 seasonal workers to sort, load, and deliver packages, the same number that it hired last year, but 10 percent higher than in 2010.

The McGraw-Hill Companies, Inc./Andrew Resek, photographer

NOTE: Some jobs are inherently seasonal. What happens to these UPS workers after the Christmas rush?

continue to grow crops, build houses, go skiing, or send holiday gifts (see News Wire) during certain seasons of the year. At the end of each of these seasons, thousands of workers must search for new jobs, experiencing some seasonal unemployment in the process.

Seasonal fluctuations also arise on the supply side of the labor market. Teenage unemployment rates, for example, rise sharply in the summer as students look for temporary jobs. To avoid such unemployment completely, we would either have to keep everyone in school or ensure that all students go immediately from the classroom to the workroom. Neither alternative is likely, much less desirable.

FRICTIONAL UNEMPLOYMENT   There are other reasons for prescribing some amount of unemployment. Many workers have sound financial or personal reasons for leaving one job to look for another. In the process of moving from one job to another, a person may well miss a few days or even weeks of work without any serious personal or social consequences. On the contrary, people who spend more time looking for work may find *better* jobs.

The same is true of students first entering the labor market. It is not likely that you will find a job the moment you leave school. Nor should you necessarily take the first job offered. If you spend some time looking for work, you are more likely to find a job you like. The job search period gives you an opportunity to find out what kinds of jobs are available, what skills they require, and what they pay. Accordingly, a brief period of job search for persons entering the labor market may benefit both the individual involved and the larger economy. The unemployment associated with this kind of job search is referred to as *frictional* unemployment.

STRUCTURAL UNEMPLOYMENT   For many job seekers, the period between jobs may drag on for months or even years because they do not have the skills that employers require. In the early 1980s, the steel and auto industries downsized, eliminating over half a million jobs. The displaced workers had years of work experience. But their specific skills were no longer in demand. They were *structurally* unemployed. The same fate befell programmers and software engineers when the "dot.com" boom burst in 2000–2001, and then skilled craft workers in the 2006–2008 housing contraction.

High school dropouts suffer similar structural problems. They simply don't have the skills that today's jobs require. When such structural unemployment exists, more job creation alone won't necessarily reduce unemployment. On the contrary, more job demand might simply push wages higher for skilled workers, leaving unskilled workers unemployed.

CYCLICAL UNEMPLOYMENT   There is a fourth kind of unemployment that is more worrisome to the macroeconomic doctors. *Cyclical* unemployment refers to the joblessness that occurs when there are simply not enough jobs to go around. Cyclical unemployment exists when the number of workers demanded falls short of the number of persons in the labor force. This is not a case of mobility between jobs (frictional unemployment) or even of job seekers' skills (structural unemployment). Rather, it is simply an inadequate level of demand for goods and services and thus for labor.

The Great Depression is the most striking example of cyclical unemployment. The dramatic increase in unemployment rates that began in 1930 (see Figure 10.4) was not due to any increase in friction or sudden decline in workers' skills. Instead the high rates of unemployment that persisted for a *decade* were due to a sudden decline in the market demand for goods and services. How do we know? Just notice what happened to our unemployment rate when the demand for military goods and services increased in 1941!

THE POLICY GOAL   In later chapters we examine the causes of cyclical unemployment and explore some potential policy responses. At this point, all we want to do is to set some goals for macro policy. We have seen that *zero unemployment is not an appropriate goal: some seasonal, frictional, and structural unemployment is both inevitable and desirable.* But what, then, is a desirable level of *low* unemployment? If we want to assess macro policy, we need to know what specific rate of unemployment to shoot for.

There is some disagreement about the level of unemployment that constitutes **full employment.** Most macro economists agree, however, that the optimal unemployment rate lies somewhere between 4 and 6 percent.

full employment The lowest rate of unemployment compatible with price stability, variously estimated at between 4 and 6 percent unemployment.

INFLATION

When the unemployment rate falls to its full employment level, you might expect everyone to cheer. This rarely happens, though. Indeed, when the jobless rate declines, a lot of macro economists start to fret. Too much of a good thing, they worry, might cause some harm. The harm they fear is *inflation.*

The fear of inflation is based on the price pressures that accompany capacity production. When the economy presses against its production possibilities, idle resources are hard to find. An imbalance between the demand and supply of goods may cause prices to start rising. The resulting inflation may cause a whole new type of pain. Even a low level of inflation pinches family pocketbooks, upsets financial markets, and ignites a storm of political protest. Runaway inflations do even more harm; they crush whole economies and topple governments. In Germany prices rose more than twenty-five-fold in only one month during the

NEWS WIRE	HYPERINFLATION

Inflation and the Weimar Republic

At the beginning of 1921 in Germany, the cost-of-living index was 18 times higher than its 1913 prewar base, while wholesale prices had mushroomed by 4,400 percent. Neither of these increases are negligible, but inflation and war have always been bedfellows. Normally, however, war ends and inflation recedes. By the end of 1921, it seemed that way; prices rose more modestly. Then, in 1922, inflation erupted.

Zenith of German Hyperinflation

Wholesale prices rose fortyfold, an increase nearly as large as during the prior eight years, while retail prices rose even more rapidly. The hyperinflation reached its zenith during 1923. Between May and June 1923, consumer prices more than quadrupled; between July and August, they rose more than 15 times; in the next month, over 25 times; and between September and October, by 10 times the previous month's increase. . . .

The German economy was thoroughly disrupted. Businessmen soon discovered the impossibility of rational economic planning. Profits fell as employees demanded frequent wage adjustments. Workers were often paid daily and sometimes two or three times a day, so that they could buy goods in the morning before the inevitable afternoon price increase. . . .

In an age that preceded the credit card, businessmen traveling around the country found themselves borrowing funds from their customers each stage of the way. The cash they'd allocated for the entire trip barely sufficed to pay the way to the next stop. Speculation began to dominate production.

As a result of the decline in profitability, the inability to plan ahead, and the concern with speculation rather than production, unemployment rose, increasing by 600 percent between September 1 and December 15, 1923. And as the hyperinflation intensified, people found goods unobtainable.

Hyperinflation crushed the middle class. Those thrifty Germans who had placed their savings in corporate or government bonds saw their lifetime efforts come to naught. Debtors sought out creditors to pay them in valueless currency.

—Jonas Prager

Source: *The Wall Street Journal*, Midwest edition, 1980. Used with permission of Dow Jones & Company, Inc., via Copyright Clearance Center, Inc.

NOTE: When prices are rising quickly, people are forced to change their market behavior. Runaway inflation can derail an economy.

---

hyperinflation of 1922–1923. As the News Wire describes, those runaway prices forced people to change their market behavior radically. After the Soviet Union collapsed in 1989, Russia also experienced price increases that exceeded 2,000 percent a year. Such uncontrolled inflation sent consumers scrambling for goods that became increasingly hard to find at "reasonable" prices. In 2009 prices rose an incomprehensible 231 *million* percent in Zimbabwe. At the height of Zimbabwe's inflation, prices were rising by a factor of 10 per day. That means that a Starbucks latte that cost $4 today would cost $40 tomorrow. Such runaway inflation caused an economic and political crisis that shrank Zimbabwe's output by 30 percent. To avoid that kind of economic disruption, every American president since Franklin Roosevelt has expressed a determination to keep prices from rising.

Relative versus Average Prices

inflation An increase in the average level of prices of goods and services.

Although most people worry about inflation, few understand it. Most people associate **inflation** with price increases on specific goods and services. The economy is not necessarily experiencing inflation, however, every time the price of a cup of coffee goes up. We must be careful to distinguish the phenomenon of inflation from price increases for specific goods. ***Inflation is an increase in the average level of prices, not a change in any specific price.***

Suppose you wanted to know the average price of fruit in the supermarket. Surely you would not have much success in seeking out an average fruit—nobody would be quite sure what you had in mind. You might have some success, however, if you sought the prices of apples, oranges, cherries, and peaches. Knowing the price of each kind of fruit, you could then compute the average price of fruit. The resultant figure would not refer to any particular product but would convey a sense of how much a typical basket of fruit might cost. By repeating these calculations every day, you could then determine whether fruit prices, *on average,* were changing. On occasion, you might even notice that apple prices rose while orange prices fell, leaving the *average* price of fruit unchanged.

The same kinds of calculations are made to measure inflation in the entire economy. We first determine the average price of all output—the average price level—then look for changes in that average. A rise in the average price level is referred to as inflation.

The average price level may fall as well as rise. A decline in average prices—**deflation**—occurs when price decreases on some goods and services outweigh price increases on all others. Although we have not experienced any general deflation since 1940, general price declines were common in earlier periods.

Because inflation and deflation are measured in terms of average price levels, it is possible for individual prices to rise or fall continuously without changing the average price level. We already noted, for example, that the price of apples can rise without increasing the average price of fruit, so long as the price of some other fruit (e.g., oranges) falls. In such circumstances, **relative prices** are changing, but not average prices. An increase in the relative price of apples, for example, simply means that apples have become more expensive in comparison with other fruits (or any other goods or services).

Changes in relative prices may occur in a period of stable average prices or in periods of inflation or deflation. In fact, in an economy as vast as ours—where literally millions of goods and services are exchanged in the factor and product markets—relative prices are always changing. Indeed, relative price changes are an essential ingredient of the market mechanism. If the relative price of apples increases, that is a signal to farmers that they should grow more apples and fewer of other fruits.

General inflation—an increase in the *average* price level—does not perform this same market function. If all prices rise at the same rate, price increases for specific goods are of little value as market signals. In less extreme cases, when most but not all prices are rising, changes in relative prices do occur but are not so immediately apparent.

deflation A decrease in the average level of prices of goods and services.

relative price The price of one good in comparison with the price of other goods.

Redistributions

The distinction between relative and average prices helps us determine who is hurt by inflation—and who is helped. Popular opinion notwithstanding, it is simply not true that everyone is worse off when prices rise. ***Although inflation makes some people worse off, it makes other people better off.*** Some people even get rich when prices rise! These redistributions of income and wealth occur because people buy different combinations of goods and services, own different assets, and sell distinct goods or services (including labor). The impact of inflation on individuals, therefore, depends on how the prices of the goods and services each person buys or sells actually change. In this sense, ***inflation acts just like a tax, taking income or wealth from some people and giving it to others.*** This "tax" is levied through changes in prices, changes in incomes, and changes in wealth.

NEWS WIRE	PRICE EFFECTS

U.S. Colleges Raise Tuition 4.8 Percent, Outpacing Inflation

Tuition and fees at U.S. public universities rose 4.8 percent this year to an average $8,655, as the smallest increase in 12 years still outpaced inflation, a College Board report found.

"It's an improvement in a bad story," said Sandy Baum, an independent policy analyst for the College Board.

Nonprofit private colleges increased tuition and fees 4.2 percent to $29,056. The public college increase outstripped inflation of about 2 percent.

—John Hechinger

Source: *Bloomberg.com*, October 23, 2012. Used with permission of Bloomberg L.P. Copyright © 2012. All rights reserved.

NOTE: An increase in tuition reduces the real income of college students, forcing them to reduce spending on other goods and services.

PRICE EFFECTS   Price changes are the most familiar of inflation's pains. If you have been paying tuition, you know how the pain feels. In 1975 the average tuition at public colleges and universities was $400 per year. In 2013, in-state tuition was $8,665 and still rising (see News Wire). At private universities, tuition has increased eightfold in the last 10 years, to roughly $28,000. You don't need a whole course in economics to figure out the implications of these tuition hikes. To stay in college, you (or your parents) must forgo increasing amounts of other goods and services. You end up being worse off, because you cannot buy as many goods and services as you were able to buy before tuition went up.

The effect of tuition increases on your economic welfare is reflected in the distinction between nominal income and real income. **Nominal income** is the amount of money you receive in a particular time period; it is measured in current dollars. **Real income,** by contrast, is the purchasing power of that money, as measured by the quantity of goods and services your dollars will buy. If the number of dollars you receive every year is always the same, your *nominal income* doesn't change, but your *real income* will fall if prices increase.

Suppose you have an income of $6,000 a year while you're in school. Out of that $6,000 you must pay for your tuition, room and board, books, and everything else. The budget for your first year at school might look like this:

nominal income The amount of money income received in a given time period, measured in current dollars.

real income Income in constant dollars; nominal income adjusted for inflation.

First Year's Budget	
Nominal income	$6,000
Consumption	
Tuition	$3,000
Room and board	2,000
Books	300
Everything else	700
Total	$6,000

After paying for all your essential expenses, you have $700 to spend on "everything else"—the clothes, entertainment, or whatever else you want.

Now suppose tuition increases to $3,500 in your second year, while all other prices remain the same. What will happen to your nominal income? Nothing. You're still getting $6,000 a year. Your *real* income, however, will suffer. This is evident in the second year's budget:

Second Year's Budget	
Nominal income	$6,000
Consumption	
Tuition	$3,500
Room and board	2,000
Books	300
Everything else	200
Total	$6,000

You now have to use more of your income to pay tuition. This means you have less income to spend on other things. After paying for room, board, books, and the increased tuition, only $200 is left for everything else. That means fewer pizzas, movies, dates, or anything you'd like to buy. The pain of higher tuition will soon be evident; your *nominal income* hasn't changed, but your *real income* has.

There are two basic lessons about inflation to be learned from this sad story:

- *Not all prices rise at the same rate during inflation.* In our example, tuition increased substantially while other prices remained steady. Hence the "average" rate of price increase was not representative of any particular good or service. Typically some prices rise rapidly, others rise only modestly, and some may actually fall. Table 10.2 illustrates some recent variations in price changes. In 2012 average prices rose by 1.6 percent. But the average rate of inflation disguised very steep price hikes for apples, donuts, college tuition, and textbooks (sorry!).

- *Not everyone suffers equally from inflation.* This follows from our first observation. Those people who consume the goods and services that are rising faster in price bear a greater burden of inflation; their real incomes fall more. In 2012 people who ate "an apple a day to keep the doctor away" were hurt badly by changing food prices. People who preferred a diet of bananas, eggs, and coffee scored real gains from falling prices. By contrast, students got ripped by rising tuition and textbook prices.

We conclude, then, that **the price increases associated with inflation redistribute real income.** In the example we have discussed, college students end up with fewer goods and services than they had before. Other consumers can continue to purchase at least as many goods as before, perhaps even more. Thus output is effectively *redistributed*

Item	Price Change in 2012 (Percent)
Apples	+11.5
Textbooks	+8.0
Chicken	+6.1
College tuition	+4.5
Donuts	+4.0
Average price level	**+1.6**
Fresh fish	−0.6
Bananas	−0.8
Gasoline	−1.5
Eggs	−2.2
Coffee	−5.0

Source: U.S. Bureau of Labor Statistics.

TABLE 10.2
Not All Prices Rise at the Same Rate
The average rate of inflation conceals substantial differences in the price changes of specific goods and services. The impact of inflation on individuals depends in part on which goods and services are consumed. People who buy goods whose prices are rising fastest lose more real income. In 2012 college students were particularly hard hit by inflation.

from college students to others. Naturally, most college students aren't happy with this outcome. Fortunately for you, inflation doesn't always work out this way.

INCOME EFFECTS   The redistributive effects of inflation are not limited to changes in prices. Changes in prices automatically influence nominal incomes also.

If the price of tuition does in fact rise faster than all other prices, we can safely make three predictions:

- The *real income* of college students will fall relative to that of nonstudents (assuming constant nominal incomes).
- The *real income* of nonstudents will rise relative to that of students (assuming constant nominal incomes).
- The *nominal income* of colleges and universities will rise.

This last prediction simply reminds us that someone always pockets higher prices. ***What looks like a price to a buyer looks like income to a seller.*** If students all pay higher tuition, the university will take in more income. It will end up being able to buy *more* goods and services (including faculty, buildings, and library books) after the price increase than it could before. Both its nominal income and its real income have risen.

Not everyone gets more nominal income when prices rise. But you may be surprised to learn that *on average* people's incomes *do* keep pace with inflation. Again, this is a direct consequence of the circular flow: what one person pays out, someone else takes in. ***If prices are rising, incomes must be rising, too.*** Notice in Figure 10.5 that nominal wages have pretty much risen in step with prices. As a

FIGURE 10.5
Nominal Wages and Prices

Inflation implies not only higher prices but higher wages as well. What is a price to one person is income to someone else. Hence inflation cannot make *everyone* worse off. This graph confirms that average hourly wages have risen along with average prices. When nominal wages rise faster than prices, *real* wages are increasing. Higher real wages reflect higher productivity (more output per worker).

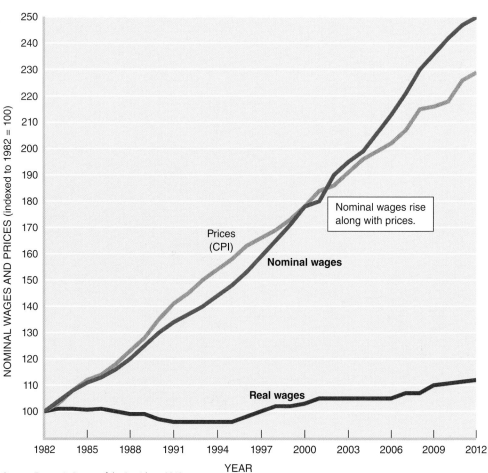

Source: *Economic Report of the President, 2013.*

	Annual Inflation Rate				
Year	2 Percent	4 Percent	6 Percent	8 Percent	10 Percent
2013	$1,000	$1,000	$1,000	$1,000	$1,000
2014	980	962	943	926	909
2015	961	925	890	857	826
2016	942	889	840	794	751
2017	924	855	792	735	683
2018	906	822	747	681	621
2019	888	790	705	630	564
2020	871	760	665	584	513
2021	853	731	627	540	467
2022	837	703	592	500	424
2023	820	676	558	463	386

TABLE 10.3

Inflation's Impact, 2013–2023

In the 1990s, the U.S. rate of inflation ranged from a low of 1.6 percent to a high of 6.1 percent. Does a range of 4–5 percentage points really make much difference? One way to find out is to see how a specific sum of money will shrink in real value.

Here's what would happen to the *real* value of $1,000 from January 1, 2013, to January 1, 2023, at different inflation rates. At 2 percent inflation, $1,000 held for 10 years would be worth $820. At 10 percent inflation that same $1,000 would buy only $386 worth of goods in the year 2023.

result, *real* wages have been fairly stable. From this perspective, it makes no sense to say that "inflation hurts everybody." On *average*, at least, we are no worse off when prices rise, because our (average) incomes increase at the same time.

No one is exactly "average," of course. In reality, some people's incomes rise faster than inflation while others' increase more slowly. Hence the redistributive effects of inflation also originate in varying rates of growth in nominal income.

WEALTH EFFECTS   The same kind of redistribution occurs between those who hold some form of wealth and those who do not. Suppose that on January 1 you deposit $100 in a savings account, where it earns 5 percent interest until you withdraw it on December 31. At the end of the year you will have more nominal wealth ($105) than you started with ($100). But what if all prices have doubled in the meantime? At the end of the year, your accumulated savings ($105) buy less than they would have at the start of the year. In other words, inflation in this case reduces the *real* value of your savings. You end up with fewer goods and services than those individuals who spent all their income earlier in the year! Table 10.3 shows how even modest rates of inflation alter the real value of money hidden under the mattress for 10 years. German households saw the value of their savings approach zero when *hyper*inflation set in (see the News Wire on page 212).

Table 10.4 shows how the value of various assets actually changed in the 1990s. Between 1991 and 2001, the average price level rose by 32 percent. The price of stocks increased much faster, however, while the price of gold fell. Hence people

Asset	Change in Value, 1991–2001
Stocks	+250%
Diamonds	+71
Oil	+66
Housing	+56
U.S. farmland	+49
Average price of goods	**+32**
Silver	+22
Bonds	+20
Stamps	−9
Gold	−29

TABLE 10.4

The Real Story of Wealth

As the value of various assets changes, so does a person's wealth. Between 1991 and 2001, prices rose an average of 32 percent. But the prices of stocks, diamonds, and oil rose even faster. People who held these assets gained in *real* (inflation-adjusted) wealth. Home prices also rose more than average prices. Hence the *real* value of homes also increased in the 1990s. Investors in silver, bonds, and gold did not fare as well.

who held their wealth in the form of stocks rather than gold came out far ahead. The *nominal* values of bonds and silver rose as well, but their *real* value fell.

ROBIN HOOD?   By altering relative prices, incomes, and the real value of wealth, then, inflation turns out to be a mechanism for redistributing incomes. *The redistributive mechanics of inflation include*

- *Price effects.* People who prefer goods and services that are increasing in price least quickly end up with a larger share of real income.
- *Income effects.* People whose nominal incomes rise faster than the rate of inflation end up with a larger share of total income.
- *Wealth effects.* People who own assets that are increasing in real value end up better off than others.

On the other hand, people whose nominal incomes do not keep pace with inflation end up with smaller shares of total output. The same thing is true of those who enjoy goods that are rising fastest in price or who hold assets that are declining in real value. In this sense, *inflation acts like a tax, taking income or wealth from one group and giving it to another.* But we have no assurance that this particular tax will behave like Robin Hood, taking from the rich and giving to the poor. It may do just the opposite. Not knowing who will win or lose the inflation sweepstakes may make everyone fear rising price levels.

Uncertainty

The uncertainties of inflation may also cause people to change their consumption, saving, or investment behavior. When average prices are changing rapidly, economic decisions become increasingly difficult. Should you commit yourself to four years of college, for example, if you are not certain that you or your parents will be able to afford the full costs? In a period of stable prices you can at least be fairly certain of what a college education will cost over a period of years. But if prices are rising, you can no longer be sure how large the bill will be. Under such circumstances, many individuals may decide not to enter college rather than risk the possibility of being driven out later by rising costs. In extreme cases, fear of rapidly increasing prices may even deter diners from ordering a meal (see cartoon).

consumer price index (CPI) A measure (index) of changes in the average price of consumer goods and services.

The uncertainties created by changing price levels affect production decisions as well. Imagine a firm that is considering building a new factory. Typically the construction of a factory takes two years or more, including planning, site selection, and actual construction. If construction costs change rapidly, the firm may find that it is unable to complete the factory or to operate it profitably. Confronted with this added uncertainty, the firm may decide to do without a new plant or at least to postpone its construction until a period of stable prices returns.

Measuring Inflation

Given the pain associated with inflation, it's no wonder that inflation rates are a basic barometer of macroeconomic health. To gauge that dimension of well-being, the government computes several price indexes. Of these indexes, the **consumer price index (CPI)** is the most familiar. As its name suggests, the CPI is a mechanism for measuring changes in the average price of consumer goods and services. It is analogous to the fruit price index we discussed earlier. The CPI refers not to the price of any particular good but, rather, to the average price of all consumer goods.

"Do I have your assurance that prices will not be increased before we are served?"

Fear of rising prices may alter production, consumption, and investment behavior.

From *The Wall Street Journal,* permission by Cartoon Features Syndicate.

By itself, the "average price" of consumer goods is not a useful number. Once we know the average price of consumer goods, however, we can observe whether that average rises—that is, whether inflation is occurring. By observing how prices change, we can calculate the **inflation rate**—that is, the annual percentage increase in the average price level.

To compute the CPI, the Bureau of Labor Statistics periodically surveys families to determine what goods and services consumers actually buy. The Bureau of Labor Statistics then goes shopping in various cities across the country, recording the prices of 184 items that make up the typical market basket. This shopping survey is undertaken every month, in 85 areas and at a variety of stores in each area.

As a result of its surveys, the Bureau of Labor Statistics can tell us what's happening to consumer prices. Suppose, for example, that the market basket cost $100 last year and that the *same* basket of goods and services cost $110 this year. On the basis of those two shopping trips, we could conclude that consumer prices had risen by 10 percent in one year—that is, that the rate of inflation was 10 percent.

In practice, the CPI is usually expressed in terms of what the market basket cost in 1982–1984. For example, the CPI stood at 230 in January 2013. In other words, it cost $230 in 2013 to buy the same market basket that cost only $100 in the base period (1982–1984). Thus prices had more than doubled, on average, over that period. Each month the Bureau of Labor Statistics updates the CPI, telling us the current cost of that same market basket.

The Price Stability Goal

In view of the inequities, anxieties, and real losses caused by inflation, it is not surprising that price stability is a major goal of economic policy. As we observed at the beginning of this chapter, every American president since Franklin Roosevelt has decreed price stability to be a foremost policy goal. Unfortunately, few presidents (or their advisers) have stated exactly what they mean by *price stability*. Do they mean *no* change in the average price level? Or is some upward creep in the CPI consistent with the notion of price stability?

THE POLICY GOAL An explicit numerical goal for **price stability** was established for the first time in the Full Employment and Balanced Growth Act of 1978. According to that act, the goal of economic policy is to hold the rate of inflation at under 3 percent.

Why did Congress choose 3 percent inflation rather than zero inflation as the benchmark for price stability? Two considerations were important. First, Congress recognized that efforts to maintain absolutely stable prices (zero inflation) might threaten full employment. Recall that our goal of full employment is defined as the lowest rate of unemployment *consistent with stable prices.* The same kind of thinking is apparent here. The amount of inflation regarded as tolerable depends in part on how anti-inflation strategies affect unemployment. If policies that promise zero inflation raise unemployment rates too high, people may prefer to accept a little inflation. After reviewing our experiences with both unemployment and inflation, Congress concluded that 3 percent inflation was a safe target.

QUALITY IMPROVEMENTS The second argument for setting our price stability goal above zero inflation relates to our measurement capabilities. Although the consumer price index is very thorough, it is not a perfect measure of inflation. In essence, the CPI simply monitors the price of specific goods over time. Over time, however, the goods themselves change, too. Old products become better as a result of *quality improvements*. A television set costs more today than

inflation rate The annual rate of increase in the average price level.

price stability The absence of significant changes in the average price level; officially defined as a rate of inflation of less than 3 percent.

it did in 1955, but today's TV also delivers a bigger, clearer picture—in digital images, stereo sound, and even 3D. Hence increases in the price of television sets tend to exaggerate the true rate of inflation: part of the higher price represents more product.

The same kind of quality changes distort our view of how car prices have changed. Since 1958 the average price of a new car has risen from $2,867 to roughly $20,000. But today's cars aren't really comparable to those of 1958. Since that time, the quality of cars has been improved with electronic ignitions, emergency flashers, rear window defrosters, crash-resistant bodies, air bags, antilock brakes, remote-control mirrors, seat belts, variable-speed windshield wipers, radial tires, a doubling of fuel mileage, and a hundredfold decrease in exhaust pollutants. Accordingly, the sixfold increase in average car prices since 1958 greatly overstates the true rate of inflation.

NEW PRODUCTS   The problem of measuring quality improvements is even more apparent in the case of new products. The smartphones most people have today did not exist when the Census Bureau conducted its 1982–1984 survey of consumer expenditures. The 2013 survey did include smartphones, but couldn't fully capture the effects of their changing features. The same thing is happening now: new products and continuing quality improvements are enriching our consumption, even though they are not reflected in the CPI. Hence there is a significant (though unmeasured) element of error in the CPI insofar as it is intended to gauge changes in the average prices paid by consumers. The goal of 3 percent inflation allows for such errors.

POLICY PERSPECTIVES

Is Another Recession Coming?

The simple answer to the above question is yes. There have been at least 47 recessions in the United States since 1790, 14 of them since 1944. So if history is any guide, we should expect to experience another recession.

But recessions don't occur on a regular schedule. Nor are they all equally severe. Recessions are like earthquakes: we know they will happen again but don't know exactly when, much less how severe the next one will be. Scientists (seismologists) who study the causes, magnitude, and timing of earthquakes have given us great insights into that natural phenomenon. But seismologists still aren't able to predict exactly when or where the next quake will erupt.

So it is with the economics profession. Economists have studied the origins, the magnitude, and the timing of past recessions. They have isolated a variety of factors (e.g., financial crises, natural disasters) that cause production to decline. And we know a lot about how production cutbacks spread from one industry to another, just like the flu. We even have a pretty good idea about how to contain and ultimately end recessions, as we'll see in later chapters. But we still don't know how to avoid them completely. The next one will probably surprise us.

Although recessions may be inevitable, the challenge for economic policy is to postpone, mitigate, and bring a quick end to future recessions. When we talk about business cycles, we are simply recognizing the inevitability of future downturns. We are not suggesting that they will occur on a set schedule or with consistent force. On the contrary, we continue to develop policy tools for taming the business cycle, even if we can't eliminate it. Our experience since the Great Depression of the 1930s suggests we are making progress in that regard.

SUMMARY

- The health of the macro economy is gauged by three measures: real GDP growth, the unemployment rate, and the inflation rate.   **LO1**
- The long-term growth rate of the U.S. economy is 3 percent a year. But output doesn't increase by 3 percent every year. In some years real GDP grows faster; in other years growth is slower. Sometimes total output actually declines (recession).   **LO5**
- These short-run variations in GDP growth are the focus of macroeconomics. Macro theory tries to explain the alternating periods of growth and contraction that characterize the business cycle; macro policy attempts to control the cycle.   **LO1**
- To understand unemployment, we need to distinguish the labor force from the larger population. Only people who are working (employed) or spend some time looking for a job (unemployed) are participants in the labor force. People who are neither working nor looking for work are outside the labor force.   **LO2**
- The most visible loss imposed by unemployment is reduced output of goods and services. Those individuals actually out of work suffer lost income, heightened insecurity, and even reduced longevity.   **LO2**
- There are four types of unemployment: seasonal, frictional, structural, and cyclical. Because some seasonal and frictional unemployment is inevitable, and even desirable, full employment is not defined as zero unemployment. These considerations, plus fear of inflation, result in full employment being defined as an unemployment rate of 4–6 percent.   **LO4**
- Inflation is an increase in the average price level. Typically it is measured by changes in a price index such as the consumer price index (CPI).   **LO3**
- Inflation redistributes income by altering relative prices, incomes, and wealth. Because not all prices rise at the same rate and because not all people buy (and sell) the same goods or hold the same assets, inflation does not affect everyone equally. Some individuals actually gain from inflation, whereas others suffer a drop in real income.   **LO3**
- Inflation threatens to reduce total output because it increases uncertainties about the future and thereby inhibits consumption and production decisions.   **LO3**
- The U.S. goal of price stability is defined as an inflation rate of less than 3 percent per year. This goal recognizes potential conflicts between zero inflation and full employment, as well as the difficulties of measuring quality improvements and new products.   **LO4**

TERMS TO REMEMBER

Define the following terms:

macroeconomics	nominal GDP	unemployment	nominal income
business cycle	real GDP	full employment	real income
production possibilities	recession	inflation	consumer price index (CPI)
gross domestic product (GDP)	labor force	deflation	inflation rate
	unemployment rate	relative price	price stability

QUESTIONS FOR DISCUSSION

1. Microsoft sells operating systems, applications software, and technical services. How would you compute changes in Microsoft's *volume* of output from one year to the next? How would price changes affect your computations?   **LO1**
2. Could we ever achieve an unemployment rate *below* full employment? What problems might we encounter if we did?   **LO2**
3. Have you ever had difficulty finding a job? Why didn't you get one right away? What kind of unemployment did you experience?   **LO2**
4. Why might inflation accelerate as the unemployment rate declines?   **LO4**
5. During the period shown in Table 10.4, what happened to the wealth of people holding hordes of silver?   **LO3**

6. According to Table 10.2, how might the diet of the average consumer have been altered by relative price changes in 2012? **LO3**

7. Which of the following people would we expect to be hurt by an increase in the rate of inflation from 3 percent to 6 percent? **LO3**
   (a) A homeowner with a $50,000 fixed-rate mortgage on his home.
   (b) A retired person who receives a monthly pension of $600 from her former employer.
   (c) An automobile worker with a cost-of-living provision in his employment contract.
   (d) A wealthy individual who owns corporate bonds that pay her an interest rate of 7 percent per year.

8. Would it be advantageous to borrow money if you expected prices to rise? Why or why not? **LO3**

9. **POLICY PERSPECTIVES** Why did the Great Depression last so long? What happened to all the jobs? **LO5**

PROBLEMS

▦ connect

1. How much *more* output will the average American have next year if the $16 trillion U.S. economy grows by **LO1**
   (a) 2 percent?
   (b) 5 percent?
   (c) −1.0 percent?
   Assume a population of 320 million.

2. Suppose the following data describe a nation's population: **LO2**

	Year 1	Year 2
Population	300 million	305 million
Labor force	150	160
Unemployed	7	7.2

   (a) What is the unemployment rate in each year?
   (b) How has the *number* of unemployed changed from Year 1 to Year 2?
   (c) How is the apparent discrepancy between (a) and (b) explained?

3. If the average worker produces $100,000 of GDP, by how much will GDP increase if there are 150 million labor force participants and the unemployment rate drops from 7.0 to 5.5 percent? **LO1, LO2**

4. In 2012–2013 by what percentage did (a) the nominal price and (b) the real price of tuition at public colleges increase (News Wire, p. 214)? **LO3**

5. Nominal GDP increased from roughly $10 trillion in 2000 to $15 trillion in 2011. In the same period prices rose on average by roughly 30 percent. By how much did *real* GDP increase? **LO3**

6. What would the *real* value be in 10 years of $100 you hid under your mattress if the inflation rate is **LO3**
   (a) 2%   (b) 8%
   (*Hint:* Table 10.3 provides clues.)

7. According to the following data by what percentage, **LO3**
   (a) Did nominal wages increase between 2000 and 2010?
   (b) Did real wages increase?

	2000	2010
Average weekly wage	$500	$750
CPI	170	220

8. In Zimbabwe the rate of inflation hit 90 sextillion percent in 2009, with prices increasing tenfold every day. At that rate, how much would a $100 textbook cost one week later? **LO3**

9. The following table lists the prices of a small market basket purchased in both 2000 and 2010. Assuming that this basket of goods is representative of all goods and services, **LO3**
   (a) Compute the cost of the market basket in 2000.
   (b) Compute the cost of the market basket in 2010.
   (c) By how much has the average price level risen between 2000 and 2010?
   (d) The average household's nominal income increased from $30,000 to $60,000 between 2000 and 2010. What happened to its real income?

		Price (per Unit)	
Item	Quantity	2000	2010
Coffee	20 pounds	$ 4	$ 5
Tuition	1 year	4,000	7,000
Pizza	100 pizzas	8	10
DVD rental	90 days	10	5
Gasoline	1,000 gallons	2	3

10. **POLICY PERSPECTIVES** What was the average duration
    of recessions in
    (*a*) The 1930s?
    (*b*) The 1970s?
    (*c*) The 1980s?
    (See Table 10.1 on page 207.)   **LO5**

◄ Practice quizzes, student PowerPoints, author podcasts, web activities, and additional materials available at **www.mhhe.com/schilleressentials9e**, or scan here. Need a barcode reader? Try ScanLife, available in your app store.

11 Aggregate Supply and Demand

◀ Practice quizzes, student PowerPoints, author podcasts, web activities, and additional materials available at www.mhhe.com/ schilleressentials9e, or scan here. Need a barcode reader? Try ScanLife, available in your app store.

LEARNING OBJECTIVES

After reading this chapter, you should be able to:

1 Cite the major macro outcomes and their determinants.
2 Explain how classical and Keynesian macro views differ.
3 Illustrate the shapes of the aggregate demand and supply curves.
4 Tell how macro failure occurs.
5 Outline the major policy options for macro government intervention.

Recurrent recessions, unemployment, and inflation indicate that the economy isn't always in perfect health. Now it's time to start thinking about causes and cures. Why does the economy slip into recession? What causes unemployment or inflation rates to flare up? And what, if anything, can the government do to cure these ailments?

The central focus of **macroeconomics** is on these questions—that is, what causes business cycles and what, if anything, the government can do about them. Can government intervention prevent or correct market excesses? Or is government intervention likely to make things worse?

macroeconomics The study of aggregate economic behavior, of the economy as a whole.

To answer these questions, we need a model of how the economy works. The model must show how the various pieces of the economy interact. The model must not only show how the macro economy works but also pinpoint potential causes of macro failure.

To develop such a macro model, some basic questions must be answered:

- What are the major determinants of macro outcomes?
- How do the forces of supply and demand fit into the macro picture?
- Why are there disagreements about causes and cures of macro ailments?

Answers to these questions will go a long way toward explaining the continuing debates about the causes of business cycles. A macro model can also be used to identify policy options for government intervention.

A MACRO VIEW

Macro Outcomes

Figure 11.1 provides a bird's-eye view of the macro economy. The primary outcomes of the macro economy are arrayed on the right side of the figure. These basic *macro outcomes include*

- *Output:* total volume of goods and services produced (real GDP).
- *Jobs:* levels of employment and unemployment.
- *Prices:* average prices of goods and services.

FIGURE 11.1   The Macro Economy

The primary outcomes of the macro economy are output of goods and services, jobs, prices, economic growth, and international balances (trade, currency). These outcomes result from the interplay of internal market forces (e.g., population growth, innovation, spending patterns), external shocks (e.g., wars, weather, trade disruptions), and policy levers (e.g., tax and budget decisions).

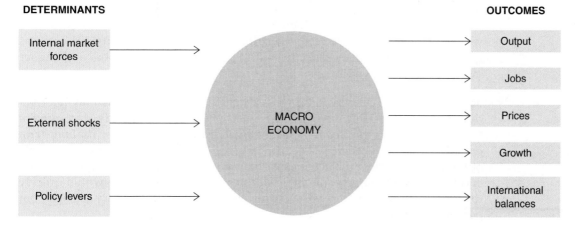

- *Growth:* year-to-year expansion in production capacity.
- *International balances:* international value of the dollar; trade and payments balances with other countries.

These macro outcomes define our nation's economic welfare. As observed in Chapter 10, we gauge the health of the macro economy by its real GDP (output) growth, unemployment (jobs), and inflation (prices). To this list we now add an international measure—the balances in our trade and financial relations with the rest of the world.

Macro Determinants

Figure 11.1 also provides an overview of the separate forces that affect macro outcomes. Three broad forces are depicted. These *determinants of macro performance include*

- *Internal market forces:* population growth, spending behavior, invention and innovation, and the like.
- *External shocks:* wars, natural disasters, terrorist attacks, trade disruptions, and so on.
- *Policy levers:* tax policy, government spending, changes in interest rates, credit availability and money, trade policy, immigration policy, and regulation.

In the absence of external shocks or government policy, an economy would still function—it would still produce output, create jobs, establish prices, and maybe even grow. The U.S. economy operated this way for much of its history. Even today, many less developed countries and areas operate in relative isolation from government and international events. In these situations, macro outcomes depend exclusively on internal market forces.

STABLE OR UNSTABLE?

The central concern of macroeconomic theory is whether the internal forces of the marketplace will generate desired outcomes. Will the market mechanism assure us full employment? Will the market itself maintain price stability? Or will the market *fail*, subjecting us to recurring bouts of unemployment, inflation, and declining output?

Classical Theory

Prior to the 1930s, macro economists thought there could never be a Great Depression. The economic thinkers of the time asserted that the economy was inherently stable. During the nineteenth century and the first 30 years of the twentieth century, the U.S. economy had experienced some bad years—years in which the nation's output declined and unemployment increased. But most of these episodes were relatively short-lived. The dominant feature of the industrial era was growth—an expanding economy, with more output, more jobs, and higher incomes nearly every year.

SELF-ADJUSTMENT In this environment, classical economists, as they later became known, propounded an optimistic view of the macro economy. *According to the classical view, the economy self-adjusts to deviations from its long-term growth trend.* Producers might occasionally reduce their output and throw people out of work. But these dislocations would cause little damage. If output declined and people lost their jobs, the internal forces of the marketplace would quickly restore prosperity. Economic downturns were viewed as temporary setbacks, not permanent problems.

FLEXIBLE PRICES   The cornerstones of classical optimism were flexible prices and flexible wages. If producers were unable to sell all their output at current prices, they had two choices. They could reduce the rate of output and throw some people out of work. Or they could reduce the price of their output, thereby stimulating an increase in the quantity demanded. According to the law of demand, price reductions cause an increase in unit sales. If prices fall far enough, all the output produced can be sold. Thus flexible prices—prices that would drop when consumer demand slowed—virtually guaranteed that all output could be sold. No one would have to lose a job because of weak consumer demand.

FLEXIBLE WAGES   Flexible prices had their counterpart in factor markets. If some workers were temporarily out of work, they would compete for jobs by offering their services at lower wages. As wage rates declined, producers would find it profitable to hire more workers. Ultimately, flexible wages would ensure that everyone who wanted a job would have a job.

SAY'S LAW   These optimistic views of the macro economy were summarized in Say's Law. **Say's Law**—named after the nineteenth-century economist Jean-Baptiste Say—decreed that "supply creates its own demand." In Say's view, if you produce something, *somebody* will buy it. All you have to do is find the right price. In this classical view of the world, unsold goods could appear in the market. But they would ultimately be sold when buyers and sellers found an acceptable price.

Say's Law Supply creates its own demand.

The same self-adjustment was expected in the labor market. Sure, some people could lose jobs, especially when output growth slowed. But they could find new jobs if they were willing to accept lower wages. With enough wage flexibility, no one would remain unemployed.

There could be no Great Depression—no protracted macro failure—in this classical view of the world. Indeed, internal market forces (e.g., flexible prices and wages) could even provide an automatic adjustment to external shocks (e.g., wars, droughts, trade disruptions) that threatened to destabilize the economy. *The classical economists saw no need for the box labeled "policy levers" in Figure 11.1; government intervention in the (self-adjusting) macro economy was unnecessary.*

The Great Depression was a stunning blow to classical economists. At the onset of the depression, classical economists assured everyone that the setbacks in production and employment were temporary and would soon vanish. Andrew Mellon, secretary of the U.S. Treasury, expressed this optimistic view in January 1930, just a few months after the stock market crash. Assessing the prospects for the year ahead, he said, "I see nothing . . . in the present situation that is either menacing or warrants pessimism . . . I have every confidence that there will be a revival of activity in the spring and that during the coming year the country will make steady progress."[1] Merrill Lynch, one of the nation's largest brokerage houses, was urging people to buy stocks. But the depression deepened. Indeed, unemployment grew and persisted *despite* falling prices and wages (see Figure 11.2). The classical self-adjustment mechanism simply did not work.

The Keynesian Revolution

The Great Depression destroyed the credibility of classical economic theory. As John Maynard Keynes wrote in 1935, classical economists

> were apparently unmoved by the lack of correspondence between the results of their theory and the facts of observation:—a discrepancy which the ordinary man has not failed to observe. . . .

[1]David A. Shannon, *The Great Depression* (Englewood Cliffs, NJ: Prentice Hall, 1960), p. 4.

FIGURE 11.2
Inflation and Unemployment, 1900–1940

In the early twentieth century, prices responded to both upward and downward changes in aggregate demand. Periods of high unemployment also tended to be brief. In the 1930s, however, unemployment rates rose to unprecedented heights and stayed high for a decade. Falling wages and prices did not restore full employment. This macro failure prompted calls for new theories and policies to control the business cycle.

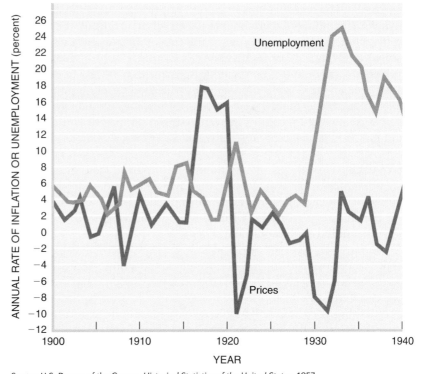

Source: U.S. Bureau of the Census, *Historical Statistics of the United States,* 1957.

The celebrated optimism of [classical] economic theory . . . is . . . to be traced, I think, to their having neglected to take account of the drag on prosperity which can be exercised by an insufficiency of effective demand. For there would obviously be a natural tendency towards the optimum employment of resources in a Society which was functioning after the manner of the classical postulates. It may well be that the classical theory represents the way in which we should like our Economy to behave. But to assume that it actually does so is to assume our difficulties away.[2]

NO SELF-ADJUSTMENT   Keynes went on to develop an alternative view of the macro economy. Whereas the classical economists viewed the economy as inherently stable, *Keynes asserted that the private economy was inherently unstable.* Small disturbances in output, prices, or unemployment were likely to be magnified, not muted, by the invisible hand of the marketplace. The Great Depression was not a unique event, Keynes argued, but a calamity that would recur if we relied on the market mechanism to self-adjust. Macro failure was the rule, not the exception, for a purely private economy.

In Keynes's view, the inherent instability of the marketplace required government intervention. When the economy falters, we cannot afford to wait for some assumed self-adjustment mechanism. We must instead intervene to protect jobs and income. Keynes concluded that policy levers (see Figure 11.1) were both effective and necessary. Without such intervention, he believed, the economy was doomed to bouts of repeated macro failure.

Modern economists hesitate to give policy intervention that great a role. Nearly all economists recognize that policy intervention affects macro outcomes. But there are great arguments about just how effective any policy lever is. A vocal minority of economists even echoes the classical notion that policy intervention may be either ineffective or, worse still, inherently destabilizing.

---

[2]John Maynard Keynes, *The General Theory of Employment, Interest and Money* (London: Macmillan, 1936), pp. 33–34.

THE AGGREGATE SUPPLY–DEMAND MODEL

These persistent debates can best be understood in the familiar framework of supply and demand—the most commonly used tools in an economist's toolbox. All of the macro outcomes depicted in Figure 11.1 are the result of market transactions—an interaction between supply and demand. Hence *any influence on macro outcomes must be transmitted through supply or demand.* In other words, if the forces depicted on the left side of Figure 11.1 affect neither supply nor demand, they will have no impact on macro outcomes. This makes our job easier. We can resolve the question about macro stability by focusing on the forces that shape supply and demand in the macro economy.

Topic Podcast:
Macro Instability

Aggregate Demand

Economists use the term "aggregate demand" to refer to the collective behavior of all buyers in the marketplace. Specifically, **aggregate demand** refers to the various quantities of output that all market participants are willing and able to buy at alternative price levels in a given period. Our view here encompasses the collective demand for *all* goods and services rather than the demand for any single good.

aggregate demand The total quantity of output demanded at alternative price levels in a given time period, *ceteris paribus.*

To understand the concept of aggregate demand better, imagine that everyone is paid on the same day. With their income in hand, people then enter the product market. The question is, How much will people buy?

To answer this question, we have to know something about prices. If goods and services are cheap, people will be able to buy more with their given income. On the other hand, high prices will limit both the ability and willingness of people to purchase goods and services. Note that we are talking here about the average price level, not the price of any single good.

REAL GDP (OUTPUT)   This simple relationship between average prices and real spending is illustrated in Figure 11.3. On the horizontal axis we depict the various quantities of output that might be purchased. We are referring here to **real GDP,** an inflation-adjusted measure of physical output.

real GDP The inflation-adjusted value of GDP; the value of output measured in constant prices.

PRICE LEVEL   On the vertical axis we measure prices. Specifically, Figure 11.3 depicts alternative levels of *average* prices. As we move up the vertical axis, the average price level rises (inflation); and as we move down, the average price level falls (deflation).

The aggregate demand curve in Figure 11.3 has a familiar shape. The message of this downward-sloping macro curve is a bit different, however. *The aggregate demand curve illustrates how the volume of purchases varies with average prices.*

REAL OUTPUT (quantity per year)

FIGURE 11.3
Aggregate Demand

Aggregate demand refers to the total output demanded at alternative price levels (*ceteris paribus*). The vertical axis here measures the average level of all prices rather than the price of a single good. Likewise, the horizontal axis refers to the real value of all goods, not the quantity of only one product.

The downward slope of the aggregate demand curve suggests that with a given (constant) level of income, people will buy more goods and services at lower prices. The curve doesn't tell us *which* goods and services people will buy; it simply indicates the total volume (quantity) of their intended purchases.

At first blush, a downward-sloping demand curve hardly seems remarkable. But because *aggregate* demand refers to the total volume of spending, Figure 11.3 requires a distinctly macro explanation. That explanation includes three separate phenomena:

- *Real balances effect:* The primary explanation for the downward slope of the aggregate demand curve is that cheaper prices make the dollars you hold more valuable. That is to say, **the real value of money is measured by how many goods and services each dollar will buy.** In this respect, lower prices make you richer: the cash balances you hold in your pocket, in your bank account, or under your pillow are worth more when the price level falls. Lower prices also increase the value of other dollar-denominated assets (e.g., bonds), thus increasing the wealth of consumers.

    When their real incomes and wealth increase because of a decline in the price level, consumers respond by buying more goods and services. They end up saving less of their incomes and spending more. This causes the aggregate demand curve to slope downward to the right.

- *Foreign trade effect:* The downward slope of the aggregate demand curve is reinforced by changes in imports and exports. When American-made products become cheaper, U.S. consumers will buy fewer imports and more domestic output. Foreigners will also step up their purchases of American-made goods when American prices are falling.

    The opposite is true as well. When the domestic price level rises, U.S. consumers are likely to buy more imports. At the same time, foreign consumers may cut back on their purchases of American-made products when American prices increase.

- *Interest rate effect:* Changes in the price level also affect the amount of money people need to borrow and so tend to affect interest rates. At lower price levels, consumer borrowing needs are smaller. As the demand for loans diminishes, interest rates tend to decline as well. This cheaper money stimulates more borrowing and loan-financed purchases.

The combined forces of these real balances, foreign trade, and interest rate effects give the aggregate demand curve its downward slope. People buy a larger volume of output when the price level falls (*ceteris paribus*). This makes perfect sense.

Aggregate Supply
While lower price levels tend to increase the volume of output *demanded*, they have the opposite effect on the aggregate quantity *supplied*.

PROFIT MARGINS   If the price level falls, producers are being squeezed. In the short run, producers are saddled with some relatively constant costs, such as rent, interest payments, negotiated wages, and inputs already contracted for. If output prices fall, producers will be hard-pressed to pay these costs, much less earn a profit. Their response will be to reduce the rate of output.

Rising output prices have the opposite effect. Because many costs are fixed in the short run, higher prices for goods and services tend to widen profit margins. As profit margins widen, producers will want to produce and sell more goods. Thus *we expect the rate of output to increase when the price level rises.* This expectation is reflected in the upward slope of the aggregate supply curve in Figure 11.4. **Aggregate supply** reflects the various quantities of real output that firms are willing and able to produce at alternative price levels in a given time period.

aggregate supply The total quantity of output producers are willing and able to supply at alternative price levels in a given time period, *ceteris paribus.*

PRICE LEVEL (average price)

Higher
prices

Aggregate
supply

Higher prices
encourage more
production.

More output
supplied

REAL OUTPUT (quantity per year)

**FIGURE 11.4
Aggregate Supply**
Aggregate supply refers to the total volume of output producers are willing and able to bring to the market at alternative price levels (*ceteris paribus*). The upward slope of the aggregate supply curve reflects the fact that profit margins widen when output prices rise (especially when short-run costs are constant). Producers respond to wider profit margins by supplying more output.

COSTS   The upward slope of the aggregate supply curve is also explained by rising costs. To increase the rate of output, producers must acquire more resources (e.g., labor) and use existing plants and equipment more intensively. These greater strains on our productive capacity tend to raise production costs. Producers must therefore charge higher prices to recover the higher costs that accompany increased capacity utilization.

Cost pressures tend to intensify as capacity is approached. If there is a lot of excess capacity, output can be increased with little cost pressure. Hence the lower end of the aggregate supply (AS) curve is fairly flat. As capacity is approached, however, business isn't so easy. Producers may have to pay overtime wages, raise base wages, and pay premium prices to get needed inputs. This is reflected in the steepening slope of the AS curve at higher output levels, as shown in Figure 11.4.

Macro Equilibrium

What we end up with here are two rather conventional-looking supply and demand curves. But these particular curves have special significance. Instead of describing the behavior of buyers and sellers in a single market, *aggregate supply and demand curves summarize the market activity of the whole (macro) economy.* These curves tell us what *total* amount of goods and services will be supplied or demanded at various price levels.

These graphic summaries of buyer and seller behavior provide some initial clues to how macro outcomes are determined. The most important clue is point E in Figure 11.5, where the aggregate demand and supply curves intersect. This is the only point at which the behavior of buyers and sellers is compatible. We know from the aggregate demand curve that people are willing and able to buy the quantity Q_E when the price level is at P_E. From the aggregate supply curve we know that businesses are prepared to sell the quantity Q_E at the price level P_E. Hence buyers and sellers are willing to trade exactly the same quantity (Q_E) at that price level. We call this situation **macro equilibrium**—the unique combination of price level and output that is compatible with both buyers' and sellers' intentions. At macro equilibrium, the rate of desired spending is exactly equal to the rate of production: everything produced is sold.

equilibrium (macro) The combination of price level and real output that is compatible with both aggregate demand and aggregate supply.

DISEQUILIBRIUM   To appreciate the significance of macro equilibrium, suppose that another price or output level existed. Imagine, for example, that prices were higher, at the level P_1 in Figure 11.5. How much output would people want to buy at that price level? How much would business want to produce and sell?

FIGURE 11.5
Macro Equilibrium

The aggregate demand and supply curves intersect at only one point (*E*). At that point, the price level (P_E) and output (Q_E) combination is compatible with both buyers' and sellers' intentions. The economy will gravitate to those equilibrium price (P_E) and output (Q_E) levels. At any other price level (e.g., P_1), the behavior of buyers and sellers is incompatible.

The aggregate demand curve tells us that people would want to buy only the quantity D_1 at the higher price level P_1. But business firms would want to sell the larger quantity, S_1. This is a *disequilibrium* situation in which the intentions of buyers and sellers are incompatible. The aggregate quantity supplied (S_1) exceeds the aggregate quantity demanded (D_1). Accordingly, a lot of the goods being produced will remain unsold at price level P_1.

MARKET ADJUSTMENTS   To unload these unsold goods, producers have to reduce their prices. As prices drop, producers will decrease the volume of goods sent to market. At the same time, the quantities consumers want to buy will increase. This adjustment process will continue until point *E* is reached and the quantities demanded and supplied are equal. At that macro equilibrium, the lower price level P_E will prevail.

The same kind of adjustment process would occur if a lower price level first existed. At lower prices, the aggregate quantity demanded would exceed the aggregate quantity supplied. As sales outpaced production, inventories would dwindle and shortages would emerge. The resulting shortages would permit sellers to raise their prices. As they did so, the aggregate quantity demanded would decrease, and the aggregate quantity supplied would increase. Eventually we would return to point *E*, where the aggregate quantities demanded and supplied are equal.

Equilibrium is unique; it is the only price–output combination that is mutually compatible with aggregate supply and demand. In terms of graphs, it is the only place where the aggregate supply and demand curves intersect. At point *E* there is no reason for the level of output or prices to change. The behavior of buyers and sellers is compatible: desired spending equals current production. By contrast, any other level of output or prices creates a *dis*equilibrium that requires market adjustments. All other price and output combinations, therefore, are unstable. They will not last. Eventually the economy will return to point *E*.

MACRO FAILURE

There are *two potential problems with the macro equilibrium* depicted in Figure 11.5:

- *Undesirability:* The price–output relationship at equilibrium may not satisfy our macroeconomic goals.
- *Instability:* Even if the designated macro equilibrium is optimal, it may be displaced by macro disturbances.

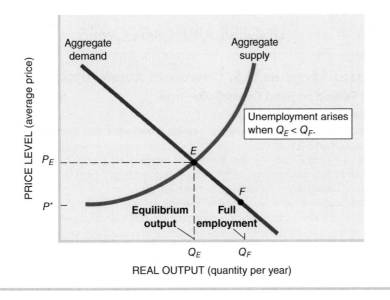

FIGURE 11.6
An Undesired Equilibrium

Equilibrium establishes the only levels of prices and output that are compatible with both buyers' and sellers' intentions. These outcomes may not satisfy our policy goals. In the case shown here, the equilibrium output rate (Q_E) falls short of full employment GDP (Q_F). Unemployment results.

Undesirable Outcomes

The macro equilibrium depicted in Figure 11.5 is simply the intersection of two curves. All we know for sure is that people want to buy the same quantity of goods and services that businesses want to sell at the price level P_E. This quantity (Q_E) may be more or less than our full employment capacity. This contingency is illustrated in Figure 11.6.

What's new in Figure 11.6 is the designation of **full employment GDP**—that is, capacity output. The output level Q_F in the figure represents society's full employment goal. Q_F *refers to the quantity of output that could be produced if the labor force were fully employed.* If we produce less output than that, some workers will remain unemployed. This is exactly what happens at the macro equilibrium depicted here: only the quantity Q_E is being produced. Since Q_E is less than Q_F, the economy is not fully utilizing its production possibilities. This is the dilemma that the U.S. economy confronted in 2008–2009 (see the following News Wire).

full employment GDP The rate of real output (GDP) produced at full employment.

UNEMPLOYMENT The shortfall in equilibrium output illustrated in Figure 11.6 implies that the economy will be burdened with cyclical **unemployment.** Full employment is attained only if we produce at Q_F. Market forces, however, lead us to the lower rate of output at Q_E. Some workers can't find jobs.

unemployment The inability of labor force participants to find jobs.

INFLATION Similar problems may arise with the equilibrium price level. Suppose that P^* represents the most desired price level. In Figure 11.6 we see that the equilibrium price level P_E exceeds P^*. If market behavior determines prices, the price level will rise above the desired level. The resulting increase in average prices is what we call **inflation.**

inflation An increase in the average level of prices of goods and services.

MACRO FAILURE It could be argued, of course, that our apparent macro failures are simply an artifact. We could have drawn our aggregate supply and demand curves to intersect at point F in Figure 11.6. At that intersection we would be assured both price stability and full employment. Why didn't we draw them there, rather than intersecting at point E?

On the graph we can draw curves anywhere we want. In the real world, however, only one set of curves will correctly express buyers' and sellers' behavior. We must emphasize here that those real-world curves may *not* intersect at point F, thus denying us price stability, full employment, or both. That is the kind of economic outcome illustrated in Figure 11.6. When that happens, we are saddled with macro failure.

NEWS WIRE | UNDESIRABLE OUTCOMES

Job Losses Surge as U.S. Downturn Accelerates

Declines Extend beyond Construction and

Manufacturing to Service Sectors

Rising unemployment across the nation reveals a pervasive downturn that is spreading at an accelerating pace.

In data released Friday by the Bureau of Labor Statistics, 12 states, including Florida, Idaho, North Carolina, and Illinois, reported a rise of at least two percentage points in unemployment rates over the past year.

For many states, the pace of decline is more severe than during the 2001 recession. Job losses have spread beyond construction and manufacturing to service sectors such as tourism, hospitality, and professional and business services.

"It's remarkable how fast the unemployment rate is increasing" in several states, said Luke Tilley, a senior economist at IHS Global Insight. "We are now seeing the full ripple effects." . . .

Unemployment generally was higher in Western states, which have been hit particularly hard by the housing bust, and the Midwest, which continues to bleed manufacturing jobs. But joblessness affected the entire country, even touching energy-producing states that had been resilient up to this point.

—Conor Dougherty

Source: *The Wall Street Journal*, November 22, 2008 p. A3. Used with permission of Dow Jones & Company, Inc., via Copyright Clearance Center, inc.

NOTE: A contraction in one industry (such as housing) can have "ripple effects" that reduce aggregate demand across the entire economy, destroying jobs.

Unstable Outcomes

Figure 11.6 is only the beginning of our macro worries. Suppose that the aggregate supply and demand curves actually intersected in the perfect spot. That is, imagine that macro equilibrium yielded the optimal levels of both employment and prices. This is pretty much the happy situation we enjoyed in 2007: we had full employment (4.6 percent unemployment), price stability (2.8 percent inflation), and decent real GDP growth (2.1 percent). With such good macro outcomes, can't we just settle back and enjoy our good fortune?

Unhappily, even a perfect macro equilibrium doesn't ensure a happy ending. The aggregate supply and demand curves that momentarily bring us macro bliss are not necessarily permanent. They can *shift*—and they will whenever the behavior of buyers and sellers changes.

SHIFT OF AD   The behavior of U.S. producers and consumers *did* change in 2007, pushing the economy out of its full employment equilibrium. The problem began in the construction industry. From 2001 to 2006 home prices rose every year. That made home-owning consumers wealthier and kept construction companies busy building new homes. The party started to peter out in July 2006, however, when home prices stopped rising. Things got worse a few months later when home prices actually started falling. By 2007 the demand for new homes began falling rapidly. As it did, the aggregate demand curve *shifted* to the left. Suddenly more output (including new homes) was being produced at Q_F than people were willing to buy. Builders responded by cutting back construction and laying off workers. As the economy moved to a new and lower equilibrium (point H in Figure 11.7a), more and more workers lost their jobs and joined the ranks of the unemployed. The economy moved from the full employment equilibrium (point F) of 2007 to the recessionary equilibrium (point H) of 2008–2009. (See the News Wire.)

FIGURE 11.7   Macro Disturbances

*(a) **Aggregate demand shifts:*** A decrease (leftward shift) in aggregate demand (AD) tends to reduce output and price levels. A fall in demand may be due to a plunge in housing prices or the stock market, an increased taste for imports, changes in expectations, higher taxes, or other events.

*(b) **Aggregate supply shifts:*** A decrease (leftward shift) of the aggregate supply (AS) curve tends to reduce real GDP and raise average prices. When supply shifts from AS_0 to AS_1, the equilibrium moves from *F* to *G*. Such a supply shift may result from natural disasters, higher import prices, changes in tax policy, or other events.

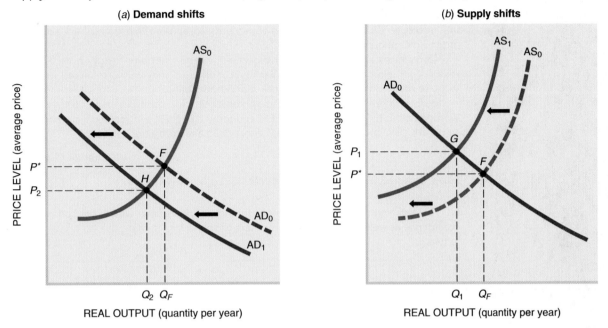

SHIFT OF AS   A shift of the AS curve can also push the economy out of full employment equilibrium. When Hurricane Sandy struck the East Coast in October 2012, it destroyed roads, bridges, and ports, making transportation of goods more expensive. Refinery shutdowns also caused the price of oil to shoot up. This oil price hike directly increased the cost of production in a wide range of U.S. industries, making producers less willing and able to supply goods at prevailing prices. Thus the aggregate supply curve *shifted to the left*, as shown in Figure 11.7*b*.

The impact of a leftward supply shift on the economy is evident. Whereas macro equilibrium was originally located at the optimal point *F*, the new equilibrium was located at point *G*. At point *G*, less output was produced, and prices were higher. Full employment and price stability vanished before our eyes. This is the kind of "external shock" that can destabilize any economy.

RECURRENT SHIFTS   The situation gets even crazier when the aggregate supply and demand curves shift repeatedly in different directions. A leftward shift of the aggregate demand curve can cause a recession as the rate of output falls. A later rightward shift of the aggregate demand curve can cause a recovery, with real GDP (and employment) again increasing. Shifts of the aggregate supply curve can cause similar upswings and downswings. Thus **business cycles** *result from recurrent shifts of the aggregate supply and demand curves.*

business cycle Alternating periods of economic growth and contraction.

Shift Factors

There is no reason to believe that the aggregate supply and demand curves will always shift in such undesired ways. However, there are lots of reasons to expect them to shift on occasion.

NEWS WIRE	SHIFTING AD

Consumer Index Sinks to All-Time Low

NEW YORK—A key measure of consumer confidence fell to an all-time low in January, according to a report released Tuesday.

The Conference Board, a New York-based business research group, said that its Consumer Confidence Index fell to 37.7 in January from the revised 38.6 reading in December. The month's reading represents an all-time low going back to the index's inception in 1967. . . .

"Consumers are losing a pretty big chunk of their net worth right now," said Adam York, economic analyst at Wachovia. York said that loss is reflected in the value of their homes and in their stock market portfolios.

"It doesn't feel good and, as a result, consumers are spending less and they are worried about the outlook for the U.S. economy and their own personal situation," said York. "We are not surprised that consumers are pretty despondent."

—Catherine Clifford

Source: CNNMoney.com, January 27, 2009, © 2009 Time Inc. Used under License.

NOTE: Declining home and stock prices sap not only consumer wealth but consumer confidence as well. This prompts consumers to spend less, shifting the AD curve leftward.

DEMAND SHIFTS   The aggregate demand curve might shift, for example, if consumer sentiment changed. As noted, a plunge in home prices would not only reduce consumers' wealth but also sap their confidence in their future. The combination of reduced wealth and shattered confidence might cause consumers to pare their spending plans—even if their current incomes were unchanged. (See News Wire.) This would shift the AD curve to the left. A tax hike might have a similar effect. Higher taxes reduce disposable (after-tax) incomes, forcing consumers to cut back spending. Higher interest rates make credit-financed spending more expensive and so might also reduce aggregate demand (especially on big-ticket items like cars and houses).

The September 2001 terrorist attacks on New York and Washington, DC, caused dramatic and abrupt shifts of aggregate demand. As fear and uncertainty gripped the nation, companies and consumers postponed spending plans. The resulting AD shift made it difficult to reach or maintain full employment.

SUPPLY SHIFTS   External forces may also shift aggregate supply. As noted earlier, rising oil prices are another brake on GDP growth. Higher oil prices raise the cost of producing goods and services (e.g., airline travel, heating, delivery services), making producers less willing to supply output at a given price level. A similar shift occurred in the wake of the September 2001 terrorist attacks. Higher costs for stepped-up security made it more expensive to produce and ship goods. As a result, a smaller quantity of goods was available at any given price level. The same kind of leftward AS shift occurred when hurricanes destroyed transportation systems (see the following News Wire).

Higher business taxes could also discourage production, thereby shifting the aggregate supply curve to the left. Tougher environmental or workplace regulations could raise the cost of doing business, inducing less supply at a given price level. On the other hand, more liberal immigration rules might increase the supply of labor and increase the supply of goods and services (a rightward shift).

NEWS WIRE	SHIFTING AS

Hurricane Damage to Gulf Ports Delays Deliveries, Raises Costs

The damage to important Gulf Coast ports and waterways from Hurricanes Katrina and Rita is delaying deliveries, sharply boosting shipping costs, and will complicate rebuilding efforts in areas devastated by the storms.

The rising costs could put more downward pressure on growth, particularly for industries dependent on key products that typically flow through the region. Bringing imported steel through substitute ports could add to the prices paid by U.S. manufacturers, said John Martin, president of Martin Associates, a maritime transportation consulting firm in Lancaster, Pa. The rising cost of forest products like lumber could add to the mounting price tag for rebuilding the region, while grain companies could see their exports become less competitive.

Ports from Houston to Mobile, Ala., that handle more than a third of U.S. cargo by tonnage were battered by the hurricanes, along with nearby shipping terminals, warehouses, navigation channels, roads, and rail lines. . . .

Barge tariff rates—the rates paid by grain companies for transportation outside longer-term shipping contracts—to move grain from St. Louis to New Orleans for export have soared by 60 percent to 100 percent since Katrina hit. . . .

Besides grain, the affected ports, terminals, and warehouses are major shipping hubs for petroleum, chemicals, lumber, paper, rubber, coffee, poultry, and other food products. Some of that cargo is being rerouted to alternative ports, but increasing the distance traveled by a shipment increases transportation costs.

—Daniel Machalaba

Source: *The Wall Street Journal*, October 3, 2005, p. A8. Used with permission of Dow Jones & Company, Inc., via Copyright Clearance Center, inc.

NOTE: If an external shock raises production costs, it reduces the willingness of producers to supply output at any given price level. This causes a leftward AS shift.

COMPETING THEORIES OF SHORT-RUN INSTABILITY

Although it is evident that either aggregate supply or aggregate demand *might* shift, economists disagree about how often such shifts might occur or what consequences they might have. What we have seen in Figures 11.6 and 11.7 is how things might go poorly in the macro economy.

Figure 11.6 suggests that the odds of the market generating an equilibrium at full employment and price stability are about the same as finding a needle in a haystack. Figure 11.7 suggests that if we are lucky enough to find the needle, we will probably drop it again when AS or AD shifts. From this perspective, it appears that our worries about the business cycle are well founded.

The classical economists had no such worries. As we saw earlier, they believed that the economy would gravitate toward full employment. Keynes, on the other hand, worried that the macro equilibrium might start out badly and get worse in the absence of government intervention.

Aggregate supply and demand curves provide a convenient framework for comparing these and other theories on how the economy works. Essentially, *macro controversies focus on the shape of aggregate supply and demand curves and the potential to shift them.* With the right shape—or the correct shift—any desired equilibrium could be attained. As we will see, there are differing views as to whether and how this happy outcome might come about. These differing views can be classified as demand-side explanations, supply-side explanations, or some combination of the two.

Demand-Side Theories

KEYNESIAN THEORY   Keynesian theory is the most prominent of the demand-side theories. *Whereas the classical economists asserted that supply creates its own demand, Keynes argued the reverse: demand it, and it will be supplied.*

The downside of this demand-driven view is that a lack of spending will cause the economy to contract. If aggregate spending isn't sufficient, some goods will remain unsold and some production capacity will be idled. This contingency is illustrated by point E_1 in Figure 11.8a. Note again that the resulting equilibrium at Q_1 falls short of full employment output (Q_F).

Keynes developed his theory during the Great Depression, when the economy seemed to be stuck at a very low level of equilibrium output, far short of full employment GDP. The only way to end the depression, he argued, was for someone to start demanding more goods. He advocated a big increase in government spending to start the economy moving toward full employment. At the time, his advice was largely ignored. When the United States mobilized for World War II, however, the sudden surge in government spending shifted the AD curve to the right, restoring full employment.

In the late 1990s, the U.S. economy didn't need that kind of surge in government spending. A spectacular rise in the stock market provided the impetus for a surge in *consumer* spending. The increase in consumption shifted the AD curve to the right, increasing GDP growth.

When consumer spending is not so buoyant, Keynesian economists might advocate tax cuts to energize consumers. With more after-tax dollars in their pockets, consumers are likely to spend more. Hence *Keynesian theory urges increased government spending or tax cuts as mechanisms for increasing (shifting) aggregate demand.* President Bush used this Keynesian argument to convince Congress to cut taxes in 2001 and again in 2003. President Obama also followed the Keynesian formula for restoring full employment, but chose more government spending rather than tax cuts to make that happen.

FIGURE 11.8   Origins of a Recession

Unemployment can result from several kinds of market phenomena, including
(a) **Demand shifts:** Total output will fall if aggregate demand (AD) declines. The shift from AD_0 to AD_1 changes equilibrium from point E_0 to E_1.
(b) **Supply shifts:** Unemployment can also emerge if aggregate supply (AS) declines, as the shift from AS_0 to AS_1 shows.
(c) **AS/AD shifts:** If aggregate demand and aggregate supply both decline, output and employment also fall (E_0 to E_3).

(a) **Demand shifts**

(b) **Supply shifts**

(c) **AS/AD shifts**

The Keynesian strategy can also be used to dampen inflation. If *too much* aggregate demand were pushing the price level up, Keynes advocated moving these policy levers in the opposite direction—that is, shifting the AD curve to the left.

MONETARY THEORIES   Another demand-side theory emphasizes the role of money in financing aggregate demand. Money and credit affect the ability and willingness of people to buy goods and services. If credit isn't available or is too expensive, consumers won't be able to buy as many cars, homes, or other expensive products. Tight money might also curtail business investment. In these circumstances, aggregate demand might prove to be inadequate. In this case, an increase in the money supply may be required to shift the aggregate demand curve into the desired position. Monetary theories thus focus on the control of money and interest rates as mechanisms for shifting the aggregate demand curve. To boost aggregate demand, the Federal Reserve cut interest rates 13 times between January 2001 and July 2003. To restrain aggregate demand, the Fed reversed course and raised interest rates throughout 2005 and early 2006. In September 2007 the Fed again reversed course, pushing interest rates down to historic lows by 2012.

Supply-Side Theories

Figure 11.8*b* illustrates an entirely different explanation of the business cycle. Notice that the aggregate *supply* curve is on the move in Figure 11.8*b*. The initial equilibrium is again at point E_0. This time, however, aggregate demand remains stationary while aggregate supply shifts. The resulting decline of aggregate supply causes output and employment to decline (to Q_2 from Q_F).

Figure 11.8*b* tells us that aggregate supply may be responsible for downturns as well. Our failure to achieve full employment may result from the unwillingness of producers to provide more goods at existing prices. That unwillingness may originate in rising costs, resource shortages, natural or terrorist disasters, or changes in government taxes and regulations. Whatever the cause, if the aggregate supply curve is AS_1 rather than AS_0, full employment will not be achieved with the demand AD_0. To get more output, the supply curve must shift back to AS_0. The mechanisms for shifting the aggregate supply curve in the desired direction are the focus of supply-side theories.

Eclectic Explanations

Not everyone blames either the demand side or the supply side exclusively. The various macro theories tell us that both supply and demand can help us achieve our policy goals—or cause us to miss them. These theories also demonstrate how various shifts of the aggregate supply and demand curves can achieve any specific output or price level. Figure 11.8*c* illustrates how undesirable macro outcomes can be caused by simultaneous shifts of both aggregate curves. Eclectic explanations of the business cycle draw from both sides of the market.

POLICY OPTIONS

Aggregate supply and demand curves not only help illustrate the causes of the business cycle; they also imply a fairly straightforward set of policy options. Essentially, *the government has three policy options:*

- *Shift the aggregate demand curve.* Find and use policy tools that stimulate or restrain total spending.

- *Shift the aggregate supply curve.* Find and implement policy levers that reduce the costs of production or otherwise stimulate more output at every price level.
- *Do nothing.* If we can't identify or control the determinants of aggregate supply or demand, we shouldn't interfere with the market.

Historically, all three approaches have been adopted.

The classical approach to economic policy embraced the "do nothing" perspective. Prior to the Great Depression, most economists were convinced that the economy would self-adjust to full employment. If the initial equilibrium rate of output was too low, the resulting imbalances would alter prices and wages, inducing changes in market behavior. The aggregate supply and demand curves would naturally shift until they reached the intersection at point E_0, where full employment (Q_F) prevails in Figure 11.8.

Recent versions of the classical theory—dubbed the new classical economics—stress not only the market's natural ability to self-adjust to *long-run* equilibrium but also the inability of the government to improve *short-run* market outcomes.

Fiscal Policy

fiscal policy The use of government taxes and spending to alter macroeconomic outcomes.

The Great Depression cast serious doubt on the classical self-adjustment concept. According to Keynes's view, the economy would *not* self-adjust. Rather, it might stagnate at point E_1 in Figure 11.8 until aggregate demand was forcibly shifted. An increase in government spending on goods and services might provide the necessary shift. Or a cut in taxes might be used to stimulate greater consumer and investor spending. These budgetary tools are the hallmark of fiscal policy. Specifically, **fiscal policy** is the use of government tax and spending powers to alter economic outcomes.

Fiscal policy is an integral feature of modern economic policy. Every year the president and the Congress debate the budget. They argue about whether the economy needs to be stimulated or restrained. They then argue about the level of spending or taxes required to ensure the desired outcome. This is the heart of fiscal policy.

Monetary Policy

monetary policy The use of money and credit controls to influence macroeconomic activity.

The government budget doesn't get all the action. As suggested earlier, the amount of money in circulation may also affect macro equilibrium. If so, the policy arsenal must include some levers to control the money supply. These are the province of monetary policy. **Monetary policy** refers to the use of money and interest rates to alter economic outcomes.

The Federal Reserve (the Fed) has direct control over monetary policy. The Fed is an independent regulatory body charged with maintaining an "appropriate" supply of money. In practice, the Fed adjusts interest rates and the money supply in accordance with its views of macro equilibrium.

Supply-Side Policy

supply-side policy The use of tax rates, (de)regulation, and other mechanisms to increase the ability and willingness to produce goods and services.

Fiscal and monetary policies focus on the demand side of the market. Both policies are motivated by the conviction that appropriate shifts of the aggregate demand curve can bring about desired changes in output or price levels. **Supply-side policies** offer an alternative; they seek to shift the aggregate supply curve.

There are scores of supply-side levers. The most famous are the tax cuts implemented by the Reagan administration in 1981. Those tax cuts were designed to increase *supply*, not just demand (as traditional fiscal policy does). By reducing tax *rates* on wages and profits, the Reagan tax cuts sought to increase the willingness to supply goods at any given price level. The promise of greater after-tax income was the key incentive for the supply shift.

Republicans used a similar argument in 2003 to reduce the tax on capital gains (profits from the sale of acquired property) from 20 percent to 15 percent. Lower capital gains tax rates encourage people to invest more in factories, equipment, and office buildings. As investment increases, so does the capacity to supply goods and services.

Other supply-side levers are less well recognized but nevertheless important. Your economics class is an example. The concepts and skills you learn here should increase your productive capabilities. This expands the economy's capacity. With a more educated workforce, a greater supply of goods and services can be produced at any given price level. Hence government subsidies to higher education might be viewed as part of supply-side policy. Government employment and training programs also shift the aggregate supply curve to the right. Immigration policies that increase the inflow of workers get even quicker supply-side effects.

Government regulation is another staple of supply-side policy. Regulations that slow innovation or raise the cost of doing business reduce aggregate supply. Removing unnecessary red tape can facilitate more output and reduce inflationary pressures.

POLICY PERSPECTIVES

Which Policy Lever to Use?

The various policy levers in our basic macro model have all been used at one time or another. The "do nothing" approach prevailed until the Great Depression. Since that devastating experience, more active policy roles have predominated.

1960s Fiscal policy dominated economic debate in the 1960s. When the economy responded vigorously to tax cuts and increased government spending, it appeared that fiscal policy might be the answer to our macro problems. Many economists even began to assert that they could fine-tune the economy—generate very specific changes in macro equilibrium with appropriate tax and spending policies.

The promise of fiscal policy was tarnished by our failure to control inflation in the late 1960s. It was further compromised by the simultaneous outbreak of both inflation and unemployment in the 1970s. This new macro failure appeared to be chronic, immune to the cures proposed by fiscal policy. Solutions to our macro problems were sought elsewhere.

1970s Monetary policy was next in the limelight. The flaw in fiscal policy, it was argued, originated in its neglect of monetary constraints. More government spending, for example, might require so much of the available money supply that private spending would be crowded out. To ensure a net boost in aggregate demand, more money would be needed—a response only the Fed could make.

In the late 1970s the Fed dominated macro policy. It was hoped that appropriate changes in the money supply would foster greater macro stability. Reduced inflation and lower interest rates were the immediate objectives. Both were to be accomplished by placing greater restraints on the supply of money.

The heavy reliance on monetary policy lasted only a short time. When the economy skidded into yet another recession, the search for effective policy tools resumed.

1980s Supply-side policies became important in 1980. In his 1980 presidential campaign, Ronald Reagan asserted that supply-side tax cuts, deregulation of markets, and other supply-focused policies would reduce both inflation and unemployment. According to Figure 11.8c, such an outcome appeared at least plausible. A rightward shift of the aggregate supply curve does reduce both prices and unemployment. Although the Reagan administration later embraced an eclectic mix of fiscal, monetary, and supply-side policies, its initial supply-side emphasis was distinctive.

1990s   The George H. Bush administration pursued a less activist approach. Bush Senior initially resisted tax increases but later accepted them as part of a budget compromise that also reduced government spending. When the economy slid into recession in 1990, President Bush maintained a hands-off policy. Like classical economists, Bush kept assuring the public that the economy would come around on its own. Not until the 1992 elections approached did he propose more active intervention. By then it was too late for him, however. Voters were swayed by Bill Clinton's promises to use tax cuts and increased government spending (fiscal policy) to create "jobs, jobs, jobs."

After he was elected, President Clinton reversed policy direction. Rather than delivering the promised tax cuts, Clinton pushed a tax *increase* through Congress. He also pared the size of his planned spending increases. This fiscal policy retreat cleared the field for the reemergence of monetary policy as the decisive policy lever.

2000s   The fiscal restraint of the late 1990s helped the federal budget move from deficits to surpluses. These budget surpluses grew so large and so fast that they prompted another turn in fiscal policy. One of the most heated issues in the 2000 presidential campaign was whether to use the federal budget surplus to cut taxes, increase government spending, or pay down the debt. By the time George W. Bush took office in January 2001, the economy had slowed so much that people feared another recession was imminent. This helped convince Congress to pull the fiscal policy lever in the direction of stimulus, with two more rounds of tax cuts in 2002 and 2003.

The fiscal stimulus and low interest rates of 2001–2004 gave the AD curve a big rightward boost. In fact, the economy started growing so fast again that people worried that inflation might accelerate. Since neither the White House nor the Congress wanted to raise taxes or cut government spending, the Federal Reserve had to take the lead role again in managing the macro economy.

OBAMANOMICS   By the time President Obama took office in January 2009 the economy was deep into another recession. Moreover, the Fed had already exhausted its arsenal of interest rate cuts. So it appeared that only a renewed emphasis on fiscal policy could save the day. President Obama preferred the option of increased government spending rather than tax cuts. When the growing federal budget deficit became a political liability in 2012, he persuaded Congress to *increase* taxes even though the economy was still far short of full employment.

Clearly past presidents have used all available macro policy tools at one time or another. They have worked well on occasion but sometimes failed also. The continuing challenge for President Obama and the U.S. Congress is to pull the right policy levers at the right time. Competing policy goals and an ever-changing economic environment make that challenge formidable. While perfection may be beyond our capabilities, the next couple of chapters offer some ideas about which policy levers to pull at any given time.

SUMMARY

- The primary outcomes of the macro economy are output, prices, jobs, and international balances. These outcomes result from the interplay of internal market forces, external shocks, and policy levers. **LO1**
- All the influences on macro outcomes are transmitted through aggregate supply or aggregate demand. Aggregate supply and demand determine the equilibrium rate of output and prices. The economy will gravitate to that unique combination of output and price levels. **LO3**
- The market's macro equilibrium may not be consistent with our nation's employment or price goals. Macro failure occurs when the economy's equilibrium is not optimal—when unemployment or inflation is too high. **LO4**
- Macro equilibrium may be disturbed by changes in aggregate supply (AS) or aggregate demand (AD). Such changes are illustrated by shifts of the AS and AD curves, and they lead to a new equilibrium. Recurring AS and AD shifts cause business cycles. **LO4**

- Competing economic theories try to explain the shape and shifts of the aggregate supply and demand curves, thereby explaining the business cycle. Specific theories tend to emphasize demand or supply influences. **LO2**
- Macro policy options range from doing nothing (the classical approach) to various strategies for shifting either the aggregate demand curve or the aggregate supply curve. **LO5**
- Fiscal policy uses government tax and spending powers to alter aggregate demand. Monetary policy uses money and credit availability for the same purpose. **LO5**
- Supply-side policies include all interventions that shift the aggregate supply curve. Examples include tax incentives, (de)regulation, immigration, and resource development. **LO5**

TERMS TO REMEMBER

Define the following terms:

macroeconomics	aggregate supply	unemployment	monetary policy
Say's Law	equilibrium (macro)	inflation	supply-side policy
aggregate demand	full-employment	business cycle	
real GDP	GDP	fiscal policy	

QUESTIONS FOR DISCUSSION

1. If the price level were below P_E in Figure 11.5, what macro problems would we observe? Why is P_E considered an equilibrium? **LO4**
2. What factors might cause a rightward shift of the aggregate demand curve? What might induce a rightward shift of aggregate supply? **LO3**
3. What kind of external shock would benefit an economy? **LO1**
4. What would a *horizontal* aggregate supply curve imply about producer behavior? How about a vertical AS curve? **LO3**
5. If equilibrium is compatible with both buyers' and sellers' intentions, how can it be undesirable? **LO4**

6. From March 2009 to 2013, the U.S. stock market more than doubled in value. How might this have affected aggregate demand? What happens to aggregate demand when the stock market plunges? **LO3**
7. **POLICY PERSPECTIVES** President George H. Bush maintained a hands-off policy during the 1990–1991 recession. How did he expect the economy to recover on its own? **LO2**
8. **POLICY PERSPECTIVES** Why did President Obama assert that government intervention was needed to get the economy out of the 2008–2009 recession? Could the economy have recovered on its own? **LO4, LO5**

PROBLEMS   ▦ connect

1. Illustrate these events with AS or AD shifts: **LO3**

   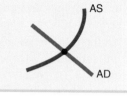

| Government increases defense spending. | The News wire on page 237. | Imported oil gets cheaper. | Taxes on the rich are increased. |

2. Based on the News Wire on page 237, **LO4**
   (a) Illustrate the AS shift that occurs.
   (b) Identify the old (E_0) and new (E_1) macro equilibrium.
   (c) What macro ailments result?
   (d) How can the economy stay healthy in this case?

3. Graph the following aggregate supply and demand curves (be sure to draw to scale). **LO3**

	Real GDP (in $ Trillions)	
Price Level	Supplied	Demanded
100	4	16
110	10	15
140	14	12
200	15	6

   (a) What is the equilibrium price level?
   (b) What is the equilibrium output?
   (c) If the quantity of output demanded at every price level increases by $2 trillion, what happens to equilibrium output and prices? Graph your answer.

4. Draw a conventional aggregate demand curve on a graph. Then add three different aggregate supply curves, labeled **LO1, LO3**
   S_1: Horizontal curve
   S_2: Upward-sloping curve
   S_3: Vertical curve
   all intersecting the AD curve at the same point. If AD were to increase (shift to the right), which AS curve would lead to
   (a) The biggest increase in output?
   (b) The largest jump in prices?
   (c) The least inflation?

5. The following schedule provides information with which to draw both an aggregate demand curve and an aggregate supply curve. Both curves are assumed to be straight lines. **LO4**

Average Price (Dollars per Unit)	Quantity Demanded (Units per Year)	Quantity Supplied (Units per Year)
$1,000	0	1,000
100	900	100

   (a) At what price level does equilibrium occur?
   (b) What curve would have shifted if a new equilibrium were to occur at an output level of 700 and a price level of $700?
   (c) What curve would have shifted if a new equilibrium were to occur at an output level of 700 and a price level of $500?
   (d) What curve would have shifted if a new equilibrium were to occur at an output level of 700 and a price level of $300?
   (e) Compared to the initial equilibrium (a), how have the outcomes in (b), (c), and (d) changed price levels or output?

6. If AD shifts by $40 for every $1,000 change in consumer wealth, by how much will AD increase when the stock market rises in value by $300 billion?   **LO3**

7. If AS decreases by $40 billion for every 1 percentage point increase in tax rates, by how much will AS shift to the left when the tax rate is raised from 35 percent to 40 percent?   **LO3**

8. **POLICY PERSPECTIVES** Suppose a nation's *maximum* GDP (with 0 percent unemployment) is $20 trillion.
   (*a*) How much is *full employment* GDP (with 5 percent unemployment)?
   (*b*) If *equilibrium* GDP is $17 trillion, how far from full employment is this economy?
   (*c*) Which of the following shifts will move this economy closer to full employment?
      i. AD shifts to the right.
      ii. AD shifts to the left.
      iii. AS shifts to the right.
      iv. AS shifts to the left.   **LO5**

◄ Practice quizzes, student PowerPoints, author podcasts, web activities, and additional materials available at **www.mhhe.com/schilleressentials9e**, or scan here. Need a barcode reader? Try ScanLife, available in your app store.

12

Fiscal Policy

◄ Practice quizzes, student PowerPoints, author podcasts, web activities, and additional materials available at www.mhhe.com/ schilleressentials9e, or scan here. Need a barcode reader? Try ScanLife, available in your app store.

LEARNING OBJECTIVES

After reading this chapter, you should be able to:

1 Define what fiscal policy is.
2 Explain why fiscal policy might be needed.
3 Illustrate what the multiplier is and how it works.
4 Tell how fiscal stimulus or restraint is achieved.
5 Specify how fiscal policy affects the federal budget.

During the Great Depression of the 1930s, as many as 13 million Americans were out of work. They were capable people and eager to work. But no one would hire them. As sympathetic as employers might have been, they simply could not use any more workers. Consumers were not buying the goods and services already being produced. Employers were more likely to cut back production and lay off still more workers than to hire any new ones. As a consequence, an "army of the unemployed" was created in 1929 and continued to grow for nearly a decade. It was not until the outbreak of World War II that enough jobs could be found for the unemployed, and most of those "jobs" were in the armed forces.

The Great Depression was the springboard for the Keynesian approach to economic policy. John Maynard Keynes concluded that the ranks of unemployed persons were growing because of problems on the *demand* side of product markets. People simply were not able and willing to buy all the goods and services the economy was capable of producing. As a consequence, producers had no incentive to increase output or to hire more labor. So long as the demand for goods and services was inadequate, unemployment was inevitable.

Keynes sought to explain how a deficiency of demand could arise in a market economy and then to show how and why the government had to intervene. Keynes was convinced that government intervention was necessary to achieve our macroeconomic goals, particularly full employment. To that end, Keynes advocated aggressive use of fiscal policy—that is, deployment of the government's tax and spending powers to alter macro outcomes. He urged policymakers to use these powers to minimize the swings of the business cycle.

In this chapter we take a closer look at what Keynes intended. We focus on the following questions:

- Why did Keynes think the market was inherently unstable?
- How can fiscal policy help stabilize the economy?
- How will the use of fiscal policy affect the government's budget deficit?

We'll also examine how the Keynesian strategy of fiscal stimulus was used to help end the Great Recession of 2008–2009.

COMPONENTS OF AGGREGATE DEMAND

The premise of **fiscal policy** is that the **aggregate demand** for goods and services will not always be compatible with economic stability. As we observed in Chapter 11 (e.g., Figure 11.7), *recessions occur when aggregate demand declines; recessions persist when aggregate demand remains below the economy's capacity to produce.* Inflation results from similar imbalances. If aggregate demand increases faster than output, prices tend to rise. The price level will keep rising until aggregate demand is compatible with the rate of production.

But why do such macro failures occur? Why wouldn't aggregate demand always reflect the economy's full employment potential?

To determine whether we are likely to have the right amount of aggregate demand, we need to take a closer look at spending behavior. Who buys the goods and services on which output decisions and jobs depend?

The four major components of aggregate demand are

C:	consumption
I:	investment
G:	government spending
X – IM:	net exports (exports minus imports)

fiscal policy The use of government taxes and spending to alter macroeconomic outcomes.

aggregate demand The total quantity of output demanded at alternative price levels in a given time period, *ceteris paribus*.

FIGURE 12.1
Components of Aggregate Demand

In 2012, the output of the U.S. economy was over $15 trillion. Over two-thirds of that output consisted of consumer goods and services. The government sectors (federal, state, and local) demanded 20 percent of total output. Investment spending took another 13 percent. Finally, because imports exceeded exports, the impact of net exports on aggregate demand was negative.

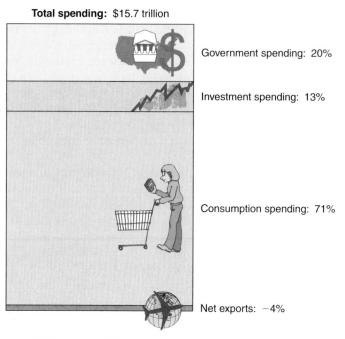

Total spending: $15.7 trillion

Government spending: 20%

Investment spending: 13%

Consumption spending: 71%

Net exports: −4%

Source: U.S. Department of Commerce.

Consumption

consumption Expenditure by consumers on final goods and services.

Consumption refers to all household expenditures on goods and services—everything from groceries to college tuition. Just look around and you can see the trappings of our consumer-oriented economy. In the aggregate, consumption spending accounts for over two-thirds of total spending in the U.S. economy (Figure 12.1).

Because consumer spending looms so large in aggregate demand, any change in consumer behavior can have a profound impact on employment and prices. Life would be simple for policymakers if consumers kept spending their incomes at the same rate. Then there wouldn't be any consumer-induced shifts of AD. But life isn't that simple: consumers *do* change their behavior. From 2002 to 2005, for example, consumers went on a buying spree, purchasing new homes, new cars, big-screen TVs, and iPods. The consumption component of AD kept the AD curve shifting rightward, increasing equilibrium GDP.

By late 2007, however, the rush to consume appeared to be slowing. Declining home sales and prices, high gasoline prices, and continuing concerns about terrorism and the war in Iraq were giving consumers pause. As the following News Wire confirms, economists feared that a slowdown in consumer spending might reverse the path of the AD curve (they were right, as the 2008–2009 recession confirmed).

To anticipate such changes in consumer behavior, the economic doctors regularly take consumers' pulse. Every month the University of Michigan and the Conference Board survey a cross-section of U.S. households to see how they are feeling. They ask how confident consumers are about their jobs and incomes and how optimistic they are about their economic future. The responses to such questions are combined into an index of consumer confidence, which is reported monthly. If confidence is rising, consumers are likely to keep spending. When consumer confidence declines, as in January 2009 (see the News Wire on page 236), the economic doctors worry that the AD curve may shift backward.

Investment

investment Expenditures on (production of) new plants and equipment (capital) in a given time period, plus changes in business inventories.

The second component of AD—investment—is similarly prone to behavioral shifts. **Investment** refers to business spending on new plants and equipment.

NEWS WIRE	AD SHIFTS

Here Comes the Recession

NEW YORK—The cash registers were ringing on Black Friday, but make no mistake: American consumers are jittery, and seem all but certain to push the U.S. economy into recession.

After years of living happily beyond their means, Americans are finally facing financial reality. A persistent rise in energy prices will mean bigger heating bills this winter and heftier tabs at the gas pump. Job growth is slowing and wage gains have been anemic. House prices are sliding, diminishing the value of the asset that's the biggest factor in Americans' personal wealth. Even the stock market, which has been resilient for so long in the face of eroding consumer sentiment, has begun pulling back amid signs of deep distress in the financial sector.

The latest evidence of the long-awaited consumer retrenchment: Chic discounter Target last week reported a weaker-than-expected third quarter, as sales of higher-margin apparel and home goods slowed. Starbucks reported for the first time that customer traffic in its stores declined in its latest quarter compared to a year earlier. Walmart shares hit a six-year low in September after the retail giant posted another wan sales increase.

With consumer spending accounting for about three-quarters of U.S. economic activity, some economists say it is inevitable that the economy will stop growing at some point in the coming year. . . . "Right now, the question is how bad it's going to get," said David Rosenberg, chief North American economist at Merrill Lynch. "The question is one of magnitude."

—Colin Barr

Source: *Fortune Magazine*, November 26, 2007, © 2007 Time Inc. Used under License.

NOTE: Consumer spending accounts for two-thirds of aggregate demand. If consumer spending slows, the AD curve shifts left, increasing the risk of recession.

When a corporation decides to build a new factory or modernize an old one, the resulting expenditure adds to aggregate demand. When farmers replace their old tractors, their purchases also increase total spending on goods and services. Construction of new homes is also counted as part of (residential) investment.

Changes in business inventory are counted as investment too. Retail stores stock their shelves with goods bought from other firms. E-commerce firms also rely on *someone* stocking goods for sale. Although they hope to resell these goods later, the inventory buildup reflects a demand for goods and services. If companies allow their inventories to shrink, then inventory investment would be negative. During the Great Depression not only was inventory investment negative but spending on plants and equipment also plummeted. As a result, total business investment plunged by 70 percent between 1929 and 1933. This plunge in investment spending wracked aggregate demand and eliminated millions of jobs.

Near the end of 2009, businesses had a more optimistic outlook. Sensing that the 2008–2009 recession was ending, businesses increased their inventories by roughly 40 percent. They wanted to be sure their shelves were stocked when consumers started shopping again. That inventory buildup added to aggregate demand and created more jobs.

Government Spending

Government spending is a third source of aggregate demand. The federal government currently spends nearly $4 trillion a year, and state and local governments collectively spend even more. Not all of that spending gets counted as part of aggregate demand, however. *Aggregate demand refers to spending on goods and services.* Much of what the government spends, however, is merely *income transfers*—payments to individuals for which no services are exchanged. Uncle Sam, for example, mails out over $700 billion a year in Social Security checks. This doesn't represent a demand for goods and services. That money will become part of aggregate demand only when the Social Security recipients spend their transfer income on goods and services.

Only that portion of government budgets that gets spent on goods and services represents part of aggregate demand. Aggregate demand includes federal, state, and local spending on highways, schools, police, national defense, and all other goods and services the public sector provides. Such spending now accounts for one-fifth of aggregate demand.

Net Exports

net exports Exports minus imports (X − IM).

The fourth component of aggregate demand, **net exports,** is the difference between export and import spending. The demand of foreigners for American-made products shows up as U.S. exports. At the same time, Americans spend some of their income on goods imported from other countries. The difference between exports and imports represents the *net* demand for domestic output.

U.S. net exports are negative. This means that Americans are buying more goods from abroad than foreigners are buying from us. The net effect of trade is thus to reduce domestic aggregate demand. That is why net exports is a negative amount in Figure 12.1.

Net export flows are also subject to abrupt changes. Strong growth in foreign nations may spur demands for U.S. exports. On the other hand, a spike in oil prices will increase the value of U.S. imports. Such changes in the flow of net exports will shift the AD curve.

Equilibrium

The four components of aggregate demand combine to determine the shape, position, and potential shifts of the aggregate demand curve. Notice that *aggregate demand is not a single number but instead a schedule of planned purchases.* The quantity of output market participants desire to purchase depends in part on the price level.

equilibrium (macro) The combination of price level and real output that is compatible with both aggregate demand and aggregate supply.

Suppose the existing price level is P_1, as seen in Figure 12.2, and the curve AS represents aggregate supply. Full employment is represented by the output level Q_F. We want to know whether aggregate demand will be just enough to ensure both price stability and full employment. This happy **equilibrium** occurs only if the aggregate demand curve intersects the aggregate supply curve at point *a*. The curve AD* achieves this goal.

FIGURE 12.2
The Desired Equilibrium

The goal of fiscal policy is to achieve price stability and full employment, the desired equilibrium represented by point *a*. This equilibrium will occur only if aggregate demand is equal to AD*. Less demand (e.g., AD₁) will cause unemployment; more demand (e.g., AD₂) will cause inflation.

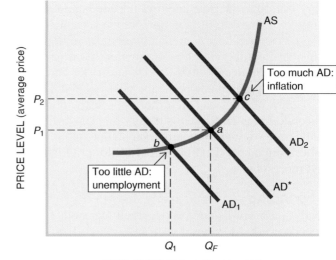

INADEQUATE DEMAND   Aggregate demand may turn out to be less than perfect, however. Keep in mind that aggregate demand includes four different types of spending:

$$AD = C + I + G + (X - IM)$$

There is no evident reason why these four distinct components of aggregate demand would generate exactly the output Q_F at the price level P_1 in Figure 12.2. They could in fact generate *less* spending, as illustrated by the curve AD_1. In this case, aggregate demand falls short, leaving some potential output unsold at the equilibrium point *b*.

EXCESSIVE DEMAND   The curve AD_2 illustrates a situation of excessive aggregate demand. The combined expenditure plans of market participants exceed the economy's full employment output. The resulting scramble for available goods and services pushes prices up to the level P_2. This inflationary equilibrium is illustrated by the AS/AD_2 intersection at point *c*.

THE NATURE OF FISCAL POLICY

Clearly, we will fulfill our macroeconomic goals only if we get the right amount of aggregate demand (the curve AD* in Figure 12.2). But what are the chances of such a fortunate event? Keynes asserted that the odds are stacked against such an outcome. Indeed, Keynes concluded that *it would be a minor miracle if C + I + G + (X − IM) added up to exactly the right amount of aggregate demand.* Consumers, investors, and foreigners all make independent decisions on how much to spend. Why should those separate decisions result in just enough demand to ensure either full employment or price stability? It is far more likely that the level of aggregate demand will turn out to be wrong. In these circumstances, government spending must be the safety valve that expands or contracts aggregate demand as needed. *The use of government spending and taxes to adjust aggregate demand is the essence of fiscal policy.* Figure 12.3 puts fiscal policy into the framework of our basic macro model. In this figure, fiscal policy appears as a policy lever for adjusting macro outcomes.

FIGURE 12.3   Fiscal Policy

Fiscal policy refers to the use of the government tax and spending powers to alter macro outcomes. Fiscal policy works principally through shifts of the aggregate demand curve.

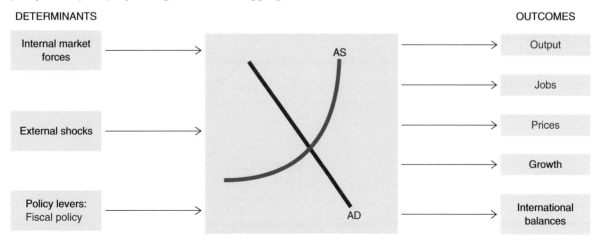

FISCAL STIMULUS

Suppose that aggregate demand has fallen short of our goals and unemployment rates are high. This scenario is illustrated again in Figure 12.4, this time with some numbers added. Full employment is reached when $6 trillion of output is demanded at current price levels, as indicated by Q_F. The quantity of output actually demanded at current price levels, however, is only $5.6 trillion ($Q_1$), as determined by the intersection at point b. Hence there is a gap between the economy's ability to produce (Q_F) and the amount of output people are willing to buy (Q_1) at the current price level (P_1). *The difference between equilibrium output and full employment output is called the GDP gap.* In Figure 12.4, this **GDP gap** amounts to $400 billion. If nothing is done, $400 billion of productive facilities will be idled and millions of workers will be unemployed.

GDP gap The difference between full employment output and the amount of output demanded at current price levels.

The goal here is to eliminate the GDP gap by *shifting* the aggregate demand curve to the right. In this case, spending has to increase by $400 billion per year to close the GDP gap. How can fiscal policy make this happen?

President Obama relied on this policy lever when he convinced Congress to pass the American Recovery and Reinvestment Act in February 2009 (see the accompanying News Wire). The largest chunk of that act was a $308.3 billion increase in government spending on goods and services (e.g., highways, bridges, railroads, energy). President Obama expected that increased spending to push the AD curve so far to the right that 3 million to 4 million jobs would be restored. He envisioned the GDP gap eventually closing.

More Government Spending

The simplest solution to the demand shortfall does appear to be increased government spending. If the government were to step up its purchases of tanks, highways, schools, and other goods, the increased spending would add directly to aggregate demand. This would shift the aggregate demand curve rightward, moving us closer to full employment. Hence *increased government spending is a form of* **fiscal stimulus.**

fiscal stimulus Tax cuts or spending hikes intended to increase (shift) aggregate demand.

MULTIPLIER EFFECTS   It isn't necessary for the federal government to fill the entire gap between desired and current spending in order to regain full employment. In

FIGURE 12.4
Deficient Demand

The aggregate demand curve AD$_1$ results in only $5.6 trillion of final sales at current price levels (P_1). This is well short of full employment (Q_F), which occurs at $6.0 trillion of output. The fiscal policy goal is to close the GDP gap by shifting the AD curve rightward until it passes through point a.

NEWS WIRE	FISCAL STIMULUS: GOVERNMENT SPENDING

Senate Passes $787 Billion Stimulus Bill

NEW YORK—It's a done deal. Still controversial, but a done deal.

The Senate on Friday evening passed the $787 billion American Recovery and Reinvestment Act of 2009, which was drawn up, amended, and negotiated in record time. . . .

President Barack Obama will sign the recently approved economic stimulus bill on Tuesday in Denver, Colorado, two senior administration officials told CNN. . . .

"The goal at the heart of this plan is to create jobs. Not just any jobs, but jobs doing the work America needs done: repairing our infrastructure, modernizing our schools and hospitals, and promoting the clean, alternative energy sources that will help us finally declare independence from foreign oil," President Obama said Friday morning.

The Obama economic team estimates the stimulus plan will create or save between 3 million and 4 million jobs. . . .

How the bill breaks down:

The package devotes $308.3 billion—or 39 percent—to appropriations spending, according to the Congressional Budget Office. That includes $120 billion on infrastructure and science and more than $30 billion on energy-related infrastructure projects, according to key congressional committees.

It devotes another $267 billion—or 34 percent—on direct spending, including increased unemployment benefits and food stamps, CBO said.

And it provides $212 billion—or 27 percent—for tax breaks for individuals and businesses, although the biggest piece of that is for individuals.

—Jeanne Sahadi

Source: From CNNMoney.com, © February 15, 2009, Time Inc. All rights reserved.

NOTE: President Obama counted on increased government spending to shift the AD curve to the right, increasing GDP and employment.

---

fact, if government spending did increase by $400 billion in Figure 12.4, aggregate demand would shift *beyond* point *a*. In that case we would quickly move from a situation of *inadequate* aggregate demand (AD_1) to a situation of *excessive* aggregate demand.

The solution to this riddle lies in the circular flow of income. According to the circular flow, *an increase in spending results in increased incomes.* When the government increases its spending, it creates additional income for market participants. The recipients of this income will in turn spend it. Hence *each dollar gets spent and respent several times.* As a result, every dollar of government spending has a *multiplied* impact on aggregate demand.

Suppose that the government decided to spend an additional $100 billion per year on a fleet of cruise missiles. This $100 billion of new defense expenditure would add directly to aggregate demand. But that is only the beginning of a long story. The people who build cruise missiles will be on the receiving end of a lot of income. Their fatter paychecks, dividends, and profits will enable them to increase their own spending.

What will the aerospace workers do with all that income? They have only two choices: *all income is either spent or saved.* Hence every dollar of income must go to consumer spending or to **saving.** From a macroeconomic perspective, the only important decision the aerospace workers have to make is what percentage of

saving Income minus consumption; that part of disposable income not spent.

FIGURE 12.5
MPC and MPS

The marginal propensity to consume (MPC) tells us what portion of an extra dollar of income will be spent. The remaining portion will be saved. The MPC and MPS help us predict consumer responses to changes in income.

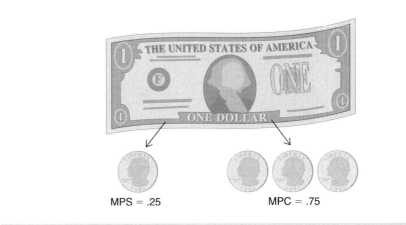

MPS = .25   MPC = .75

income to spend and what percentage to save (i.e., not spend). Any additional consumption spending contributes directly to aggregate demand. The portion of income that is saved (not spent) goes under the mattress or into banks or other financial institutions.

Suppose aerospace workers decide to spend 75 percent of any extra income they get and to save the rest (25 percent). We call these percentages the marginal propensity to consume and the marginal propensity to save, respectively. The **marginal propensity to consume (MPC)** is the fraction of additional income people spend. The **marginal propensity to save (MPS)** is the fraction of new income that is saved.

Figure 12.5 illustrates how the spending and saving decisions are connected. In this case we have assumed that the MPC equals 0.75. Hence 75 cents out of any extra dollar get spent. By definition, the remaining 25 cents get saved. The MPC and MPS tell us how the aerospace workers will behave when their incomes rise.

According to these behavioral patterns, the aerospace workers will use their additional $100 billion of income as follows:

marginal propensity to consume (MPC) The fraction of each additional (marginal) dollar of disposable income spent on consumption.

marginal propensity to save (MPS) The fraction of each additional (marginal) dollar of disposable income not spent on consumption: 1 − MPC.

Increased consumption = MPC × additional income

= 0.75 × $100 billion

= $75 billion

Increased saving = MPS × additional income

= 0.25 × $100 billion

= $25 billion

Thus all of the new income is either spent ($75 billion) or saved ($25 billion).

According to our MPC calculations, the aerospace workers increase their consumer spending by $75 billion. This $75 billion of new consumption adds directly to aggregate demand. Hence aggregate demand has now been increased *twice:* first by the government expenditure on missiles ($100 billion) and then by the additional consumption of aerospace workers ($75 billion). Thus aggregate demand has increased by $175 billion as a consequence of the stepped-up defense expenditure. *The fiscal stimulus to aggregate demand includes both the initial increase in government spending and all subsequent increases in consumer spending triggered by the government outlays.* That combined stimulus is already up to $175 billion.

The stimulus of new government spending doesn't stop with the aerospace workers. The circular flow of income is a *continuing* process. The money spent by the aerospace workers becomes income to *other* workers. As their incomes rise, we expect their spending to increase as well. In other words, *income gets spent and respent in the circular flow.* This multiplier process is illustrated in Figure 12.6.

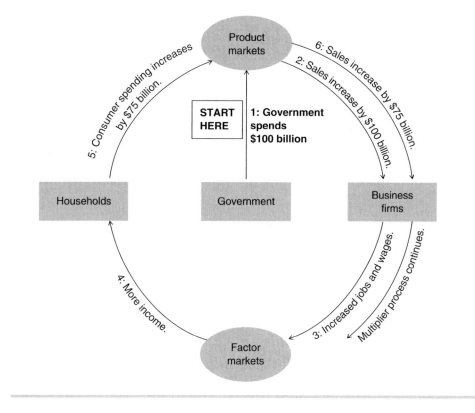

FIGURE 12.6
The Circular Flow

In the circular flow of income, money gets spent and respent multiple times. As a result of this multiplier process, aggregate demand increases by much more than the initial increase in government spending. An MPC of 0.75 is assumed here.

SPENDING CYCLES Table 12.1 fills in the details of the multiplier process. Suppose the aerospace workers spend their $75 billion on new boats. This increases the income of boat builders. They, too, are then in a position to increase *their* spending.

Spending Cycles	Change in Spending during Cycle (Billions per Year)	Cumulative Increase in Spending (Billions per Year)
First cycle: government buys $100 billion worth of missiles.	$100.00	$100.00
Second cycle: missile workers have more income, buy new boats (MPC = 0.75).	75.00	175.00
Third cycle: boat builders have more income, spend it on beer (0.75 × $75).	56.25	231.25
Fourth cycle: bartenders and brewery workers have more income ($56.25 billion), spend it on new cars (0.75 × $56.25).	42.19	273.44
Fifth cycle: autoworkers have more income, spend it on clothes (0.75 × $42.19).	31.64	305.08
Sixth cycle: apparel workers have more income, spend it on movies and entertainment (0.75 × $31.64).	23.73	328.81
Nth cycle and beyond		400.00

TABLE 12.1
The Multiplier Process at Work

Purchasing power is passed from hand to hand in the circular flow. The *cumulative* change in total expenditure that results from a new injection of spending into the circular flow depends on the MPC and the number of spending cycles that occur.

The limit to multiplier effects is established by the ratio 1/(1 − MPC). In this case MPC = 0.75, so the multiplier equals 4. That is, total spending will ultimately rise by $400 billion per year as a result of an increase in G of $100 billion per year.

Suppose the boat builders also have a marginal propensity to consume of 0.75. They will then spend 75 percent of their new income ($75 billion). This will add *another* $56.25 billion to consumption demand.

Notice in Table 12.1 what is happening to cumulative spending as the multiplier process continues. When the boat builders go on a spending spree, the cumulative increase in spending becomes:

Cycle 1: Government expenditure on cruise missiles	$100.00 billion
Cycle 2: Aerospace workers, purchase of boats	75.00 billion
Cycle 3: Boat builders' expenditure on beer	56.25 billion
Cumulative increase in spending after three cycles	$231.25 billion

As a result of the circular flow of spending and income, the impact of the initial government expenditure has already more than doubled.

Table 12.1 follows the multiplier process to its logical end. Each successive cycle entails less new income and smaller increments to spending. Ultimately the changes get so small that they are not even noticeable. By that time, however, the *cumulative* change in spending is huge. The cumulative change in spending is $400 billion: $100 billion of initial government expenditure and an additional $300 billion of consumption induced by multiplier effects. Thus *the demand stimulus initiated by increased government spending is a multiple of the initial expenditure.*

MULTIPLIER FORMULA   To compute the cumulative change in spending, we need not examine each cycle of the multiplier process. There is a shortcut. The entire sequence of multiplier cycles is summarized in a single number, aptly named the *multiplier*. The **multiplier** tells us how much *total* spending will change in response to an initial spending stimulus. The multiplier is computed as

multiplier The multiple by which an initial change in aggregate spending will alter total expenditure after an infinite number of spending cycles: $1/(1 - \text{MPC})$.

$$\text{Multiplier} = \frac{1}{1 - \text{MPC}}$$

In our case, where MPC = 0.75, the multiplier is

$$\text{Multiplier} = \frac{1}{1 - \text{MPC}}$$

$$= \frac{1}{1 - 0.75} = \frac{1}{0.25} = 4$$

Using this multiplier, we can confirm the conclusion of Table 12.1 by observing that

$$\frac{\text{Total change}}{\text{in spending}} = \text{multiplier} \times \frac{\text{initial change in}}{\text{government spending}}$$

$$= \frac{1}{1 - \text{MPC}} \times \$100 \text{ billion per year}$$

$$= \frac{1}{1 - 0.75} \times \$100 \text{ billion per year}$$

$$= 4 \times \$100 \text{ billion per year}$$

$$= \$400 \text{ billion per year}$$

The impact of the multiplier on aggregate demand is illustrated in Figure 12.7. The AD$_1$ curve represents the inadequate aggregate demand that caused the initial unemployment problem (Figure 12.4). When the government increases its defense spending, the aggregate demand curve shifts rightward by $100 billion

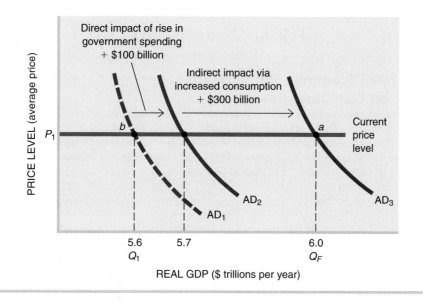

FIGURE 12.7
Multiplier Effects

A $100 billion increase in government spending shifts the aggregate demand curve to the right by a like amount (i.e., AD$_1$ to AD$_2$). Aggregate demand gets another boost from the additional consumption induced by multiplier effects. In this case, an MPC of 0.75 results in $300 billion of additional consumption.

to AD$_2$. This increase in defense expenditure sparks a consumption spree, shifting aggregate demand further to AD$_3$. This combination of increased government spending ($100 billion) and induced consumption ($300 billion) is sufficient to restore full employment.

The multiplier packs a lot of punch. *Every dollar of fiscal stimulus has a multiplied impact on aggregate demand.* This makes fiscal policy easier. The multiplier also makes fiscal policy riskier, however, by exaggerating any intervention mistakes.

Tax Cuts

Although government spending is capable of moving the economy to its full employment potential, increased G is not the only way to get there. The stimulus required to raise output and employment levels from Q_1 to Q_F could originate in C or I as well as from G. It could also come from abroad, in the form of increased demand for our exports. In other words, any Big Spender would help. Of course, the reason we are initially at Q_1 instead of Q_F in Figure 12.7 is that consumers and investors have chosen not to spend as much as is required for full employment.

The government might be able to stimulate more consumer and business spending with a tax cut. A tax cut directly increases the **disposable income** of the private sector. As soon as people get more income in their hands, they're likely to spend it. When they do, aggregate demand gets a lift. This is what happened in 2008. In February 2008 Congress approved tax rebates of $300 to $600 per person. That amounted to over $100 billion in tax cuts, paid directly to consumers. What did consumers do with that added income? Spend much of it, of course, as the following News Wire reveals. That tax-cut-induced spending shifted the AD curve to the right, increasing both GDP and employment in the spring of 2008.

disposable income After-tax income of consumers.

TAXES AND CONSUMPTION   How much of an AD shift we get from a personal tax cut depends on the marginal propensity to consume. If consumers squirreled away their entire tax cut, AD wouldn't budge. But an MPC of zero is an alien concept. People *do* increase their spending when their disposable income increases. So long as the MPC is greater than zero, a tax cut *will* stimulate more consumer spending.

NEWS WIRE	FISCAL STIMULUS: TAX CUTS

The 2008 Economic Stimulus: First Take on Consumer Response

In a new study, business school professors Christian Broda of the University of Chicago and Jonathan Parker of Northwestern University conclude the stimulus payments "are providing a substantial stimulus to the national economy, helping to ameliorate the ongoing 2008 downturn." U.S. households are "doing a significant amount of extra spending" because of the $90 billion in government payments that have gone out so far, they say.

As outlined in *The Wall Street Journal* today, the preliminary assessment found that the typical family increased its spending on food, mass merchandise, and drug products by 3.5 percent once the rebates arrived relative to a family that hadn't received its rebate yet. The average family spent about 20 percent of its rebate in the first month after receipt, a slightly faster pace than with the 2001 rebates.

The authors estimate that nondurable consumption—a piece of consumer spending that excludes big-ticket items such as refrigerators and televisions—rose by 2.4 percent in the second quarter as a direct result of the stimulus payments. It'll be boosted by 4.1 percent in the current quarter, they estimate.

—Sudeep Reddy

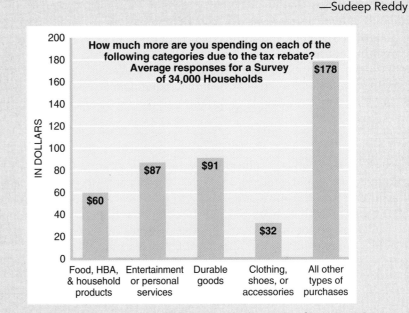

Source: *The Wall Street Journal* online blog post, July 30, 2008. Used with permission of Dow Jones & Company, Inc. via Copyright Clearance Center, Inc.

NOTE: Tax cuts increase disposable income and boost consumer spending. This shifts the AD curve rightward.

Suppose again the MPC is 0.75. If taxes are cut by $100 billion, the resulting consumption spree amounts to

$$\text{Initial increase in consumption} = \text{MPC} \times \text{tax cut}$$

$$= 0.75 \times \$100 \text{ billion}$$
$$= \$75 \text{ billion}$$

Hence *a tax cut that increases disposable incomes stimulates consumer spending.*

The initial consumption spree induced by a tax cut starts the multiplier process in motion. Once in motion, the multiplier picks up steam. The new consumer spending creates additional income for producers and workers, who will then use the additional income to increase their own consumption. This will propel us along the multiplier path already depicted in Table 12.1. The cumulative change in total spending will be

$$\text{Cumulative change in spending} = \text{multiplier} \times \frac{\text{initial change}}{\text{in consumption}}$$

In this case, the cumulative change is

$$\begin{aligned}
\text{Cumulative change in spending} &= \frac{1}{1 - \text{MPC}} \times \$75 \text{ billion} \\
&= 4 \times \$75 \text{ billion} \\
&= \$300 \text{ billion}
\end{aligned}$$

Here again we see that the multiplier increases the impact of a tax cut on aggregate demand. *The cumulative increase in aggregate demand is a multiple of the initial tax cut.* Thus the multiplier makes both increased government spending and tax cuts powerful policy levers.

TAXES AND INVESTMENT   A tax cut may also be an effective mechanism for increasing investment spending. Investment decisions are guided by expectations of future profit, particularly after-tax profits. If a cut in corporate taxes raises after-tax profits, it should encourage additional investment. Once increased investment spending enters the circular flow, it has a multiplier effect on total spending like that which follows an initial change in consumer spending. Thus tax cuts for consumers or investors provide an alternative to increased government spending as a mechanism for stimulating aggregate spending.

Tax cuts designed to stimulate C and I have been used frequently. In 1963 President John F. Kennedy announced his intention to reduce taxes in order to stimulate the economy, citing the fact that the marginal propensity to consume for the average American family at that time appeared to be exceptionally high. His successor, Lyndon Johnson, concurred with Kennedy's reasoning. Johnson agreed to "shift emphasis sharply from expanding federal expenditure to boosting private consumer demand and business investment." He proceeded to cut personal and corporate taxes by \$11 billion.

One of the largest tax cuts in history was initiated by President Ronald Reagan in 1981. The Reagan administration persuaded Congress to cut personal taxes by \$250 billion over a three-year period and to cut business taxes by another \$70 billion. The resulting increase in disposable income stimulated consumer spending and helped push the economy out of the 1981–1982 recession.

President George W. Bush proposed even larger tax cuts in 2001. He urged a \$1.6 *trillion* tax cut, spread out over 10 years. One of the principal arguments for the tax cut was the weak condition of the U.S. economy in early 2001. A tax cut, Bush argued, would not only increase disposable income but also raise expectations for future income. Congress concurred, ultimately passing a \$1.35 trillion tax cut, spread out over 10 years. Continued weakness in the U.S. economy prompted further tax cuts in 2002 and again in 2003.

Inflation Worries

President Clinton had used the same Keynesian argument when he ran for president in 1992. With the economy still far short of its productive capacity (Q_F), he called for more fiscal stimulus. After he was elected, however, President Clinton changed his mind about the need for fiscal stimulus. Rather than delivering the middle-class tax cut he had promised, Clinton instead decided to *raise* taxes. This abrupt policy U-turn was motivated in part by the recognition of how powerful the multiplier is. The economy was already expanding when Clinton was elected, and the multiplier was at work. As each successive spending cycle developed, the economy would move closer to full employment. Any *new* fiscal stimulus would accelerate that movement. As a result, the economy might end up expanding so fast that it would overshoot the full employment goal.

The pressure from any more fiscal stimulus could easily force prices higher. This risk was illustrated in Figure 12.2. *Whenever the aggregate supply curve is upward sloping, an increase in aggregate demand increases prices as well as output.* Notice in Figure 12.2 how the price level starts creeping up as aggregate demand increases from AD_1 to AD*. If aggregate demand expands further to AD_2, the price level really jumps. This suggests that the degree of inflation caused by increased aggregate demand depends on the slope of the aggregate supply curve. Only if the AS curve were horizontal would there be no risk of inflation when AD increases. Keynes thought this might have been the case during the Great Depression. With so much excess capacity available, businesses were willing and able—indeed, eager—to supply more output at the existing price level.

President Obama had a similar view. With the unemployment rate still hovering in the 8–10 percent range two years after his initial 2009 stimulus package, he believed *more* stimulus would not cause price levels to rise. He convinced Congress to pass additional tax cuts and spending increases in 2011. Were the economy closer to capacity, the risk of inflation would have been greater.

FISCAL RESTRAINT

fiscal restraint Tax hikes or spending cuts intended to reduce (shift) aggregate demand.

The threat of inflation suggests that **fiscal restraint** may be an appropriate policy strategy at times. *If excessive aggregate demand is causing prices to rise, the goal of fiscal policy will be to reduce aggregate demand, not stimulate it* (see Figure 12.8).

The means available to the federal government for restraining aggregate demand emerge again from both sides of the budget. The difference here is that we use the budget tools in reverse. We now want to *reduce* government spending or *increase* taxes.

Budget Cuts

Cutbacks in government spending on goods and services directly reduce aggregate demand. As with spending increases, the impact of spending cuts is magnified by the multiplier.

MULTIPLIER CYCLES Suppose the government cut military spending by $100 billion. This would throw a lot of aerospace employees out of work. Thousands of workers would get smaller paychecks, or perhaps none at all. These workers would be

FIGURE 12.8
Fiscal Restraint

Fiscal restraint is used to reduce inflationary pressures. The strategy is to shift the aggregate demand curve to the left with budget cuts or tax hikes.

Budget cuts and tax hikes reduce AD.

PRICE LEVEL (average price)

REAL OUTPUT (quantity per year)

forced to cut back on their own spending. Hence aggregate demand would take two hits: first a cut in government spending and then induced cutbacks in consumer spending. *The multiplier process works in both directions.*

The marginal propensity to consume again reveals the power of the multiplier process. If the MPC is 0.75, the consumption of aerospace workers will drop by $75 billion when the government cutbacks reduce their income by $100 billion. (The rest of the income loss will be covered by a reduction in savings balances.)

From this point on the story should sound familiar. As detailed in Table 12.1, the $100 billion government cutback will ultimately reduce consumer spending by $300 billion. The *total* drop in spending is thus $400 billion. Like their mirror image, *government cutbacks have a multiplied effect on aggregate demand.* The total impact is equal to

> Cumulative reduction in spending = multiplier × initial budget cut

Tax Hikes

Tax increases can also be used to shift the aggregate demand curve to the left. The direct effect of a tax increase is a reduction in disposable income. People will pay the higher taxes by reducing their consumption and depleting their savings. The reduced consumption results in less aggregate demand. As consumers tighten their belts, they set off the multiplier process, leading to a much larger cumulative shift of aggregate demand.

In 1982 there was great concern that the 1981 tax cuts had been excessive and that inflationary pressures were building up. To reduce that inflationary pressure, Congress withdrew some of its earlier tax cuts, especially those designed to increase investment spending. The net effect of the Tax Equity and Fiscal Responsibility Act of 1982 was to increase taxes by roughly $90 billion for the years 1983–1985. This shifted the aggregate demand curve leftward, reducing inflationary pressures (see Figure 12.8).

The same kind of leftward shift of the AD curve occurred in 2013 when Congress increased the payroll (FICA) tax. Raising the tax rate from 4.2 to 6.2 percent reduced consumers' disposable income by $110 billion (see the accompanying News Wire).

| NEWS WIRE | FISCAL RESTRAINT |

Payroll Tax Whacks Spending

Walmart Stores Inc. on Thursday joined a parade of retailers, restaurants, and consumer goods companies worried about the economic impact of the recently restored federal payroll tax that has left Americans with less money to spend.

The world's largest retailer, Burger King Worldwide Inc., Kraft Foods Group Inc., and others are lowering forecasts and adjusting sales and marketing strategies, expecting consumers with smaller paychecks to dine out less and trade down to less expensive purchases.

The expiration of the payroll tax cuts that knocked 2 percent off consumers' take-home pay is having an impact, these companies say. It will ding a household with $65,000 in annual income $1,300 this year, and shift $110 billion overall out of consumers' hands.

—Shelly Banjo, Annie Gasparro, and Julie Jargon

Source: *The Wall Street Journal*, February 22, 2013, p.1. Used with permission of Dow Jones & Company, Inc. via Copyright Clearance Center, Inc.

NOTE: Tax increases leave consumers with less income to spend, reducing aggregate demand.

TABLE 12.2
Fiscal Policy Guidelines

The Keynesian emphasis on aggregate demand results in simple guidelines for fiscal policy: reduce aggregate demand to fight inflation; increase aggregate demand to fight unemployment. Changes in government spending and taxes are the tools used to shift AD.

Topic Podcast:
Fiscal Policy

Problem	Solution	Policy Tools
Unemployment (recession)	Increase aggregate demand.	Increase government spending. Cut taxes.
Inflation	Reduce aggregate demand.	Cut government spending. Raise taxes.

Fiscal Guidelines

The basic rules for fiscal policy are so simple that they can be summarized in a small table. *The policy goal is to match aggregate demand with the full employment potential of the economy. The fiscal strategy for attaining that goal is to shift the aggregate demand curve.* The tools for doing so are (1) changes in government spending and (2) changes in tax rates. Table 12.2 summarizes the guidelines developed by John Maynard Keynes for using those tools.

POLICY PERSPECTIVES

Must the Budget Be Balanced?

The primary lever of fiscal policy is the federal government's budget. As we have observed, changes in either federal taxes or outlays are the mechanism for shifting the aggregate demand curve. The use of this mechanism has a troubling implication: *The use of the budget to manage aggregate demand implies that the budget will often be unbalanced.* In the face of a recession, for example, the government has sound reasons both to cut taxes and to increase its own spending. By reducing tax revenues and increasing expenditures simultaneously, however, the federal government will throw its budget out of balance.

budget deficit The amount by which government expenditures exceed government revenues in a given time period.

BUDGET DEFICIT   Whenever government expenditures exceed tax revenues, a **budget deficit** exists. The deficit is measured by the difference between expenditures and receipts

$$\text{Budget deficit} = \text{government spending} > \text{tax revenues}$$

where spending exceeds revenues. In 2012 the federal budget deficit was more than $1.1 *trillion*. To pay for such deficit spending, the government had to borrow money, either directly from the private sector or from the banking sector. As Figure 12.9 reveals, the deficits of 2009–2012 were far larger than any earlier deficits. The series of deficits from 1970 to 1997 were tiny by comparison. Yet even those deficits caused recurrent political crises. Several times the federal government had to shut down for days at a time while Republicans and Democrats in Congress battled over how to cut the deficit. A majority of citizens even supported adding an amendment to the U.S. Constitution that would *force* Congress to balance the budget every year.

BUDGET SURPLUS   Ironically, while the U.S. Congress was debating such an amendment, the deficit started shrinking. The record-breaking expansion of the U.S. economy and the stock market boom of the late 1990s swelled tax collections. The Balanced Budget Act of 1997 also slowed the growth of government spending. This combination of growing tax revenues and slower government spending shrunk the deficit dramatically.

By 1998 the deficit had completely vanished, and a **budget surplus** appeared. For the first time in 30 years, tax revenues exceeded government spending.

budget surplus An excess of government revenues over government expenditures in a given time period.

$$\text{Budget surplus} = \text{government spending} < \text{tax revenues}$$

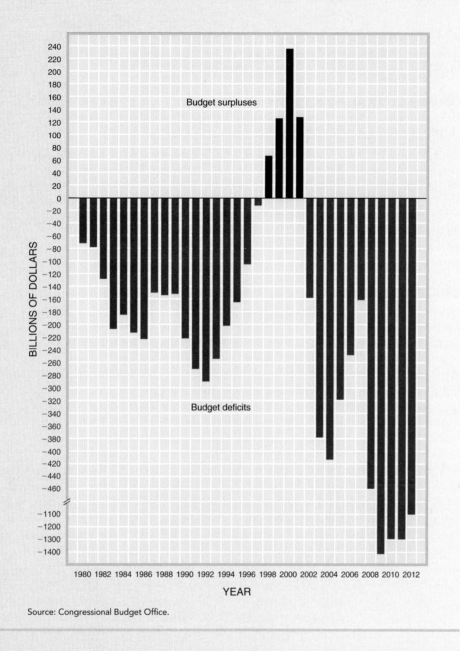

Source: Congressional Budget Office.

FIGURE 12.9
Unbalanced Budgets

From 1970 until 1997 the federal budget was in deficit every year. In the 1980s and early 1990s, federal deficits increased dramatically as a result of recessions, tax cuts, and the continued expansion of government programs.

From 1998 to 2002 the budget was in surplus due to strong GDP growth and slowed federal spending. An economic slowdown, tax cuts, and a surge in defense spending returned the budget to deficit. The recession of 2008–2009 and subsequent fiscal stimulus sent the deficit soaring to over $1 trillion.

The surpluses started out small but grew rapidly as the economy kept expanding.

The budget surpluses of 1998–2001 created a unique problem: what to do with the "extra" revenue. Should the government give it back to taxpayers? Expand government programs? Pay down accumulated debt? The government had not confronted that problem since 1969.

DEFICITS RESURFACE The problem of managing a budget surplus vanished with the surplus itself in 2002. The September 11, 2001, terrorist attacks on New York City and Washington, DC, contributed to an economic contraction that reduced tax revenues. A subsequent surge in defense spending and new tax cuts widened the deficit further.

2008–2009 RECESSION The Great Recession of 2008–2009 threw the federal budget completely out of whack. GDP growth turned negative in the last quarter of 2008 and stayed negative throughout 2009. As employment, payrolls, and profits shrank, so did tax revenues. The 2008 tax rebates took another $100 billion out of the revenue stream. Then the gigantic 2009 stimulus program ratcheted up federal spending. All these policies helped widen the annual deficit to more than $1 trillion for several years' running (2009–2012).

COUNTERCYCLICAL POLICY   For John Maynard Keynes, the 2009–2012 deficit explosion would seem perfectly normal. From a Keynesian perspective, the desirability of a budget deficit or surplus depends on the health of the economy. If the economy was ailing, an injection of government spending or a tax cut would be appropriate. On the other hand, if the economy was booming, some fiscal restraint (spending cuts, tax hikes) would be called for. Hence Keynes would first examine the economy and then prescribe fiscal restraint or stimulus. He might even prescribe neither, sensing that the economy was in optimal health. *In Keynes's view, an unbalanced budget is perfectly appropriate if macro conditions call for a deficit or surplus.* A balanced budget is appropriate only if the resulting aggregate demand is consistent with full employment equilibrium.

DEFICIT WORRIES   Not everyone is as comfortable as Keynes with soaring deficits. Most people understand that recessions can throw government budgets deep into the red. But those cyclical displacements should be *temporary*. What worried people so much in 2009–2012 was the perception that those trillion-dollar deficits would continue. The American Recovery and Reinvestment Act of 2009 authorized infrastructure and energy projects that would continue for years, long after the recession was over. Without cutbacks in other government programs or tax increases—both politically unpopular—huge deficits were bound to persist.

In early 2013 public anxiety over massive deficits triggered a heated political battle. Republicans in Congress insisted that the growth of government spending had to be reined in. President Obama, on the other hand, refused to consider cuts in spending, especially for entitlements like Social Security. He preferred additional tax increases, especially for the rich. In February 2013 the issue came to a head when Congress had to authorize additional government borrowing (the debt ceiling). Both sides dug their heels in, threatening a temporary shutdown of the federal government (as had happened in 1995 for much the same reason). In the end, both parties took the easy way out, *promising* future deficit reduction but delivering little immediate fiscal restraint. In these circumstances, future deficit reduction is almost completely dependent on faster economic growth.

SUMMARY

- The Keynesian explanation of macro instability requires government intervention to shift the aggregate demand curve to the desired rate of output.   **LO2**

- To boost aggregate demand, the government may either increase its own spending or cut taxes. To restrain aggregate demand, the government may reduce its own spending or raise taxes.   **LO4**

- Any change in government spending or taxes will have a multiplied impact on aggregate demand. The additional impact comes from changes in consumption caused by changes in disposable income.   **LO3**

- The marginal propensity to consume indicates how changes in disposable income affect consumer

- spending. The MPC is the fraction of each additional dollar spent (i.e., not saved).   **LO3**

- The size of the multiplier depends on the marginal propensity to consume. The higher the MPC, the larger the multiplier, where the multiplier $= 1/(1 - \text{MPC})$.   **LO3**

- Fiscal stimulus carries the risk of inflation. The steeper the upward slope of the AS curve, the greater the risk of inflation.   **LO4**

- A balanced budget is appropriate only if the resulting aggregate demand is compatible with full employment and price stability. Otherwise *unbalanced* budgets (deficits or surpluses) are appropriate.   **LO5**

TERMS TO REMEMBER

Define the following terms:

fiscal policy	net exports	saving	disposable income
aggregate demand	equilibrium (macro)	marginal propensity to consume (MPC)	fiscal restraint
consumption	GDP gap	marginal propensity to save (MPS)	budget deficit
investment	fiscal stimulus	multiplier	budget surplus

QUESTIONS FOR DISCUSSION

1. How was the author of the News Wire on page 249 so confident that a recession was coming?   **LO2**
2. How long does it take you to spend any income you receive? Where do the dollars you spend end up?   **LO3**
3. What is your MPC? Would a welfare recipient and a millionaire have the same MPC? What determines a person's MPC?   **LO3**
4. Why was Walmart worried about the 2013 payroll tax hike (News Wire, p. 261)?   **LO4**
5. If the guidelines for fiscal policy (Table 12.2) are so simple, why does the economy ever suffer from unemployment or inflation?   **LO2**
6. At the end of 2012 businesses bought more inventory, increasing GDP. What would happen if consumers didn't buy those goods?   **LO2**
7. What did consumers buy with their 2008 tax rebates (News Wire, p. 258)? Why did food purchases increase so little?   **LO4**
8. **POLICY PERSPECTIVES**   Would a constitutional amendment that would require the federal government to balance its budget (incur no deficits) be desirable? Explain.   **LO5**
9. **POLICY PERSPECTIVES**   What government programs would you cut in the pursuit of fiscal restraint?   **LO4**

PROBLEMS

connect

1. What was the short-run (one-month) MPC for the 2008 tax rebates (News Wire, p. 258)?   **LO3**
2. If the marginal propensity to save is 0.10, (a) What is the MPC? (b) How large is the multiplier?   **LO3**
3. If the MPC were 0.9, (a) How much spending would occur in the third cycle of Figure 12.6? (b) How many spending rounds would occur before consumer spending increased by $300 billion?   **LO3**
4. (a) The multiplier process depicted in Table 12.1 is based on an MPC of 0.75. Recompute the first five cycles using an MPC of 0.80.
   (b) How much *more* consumption occurs in the first five cycles?
   (c) What is the value of the multiplier in this case?   **LO3**
5. Suppose the government increases education spending by $30 billion. How much additional *consumption* will this increase cause?   **LO4**
6. By how much would the 2008 tax rebates have shifted AD if the MPC was 0.95? (See the News Wire, p. 258.)   **LO4**
7. If taxes were cut by $1 trillion and the MPC was 0.75, by how much would total spending   **LO3**
   (a) Increase in the first year with two spending cycles?
   (b) Increase over five years, with two spending cycles per year?
   (c) Increase over an infinite time period?
8. How much would AD eventually increase with Obama's increased appropriations spending (News Wire, p. 253) if consumers had an MPC of 0.95?   **LO3**
9. If the MPC were 0.8, (a) How much did consumer spending decline initially in response to the 2013 payroll tax hike (News Wire, p. 261)? (b) What was the ultimate decline in AD after all multiplier effects?   **LO3**
10. **POLICY PERSPECTIVES**   If an initial fiscal restraint of $100 billion is desired, by how much must
    (a) Government spending be reduced? or
    (b) Taxes be raised?
    Assume MPC = 0.80.   **LO4**

◄ Practice quizzes, student PowerPoints, author podcasts, web activities, and additional materials available at **www.mhhe.com/schilleressentials9e**, or scan here. Need a barcode reader? Try ScanLife, available in your app store.

13 Money and Banks

◄ Practice quizzes, student PowerPoints, author podcasts, web activities, and additional materials available at www.mhhe.com/schilleressentials9e, or scan here. Need a barcode reader? Try ScanLife, available in your app store.

LEARNING OBJECTIVES

After reading this chapter, you should be able to:

1   Detail what the features of "money" are.
2   Specify what is included in the "money supply."
3   Describe how a bank creates money.
4   Explain how the money multiplier works.
5   Discuss why the money supply is important.

Sophocles, the ancient Greek playwright, had strong opinions about the role of money. As he saw it, "Of evils upon earth, the worst is money. It is money that sacks cities, and drives men forth from hearth and home; warps and seduces native intelligence, and breeds a habit of dishonesty."

In modern times, people may still be seduced by the lure of money and fashion their lives around its pursuit. Nevertheless, it is hard to imagine an economy functioning without money. Money affects not only morals and ideals but also the way an economy works.

The purpose of this chapter and the following chapter is to examine the role of money in the economy today. We begin with a very simple question:

- What is money?

As we shall discover, money isn't exactly what you think it is. Once we have established the characteristics of money, we go on to ask,

- Where does money come from?
- What role do banks play in the macro economy?

In the next chapter we look at how the Federal Reserve System controls the supply of money and thereby affects macroeconomic outcomes. We will then have a second policy lever in our basic macro model.

THE USES OF MONEY

To appreciate the significance of money in a modern economy, imagine for a moment that there were no such thing as money. How would you get something for breakfast? If you wanted eggs for breakfast, you would have to tend your own chickens or go see Farmer Brown. But how would you pay Farmer Brown for her eggs? Without money, you would have to offer her goods or services that she could use. In other words, you would have to engage in primitive **barter**—the direct exchange of one good for another. You would get those eggs only if Farmer Brown happened to want the particular goods or services you had to offer and if the two of you could agree on the terms of the exchange.

barter The direct exchange of one good for another, without the use of money.

The use of money greatly simplifies market transactions. It's a lot easier to exchange money for eggs at the supermarket than to go into the country and barter with farmers. Our ability to use money in market transactions, however, depends on the grocer's willingness to accept money as a *medium of exchange*. The grocer sells eggs for money only because he can use the same money to pay his help and buy the goods he himself desires. He, too, can exchange money for goods and services. Accordingly, *money plays an essential role in facilitating the continuous series of exchanges that characterizes a market economy.*

Money has other desirable features. The grocer who accepts your money in exchange for a carton of eggs doesn't have to spend his income immediately. He can hold on to the money for a few days or months without worrying about its spoiling. Hence money is also a useful *store of value*—that is, a mechanism for transforming current income into future purchases. Finally, common use of money serves as a *standard of value* for comparing the market worth of different goods. A dozen eggs are more valuable than a dozen onions if they cost more at the supermarket.

We may identify, then, several essential characteristics of what we call money. Specifically, *anything that serves all the following purposes can be thought of as money:*

- *Medium of exchange:* is accepted as payment for goods and services.
- *Store of value:* can be held for future purchases.
- *Standard of value:* serves as a yardstick for measuring the prices of goods and services.

The great virtue of money is that it facilitates the market exchanges that permit specialization in production. In fact, efficient division of labor requires a system whereby people can exchange the things they produce for the things they desire. Money makes this system of exchange possible.

Many Types of Money

Although markets cannot function without money, they can get along without *dollars*. U.S. dollars are just one example of money. In the early days of colonial America, there were no U.S. dollars. A lot of business was conducted with Spanish and Portuguese gold coins. Later people used Indian wampum, then tobacco, grain, fish, and furs, as media of exchange. Throughout the colonies, gunpowder and bullets were frequently used for small change. These forms of money weren't as convenient as U.S. dollars, but they did the job. So long as they served as a medium of exchange, a store of value, and a standard of value, they were properly regarded as money.

The first paper money issued by the U.S. federal government consisted of $10 million worth of "greenbacks," printed in 1861 to finance the Civil War. The Confederate states also issued paper money to finance their side of the Civil War. Confederate dollars became worthless, however, when the South lost and people no longer accepted Confederate currency in exchange for goods and services.

When communism collapsed in Eastern Europe, similar problems arose. In Poland, the zloty was shunned as a form of money in the early 1980s. Poles preferred to use cigarettes and vodka as media of exchange and stores of value. So much Polish currency (zlotys) was available that its value was suspect. The same problem undermined the value of the Russian ruble in the 1990s. Russian consumers preferred to hold and use American dollars rather than the rubles that few people would accept in payment for goods and services. Cigarettes, vodka, and even potatoes were a better form of money than Russian rubles. Notice in the following News Wire how movie tickets were sold in 1997 for eggs, not cash, and workers were paid in goods, not rubles.

THE MONEY SUPPLY

Cash versus Money

In the U.S. economy today, such unusual forms of money are rarely used. Nevertheless, the concept of money includes more than the dollar bills and coins in your pocket or purse. Most people realize this when they offer to pay for goods with a check or debit card rather than cash. The money you have in a checking account can be used to buy goods and services, or it can be retained for future use. In these respects, your checking account balance is as much a part of your money as are the coins and dollars in your pocket or purse. In fact, you could get along without *any* cash if everyone accepted your checks and debit cards (and if they worked in vending machines and parking meters).

There is nothing unique about cash, then, insofar as the market is concerned. ***Checking accounts can and do perform the same market functions as cash.*** Accordingly, we must include checking account balances in our concept of **money.** The essence of money is not its taste, color, or feel but, rather, its ability to purchase goods and services.

Transactions Accounts

In their competition for customers, banks have created all kinds of different checking accounts. Credit unions and other financial institutions have also created checking account services. Although they have a variety of distinctive names, all

money Anything generally accepted as a medium of exchange.

NEWS WIRE	BARTER

Goods Replace Rubles in Russia's Vast Web of Trade
Workers, Paid in Products, Must Make Deals to Survive; Glasses, Shoes, Bras Become New Forms of Currency

GUS-KHRUSTALNY, RUSSIA—Wrapped tightly against chilling winds, Valentina Novikova, a pensioner, stood expectantly at a lonely crossroads outside this old glass- and crystal-making town, her champagne flutes tucked neatly into cardboard boxes, stacked on makeshift birch tables. . . .

The glass and crystal sold on the roadside here are the lifeblood of the local economy. Workers are paid in glass, receive their social benefits in glass, and must sell the glass to stay alive. The glass has become a kind of substitute money.

The workers and their glass factory are part of a vast transactional web of barter, trading, and debt—all using surrogates for the Russian ruble—that by some estimates now accounts for more than half of the Russian economy.

Virtually every sector, every factory, and every worker in Russia has been touched by the flood of surrogate money. What began a few years ago at a time of runaway inflation has persisted and become even more widespread as inflation has cooled yet industry has remained moribund. From sheet metal to finished cars, from champagne glasses to shoes, goods are traded around Russia in lieu of money.

In Volgograd, workers at the Armina factory decided to go on strike this month, according to the newspaper Izvestia. The reason: their monthly wage of about $50 is paid in brassieres. . . .

Movie theaters in the Siberian city of Altai started charging two eggs for admission because people had no cash to spare. But the theaters hit a problem in the winter, when hens lay fewer eggs and audiences began to dwindle. So now the movie houses are taking empty bottles as payment, turning them back in to the bottlers for cash. . . .

—David Hoffman

Source: *The Washington Post*, © January 31, 1997, The Washington Post. All rights reserved.

NOTE: When people lose faith in a nation's currency, they must use something else as a medium of exchange. This greatly limits market activity.

checking accounts have a common feature: they permit depositors to spend their deposit balances easily without making a special trip to the bank to withdraw funds. All you need is a checkbook, a debit card, an ATM card, or a payment app on your smartphone.

Because all such checking account balances can be used directly in market transactions (without a trip to the bank), they are collectively referred to as *transactions accounts*. The distinguishing feature of all **transactions accounts** is that they permit direct payment to a third party without requiring a trip to the bank to make a withdrawal. The payment itself may be in the form of a check, a debit card transfer, or an automatic payment transfer. In all such cases, *the balance in your transactions account substitutes for cash, and is therefore a form of money.*

transactions account A bank account that permits direct payment to a third party (e.g., with a check).

Basic Money Supply

Because all transactions accounts can be spent as readily as cash, they are counted as part of our money supply. Adding transactions account balances to the quantity of coins and currency held by the public gives us one measure of the amount of "money" available—that is, the basic **money supply.** The basic money supply is typically referred to by the abbreviation **M1.**

money supply (M1) Currency held by the public, plus balances in transactions accounts.

FIGURE 13.1
Composition of the
Basic Money Supply
(M1)

The money supply (M1) includes
all cash held by the public plus
balances people hold in
transactions accounts (e.g.,
checking, ATS, and credit union
share draft accounts). Cash is
only part of our money supply.

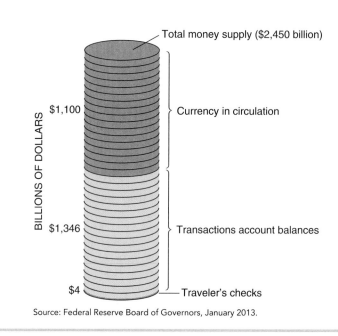

Source: Federal Reserve Board of Governors, January 2013.

Topic Podcast:
Money

Figure 13.1 illustrates the actual composition of our money supply. The first component of M1 is the cash people hold (currency in circulation outside of commercial banks). Clearly, ***cash is only part of the money supply; a lot of "money" consists of balances in transactions accounts.*** This really should not come as too much of a surprise. Most market transactions are still conducted in cash. But those cash transactions are typically small (e.g., for coffee, lunch, small items). They are vastly outspent by the 80 billion *non*cash retail payments made each year. People prefer to use checks rather than cash for most large market transactions and to use debit cards just about everywhere (see the following News Wire). Checks and debit cards are more convenient than cash because they eliminate trips to the bank. Checks and debit cards are also safer: lost or stolen cash is gone forever; checkbooks and debit cards are easily replaced at little or no cost.

Credit cards are another popular medium of exchange. People use credit cards for about one-third of all purchases. This use is not sufficient, however, to qualify credit cards as a form of money. Credit card balances must be paid by check or cash. Hence credit cards are simply a payment *service*, not a final form of payment (credit card companies charge fees and interest for this service). The cards themselves are not a store of value, in contrast to cash or bank account balances.

The last component of our basic money supply consists of traveler's checks issued by nonbank firms (e.g., American Express). These, too, can be used directly in market transactions, just like cash.

Near Money

Transactions accounts are not the only substitute for cash. Even a conventional savings account can be used to finance market purchases. This use of a savings account may require a trip to the bank for a special withdrawal. But that is not too great a barrier to consumer spending. Many savings banks make that trip unnecessary by offering computerized withdrawals and transfers from their savings accounts, some even at supermarket service desks or cash machines. Others offer to pay your bills if you phone in instructions.

NEWS WIRE | MEDIA OF EXCHANGE

How Would You Like to Pay for That?

As new payment technologies have developed, consumers have changed the way they pay for the goods and services they buy. Although the number and volume of consumers' cash transactions cannot be measured accurately, indirect evidence suggests that cash transactions have declined. It is certain that the use of checks as a form of payment has declined substantially. The decline was accompanied by an increase in the use of debit cards and the number of preauthorized payments.

Payment Method	Number of Transactions (in Billions)	Total Dollar Value (in Trillions)
Checks	33	$54.9
Credit cards	23	2.8
Debit cards	27	1.3
Preauthorized payments	16	40.9

Source: *Federal Reserve Bulletin*, July 2009.

NOTE: People increasingly pay for their purchases electronically with debit or credit cards. Checks are still used for larger purchases and to pay credit card balances.

Not all savings accounts are so easily spendable. Certificates of deposit, for example, require a minimum balance to be kept in the bank for a specified number of months or years; early withdrawal results in a loss of interest. Funds held in certificates of deposit cannot be transferred automatically to a checking account (like passbook savings balances) or to a third party. As a result, certificates of deposit are seldom used for everyday market purchases. Nevertheless, such accounts still function like "near money" in the sense that savers can go to the bank and withdraw cash if they really want to buy something.

Another popular way of holding money is to buy shares of money market mutual funds. Deposits into money market mutual funds are pooled and used to purchase interest-bearing securities (e.g., Treasury bills). The resultant interest payments are typically higher than those paid on regular checking accounts. Moreover, money market funds can often be withdrawn *immediately,* just like those in transactions accounts. However, such accounts allow only a few checks to be written each month without paying a fee. Hence consumers don't use money market funds as readily as other transactions accounts to finance everyday spending.

Additional measures of the money supply (M2, M3, etc.) have been constructed to account for the possibility of using money market mutual funds and various other deposits to finance everyday spending. At the core of all such measures, however, are cash and transactions account balances, the key elements of the basic money supply (M1). Accordingly, we limit our discussion to just M1.

Aggregate Demand

Why do we care so much about the specifics of money? Who cares what forms money comes in or how much of it is out there?

aggregate demand The total quantity of output demanded at alternative price levels in a given time period, *ceteris paribus*.

Our concern about the specific nature of money stems from our broader interest in macro outcomes. As we have observed, total output, employment, and prices are all affected by changes in **aggregate demand.** How much money people have (in whatever form) directly affects their spending behavior. That's why it's important to know what "money" is and where it comes from.

CREATION OF MONEY

When people ponder where money comes from, they often have a simple answer: the government prints it. They may even have toured the Bureau of Engraving and Printing in Washington, DC, and seen dollar bills running off the printing presses. Or maybe they visited the U.S. Mint in Denver or Philadelphia and saw coins being stamped.

There is something wrong with this explanation of the origin of money, however. As Figure 13.1 illustrates, *most of what we call money is not cash but bank balances.* Hence the Bureau of Engraving and the two surviving U.S. mints play only a minor role in creating money. The real power over the money supply lies elsewhere.

Deposit Creation

To understand the origins of money, think about your own bank balance. How did you acquire a balance in your checking account? Did you deposit cash? Did you deposit a check? Or did you receive an automatic payroll transfer?

If you typically make *non*cash deposits, your behavior is quite typical. Most deposits into transactions accounts are checks or computer transfers; hard cash is seldom used. When people get paid, for example, they typically deposit their paychecks at the bank. Some employers even arrange automatic payroll deposits, thereby eliminating the need for employees to go to the bank at all. The employee never sees or deposits cash in these cases (see cartoon).

If checks are used to make deposits, then the supply of checks provides an initial clue about where money comes from. Anyone can buy blank checks and sign them, of course. But banks won't cash checks unless there are funds on deposit to make the check good. Banks, in fact, hold checks for a few days to confirm the existence of sufficient account balances to cover the checks. Likewise, retailers won't accept checks unless they get some deposit confirmation or personal identification. The constraint on check writing, then, is not the supply of paper but the availability of transactions account balances. The same is true of debit cards: if you don't have enough funds in your bank account, the purchase will be rejected.

Less than half of our money supply consists of coins and currency. Most banking transactions entail check or electronic deposits and payments, not cash.

FRANK & ERNEST © (2007) Thaves Reprinted by permission of Universal Uclick for UFS. All rights reserved.

Like a good detective novel, the search for the origins of money seems to be going in a circle. It appears that transactions account deposits come from transactions account balances. This seeming riddle suggests that money creates money. But it offers no clue to us to how the money got there in the first place. Who created the first transactions account balance? What was used as a deposit?

The solution to this mystery is totally unexpected: banks themselves create money. They don't print dollar bills. But they do make loans. The loans, in turn, become transactions account balances and therefore part of the money supply. This is the answer to the riddle. Quite simply, *in making a loan, a bank effectively creates money because the resulting transactions account balance is counted as part of the money supply.* And you are free to spend that money, just as if you had earned it yourself.

To understand where money comes from, then, we must recognize two basic principles:

- Transactions account balances are the largest part of the money supply.
- Banks create transactions account balances by making loans.

In the following two sections we examine this process of creating money—**deposit creation**—more closely.

deposit creation The creation of transactions deposits by bank lending.

A Monopoly Bank

Suppose, to keep things simple, that there is only one bank in town, University Bank, and no one regulates bank behavior. Imagine also that you have been saving some of your income by putting loose change into a piggy bank. Now, after months of saving, you break the bank and discover that your thrift has yielded $100. You immediately deposit this money in a new checking account at University Bank.

Your initial deposit will have no immediate effect on the money supply (M1). The coins in your piggy bank were already counted as part of the money supply because they represented cash held by the public (see Figure 13.1 again). *When you deposit cash or coins in a bank, you are changing the composition of the money supply, not its size.* The public (you) now holds $100 less of coins but $100 more of transactions deposits. Accordingly, no money is lost or created by the demise of your piggy bank (the initial deposit).

What will University Bank do with your deposit? Will it just store the coins in its safe until you withdraw them (in person or by check)? That doesn't seem likely. After all, banks are in business to earn a profit. And University Bank won't make much profit just storing your coins. To earn a profit on your deposit, University Bank will have to put your money to work. This means using your deposit as the basis for making a loan to someone else—someone who wants to buy something but is short on cash *and* is willing to pay the bank interest for the use of money.

Typically a bank does not have much difficulty finding someone who wants to borrow money. Many firms and individuals have spending plans that exceed their current money balances. These market participants are eager to borrow whatever funds banks are willing to lend. The question is, How much money can a bank lend? Can it lend your entire deposit? Or must University Bank keep some of your coins in reserve, in case you want to withdraw them? The answer may surprise you.

AN INITIAL LOAN   Suppose that University Bank decided to lend the entire $100 to Campus Radio. Campus Radio wants to buy a new antenna but doesn't have any money in its own checking account. To acquire the antenna, Campus Radio must take out a loan from University Bank.

How does University Bank lend $100 to Campus Radio? The bank doesn't hand over $100 in cash. Instead it credits the account of Campus Radio. University Bank simply adds $100 to Campus Radio's checking account balance. That is to say, the loan is made electronically with a simple book-keeping entry.

This simple bookkeeping entry is the key to creating money. At the moment University Bank lends $100 to the Campus Radio account, it creates money. Keep in mind that transactions deposits are counted as part of the money supply. Once the $100 loan is credited to its account, Campus Radio can use this new money to purchase its desired antenna without worrying that its check will bounce.

Or can it? Once University Bank grants a loan to Campus Radio, both you and Campus Radio have $100 in your checking accounts to spend. But the bank is holding only $100 of **reserves** (your coins). Yet the increased checking account balance obtained by Campus Radio does not limit *your* ability to write checks. There has been a net *increase* in the value of transactions deposits, but no increase in bank reserves. How is that possible?

USING THE LOAN   What happens if Campus Radio actually spends the $100 on a new antenna? Won't this use up all the reserves held by the bank and endanger your check-writing privileges? Happily, the answer is no.

Consider what happens when Atlas Antenna receives the check from Campus Radio. What will Atlas do with the check? Atlas could go to University Bank and exchange the check for $100 of cash (your coins). But Atlas probably doesn't have any immediate need for cash. Atlas may prefer to deposit the check in its own checking account at University Bank (still the only bank in town). In this way, Atlas not only avoids the necessity of going to the bank (it can deposit the check by mail, ATM, or smartphone) but also keeps its money in a safe place. Should Atlas later want to spend the money, it can simply write a check or use a debit card. In the meantime, the bank continues to hold its entire reserves (your coins), and both you and Atlas have $100 to spend.

FRACTIONAL RESERVES   Notice what has happened here. The money supply has increased by $100 as a result of deposit creation (the loan to Campus Radio). Moreover, the bank has been able to support $200 of transaction deposits (your account and either the Campus Radio or Atlas account) with only $100 of reserves (your coins). In other words, *bank reserves are only a fraction of total transactions deposits.* In this case, University Bank's reserves (your $100 in coins) are only 50 percent of total deposits. Thus the bank's **reserve ratio** is 50 percent—that is,

bank reserves Assets held by a bank to fulfill its deposit obligations.

reserve ratio The ratio of a bank's reserves to its total transactions deposits.

$$\text{Reserve ratio} = \frac{\text{bank reserves}}{\text{total deposits}}$$

The ability of University Bank to hold reserves that are only a fraction of total deposits results from two facts: (1) people use checks for most transactions, and (2) there is no other bank. Accordingly, reserves are rarely withdrawn from this monopoly bank. In fact, if people *never* withdrew their deposits in cash and *all* transactions accounts were held at University Bank, University Bank would not really need any reserves. Indeed, it could melt your coins and make a nice metal sculpture. So long as no one ever came to see or withdraw the coins, everybody would be blissfully ignorant. Merchants and consumers would just continue using checks, presuming that the bank could cover them when necessary. In this most unusual case, University Bank could continue to make as many loans as it wanted. Every loan made would increase the supply of money.

Reserve Requirements

If a bank could create money at will, if would have a lot of control over aggregate demand. In reality, no private bank has that much power. First, there are many banks available, not just a single monopoly bank. Hence *the power to create money resides in the banking system, not in any single bank.* Each of the thousands of banks in the system plays a relatively small role.

The second constraint on bank power is government regulation. The Federal Reserve System (the Fed) regulates bank lending. The Fed decides how many loans banks can make with their available reserves. Hence even an assumed monopoly bank could not make unlimited loans with your piggy bank's coins. *The Federal Reserve System requires banks to maintain some minimum reserve ratio.* The reserve requirement directly limits the ability of banks to grant new loans.

To see how Fed regulations limit bank lending (money creation), we have to do a little accounting. Suppose the Federal Reserve had imposed a minimum reserve requirement of 75 percent on University Bank. That means the bank must hold reserves equal to at least 75 percent of total deposits.

A 75 percent reserve requirement would have prohibited University Bank from lending $100 to Campus Radio. That loan would have brought *total* deposits up to $200 (your $100 plus the $100 Campus Radio balance). But reserves (your coins) would still be only $100. Hence the ratio of reserves to deposits would have been 50 percent ($100 of reserves ÷ $200 of deposits). That would have violated the Fed's assumed 75 percent reserve requirement. A 75 percent reserve requirement means that University Bank must hold at all times **required reserves** equal to 75 percent of *total* deposits, including those created through loans.

> **required reserves** The minimum amount of reserves a bank is required to hold by government regulation; equal to required reserve ratio times transactions deposits.

The bank's dilemma is evident in the following equation:

$$\text{Required reserves} = \text{required reserve ratio} \times \text{total deposits}$$

To support $200 of total deposits, University Bank would need to satisfy this equation:

$$\text{Required reserves} = 0.75 \times \$200 = \$150$$

But the bank has only $100 of reserves (your coins) and so would violate the reserve requirement if it increased total deposits to $200 by lending $100 to Campus Radio.

University Bank can still issue a loan to Campus Radio. But the loan must be less than $100 to keep the bank within the limits of the required reserve formula. Thus *a minimum reserve requirement directly limits deposit creation possibilities.*

Excess Reserves

Banks will sometimes hold reserves in excess of the minimum required by the Fed. Such reserves are called **excess reserves** and are calculated as

> **excess reserves** Bank reserves in excess of required reserves.

$$\text{Excess reserves} = \text{total reserves} - \text{required reserves}$$

Suppose again that University Bank's only asset is the $100 in coins you deposited. Assume also a Fed reserve requirement of 75 percent. In this case, the initial ledger of the bank would look like this:

Assets		Liabilities	
Required reserves	$75	Your account balance	$100
Excess reserves	$25		
Total assets (your coins)	$100		

Notice two things in this "T-account" ledger. First, total assets equal total liabilities: there are $100 in total assets on the left side of the T-account and $100 on the right. This equality must always exist because someone must own every asset. Second, the bank has $25 of excess reserves. It is *required* to hold only $75 (.75 × $100); the remainder of its reserves ($25) are thus excess.

This bank is not fully using its lending capacity. *So long as a bank has excess reserves, it can make additional loans.* If it does, the nation's money supply will increase.

A Multibank World

In reality, there is more than one bank in town. Hence any loan University Bank makes may end up as a deposit in another bank rather than at its own. This complicates the arithmetic of deposit creation but doesn't change its basic character. Indeed, the existence of a multibank system makes the money creation process even more powerful.

In a multibank world, *the key issue is not how much excess reserves any specific bank holds but how much excess reserves exist in the entire banking system.* If excess reserves exist anywhere in the system, then some banks still have unused lending authority.

THE MONEY MULTIPLIER

Excess reserves are the source of bank lending authority. If there are no excess reserves in the banking system, banks can't make any more loans.

Although an *absence* of excess reserves precludes further lending activity, the *amount* of excess reserves doesn't define the limit to further loans. This surprising conclusion emerges from the way a multibank system works. Consider again what happens when someone borrows all of a bank's excess reserves. Suppose University Bank uses its $25 excess reserves to support a loan. If someone borrows that much money from University Bank, those excess reserves will be depleted. The money won't disappear, however. Once the borrower *spends* the money, someone else will *receive* $25. If that person deposits the $25 elsewhere, then another bank will acquire a new deposit.

If another bank gets a new deposit, the process of deposit creation will continue. The new deposit of $25 increases the second bank's *required* reserves as well as its *excess* reserves. We're talking about a $25 deposit. If the Federal Reserve minimum is 75 percent, then *required* reserves increase by $18.75. The remaining $6.25, therefore, represents *excess* reserves. This second bank can now make additional loans in the amount of $6.25.

Perhaps you are beginning to get a sense that the process of deposit creation will not come to an end quickly. On the contrary, it can continue indefinitely as loans get made and the loans are spent—over and over again. *Each loan made creates new excess reserves, which help fund the next loan.* This recurring

FIGURE 13.2   The Money Multiplier Process

Each bank can use its excess reserves to make a loan. The loans will end up as deposits at other banks. These banks will then have some excess reserves and lending capacity of their own. If the required reserve ratio is .75, Bank #2 can lend 25 percent of the $25 deposit it receives. In this case, it lends $6.25, continuing the deposit creation process.

sequence of loans and spending is much like the income multiplier, which creates additional income every time income is spent. People often refer to deposit creation as the money multiplier process, with the **money multiplier** expressed as the reciprocal of the required reserve ratio:

$$\text{Money multiplier} = \frac{1}{\text{required reserve ratio}}$$

money multiplier The number of deposit (loan) dollars that the banking system can create from $1 of excess reserves; equal to 1 ÷ required reserve ratio.

The money multiplier process is illustrated in Figure 13.2. When a new deposit enters the banking system, it creates both excess and required reserves. The required reserves represent leakage from the flow of money because they cannot be used to create new loans. Excess reserves, on the other hand, can be used for new loans. Once those loans are made, they typically become transactions deposits elsewhere in the banking system (Bank #2 in Figure 13.2). Then some additional leakage into required reserves occurs, and further loans are made (Banks #3 and #4). The process continues until all excess reserves have leaked into required reserves. Once excess reserves have all disappeared, the total value of new loans will equal initial excess reserves multiplied by the money multiplier.

Limits to Deposit Creation

The potential of the money multiplier to create loans is summarized by the equation

$$\begin{array}{c}\text{Excess reserves of} \\ \text{banking system}\end{array} \times \begin{array}{c}\text{money} \\ \text{multiplier}\end{array} = \begin{array}{c}\text{potential} \\ \text{deposit creation}\end{array}$$

Notice how the money multiplier worked in our previous example. The value of the money multiplier was equal to 1.33, which is 1.0 divided by the required reserve ratio of 0.75. The banking system started out with the $25 of excess reserves created by your initial $100 deposit. According to the money multiplier, then, the deposit creation potential of the banking system was

$$\begin{array}{c}\text{Excess reserves} \\ (\$25)\end{array} \times \begin{array}{c}\text{money multiplier} \\ (1.33)\end{array} = \begin{array}{c}\text{potential deposit} \\ \text{creation (\$33.25)}\end{array}$$

If all the banks fully utilize their excess reserves at each step of the money multiplier process, the banking system could make loans in the amount of $33.25. Not very impressive, but in the real world all these numbers would be in the billions—and that would be impressive.

Excess Reserves as Lending Power

While you are reviewing the arithmetic of deposit creation, notice the critical role that excess reserves play in the process. A bank can make loans only if it has excess reserves. Without excess reserves, all of a bank's reserves are required, and no further liabilities (transactions deposits) can be created with new loans. On the other hand, a bank with excess reserves can make additional loans. In fact,

   • *Each bank may lend an amount equal to its excess reserves and no more.*

As such loans enter the circular flow and become deposits elsewhere, they create new excess reserves and further lending capacity. As a consequence,

   • *The entire banking system can increase the volume of loans by the amount of excess reserves multiplied by the money multiplier.*

By keeping track of excess reserves, then, we can gauge the lending capacity of any bank or, with the aid of the money multiplier, the entire banking system.

THE MACRO ROLE OF BANKS

The bookkeeping details of bank deposits and loans are complex, frustrating, and downright boring. But they demonstrate convincingly that *banks can create money.* Since virtually all market transactions involve the use of money, banks must have some influence on macro outcomes.

Financing Aggregate Demand

What we have demonstrated in this chapter is that banks perform two essential functions:

   • Banks transfer money from savers to spenders by lending funds (reserves) held on deposit.
   • The banking system creates additional money by making loans in excess of total reserves.

In performing these two functions, banks change not only the size of the money supply but aggregate demand as well. The loans banks offer to their customers will be used to purchase new cars, homes, business equipment, and other output. All of these purchases will add to aggregate demand. Hence *increases in the money supply tend to increase aggregate demand.*

When banks curtail their lending activity, the opposite occurs. People can't get the loans or credit they need to finance desired consumption or investment. As a result, *aggregate demand declines when the money supply shrinks.*

The central role of the banking system in the economy is emphasized in Figure 13.3. In this depiction of the circular flow, income flows from product markets through business firms to factor markets and returns to consumers in the form of disposable income. Consumers spend most of their income but also save (don't spend) some of it. This consumer saving could pose a problem for the economy if no one else were to step up and buy the goods and services consumers leave unsold.

The banking system is the key link between consumer savings and the demand originating in other sectors of the economy. To see how important that link is, imagine that *all* consumer saving was deposited in piggy banks rather than depository institutions (banks) and that no one used checks. Under these circumstances, banks could not transfer money from savers to spenders by holding deposits and making loans. The banks could not create the money needed to boost aggregate demand.

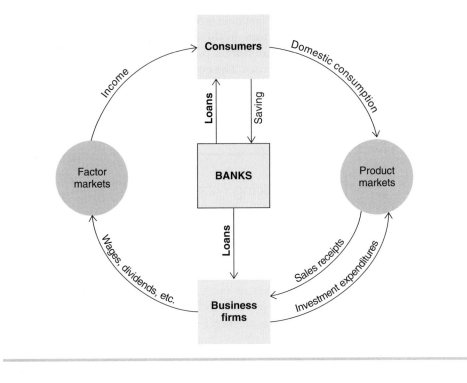

FIGURE 13.3
Banks in the Circular Flow
Banks help transfer income from savers to spenders. They do this by using their deposits to make loans to business firms and consumers who desire to spend more money than they have. By lending money, banks help maintain any desired rate of aggregate spending.

In reality, a substantial portion of consumer saving *is* deposited in banks. These and other bank deposits can be used as the bases of loans, thereby returning purchasing power to the circular flow. Moreover, because the banking system can make *multiple* loans from available reserves, banks don't have to receive all consumer saving in order to carry out their function. On the contrary, *the banking system can create any desired level of money supply if allowed to expand or reduce loan activity at will.*

Constraints on Money Creation

If banks had unlimited power to create money (make loans), they could control aggregate demand. Their power isn't quite so vast, however. There are four major constraints on their lending activity.

BANK DEPOSITS   The first constraint on the lending activity of banks is the willingness of people to keep deposits in the bank. If people preferred to hold cash rather than debit cards and checkbooks, banks would not be able to acquire or maintain the reserves that are the foundation of bank lending activity.

WILLING BORROWERS   The second constraint on deposit creation is the willingness of consumers, businesses, and governments to borrow the money that banks make available. If no one wanted to borrow any money, deposit creation would never begin.

WILLING LENDERS   The banks themselves may not be willing to satisfy all credit demands. This was the case in the 1930s when the banks declined to use their excess reserves for loans they perceived to be too risky. In the recession of 2008–2009 many banks again closed their loan windows. Consumers couldn't get mortgages to buy new homes; businesses couldn't get loans to purchase equipment or inventory.

GOVERNMENT REGULATION The last and most important constraint on deposit creation is the Federal Reserve System. In the absence of government regulation, individual banks would have tremendous power over the money supply and therewith all macroeconomic outcomes. The government limits this power by regulating bank lending practices. The levers of Federal Reserve policy are examined in the next chapter.

POLICY PERSPECTIVES

Are Mobile Payments Replacing Money?

The Internet has created a virtual mall that millions of people visit every day. In 2013 $250 *billion* of goods and services were sold at that mall. Yet experts say the sales potential of the Internet has barely been tapped. Only a tiny fraction of the consumers who browse through the Internet mall actually buy something. As a result, Internet sales remain a small fraction of gross domestic product.

E-retailers say *money* is the problem. You can't pay cash at the Internet mall. And you can't hand over a check in cyberspace. So the most common forms of money used in bricks-and-mortar malls can't serve as a medium of exchange in electronic malls.

CREDIT CARDS Because cash and checks don't work in cyberspace, almost all Internet purchases are completed with credit cards. But dependence on credit cards limits the potential of e-commerce. To begin with, there is the question of security. Once you transmit your credit card number into cyberspace, you can't be 100 percent confident about its use. There are thousands of credit card thefts on the Internet. Hackers have even broken into databases that were supposed to provide security for credit card transactions.

NEWS WIRE	PAYMENT SERVICES

Starbucks to Accept Square Mobile Payments

NEW YORK (AP)—Starbucks Corp. will soon be the first national chain to let customers pay with Square's mobile payment application . . .

The Seattle-based coffee company says it will start accepting payments from Square's app this fall, in addition to the Starbucks payment app it rolled out a year and a half ago.

The McGraw-Hill Companies, Inc./Jill Braaten, photographer

To use either of the programs, customers download the apps then link a credit or debit card to the account. When it comes time to pay at the register, they open the app and wave their phone in front of the scanner.

Source: Associated Press, August 8, 2012. Used with permission of The Associated Press. Copyright © 2012. All rights reserved.

Consumers also worry about privacy. Retail merchants compile databases on credit card purchasers. They sell these data files to other merchants, unleashing a barrage of targeted advertising. Consumers don't want those marketing intrusions. And they don't want the world to know the details of their private web browsing and purchases.

MOBILE PAYMENTS   Dozens of Internet companies have tried to create alternative means of payment for cybershoppers. The latest craze is mobile payments—software programs that permit you to make payment directly to the seller from your smartphone or tablet. You don't have to wait in line to place your order or to pay for it; the entire transaction occurs in the cloud. Starbucks introduced this payment system in 2012 using Square's technology (see the accompanying News Wire). Retail analysts expect mobile payments to skyrocket from $640 million in 2012 to $64 *billion* in 2016.

As convenient as mobile payments are, they are *not* money. Notice in the News Wire how you actually *pay* for those mobile transactions: your purchases are debited to your bank or credit account. Mobile payments are a *service*, not a new form of money. M1 still reigns supreme.

SUMMARY

- In a market economy, money serves a critical function in facilitating exchanges and specialization, thus permitting increased output. "Money" refers to anything that serves as a medium of exchange, store of value, and standard of value.   **LO1**

- The most common measure of the money supply (M1) includes both cash and balances people hold in transactions accounts (e.g., checking accounts).   **LO2**

- Banks have the power to create money simply by making loans. In making loans, banks create new transactions deposits (bank balances), which become part of the money supply.   **LO3**

- The ability of banks to make loans—create money— depends on their reserves. Only if a bank has excess reserves—reserves greater than those required by federal regulation—can it make new loans.   **LO3**

- As loans are spent, they create deposits elsewhere, making it possible for other banks to make additional loans. The money multiplier (1 ÷ required reserve ratio) indicates the total value of deposits that can be created by the banking system from excess reserves.   **LO4**

- The role of banks in creating money includes the transfer of money from savers to spenders as well as deposit creation in excess of deposit balances. Taken together, these two functions give banks direct control over the amount of purchasing power available in the marketplace.   **LO5**

- The deposit creation potential of the banking system is limited by government regulation. It is also limited by the willingness of market participants to hold deposits or borrow money. At times, banks themselves may be unwilling to use all their lending ability.   **LO4**

TERMS TO REMEMBER

Define the following terms:

barter	money supply (M1)	bank reserves	excess reserves
money	aggregate demand	reserve ratio	money multiplier
transactions account	deposit creation	required reserves	

QUESTIONS FOR DISCUSSION

1. Do eggs satisfy the three conditions for money? Did barter make it easier or more difficult to go to the movies in Russia? (See the News Wire on p. 269.)   **LO1**

2. If a friend asked you how much money you had to spend, what items would you include in your response?   **LO2**

3. Does money have any intrinsic value? If not, why are people willing to accept money in exchange for goods and services?   **LO1**

4. Have you ever borrowed money to buy a car, pay tuition, or for any other purpose? In what form did you receive the money? How did your loan affect the money supply? Aggregate demand?   **LO3**

5. Does the fact that your bank keeps only a fraction of your account balance in reserve worry you? Why don't people rush to the bank and retrieve their money? What would happen if they did?   **LO3**

6. If all banks heeded Shakespeare's admonition "Neither a borrower nor a lender be," what would happen to the supply of money?   **LO3**

7. Why would a bank ever hold excess reserves rather than make new loans?   **LO3**

8. If banks stopped making new loans, how would aggregate demand be affected?   **LO5**

9. **POLICY PERSPECTIVES** Why aren't mobile payments counted as money (News Wire, p. 280)?   **LO2**

PROBLEMS   connect

1. What percentage of your monthly spending do you pay with (*a*) cash, (*b*) check, (*c*) credit card, or (*d*) automatic transfers? How do you pay off the credit card balance? How does your use of cash compare with the composition of the money supply (Figure 13.1)?   **LO2**

2. If a bank has $100 million in deposits and $16 million in reserves with a reserve requirement of 0.15,   **LO3**
   (*a*) How much are its required reserves?
   (*b*) How much excess reserves does it have?
   (*c*) How much can it lend?

3. How large is the money multiplier when the required reserve ratio is 0.10? If the required reserve ratio increases to 0.125, what happens to the money multiplier?   **LO4**

4. If a bank has total reserves of $400,000 and $1 million in deposits, how much money can it lend if the required reserve ratio is   **LO3**
   (*a*) 5 percent?
   (*b*) 10 percent?

5. How large a loan can Bank #2 in Figure 13.2 make?   **LO3**

6. What volume of loans can the banking system in Figure 13.2 support? If the reserve requirement were 50 percent rather than 75 percent, what would the system's lending capacity be?   **LO3, LO4**

7. Suppose that an Irish Sweepstakes winner deposits $10 million in cash into her transactions account at the Bank of America. Assume a reserve requirement of 20 percent and no excess reserves in the banking system prior to this deposit. Show the changes on the Bank of America balance sheet when the $10 million is initially deposited.   **LO3**

8. In December 1994 a man in Ohio decided to deposit all of the *8 million* pennies he had been saving for nearly 65 years. (His deposit weighed over 48,000 pounds!) With a reserve requirement of 5 percent, how did his deposit change the lending capacity of   **LO3, LO4**
   (*a*) His bank?
   (*b*) The banking system?

9. **POLICY PERSPECTIVES** If mobile payments increase by $3 billion this year, by how much will M1 increase?   **LO2**

◄ Practice quizzes, student PowerPoints, author podcasts, web activities, and additional materials available at **www.mhhe.com/schilleressentials9e**, or scan here. Need a barcode reader? Try ScanLife, available in your app store.

14 Monetary Policy

◄ Practice quizzes, student PowerPoints, author podcasts, web activities, and additional materials available at www.mhhe.com/schilleressentials9e, or scan here. Need a barcode reader? Try ScanLife, available in your app store.

LEARNING OBJECTIVES

After reading this chapter, you should be able to:

1 Describe how the Federal Reserve is organized.
2 Identify the Fed's three primary policy tools.
3 Explain how open market operations work.
4 Tell how monetary stimulus or restraint is achieved.
5 Discuss how monetary policy affects macro outcomes.

Rarely do all the members of a congressional committee attend a committee hearing. But when the chairman of the Fed is the witness, all 21 members of the U.S. Senate Committee on Banking, Housing, and Urban Affairs typically show up. So do staffers, lobbyists, and a throng of reporters and camera crews from around the world. They don't want to miss a word that the Chairman utters.

Tourists visiting the U.S. Capitol are often caught up in the excitement. Seeing all the press and the crowds, they assume some movie star is testifying. Maybe George Clooney is pleading for humanitarian aid for Sudan. Or Lars Ulrich, the drummer for Metallica, is asking for more copyright protection for music. Maybe Angelina Jolie is urging Congress to increase funding for AIDS research and global poverty. Or Clint Eastwood is asking Congress to ease the requirements of the Americans with Disabilities Act. Curious to see who's getting all the attention, the tourists often stand in line to get a brief look into the hearing room. Imagine their bewilderment when they finally get in: the star witness is an economics professor droning on about economic statistics. Who is *this* person? they wonder, as they head for the exit.

Why did so many people listen intently to the former Fed chairman, Ben Bernanke?
© AP Photo/Dennis Cook

"This person" is often described as the most powerful person in the U.S. economy. Even the president seeks his advice and approval. Why? Because this is the chairman of the Federal Reserve—the government agency that controls the nation's money supply. As we saw in the previous chapter, changes in the money supply can alter aggregate demand. So whoever has a hand on the money supply lever has a lot of power over macroeconomic outcomes—which explains why so many people want to know what the Fed chairman thinks about the health of the economy.

Figure 14.1 offers a bird's-eye view of how **monetary policy** fits into our macro model. Clearly a lot of people think the monetary policy lever is important. Otherwise no one would be attending those boring congressional hearings at which the Fed chairman testifies. To understand why monetary policy is so important, we must answer two basic questions:

monetary policy The use of money and credit controls to influence macroeconomic activity.

- How does the government control the amount of money in the economy?
- How does the money supply affect macroeconomic outcomes?

FIGURE 14.1   Monetary Policy

Monetary policy tries to alter macro outcomes by managing the amount of money available in the economy. By changing the money supply and/or interest rates, monetary policy seeks to shift aggregate demand.

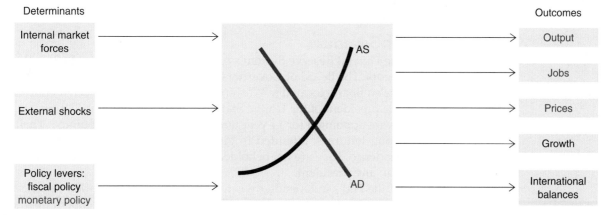

THE FEDERAL RESERVE SYSTEM

Control of the money supply in the United States starts with the Fed. The Federal Reserve System is actually a system of regional banks and central controls, headed by a chairman of the board.

Federal Reserve Banks

The core of the Federal Reserve System consists of 12 Federal Reserve banks, located in the various regions of the country. Each of these banks acts as a central banker for the private banks in its region. In this role, the regional Fed banks perform many critical services, including the following:

- *Clearing checks between private banks.* Suppose the Bank of America in San Francisco receives a deposit from one of its customers in the form of a check written on a Chase Manhattan bank branch in New York. The Bank of America doesn't have to go to New York to collect the cash or other reserves that support that check. Instead the Bank of America can deposit the check at its account with the Federal Reserve Bank of San Francisco. The Fed then collects from Chase Manhattan. This vital clearinghouse service saves the Bank of America and other private banks a great deal of time and expense. In view of the fact that over 35 *billion* checks are written every year, this clearinghouse service is an important feature of the Federal Reserve System.

- *Holding bank reserves.* What makes the Fed's clearinghouse service work is the fact that the Bank of America and Chase Manhattan both have their own accounts at the Fed. Recall from Chapter 13 that banks are *required* to hold some minimum fraction of their transactions deposits in reserve. Nearly all these reserves are held in accounts at the regional Federal Reserve banks. Only a small amount of reserves is held as cash in a bank's vaults. The accounts at the regional Fed banks provide greater security and convenience for bank reserves. They also enable the Fed to monitor the actual level of bank reserves.

- *Providing currency.* Because banks hold little cash in their vaults, they turn to the Fed to meet sporadic cash demands. A private bank can simply call the regional Federal Reserve bank and order a supply of cash to be delivered (by armored truck) before a weekend or holiday. The cash will be deducted from the bank's own account at the Fed. When all the cash comes back in after the holiday, the bank can reverse the process, sending the unneeded cash back to the Fed.

- *Providing loans.* The Federal Reserve banks may also lend reserves to private banks. This practice, called *discounting,* will be examined more closely in a moment.

The Board of Governors

At the top of the Federal Reserve System's organization chart (Figure 14.2) is the Board of Governors. The Board of Governors is the key decision maker for monetary policy. The Fed Board, located in Washington, DC, consists of seven members appointed by the president of the United States and confirmed by the U.S. Senate. Board members are appointed for 14-year terms and cannot be reappointed. Their exceptionally long tenure is intended to give the Fed governors a measure of political independence. They are not beholden to any elected official and will hold office longer than any president.

The intent of the Fed's independence is to keep control of the nation's money supply beyond the immediate reach of politicians (especially members of the

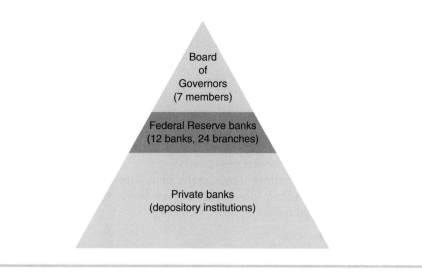

FIGURE 14.2
Structure of the
Federal Reserve System
The broad policies of the Fed
are determined by the seven-
member Board of Governors.
Ben Bernanke is the chairman
of the Fed Board.
The 12 Federal Reserve
banks provide central banking
services to individual banks in
their respective regions.
The private banks must follow
Fed rules on reserves and
loan activity.

House of Representatives, elected for two-year terms). The designers of the Fed system feared that political control of monetary policy would cause wild swings in the money supply and macro instability. Critics argue, however, that the Fed's independence makes it unresponsive to the majority will.

The Fed Chairman

The most visible member of the Fed system is the Board's chairman. The chairman is selected by the president of the United States, subject to congressional approval. The chairman is appointed for four years but may be reappointed for successive terms. Alan Greenspan was first appointed chairman by President Reagan, then reappointed by Presidents George H. Bush, Bill Clinton, and George W. Bush. When his term as a governor expired on January 31, 2006, he was replaced by Ben Bernanke, a former economics professor from Princeton University. President Obama reappointed Bernanke for another four-year term in January 2010. In 2014 the president appointed a new chairman.

MONETARY TOOLS

Our immediate interest is not in the structure of the Federal Reserve System but in the way the Fed can use its powers to alter the **money supply (M1)**. *The basic tools of monetary policy are*

- *Reserve requirements.*
- *Discount rates.*
- *Open market operations.*

money supply (M1) Currency held by the public, plus balances in transactions accounts.

Reserve Requirements

In Chapter 13 we emphasized the need for banks to maintain some minimal level of reserves. The Fed requires private banks to keep a certain fraction of their deposits in reserve. These **required reserves** are held either in the form of actual vault cash or, more commonly, as credits (deposits) in a bank's reserve account at a regional Federal Reserve bank.

The Fed's authority to set reserve requirements gives it great power over the lending behavior of individual banks. *By changing the reserve requirement, the Fed can directly alter the lending capacity of the banking system.*

required reserves The minimum amount of reserves a bank is required to hold by government regulation; equal to required reserve ratio times transactions deposits.

Recall that the ability of the banking system to make additional loans—create deposits—is determined by two factors: (1) the amount of excess reserves banks hold and (2) the money multiplier:

$$\text{Available lending capacity of banking system} = \text{excess reserves} \times \text{money multiplier}$$

Changes in reserve requirements affect both variables on the right side of this equation, giving this policy tool a one–two punch.

The impact of reserve requirements on the first of these variables is straightforward. **Excess reserves** are simply the difference between total reserves and the amount required by Fed rules:

$$\text{Excess reserves} = \text{total reserves} - \text{required reserves}$$

excess reserves Bank reserves in excess of required reserves.

Accordingly, with a given amount of total reserves, *a decrease in required reserves directly increases excess reserves.* The opposite is equally apparent: an increase in the reserve requirement reduces excess reserves.

A change in the reserve requirement also increases the *money multiplier.* Recall that the **money multiplier** is the reciprocal of the reserve requirement (i.e., $1 \div$ reserve requirement). Hence *a lower reserve requirement increases the value of the money multiplier.* Both determinants of bank lending capacity thus are affected by reserve requirements.

money multiplier The number of deposit (loan) dollars that the banking system can create from $1 of excess reserves; equal to $1 \div$ required reserve ratio.

A DECREASE IN REQUIRED RESERVES The impact of a decrease in the required reserve ratio is summarized in Table 14.1. In this case, the required reserve ratio is decreased from 25 to 20 percent. Notice that this change in the reserve requirement has no effect on the amount of initial deposits in the banking system (row 1 of Table 14.1) or the amount of *total* reserves (row 2). They remain at $100 billion and $30 billion, respectively.

What the decreased reserve requirement *does* affect is the way those reserves can be used. Before the increase, $25 billion in reserves was *required* (row 3) leaving $5 billion of *excess* reserves (row 4). Now, however, banks are required to hold only $20 billion (0.20 × $100 billion) in reserves, leaving them with $10 billion in excess reserves. Thus a decrease in the reserve requirement immediately increases excess reserves, as illustrated in row 4 of Table 14.1.

There is a second effect also. Notice in row 5 of Table 14.1 what happens to the money multiplier ($1 \div$ reserve ratio). Previously it was 4 (= $1 \div 0.25$); now it is 5 (= $1 \div 0.20$). Consequently, a lower reserve requirement not only increases excess reserves but boosts their lending power as well.

TABLE 14.1
The Impact of a Decreased Reserve Requirement

A decrease in the required reserve ratio raises both excess reserves (row 4) and the money multiplier (row 5). As a consequence, changes in the reserve requirement have a huge impact on the lending capacity of the banking system (row 6).

	Required Reserve Ratio	
	25 Percent	20 Percent
1. Total deposits	$100 billion	$100 billion
2. Total reserves	30 billion	30 billion
3. Required reserves	25 billion	20 billion
4. Excess reserves	5 billion	10 billion
5. Money multiplier	4	5
6. Unused lending capacity	$20 billion	$50 billion

| NEWS WIRE | RESERVE REQUIREMENTS |

Beijing Seeks to Cool Prices by Reining In Bank Lending

BEIJING—China announced an increase in the share of deposits banks must hold in reserve, its fourth such move this year, a fresh step in its battle against inflation that came after data showed consumer prices rising at their fastest clip in nearly three years in March.

The People's Bank of China said Sunday that it will raise banks' reserve requirement ratio by a half percentage point, effective from Thursday. . . .

China's official reserve requirement ratio for most banks will be 20.5 percent after the latest increase takes effect.

Source: *The Wall Street Journal*, April 18, 2011. Used with permission of Dow Jones & Company, Inc. via Copyright Clearance Center, Inc.

NOTE: A change in reserve requirements is such a powerful monetary lever that it is rarely used. A change in the reserve requirements immediately changes both the amount of excess reserves and the money multiplier.

A change in the reserve requirement, therefore, hits banks with a double whammy. *A change in the reserve requirement causes*

- *A change in excess reserves.*
- *A change in the money multiplier.*

These changes lead to a sharp rise in bank lending power. Whereas the banking system initially had the power to increase the volume of loans by only $20 billion (= $5 billion of excess reserves × 4), it now has $50 billion (= $10 billion × 5) of unused lending capacity, as noted in row 6 of Table 14.1. Were all this extra lending capacity put to use, the AD curve would shift noticeably to the right.

Changes in reserve requirements are a powerful weapon for altering the lending capacity of the banking system. The Fed uses this power sparingly, so as not to cause abrupt changes in the money supply and severe disruptions of banking activity. From 1970 to 1980, for example, reserve requirements were changed only twice, and then by only half a percentage point each time (e.g., from 12.0 to 12.5 percent). In December 1990 the Fed lowered reserve requirements, hoping to create enough extra lending power to push the stalled U.S. economy out of recession.

The central bank of China pushed this policy lever in the opposite direction in 2011. Fearful that excessive bank lending was overheating the economy, China *raised* the reserve requirement (see the accompanying News Wire). In so doing, it *reduced* the lending capacity of Chinese banks and helped rein in AD before inflation got out of control.

The Discount Rate

The second tool in the Fed's monetary policy toolbox is the **discount rate**. This is the interest rate the Fed charges for *lending* reserves to private banks.

To understand how this policy tool is used, you have to recognize that banks are profit seekers. They don't want to keep idle reserves; they want to use all available reserves to make interest-bearing loans. In their pursuit of profits, banks try to keep reserves at or close to the bare minimum established by the Fed. In fact, banks have demonstrated an uncanny ability to keep their reserves close to the minimum federal requirement. As Figure 14.3 illustrates, the only two times banks held huge excess reserves were during the Great Depression of the 1930s and again in 2008–2012. Banks didn't want to make any more loans during the Depression and were fearful of panicky customers withdrawing their deposits. Excess

discount rate The rate of interest charged by the Federal Reserve banks for lending reserves to private banks.

reserves spiked up briefly again after the terrorist attacks of September 2001, when the future looked unusually uncertain. In 2008–2012 excess reserves flew off the charts (see Figure 14.3) as banks were waiting for clarity about the economic outlook and government regulation of lending practices.

FIGURE 14.3   Excess Reserves and Borrowings

Excess reserves represent unused lending capacity. Hence banks strive to keep excess reserves at a minimum. The only exception to this practice occurred during the Great Depression, when banks were hesitant to make any loans, and again in 2008–2012, when both the economic and regulatory outlooks were uncertain.

In trying to minimize excess reserves, banks occasionally fall short of required reserves. At such times they may borrow from other banks (the federal funds market), or they may borrow reserves from the Fed. Borrowing from the Fed is called *discounting*.

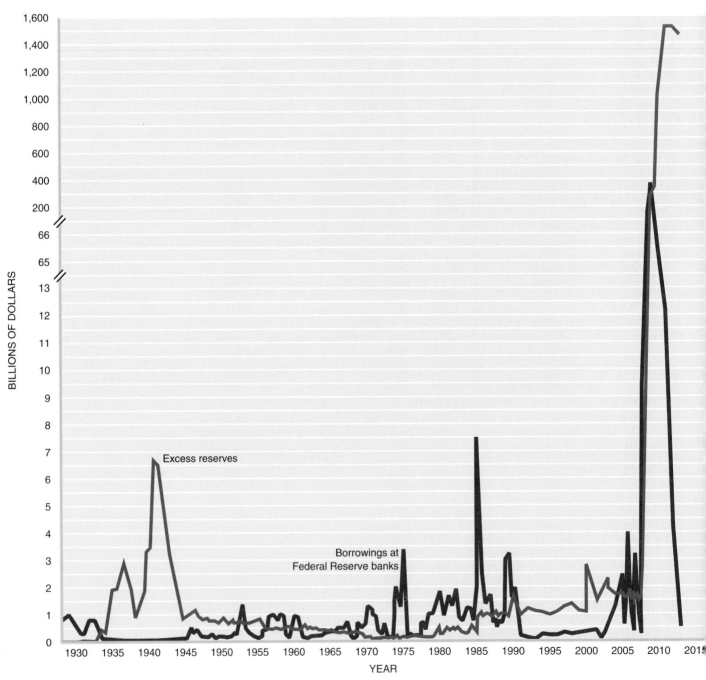

Source: Federal Reserve System.

Because banks continually seek to keep excess reserves at a minimum, they run the risk of occasionally falling below reserve requirements. A large borrower may be a little slow in repaying a loan, or deposit withdrawals may exceed expectations. At such times a bank may find that it doesn't have enough reserves to satisfy Fed requirements.

Banks could ensure continual compliance with reserve requirements by maintaining large amounts of excess reserves. But that is an unprofitable practice. On the other hand, a strategy of maintaining minimum reserves runs the risk of violating Fed rules. Banks can pursue this strategy only if they have some last-minute source of extra reserves.

FEDERAL FUNDS MARKET   There are three possible sources of last-minute reserves. A bank that finds itself short of reserves can turn to other banks for help. If a reserve-poor bank can borrow some reserves from a reserve-rich bank, it may be able to bridge its temporary deficit and satisfy the Fed. Interbank borrowing is referred to as the *federal funds market*. The interest rate banks charge each other for lending reserves is called the **federal funds rate.**

federal funds rate The interest rate banks charge each other for reserves loans.

SECURITIES SALES   Another option available to reserve-poor banks is the sale of securities. Banks use some of their excess reserves to buy government bonds, which pay interest. If a bank needs more reserves to satisfy federal regulations, it may sell these securities and deposit the proceeds at the regional Federal Reserve bank. Its reserve position is thereby increased.

DISCOUNTING   A third option for avoiding a reserve shortage is to *borrow* reserves from the Federal Reserve System itself. The Fed not only establishes rules of behavior for banks but also functions as a central bank, or banker's bank. Banks maintain accounts with the regional Federal Reserve banks, much the way you and I maintain accounts with a local bank. Individual banks deposit and withdraw *reserve credits* from these accounts, just as we deposit and withdraw dollars. Should a bank find itself short of reserves, it can go to the Fed's *discount window* and *borrow* some reserves.

The discounting operation of the Fed provides private banks with an important source of reserves, but not without cost. The Fed, too, charges interest on the reserves it lends to banks, a rate of interest referred to as the *discount rate*.

The discount window provides a mechanism for directly influencing the size of bank reserves. ***By raising or lowering the discount rate, the Fed changes the cost of money for banks and therewith the incentive to borrow reserves.*** At high discount rates, borrowing from the Fed is expensive. High discount rates also signal the Fed's desire to restrain money supply growth. Low discount rates, on the other hand, make it profitable for banks to borrow additional reserves and to exploit one's lending capacity to the fullest. This was the objective of the Fed's October 2008 discount rate reduction (see the accompanying News Wire), which was intended to increase aggregate demand. Notice in Figure 14.3 how bank borrowing from the Fed jumped after the discount rate was cut.

Open Market Operations

Reserve requirements and discount rates are important tools of monetary policy. But they do not come close to open market operations in terms of day-to-day impact on the money supply. ***Open market operations are the principal mechanism for directly altering the reserves of the banking system.*** Since reserves are the lifeblood of the banking system, open market operations have an immediate and direct impact on lending capacity. They are more flexible than changes in reserve requirements, thus permitting minor adjustments to lending capacity (and ultimately aggregate demand).

NEWS WIRE	DISCOUNT RATES

Fed Cuts Key Interest Rate Half-Point to 1 Percent

WASHINGTON—The Federal Reserve has slashed a key interest rate by half a percentage point as it seeks to revive an economy hit by a long list of maladies stemming from the most severe financial crisis in decades.

The central bank on Wednesday reduced its target for the federal funds rate, the interest banks charge on overnight loans, to 1 percent, a low last seen in 2003–2004. The funds rate has not been lower since 1958, when Dwight Eisenhower was president. . . .

The central bank also announced that it was lowering its discount rate, the interest it charges to make direct loans to banks, by a half-point to 1.25 percent. This rate has become increasingly important as the central bank has dramatically increased direct loans to banks in an effort to break the grip of the credit crisis.

Bernanke pledged in a speech earlier this month that the Fed "will not stand down until we have achieved our goals of repairing and reforming our financial system and restoring prosperity."

In addition to the rate cuts, the Fed has been moving to pump billions of dollars into the banking system to help unfreeze markets that seized up in dramatic fashion last month. The ensuing meltdown of financial markets caused the Bush administration to successfully lobby Congress to pass on Oct. 3 a $700 billion rescue package to make direct purchases of bank stock and buy up bad assets as a way of getting financial institutions to start lending again.

—Martin Crutsinger, AP Economics Writer

Source: Associated Press, October 29, 2008. Used with permission of The Associated Press Copyright © 2008. All rights reserved.

NOTE: A cut in the discount rate lowers the cost of bank borrowing. By cutting both the discount and federal funds rates, the Fed sought to reduce interest rates to consumers and business, thereby stimulating more spending.

PORTFOLIO DECISIONS   To appreciate the impact of open market operations, you have to think about the alternative uses for idle funds. Just about everybody has some idle funds, even if they amount to a few dollars in your pocket or a minimal balance in your checking account. Other consumers and corporations have great amounts of idle funds, even millions of dollars at any time. What we're concerned with here is what people decide to do with such funds.

People, and corporations, do not hold all of their idle funds in transactions accounts or cash. Idle funds are also used to purchase stocks, build up savings account balances, and purchase bonds. These alternative uses of idle funds are attractive because they promise some additional income in the form of interest, dividends, or capital appreciation (e.g., higher stock prices).

HOLD MONEY OR BONDS?   *The open market operations of the Federal Reserve focus on one of the portfolio choices people make—whether to deposit idle funds in transactions accounts (banks) or to purchase government bonds* (see Figure 14.4). In essence, the Fed attempts to influence this choice by making bonds more or less attractive as circumstances warrant. It thereby induces people to move funds from banks to bond markets, or vice versa. In the process, reserves either enter or leave the banking system, thereby altering the lending capacity of banks. Hence the size of potential deposits depends on how much of their wealth people hold in the form of *money* and how much in the form of bonds.

FIGURE 14.4
Portfolio Choice
People holding extra funds have to place them somewhere. If the funds are deposited in the bank, lending capacity increases.

OPEN MARKET ACTIVITY   The Fed's interest in these portfolio choices originates in its concern over bank reserves. The more money people hold in the form of bank deposits, the greater the reserves and lending capacity of the banking system. If people hold more bonds and smaller bank balances, banks will have fewer reserves and less lending power. Recognizing this, *the Fed buys or sells bonds to alter the level of bank reserves.* This is the purpose of the Fed's bond market activity. In other words, **open market operations** entail the purchase and sale of government securities (bonds) for the purpose of altering the flow of reserves into and out of the banking system.

BUYING BONDS   Suppose the Fed wants to increase the money supply. To do so, it must persuade people to deposit a larger share of their financial assets in banks and hold less in other forms, particularly government bonds. How can the Fed do this? The solution lies in bond prices. If the Fed offers to pay a high price for bonds, people will sell some of their bonds to the Fed. They will then deposit the proceeds of the sale in their bank accounts. This influx of money into bank accounts will directly increase bank reserves.

Figure 14.5 shows how this process works. Notice in step 1 that when the Fed buys a bond from the public, it pays with a check written on itself. The bond seller must deposit the Fed's check in a bank account (step 2) if she wants to use the proceeds or simply desires to hold the money for safekeeping. The bank, in turn, deposits the check at a regional Federal Reserve bank, in exchange for a reserve credit (step 3). The bank's reserves are directly increased by the amount of the check. Thus *by buying bonds, the Fed increases bank reserves.* These reserves can be used to expand the money supply as banks put their newly acquired reserves to work making loans.

SELLING BONDS   Should the Fed desire to slow the growth in the money supply, it can reverse the whole process. Instead of offering to *buy* bonds, the Fed in this

open market operations
Federal Reserve purchases and sales of government bonds for the purpose of altering bank reserves.

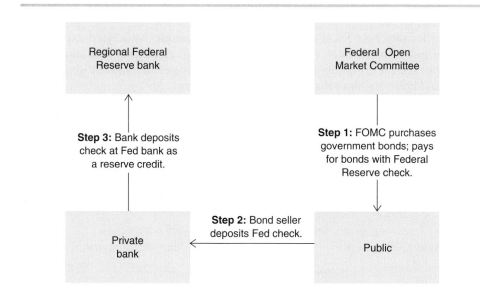

FIGURE 14.5
An Open Market Purchase
The Fed can increase bank reserves by buying government securities from the public. The Fed check used to buy securities (step 1) gets deposited in a private bank (step 2). The bank returns the check to the Fed (step 3), thereby obtaining additional reserves (and lending capacity).

To decrease bank reserves, the Fed would sell securities, thus reversing the flow of reserves.

case will try to *sell* bonds. If it sets the price sufficiently low, individuals, corporations, and government agencies will want to buy them. When they do so, they write a check, paying the Fed for the bonds. The Fed then returns the check to the depositor's bank, taking payment through a reduction in the bank's reserve account. The reserves of the banking system are thereby diminished. So is the capacity to make loans. Thus *by selling bonds, the Fed reduces bank reserves.*

To appreciate the significance of open market operations, one must have a sense of the magnitudes involved. The volume of trading in U.S. government securities exceeds $1 *trillion* per day. The Fed alone owned over 1.5 *trillion* worth of government securities at the beginning of 2013 and bought or sold enormous sums daily. Thus open market operations involve tremendous amounts of money and, by implication, potential bank reserves.

Powerful Levers

What we have seen in these last few pages is how the Fed can regulate the lending behavior of the banking system. By way of summary, we observe that the three levers of monetary policy are

- Reserve requirements.
- Discount rates.
- Open market operations.

By using these levers, the Fed can change the level of bank reserves and banks' lending capacity. Since bank loans are the primary source of new money, *the Fed has effective control of the nation's money supply.* The question then becomes, What should the Fed do with this policy lever?

SHIFTING AGGREGATE DEMAND

The ultimate goal of all macro policy is to stabilize the economy at its full employment potential. Monetary policy contributes to the goal by increasing or decreasing the money supply as economic conditions require. Table 14.2 summarizes the tools the Fed uses to pursue this goal.

Expansionary Policy

Suppose the economy is in recession, producing less than its full employment potential. Such a situation is illustrated by the equilibrium point E_1 in Figure 14.6. The objective in this situation is to stimulate the economy, increasing the rate of output from Q_1 to Q_F.

We earlier saw how fiscal policy can help bring about the desired expansion. Were the government to increase its own spending, **aggregate demand** would shift to the right. A tax cut would also stimulate aggregate demand by giving consumers and business more disposable income to spend.

aggregate demand The total quantity of output demanded at alternative price levels in a given time period, *ceteris paribus.*

TABLE 14.2
Monetary Policy Guidelines
Monetary policy works by increasing or decreasing aggregate demand, as macro conditions warrant. The tools for shifting AD include open market bond activity, the discount rate, and bank reserve requirements.

Problem	Solution	Policy Tools
Unemployment (slow GDP growth)	Increase aggregate demand.	Buy bonds. Lower discount rate. Reduce reserve requirement.
Inflation (excessive GDP growth)	Decrease aggregate demand.	Sell bonds. Raise discount rate. Increase reserve requirement.

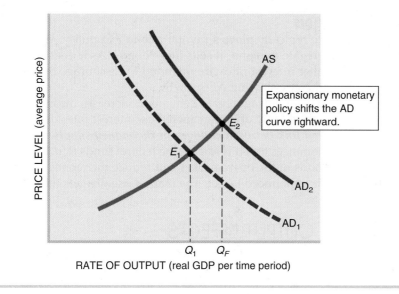

FIGURE 14.6
Demand-Side Focus

Monetary policy tools change the size of the money supply. Changes in the money supply, in turn, shift the aggregate demand curve. In this case, an increase in M1 shifts demand from AD_1 to AD_2 restoring full employment (Q_F).

Monetary policy may be used to shift aggregate demand as well. If the Fed lowers reserve requirements, drops the discount rate, or buys more bonds, it will increase bank lending capacity. The banks in turn will try to use that expanded capacity and make more loans. By offering lower interest rates or easier approvals, the banks can encourage people to borrow and spend more money. In this way, an increase in the money supply will result in a rightward shift of the aggregate demand curve. In Figure 14.6 the resulting shift propels the economy out of recession (Q_1) to its full employment potential (Q_F).

Topic Podcast:
Interest Rates

Restrictive Policy

Monetary policy may also be used to cool an overheating economy. Excessive aggregate demand may put too much pressure on our production capacity. As market participants bid against each other for increasingly scarce goods, prices will start rising.

The goal of monetary policy in this situation is to reduce aggregate demand—that is, to shift the AD curve leftward. To do this, the Fed can reduce the money supply by (1) raising reserve requirements, (2) increasing the discount rate, or (3) selling bonds in the open market. All of these actions will reduce bank lending capacity. The competition for this reduced pool of funds will drive up interest rates. The combination of higher interest rates and lessened loan availability will curtail investment, consumption, and even government spending. This was the intent of China's monetary restraint in 2011 (see the News Wire on page 289). Worried that the Chinese economy was pressing against its production possibilities, the People's Bank of China moved to slow money supply growth and nudge interest rates up a bit. The essence of this restrictive policy is captured in the accompanying cartoon.

Tight monetary policy reduces aggregate demand and inflationary pressures.

The Dropouts—Used by permission of Howard Post.

Interest Rate Targets

The federal funds rate typically plays a pivotal role in Fed policy. When the Fed wants to restrain aggregate demand, it sells more bonds. As it does so, it pushes interest rates up. Higher interest rates are intended to discourage consumer and investor borrowing, thereby slowing AD growth.

If the Fed wants to stimulate aggregate demand, it increases the money supply by buying bonds. As the supply of money increases, interest rates decline. Hence *interest rates are a key link between changes in the money supply and shifts of AD.* When the Fed announces that it is raising the federal funds rate, it is signaling its intention to sell bonds in the open market and reduce the money supply until interest rates rise to its announced target. The market usually gets the message.

PRICE VERSUS OUTPUT EFFECTS

The successful execution of monetary policy depends on two conditions. The first condition is that aggregate *demand* will respond (shift) to changes in the money supply. The second prerequisite for success is that the aggregate *supply* curve have the right shape.

Aggregate Demand

The first prerequisite—responsive aggregate demand—usually isn't a problem. An increase in the money supply is typically gobbled up by consumers and investors eager to increase their spending. Only in rare times of economic despair (e.g., the Great Depression of the 1930s, the credit crisis of 2008–2009) do banks or their customers display a reluctance to use available lending capacity. In such situations, anxieties about the economy may overwhelm low interest rates and the ready availability of loans. If this happens, monetary policy will be no more effective than pushing on a string. In more normal times, however, increases in the money supply can shift aggregate demand rightward.

Aggregate Supply

aggregate supply The total quantity of output producers are willing and able to supply at alternative price levels in a given time period, *ceteris paribus.*

The second condition for successful monetary policy is not so assured. As we first observed in Chapter 12, an increase in aggregate demand affects not only output but prices as well. How fast prices rise depends on **aggregate supply.** *Specifically, the effects of an aggregate demand shift on prices and output depend on the shape of the aggregate supply curve.*

Notice in Figure 14.6 what happened to output and prices when aggregate demand shifted rightward. This expansionary monetary policy *did* succeed in increasing output to its full employment level. In the process, however, prices also rose. The price level of the new macro equilibrium (E_2) is higher than it was before the monetary stimulus (E_1). Hence the economy suffers from inflation as it moves toward full employment. The monetary policy intervention is not an unqualified success.

Figure 14.7 illustrates how different slopes of the aggregate supply curve could change the impact of monetary policy. Figure 14.7*a* depicts the shape often associated with Keynesian theory. In Keynes's view, producers would not need the incentive of rising prices during a recession. They would willingly supply more output at prevailing prices, just to get back to full production. Only when capacity was reached would producers start raising prices. In this view, the aggregate supply curve is horizontal until full employment is reached, at which time it shoots up.

The horizontal aggregate supply curve in Figure 14.7*a* creates an ideal setting for monetary policy. If the economy is in recession (e.g., Q_1), expansionary policy

(a) **The Keynesian view**

(b) **The monetarist view**

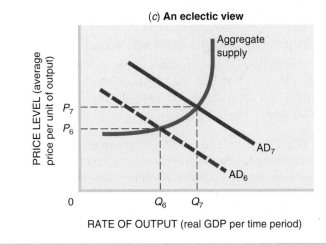

(c) **An eclectic view**

FIGURE 14.7
Contrasting Views of
Aggregate Supply

The impact of increased demand on output and prices depends on the shape of the aggregate supply curve.

(a) Horizontal AS: In the simple Keynesian model, the rate of output responds fully and automatically to increases in demand until full employment (Q_F) is reached. If demand increases from AD_1 to AD_2, output will expand from Q_1 to Q_F without any inflation. Inflation becomes a problem only if aggregate demand increases beyond capacity—to AD_3, for example.

(b) Vertical AS: Some critics assert that changes in the money supply affect prices but not output. They regard aggregate supply as a fixed rate of output, positioned at the long-run, "natural" rate of unemployment (here noted as Q_N). Accordingly, a shift of demand (from AD_4 to AD_5) can affect only the price level (from P_4 to P_5).

(c) Sloped AS: The eclectic view concedes that the AS curve may be horizontal at low levels of output and vertical at capacity. In the middle, however, the AS curve is upward-sloping. In this case, both prices and output are affected by monetary policy.

(e.g., AD_1 to AD_2) increases output but not prices. If the economy is overheated, restrictive policy (e.g., AD_3 to AD_2) lowers prices but not output. In each case, the objectives of monetary policy are painlessly achieved.

Although a horizontal AS curve is ideal, there is no guarantee that producers and workers will behave in that way. The relevant AS curve is the one that mirrors producer behavior. Economists disagree, however, about the true shape of the AS curve.

Figure 14.7b illustrates a different theory about the shape of the AS curve, a theory that gives the Fed nightmares. The AS curve is completely vertical in this case. The argument here is that the quantity of goods produced is primarily dependent on production capacity, labor market efficiency, and other structural forces. These structural forces establish a "natural rate" of unemployment that is fairly immune to short-run policy intervention. From this perspective, there is no reason for producers to depart from this natural rate of output when the money supply increases. Producers are smart enough to know that both prices and costs will rise when spending increases. Hence rising prices will not create any new profit incentives for increasing output. Firms will just continue producing at the natural rate, with higher (nominal) prices and costs. As a result, increases in aggregate demand (e.g., AD_4 to AD_5) are not likely to increase output levels. Expansionary monetary policy causes only inflation in this case; the rate of output is unaffected.

The third picture in Figure 14.7 is much brighter. The AS curve in Figure 14.7c illustrates a middle ground between the other two extremes. This upward-sloping AS curve renders monetary policy effective but not perfectly so. **With an upward-sloping AS curve, expansionary policy causes some inflation, and restrictive policy causes some unemployment.** There are no clear-cut winners or losers here. Rather, monetary (and fiscal) policy confronts a trade-off between the goals of full employment and price stability.

Many economists believe Figure 14.7c best represents market behavior. The Keynesian view (horizontal AS) assumes more restraint in raising prices and wages than seems plausible. The monetarist vision (vertical AS) assumes instantaneous wage and price responses. The eclectic view (upward-sloping AS), on the other hand, recognizes that market behavior responds gradually and imperfectly to policy interventions.

POLICY PERSPECTIVES

How Much Discretion Should the Fed Have?

The debate over the shape of the aggregate supply curve spotlights a central policy debate. Should the Fed try to fine-tune the economy with constant adjustments of the money supply? Or should the Fed instead simply keep the money supply growing at a steady pace?

DISCRETIONARY POLICY The argument for active monetary intervention rests on the observation that the economy itself is constantly beset by positive and negative shocks. In the absence of active discretionary policy, it is feared, the economy would tip first one way and then the other. To reduce such instability, the Fed can lean against the wind, restraining the economy when the wind accelerates, stimulating the economy when it stalls. This view of market instability and the attendant need for active government intervention reflects the Keynesian perspective. Applied to monetary policy, it implies the need for continual adjustments to the money supply.

FIXED RULES Critics of discretionary monetary policy raise two objections. Their first argument relies on the vertical AS curve (Figure 14.7b). They contend that expansionary monetary policy inevitably leads to inflation. Producers and workers can't be fooled into believing that more money will create more goods. With a little experience, they'll soon realize that when more money chases available goods, prices rise. To protect themselves against inflation, they will demand higher prices and wages whenever they see the money supply expanding. Such defensive behavior will push the AS curve into a vertical position.

Even if one concedes that the AS curve isn't necessarily *vertical,* one still has to determine how much slope it has. This inevitably entails some guesswork and the potential for policy mistakes. If the Fed thinks the AS curve is less vertical than it really is, its expansionary policy might cause too much inflation. Hence discretionary policy is as likely to cause macro problems as to cure them. Critics conclude that fixed rules for money supply management are less prone to error. These critics, led by Milton Friedman, urge the Fed to increase M1 by a constant (fixed) rate each year.

THE FED'S ECLECTICISM   For a brief period (1979–1982) the Fed adopted the policy of fixed money supply targets. On October 6, 1979, the chairman of the Fed (Paul Volcker) announced that the Fed would begin focusing on the money supply, seeking to keep its growth within tight limits. The Fed's primary goal was to reduce inflation, which was then running at close to 14 percent a year. To slow the inflationary spiral, the Fed decided to limit sharply the growth of the money supply.

The Fed succeeded in reducing money supply growth and the inflationary spiral. But its tight money policies sent interest rates soaring and pushed the economy into a deep recession (1981–1982). Exactly three years after adopting fixed rules, the Fed abandoned them.

Instead of fixed rules for money supply growth, the Fed then adopted an eclectic combination of (flexible) rules and (limited) discretion. Each year the Fed used to announce targets for money supply growth. But the targets were broad and not stable. At the beginning of 1986, for example, the Fed set a target of 3 to 8 percent growth for M1. That wide target gave it plenty of room to adjust to changing interest rates and cyclical changes. Chairman Volcker emphasized pragmatism. "Success in my mind," he asserted, "will not be measured by whether or not we meet some preordained, arbitrary target" but by our macroeconomic performance. Since the economy was growing steadily in 1987, and inflation was not increasing, he concluded that monetary policy had been a success.

Alan Greenspan was committed to the same brand of eclecticism. In early 1992 he refused to set a target for growth of the narrowly defined money supply (M1) and set very wide targets (2.5–6.5 percent) for broader measures of the money supply (M2). He wanted to stimulate the economy but also to keep a rein on inflation. To achieve this balancing act, Greenspan proclaimed that the Fed could not be bound to any one theory but must instead use a mix of money supply and interest rate adjustments to attain desired macro outcomes.

INFLATION TARGETING   Ben Bernanke, the current Fed chairman, has been a bit more specific about the Fed's policy. He believes the Fed should set an upper limit on inflation and then manipulate interest rates and the money supply to achieve it. Such "inflation targeting," Bernanke believes, would make market participants more confident in the Fed's intentions. However, even he concedes that the Fed could not adhere to a strict set of intervention rules every time the monthly inflation rate inched above a set target. Someone would still have to make a judgment call about whether an uptick in reported inflation was a temporary fluke or a real cause for concern. In other words, the Fed would still have to engage in a little guesswork.

The Fed's guesswork approach was severely criticized when the economy stumbled into the September 2008 credit crisis. Critics blamed the wave of bank failures on the Fed's decision to keep interest rates too low for too long. That "easy money" had encouraged people to borrow way too much money. When borrowers no longer could pay their debts on time, a wave of home foreclosures and bankruptcies stopped the flow of credit in its tracks and knocked the economy into the 2008–2009 recession. Critics claimed that stricter (fixed) rules for money creation would have prevented such a crisis.

UNEMPLOYMENT TARGETING   In December 2012 the Fed announced a new policy of *unemployment* targeting. Market participants wanted to know how long the Fed would keep interest rates at rock-bottom levels in an effort to stimulate the economy. Chairman Bernanke declared that the Fed would continue its monetary stimulus until the national unemployment rate fell to 6.5 percent.

This declaration was intended to give market participants more certainty about the monetary outlook. But it didn't resolve the question about Fed discretion. Critics wanted more certainty about Fed *actions*, not just its goals; they wanted fixed rates of money growth. Fed defenders responded that discretion was still the better part of valor.

SUMMARY

- The Federal Reserve System controls the nation's money supply by regulating the loan activity (deposit creation) of private banks (depository institutions). **LO2**

- The core of the Federal Reserve System is the 12 regional Federal Reserve banks, which provide check clearance, reserve deposit, and loan (discounting) services to individual banks. Private banks are required to maintain minimum reserves on deposit at one of the regional Federal Reserve banks. **LO1**

- The general policies of the Fed are set by its Board of Governors. The Board's chairman is selected by the U.S. president and confirmed by Congress. The chairman serves as the chief spokesperson for monetary policy. **LO1**

- The Fed has three basic tools for changing the money supply: reserve requirements, discount rates, and open market operations (buying and selling of Treasury bonds). With these tools, the Fed can change bank reserves and their lending capacity. **LO2**

- By buying or selling bonds in the open market, the Fed alters bank reserves and interest rates. **LO3**

- Changes in the money supply directly affect aggregate demand. Increases in M1 shift the aggregate demand curve rightward; decreases shift it to the left. **LO5**

- The impact of monetary policy on macro outcomes depends on the slope of the aggregate supply curve. If the AS curve has an upward slope, a trade-off exists between the goals of full employment and price stability. **LO5**

- Advocates of discretionary monetary policy say the Fed must counter market instabilities. Advocates of fixed policy rules warn that discretionary policy may do more harm than good. **LO5**

TERMS TO REMEMBER

Define the following terms:

monetary policy	excess reserves	federal funds rate	aggregate demand
money supply (M1)	money multiplier	open market	aggregate supply
required reserves	discount rate	operations	

QUESTIONS FOR DISCUSSION

1. Why do banks want to maintain as little excess reserves as possible? Under what circumstances might banks desire to hold excess reserves? (*Hint:* see Figure 14.3.) **LO4**

2. Why do people hold bonds rather than larger savings account or checking account balances? Under what circumstances might they change their portfolios, moving their funds out of bonds into bank accounts? **LO3**

3. If the Federal Reserve banks mailed everyone a brand-new $100 bill, what would happen to prices, output, and income? Illustrate with aggregate demand and supply curves. **LO5**

4. How does an increase in the money supply get into the hands of consumers? What do they do with it? **LO4**

5. Is a reduction in interest rates likely to affect spending on pizza? What kinds of spending are sensitive to interest rate fluctuations? **LO5**

6. Which aggregate supply curve in Figure 14.6 does the Fed chairman fear the most? Why?   **LO5**

7. Would you advocate monetary restraint or stimulus for today's economy? Who would disagree with you?   **LO5**

8. **POLICY PERSPECTIVES** Like all human institutions, the Fed makes occasional errors in altering the money supply. Would a constant (fixed) rate of money supply growth eliminate errors?   **LO5**

9. **POLICY PERSPECTIVES** Congress sometimes demands more control of monetary policy. Is this a good idea? Why is fiscal policy, but not monetary policy, entrusted to elected politicians?   **LO5**

PROBLEMS

　 connect

1. Suppose the following data apply: **LO2**

Total bank reserves:	$ 34 billion
Total bank deposits:	$600 billion
Cash held by public:	$200 billion
Bonds held by public:	$220 billion
Stocks held by public:	$140 billion
Gross domestic product:	$ 6 trillion
Interest rate:	6 percent
Required reserve ratio:	0.05

   (a) How large is the money supply?
   (b) How much excess reserves are there?
   (c) What is the money multiplier?
   (d) What is the available lending capacity?

2. Assume that the following data describe the condition of the commercial banking system: **LO2**

Total reserves:	$ 80 billion
Transactions deposits:	$700 billion
Cash held by public:	$300 billion
Reserve requirement:	0.10

   (a) How large is the money supply (M1)?
   (b) Are the banks fully utilizing their lending capacity?
   (c) What would happen to the money supply *initially* if the public deposited another $20 billion in cash in transactions accounts?
   (d) What would the lending capacity of the banking system be after such a portfolio switch?
   (e) How large would the money supply be if the banks fully utilized their lending capacity?
   (f) What three steps could the Fed take to offset that potential growth in M1?

3. Suppose the Federal Reserve decided to purchase $20 billion worth of government securities in the open market.   **LO3**
   (a) By how much will M1 change initially?
   (b) How will the lending capacity of the banking system be affected if the reserve requirement is 10 percent?
   (c) How will banks induce investors to utilize this expanded lending capacity?

4. Suppose the economy is initially in equilibrium at an output level of 100 and price level of 100. The Fed then manages to shift aggregate demand rightward by 20.   **LO4**
   (a) Illustrate the initial equilibrium (E_1) and the shift of AD.
   (b) Show what happens to output and prices if the aggregate supply curve is (i) horizontal, (ii) vertical, and (iii) upward-sloping.

5. What was the money multiplier in China
   (a) Before the change in reserve requirements?
   (b) After the change in reserve requirements? (See the News Wire on p. 289.)   **LO2**

6. If every one-point change in the federal funds rate alters aggregate demand by $300 billion, how far did AD shift in response to the News Wire on page 292?   **LO5**

7. **POLICY PERSPECTIVES** From June 2008 to June 2009, M1 increased from $1,400 billion to $1,656 billion.
   (a) By what percentage did M1 increase?
   (b) If the Fed had used the fixed rule of 3 percent growth, how large would M1 have been in 2009?   **LO5**

◄ Practice quizzes, student PowerPoints, author podcasts, web activities, and additional materials available at **www.mhhe.com/schilleressentials9e**, or scan here. Need a barcode reader? Try ScanLife, available in your app store.

15 Economic Growth

◀ Practice quizzes, student PowerPoints, author podcasts, web activities, and additional materials available at www.mhhe.com/ schilleressentials9e, or scan here. Need a barcode reader? Try ScanLife, available in your app store.

LEARNING OBJECTIVES

After reading this chapter, you should be able to:

1   Specify how economic growth is measured.
2   Describe what GDP per capita and GDP per worker measure.
3   Illustrate how productivity increases.
4   Explain how government policy affects growth.
5   Discuss why economic growth is desirable.

Forty years ago there were no fax machines, no cell phones, no satellite TVs, and no iPods. Personal computers were still on the drawing board, and laptops weren't even envisioned. Home video didn't exist, and no one had yet produced microwave popcorn. Biotechnology hadn't yet produced any blockbuster drugs, and people used the same pair of athletic shoes for most sports.

New products are symptoms of our economic progress. Over time, we produce not only *more* goods and services but also *new* and *better* goods and services. In the process, we get richer: our material living standards rise.

Rising living standards are not inevitable, however. According to World Bank estimates, nearly 3 *billion* people—close to half the world's population—continue to live in abject poverty (incomes of less than $3 per day). Worse still, living standards in many of the poorest countries have *fallen* in the last decade. Living standards also fell in Eastern Europe when communism collapsed and a painful transition to market economies began. The former communist bloc countries, including China, are counting on the power of free markets to jump-start their economies and raise living standards.

The purpose of this chapter is to take a longer-term view of economic performance. Most macro policy focuses on the *short-run* variations in output and prices we refer to as business cycles. There are *long-run* concerns as well. As we ponder the future of the economy beyond the next business cycle, we have to confront the prospects for economic growth. In that longer-run context three questions stand out:

- How important is economic growth?
- How does an economy grow?
- What policies promote economic growth?

We develop answers to these questions by first examining the nature of economic growth and then examining its sources and potential.

THE NATURE OF GROWTH

Economic growth refers to increases in the output of goods and services. But there are two distinct ways in which output increases, and they have different implications for our economic welfare.

Short-Run Changes in Capacity Use

The easiest kind of growth comes from increased use of our productive capabilities. In any given year there is a limit to an economy's potential output. This limit is determined by the quantity of resources available and our technological know-how. We have illustrated these short-run limits to output with a **production possibilities** curve, as shown in Figure 15.1a. By using all of our available resources and our best expertise, we can produce any combination of goods on the production possibilities curve.

We do not always take full advantage of our productive capacity, however. The economy often produces a mix of output that lies *inside* our production possibilities, like point *A* in Figure 15.1a. When this happens, the short-run goal of macro policy is to achieve full employment—to move us from point *A* to some point on the production possibilities curve (e.g., point *B*). This was the focus of macro policy during the 2008–2009 recession. The fiscal and monetary policy levers for attaining full employment were the focus of Chapters 12 to 14.

Long-Run Changes in Capacity

As desirable as full employment is, there is an obvious limit to how much additional output we can obtain in this way. Once we are fully utilizing our productive capacity, further increases in output are attainable only if we *expand* that capacity. To do so, we have to *shift* the production possibilities curve outward, as shown in Figure 15.1b. Such shifts imply an increase in *potential* GDP—that is, our productive capacity.

production possibilities The alternative combinations of goods and services that could be produced in a given time period with all available resources and technology.

FIGURE 15.1
Two Types of Growth

Increases in output may result from increased use of existing capacity or from increases in that capacity itself. In part *a* the mix of output at point *A* does not make full use of production possibilities. Hence we can grow—get more output—by employing more of our available resources or using them more efficiently. This is illustrated by point *B* (or any other point on the curve).

Once we are on the production possibilities curve, we can increase output further only by *increasing* our productive capacity. This is illustrated by the outward *shift* of the production possibilities curve in part *b*.

economic growth An increase in output (real GDP); an expansion of production possibilities.

(*a*) **The short run: increased capacity utilization**

(*b*) **The long run: expanded capacity**

Over time, increases in capacity are critical. Short-run increases in the utilization of existing capacity can generate only modest increases in output. Even high unemployment rates (e.g., 7 percent) leave little room for increased output. *To achieve large and lasting increases in output we must push our production possibilities outward.* For this reason, economists tend to define **economic growth** in terms of changes in *potential* GDP.

AGGREGATE SUPPLY FOCUS   The unique character of economic growth can also be illustrated with aggregate supply and demand curves. Short-run macro policies focus on aggregate demand. Fiscal and monetary policy levers are used to shift the AD curve, trying to achieve the best possible combination of full employment and price stability. As we have observed, however, the aggregate supply (AS) curve sets a limit to demand-side policy. In the short run, the slope of the aggregate supply curve determines how much inflation we have to experience to get more output. In the long run, the position of the AS curve limits total output. To get a long-run increase in output, we must move the AS curve.

Figure 15.2 illustrates the supply-side focus of economic growth. Notice that *economic growth—sustained increases in total output—is possible only if the AS curve shifts rightward.*

FIGURE 15.2   Supply-Side Focus

Short-run macro policy uses shifts of the aggregate demand curve to achieve economic stability. To achieve long-run *growth*, however, the aggregate supply curve must be shifted as well.

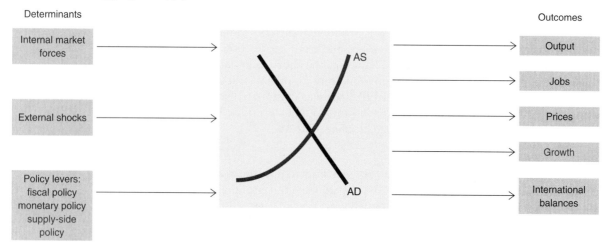

Nominal versus Real GDP

We refer to *real* GDP, not *nominal* GDP, in our concept of economic growth. **Nominal GDP** is the current dollar value of output—that is, the average price level (*P*) multiplied by the quantity of goods and services produced (*Q*). Accordingly, increases in nominal GDP can result from either increases in the price level or increases in the quantity of output. In fact, nominal GDP can rise even when the quantity of goods and services falls. This was the case in 1991, for example. The total quantity of goods and services produced in 1991 was less than the quantity produced in 1990. Nevertheless, prices rose enough during 1991 to keep nominal GDP growing.

nominal GDP The total value of goods and services produced within a nation's borders, measured in current prices.

Real GDP refers to the actual quantity of goods and services produced. Real GDP avoids the distortions of inflation by valuing output in *constant* prices.

real GDP The inflation-adjusted value of GDP; the value of output measured in constant prices.

GROWTH INDEXES

The GDP Growth Rate

Typically changes in real GDP are expressed in percentage terms as a growth *rate.* The **growth rate** is simply the change in real output between two periods divided by total output in the base period. In 2008, for example, real GDP was $13.162 trillion when valued in constant (2005) prices. Real GDP fell to $12.758 trillion in 2009, again measured in constant prices. Hence the growth rate between 2008 and 2009 was

growth rate Percentage change in real GDP from one period to another.

$$\text{Growth rate} = \frac{\text{change in real GDP}}{\text{base period GDP}}$$

$$= \frac{-.404 \text{ trillion}}{13.162 \text{ trillion}} = -3.1\%$$

The negative growth rate in 2009 was an exception, not the rule. As Figure 15.3 illustrates, U.S. growth rates are usually positive, averaging about 3 percent a year. Although there is a lot of year-to-year variation around that average, years of actual decline in real GDP (e.g., 1974, 1975, 1980, 1982, 1991, 2009) are relatively rare.

The challenge for the future is to maintain higher rates of economic growth. After the recession of 1990–1991, the U.S. economy got back on its long-term growth track. The growth rate even moved a bit above the long-term average for several years (1997–1999). A brief recession and the 9/11 terrorist attacks put the brakes on economic growth in 2001. Then the economy really stalled in 2008–2009. Once again, policymakers were challenged to restore the GDP growth rate to 3 percent or better. That was President Obama's primary macro challenge.

THE EXPONENTIAL PROCESS   At first blush, the challenge of raising the growth rate from −2.4 percent to 3 percent may appear neither difficult nor important. Indeed, the whole subject of economic growth looks rather dull when you discover that big gains in economic growth are measured in fractions of a percent. However, this initial impression is not fair. First, even one year's low growth implies lost output. Consider the recession of 2009 (see Figure 15.3). If we had just *maintained* the rate of total ouput in 2009—that is, achieved a *zero* growth rate rather than a 3.1 percent decline—we would have had $404 billion more worth of goods and services. That works out to nearly $1,400 worth of goods and services per person for 300 million Americans. Lots of people would have liked that extra output.

Second, economic growth is a *continuing* process. Gains made in one year accumulate in future years. It's like interest you earn at the bank. The interest you earn

FIGURE 15.3   Recent U.S. Growth Rates

Total output typically increases from one year to another. The focus of policy is on the growth rate—that is, how fast real GDP increases from one year to the next. Historically, growth rates have varied significantly from year to year and even turned negative on occasion. The policy challenge is to foster faster, steadier GDP growth. Is this possible?

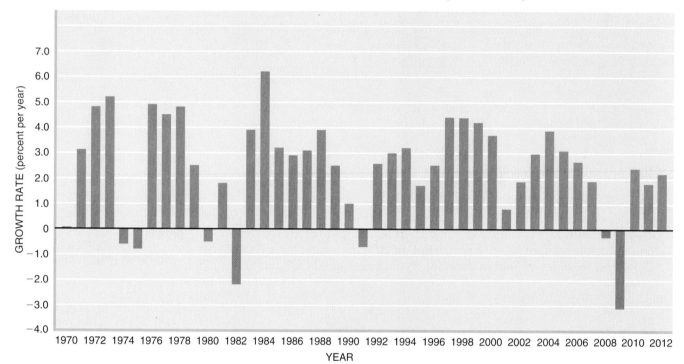

in a single year doesn't amount to much. But if you leave your money in the bank for several years, you begin to earn interest on your interest. Eventually you accumulate a nice little bankroll.

The process of economic growth works the same way. Each little shift of the production possibilities curve broadens the base for future GDP. As shifts accumulate over many years, the economy's productive capacity is greatly expanded. Ultimately we discover that those little differences in annual growth rates generate tremendous gains in GDP.

This cumulative process, whereby interest or growth is compounded from one year to the next, is called an *exponential process.* To get a feel for its impact, consider the longer-run difference between annual growth rates of 3 percent and 5 percent. In 30 years, a 3 percent growth rate will raise our GDP to $40 trillion (in 2013 dollars). But a 5 percent growth rate would give us $70 trillion of goods and services in the same amount of time. Thus, in a single generation, 5 percent growth translates into a standard of living that is 75 percent higher than 3 percent growth. From this longer-term perspective, little differences in annual growth rates look big indeed.

GDP per Capita: A Measure of Living Standards

GDP per capita Total GDP divided by total population; average GDP.

The exponential process looks even more meaningful when translated into *per capita* terms. **GDP per capita** is simply total output divided by total population. In 2013 the total output of the U.S. economy was about $16 trillion. Since there were 320 million of us to share that output, GDP per capita was

$$2013 \text{ GDP per capita} = \frac{\$16 \text{ trillion of output}}{320 \text{ million people}} = \$50,000$$

NEWS WIRE	IMPROVED LIVING STANDARDS

What Economic Growth Has Done for U.S. Families

As the economy grows, living standards rise. The changes are so gradual, however, that few people notice. After 20 years of growth, though, some changes are remarkable. We now live longer, work less, and consume a lot more. Some examples:

	1970	1990
Average size of a new home (square feet)	1,500	2,080
New homes with central air conditioning	34%	76%
People using computers	<100,000	75.9 million
Households with color TV	33.9%	96.1%
Households with cable TV	4 million	55 million
Households with VCRs	0	67 million
Households with two or more vehicles	29.3%	54%
Median household net worth (real)	$24,217	$48,887
Households owning a microwave oven	<1%	78.8%
Heart transplant procedures	<10	2,125
Average workweek	37.1 hours	34.5 hours
Average daily time working in the home	3.9 hours	3.5 hours
Annual paid vacation and holidays	15.5 days	22.5 days
Women in the workforce	31.5%	56.6%
Recreational boats owned	8.8 million	16 million
Manufacturers' shipments of RVs	30,300	226,500
Adult softball teams	29,000	188,000
Recreational golfers	11.2 million	27.8 million
Attendance at symphonies and orchestras	12.7 million	43.6 million
Americans finishing high school	51.9%	77.7%
Americans finishing four years of college	13.5%	24.4%
Employee benefits as a share of payroll	29.3%	40.2%
Life expectancy at birth (years)	70.8	75.4
Death rate by natural causes (per 100,000)	714.3	520.2

Source: Federal Reserve Bank of Dallas, *1993 Annual Report.*

NOTE: Economic growth not only generated more and better output but also improved health and provided more leisure.

This does not mean that every man, woman, and child in the United States received $50,000 worth of goods and services in 2013. Rather, it simply indicates how much output was potentially available to the average person.

Growth in GDP per capita is attained only when the growth of output exceeds population growth. In the United States, this condition is usually achieved. Our population grows by an average of only 1 percent a year. Hence our average economic growth rate of 3 percent is more than sufficient to ensure steadily rising living standards.

The accompanying News Wire illustrates some of the ways rising per capita GDP has changed our lives. In the 20-year period between 1970 and 1990, the size of the average U.S. house increased by a third. Air conditioning went from the exception to the rule. And the percentage of college graduates nearly doubled.

FIGURE 15.4
The History of World Growth

GDP per capita was stagnant for centuries. Living standards started rising significantly around 1820. Even then, most growth in per capita GDP occurred in the West.

Growth Explosion

GDP per Capita in 1990 International Dollars

Year	0	1000	1500	1820	1995
World	$425	$420	$545	$675	$5,188
The West	$439	$406	$624	$1,149	$19,990
West Europe	450	400	670	1,269	17,456
North America	400	400	400	1,233	22,933
Japan	400	425	525	675	19,720
The Rest	$423	$424	$532	$594	$2,971
Other Europe	400	400	597	803	5,147
Latin America	400	415	415	671	5,031
China	450	450	600	600	2,653
Other Asia	425	425	525	560	2,768
Africa	400	400	400	400	1,221

Source: Angus Maddison, "Poor Until 1820," *The Wall Street Journal*, January 11, 1999. Used with permission of Dow Jones & Company, Inc., via Copyright Clearance Center.

Topic Podcast:
Growing Prosperous

Had the economy grown more slowly, we wouldn't have gotten all these additional goods and services.

It's tempting to take the benefits of growth for granted. But that would be a serious mistake. As Figure 15.4 shows, rising GDP per capita is a relatively new phenomenon in the long course of history. World GDP per capita hardly grew at all for 1,500 years or so. It is only since 1820 that world output has grown significantly faster than the population.

Figure 15.4 also reveals that most of the non-Western world has not enjoyed the robust GDP growth we have experienced. Even today, many poor countries continue to suffer from a combination of slow GDP growth and fast population growth. Madagascar, for example, is one of the poorest countries in the world, with GDP per capita of less than $900. Yet its population continues to grow more rapidly (2.9 percent per year) than GDP (2.0 percent growth), further depressing living standards. The population of Niger grew by 3.3 percent per year from 1990 to 2005 while GDP grew at a slower rate of only 2.8 percent. As a consequence, GDP per capita *declined* by more than 0.4 percent per year. Even that dismal record outstripped Haiti, where GDP itself *declined* by 0.8 percent a year from 1990 to 2005 while the population continued to grow at 1.4 percent a year. Haitians were desperately poor even before the January 2010 earthquake. Their low living standards and primitive infrastructure made them more vulnerable to earthquake damage and less able to recover.

By comparison with these countries, the United States has been most fortunate. Our GDP per capita has more than doubled since Ronald Reagan was elected president. This means that the average person today has twice as many goods and services as the average person had only a generation ago.

What about the future? Will we continue to enjoy substantial gains in living standards? It all depends on how fast output continues to grow in relation to population. Table 15.1 indicates some of the possibilities. If GDP per capita continues to grow at 2.0 percent per year—as it did in the 1990s—our average income will double again in 36 years.

Growth Rate (Percent)	Doubling Time (Years)
0.0	Never
0.5	144
1.0	72
1.5	48
2.0	36
2.5	29
3.0	24
3.5	21
4.0	18
4.5	16
5.0	14

TABLE 15.1
The Rule of 72
Small differences in annual growth rates cumulate into large differences in GDP. Shown here are the number of years it would take to double GDP at various growth rates.

Doubling times can be approximated by the rule of 72. Seventy-two divided by the growth rate equals the number of years it takes to double.

GDP per Worker: A Measure of Productivity

As the people in Madagascar, Haiti, and Niger know, these projected increases in total output may never occur. Someone has to *produce* more output if we want GDP per capita to rise. One reason our living standard rose so nicely in the 1990s is that the **labor force** grew faster than the population. The baby boomers born after World War II had completed college, raised families, and were fully committed to the workforce. The labor force also continued to expand with a steady stream of immigrants and women taking jobs outside the home. The **employment rate**—the percentage of the adult population actually working—rose from under 60 percent in 1980 to over 62 percent in 2005.

The employment rate cannot increase forever. At the limit, everyone would be in the labor market, and no further workers could be found. Sustained increases in GDP per capita are more likely to come from increases in output *per worker*. The total quantity of output produced depends not only on how many workers are employed but also on how productive each worker is. If **productivity** is increasing, then GDP per capita is likely to rise as well.

Historically, productivity gains have been the major source of economic growth. The average worker today produces *twice* as much output as his or her parents did. The consequences of this productivity gain are evident in Figure 15.5. Between 1992 and 2012, the amount of labor employed in the U.S. economy increased

labor force All persons over age 16 who are either working for pay or actively seeking paid employment.

employment rate The proportion of the adult population that is employed.

productivity Output per unit of input, such as output per labor-hour.

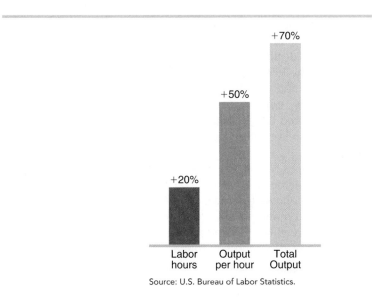

Source: U.S. Bureau of Labor Statistics.

FIGURE 15.5
Rising Productivity and Living Standards

From 1992 to 2012, work hours increased by only 20 percent but output increased by 70 percent. Rising output per worker (productivity) is the key to increased living standards (GDP per capita).

by only 20 percent. If productivity hadn't increased, total output would have grown by the same percentage. But productivity *wasn't* stagnant; output per labor hour increased by 50 percent during that period. As a consequence, total output jumped by 70 percent. We are now able to *consume* more goods and services than our parents did because the average worker *produces* more.

SOURCES OF PRODUCTIVITY GROWTH

If we want consumption levels to keep rising, individual workers will have to produce still more output each year. How is this possible?

To answer this question, we need to examine how productivity increases. *The sources of productivity gains include*

- *Higher skills*—an increase in labor skills.
- *More capital*—an increase in the ratio of capital to labor.
- *Improved management*—better use of available resources in the production process.
- *Technological advance*—the development and use of *better* capital equipment.

Labor Quality

As recently as 1950, less than 8 percent of all U.S. workers had completed college. Today over 30 percent of the workforce has completed four years of college. As a result, today's workers enter the labor market with much more knowledge. Moreover, they keep acquiring new skills through company-paid training programs, adult education classes, and distance learning options on the Internet. As education and training levels rise, so does productivity.

Capital Investment

investment Expenditures on (production of) new plant and equipment (capital) in a given time period, plus changes in business inventories.

No matter how educated workers are, they need tools, computers, and other equipment to produce most goods and services. Thus *capital* **investment** *is a prime determinant of both productivity and growth.* More investment gives the average worker more and better tools to work with.

While labor force growth accelerated in the 1970s, the growth of capital slowed. The capital stock increased by 4.1 percent per year in the late 1960s but by only 2.5 percent per year in the 1970s and early 1980s. The stock of capital was still growing faster than the labor force, but the difference was getting smaller. This means that although the average worker was continuing to get more and better machines, the rate at which he or she was getting them was slower. As a consequence, productivity growth declined.

These trends reversed in the 1990s. Capital investment accelerated, with investments in computer networks and telecommunications surging by 10–12 percent a year. As a result, productivity gains accelerated into the 2.5–2.7 percent range. Those productivity gains shifted the production possibilities curve outward, permitting output to expand with less inflationary pressure.

Management

The quantity and quality of factor inputs do not completely determine the rate of economic growth. Resources, however good and abundant, must be organized into a production process and managed. Hence entrepreneurship and the quality of continuing management are major determinants of economic growth.

It is difficult to characterize differences in management techniques or to measure their effectiveness. However, much attention has been focused in recent years on the potential conflict between short-term profits and long-term productivity gains. By cutting investment spending (a cost to the firm), a firm can increase short-run profits. In doing so, however, a firm may also reduce its growth potential and ultimately its long-term profitability. When corporate managers become fixated on short-run fluctuations in the price of corporate stock, the risk of such a trade-off increases.

Managers must also learn to motivate employees to their maximum potential. Workers who are disgruntled or alienated aren't likely to put out much effort. To maximize productivity, managers must develop personnel structures and incentives that make employees want to contribute to production.

Research and Development

A fourth and vital source of productivity advance is research and development (R&D). R&D is a broad concept that includes scientific research, product development, innovations in production technique, and the development of management improvements. R&D activity may be a specific, identifiable activity (e.g., in a research lab), or it may be part of the process of learning by doing. In either case, the insights developed from R&D generally lead to new products and cheaper ways of producing them. Over time, R&D is credited with the greatest contributions to economic growth. In his study of U.S. growth during the period 1929–1982, Edward Denison concluded that 26 percent of *total* growth was due to "advances in knowledge." The relative contribution of R&D to productivity (output per worker) was probably twice that much.

There is an important link between R&D and capital investment. A lot of investment is needed to replace worn and aging equipment. However, new machines are rarely identical to the ones they replace. When you get a new computer, you're not just *replacing* an old one; you're *upgrading* your computing capabilities with more memory, greater speed, and a lot of new features. Indeed, the availability of *better* technology is often the motivation for such capital investment. The same kind of motivation spurs businesses to upgrade machines and structures. Hence advances in technology and capital investment typically go hand in hand.

The fruits of research and development don't all reside in new machinery. New ideas may nurture products and processes that expand production possibilities even without additional capital equipment. Biotechnology has developed strains of wheat and rice that have multiplied the size of harvests, with no additional farm machinery. The development of nonhierarchical databases revolutionized information technology, making it far less time-consuming to access and transmit data, with *less* hardware.

POLICY LEVERS

To a large extent, the pace of economic growth is set by market forces—by the education, training, and investment decisions of market participants. Government policy plays an important role as well. Indeed, *government policies can have a major impact on whether and how far the aggregate supply curve shifts.*

Education and Training

As noted earlier, the quality of labor largely depends on education and training. Accordingly, government policies that support education and training contribute directly to growth and productivity. From a fiscal policy perspective, money spent on schools and training has a dual payoff: it stimulates the economy in the *short* run (like all other spending) and increases the *long*-run capacity to produce. Hence we get positive AD and AS shifts. Tax incentives for training have the same effects.

Immigration Policy

Both the quality and the quantity of labor are affected by immigration policy. Close to a million people immigrate to the United States each year. This influx of immigrants has been a major source of growth in the U.S. labor force—and thus a direct contributor to an outward shift of our production possibilities.

The impact of immigration on our productive capacity is a question not just of numbers but also of the quality of these new workers. Recent immigrants have much lower educational attainment than native-born Americans and are less able to fill job vacancies in growing industries. This is largely due to immigration policy, which sets only country-specific quotas and gives preference to relatives of U.S. residents. Some observers have suggested that the United States should pay more attention to the educational and skill levels of immigrants and set preferences on the basis of potential productivity, as Canada and many other nations do. In December 2012 the U.S. House of Representatives proposed to set aside 55,000 visas for foreign students graduating with degrees in science, technology, engineering, and math, the so-called STEM fields (see the accompanying News Wire). To make room for the additional STEM visas, the House voted to eliminate the 55,000 "diversity" visas reserved for foreigners from nations with low immigration rates to the United States. Although high-tech industries lobbied hard for this policy change, President Obama rejected the idea, saying he wanted more comprehensive immigration reforms, not just piecemeal changes. Whatever the outcome, we have to recognize that the sheer number of people entering the country makes immigration policy an important growth policy lever.

Investment Incentives

Government policy also affects the supply of capital. As a rule, lower tax rates encourage people to invest more—to build factories, purchase new equipment, and construct new offices. Hence *tax policy is not only a staple of short-term stabilization policy but a determinant of long-run growth as well.*

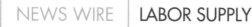

| NEWS WIRE | LABOR SUPPLY |

House Poised to Pass STEM Immigration Bill

Despite White House opposition, the House appears likely to pass a bill this week that would allow more foreign students who graduate from U.S. schools with advanced technical degrees to stay in the country. . . .

The bill would eliminate the Diversity Visa Program and shift up to 55,000 green cards a year to foreign students who graduate from qualified U.S. schools with a doctorate or master's degree in the "STEM" disciplines: science, technology, engineering, and math. . . .

Tech firms and lawmakers argue that immigrants have been responsible for helping to start some of the most successful tech firms in the United States, including Google and Yahoo, and that it makes no sense to educate foreign students in the key STEM fields and then force them to leave the United States when they graduate.

—Juliana Gruenwald

Source: *National Journal*, November 28, 2012. Used with permission by Wrights Media.

NOTE: Immigrants are an important source of human capital. Should immigrants be selected on the basis of skills instead of family ties or country of origin?

The tax treatment of capital gains is one of the most debated supply-side policy levers. Capital gains are increases in the value of assets. When stocks, land, or other assets are sold, any resulting gain is counted as taxable income. Many countries—including Japan, Italy, South Korea, Taiwan, and the Netherlands—do not levy any taxes on capital gains. The rest of the European Union and Canada impose lower capital gains taxes than does the United States. Lowering the tax rate on capital gains might stimulate more investment and encourage people to reallocate their assets to more productive uses. When the capital gains tax rate was cut from 28 to 20 percent in 1997, U.S. investment accelerated. That experience prompted President George W. Bush to push for further tax cuts in 2003. After the capital gains tax rate was cut to 15 percent (May 2003), nonresidential investment increased significantly. That pickup in investment may have accelerated GDP growth by as much as 2 percent in 2004.

Critics argue that a capital gains tax cut overwhelmingly favors the rich, who own most stocks, property, and other wealth. This inequity, they assert, outweighs any efficiency gains. That's why President Obama pushed Congress to increase the capital gains tax from 15 to 20 percent in 2013. Critics worried that the higher tax rates might slow capital investment and economic growth.

Savings Incentives

Another prerequisite for faster growth is more **saving.** At full employment, a greater volume of investment is possible only if the rate of consumption is cut back. In other words, additional investment requires additional saving. Hence *supply-side economists favor tax incentives that encourage saving as well as greater tax incentives for investment.* This kind of perspective contrasts sharply with the Keynesian emphasis on stimulating consumption.

saving Income minus consumption; that part of disposable income not spent.

In the early 1980s Congress greatly increased the incentives for saving. First, banks were permitted to increase the rate of interest paid on various types of savings accounts. Second, the tax on earned interest was reduced. And third, new forms of tax-free saving were created (e.g., Individual Retirement Accounts [IRAs]).

Despite these incentives, the U.S. saving rates declined during the 1980s. Household saving dropped from 6.2 percent of disposable income in 1981 to a low of 2.5 percent in 1987. Neither the tax incentives nor the high interest rates that prevailed in the early 1980s convinced Americans to save more. As a result, the U.S. saving rate fell considerably below that of other nations. By 2006 the U.S. saving rate was actually *negative:* consumers were spending more than they were earning (see the accompanying News Wire). As a consequence, the United States is heavily dependent on foreign saving (deposited in U.S. banks and bonds) to finance investment and growth.

Government Finances

The dependence of economic growth on investment and savings adds an important dimension to the debate over budget deficits. When the government borrows money to finance its spending, it dips into the nation's savings pool. Hence the government ends up borrowing funds that could have been used to finance investment. If this happens, the government deficit effectively crowds out private investment. This process of **crowding out**—of diverting available savings from investment to government spending—directly limits private investment. From this perspective, government budget deficits act as a constraint on economic growth.

crowding out A reduction in private sector borrowing (and spending) caused by increased government borrowing.

From 1998 until 2001 the federal government generated a budget *surplus* every year. These surpluses turned the situation around. The surpluses not only eliminated

NEWS WIRE	SAVING RATES

Americans Save Little

American households save very little. In 2006 the average American actually spent *more* income than he or she earned—the saving rate was *negative*. As shown here, the United States continues to rank near the bottom of the savers' list in 2012.

Supply-siders are especially concerned about low saving rates. They argue that Americans must save more to finance increased investment and economic growth. Otherwise, they fear, the United States will fall behind other countries in the progression toward higher productivity levels and living standards.

Country	Saving Rate (2012)
Switzerland	13.2
Germany	10.1
Netherlands	9.0
Australia	8.9
Czech Republic	6.8
United States	**3.7**
Japan	1.9

Note: Saving rate equals household saving divided by disposable income.

Source: oecd.org, Economic Outlook, 2012. Statistical Annex Table 23.

NOTE: Savings are a primary source of investment financing. Higher saving rates imply proportionately less consumption and more investment and growth.

crowding in An increase in private sector borrowing (and spending) caused by decreased government borrowing.

government borrowing but also *added* funds to money markets. This tended to drive down interest rates, stimulating private investment. In other words, crowding out was transformed to **crowding in.**

As we saw in earlier chapters, budget deficits aren't always bad. Nor are budget surpluses always good. Short-run cyclical instability may require fiscal policies that unbalance the federal budget. The concern for long-run growth simply adds another wrinkle to fiscal policy decisions: *fiscal and monetary policies must be evaluated in terms of their impact not only on short-run aggregate demand but also on long-run aggregate supply.* This was a major concern in 2009–2012 when massive federal government fiscal stimulus packages pushed the government's budget deficit into the trillion-dollar stratosphere.

Deregulation

There are still other mechanisms for stimulating economic growth. The government intervenes directly in supply decisions by *regulating* employment and output behavior. In general, such regulations limit the flexibility of producers to respond to changes in demand. Government regulation also tends to raise production costs. The higher costs result not only from required changes in the production process but also from the expense of monitoring government regulations. The budget costs and the burden of red tape discourage production and so limit aggregate supply. From this perspective, deregulation would shift the AS curve rightward.

FACTOR MARKETS   Minimum wage laws are one of the most familiar forms of factor market regulation. The Fair Labor Standards Act of 1938 required employers to pay workers a minimum of 25 cents per hour. Over time, Congress has increased the minimum wage repeatedly (see the News Wire in Chapter 8, page 171), up to $7.25 as of July 2009.

The goal of the minimum wage law is to ensure workers a decent standard of living. But the law has other effects as well. By prohibiting employers from using lower-paid workers, it limits the ability of employers to hire additional workers. This hiring constraint limits job opportunities for immigrants, teenagers, and low-skill workers. Without that constraint, more of these workers would find jobs, gain valuable experience, and attain higher wages—shifting the AS curve rightward.

The government also sets standards for workplace safety and health. The Occupational Safety and Health Administration (OSHA), for example, sets limits on the noise levels at work sites. If noise levels exceed these limits, the employer is required to adopt administrative or engineering controls to reduce the noise level. Personal protection of workers (e.g., earplugs or earmuffs), though much less costly, will suffice only if source controls are not feasible. All such regulations are intended to improve the welfare of workers. In the process, however, these regulations raise the costs of production and inhibit supply responses.

PRODUCT MARKETS   The government's regulation of factor markets tends to raise production costs and inhibit supply. The same is true of regulations imposed directly on product markets. A few examples illustrate the impact.

Transportation Costs   At the federal level, various agencies regulate the output and prices of transportation services. Until 1984 the Civil Aeronautics Board (CAB) determined which routes airlines could fly and how much they could charge. The Interstate Commerce Commission (ICC) has had the same kind of power over trucking, interstate bus lines, and railroads. The routes, services, and prices for ships (in U.S. coastal waters and foreign commerce) have been established by the Federal Maritime Commission. In all these cases the regulations constrained the ability of producers to respond to increases in demand. Existing producers could not increase output at will, and new producers were excluded from the market. The easing of these restrictive regulations spurred more output, lower prices, and innovation in air travel, telecommunications, and land transportation. In the process, the AS curve shifted to the right.

Food and Drug Standards   The Food and Drug Administration (FDA) has a broad mandate to protect consumers from dangerous products. In fulfilling this responsibility, the FDA sets health standards for the content of specific foods. A hot dog, for example, can be labeled as such only if it contains specific mixtures of skeletal meat, pig lips, snouts, and ears. By the same token, the FDA requires that chocolate bars must contain no more than 60 microscopic insect fragments per 100 grams of chocolate. The FDA also sets standards for the testing of new drugs and evaluates the test results. In all three cases, the goal of regulation is to minimize health risks to consumers.

Like all regulation, the FDA standards entail real costs. The tests required for new drugs are expensive and time-consuming. Getting a new drug approved for sale can take years of effort and require a huge investment. The net results are that (1) fewer new drugs are brought to market and (2) those that do reach the market are more expensive than they would be in the absence of regulation. In other words, the aggregate supply of goods is shifted to the left.

FINANCIAL MARKETS   The Great Recession of 2008–2009 prompted a huge increase in federal regulation of financial markets. In the quest to avoid another financial crisis, Congress in 2010 approved sweeping new powers for federal regulators of banks, credit card companies, and other financial institutions (the Dodd-Frank

Wall Street Reform and Consumer Protection Act). The act was so complex that it took federal regulators three years just to spell out the new regulations that would affect financial institutions. The uncertainties associated with that process made banks less willing to make new loans; excess reserves of the banking system skyrocketed (Figure 14.3, page 290), while new loan activity stagnated. That kept recovery from the recession in check. Critics worry that the final regulations will make loans more costly and more difficult to get, continuing to dampen economic growth.

Many—perhaps most—of these regulatory activities are beneficial. In fact, all were originally designed to serve specific public purposes. As a result of such regulation, we get safer drugs, cleaner air, less deceptive advertising, and more secure loans. We must also consider the costs involved, however. All regulatory activities impose direct and indirect costs. These costs must be compared to the benefits received. *The basic contention of supply-side economists is that regulatory costs are too high.* To improve our economic performance, they assert, we must *deregulate* the production process, thereby shifting the aggregate supply curve to the right again. At a minimum, *we should at least consider potential trade-offs between increased regulation and increased growth.*

Economic Freedom

Regulation and taxes are just two forms of government intervention that affect production possibilities. Governments also establish and enforce property rights, legal rights, and political rights. One of the greatest obstacles to postcommunist growth in Russia was the absence of legal protection. Few people wanted to invest in businesses that could be stolen or confiscated, with little hope of judicial redress. Nor did producers want to ship goods without ironclad payment guarantees.

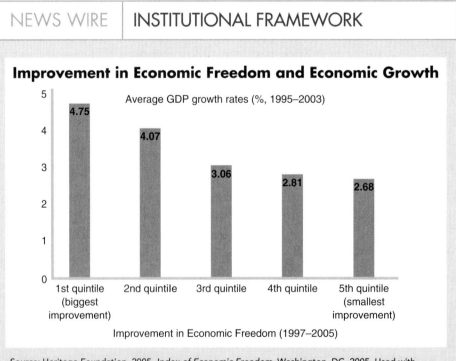

NEWS WIRE | INSTITUTIONAL FRAMEWORK

Improvement in Economic Freedom and Economic Growth

Average GDP growth rates (%, 1995–2003)

Improvement in Economic Freedom (1997–2005)	value
1st quintile (biggest improvement)	4.75
2nd quintile	4.07
3rd quintile	3.06
4th quintile	2.81
5th quintile (smallest improvement)	2.68

Source: Heritage Foundation, 2005. *Index of Economic Freedom*, Washington, DC, 2005. Used with permission.

NOTE: As nations give more rein to market forces, they tend to grow faster. These data compare changes in the degree of market freedom (from government regulation) with GDP growth rates.

By contrast, producers in the United States are willing to produce and ship goods without prepayment, knowing that the courts, collection agencies, and insurance companies can help ensure payment, if necessary.

It is difficult to identify all of the institutional features that make an economy business friendly. The Heritage Foundation, a conservative think tank, has constructed an index of economic freedom, using 50 different measures of government policy. Each year it ranks the world's countries on this index, thereby identifying the most "free" economies (least government control) and the most "repressed" (most government control). According to Heritage, the nations with the most economic freedom not only have the highest GDP per capita but continue to grow the fastest. As the accompanying News Wire illustrates, the countries that moved the furthest toward free markets also grew the fastest from 1995 to 2003. Their average annual GDP growth rate (4.75 percent) greatly exceeded that (2.68 percent) of nations that made little progress toward free markets—or that actually *increased* government regulation of resource and product markets (e.g., Venezuela, Uganda, Cuba, Morocco).

The Heritage study doesn't imply that we should rely exclusively on private markets to resolve the WHAT, HOW, and FOR WHOM questions. But it does reinforce the notion that an economy's institutional framework—particularly the extent of market freedom—plays a critical role in its growth potential. We have to ask whether any specific government intervention promotes economic growth or slows it.

POLICY PERSPECTIVES

Is More Growth Desirable?

The government clearly has a powerful set of levers for promoting faster economic growth. Many people wonder, though, whether more economic growth is really *desirable*. Those of us who commute on congested highways, worry about climate change, breathe foul air, and can't find a secluded camping site may raise a loud chorus of nos. But before reaching a conclusion, let us at least determine what it is people don't like about the prospect of continued growth. Is it really economic growth per se that people object to or, instead, the specific ways GDP has grown in the past?

First of all, let us distinguish clearly between economic growth and population growth. Congested neighborhoods, dining halls, and highways are the consequence of too many people, not of too many goods and services. And there's no indication that population growth will cease any time soon. The world's population of 7 billion people is likely to increase by another 2 billion people by the year 2050. The United States alone harbors another 3 million or so more people every year.

Who's going to feed, clothe, and house all these people? Are we going to redistribute the current level of output, leaving everyone with less? Or should we try to produce *more* output so living standards don't fall? If we had *more* goods and services—if we had more houses and transit systems—much of the population congestion we now experience might be relieved. Maybe if we had enough resources to meet our existing demands *and* to build a solar-generated "new town" in the middle of Montana, people might move out of the crowded neighborhoods of Chicago and St. Louis. Well, probably not, but at least one thing is certain: with fewer goods and services, more people will have to share any given quantity of output.

Which brings us back to the really essential measure of growth, GDP per capita. Are there any serious grounds for desiring *less* GDP per capita—a reduced standard of living? Don't say yes just because you think we already have too many cars on our roads or calories in our bellies. That argument refers to the *mix* of output again and does not answer the question of whether we want *any* more goods or services per person. Increasing GDP per capita can take a million forms, including the educational services you are now consuming. The rejection of economic growth per se implies that none of those forms is desirable.

We could, of course, acquire more of the goods and services we consider beneficial simply by cutting back on the production of the things we consider unnecessary. But who is to say which mix of output is best? The present mix of output may be considered bad because it is based on a maldistribution of income, deceptive advertising, or failure of the market mechanism to account for external costs. If so, it would seem more efficient (and politically more feasible) to address those problems directly rather than to attempt to lower our standard of living.

SUMMARY

- Economic growth refers to increases in real GDP. Short-run growth may result from increases in capacity utilization (e.g., less unemployment). In the long run, however, growth requires increases in capacity itself—rightward shifts of the long-run aggregate supply curve. **LO1**
- GDP per capita is a basic measure of living standards. By contrast, GDP per worker gauges our productivity. Over time, increases in productivity have been the primary cause of rising living standards. **LO2**
- Productivity gains can originate in a variety of ways. These sources include better labor quality, increased capital investment, research and development, and improved management. **LO3**
- The policy levers for increasing growth rates include education and training, immigration,

investment and saving incentives, and the broader institutional framework. All of these levers may increase the quantity or quality of resources. **LO4**
- Budget deficits may inhibit economic growth by crowding out investment—that is, absorbing savings that would otherwise finance investment. Budget surpluses can have the opposite (crowding in) effect. **LO4**
- The goal of economic growth implies that macroeconomic policies must be assessed in terms of their long-run supply impact as well as their short-term demand effects. **LO4**
- Continued economic growth is desirable as long as it brings a higher standard of living for people and an increased ability to produce and consume socially desirable goods and services. **LO5**

TERMS TO REMEMBER

Define the following terms:

production possibilities	growth rate	productivity	crowding out
economic growth	GDP per capita	investment	crowding in
nominal GDP	labor force	saving	
real GDP	employment rate		

QUESTIONS FOR DISCUSSION

1. In what specific ways (if any) does a college education increase a worker's productivity? **LO3**
2. What's wrong with a negative saving rate, as the United States had in 2006? **LO3**
3. Notice in the News Wire on page 307 how the time spent working on the job and at home has declined. How are these changes indicative of economic growth? **LO5**
4. How would the following factors affect a nation's growth potential? **LO4**
   (*a*) Legal protection of private property.
   (*b*) High tax rates.
   (*c*) Judicial corruption.
   (*d*) Government price controls.
   (*e*) Free trade.

5. Should the United States adopt a skill-based immigration policy (News Wire, p. 312) or continue to give preference to family members?   **LO4**

6. Is limitless growth really possible? What forces do you think will be most important in slowing or halting economic growth?   **LO5**

7. **POLICY PERSPECTIVES** How did GDP growth contribute to the last two items in the News Wire on page 307?   **LO5**

8. **POLICY PERSPECTIVES** Suppose that economic growth could be achieved only by increasing inequality (e.g., via tax incentives for investment). Would economic growth still be desirable?   **LO4**

PROBLEMS

connect

1. How many years will it take for GDP to double if GDP growth is   **LO1**
   (*a*) 4 percent?
   (*b*) 2 percent?
   (*c*) 1 percent?

2. China's output grew at an amazing rate of 10 percent per year from 2000 to 2008. At that rate how long would it take for China's GDP to double? (See Table 15.1.) With its population increasing at 0.6 percent per year, how long will it take for *per capita* GDP to double?   **LO2**

3. In 2013, approximately 58 percent of the adult population (245 million) was employed, the lowest employment rate in 20 years. If the employment rate increased to the prerecession level of 62 percent,   **LO2**
   (*a*) How many more people would be working?
   (*b*) By how much would output increase if per worker GDP is $100,000?

4. According to the data in Figure 15.4, how fast did world GDP per capita grow annually from   **LO1**
   (*a*) 1000 to 1500?
   (*b*) 1500 to 1820?
   (*c*) 1820 to 1995?

5. According to Figure 15.4, by what percentage did GDP per capita increase between 1820 and 1995 in   **LO5**
   (*a*) North America?
   (*b*) Latin America?
   (*c*) Africa?

6. Zimbabwe's GDP shrank by an average of 5 percent a year from 2000 to 2010.   **LO2**
   (*a*) What was the cumulative GDP decline in that decade?
   (*b*) If the population grew by 0.8 percent a year, by how much did per capita GDP decline in that decade?

7. Suppose that every additional 3 percentage points in the investment rate (I ÷ GDP) boost GDP growth by 1 percentage point. Assume also that all investment must be financed with consumer saving. The economy is now characterized by

GDP:	$10 trillion
Consumption:	9 trillion
Saving:	1 trillion
Investment:	1 trillion

   If the goal is to raise the growth rate by 2 percentage points,   **LO3**
   (*a*) By how much must investment increase?
   (*b*) By how much must consumption decline for this to occur?

8. **POLICY PERSPECTIVES** The World Bank projects that the world's population will increase from 7 billion today to 8 billion in 2025. World output today is roughly $80 trillion.   **LO5**
   (*a*) What is global per capita income today?
   (*b*) What will per capita income be in 2025 if the world's economy doesn't grow?
   (*c*) By what percentage must the world economy grow by 2025 to maintain current living standards?

◀ Practice quizzes, student PowerPoints, author podcasts, web activities, and additional materials available at **www.mhhe.com/schilleressentials9e**, or scan here. Need a barcode reader? Try ScanLife, available in your app store.

16 Theory and Reality

 ◄ Practice quizzes, student PowerPoints, author podcasts, web activities, and additional materials available at www.mhhe.com/ schileressentials9e, or scan here. Need a barcode reader? Try ScanLife, available in your app store.

LEARNING OBJECTIVES

After reading this chapter, you should be able to:

1 Identify the major tools of macro policy.
2 Explain how macro tools can fix macro problems.
3 Depict the track record of macro outcomes.
4 Describe major impediments to policy success.
5 Discuss the pros and cons of discretionary policy.

Macroeconomic theory is supposed to explain the business cycle and show policymakers how to control it. But something is obviously wrong. Despite our relative prosperity, we have not consistently achieved the goals of full employment, price stability, and vigorous economic growth. All too often, either unemployment or inflation jumps unexpectedly or economic growth slows down. No matter how hard we try, the business cycle seems to persist.

What accounts for this gap between the promises of economic theory and the reality of economic performance? Are the theories inadequate? Or is sound economic advice being ignored? Many people blame the economists. They point to the conflicting theories and advice that economists offer and wonder what theory is supposed to be followed. If economists themselves can't agree, it is asked, why should anyone else listen to them?

Not surprisingly, economists see things a bit differently. First, they point out, the business cycle isn't as bad as it used to be. Since World War II, the economy has had many ups and downs, but none as severe as the Great Depression. In recent decades, the U.S. economy has enjoyed several long and robust economic expansions, even in the wake of recession, terrorist attacks, and natural disasters. The recession and recovery of 2008–2010 was no exception. So the economic record contains more wins than losses.

Second, economists place most of the blame for occasional losses on the real world, not on their theories. They complain that politics takes precedence over good economic advice. Politicians are reluctant, for example, to raise taxes or cut spending to control inflation. Their concern is winning the next election, not solving the country's economic problems.

President Jimmy Carter anguished over another problem—the complexity of economic decision making. In the real world, neither theory nor politics can keep up with all our economic goals. As President Carter observed,

> We cannot concentrate just on inflation or just on unemployment or just on deficits in the federal budget or our international payments. Nor can we act in isolation from other countries. We must deal with all of these problems simultaneously and on a worldwide basis.

That's a message that rang in President Obama's ears when he started to grapple with an array of short- and long-term economic problems (see cartoon).

The purpose of this chapter is to confront these and other frustrations of the real world. In so doing, we will try to provide answers to the following questions:

- What is the ideal package of macro policies?
- How well does our macro performance live up to the promises of that package?
- What kinds of obstacles prevent us from doing better?

POLICY TOOLS

The macroeconomic tools available to policymakers for combating **business cycles** and fostering GDP growth are summarized in Table 16.1. Although this list is brief, we hardly need a reminder at this point of how powerful each instrument can be. Every one of these major policy instruments can significantly change our answers to the basic economic questions of WHAT, HOW, and FOR WHOM to produce.

Fiscal Policy

The basic tools of **fiscal policy** are contained in the federal budget. Tax cuts are supposed to stimulate spending by putting more income in the hands of

The economist in chief must deal with an array of economic problems—often all at the same time.

Source: "First 100 Daze" © 2009 John Darkow, Columbia Daily Tribune, Missouri, and PoliticalCartoons.com.

business cycle Alternating periods of economic growth and contraction.

fiscal policy The use of government taxes and spending to alter macroeconomic outcomes.

TABLE 16.1
The Policy tools

Economic policymakers have access to a variety of policy instruments. The challenge is to choose the right tools at the right time. The mix of tools required may vary from problem to problem.

Type of Policy	Policy Tools
Fiscal	Tax cuts and increases Changes in government spending
Monetary	Open market operations Reserve requirements Discount rates
Supply side	Tax incentives for investment and saving Deregulation Education and training Immigration Trade policy

consumers and businesses. Tax increases are intended to curtail spending and thus reduce inflationary pressures. Some of the major tax changes implemented in recent years are summarized in Table 16.2.

The expenditure side of the federal budget provides another fiscal policy tool. Increases in government spending raise aggregate demand and so encourage more production. A slowdown in government spending restrains aggregate demand, lessening inflationary pressures. With federal spending approaching $4 trillion a year, changes in Uncle Sam's budget can influence aggregate demand significantly. That was the intent, of course, of President Obama's massive 2009 fiscal stimulus package. The $787 billion of increased federal spending, income transfers, and tax cuts were intended to give a big push to aggregate demand.

TABLE 16.2
Fiscal Policy Milestones

1981	Economic Recovery Tax Act	Three-year consumer tax cut of $213 billion plus $59 billion of business tax cuts.
1982	Tax Equity and Fiscal Responsibility Act	Raised business, excise, and income taxes by $100 billion over three years.
1985	Gramm-Rudman-Hollings Act	Required a balanced budget by 1991 and authorized automatic spending cuts.
1986	Tax Reform Act	Major reduction in tax rates coupled with broader tax base.
1990	Budget Enforcement Act	Imposed limits on discretionary spending; required PAYGO.
1993	Clinton's "New Direction"	Tax increases and spending cuts to reduce deficit, 1994–1997.
2001	Economic Growth and Tax Relief Reconciliation Act	$1.35 trillion in personal tax cuts spread over 10 years.
2003	Jobs and Growth Tax Relief Act	$350 billion tax cut, including reduced dividend and capital gains taxes.
2008	Tax rebates	$160 billion in $600 rebates and business tax cuts.
2009	American Recovery and Reinvestment Act	$787 billion package of increased spending and tax cuts.
2012	American Taxpayer Relief Act	Raised top tax rate to 39.6 percent; ended payroll tax cut.

AUTOMATIC STABILIZERS Changes in the budget don't necessarily originate in presidential decisions or congressional legislation. Tax revenues and government outlays also respond to economic events. *When the economy slows, tax revenues decline, and government spending increases automatically.* The 2008–2009 recession, for example, displaced 8 million workers and reduced the incomes of millions more. As their incomes fell, so did their tax liabilities. As a consequence, government tax revenues fell.

The recession also caused government spending to *rise*. The swollen ranks of unemployed workers increased outlays for unemployment insurance benefits, welfare, food stamps, and other transfer payments. None of this budget activity required new legislation. Instead the benefits were increased *automatically* under laws already written. No *new* policy was required.

These recession-induced changes in tax receipts and budget outlays are referred to as **automatic stabilizers.** Such budget changes help stabilize the economy by increasing after-tax incomes and spending when the economy slows. Specifically, *recessions automatically*

automatic stabilizer Federal expenditure or revenue item that automatically responds counter-cyclically to changes in national income—such as unemployment benefits, income taxes.

- *Reduce tax revenues.*
- *Increase government outlays.*
- *Widen budget deficits.*

Economic expansions have the opposite effect on government budgets. When the economy booms, people have to pay more taxes on their rising incomes. They also have less need for government assistance. Hence tax receipts rise and government spending drops automatically when the economy heats up. These changes tend to shrink the budget deficit. This is exactly the kind of automatic deficit reduction that occurred in the late 1990s. While President Clinton and congressional Republicans were squabbling about how to reduce the federal deficit, the economy kept growing. Indeed, it grew so fast that the budget *deficit* turned into a budget *surplus* in 1998. Soon thereafter both the Democrats and the Republicans claimed credit for that turn of events.

DISCRETIONARY POLICY To assess political claims for deficit reduction, we need to distinguish *automatic* changes in the budget from *policy-induced* changes. Automatic changes in taxes and spending do not reflect current fiscal policy decisions; they reflect laws already on the books. Discretionary fiscal policy entails only *new* tax and spending decisions. Specifically, *fiscal policy refers to deliberate changes in tax or spending legislation.* These changes can be made only by the U.S. Congress. Every year the president proposes specific budget and tax changes, negotiates with Congress, and then accepts or vetoes specific acts that Congress has passed. The resulting policy decisions represent discretionary fiscal policy. Policymakers deserve credit (or blame) only for the effects of the discretionary policy decisions they make (or fail to make).

The distinction between automatic stabilizers and discretionary spending helps explain why the federal budget deficit jumped from $221 billion in **fiscal year** 1991 to nearly $270 billion in fiscal 1992. Ironically, Congress had *increased* tax rates in fiscal 1992, hoping to trim the deficit. Congress had also planned to slow the growth of government spending. Hence discretionary fiscal policy was slightly restrictive. These discretionary policies were overwhelmed, however, by the force of the 1990–1991 recession. Automatic stabilizers caused tax revenues to fall and government transfer payments to rise. The net result was a much *larger* budget deficit in fiscal 1992, the opposite of what Congress had intended. The swollen deficit was a symptom of the economy's weakness, not a measure of fiscal policy stimulus.

fiscal year The 12-month period used for accounting purposes; begins October 1 for the federal government.

NEWS WIRE   ORIGINS OF DEFICITS

Budget Deficit Sets Record in February

WASHINGTON—The government ran up the largest monthly deficit in history in February, keeping the flood of red ink on track to top last year's record for the full year.

The Treasury Department said Wednesday that the February deficit totaled $220.9 billion, 14 percent higher than the previous record set in February of last year. . . .

The Obama administration is projecting that the deficit for the 2010 budget year will hit an all-time high of $1.56 trillion, surpassing last year's $1.4 trillion total. The administration is forecasting that the deficit will remain above $1 trillion in 2011, giving the country three straight years of $1 trillion-plus deficits.

The administration says the huge deficits are necessary to get the country out of the deepest recession since the 1930s. But Republicans have attacked the stimulus spending as wasteful and a failure at the primary objective of lowering unemployment. . . .

The administration has maintained that the country must run large budget deficits until the economy has begun to grow at a sustainable pace that is bringing the unemployment rate down. Only then, the administration says, should the government focus on getting control of the deficits.

—Martin Crutsinger

Source: Associated Press, March 11, 2010. Used with permission of The Associated Press Copyright © 2008. All rights reserved.

NOTE: The budget deficit is affected by both deliberate fiscal policy and cyclical changes in the economy. A recession, combined with a huge fiscal stimulus, caused deficits to soar in 2009–2012.

A similar chain of events plunged the federal budget into an enormous deficit in 2009 (see the accompanying News Wire). From 2008 to 2009 the government's budget deficit soared from $459 billion to over $1.4 trillion. President Obama blamed that trillion-dollar jump in the deficit on the 2008–2009 recession—that is, the automatic stabilizers. His critics blamed Obama's enormous spending plans—that is, policy decisions. The Congressional Budget Office studied the situation and concluded that only a quarter of the trillion-dollar deficit increase was caused by the recession. The remaining three-quarters was due to the federal government's fiscal policy.

Monetary Policy

monetary policy The use of money and credit controls to influence macroeconomic activity.

money supply (M1) Currency held by the public, plus balances in transactions accounts.

The policy arsenal described in Table 16.1 also contains monetary tools. The tools of **monetary policy** include open market operations, discount rate change, and reserve requirements. The Federal Reserve uses these tools to change the **money supply.** In so doing, the Fed strives to change interest rates and shift the aggregate demand curve in the desired direction.

The effectiveness of both fiscal policy and monetary policy depends on the shape of the aggregate supply (AS) curve. If the AS curve is horizontal, changes in the money supply (and related aggregate demand shifts) affect output only. If the AS curve is vertical, money supply changes will affect prices only. In the typical case of an upward-sloping AS curve, changes in the money supply affect both prices and output (review Figure 14.7 on page 297).

RULES VERSUS DISCRETION Disagreements about the actual shape of the AS curve raise questions about how to conduct monetary policy. As discussed in Chapter 14, some economists urge the Fed to play an active role in adjusting the money supply to changing economic conditions. Others suggest that we would be better served by fixed rules for money supply growth. Fixed rules would make the Fed more of a passive mechanic rather than an active policymaker.

There are clear risks of error in discretionary policy. In 1979 and again in 1989 the Fed pursued restrictive policies that pushed the economy into recessions. In both cases, the Fed had to reverse its policies. (In Table 16.3 compare October 1982 to October 1979 and the year 1991 to 1989.) In 1999–2000 the Fed again raised interest rates substantially, in six separate steps. When the economy slowed abruptly at the end of 2000, critics said the Fed had again stepped too hard on the monetary brake. The Fed was forced to reverse course again in 2001.

Critics say the stimulative monetary policy (low interest rates) after 2001 fueled the rapid rise in home prices that proved to be excessive. When the Fed later started exercising some monetary restraint, the housing bubble burst, pushing the economy into the 2008–2009 recession.

Critics charge that these repeated U-turns in monetary policy have *destabilized* the economy rather than stabilizing it. They contend that strict rules for money management would be better than Fed discretion. It certainly looks that way at times, especially in hindsight. But fixed rules might not work better. The September 11 terrorist attacks and a subsequent plunge in consumer confidence forced the Fed to respond quickly and with more forcefulness than fixed policy rules would have permitted.

October 1979	Fed adopts monetarist approach, tightening money supply; interest rates soar.	**TABLE 16.3** Monetary Policy Milestones
October 1982	Fed abandons pure monetarist approach and expands money supply rapidly.	
May 1987	Fed abandons money supply targets as policy guides.	
June 1987	Alan Greenspan appointed chairman; money supply growth decreases; discount rate increased.	
1989	Greenspan announces goal of zero inflation, slows money supply growth.	
1991	In midst of recession Fed reverses monetary policy; interest rates fall to their lowest level in decades.	
1994	As growth accelerates and unemployment dips, Fed raises interest rates substantially.	
1995	Fed reduces interest rates slightly when economy stalls in first quarter.	
1997	When unemployment rate drops below 5 percent, Fed nudges interest rates higher.	
1998	Fed cuts interest rates to offset shock of Asian crisis.	
1999–2000	Fed increases interest rates six times in one year.	
2001–2003	Fed reverses policy, cuts interest rates; continues cutting interest rates repeatedly until mid-2003.	
2004–2006	Fearing inflationary pressures, the Fed raises interest rates 17 times.	
2006	Alan Greenspan retires; Ben Bernanke becomes Fed chairman.	
2008–2009	Battling recession, Fed cuts interest rates sharply and repeatedly.	
2010–2013	Fed engages in "quantitative easing," buying huge quantities of bonds and mortgage-backed securities.	

The September 2008 credit crisis required even more discretionary intervention. The Fed had to act quickly and boldly—more quickly than fixed rules would permit—to pump reserves into the banking system. Without such dramatic discretionary action by the Fed, the credit crisis could have brought the economy to a complete standstill.

Supply-Side Policy

Supply-side theory offers the third major set of policy tools. We have seen how *the shape of the aggregate supply curve limits the effectiveness of fiscal and monetary policies* (Figure 14.7). Shifts of the aggregate supply curve are also a prerequisite for economic growth. **Supply-side policy** focuses directly on these constraints. The goal of supply-side policy is to shift the aggregate supply curve to the right. Such rightward shifts not only promote long-term growth but also make short-run demand-side intervention more successful.

supply-side policy The use of tax rates, (de)regulation, and other mechanisms to increase ability and willingness to produce goods and services.

The supply-side toolbox is filled with tools. Tax cuts designed to stimulate work effort, saving, and investment are among the most popular and powerful supply-side tools. Deregulation may also reduce production costs and stimulate investment. Expenditure on education, training, and research expands our capacity to produce. Immigration policy alters the size and skills of the labor force and thus affects aggregate supply as well.

In the 1980s tax rates were reduced dramatically. The maximum marginal tax rate on individuals was cut from 70 percent to 50 percent in 1981, and then still further, to 28 percent, in 1987. The 1980s also witnessed major milestones in the deregulation of airlines, trucking, telephone service, and other industries (see Table 16.4). All of these policies helped shift the AS curve rightward.

Government policies can also shift the AS curve leftward. When the minimum wage jumped to $7.25 an hour in 2009, the cost of supplying goods and services went up. A 1990 increase in the payroll tax boosted production costs as well. In the early 1990s, private employers also incurred higher labor costs associated with government-mandated benefits (Family Leave Act of 1993) and accommodations

TABLE 16.4   Supply-Side Milestones

1978	Airline Deregulation Act	Phased out federal regulations of airline routes, fares, and entry.
1980	Motor Carrier Act	Eliminated federal restrictions on entry, routes, and fares in the trucking industry.
1981	Economic Recovery Tax Act	Decreased marginal tax rates by 30 percent.
1986	Tax Reform Act	Eliminated most tax preferences for investment and saving but sharply reduced marginal tax rates.
1990	Social Security Act amendments	Increased payroll tax to 7.65 percent.
1990	Americans with Disabilities Act	Required employers to provide more universal access.
1990	Clean Air Act	Toughened pollution standards.
1993	Family Leave Act	Required employers to offer unpaid leave.
1994	NAFTA	Lowered North American trade barriers.
2001	Economic Growth and Tax Relief Reconciliation Act	Reduced marginal tax rates over 10 years.
2002	Job Creation and Worker Assistance Act	Provided business tax cuts and incentives.
2003	Jobs and Growth Tax Relief Act	Reduced taxes on dividends and capital gains.
2007–2009	Minimum wage	Increased minimum wage from $5.15 to $7.25 per hour.
2009	American Recovery and Reinvestment Act	Sharply increased infrastructure and energy development.
2012	American Taxpayer Relief Act	Raised tax rates on high incomes and investment income.

for handicapped workers (Americans with Disabilities Act). In 2013 marginal tax rates were increased for wealthy individuals and many small businesses. All of these policies restrained aggregate supply.

Even welfare reform has supply-side implications. The 1996 Personal Responsibility and Work Opportunity Act established time limits for welfare dependence. When those limits were reached in 1998–1999, more welfare recipients had to enter the labor market. When they did, aggregate supply shifted rightward. The extension of unemployment benefits in 2009–2011 had the opposite effect.

Because tax rates are a basic tool of supply-side policy, fiscal and supply-side policies are often interwined. When Congress changes the tax laws, it almost always alters marginal tax rates and thus changes production incentives. Notice, for example, that tax legislation appears in Table 16.4 as well as in Table 16.2. The American Taxpayer Relief Act of 2012 not only changed total tax revenues (fiscal policy) but also restructured production and investment incentives (supply-side policy).

IDEALIZED USES

These fiscal, monetary, and supply-side tools are potentially powerful levers for controlling the economy. In principle, they can cure the excesses of the business cycle. To see how, let us review their use in three distinct macroeconomic settings.

Case 1: Recession

When output and employment levels fall far short of the economy's full-employment potential, the mandate for public policy is clear. The **GDP gap** must be closed. Total spending must be increased so that producers can sell more goods, hire more workers, and move the economy toward its productive capacity. At such times the most urgent need is to get people back to work.

GDP gap The difference between full employment output and the amount of output demanded at current price levels.

How can a recession be ended? Keynesians emphasize the need to stimulate aggregate demand. They seek to shift the aggregate demand curve rightward by cutting taxes or boosting government spending. The resulting stimulus will set off a **multiplier** reaction, propelling the economy to full employment.

Modern Keynesians acknowledge that monetary policy might also help. Specifically, increases in the money supply may lower interest rates and give investment spending a further boost. To give the economy a really powerful stimulus, we might want to do everything at the same time—that is, cut taxes, increase government spending, and expand the money supply simultaneously (as in 2001–2003 and again in 2008–2009). By taking such convincing action, we might also increase consumer confidence, raise investor expectations, and induce still greater spending and output.

multiplier The multiple by which an initial change in aggregate spending will alter total expenditure after an infinite number of spending cycles; $1/(1 - MPC)$.

Other economists offer different advice. So-called monetarists and other critics of government intervention see no point in these discretionary policies. As they see it, the aggregate supply curve is vertical at the natural rate of unemployment (see Figure 14.7, page 297). Quick fixes of monetary or fiscal policy may shift the aggregate demand curve but won't change the aggregate supply curve. Monetary or fiscal stimulus will only push the price level up (more inflation) without reducing unemployment. In this view, the appropriate policy response to a recession is patience. As sales and output slow, interest rates will decline, and new investment will be stimulated.

Supply-siders confront these objections head-on. In their view, policy initiatives should focus on changing the shape and position of the aggregate supply curve. Supply-siders emphasize the need to improve production incentives. They urge cuts in marginal tax rates on investment and labor. They also look for ways to reduce government regulation.

Different macro theories offer alternative explanations and policy options for macro failures.

By MAL, Associated Features, Inc.

Case 2: Inflation

An overheated economy elicits a similar assortment of policy prescriptions. In this case the immediate goal is to restrain aggregate demand—that is, shift the aggregate demand curve to the left. Keynesians would do this by raising taxes and cutting government spending, relying on the multiplier to cool down the economy.

The monetary policy response to inflation would be a hike in interest rates. By making credit more expensive, the Fed would discourage some investment and consumption, shifting the AD curve leftward. Pure monetarists would simply cut the money supply, expecting the same outcome. The Fed might even seek to squeeze AD extra hard just to convince market participants that the inflation dragon was really slain.

Supply-siders would point out that inflation implies both too much money and not enough goods. They would look at the supply side of the market for ways to expand productive capacity. In a highly inflationary setting, they would propose more incentives to save. The additional savings would automatically reduce consumption while creating a larger pool of investable funds. Supply-siders would also cut taxes and regulations, encourage more immigration, and lower import barriers that keep out cheaper foreign goods.

Case 3: Stagflation

Although serious inflations and recessions provide reasonably clear options for economic policy, there is a vast gray area between these extremes. Occasionally the economy suffers from both inflation and unemployment at the same time—a condition called **stagflation.** In 1975, for example, the unemployment rate (8.5 percent) and the inflation rate (9.1 percent) were both far too high. With an upward-sloping aggregate supply curve, there is no easy way to bring both rates down at the same time. Any demand-side stimulus to attain full employment worsens inflation. Likewise, restrictive demand policies increase unemployment. Although any upward-sloping AS curve poses such a trade-off, the position of the curve also determines how difficult the choices are. Figure 16.1 illustrates this stagflation problem.

stagflation The simultaneous occurrence of substantial unemployment and inflation.

FIGURE 16.1
Stagflation

Both unemployment and inflation may occur at the same time. This is always a potential problem with an upward-sloping AS curve. The farther the AS curve is to the left, the worse the stagflation problem is likely to be. The curve AS_1 implies higher prices and more unemployment than AS_2 for any given level of aggregate demand.

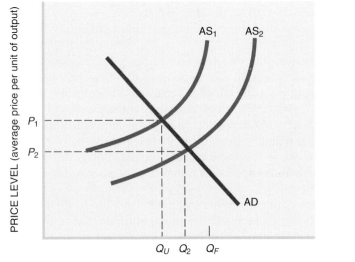

There are no simple solutions for stagflation. Any demand-side initiatives must be designed with care, seeking to balance the competing threats of inflation and unemployment. This requires more attention to the specific nature of the supply constraints. Perhaps the early rise in the AS curve is due to **structural unemployment.** Prices may be rising in the auto industry, for example, while unemployed workers are abundant in the housing industry. The higher prices and wages in the auto industry function as a signal to transfer resources from the construction industry into autos. Such resource shifts, however, may not occur smoothly or quickly. In the interim, public policy can be developed to facilitate interindustry mobility or to alter the structure of supply or demand.

structural unemployment Unemployment caused by a mismatch between the skills (or location) of job seekers and the requirements (or location) of available jobs.

On the demand side, the government could reduce the demand for new cars by increasing interest rates. The government could also cut back on its fleet purchases. It could increase the demand for construction workers by offering larger tax deductions for new home purchases. On the supply side, the government could offer tax credits or skill classes, teach construction workers how to build cars, or speed up the job search process.

High tax rates or costly regulations might also contribute to stagflation. If either of these constraints exists, high prices (inflation) may not be a sufficient incentive for increased output. In this case, reductions in tax rates and regulation could shift the AS curve rightward, easing stagflation pressures.

Stagflation may have arisen from a temporary contraction (leftward shift) of aggregate supply that both reduces output and drives up prices. In this case, neither structural unemployment nor excessive demand is the culprit. Rather, an external shock (such as a natural disaster) or an abrupt change in world trade (such as higher oil prices) is the cause of stagflation. The high oil prices and supply disruptions caused by Hurricanes Katrina and Rita (2005) illustrate this problem. In such circumstances, conventional policy tools are unlikely to provide a complete cure. In most cases the economy simply has to adjust to a temporary setback.

Fine-Tuning

Everything looks easy on the blackboard. Indeed, economic theory seems to have all the answers for our macro problems. Some people even imagine that economic theory has the potential to fine-tune the economy—that is, to correct any and all macro problems that arise. Such **fine-tuning** would entail continual adjustments to policy levers. When unemployment is the problem, simply give the economy a jolt of fiscal or monetary stimulus; when inflation is worrisome, simply tap on the fiscal or monetary brakes. To fulfill our goals for content and distribution, we simply pick the right target for stimulus or restraint. With a little attention and experience, the right speed could be found and the economy guided successfully down the road to prosperity.

fine-tuning Adjustments in economic policy designed to counteract small changes in economic outcomes; continuous responses to changing economic conditions.

THE ECONOMIC RECORD

The economy's track record does not live up to these high expectations. To be sure, the economy has continued to grow, and we have attained an impressive standard of living. We have also had some great years when both unemployment and inflation rates were low, as in 1994–2000 and again in 2004–2007. Nor can we lose sight of the fact that even in a bad year our per capita income greatly exceeds the realities and even the expectations in most other countries of the world. Nevertheless, we must also recognize that our economic history is punctuated by periods of recession, high unemployment, inflation, and recurring concern for the distribution of income and mix of output.

FIGURE 16.2

The Economic Record

The Full Employment and Balanced Growth Act of 1978 established specific goals for unemployment (4 percent), inflation (3 percent), and economic growth (4 percent). We have rarely attained all those goals, however, as these graphs illustrate. Measurement, design, and policy implementation problems help explain these shortcomings.

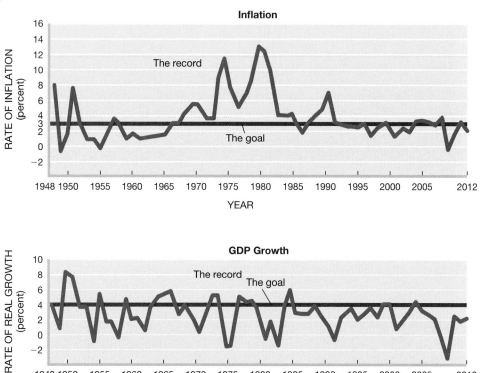

Source: *Economic Report of the President*, 2013.

The graphs in Figure 16.2 provide a quick summary of our experiences since 1946, the year the Employment Act committed the federal government to macro stability. It is evident that our economic track record is far from perfect. In the 1970s the record was particularly bleak: two recessions, high inflation, and persistent unemployment. The 1980s were better but still marred by two recessions, one of which sent the unemployment rate to a post–World War II record.

In terms of real economic growth, the record is equally spotty. Output actually declined (i.e., recessions) in 10 years and grew less than 3 percent in another 23. The Great Recession of 2008–2009 caused the largest annual contraction of GDP (−3.1 percent) in over 50 years.

The economic performance of the United States is similar to that of other Western nations. The economies of most countries did not grow as fast as the U.S. economy from 2000 to 2010. But as the accompanying News Wire shows, some countries did a better job of restraining prices.

NEWS WIRE	COMPARATIVE PERFORMANCE

Macro Performance, 2000–2010

The 2000–2010 performance of the U.S. economy was better than that of most developed economies. Japan had the greatest success in restraining inflation (−0.2 percent) but suffered from sluggish growth (0.5 percent per year). The United States grew faster and had less unemployment than Europe.

Performance (Annual Average Percentage)	U.S.	Japan	Germany	United Kingdom	France	Italy	Canada
Real growth	1.9	0.8	0.9	1.7	1.4	0.5	2.2
Inflation	2.5	−0.2	1.5	1.9	1.7	2.2	2.1
Unemployment	6.0	4.7	8.9	5.7	8.6	8.2	7.3

Source: United Nations.

NOTE: No nation gets a gold medal in all macro dimensions. Inflation, unemployment, and growth records reveal uneven performance.

WHY THINGS DON'T ALWAYS WORK

We have already noted the readiness of economists and politicians to blame each other for the continuing gap between our economic goals and performance. Rather than taking sides, however, we may note some general constraints on successful policymaking. In this regard, we can distinguish *four obstacles to policy success:*

- *Goal conflicts.*
- *Measurement problems.*
- *Design problems.*
- *Implementation problems.*

Goal Conflicts

The first factor to note is potential conflicts in policy priorities. Suppose that the economy was suffering from stagflation and, further, that all macro policies involved some trade-off between unemployment and inflation. Should fighting inflation or fighting unemployment get priority? Unemployed people will put the highest priority on attaining full employment. Labor unions and advocates for the poor will press for faster economic growth. Bankers, creditors, and people on fixed incomes will worry more about inflation. They will lobby for more restrictive fiscal and monetary policies. There is no way to satisfy everyone in such a situation.

In practice, these goal conflicts are often institutionalized in the decision-making process. The Fed is traditionally viewed as the guardian of price stability and tends to favor policy restraint. The president and Congress worry more about people's jobs and government programs, so they lean toward policy stimulus. The end result may entail a mix of contradictory policies.

Distributional goals may also conflict with macro objectives. Anti-inflationary policies may require cutbacks in programs for the poor, the elderly, or needy students. These cutbacks may be politically impossible. Likewise, tight money policies may be viewed as too great a burden for small businesses.

Although the policy levers listed in Table 16.1 are powerful, they cannot grant all our wishes. Since we still live in a world of scarce resources, ***all policy decisions entail opportunity costs.*** This means that we will always be confronted with trade-offs: the best we can hope for is a set of compromises that yields optimal outcomes, not ideal ones.

Even if we all agreed on policy priorities, success would not be assured. We would still have to confront the more mundane problems of measurement, design, and implementation.

Measurement Problems

One reason firefighters are pretty successful in putting out fires before whole cities burn down is that fires are highly visible phenomena. Economic problems are rarely so visible. An increase in the unemployment rate from 5 percent to 6 percent, for example, is not the kind of thing you notice while crossing the street. Unless you lose your own job, the increase in unemployment is not likely to attract your attention. The same is true of prices; small increases in product prices are unlikely to ring many alarms. Hence both inflation and unemployment may worsen considerably before anyone takes serious notice. Were we as slow and ill equipped to notice fires, whole neighborhoods would burn before someone rang the alarm.

To formulate good economic policy, we must be able to see the scope of our economic problems. To do so, we must measure employment changes, output changes, price changes, and other macro outcomes. Although the government spends vast sums of money to collect and process such data, the available information is always dated and incomplete. ***At best, we know what was happening in the economy last month or last week.*** The processes of data collection, assembly, and presentation take time, even in this age of high-speed computers. The average recession lasts about 11 months, but official data generally do not even confirm the existence of a recession until 8 months after a downturn starts! The recession of 2008–2009 was no exception, as the accompanying News Wire shows. Notice that it took an entire year before the onset of that recession was officially recognized.

FORECASTS   In an ideal world, policymakers would not only respond to economic problems that occur but also *anticipate* their occurrence and act to avoid them. If we foresee an inflation emerging, for example, we want to take immediate action to restrain aggregate demand. That is to say, the successful firefighter not only responds to fires but also looks for hazards that might start one.

Unfortunately, economic policymakers are again at a disadvantage. Their knowledge of future problems is even worse than their knowledge of current problems. ***In designing policy, policymakers must depend on economic forecasts—*** informed guesses about what the economy will look like in future periods.

MACRO MODELS   Those guesses are often based on complex computer models of how the economy works. These models—referred to as *econometric macro models*— are mathematical summaries of the economy's performance. The models try to identify the key determinants of macro performance and then show what happens to macro outcomes when they change. As the accompanying News Wire suggests, the apparent precision of such computer models may disguise "a black art."

An economist feeds the computer two essential inputs. One is a model of how the economy allegedly works. Such models are quantitative summaries of one or more macro theories. A Keynesian model, for example, will include equations that show multiplier spending responses to tax cuts. A monetarist model will show that tax cuts raise interest rates (crowding out), not total spending. And a supply-side model stipulates labor supply and production responses. The computer can't tell which theory is right; it just predicts what it is programmed to see. In other words, the computer sees the world through the eyes of its economic master.

NEWS WIRE	MEASUREMENT PROBLEMS

NBER Makes It Official: Recession Started in December 2007

Official recession watchers at the NBER said today that the U.S. is in recession, and it began in December 2007. Here is the text of their statement.

The Business Cycle Dating Committee of the National Bureau of Economic Research met by conference call on Friday, November 28. The committee maintains a chronology of the beginning and ending dates (months and quaters) of U.S. recessions. The committee determined that a peak in economic activity occurred in the U.S. economy in December 2007. The peak marks the end of the expansion that began in November 2001 and the beginning of a recession. The expansion lasted 73 months; the previous expansion of the 1990s lasted 120 months.

A recession is a significant decline in economic activity spread across the economy, lasting more than a few months, normally visible in production, employment, real income, and other indicators. A recession begins when the economy reaches a peak of activity and ends when the economy reaches its trough. Between trough and peak, the economy is in an expansion.

Source: *The Wall Street Journal* online blog post, December 1, 2008. Used with permission of Dow Jones & Company, Inc., via Copyright Clearance Center, Inc.

NOTE: Successful macro policy requires timely and accurate data on the economy. The measurement process is slow and imperfect, however.

The second essential input in a computer forecast is the assumed values for critical economic variables. A Keynesian model, for example, must specify how large a multiplier to expect. All the computer does is carry out the required mathematical routines once it is told that the multiplier is relevant and what its value is. It cannot discern the true multiplier any better than it can pick the right theory.

Given the dependence of computers on the theories and perceptions of their economic masters, it is not surprising that computer forecasts often differ greatly. It's also not surprising that they are often wrong.

Even policymakers who are familiar with both economic theory and computer models can make bad calls. In January 1990 Fed chairman Alan Greenspan assured Congress that the risk of a recession was as low as 20 percent. Although he said he "wouldn't bet the ranch" on such a low probability, he was confident that the odds of a recession were below 50 percent. Five months after his testimony, the 1990–1991 recession began.

Martin Baily, chairman of President Clinton's Council of Economic Advisers, made the same mistake in January 2001. "Let me be clear," he told the press, "we don't think that we're going into recession." President Clinton echoed this optimism, projecting growth of 2–3 percent in 2001 (see the accompanying News Wire). Two months later the U.S. economy fell into another recession.

President Obama made a similarly bad forecast. In January 2009 he predicted that his $787 billion fiscal stimulus would create so many jobs that the national unemployment rate, then at 7.7 percent, would not rise above 8 percent and would fall to 5 percent by 2012. In fact, the unemployment rate jumped to 10 percent in 2009 and was still at 7.8 percent at the beginning of 2013.

Design Problems

Forget all these bad forecasts for a moment and just pretend that we can somehow get a reliable forecast of where the economy is headed. The outlook, let us suppose, is bad. Now we are in the driver's seat, trying to steer the economy past looming

NEWS WIRE	MACRO MODELS

Tough Calls in Economic Forecasting
Seers Often Peer into Cracked Crystal Balls

In presenting his annual economic outlook last Thursday, the chairman of President Clinton's Council of Economic Advisers was having nothing to do with all the recession talk going around.

"Let me be clear," Martin Baily said, "we don't think that we're going into recession."

The same message was delivered the next day by Clinton in a Rose Garden economic valedictory. Citing the predictions of 50 private forecasters known as the Blue Chip Consensus—"the experts who make a living doing this," as he put it—Clinton assured Americans that the economy would continue to grow this year at an annual rate of 2 percent to 3 percent.

What the president and his adviser failed to mention was that "the experts" have not predicted any of the nine recessions since the end of World War II. . . .

"A recession, by its nature, is a speculative call."

On first blush, such humility may seem at odds with the aura surrounding the modern day forecaster. Using high-speed computers and sophisticated models of the U.S. economy, they constantly revise their two-year predictions for everything from unemployment to business investment to long-term interest rates, expressed numerically to the first decimal point.

But according to the forecasters themselves, what may appear to be a precise science is a black art, one that is constantly confounded by the changing structure of the economy and the refusal of investors, consumers, and business executives to behave as rationally and predictably in real life as they do in the economic models.

"The reason we have trouble calling recessions is that all recessions are anomalies," said Joel Prakken, president of Macroeconomic Advisers of St. Louis, one of the nation's leading forecasting firms. . . .

—Steven Pearlstein

Source: *The Washington Post*, © January 15, 2001, The Washington Post. All rights reserved.

NOTE: Even the most sophisticated computer models rely on basic assumptions about consumer and investor behavior. If the assumptions are wrong, the forecast will likely be wrong as well.

dangers. We need to chart our course—to design an economic plan. What action should we take? How will the marketplace respond to any specific action we take? Will the aggregate demand curve respond as expected? What shape will the aggregate supply curve have? Which macro theory should we use to guide policy decisions?

Suppose we adopt a Keynesian approach to fighting recession. Specifically, we cut income taxes to stimulate consumer spending. How do we know that consumers will respond as anticipated? Perhaps the marginal propensity to consume has changed. Maybe the level of consumer confidence has dropped. Any of these changes could frustrate even the best-intentioned policy, as Japanese policymakers learned in 1998–1999. Japanese consumers *saved* their tax cuts rather than *spending* them, nullifying the intended policy stimulus. Who would have foreseen such a response?

Implementation Problems

Suppose our crystal ball foresees all these problems, allowing us to design a "perfect" policy package. How will we implement the package? To understand fully why things go wrong, we must also consider the difficulties of implementing a well-designed (and credible) policy initiative.

CONGRESSIONAL DELIBERATIONS   Suppose the president and his Council of Economic Advisers (perhaps in conjunction with the secretary of the Treasury and the director of the Office of Management and Budget) correctly foresee that aggregate demand is slowing. A tax cut, they believe, is necessary to stimulate demand for goods and services. Can they simply cut tax rates? No, because all tax changes must be legislated by Congress. Once the president decides on the appropriate policy initiative, he must ask Congress for authority to take the required action. This means a delay in implementing policy, and possibly no policy at all.

At the very least, the president must convince Congress of the desirability of his suggested action. The tax proposal must work its way through separate committees of both the House of Representatives and the Senate, get on the congressional calendar, and be approved in each chamber. If there are important differences in Senate and House versions of the tax cut legislation, they must be compromised in a joint conference. The modified proposal must then be returned to each chamber for approval.

The same kind of process applies to the outlay side of the budget. Once the president has submitted his budget proposals (in January), Congress reviews them and then sets its own spending goals. After that the budget is broken down into 13 different categories, and a separate appropriations bill is written for each one. These bills spell out in detail how much can be spent and for what purposes. Once Congress passes them, they go to the president for acceptance or veto.

In theory, all of these budget deliberations are to be completed in nine months. Budget legislation requires Congress to finish the process by October 1 (the beginning of the federal fiscal year). Congress rarely meets this deadline, however. In most years the budget debate continues well into the fiscal year. In some years, the budget debate is not resolved until the fiscal year is nearly over! The final budget legislation is typically over 1,000 pages long and so complex that few people understand all its dimensions.

This description of congressional activity is not an outline for a civics course; rather, it explains why economic policy is not fully effective. *Even if the right policy is formulated to solve an emerging economic problem, there is no assurance that it will be implemented. And if it is implemented, there is no assurance that it will take effect at the right time.* One of the most frightening prospects for economic policy is that a policy design intended to serve a specific problem will be implemented much later, when economic conditions have changed. The policy's effect on the economy may then be the opposite of what was intended.

Figure 16.3 is a schematic view of why things don't always work out as well as economic theory suggests they might. There are always delays between the time a problem emerges and the time it is recognized. There are additional delays between recognition and response design, between design and implementation, and finally between implementation and impact. Not only may mistakes be made at each juncture, but even correct decisions may be overcome by changing economic conditions.

FIGURE 16.3   Policy Response: A Series of Time Lags

Even the best-intentioned economic policy can be frustrated by time lags. It takes time for a problem to be recognized, time to formulate a policy response, and still more time to implement that policy. By the time the policy begins to affect the economy, the underlying problem may have changed.

© 1989 Tribune Media Services, Inc
All Rights Reserved

Budget cuts are not popular with voters—even when economic conditions warrant fiscal restraint.

Source: SHOE-NEW BUSINESS © 1989 Macnelly. Distributed BY King Features.

POLITICS VERSUS ECONOMICS   Last but not least, we must confront the politics of economic policy. Tax hikes and budget cuts rarely win votes (see the accompanying cartoon). On the other hand, tax cuts and pork-barrel spending are always popular. Accordingly, savvy politicians tend to stimulate the economy before elections, then tighten the fiscal restraints afterward. This creates a kind of *political business cycle*—a two-year pattern of short-run stops and starts. The conflict between the urgent need to get reelected and the necessity to manage the economy results in a seesaw kind of instability.

Fiscal Policy   The politics of fiscal policy were clearly visible in the policy response to the 2008–2009 recession. Democrats preferred to rely on increases in government spending to stimulate aggregate demand. Republicans preferred tax cuts to expand the private sector while limiting the size of government. Democrats wanted more stimulus; Republicans worried that too much stimulus would widen the deficit and increase inflation. No Republican in the House of Representatives and only three Republicans in the Senate voted for President Obama's massive fiscal stimulus package. When the stimulus didn't deliver the AD shift promised, Republicans were quick to label the fiscal package wasteful and ineffective.

The politics of fiscal policy were equally apparent in the 2012–2013 debate over the national debt. Four consecutive years of trillion-dollar-plus deficits had aroused public anxiety. Voters demanded that Washington "do something" about the skyrocketing debt. But what kind of fiscal restraint should be pursued? Republicans opposed any tax increases, and Democrats opposed any spending cuts. That didn't leave many tools in the fiscal policy toolbox. A series of budget-related deadlines failed to spur a compromise (see the accompanying News Wire). In the end, the president and the Congress made vague promises to reduce *future* deficits but adopted little immediate fiscal restraint. So the national debt continued to rise at alarming rates. Both sides were hoping that stronger economic growth (automatic stabilizers) would somehow substitute for politically tough policy decisions.

Monetary Policy   In theory, the political independence of the Fed's Board of Governors provides some protection from ill-advised but politically advantageous policy decisions. In practice, however, the Fed's relative obscurity and independence may backfire. The president and the Congress know that if they don't take action against inflation—by raising taxes or cutting government spending—the Fed can and will take stronger action to restrain aggregate demand. This is a classic case of having one's cake and eating it too. Elected officials win votes for not raising taxes or not cutting some constituent's favorite spending program. They also take credit for any reduction in the rate of inflation brought about by Federal

NEWS WIRE	THE POLITICS OF POLICY

House Votes to Extend Debt Ceiling; Senate Expected to Follow

The House of Representatives voted overwhelmingly Wednesday to suspend the nation's debt limit until May, allowing the federal government to continue to pay its bills and removing an immediate threat to the economy as it struggles to gain strength. . . .

But economists stressed that a short-term debt limit extension is only a bandage covering a festering long-term fiscal problem that Congress and the White House need to get a handle on to better instill confidence in the U.S economy. . . .

The extension prolongs the uncertainty over Washington's eventual decision on fiscal matters, said Steven Ricchiuto, chief economist for Mizuho Securities USA in New York. "There is going to be no certainty until somebody blinks here on spending and taxes," he said.

—William Douglas and Kevin G. Hall

Source: McClatchy DC, January 23, 2013 © 2013 The McClatchy Company. All rights reserved.

NOTE: Fiscal restraint requires policy choices that no politician wants to make.

Reserve policies. To top it off, Congress and the president can also blame the Fed for driving up interest rates or starting a recession if monetary policy becomes too restrictive.

Finally, we must recognize that policy design is obstructed by a certain lack of will. Neither the person in the street nor the elected public official is constantly attuned to economic goals and activities. Even students enrolled in economics courses have a hard time keeping their minds on the economy and its problems. The executive and legislative branches of government, for their part, are likely to focus on economic concerns only when economic problems become serious or voters demand action. Otherwise policymakers are apt to be complacent about economic policy as long as economic performance is within a tolerable range of desired outcomes.

Topic Podcast:
Policy Constraints

POLICY PERSPECTIVES

Hands Off or Hands On?

In view of the goal conflicts and the measurement, design, and implementation problems that policymakers confront, it is less surprising that things sometimes go wrong than that things often work out right. The maze of obstacles through which theory must pass before it becomes policy explains many economic disappointments. On this basis alone, we may conclude that *consistent fine-tuning of the economy is not compatible with either our design capabilities or our decision-making procedures.*

HANDS-OFF POLICY   Some critics of economic policy take this argument a few steps further. If fine-tuning isn't really possible, they say, we should abandon discretionary policies altogether. Typically policymakers seek minor adjustments in interest rates, unemployment, inflation, and growth. The pressure to do something is particularly irresistible in election years. In so doing, however, policymakers are as likely to worsen the economic situation as to improve it. Moreover, the potential for such short-term discretion undermines people's confidence in the economy's future.

Critics of discretionary policies say we would be better off with fixed policy rules. They would require the Fed to increase the money supply at a constant rate. Congress would be required to maintain balanced budgets or at least to offset deficits in sluggish years with surpluses in years of high growth. Such rules would prevent policymakers from over- or understimulating the economy. They would also add a dose of certainty to the economic outlook.

Milton Friedman has been one of the most persistent advocates of fixed policy rules instead of discretionary policies. With discretionary authority, Friedman argues,

> the wrong decision is likely to be made in a large fraction of cases because the decision makers are examining only a limited area and not taking into account the cumulative consequences of the policy as a whole. On the other hand, if a general rule is adopted for a group of cases as a bundle, the existence of that rule has favorable effects on people's attitudes and beliefs and expectations that would not follow even from the discretionary adoption of precisely the same policy on a series of separate occasions.[1]

The case for a hands-off policy stance is based on practical, not theoretical, arguments. Everyone agrees that flexible, discretionary policies *could* result in better economic performance. But Friedman and others argue that the practical requirements of monetary and fiscal management are too demanding and thus prone to failure. Moreover, required policies may be compromised by political pressures.

HANDS-ON POLICY   Critics of fixed rules acknowledge occasional policy blunders but emphasize that the historical record of prices, employment, and growth has improved since active fiscal and monetary policies were adopted. Without flexibility in the money supply and the budget, they argue, the economy would be less stable and our economic goals would remain unfulfilled. They say the government must maintain a hands-on policy of active intervention.

The historical evidence does not provide overwhelming support for either policy stance. Victor Zarnowitz showed that the U.S. economy has been much more stable since 1946 than it was in earlier periods (1875–1918 and 1919–1945). Recessions have gotten shorter and economic expansions longer. But a variety of factors—including a shift from manufacturing to services, a larger government sector, and automatic stabilizers—have contributed to this improved macro performance. The contribution of discretionary macro policy is less clear. It is easy to observe what actually happened but almost impossible to determine what would have occurred in other circumstances. It is also evident that there have been noteworthy occasions—the September 11 terrorist attacks, for example—when something more than fixed rules for monetary and fiscal policy was called for, a contingency even Professor Friedman acknowledges. Thus occasional flexibility is required, even if a nondiscretionary policy is appropriate in most situations.

Finally, one must contend with the difficulties inherent in adhering to any fixed rules. How is the Fed, for example, supposed to maintain a steady rate of growth in M1? The supply of money (M1) is not determined exclusively by the Fed. It also depends on the willingness of market participants to buy and sell bonds, maintain bank balances, and borrow money. Since all of this behavior is subject to change at any time, maintaining a steady rate of M1 growth is an impossible task.

---

[1]Milton Friedman, *Capitalism and Freedom* (Chicago: University of Chicago Press, 1962), p. 53.

The same is true of fiscal policy. Policymakers can't control deficits completely. Government spending and taxes are directly affected by the business cycle—by changes in unemployment, inflation, interest rates, and growth. These automatic stabilizers make it virtually impossible to maintain any fixed rule for budget balancing. Moreover, if we eliminated the automatic stabilizers, we would risk greater instability.

MODEST EXPECTATIONS The clamor for fixed policy rules is more a rebuke of past policy than a viable policy alternative. We really have no choice but to pursue discretionary policies. Recognition of measurement, design, and implementation problems is important for an understanding of the way the economy functions. But even though it is impossible to reach all our goals, we cannot abandon the pursuit. If public policy can create a few more jobs, a better mix of output, a little more growth and price stability, or an improved distribution of income, those initiatives are worthwhile.

SUMMARY

- The government possesses an array of policy levers for altering macroeconomic outcomes. To end a recession, we can cut taxes, expand the money supply, or increase government spending. To curb inflation, we can reverse each of these policy levers. To overcome stagflation, we can combine fiscal and monetary levers with improved supply-side incentives. **LO2**

- Although the potential of economic theory is impressive, the economic record does not look as good. Persistent unemployment, recurring economic slowdowns, and nagging inflation suggest that the realities of policymaking are more difficult than theory implies. **LO3**

- To a large extent, the failures of economic policy are a reflection of scarce resources and competing goals. Even when consensus exists, however, serious obstacles to effective economic policy remain:

  (a) *Measurement problems.* Our knowledge of economic performance is always dated and incomplete. We must rely on forecasts of future problems.

  (b) *Design problems.* We don't know exactly how the economy will respond to specific policies.

  (c) *Implementation problems.* It takes time for Congress and the president to agree on an appropriate plan of action. Moreover, the agreements reached may respond more to political needs than to economic needs.

  For all these reasons, fine-tuning of economic performance rarely lives up to its theoretical potential. **LO4**

- Many people favor rules rather than discretionary macro policies. They argue that discretionary policies are unlikely to work and risk being wrong. Critics respond that discretionary policies are needed to cope with ever-changing economic circumstances. **LO5**

TERMS TO REMEMBER

Define the following terms:

business cycle	monetary policy	GDP gap	structural
fiscal policy	money supply (M1)	multiplier	unemployment
automatic stabilizer	supply-side policy	stagflation	fine-tuning
fiscal year (FY)			

QUESTIONS FOR DISCUSSION

1. What policies would Keynesian, monetarists, and supply-siders advocate for **LO2**
   (a) Restraining inflation?
   (b) Reducing unemployment?

2. Suppose it is an election year and aggregate demand is growing so fast that it threatens to set off an inflationary movement. Why might Congress and the president hesitate to cut back on government spending or raise taxes, as economic theory suggests is appropriate? **LO4**

3. Should military spending be subject to macroeconomic constraints? What programs should be expanded or contracted to bring about needed changes in the budget? **LO4**

4. Why does it take so long to recognize that a recession has begun (News Wire, p. 333)? **LO4**

5. Republicans asserted that many of President Obama's fiscal spending projects were "wasteful and ineffective." Does the *content* of fiscal stimulus spending matter? **LO4**

6. Outline a macro policy package for attaining full employment and price stability in the next 12 months. What obstacles, if any, will impede attainment of these goals? **LO2**

7. Which nation had the best macro performance in 2000–2010 (News Wire, p. 331)? **LO3**

8. In the News Wire on page 337, why didn't anyone "blink"? Who should have?

9. **POLICY PERSPECTIVES** Should economic policies respond immediately to any changes in reported unemployment or inflation rates? When should a response be undertaken? **LO5**

PROBLEMS   ▓ connect

1. The 2008 fiscal policy package included roughly $100 billion in tax rebates that were mailed to taxpayers. By how much would aggregate demand shift (a) initially and (b) ultimately as a result of these rebates? **LO2**

2. Suppose the federal budget is balanced but automatic stabilizers increase tax revenues by $80 billion per year and decrease transfer payments (e.g., welfare, unemployment benefits) by $20 billion per year for every 1 percentage point change in the real GDP growth. Using this information, complete the following table: **LO4**

Change in GDP Growth Rate	Change in Tax Revenue	Change in Transfer Payments	Change in Budget Balance
−2%			
+1%			
+3%			

3. If automatic stabilizers change the federal budget balance by $70 billion for every 1 percent change in real GDP growth, what will happen to the federal budget balance if the economy falls into a recession of −3 percent from a growth path of +2 percent? **LO4**

4. The following table presents hypothetical data on government expenditure, taxes, inflation, unemployment, and pollution for three levels of equilibrium income (GDP). A government decision maker is trying to determine the optimal level of government expenditures, with each of the three columns being a possible choice. **LO4**

	Nominal GDP (Billions)		
	A: $8,000	B: $9,000	C: $10,000
Government expenditure	$700	$800	$900
Taxes	$600	$800	$1,000
Inflation (index)	1.00	1.04	1.15
Unemployment rate	10%	4%	3.5%
Pollution index	1.00	1.80	2.00

   (a) Compute the federal budget balance for each level of nominal GDP.
   (b) What government expenditure level would best accomplish each of the following goals?
   Lowest taxes
   Lowest pollution
   Lowest inflation rate
   Lowest unemployment rate
   A balanced federal budget

5. **POLICY PERSPECTIVES**   Monetary stimulus in the
form of lower interest rates is an alternative to
fiscal stimulus. If a 0.1 point change in interest
rates has the stimulus impact of $10 billion in
spending, what is the monetary equivalent of a
$800 billion spending stimulus?   **LO2**

◄ Practice quizzes, student PowerPoints, author podcasts, web activities, and additional materials available at
www.mhhe.com/schilleressentials9e, or scan here. Need a barcode reader? Try ScanLife, available in your
app store.

17

International Trade

◄ Practice quizzes, student PowerPoints, author podcasts, web activities, and additional materials available at www.mhhe.com/ schilleressentials9e, or scan here. Need a barcode reader? Try ScanLife, available in your app store.

LEARNING OBJECTIVES

After reading this chapter, you should be able to:

1 Summarize U.S. trade patterns.
2 Explain how trade increases total output.
3 Tell how the terms of trade are established.
4 Discuss how trade barriers affect market outcomes.
5 Describe how currency exchange rates affect trade flows.

Worg ld travelers have discovered that Big Macs taste pretty much the same everywhere, but a Big Mac's price can vary tremendously. In 2012 a Big Mac was priced at 22,534 rupiah at the McDonald's in Jakarta, Indonesia. That sounds really expensive! The same Big Mac cost only 3.49 euros in Rome, 78 baht in Bangkok, and 15.4 yuan in Beijing. But what do all these foreign prices mean in American dollars? If you want a Big Mac in a foreign country, you need to figure out foreign prices.

Similar problems affect even consumers who stay at home. In 2012 American kids were clamoring for Nintendo's Wii game consoles produced in Japan. But how much would they have to pay? In Japan the machines were selling for 20,000 yen. What did that translate into in American dollars? In the same year American steel, textile, and lumber companies were complaining that Chinese producers were selling their products too cheaply. They wanted the government to protect them from unfair foreign competition. President Obama promised to help, seeking ways to *double* U.S. exports within five years, creating millions of American jobs in the process.

Why does life have to be so complicated? Why doesn't everyone just use American dollars? For that matter, why can't each nation simply produce for its own consumption so we don't have to worry about foreign competition?

This chapter takes a bird's-eye view of how America interacts with the rest of the world. Of particular interest are the following questions:

- Why do we trade so much?
- Who benefits and who loses from imports, exports, and changes in the value of the dollar?
- How is the international value of the dollar established?

As we'll see, international trade *does* diminish the job and income opportunities for specific industries and workers. But those individual losses are overwhelmed by the gains the average consumer gets from international trade.

U.S. TRADE PATTERNS

To understand how international trade affects our standard of living, it's useful to have a sense of *how much* we actually trade.

Imports

Baseball is often called the all-American sport. But the balls used in professional baseball are made in Costa Rica. The same is true of coffee. Only a tiny fraction of the beans used to brew American coffee are grown in the United States (in Hawaii). All our Wii machines and Apple iPhones are also produced abroad. The fact is that many of the products we consume are produced primarily or exclusively in other nations. All these products are part of America's **imports.**

imports Goods and services purchased from foreign sources.

All told, America imports nearly $3 trillion worth of products from the rest of the world. Most of these products are *goods* like coffee, baseballs, and steel. The rest of the imports are *services*, like travel (on Air France or Aero Mexico), insurance (Lloyds of London), or entertainment (foreign movies). Together our imports account for about 14 percent of U.S. GDP.

Exports

While we are buying baseballs, coffee, video game machines, and oil from the rest of the world, foreigners are buying our **exports.** In 2012 we exported over $1.5 trillion of *goods*, including farm products (wheat, corn, soybeans, tobacco), machinery (computers, aircraft, automobiles, and auto parts), and raw materials (lumber, iron ore, and chemicals). We also exported over $600 billion of *services* such as tourism, insurance, and software.

exports Goods and services sold to foreign buyers.

NEWS WIRE | EXPORT RATIOS

Exports in Relation to GDP

Exports of goods and services account for 14 percent of total U.S. output. This export ratio is very low by international standards. China, for example, exports one-third of its total output, while Belgium exports nearly 90 percent of its annual production (especially diamonds and chocolates). Myanmar, by contrast, is virtually a closed economy.

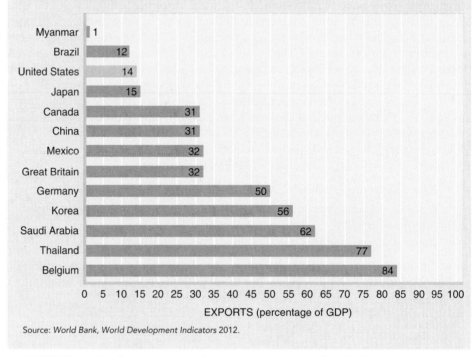

Source: *World Bank, World Development Indicators 2012.*

NOTE: The ratio of exports to total output is a measure of trade dependence. Most countries are much more dependent on trade than is the United States.

As with our imports, our exports represent a relatively modest fraction of total GDP. Whereas we export 12–14 percent of total output, other developed countries export as much as 25–45 percent of their output (see the accompanying News Wire). Saudi Arabia, for example, is considered a relatively prosperous nation, with a GDP per capita twice that of the world average. But how prosperous would it be if no one bought the oil exports that now account for more than half of its output?

Even though the United States has a low export ratio, many American industries depend on export sales. We export 25 to 50 percent of our rice, corn, and wheat production each year and still more of our soybeans. Clearly a decision by foreigners to stop eating American agricultural products would devastate a lot of American farmers. Companies such as Boeing (planes), Caterpillar Tractor (construction and farm machinery), Weyerhaeuser (logs, lumber), Eastman Kodak (cameras), Dow (chemicals), and Sun Microsystems (computer workstations) sell over one-fourth of their output in foreign markets. Pepsi and Coke are battling it out in the soft drink markets of such unlikely places as Egypt, Abu Dhabi, Burundi, and Kazakhstan.

Product Category	Exports	(In Billions of Dollars) Imports	Surplus (Deficit)
Goods	$1,564	$2,299	$ (735)
Services	630	435	195
Total trade	$2,194	$2,734	$(540)

Source: U.S. Department of Commerce.

TABLE 17.1
Trade Balances
Both merchandise (goods) and services are traded between countries. The United States typically has a merchandise *deficit* and a services *surplus*. When combined, an overall trade deficit remained in 2012.

Trade Balances

As the figures indicate, our imports and exports were not equal in 2012. Quite the contrary: we had a large imbalance in our trade flows, with many more imports than exports. The trade balance is computed simply as the difference between exports and imports:

$$\text{Trade balance} = \text{exports} - \text{imports}$$

During 2012 we imported more than we exported and so had a negative trade balance. A negative trade balance is called a **trade deficit.** In 2012 the United States had a negative trade balance of $540 billion. As Table 17.1 shows, this overall trade deficit reflected divergent patterns in goods and services. The United States had a large deficit in *merchandise* trade, mostly due to auto and oil imports. In *services* (e.g., travel, finance, consulting), however, the United States enjoyed a modest surplus. When the merchandise and services accounts are combined, the United States ends up with a trade deficit.

If the United States has a trade deficit with the rest of the world, then other countries must have an offsetting **trade surplus.** On a global scale, imports must equal exports, since every good exported by one country must be imported by another. Hence *any imbalance in America's trade must be offset by reverse imbalances elsewhere.*

Whatever the overall balance in our trade accounts, bilateral balances vary greatly. For example, our trade deficit incorporated a huge bilateral trade deficit with China and also large deficits with Mexico, Germany, and Japan. As Table 17.2 shows, however, we had trade surpluses with Australia, the Netherlands, Hong Kong, and the United Arab Emirates.

trade deficit The amount by which the value of imports exceeds the value of exports in a given time period.

trade surplus The amount by which the value of exports exceeds the value of imports in a given time period.

Country	Trade Balance (Billions of Dollars)
Top deficit countries	
China	−315
Japan	−76
Mexico	−61
Germany	−60
Saudi Arabia	−38
Top surplus countries	
Hong Kong	+32
Australia	+22
United Arab Emirates	+20
Netherlands	+18
Belgium	+12

Source: U.S. Department of Commerce (2012 data).

TABLE 17.2
Bilateral Trade Balances
The U.S. trade deficit in 2012 was the net result of bilateral deficits and surpluses. We had a huge trade deficit with China but small trade surpluses with the Netherlands, Australia, and Hong Kong. International trade is *multi*national, with surpluses in some countries being offset by trade deficits elsewhere.

MOTIVATION TO TRADE

Many people wonder why we trade so much, particularly since (1) we import many of the things we also export (e.g., computers, airplanes, clothes), (2) we *could* produce many of the other things we import, and (3) we seem to worry so much about imports and trade deficits. Why not just import those few things that we cannot produce ourselves and export just enough to balance that trade?

Although it might seem strange to be importing goods we could produce ourselves, such trade is entirely rational. Indeed, our decision to trade with other countries arises from the same considerations that motivate individuals to specialize in production. Why don't you grow your own food, build your own shelter, and record your own songs? Presumably because you have found that you can enjoy a much higher standard of living (and better music) by working at just one job and then buying other goods in the marketplace. When you do so, you're no longer self-sufficient. Instead you are *specializing* in production, relying on others to produce the array of goods and services you want. When countries trade goods and services, they are doing the same thing—*specializing* in production and then *trading* for other desired goods. Why do they do this? Because *specialization increases total output.*

To demonstrate the economic gains from international trade, we examine the production possibilities of two countries. We want to demonstrate that two countries that trade can together produce *more* total output than they could in the absence of trade. If they can produce more, *the gain from trade will be increased world output and thus a higher standard of living in both countries.*

Production and Consumption without Trade

Consider the production possibilities of just two countries—say, the United States and France. For the sake of illustration, we assume that both countries produce only two goods, bread and wine. To keep things simple, we also transform the familiar **production possibilities** curve into a straight line, as shown in Figure 17.1.

The curves in Figure 17.1 suggest that the United States is capable of producing much more bread than France is. After all, we have a greater abundance of land, labor, and other factors of production. With these resources, we assume the United States is capable of producing up to 100 zillion loaves of bread per year if we devote *all* of our resources to that purpose. This capability is indicated by point *A* in Figure 17.1*a* and row *A* in the accompanying production possibilities schedule. France (Figure 17.1*b*), on the other hand, confronts a *maximum* bread production of only 15 zillion loaves per year (point *G*) because it has little available land, less fuel, and fewer potential workers.

The assumed capacities for wine production are also illustrated in Figure 17.1. The United States can produce *at most* 50 zillion barrels (point *F*), while France can produce a maximum of 60 zillion (point *L*), reflecting France's greater experience in tending vines. Both countries are also capable of producing alternative *combinations* of bread and wine, as evidenced by their respective production possibilities curves (points *B–E* for the United States and *H–K* for France).

We have seen production possibilities curves (PPCs) before. We are looking at them again to emphasize that

- The production possibilities curve defines the limits to what a country can produce.
- *In the absence of trade, a country cannot consume more than it produces.*

Accordingly, a production possibilities curve also defines the **consumption possibilities** for a country that does not engage in international trade. Like a truly

production possibilities The alternative combinations of goods and services that could be produced in a given time period with all available resources and technology.

consumption possibilities The alternative combinations of goods and services that a country could consume in a given time period.

FIGURE 17.1   Consumption Possibilities Without Trade

In the absence of trade, a country's *consumption* possibilities are identical to its *production* possibilities. The assumed production possibilities of the United States and France are illustrated in the graphs and the corresponding schedules. Before entering into trade, the United States chose to produce and consume at point *D*, with 40 zillion loaves of bread and 30 zillion barrels of wine. France chose point *I* on its own production possibilities curve. By trading, each country hopes to increase its consumption beyond these levels.

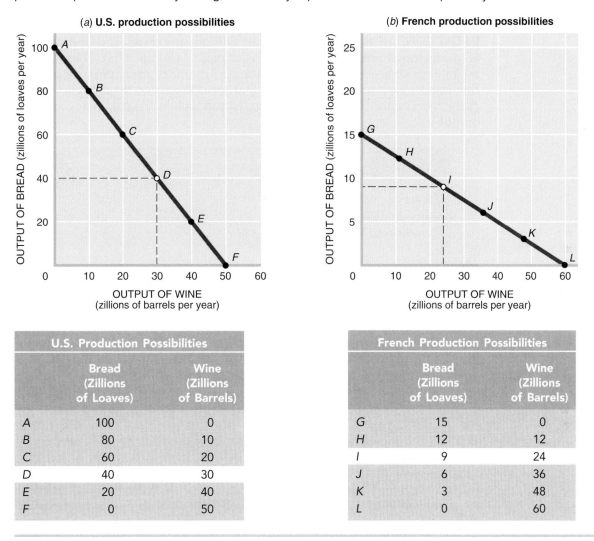

(a) **U.S. production possibilities**

(b) **French production possibilities**

U.S. Production Possibilities		
	Bread (Zillions of Loaves)	Wine (Zillions of Barrels)
A	100	0
B	80	10
C	60	20
D	40	30
E	20	40
F	0	50

French Production Possibilities		
	Bread (Zillions of Loaves)	Wine (Zillions of Barrels)
G	15	0
H	12	12
I	9	24
J	6	36
K	3	48
L	0	60

self-sufficient person, a nation that doesn't trade can consume only the goods and services it produces. If the United States closed its trading windows and produced the mix of output at point *D* in Figure 17.1, that is the combination of wine and bread we would have to consume. If a self-sufficient France produced at point *I*, that is the mix of output it would have to consume.

International trade opens new options. ***International trade breaks the link between production possibilities and consumption possibilities.*** Nations no longer have to consume exactly what they produce. Instead they can *export* some goods and *import* others. This will change the mix of goods *consumed* even if the mix *produced* stays the same.

Now here's the real surprise. When nations specialize in production, not only does the *mix* of consumption change—the *quantity* of consumption *increases* as well.

Both countries end up consuming *more* output by trading than by being self-suffi-cient. In other words,

- *With trade, a country's consumption possibilities exceed its production possibilities.*

To see how this startling outcome emerges, we'll examine how countries operate without trade and then with trade.

INITIAL CONDITIONS   Assume we start without any trade. The United States is producing at point *D*, and France is at point *I* (Figure 17.1). These output mixes have no special significance; they are just one of many possible produc-tion choices each nation could make. Our focus here is on the *combined* output of the two countries. Given their assumed production choices, their combined output is

	Bread Output (Zillions of Loaves)	Wine Output (Zillions of Barrels)
U.S. (at point *D*)	40	30
France (at point *I*)	9	24
World total	**49**	**54**

Trade Increases Specialization and World Output

Now comes the tricky part. We increase total (combined) output of these two countries by trading.

At first blush, increasing total output might seem like an impossible task. Both countries, after all, are already fully using their limited production possi-bilities. But look at the U.S. PPC. Suppose the United States were to produce at point *C* rather than point *D* in Figure 17.1*a*. At point *C* we could produce 60 zillion loaves of bread and 20 zillion barrels of wine. That combination is clearly possible since it lies on the U.S. production possibilities curve. We didn't start at point *C* earlier because consumers preferred the output mix at point *D*. *Now*, however, we can use trade to break the link between production and consumption.

Suppose the French also change their mix of output. The French earlier pro-duced at point *I*. Now we will move them to point *K*, where they can produce 48 zillion barrels of wine and 3 zillion loaves of bread. France might not want to consume this mix of output, but it clearly can produce it.

Now consider the consequences of these changes in each nation's *production* for combined (total) output. Like magic, total output of both goods has in-creased. This is illustrated in Table 17.3. Both the old (pretrade) and new output mixes in each country are shown, along with their combined totals. The com-

TABLE 17.3
Gains from Specialization

The combined total output of two countries can increase by simply altering the mix of output in each country. Here world output increases by 14 zillion loaves of bread and 14 zillion barrels of wine when nations specialize in production.

	Pretrade Mix of Output		New Mix of Output	
	Bread	Wine	Bread	Wine
United States	40	30	60	20
	(point *D*)		(point *C*)	
France	9	24	3	48
	(point *I*)		(point *K*)	
World total	49	54	63	68
World gain			**+14**	**+14**

bined output of bread has increased from 49 to 63 zillion loaves. And combined output of wine has increased from 54 to 68 zillion barrels. Just by changing the mix of output produced in each country, we have increased *total* world output. Nice trick, isn't it?

The reason the United States and France weren't producing at points C and K before is that they simply didn't want to *consume* those particular combinations of output. The United States wanted a slightly more liquid combination than point C, and the French could not survive long at point K. Hence they chose points D and I. Nevertheless, our discovery that points C and K result in greater *total* output suggests that everybody can be happier if we all cooperate. The obvious thing to do is to *specialize* in production and then start exchanging wine for bread in international trade. In this case the United States specialized in bread production when it moved from point D to point C. France specialized in wine production when it moved from point I to point K.

The increase in the combined output of both countries is the gain from trading. In this case the net gain is 14 zillion loaves of bread and 14 zillion barrels of wine (Table 17.3). By trading, the United States and France can divide up this increase in output and end up consuming *more* goods than they did before.

There is no sleight of hand going on here. Rather, ***the gains from trade are due to specialization in production.*** When each country goes it alone, it is a prisoner of its own production possibilities curve; it must make its production decisions on the basis of its own consumption desires. When international trade is permitted, however, each country can concentrate on those goods it makes best. Then the countries trade with each other to acquire the goods they desire to consume.

COMPARATIVE ADVANTAGE

By now it should be apparent that international trade *can* generate increased output. But how do we get from here to there? Which products should countries specialize in? How much should they trade?

Opportunity Costs

In the previous example, the United States specialized in bread production and France specialized in wine production. This wasn't an arbitrary decision. Rather, those decisions were based on the relative costs of producing both products in each nation. Bread production was relatively cheap in the United States but expensive in France. Wine production was more costly in the United States but relatively cheap in France.

How did we reach such conclusions? There is nothing in Figure 17.1 that reveals actual production costs, as measured in dollars or euros. That doesn't matter, however, because economists measure costs not in *dollars* but in terms of *goods* given up.

Reexamine America's PPC (Figure 17.1) from this basic economic perspective. Notice again that the United States can produce a maximum of 100 zillion loaves of bread. To do so, however, we must sacrifice the opportunity of producing 50 zillion barrels of wine. Hence the true cost—the **opportunity cost**—of 100 zillion bread loaves is 50 zillion barrels of wine. In other words, we're paying half a barrel of wine for every loaf of bread.

Although the opportunity costs of bread production in the United States might appear outrageous, note the even higher opportunity costs that prevail in France. According to Figure 17.1b, the opportunity cost of producing a loaf of bread in France is a staggering four barrels of wine. To produce a loaf of bread, the French must use factors of production that could have been used to produce four barrels of wine.

opportunity cost The most desired goods or services that are forgone in order to obtain something else.

comparative advantage The ability of a country to produce a specific good at a lower opportunity cost than its trading partners.

A comparison of the opportunity costs prevailing in each country exposes the nature of what we call **comparative advantage.** The United States has a *comparative* advantage in bread production because less wine has to be given up to produce bread in the United States than in France. In other words, the opportunity costs of bread production are lower in the United States than in France. *Comparative advantage refers to the relative (opportunity) costs of producing particular goods.*

A country should specialize in what it is *relatively* efficient at producing—that is, goods for which it has the lowest opportunity costs. In this case, the United States should produce bread because its opportunity cost (a half barrel of wine) is less than France's (four barrels of wine). Were you the production manager for the whole world, you would certainly want each country to exploit its relative abilities, thus maximizing world output. Each country can arrive at that same decision itself by comparing its own opportunity costs to those prevailing elsewhere. *World output, and thus the potential gains from trade, will be maximized when each country pursues its comparative advantage.* It does so by exporting goods that entail low domestic opportunity costs and importing goods that involve higher domestic opportunity costs.

Absolute Costs Don't Count

In assessing the nature of comparative advantage, notice that we needn't know anything about the actual costs involved in production. Have you seen any data suggesting how much labor, land, or capital is required to produce a loaf of bread in either France or the United States? For all you and I know, the French may be able to produce both goods with fewer resources than we are using. Such an **absolute advantage** in production might exist because of their much longer experience in cultivating both grapes and wheat or simply because they have more talent.

absolute advantage The ability of a country to produce a specific good with fewer resources (per unit of output) than other countries.

We can envy such productivity, but it should not alter our production and trade decisions. *All we really care about are opportunity costs—what we have to give up in order to get more of a desired good.* If we can get a barrel of imported wine for less bread than we have to give up to produce that wine ourselves, we should *import* it, not *produce* it. In other words, as long as we have a *comparative* advantage in bread production, we should exploit it. It doesn't matter to us whether France uses a lot of resources or very few to produce the wine. The absolute costs of production were omitted from the previous illustration because they are irrelevant.

To clarify the distinction between absolute advantage and comparative advantage, consider this example. When Charlie Osgood joined the Willamette Warriors' football team, he was the fastest runner ever to play football in Willamette. He could also throw the ball farther than most people could see. In other words, he had an *absolute advantage* in both throwing and running. Charlie would have made the greatest quarterback *or* the greatest end ever to play football. *Would have.* The problem was that he could play only one position at a time. Thus the Willamette coach had to play Charlie either as a quarterback or as an end. He reasoned that Charlie could throw only a bit farther than some of the other top quarterbacks but could far outdistance all the other ends. In other words, Charlie had a *comparative advantage* in running and was assigned to play as an end.

TERMS OF TRADE

The principle of comparative advantage tells nations how to specialize in production. As we saw, the United States specialized in bread production, and France specialized in wine. We haven't yet determined, however, how much output each country should *trade*. How much bread should the United States export? How much wine should it expect to get in return? Is there any way to determine the **terms of trade,** the quantity of good *A* that must be given up in exchange for good *B*?

terms of trade The rate at which goods are exchanged; the amount of good *A* given up for good *B* in trade.

Limits to the Terms of Trade

Our first clue to the terms of trade lies in each country's domestic opportunity costs. *A country will not trade unless the terms of trade are superior to domestic opportunity costs.* In our example, the opportunity cost of a barrel of wine in the United States is two loaves of bread. Accordingly, we will not export bread unless we get at least one barrel of wine in exchange for every two loaves of bread we ship overseas. In other words, we will not play the game unless the terms of trade are superior to our own opportunity costs. Otherwise we get no benefit.

No country will trade unless the terms of exchange are better than its domestic opportunity costs. Hence we can predict that *the terms of trade between any two countries will lie somewhere between their respective opportunity costs in production.* That is to say, a loaf of bread in international trade will be worth at least a half-barrel of wine (the U.S. opportunity cost) but no more than four barrels (the French opportunity cost).

The Market Mechanism

Exactly where the terms of trade end up in the range of 0.5–4.0 barrels of wine per loaf of bread will depend on how market participants behave. Suppose that Henri, an enterprising Frenchman, visited the United States before the advent of international trade. He noticed that bread was relatively cheap, while wine was relatively expensive, the opposite of the price relationship prevailing in France. These price comparisons brought to his mind the opportunity for making an easy euro. All he had to do was bring over some French wine and trade it in the United States for a large quantity of bread. Then he could return to France and exchange the bread for a greater quantity of wine. Were he to do this a few times, he would amass substantial profits.

Our French entrepreneur's exploits will not only enrich him but will also move each country toward its comparative advantage. The United States ends up exporting bread to France, and France ends up exporting wine to the United States. The activating agent is not the Ministry of Trade and its 620 trained economists, however, but simply one enterprising French trader. He is aided and encouraged by the consumers and producers in each country. American consumers are happy to trade their bread for his wines. They thereby end up paying less for wine (in terms of bread) than they would otherwise have to. In other words, the terms of trade Henri offers are more attractive than prevailing (domestic) relative prices. On the other side of the Atlantic, Henri's welcome is equally warm. French consumers get a better deal by trading their wine for his imported bread than by trading with the local bakers.

Even some producers are happy. The wheat farmers and bakers in America are eager to deal with Henri. He is willing to buy a lot of bread and even to pay a premium price for it. Indeed, bread production has become so profitable that a lot of farmers who used to cultivate grapes are now starting to grow wheat. This alters the mix of U.S. output in the direction of more bread, exactly as suggested earlier in Figure 17.1.

In France the opposite kind of production shift is taking place. French wheat farmers start to plant grapes so they can take advantage of Henri's generous purchases. Thus Henri is able to lead each country in the direction of its comparative advantage—raking in a substantial profit for himself along the way.

Where the terms of trade end up depends in part on how good a trader Henri is. It will also depend on the behavior of the thousands of consumers and producers who participate in the market exchanges. In other words, trade flows depend on both the supply of and the demand for bread and wine in each country. ***The terms of trade, like the price of any good, will depend on the willingness of market participants to buy or sell at various prices.*** All we know for sure is that the terms of trade will end up somewhere between the limits set by each country's opportunity costs.

PROTECTIONIST PRESSURES

Although the potential gains from world trade are impressive, not everyone will be smiling at the Franco-American trade celebration. On the contrary, some people will be upset about the trade routes that Henri has established. They will seek to discourage us from continuing to trade with France.

Microeconomic Losers

Consider, for example, the wine growers in western New York State. Do you think they are going to be happy about Henri's entrepreneurship? Americans can now buy wine more cheaply from France than they can from New York. Before long we may hear talk about unfair foreign competition or about the greater nutritional value of American grapes (see the accompanying News Wire). The New York wine growers may also emphasize the importance of maintaining an adequate grape supply and a strong wine industry at home.

Joining with the growers will be the farmworkers and all the other workers, producers, and merchants whose livelihood depends on the New York wine industry. If they are aggressive and clever enough, the growers will also get the governor of the state to join their demonstration. After all, the governor must recognize the needs of his people, and his people definitely don't include the

---

NEWS WIRE	IMPORT COMPETITION

California Grape Growers Protest Mixing Foreign Wine
California wine grape growers are growing increasingly frustrated and angry at each market percentage point gain of foreign wine in the U.S. wine market.

By the end of the year, burgeoning wine imports are expected to account for 30 percent of the U.S. market.

As the overall wine market in the U.S. grows at a healthy 2 percent to 5 percent annual clip, California grape growers continue to rip out vineyards. More than 100,000 acres in the Central Valley have been destroyed in the past five years. Growers are beyond weary of prices offered less than production costs. . . .

Rubbing salt into the open economic sore this season includes record bulk, inexpensive wine imports that are being blended with California wines and sold by California wineries as "American" appellation wine. . . .

"California grape growers made a significant investment in wine grape vineyards on the signals from wineries that there was a bright future in California wine." Those same growers are seeing at least some of that bright future being taken by imports.

—Harry Cline

Source: WesternFarmPress.com, December 6, 2006. Used with permission of Penton Media, Inc.

NOTE: Imports reduce sales, jobs, profits, and wages in import-competing industries. This is the source of micro resistance to international trade.

wheat farmers in Kansas who are making a bundle from international trade. New York consumers are, of course, benefiting from lower wine prices, but they are unlikely to demonstrate over a few cents a bottle. On the other hand, those few extra pennies translate into millions of dollars for domestic wine producers.

The wheat farmers in France are no happier about international trade. They would love to sink all those boats bringing wheat from America, thereby protecting their own market position.

If we are to make sense of international trade policies, we must recognize one central fact of life: some producers have a vested interest in restricting international trade. In particular, ***workers and producers who compete with imported products—who work in import-competing industries—have an economic interest in restricting trade.*** This helps to explain why GM, Ford, and Chrysler are unhappy about auto imports and why workers in Massachusetts want to end the importation of Italian shoes. It also explains why the textile producers in South Carolina think China is behaving irresponsibly when it sells cotton shirts and dresses in the United States. Complaints of other losers from trade appear in the accompanying News Wire.

Although imports typically mean fewer jobs and less income for some domestic industries, exports represent increased jobs and incomes for other industries. Producers and workers in export industries gain from trade. Thus on a microeconomic

NEWS WIRE	TRADE RESISTANCE

A Litany of Losers

Some excerpts from congressional hearings on trade:

In the past few years, sales of imported table wines . . . have soared at an alarming rate. . . . Unless this trend is halted immediately, the domestic wine industry will face economic ruin. . . . Foreign wine imports must be limited.

—Wine Institute

The apparel industry's workers have few other alternative job opportunities. They do want to work and earn a living at their work. Little wonder therefore that they want their jobs safeguarded against the erosion caused by the increasing penetration of apparel imports.

—International Ladies' Garment Workers' Union

We are never going to strengthen the dollar, cure our balance of payments problem, lick our high unemployment, eliminate an ever-worsening inflation, as long as the U.S. sits idly by as a dumping ground for shoes, TV sets, apparel, steel and automobiles, etc. It is about time that we told the Japanese, the Spanish, the Italians, the Brazilians, and the Argentinians, and others who insist on flooding our country with imported shoes that enough is enough.

—United Shoe Workers of America

We want to be friends with Mexico and Canada. . . . We would like to be put in the same ball game with them. . . . We are not trying to hinder foreign trade . . . (but) plants in Texas go out of business (17 in the last 7 years) because of the continued threat of fly-by-night creek bed, river bank Mexican brick operations implemented overnight.

—Brick Institute of America

Trade policy should not be an absolute statement of how the world ought to behave to achieve a textbook vision of "free trade" or "maximum efficiency." It should . . . attempt to achieve the best results for Americans.

—United Auto Workers

NOTE: Workers and owners in import-competing industries always depict imports as a threat to the American way of life. In reality, trade raises American living standards.

level, there are identifiable gainers and losers from international trade. *Trade not only alters the mix of output but also redistributes income from import-competing industries to export industries.* This potential redistribution is the source of political and economic friction.

The Net Gain

We must be careful to note, however, that the microeconomic gains from trade are greater than the microeconomic losses. It's not simply a question of robbing Peter to enrich Paul. On the contrary, consumers in general enjoy a higher standard of living as a result of international trade. As we saw earlier, trade increases world efficiency and total output. Accordingly, we end up slicing up a larger pie rather than just reslicing the same smaller pie.

BARRIERS TO TRADE

The microeconomic losses associated with imports give rise to a constant clamor for trade restrictions. People whose jobs and incomes are threatened by international trade tend to organize quickly and air their grievances. Moreover, they are assured of a reasonably receptive hearing, both because of the political implications of well-financed organizations and because the gains from trade are widely diffused. If successful, such efforts can lead to a variety of trade restrictions.

Tariffs

tariff A tax (duty) imposed on imported goods.

One of the most popular and visible restrictions on trade is a **tariff,** a special tax imposed on imported goods. Tariffs, also called *customs duties,* were once the principal source of revenue for governments. In the eighteenth century, tariffs on tea, glass, wine, lead, and paper were imposed on the American colonies to provide extra revenue for the British government. The tariff on tea led to the Boston Tea Party in 1773 and gave added momentum to the American independence movement. In modern times, tariffs have been used primarily as a means of import protection to satisfy specific microeconomic or macroeconomic interests. The current U.S. tariff code specifies tariffs on over 9,000 different products—nearly 50 percent of all U.S. imports. Although the average tariff is only 3 percent, individual tariffs vary widely. The tariff on cars, for example, is only 2.5 percent, while wool sweaters confront a 17 percent tariff.

The attraction of tariffs to import-competing industries should be obvious. *A tariff on imported goods makes them more expensive to domestic consumers, and thus less competitive with domestically produced goods.* Among familiar tariffs in effect in 2013 were $0.20 per gallon on Scotch whiskey and $0.76 per gallon on imported champagne. These tariffs made American-produced spirits look like relatively good buys and thus contributed to higher sales and profits for domestic distillers and grape growers. In the same manner, imported baby food is taxed at 34.6 percent, imported footwear at 20 percent, and imported stereos at rates ranging from 4 to 6 percent. In 2009 President Obama imposed a 35 percent tariff on imported Chinese tires, and in 2012 he set a 31 percent tariff on Chinese solar panels (see News Wire). In each of these cases, domestic producers in import-competing industries gain. The losers are domestic consumers, who end up paying higher prices; foreign producers, who lose business; and world efficiency, as trade is reduced.

Quotas

quota A limit on the quantity of a good that may be imported in a given time period.

Tariffs reduce the flow of imports by raising import prices. As an alternative barrier to trade, a country can impose import **quotas,** numerical restrictions on the quantity of a particular good that may be imported. The United States maintains

NEWS WIRE	TARIFF PROTECTION

U.S. Slaps Tariffs on Chinese Panels. Is This the End of Cheap Solar?

Over the past few years, the price of solar power in the United States has been dropping at a dramatic pace. Part of the reason for the drop: China has been flooding the U.S. market with dirt-cheap solar panels. But that's all about to change. . . .

On Thursday the Commerce Department ruled that China's solar manufacturers are engaged in "dumping"—that is, they're selling their panels for below-market rates in order to drive their competitors out of business. In response, the Commerce Department has slapped a 31 percent tariff on imports of silicon photovoltaic cells from many major Chinese manufacturers. . . .

Domestic manufacturers of solar panels—such as Solar World—say that they're being stomped out of business by Chinese competitors who are unfairly subsidized by the government. But companies that *install* solar panels, represented by the Coalition for Affordable Solar Energy, oppose import tariffs on the grounds that they make solar panels more expensive.

"The decision will increase solar electricity prices in the U.S. precisely at the moment solar power is becoming competitive with fossil fuel–generated electricity," said Jigar Shah, president of CASE, in a statement.

—Brad Plumer

Source: *The Washington Post*, May 17, 2012. © 2012 Washington Post Company. All rights reserved.

NOTE: Tariffs protect *some* domestic manufacturers but hurt other domestic producers, foreign manufacturers, and domestic consumers.

---

import quotas on sugar, meat, dairy products, textiles, cotton, peanuts, steel, cloth diapers, and even ice cream. According to the U.S. Department of State, approximately 12 percent of our imports are subject to import quotas.

Quotas, like all barriers to trade, reduce world efficiency and invite retaliatory action. Moreover, quotas are especially harmful because of their impact on competition and prices. Figure 17.2 shows how this works.

Figure 17.2*a* depicts the supply-and-demand relationships that would prevail in a closed (no-trade) economy. In this situation, the **equilibrium price** of textiles is completely determined by domestic demand and supply curves. The equilibrium price is p_1, and the quantity of textiles consumed is q_1.

Suppose now that trade begins and foreign producers are allowed to sell textiles in the American market. The immediate effect of this decision will be a rightward shift of the market supply curve as foreign supplies are added to domestic supplies (Figure 17.2*b*). If an unlimited quantity of textiles can be bought in world markets at a price of p_2, the new supply curve will look like S_2 (infinitely elastic at p_2). The new supply curve (S_2) intersects the old demand curve (D_1) at a new equilibrium price of p_2 and an expanded consumption of q_2. At this new equilibrium, domestic producers are supplying the quantity q_d, while foreign producers are supplying the rest ($q_2 - q_d$). Comparing the new equilibrium to the old one, we see that *trade results in reduced prices and increased consumption.*

Domestic textile producers are unhappy, of course, with their foreign competition. In the absence of trade, the domestic producers would sell more output (q_1) and get higher prices (p_1). Once trade is opened up, the willingness of foreign producers to sell unlimited quantities of textiles at the price p_2 puts a limit on the price behavior of domestic producers. Accordingly, we can anticipate some lobbying for trade restrictions.

equilibrium price The price at which the quantity of a good demanded in a given time period equals the quantity supplied.

FIGURE 17.2
The Impact of Trade Restrictions

In the *absence of trade,* the domestic price and sales of a good will be determined by domestic supply and demand curves (point A in part a). Once trade is permitted, the market supply curve will be altered by the availability of imports. With *free trade* and unlimited availability of imports at price p_2, a new market equilibrium will be established at world prices (point B in part b). At that equilibrium, domestic *consumption* is higher (q_2) but *production* is lower (q_d).

Tariffs raise domestic prices and reduce the quantity sold. In graph (c) a tariff that increases the import price from p_2 to p_3 reduces imports and increases domestic sales (from q_2 to q_t) and price.

Quotas put an absolute limit on imported sales and thus give domestic producers a great opportunity to raise the market price. In graph (d), the quota Q limits how far market supply can shift to the right, pushing the price up from P_2 to P_4.

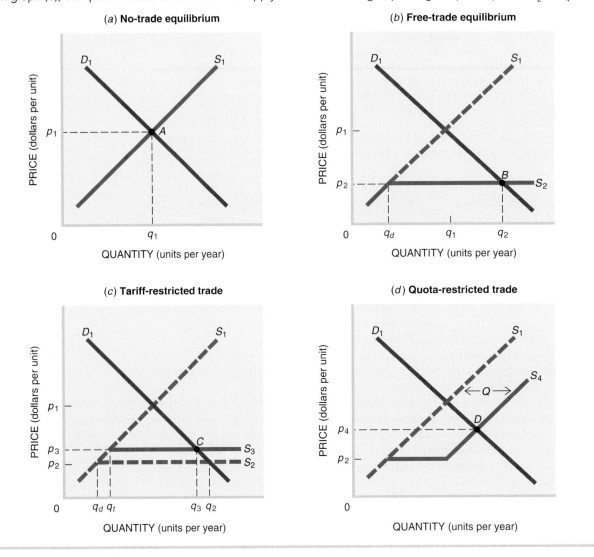

TARIFF EFFECTS Figure 17.2c illustrates what would happen to prices and sales if the United Textile Producers were successful in persuading the government to impose a tariff. Assume the tariff raises imported textile prices from p_2 to p_3. The higher price p_3 makes it more difficult for foreign producers to undersell domestic producers. Domestic production expands from q_d to q_t, imports are reduced from $q_2 - q_d$ to $q_3 - q_t$, and the market price of textiles rises. Domestic textile producers are clearly better off, whereas domestic consumers and foreign producers are worse off.

QUOTA EFFECTS   Now consider the impact of a textile *quota*. Suppose that we eliminate tariffs but decree that imports cannot exceed the quantity Q. Because the quantity of imports can never exceed Q, the supply curve is effectively shifted to the right by that amount. The new curve S_4 (Figure 17.2d) indicates that no imports will occur below the world price p_2 and that above that price the quantity Q will be imported. Thus the *domestic* supply curve determines subsequent prices. Foreign producers are precluded from selling greater quantities as prices rise further. This outcome is in marked contrast to that of tariff-restricted trade (Figure 12.3c), which at least permits foreign producers to respond to rising prices. Accordingly, *quotas are a much greater threat to competition than tariffs because quotas preclude additional imports at any price.*

Quotas have long been maintained on sugar coming into the United States. By keeping cheap imported sugar out, these quotas have permitted beet farmers in Nebraska and sugarcane farmers in Florida to reap economic profits. American consumers have paid for that protection, however, in the form of higher prices for candy, sodas, and sugar—about $2 billion year. Foreign sugar producers have also lost sales, jobs, and profits. Confronted with higher input costs, U.S. candy and soda manufacturers have shut down U.S. plants and relocated elsewhere, taking thousands of U.S. jobs (see the accompanying News Wire).

Nontariff Barriers

Tariffs and quotas are the most visible barriers to trade, but they are only the tip of the iceberg. Indeed, the variety of protectionist measures that have

Import quotas tend to push both domestic and import prices higher, making consumers worse off.

© The Herb Block Foundation

NEWS WIRE	IMPORT QUOTAS

Obama Cuts Sour Deal on Sugar

President Barack Obama has kept a campaign promise to the sugar lobby at the expense of American families struggling to pay their grocery bills and U.S. manufacturing workers fighting to keep their jobs. . . .

Since the early 1980s, the domestic U.S. sugar industry has enjoyed cartel-like control of the domestic market. A system of price supports and import quotas virtually guarantees domestic beet and cane growers an 80 percent market share. At times, this has forced American families and sugar-consuming industries to pay prices two or three times the spot world price.

This has been bad news for families, who must pay higher prices at the grocery store, but equally bad for a segment of American workers. Artificially high domestic sugar prices raise the cost of production for refined sugar, candy and other confectionary products, chocolate and cocoa products, chewing gum, bread and other bakery products, cookies and crackers, and frozen bakery goods. Higher costs cut into profits and competitiveness, putting thousands of jobs in jeopardy. . . .

In all, 6,400 workers in the sugar-processing industry have lost their jobs because of their own government's deliberate policy to drive up the cost of their major input. According to the U.S. International Trade Commission, the sugar program "saves" only 2,200 jobs in the sugar growing and harvesting industry. So our sugar policy eliminates three jobs for every one it saves.

—Daniel Griswold, Cato Institute

Source: October 8, 2009, from the archives of *The Detroit News*.

NOTE: Import restrictions raise domestic prices, making both domestic consumers and foreign producers worse off. They enrich domestic producers, however.

been devised is testimony to human ingenuity. At the turn of the century, the Germans were officially committed to a policy of extending equal treatment to all trading partners. They wanted, however, to lower the tariff on cattle imports from Denmark without extending the same break to Switzerland. Accordingly, the Germans created a new and higher tariff on "brown and dappled cows reared at a level of at least 300 meters above sea level and passing at least one month in every summer at an altitude of at least 800 meters." The new tariff was, of course, applied equally to all countries. But Danish cows never climb that high, so they were not burdened with the new tariff.

With the decline in tariffs over the last 20 years, nontariff barriers have increased. The United States uses product standards, licensing restrictions, restrictive procurement practices, and other nontariff barriers to restrict roughly 15 percent of imports. Japan makes even greater use of nontariff barriers, restricting nearly 30 percent of imports in such ways.

In 1999–2000 the European Union banned imports of U.S. beef, arguing that the use of hormones on U.S. ranches created a health hazard for European consumers. Although both the U.S. government and the World Trade Organization disputed that claim, the ban was a highly effective nontariff trade barrier. The United States responded by slapping 100 percent tariffs on dozens of European products.

EXCHANGE RATES

Up until now, we've made no mention of how people *pay* for goods and services produced in other countries. In fact, the principle of comparative advantage is based only on opportunity costs; it makes no reference to monetary prices. Yet when France and the United States started specializing in production, market participants had to *purchase* wine and bread to get trade flows started. Remember Henri, the mythical French entrepreneur? He got trade started by buying bread in the United States for export to France. That meant he had to make purchases in *dollars* and sales in *euros*. **So long as each nation has its own currency, every trade will require use of two different currencies at some point.**

If you've ever traveled to a foreign country, you know the currency problem. Stores, hotels, vending machines, and restaurants price their products in local currency. So you've got to exchange your dollars for local currency when you travel (a service import). That's when you learn how important the **exchange rate** is. The exchange rate refers to the value of one currency in terms of another currency. If $1 exchanges for 2 euros, then a euro is worth 50 cents.

exchange rate The price of one country's currency expressed in terms of another country's currency.

Global Pricing

Exchange rates are a critical link in the global pricing of goods and services. Whether a bottle of French wine is expensive depends on two factors: (1) the French price of the wine, expressed in euros, and (2) the dollar–euro exchange rate. Specifically,

$$\text{Dollar price of imported good} = \text{foreign price of good} \times \text{dollar price of foreign currency}$$

Hence if French wine sells for 60 euros per bottle in France and the dollar price of a euro is $1.50, the American price of imported French wine is

$$= 60 \text{ euros} \times \$1.50 \text{ per euro}$$
$$= \$90.00$$

NEWS WIRE	CURRENCY APPRECIATION

Travelers Flock to Europe as Dollar Gets Stronger
**With U.S. Currency Near Two-Year High against Euro,
Hotels, Dining Get Cheaper**

European vacations are getting cheaper than they have been in years.

With the dollar gaining 14.6 percent on the euro and 12.1 percent on the British pound over the past 12 months, large numbers of U.S. tourists are already booking vacations to Europe for the coming year.

The stronger dollar means prices on everything from French hotel rooms to Italian wine are falling for U.S. travelers. Airline fares, too, are easing, as more trans-Atlantic flights are scheduled and fuel costs start to come down. As a result travel agents are seeing a sharp rise in advance bookings to Britain and the Continent. AAA Travel, a national agency, says its advance bookings to Europe are up 116 percent over last year. (Italy's bookings are up 236 percent, England's are 79 percent higher and Spain's have climbed 170 percent.)

—Avery Johnson

Source: *The Wall Street Journal*, Midwest Edition, December 8, 2005. Used with permission of Dow Jones & Company, Inc., via Copyright Clearance Center, Inc.

NOTE: When the dollar appreciates (rises in value), the euro simultaneously depreciates (falls in value). This makes European vacations cheaper for American college students.

Appreciation/Depreciation

The formula for global pricing highlights how important exchange rates are for trade flows. *Whenever exchange rates change, so do the global prices of all imports and exports.*

Suppose the dollar were to get stronger against the euro. That means the dollar price of a euro would decline. Suppose the dollar price of a euro fell from $1.50 to only $1.20. That **currency appreciation** of the dollar would cut the dollar price of French wine by 20 percent. Americans would respond by buying more imported wine. In 2005–2006 Americans took advantage of the dollar's appreciation to book more travel to Europe (see the accompanying News Wire).

If the dollar is *rising* in value, another currency must be *falling*. Specifically, the appreciation of the dollar implies a **currency depreciation** for the euro. If the dollar price of a euro declines from $1.50 to $1.20, that implies an *increase* in the *euro* price of a *dollar* (from .67 euros to .83 euros). Hence French consumers will have to pay more euros for an American loaf of bread. Stuck with a depreciated currency, they may decide to buy fewer imported loaves of bread. As the previous equation implies, *if the value of a nation's currency declines,*

- *Its exports become cheaper.*
- *Its imports become more expensive.*

Imagine how Argentinians felt in January 2001 when their currency (the peso) depreciated by nearly 70 percent. That abrupt depreciation made all foreign-made products too expensive for Argentinians. But it made Argentina a bargain destination for U.S. travelers.

A WEAKER DOLLAR   In 2009 the United States enjoyed a similar tourist influx. The dollar *depreciated* by nearly 10 percent against the euro in early 2009. This dollar depreciation dropped the *euro* price of a ticket to Disney World by 10 percent. Europeans responded by flocking to Florida.

currency appreciation An increase in the value of one currency relative to another.

currency depreciation A decrease in the value of one currency relative to another.

FIGURE 17.3
The Euro Market

FIGURE 17.3
The Euro Market

Exchange rates are set in foreign exchange markets by the international supply of and demand for a currency. In this case the equilibrium price is 110 U.S. cents for one euro.

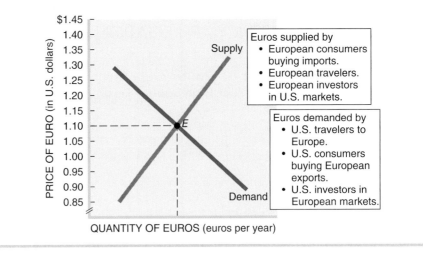

Foreign Exchange Markets

The changes in exchange rates that alter global prices are really no different in principle from other price changes. An exchange rate is, after all, simply the *price* of a currency. Like other market prices, an exchange rate is determined by supply and demand.

Figure 17.3 depicts a foreign exchange market. In this case, the supply and demand for euros is the focus. On the demand side of the market is everyone who has some use of euros, including U.S. travelers to Europe, U.S. importers of European products, and foreign investors who want to buy European stocks, bonds, and factories. The cheaper the euro, the greater the quantity of euros demanded.

The supply of euros comes from similar sources. German tourists visiting Disney World *supply* euros when they *demand* U.S. dollars. European consumers who buy American-made products set off a chain of transactions that *supplies* euros in exchange for dollars. The higher the price of the euro, the more they are willing to supply.

The intersection of the supply and demand curves in Figure 17.3 establishes the equilibrium price of the euro—that is, the prevailing exchange rate. As we have seen, however, exchange rates change. As with other prices, *exchange rates change when either the supply of or the demand for a currency shifts.* If American students suddenly decided to enroll in European colleges, the demand for euros would increase. This rightward shift of the euro demand curve would cause the euro to *appreciate* (go up), as shown in Figure 17.4. Such a euro appreciation would increase the cost of studying in Europe. But the euro appreciation would make it cheaper for European students to attend U.S. colleges.

Topic Podcast:
Value of the Dollar

FIGURE 17.4
Currency Appreciation

If the demand for a currency increases, its value will rise (appreciate). Shifts of a currency's demand or supply curve will alter exchange rates.

NEWS WIRE	CURRENCY REVALUATION

China Ends Fixed-Rate Currency

SHANGHAI, July 21—China on Thursday took an important step forward in its move toward a market economy, announcing it would increase the value of its currency, the yuan, and abandon its decade-old fixed exchange rate to the U.S. dollar in favor of a link to a basket of world currencies.

The evening announcement on state television delivered China's first concrete move toward allowing the yuan—also known as the renminbi—to eventually float freely at the whim of global traders.

The move eased tensions between China and the United States on a key source of trade friction. The White House, pressured by manufacturers and vocal members of Congress, has lobbied China to raise the value of its currency, arguing that a low-priced yuan has unfairly kept Chinese goods artificially cheap. . . .

The details of China's announced shift fell short of their demands. In a statement posted on its website, China's central bank said it would on Friday free the yuan to rise to 8.11 from its current 8.28 to the dollar—an increase of about 2.1 percent. The bank also said it would allow the yuan to move within a trading range of 0.3 percent above or below the previous day's closing price, continuing its "managed float" policy. . . .

—Peter S. Goodman

Source: *The Washington Post*, © July 22, 2005, The Washington Post. All rights reserved.

NOTE: When a nation keeps its currency cheap, it gains an export advantage. China manages its currency to keep exports strong.

China's government has used a cheap currency to increase its exports. By keeping the dollar price of the yuan low, China effectively lowers the price of its exports and raises the price of its imports. This helps China achieve huge export surpluses (see Table 17.2) but angers U.S. and European producers who must compete against cheap Chinese products. In response to political pressure from the United States and other trading partners, China increased the value of the yuan slightly in 2005 (see the accompanying News Wire). President Obama wanted the Chinese to revalue their currency more so they would buy more U.S. exports.

POLICY PERSPECTIVES

Who Enforces World Trade Rules?

Trade policy is a continuing conflict between the benefits of comparative advantage and pleadings of protectionists. Free trade promises more output, greater efficiency, and lower prices. At the same time, free trade threatens profits, jobs, and wealth in specific industries.

Politically, the battle over trade policy favors protectionist interests over consumer interests. Few consumers understand how free trade affects them. Moreover, consumers are unlikely to organize political protests just because the price of orange juice is 35 cents per gallon higher. By contrast, import-competing industries have a large economic stake in trade restrictions and can mobilize political support easily. After convincing Congress to pass new quotas on textiles in 1990, the Fiber Fabric Apparel Coalition for Trade (FFACT) mustered 250,000 signatures and 4,000 union members to march on the White House demanding that President Bush sign the legislation.

President Clinton faced similar political resistance when he sought congressional approval of NAFTA in 1993 and GATT in 1994. Indeed, the political resistance to free trade was so intense that Congress delayed a vote on GATT until after the November 1994 elections. This forced President Clinton to convene a special post-election session of Congress for the sole purpose of ratifying the GATT agreement.

President Obama confronted the same kind of political power in 2009. The president was committed to a massive fiscal stimulus program that would help end the 2008–2009 recession. The labor unions that had helped elect him wanted to be sure that the stimulus money benefited them, so they convinced Obama to include a "Buy American" provision in the stimulus bill. That provision created a few more jobs in the auto and steel industries but raised the specter of retaliation by foreign nations (see the accompanying News Wire).

GATT   The political resistance to free trade is not unique to the United States. International trade creates winners and losers in every trading nation. Recognizing this, the countries of the world decided long ago that multinational agreements were the most effective way to overcome domestic protectionism. Broad trade agreements can address the entire spectrum of trade restrictions rather than focusing on one industry at a time. Multinational agreements can also muster political support by offering greater *export* opportunities as *import* restrictions are lifted.

In 1947, 23 of the world's largest trading nations signed the General Agreement on Tariffs and Trade (GATT). The GATT pact committed these nations to pursue

---

NEWS WIRE	THE POLITICS OF TRADE

U.S. Trade Restrictions Draw Warning

The nation's largest trading partners are warning that protectionist moves by Congress could poison global trade relations despite President Obama's assurances that he wants to keep U.S. markets open.

Businesses in the European Union and Canada complain that they have been shut out of U.S. markets because of the "Buy American" provision in the massive stimulus bill, passed in February, which requires the use of U.S.-manufactured products. . . .

Buy American supporters want to make sure the billions of U.S. taxpayer dollars being spent to revive the economy create jobs at home. . . .

Many U.S. exporters fear the provisions will backfire, costing American jobs as other countries retaliate. Some municipalities in Canada have begun organizing boycotts of U.S. products, and EU and Canadian officials say they are reviewing their options. . . .

In the United States, the Buy American provisions are supported by labor groups that have long been among the most important constituencies for Democrats, who control both chambers of Congress as well as the White House.

The Democratic lawmaker behind the Buy American provision in the schools bill, Rep. Peter J. Visclosky of Indiana, said it will be a big boost to U.S. steelworkers, whose industry has been hit hard.

"We must do everything possible to ensure that American taxpayer dollars are going to build American schools with American steel," Mr. Visclosky said in a statement he issued after the bill passed the House last month.

—Desmond Butler, Associated Press

Source: Associated Press, July 9, 2009. Used with permission of The Associated Press Copyright © 2008. All rights reserved.

NOTE: Trade restrictions benefit specific import-competing industries. But they raise costs and invite retaliation that hurts domestic export industries.

free trade policies and to extend equal access ("most favored nation" status) to domestic markets for all GATT members. This goal was pursued with periodic rounds of multilateral trade agreements. Because each round of negotiations entailed hundreds of industries and products, the negotiations typically dragged on for 6 to 10 years. At the end of each round, however, trade barriers were always lower. When GATT was first signed in 1947, tariff rates in developed countries averaged 40 percent. The first seven GATT rounds pushed tariffs down to an average of 6.3 percent, and the 1986–1994 Uruguay Round lowered them further to 3.9 percent.

WTO   The 117 nations that signed the 1994 Uruguay agreement also decided that a stronger mechanism was needed to enforce free trade agreements. To that end, the World Trade Organization (WTO) was created to replace GATT. If a nation feels its exports are being unfairly excluded from another country's market, it can file a complaint with the WTO. This is exactly what the United States did when the European Union (EU) banned U.S. beef imports. The WTO ruled in favor of the United States. When the EU failed to lift its import ban, the WTO authorized the United States to impose retaliatory tariffs on European exports.

The European Union turned the tables on the United States in 2003. It complained to the WTO that U.S. tariffs on steel violated trade rules. The WTO agreed and gave the EU permission to impose retaliatory tariffs on $2.2 billion of U.S. exports. That prompted the Bush administration to scale back the tariffs in December 2003. In 2009 China petitioned the WTO to force the United States to repeal the tariff on Chinese tires (page 354).

In effect, the WTO is now the world's trade police force. It is empowered to cite nations that violate trade agreements and even to authorize remedial action when violations persist. Why do sovereign nations give the WTO such power? Because they are convinced that free trade is the surest route to GDP growth.

SUMMARY

- A trade *deficit* arises when imports exceed exports; a trade *surplus* is the reverse.   **LO1**

- Trade breaks the link between a nation's *consumption* possibilities and its *production* possibilities.   **LO2**

- Trade permits each country to concentrate its resources on those goods it can produce most efficiently. This kind of productive specialization increases world output.   **LO2**

- In determining what to produce and offer in trade, each country will exploit its *comparative* advantage— its *relative* efficiency in producing various goods. One way to determine where comparative advantage lies is to compare the quantity of good *A* that must be given up in order to *produce* a given quantity of good *B*. If the same quantity of *B* can be obtained for less *A* by *trading*, we have a comparative advantage in the production of good *A*. Comparative advantage rests on a comparison of relative opportunity costs (domestic versus international).   **LO2**

- The terms of trade—the rate at which goods are exchanged—are subject to the forces of international supply and demand. The terms of trade will lie somewhere between the opportunity costs of the trading partners.   **LO3**

- Resistance to trade emanates from workers and firms that must compete with imports. Even though the country as a whole stands to benefit from trade, these individuals and companies may lose jobs and incomes in the process.   **LO4**

- The means of restricting trade are many and diverse. Tariffs discourage imports by making them more expensive. Quotas limit the quantity of a good that may be imported. Nontariff barriers are less visible but also effective in curbing imports.   **LO4**

- International trade requires converting one nation's currency into that of another. The exchange rate is the price of one currency in terms of another.   **LO5**

- Changes in exchange rates (currency appreciation and depreciation) occur when supply or demand for a currency shifts. When a nation's currency appreciates, its exports become more expensive and its imports cheaper.   **LO5**

- The World Trade Organization (WTO) polices multilateral trade agreements to keep trade barriers low.   **LO4**

TERMS TO REMEMBER

Define the following terms:

imports	consumption	absolute advantage	equilibrium price
exports	possibilities	terms of trade	exchange rate
trade deficit	opportunity cost	tariff	currency appreciation
trade surplus	comparative	quota	currency depreciation
production possibilities	advantage		

QUESTIONS FOR DISCUSSION

1. Suppose a lawyer can type faster than any secretary. Should the lawyer do her own typing?   **LO2**
2. Can you identify three services Americans import? How about three exported services?   **LO1**
3. If a nation exported much of its output but imported little, would it be better or worse off? How about the reverse—that is, exporting little but importing a lot?   **LO1**
4. Were the 2009 "Buy American" provisions (News Wire, p. 362) good for (a) U.S. consumers, (b) U.S. producers, (c) Congressman Visclosky?   **LO4**
5. Why did solar panel installers object to tariffs on Chinese-made solar panels (News Wire, p. 355)?   **LO2**
6. How would each of these events affect the supply or demand for Japanese yen?   **LO5**
   (a) Stronger U.S. economic growth.
   (b) A decline in Japanese interest rates.
   (c) Higher inflation in the United States.
7. Is a stronger dollar good or bad for America? Explain.   **LO5**
8. How did China's yuan revaluation (News Wire, p. 361) affect U.S.–China trade? Who gained? Who lost?   **LO5**
9. **POLICY PERSPECTIVES** If another nation raises tariffs on U.S. products, should the United States retaliate with similar trade barriers?

PROBLEMS

≋ connect

1. Suppose the following table reflects the domestic supply and demand for compact disks (CDs):   **LO4**

Price ($)	15	13	11	9	7	5	3	1
Quantity supplied	8	7	6	5	4	3	2	1
Quantity demanded	2	4	6	8	10	12	14	16

   (a) Graph these market conditions and identify the equilibrium price and sales.
   (b) Now suppose that foreigners enter the market, offering to sell an unlimited supply of CDs for $7 apiece. Illustrate and identify (1) the market price, (2) domestic consumption, and (3) domestic production.
   (c) If a tariff of $2 per CD is imposed, what will happen to (i) the market price, (ii) domestic consumption, and (iii) domestic production?

2. Alpha and Beta, two tiny islands off the east coast of Tricoli, produce pearls and pineapples. The production possibilities schedules in the table below describe their potential output in tons per year.   **LO3**
   (a) Graph the production possibilities confronting each island.
   (b) What is the opportunity cost of pineapples on each island (before trade)?
   (c) Which island has a comparative advantage in pearl production?

Alpha		Beta	
Pearls	Pineapples	Pearls	Pineapples
0	30	0	20
2	25	10	16
4	20	20	12
6	15	30	8
8	10	40	4
10	5	45	2
12	0	50	0

3. Suppose the two islands in Problem 2 agree that the terms of trade will be 1 pineapple for 1 pearl and that trade soon results in an exchange of 10 pearls for 10 pineapples. **LO2**
   (*a*) If Alpha produced 6 pearls and 15 pineapples and Beta produced 30 pearls and 8 pineapples before they decided to trade, how much would each be producing after trade became possible? Assume that the two countries specialize just enough to maintain their consumption of the item they export, and make sure each island trades the item for which it has a comparative advantage.
   (*b*) How much would the combined production of pineapples increase for the two islands due to trade? How much would the combined production of pearls increase?
   (*c*) How could both countries produce and consume even more?
4. What is the equilibrium euro price of the U.S. dollar **LO5**
   (*a*) In Figure 17.3?
   (*b*) In Figure 17.4?
   (*c*) Did the dollar appreciate or depreciate in Figure 17.4?

5. In what country is the U.S. dollar price of a Big Mac (p. 343) the highest with the following exchange rates? **LO5**
   (*a*) 9,160 rupiah = $1
   (*b*) .79 euros = $1
   (*c*) 31.8 baht = $1
   (*d*) 6.32 yuan = $1
6. If a Nintendo Wii 3 costs 24,000 yen in Japan, how much will it cost in U.S. dollars if the exchange rate is as follows? **LO5**
   (*a*) 120 yen = $1
   (*b*) 1 yen = $0.00833
   (*c*) 100 yen = $1
7. How much cheaper, in U.S. dollars, did a 100-euro-per-night Paris hotel become in 2005, according to the News Wire on page 359? **LO5**
8. According to the News Wire on page 357, what is the *net* U.S. job loss from sugar quotas? **LO4**
9. **POLICY PERSPECTIVES** How would you illustrate the effects of the 2009 "Buy American" policy (News Wire, p. 362) in Figure 17.2? **LO4**

◄ Practice quizzes, student PowerPoints, author podcasts, web activities, and additional materials available at **www.mhhe.com/schilleressentials9e**, or scan here. Need a barcode reader? Try ScanLife, available in your app store.

GLOSSARY

Numbers in parentheses indicate the chapters in which the definitions appear.

A

absolute advantage The ability of a country to produce a specific good with fewer resources (per unit of output) than other countries. (*17*)

aggregate demand The total quantity of output demanded at alternative price levels in a given time period, *ceteris paribus.* (*11*) (*12*) (*13*) (*14*)

aggregate supply The total quantity of output producers are willing and able to supply at alternative price levels in a given time period, *ceteris paribus.* (*11*) (*14*)

antitrust Government intervention to alter market structure or prevent abuse of market power. (*9*)

automatic stabilizer Federal expenditure or revenue item that automatically responds countercyclically to changes in national income—e.g., unemployment benefits, income taxes. (*16*)

average total cost (ATC) Total cost divided by the quantity produced in a given time period. (*5*)

B

bank reserves Assets held by a bank to fulfill its deposit obligations. (*13*)

barriers to entry Obstacles that make it difficult or impossible for would-be producers to enter a particular market, e.g., patents. (*6*) (*7*)

barter The direct exchange of one good for another, without the use of money. (*3*) (*13*)

budget deficit The amount by which government expenditures exceed government revenues in a given time period. (*12*)

budget surplus An excess of government revenues over government expenditures in a given time period. (*12*)

business cycle Alternating periods of economic growth and contraction. (*10*) (*11*) (*16*)

C

capital intensive Production processes that use a high ratio of capital to labor inputs. (*2*)

ceteris paribus The assumption of nothing else changing. (*1*) (*3*) (*4*)

comparative advantage The ability of a country to produce a specific good at a lower opportunity cost than its trading partners. (*17*)

competitive firm A firm without market power, with no ability to alter the market price of the goods it produces. (*6*)

competitive market A market in which no buyer or seller has market power. (*6*)

competitive profit-maximization rule Produce at that rate of output where price equals marginal cost. (*6*)

Consumer Price Index (CPI) A measure (index) of changes in the average price of consumer goods and services. (*10*)

Consumption Expenditure by consumers on final goods and services. (*12*)

consumption possibilities The alternative combinations of goods and services that a country could consume in a given time period. (*17*)

contestable market An imperfectly competitive industry subject to potential entry if prices or profits increase. (*7*)

crowding in An increase in private-sector borrowing (and spending) caused by decreased government borrowing. (*15*)

crowding out A reduction in private-sector borrowing (and spending) caused by increased government borrowing. (*15*)

currency appreciation An increase in the value of one currency relative to another. (*17*)

currency depreciation A decrease in the value of one currency relative to another. (*17*)

D

deflation A decrease in the average level of prices of goods and services. (*10*)

demand The ability and willingness to buy specific quantities of a good at alternative prices in a given time period, *ceteris paribus.* (*3*) (*4*)

demand curve A curve describing the quantities of a good a consumer is willing and able to buy at alternative prices in a given time period, *ceteris paribus.* (*3*) (*4*)

demand for labor The quantities of labor employers are willing and able to hire at alternative wage rates in a given time period, *ceteris paribus.* (*8*)

demand schedule A table showing the quantities of a good a consumer is willing and able to buy at alternative prices in a given time period, *ceteris paribus.* (*3*)

deposit creation The creation of transactions deposits by bank lending. (*13*)

derived demand The demand for labor and other factors of production results from (depends on) the demand for final goods and services produced by these factors. (*8*)

discount rate The rate of interest charged by the Federal Reserve banks for lending reserves to private banks. (*14*)

disposable income After-tax income of consumers. (*12*)

E

economic cost The value of all resources used to produce a good or service; opportunity cost. (*5*)

economic growth An increase in output (real GDP); an expansion of production possibilities. (*1*) (*2*) (*15*)

economics The study of how best to allocate scarce resources among competing uses. (*1*)

economies of scale Reductions in minimum average costs that come about through increases in the size (scale) of plant and equipment. (*7*)

emission charge A fee imposed on polluters, based on the quantity of pollution. (*9*)

employment rate The proportion of the adult population that is employed. (*15*)

equilibrium (macro) The combination of price level and real output that is compatible with both aggregate demand and aggregate supply. (*11*) (*12*)

equilibrium price The price at which the quantity of a good demanded in a given time period equals the quantity supplied. (*3*) (*6*) (*17*)

equilibrium wage The wage at which the quantity of labor supplied in a given time period equals the quantity of labor demanded. (*8*)

excess reserves Bank reserves in excess of required reserves. (*13*) (*14*)

exchange rate The price of one country's currency expressed in terms of another country's currency. (*17*)

exports Goods and services sold to foreign buyers. (*2*) (*17*)

externalities Costs (or benefits) of a market activity borne by a third party; the difference between the social and private costs (or benefits) of a market activity. (*2*) (*9*)

F

factor market Any place where factors of production (e.g., land, labor, capital, entrepreneurship) are bought and sold. (*3*)

factors of production Resource inputs used to produce goods and services, e.g., land, labor, capital, entrepreneurship. (*1*) (*2*) (*5*)

federal funds rate The interest rate banks charge each other for reserves loans. (*14*)

fine-tuning Adjustments in economic policy designed to counteract small changes in economic outcomes; continuous responses to changing economic conditions. (*16*)

fiscal policy The use of government taxes and spending to alter macroeconomic outcomes. (*11*) (*12*) (*16*)

fiscal restraint Tax hikes or spending cuts intended to reduce (shift) aggregate demand. (*12*)

fiscal stimulus Tax cuts or spending hikes intended to increase (shift) aggregate demand. (*12*)

fiscal year (FY) The 12-month period used for accounting purposes; begins October 1 for the federal government. (*16*)

fixed costs Costs of production that do not change when the rate of output is altered, e.g., the cost of basic plant and equipment. (*5*)

free rider An individual who reaps direct benefits from someone else's purchase (consumption) of a public good. (*9*)

full employment The lowest rate of unemployment compatible with price stability; variously estimated at between 4 and 6 percent unemployment. (*10*)

full-employment GDP The rate of real output (GDP) produced at full employment. (*11*)

G

GDP gap The difference between full-employment output and the amount of output demanded at current price levels. (*12*) (*16*)

GDP per capita Total GDP divided by total population; average GDP. (*15*)

government failure Government intervention that fails to improve economic outcomes. (*1*) (*3*) (*9*)

gross domestic product (GDP) The total value of goods and services produced within a nation's borders in a given time period. (*2*) (*10*)

growth rate Percentage change in real GDP from one period to another. (*15*)

H

human capital The knowledge and skills possessed by the workforce. (*2*)

I

imports Goods and services purchased from foreign sources. (*2*) (*17*)

income transfers Payments to individuals for which no current goods or services are exchanged, e.g., Social Security, welfare, unemployment benefits. (*2*) (*9*)

inflation An increase in the average level of prices of goods and services. (*10*) (*11*)

inflation rate The annual rate of increase in the average price level. (*10*)

investment Expenditures on (production of) new plant and equipment (capital) in a given time period, plus changes in business inventories. (*1*) (*2*) (*12*) (*15*)

investment decision The decision to build, buy, or lease plant and equipment; to enter or exit an industry. (*5*)

L

labor force All persons over age 16 who are either working for pay or actively seeking paid employment. (*10*) (*15*)

labor supply The willingness and ability to work specific amounts of time at alternative wage rates in a given time period, *ceteris paribus*. (*8*)

laissez faire The doctrine of "leave it alone," of nonintervention by government in the market mechanism. (*1*) (*3*) (*9*)

law of demand The quantity of a good demanded in a given time period increases as its price falls, *ceteris paribus*. (*3*) (*4*)

law of diminishing marginal utility The marginal utility of a good declines as more of it is consumed in a given time period. (*4*)

law of diminishing returns The marginal physical product of a variable input declines as more of it is employed with a given quantity of other (fixed) inputs. (*5*) (*8*)

law of supply The quantity of a good supplied in a given time period increases as its price increases, *ceteris paribus*. (*3*)

long run A period of time long enough for all inputs to be varied (no fixed costs). (*5*)

M

macroeconomics The study of aggregate economic behavior, of the economy as a whole. (*1*) (*10*) (*11*)

macro equilibrium The combination of price level and real output that is compatible with both aggregate demand and aggregate supply. (*11*)

marginal cost (MC) The increase in total cost associated with a one-unit increase in production. (*5*) (*6*)

marginal cost pricing The offer (supply) of goods at prices equal to their marginal cost. (7)

marginal physical product (MPP) The change in total output associated with one additional unit of input. (5) (8)

marginal propensity to consume (MPC) The fraction of each additional (marginal) dollar of disposable income spent on consumption. (12)

marginal propensity to save (MPS) The fraction of each additional (marginal) dollar of disposable income not spent on consumption; $1 - \text{MPC}$. (12)

marginal revenue (MR) The change in total revenue that results from a one-unit increase in quantity sold. (7)

marginal revenue product (MRP) The change in total revenue associated with one additional unit of input. (8)

marginal utility The change in total utility obtained by consuming one additional (marginal) unit of a good or service consumed. (4)

market Any place where goods are bought and sold. (3)

market demand The total quantities of a good or service people are willing and able to buy at alternative prices in a given time period; the sum of individual demands. (3) (4) (7)

market failure An imperfection in the market mechanism that prevents optimal outcomes. (1) (9)

market mechanism The use of market prices and sales to signal desired outputs (or resource allocations). (1) (3) (6) (9)

market power The ability to alter the market price of a good or service. (6) (7) (9)

market shortage The amount by which the quantity demanded exceeds the quantity supplied at a given price; excess demand. (3)

market structure The number and relative size of firms in an industry. (6)

market supply The total quantities of a good that sellers are willing and able to sell at alternative prices in a given time period, *ceteris paribus*. (3) (6)

market supply of labor The total quantity of labor that workers are willing and able to supply at alternative wage rates in a given time period, *ceteris paribus*. (8)

market surplus The amount by which the quantity supplied exceeds the quantity demanded at a given price; excess supply. (3)

microeconomics The study of individual behavior in the economy, of the components of the larger economy. (1)

mixed economy An economy that uses both market and nonmarket signals to allocate goods and resources. (1)

monetary policy The use of money and credit controls to influence macroeconomic activity. (11) (14) (16)

money Anything generally accepted as a medium of exchange. (13)

money multiplier The number of deposit (loan) dollars that the banking system can create from $1 of excess reserves; equal to $1 \div$ required reserve ratio. (13) (14)

money supply (M1) Currency held by the public, plus balances in transactions accounts. (13) (14) (16)

monopoly A firm that produces the entire market supply of a particular good or service. (2) (6) (7)

multiplier The multiple by which an initial change in aggregate spending will alter total expenditure after an infinite number of spending cycles; $1/(1 - \text{MPC})$. (12) (16)

N

natural monopoly An industry in which one firm can achieve economies of scale over the entire range of market supply. (7)

net exports Exports minus imports $(X - IM)$. (12)

nominal GDP The total value of goods and services produced within a nation's borders, measured in current prices. (2) (10) (15)

nominal income The amount of money income received in a given time period, measured in current dollars. (10)

O

open-market operations Federal Reserve purchases and sales of government bonds for the purpose of altering bank reserves. (14)

opportunity cost The most desired goods and services that are forgone in order to obtain something else. (1) (3) (8) (17)

opportunity wage The highest wage an individual would earn in his or her best alternative job. (8)

optimal mix of output The most desirable combination of output attainable with existing resources, technology, and social values. (9)

P

patent Government grant of exclusive ownership of an innovation. (7)

per capita GDP Total GDP divided by total population; average GDP. (2)

personal distribution of income The way total personal income is divided up among households or income classes. (2)

predatory pricing Temporary price reductions designed to drive out competition. (7)

price ceiling Upper limit imposed on the price of a good. (3)

price elasticity of demand The percentage change in quantity demanded divided by the percentage change in price. (4)

price floor Lower limit imposed on the price of a good. (3)

price stability The absence of significant changes in the average price level; officially defined as a rate of inflation of less than 3 percent. (10)

private costs The costs of an economic activity directly borne by the immediate producer or consumer (excluding externalities). (9)

private good A good or service whose consumption by one person excludes consumption by others. (9)

product market Any place where finished goods and services (products) are bought and sold. (3)

production decision The selection of the short-run rate of output (with existing plant and equipment). (5) (6) (7)

production function A technological relationship expressing the maximum quantity of a good attainable from different combinations of factor inputs. (5)

production possibilities The alternative combinations of goods and services that could be produced in a given time period with all available resources and technology. (1) (10) (15) (17)

productivity Output per unit of input, e.g., output per labor-hour. (2) (15)

profit The difference between total revenue and total cost. (5) (6)

profit-maximization rule   Produce at that rate of output where marginal revenue equals marginal cost. (7)

progressive tax   A tax system in which tax rates rise as incomes rise. (2)

public good   A good or service whose consumption by one person does not exclude consumption by others. (9)

Q

quota   A limit on the quantity of a good that may be imported in a given time period. (17)

R

real GDP   The inflation-adjusted value of GDP; the value of output measured in constant prices. (10) (11) (15)

real income   Income in constant dollars; nominal income adjusted for inflation. (10)

recession   A decline in total output (real GDP) for two or more consecutive quarters. (10)

relative price   The price of one good in comparison with the price of other goods. (10)

required reserves   The minimum amount of reserves a bank is required to hold by government regulation; equal to required reserve ratio times transactions deposits. (13) (14)

reserve ratio   The ratio of a bank's reserves to its total transactions deposits. (13)

S

saving   Income minus consumption; that part of disposable income not spent. (12) (15)

Say's Law   Supply creates its own demand. (11)

scarcity   Lack of enough resources to satisfy all desired uses of those resources. (1)

shift in demand   A change in the quantity demanded at any (every) given price. (3)

short run   The period in which the quantity (and quality) of some inputs cannot be changed. (5)

social costs   The full resource costs of an economic activity, including externalities. (9)

stagflation   The simultaneous occurrence of substantial unemployment and inflation. (16)

structural unemployment   Unemployment caused by a mismatch between the skills (or location) of job seekers and the requirements (or location) of available jobs. (16)

supply   The ability and willingness to sell (produce) specific quantities of a good at alternative prices in a given time period, *ceteris paribus*. (3) (5) (6)

supply-side policy   The use of tax rates, (de)regulation, and other mechanisms to increase the ability and willingness to produce goods and services. (11) (16)

T

tariff   A tax (duty) imposed on imported goods. (17)

terms of trade   The rate at which goods are exchanged; the amount of good *A* given up for good *B* in trade. (17)

total cost   The market value of all resources used to produce a good or service. (5)

total revenue   The price of a product multiplied by the quantity sold in a given time period, $p \times q$. (4) (6)

total utility   The amount of satisfaction obtained from entire consumption of a product. (4)

trade deficit   The amount by which the value of imports exceeds the value of exports in a given time period. (17)

trade surplus   The amount by which the value of exports exceeds the value of imports in a given time period. (17)

transactions account   A bank account that permits direct payment to a third party (e.g., with a check). (13)

transfer payments   See *income transfers*.

U

unemployment   The inability of labor-force participants to find jobs. (10) (11)

unemployment rate   The proportion of the labor force that is unemployed. (10)

utility   The pleasure or satisfaction obtained from a good or service. (4)

V

variable costs   Costs of production that change when the rate of output is altered, e.g., labor and material costs. (5)

PHOTO CREDITS

Page 2: Public Domain, Library of Congress
Page 26: © Digital Vision/PunchStock/DAL
Page 46: © IMS Communications, Ltd. All Rights Reserved/DAL
Page 74: © PLC/Alamy
Page 94: © The McGraw-Hill Companies, Inc./Andrew Resek, photographer/DAL
Page 112: © TongRo Image Stock/Alamy/DAL
Page 136: © Bettmann/Corbis
Page 158: © Patrick Smith/Stringer/Getty Images

Page 178: © Brand X Pictures/PunchStock/DAL
Page 200: © Topham/The Image Works
Page 224: © Flat Earth Images/DAL
Page 246: © Shawn Thew/epa/Corbis
Page 266: © Royalty-Free/Corbis/DAL
Page 284: © Eyewire/Photodisc/PunchStock/DAL
Page 302: © Royalty-Free/Corbis/DAL
Page 320: © Comstock/PictureQuest/DAL
Page 342: © Roslan Rahman/AFP/Getty Images

INDEX

Note: **Boldface** indicates glossary terms defined in the text; page numbers followed by n indicate footnotes.